THE HERMENEUTICAL SPIRAL

A Comprehensive Introduction to Biblical Interpretation

GRANT R. OSBORNE

InterVarsity Press
Downers Grove, Illinois

InterVarsity Press® is the book-publishing division of InterVarsity Christian Fellowship®, a student movement active on campus at hundreds of universities, colleges and schools of nursing in the United States of America, and a member movement of the International Fellowship of Evangelical Students. For information about local and regional activities, write Public Relations Dept., InterVarsity Christian Fellowship, 6400 Schroeder Rd., P.O. Box 7895, Madison, WI 53707-7895.

All Scripture quotations, unless otherwise indicated, are from the HOLY BIBLE, NEW INTERNATIONAL VERSION. Copyright 1973, 1978, 1984 by International Bible Society. Used by permission of Zondervan Publishing House. All rights reserved.

ISBN 0-8308-1288-1

Printed in the United States of America ♾

Library of Congress Cataloging-in-Publication Data

Osborne, Grant R.
    The hermeneutical spiral: a comprehensive introduction to
biblical interpretation/Grant R. Osborne.
        p.   cm.
    Includes bibliographical references.
    ISBN 0-8308-1272-5 (hdbk.)
    ISBN 0-8308-1288-1 (pbk.)
    1. Bible—Hermeneutics.   I. Title.
BS476.079   1991
220.6'01—dc20   91-31967
                                                                          CIP

20	19	18	17	16	15	14	13	12	11	10	9	8	7	6	5	4	3	2
15	14	13	12	11	10	09	08	07	06	05	04	03	02	01	00	99	98	97

To
Amber and Susanne
Our gift from God
Our reward from him
(Psalm 127:3)

Acknowledgments

When a book is written over a period of seven years, many of those who helped in the early years unfortunately slip one's memory. Therefore I apologize to any who are not mentioned here due to my human frailty. So many have contributed to this work that I can only hope that most are mentioned. Secretaries who have typed portions of the manuscript are Sherry Kull, Ruth Jones and Ingrid Chitwood. Graduate assistants who have helped with research are Lois Fuller, Bruce Fisk, Dennis Fisher, Gerald Barber, David Palm and Andreas Kostenberger. Special thanks are due Andreas, who prepared the indexes and went the second mile in terms of meeting deadlines. A further word of thanks is due Mark Hendricksen, whose gift in graphic illustration was the major force in helping me to visualize my material and to prepare many of the charts used in this book. Appreciation is also due my colleagues who have critiqued portions and increased the quality of this work many-fold: Dennis Magary, David Howard, Kevin Vanhoozer and John Feinberg. Any errors in this book are mine and not theirs! Finally, two marvelous sabbaticals greatly aided my research—a year at the University of Marburg in Germany and five months at Tyndale House in Cambridge, England. The excellent libraries at both institutions were a privilege and a joy in which to do research. In addition, my profound gratitude is due Trinity Evangelical Divinity School for granting me the sabbaticals.

The abbreviations used throughout this work are in conformity with those of the *Journal of Biblical Literature* and *New Testament Abstracts.*

Introduction

Hermeneutics is derived from the Greek word meaning "to interpret." Traditionally it has meant "that science which delineates principles or methods for interpreting an individual author's meaning." However, this is being challenged, and the tendency in many circles today is to restrict the term to an elucidation of a text's present meaning rather than of its original intent. This is the subject of the two appendices, where I will argue that the original meaning is a legitimate, even necessary, concern and that hermeneutics encompasses both what it meant and what it means. I would oppose even the practice today of using "exegesis" for the study of the text's meaning and "hermeneutics" for its significance in the present. Rather, hermeneutics is the overall term while exegesis and "contextualization" (the crosscultural communication of a text's significance for today) are the two aspects of that larger task.

Three perspectives are critical to a proper understanding of the interpretive task. First, hermeneutics is a science, since it provides a logical, orderly classification of the laws of interpretation. In the first part, which constitutes the bulk of this book, I will seek to rework the "laws" of interpretation in light of the enormous amount of material from related disciplines such as linguistics or literary criticism. Second, hermeneutics is an art, for it is an acquired skill demanding both imagination and an ability to apply the "laws" to selected passages or books. Such can never be merely learned in the classroom but must result from extensive practice in the field. I will try to demonstrate the hermeneutical "art" with numerous examples drawn from Scripture itself. Third and most important, hermeneutics when utilized to interpret Scripture is a spiritual act, depending upon the leading of the Holy Spirit. Modern scholars too often ignore the sacred dimension and approach the Bible purely as literature, considering the sacral aspect to be almost a genre. Yet human efforts can never properly divine the true message of the Word of God. While Karl Barth wrongly taught that Scripture possesses only instrumental authority, he was certainly correct that it speaks to humanity through divinely controlled "flashes of insight." We must depend upon God and not just upon humanly derived hermeneutical principles when studying the Bible. The doctrine of "illumination" will be explored further in a later chapter.

The hermeneutical enterprise also has three levels. I will discuss them from the standpoint of the personal pronoun that defines the thrust. We begin with a third-person approach, asking "what *it* meant" (exegesis), then passing to a first-person approach, querying "what it means for *me*" (devotional) and finally taking a second-person approach, seeking "how to share with *you* what it means to me" (sermonic).

These levels are interdependent rather than exclusive. Evangelical hermeneutics has consistently centered upon the first, leaving the others to homileticians. Existential hermeneutics has always centered upon the second or third, with some arguing that the first no longer has relevance for today. In actuality all three are essential to a wholistic methodology. To ignore the first is to enter a subjective world without controls, so that anyone's opinion is as good as another person's (the "polyvalence" of appendix one). To ignore the second is to remove the very basis of Scripture, an individual's encounter with the divine, which demands a changed life. To ignore the third is to remove the other biblical imperative that the divine revelation must be shared as the good news, not kept to oneself for personal gratification. Interpreters must follow this order to treat Scripture properly: the original meaning of Scripture provides the necessary foundation upon which we build the significance first for ourselves and then for those to whom we minister. For instance, if I move from the first to the third steps I become a hypocrite, for I have never put into practice what I am demanding of my congregation or audience.

The major premise of this book is that biblical interpretation entails a "spiral" from text to context, from its original meaning to its contextualization or significance for the church today. Scholars since the New Hermeneutic have been fond of describing a "hermeneutical circle" within which our interpretation of the text leads to its interpreting us. However, such a closed circle is dangerous because the priority of the text is lost in the shared gestalt of the "language event" (see Packer 1983:325-27). A "spiral" is a better metaphor because it is not a closed circle but rather an open-ended movement from the horizon of the text to the horizon of the reader. I am not going round and round a closed circle that can never detect the true meaning but am spiralling nearer and nearer to the text's intended meaning as I refine my hypotheses and allow the text to continue to challenge and correct those alternative interpretations, then to guide my delineation of its significance for my situation today. The sacred author's intended meaning is the critical starting-point but not an end in itself. The task of hermeneutics must begin with exegesis but is not complete until one notes the contextualization of that meaning for today. These are the two aspects, entailing what Hirsch calls "meaning" and "significance" or the original intended meaning for the author and his readers (called "audience criticism") as well as its significance for the modern reader (1967:103-26).

Hermeneutics is important because it enables one to move from text to context, to allow the God-inspired meaning of the Word to speak today with as fresh and dynamic a relevance as it had in its original setting. Moreover, preachers or teachers must proclaim the Word of God rather than their own subjective religious opinions. Only a carefully defined hermeneutic can keep one wedded to the text. The basic evangelical fallacy of our generation is "proof-texting," that process whereby a person "proves" a doctrine or practice merely by alluding to a text without considering its original inspired meaning. Many memory-verse programs, while valuable in themselves, virtually encourage people to ignore the context and meaning of a passage and apply it on the surface to current needs. Bridging the gap between these two aspects, foundational meaning and contemporary relevance, demands sophistication.

I have adopted a meaning-significance format in this book. The concept builds upon E. D. Hirsch's distinction between the author's intended meaning of a text, a core that is unvarying, and the multiform significance or implications of a text for individual readers, an application of the original meaning that varies depending upon the diverse circumstances (1976:1-13). The issue is highly debated today and challenges widespread assumptions. Brueggemann observes, "The distinction of 'what it meant' and 'what it means' . . . is increasingly disregarded, overlooked or denied" because the preunderstanding, or "hermeneutical self-awareness," of the interpreter makes it so difficult (and to many, so irrelevant) to get back to that original meaning (1984:1). Nevertheless, the arguments in appendices one and two as well as the entire development of this book, I believe, justify this format as best expressing the task of hermeneutics.

The Bible was not revealed via "the tongues of angels." Though inspired of God, it was written in human language and within human cultures. By the very nature of language the Bible's univocal truths are couched in analogical language, that is, the absolute truths of Scripture were encased in the human languages and cultures of the ancient Hebrews and Greeks, and we must understand those cultures in order to interpret the biblical texts properly. Therefore Scripture does not automatically cross cultural barriers to impart its meaning. Moreover, by the very fact that scholars differ so greatly when interpreting the same passage, we know that God does not miraculously reveal the meaning of passages whenever they are read. While gospel truths are simple, the task of uncovering the original meaning of specific texts is complex and demands hard work. We can fulfill this enormous responsibility only when we develop and apply a consistent hermeneutic. Several issues should be highlighted before we begin our task.

Hermeneutics and Intended Meaning

Modern critics increasingly deny the very possibility of discovering the original, or intended, meaning of a text. The problem is that while the original authors had a definite meaning in mind when they wrote, that is now lost to us because they are no longer present to clarify and explain what they wrote. The modern reader cannot study the text from the ancient perspective but constantly reads into that passage modern perspectives. Therefore, critics argue, objective interpretation is impossible and the author's intended meaning is forever lost to us. Every community provides traditions to guide the reader in comprehending a text, and these produce the meaning. That "meaning" differs from community to community, so in actuality any passage might have multiple meanings, and each is valid for a particular reading perspective or community.

These problems are indeed very real and complex. Due to the difficult philosophical issues involved, I do not discuss them in detail until the appendices. In another sense, however, every chapter in this book is a response to this issue, for the very process of interpretation builds a base for discovering the original intended meaning of the biblical text. The appendices discuss the theoretical answer, while the book as a whole attempts to provide the practical solution to this dilemma.

The Inspiration and Authority of Scripture

The Bible has an inherent sense of authority, seen in the constant use of "Yahweh says" in the Old Testament and the aura of divinely bestowed apostolic authority in the New Testament (see Grudem 1983:19-59). Of course, the exact parameters are widely debated, but I would affirm a carefully nuanced form of inerrancy (see Feinberg 1979) rather than the more dynamic model of Achtemeier (1980), who says that not only are the original events inspired, but also the meanings added by later communities and the canonical finalization are likewise inspired. Moreover, he affirms, we ourselves are inspired as we read it today. The chart below has important implications for hermeneutics, for it means that there is an authority gap the further we remove ourselves from the intended meaning of the Word.

As we can see from the flow chart in figure 0.1, the level of authority moves down as we go from text to reading to application; therefore, we must move upward as we make certain that our contextualization approximates as closely as possible our interpretation, and that this in turn coheres to the original/intended meaning of the text/author. The only means for true authority in preaching and daily Christian living is to utilize hermeneutics to wed our application as closely as possible to our interpretation and to make certain that our interpretation coheres with the thrust of the text. Achtemeier's claim that the historical tradition of the church and contemporary interpretations are also inspired does injustice to the priority of the text, which alone contains the Word of God.

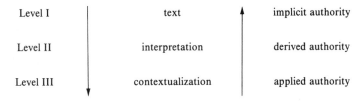

Level I	text	implicit authority
Level II	interpretation	derived authority
Level III	contextualization	applied authority

Fig. 0.1. Flow Chart on Authority.

Meaning Is Genre-Dependent

As I will argue in appendix two and in the section on special hermeneutics below, the genre or type of literature in which a passage is found provides the "rules of the language game" (Wittgenstein), that is, the hermeneutical principles by which one understands it. Obviously, we do not interpret fiction the same way as we understand poetry. Nor will a person look for the same scheme in biblical wisdom as in the prophetic portions. Yet this also occasions great debate, for there is significant overlap. For instance, large portions of the prophetic books contain poetry and other portions contain apocalyptic.

There is epistolary material in apocalyptic (such as Rev 2—3) and apocalyptic material in the Gospels (for example, the Olivet Discourse, Mk 13 and parallels) and Epistles (such as 2 Thess 2).[1] For this reason some doubt the validity of genre as an interpretive device, arguing that the intermixture of genres makes it impossible to identify genres with sufficient clarity to make them useful as hermeneutical tools. However, the very fact that we can identify apocalyptic or poetic portions within other genres demonstrates the viability of the approach (see Osborne 1984 for more detailed argumentation).

The presence of genre is an important point in the debate as to whether one can recover the author's intended meaning (Hirsch calls this "intrinsic genre"). Every writer couches his message in a certain genre in order to give the reader sufficient rules by which to decode that message. These hints guide the reader (or hearer) and provide clues for interpretation. When Mark recorded Jesus' parable of the sower (4:1-20) he placed it in a context and within a medium that would communicate properly to his readers. We can recover that meaning by understanding how parables function (see chap. eleven) and by noting how the symbols function within the Markan context.

The Simplicity and Clarity of Scripture

Since the late patristic period with its *regula fidei* ("rule of faith"), the church has wrestled with the "perspicuity of Scripture," that is, whether or not it is actually open or plain to one's understanding. It is not without reason that the biblical scholar is often charged with removing the Scriptures from the average person. After a text has been dissected and subjected to the myriad theories of academia, the layperson cries plaintively, "Yes, but what does it say to *me?* Can *I* study it?" Certainly, the very discovery of the multitudinous options for the interpretation of biblical passages is the greatest single shock to new students in college or seminary. People can hardly be blamed if, after noting the numerous possible interpretations of virtually every biblical statement, they cease to affirm the principle that the Bible is easy to understand! However, this is to confuse hermeneutical principles with the gospel message itself. It is the task of bridging the cultural gap from the original situation to our day that is complex, not the resultant meaning.

Luther (in *The Bondage of the Will*) proclaimed the basic clarity of Scripture in two areas: external clarity, which he called the grammatical aspect, attained by applying the laws of grammar (hermeneutical principles) to the text; and internal clarity, which he called the spiritual aspect, attained when the Holy Spirit illumines the reader in the act of interpretation. It is clear that Luther meant the final product (the gospel message) rather than the process (recovering the meaning of individual texts) when he spoke of clarity. In the last century, however, the application of Scottish Common Sense Realism to Scripture has led many to assume that everyone can understand the Bible for themselves, that the surface of the text is sufficient to produce meaning in and of itself. Therefore, the need for hermeneutical principles to bridge the cultural gap was ignored, and individualistic interpretations abounded. For some reason, no one seemed to notice that this led to multiple meanings. The principle of perspicuity was extended to the hermeneutical process as well, leading to misunderstanding in popular interpretation of

Scripture and a very difficult situation today. Hermeneutics as a discipline demands a complex interpretive process in order to uncover the original clarity of Scripture.

Yet this in itself causes confusion, and the average person is again justified in asking whether biblical understanding is increasingly being reserved for the academic elite. I would argue that it is not. First, there are many levels of understanding: devotional, basic Bible study, sermonic, term paper or dissertation. Each level has its own validity and its own process. Furthermore, those who wish to learn the hermeneutical principles that pertain to these various levels may do so. They are not restricted to any "elite" but are available to all who have the interest and energy to learn them. Basic hermeneutics can and should be taught at the level of the local church. I hope to address these various levels throughout this book.

The Unity and Diversity of Scripture

A failure to grasp the balance between these two interdependent aspects has caused both evangelicals (stressing the unity) and nonevangelicals (stressing the diversity) to misread the Scriptures. Diversity is demanded by the analogical cast of biblical language. Since few books in Scripture were addressed to similar situations, there is great variety in wording and emphasis. Moreover, the doctrine of inspiration itself demands that we recognize the personalities of the sacred authors behind their works. Each writer expressed himself in different ways, with different emphases and quite different figures of speech. For instance, John used "new birth" language to express the concept of regeneration, while Paul used the image of adoption. Also, Paul stressed the faith that alone could lead to regeneration, while James emphasized the works that alone could point to a valid faith. These are not contradictory but diverse emphases of individual writers.

The issue is whether the differences are irreconcilable, or whether a deeper unity underlies the diverse expressions of the various traditions in Israel and the early church. J. D. G. Dunn in *Unity and Diversity in the New Testament* argues for the almost complete diversity of the early church, saying the one unifying thread is the continuity between the historical Jesus and the exalted Lord. However, the very evidence he adduces points to a far greater unity. This unity began with Christology *(contra* Dunn's later *The Making of Christology)* and went beyond to bibliology (adherence to the early church's creeds and the *logia Jesu*) and even to ecclesiology (as Paul stressed in Eph 2).

Yet we dare not overstate the unity of Scripture, so as to remove John's or Paul's individual emphases. Such can lead to a misuse of parallels, so that one author (say, Paul) is interpreted on the basis of another (John), resulting in an erroneous interpretation. Nevertheless, behind the different expressions is a critical unity. The concept of diversity is the backbone of biblical theology, which I believe is the necessary link between exegesis and systematic theology (centering upon the unity). Before we can develop a comprehensive doctrine of perseverance, for instance, we must allow John's Gospel and the Epistle to the Hebrews to speak for themselves and only then put them together. At the same time the concept of unity provides the basis for systematic theology. While it is true that the finite human can never produce a final "system" of biblical truth, it is not true that one can never "systematize" biblical truth. The key is to allow the system to emerge from the text via biblical theology, to seek biblical categories that summarize the unity behind the diverse expressions of Scripture.

The Analogy of Scripture

In contrast to the *regula fidei* ("rule of faith") of the Roman Catholic Church, Luther propounded the *analogia fidei* ("analogy of faith"). Luther opposed the centrality of ecclesial tradition and believed that Scripture alone should determine dogma. On the basis of the unity and clarity of Scripture, he proposed that the basic doctrines must cohere with and cannot contradict the holistic teaching of Scripture. However, for Luther the system still had a certain predominance. Therefore, I would suggest the *analogia scriptura* ("analogy of Scripture") as an alternative. Terry's dictum still stands: "No single statement or obscure passage of one book can be allowed to set aside a doctrine which is clearly established by many passages" (1890:579). I would strengthen this by adding that doctrines should not be built upon a single passage but rather should summarize all that Scripture says on that topic. If there are no clarifying passages (for example, on baptism for the dead in 1 Cor 15:29 or a compartmentalized Hades in Lk 16:22-26), we must be careful about seeing a statement of dogma.

Moreover, all such doctrinal statements (for instance, on the lordship of Christ or on eternal security) should be made on the basis of all the texts that speak to the issue rather than on the basis of proof-texts or "favorite" passages. Such an approach results in a "canon within a canon," a phenomenon in which certain passages are subjectively favored over others because they fit a system that is imposed on Scripture rather than drawn from it. This is a dangerous situation, for it assumes that one's preconceived ideas are more important than is the text. Also, it misinterprets Scripture. Few biblical statements are theoretical—that is, holistic—descriptions of dogma. Rather, a biblical author's statements apply a larger doctrine to a particular issue in a specific church setting and stress whatever aspect of the larger teaching applies to that situation. For instance, Paul's epistles are occasional letters addressing problems and issues in local communities rather than theological treatises summarizing doctrine. This does not mean that they are not theological; rather, the epistles take one aspect of a larger theology (which we derive from a "biblical theology" approach; see chapter thirteen) and apply it to the situation addressed. Therefore, to establish a doctrine we must place all the statements on the issue side by side and work out how best to summarize scriptural teaching on the topic. The *analogia scriptura* is the method by which we do this.

The Progress of Revelation

It has long been realized that God revealed himself in stages to his people. An important correlative to the *analogia scriptura* is the delineation of further revelation developed throughout the biblical period. When we trace the biblical teaching on subjects like polygamy or slavery, it is critical to recognize the historical development of those doctrines in Scripture. However, the later passages do not replace the earlier; rather, they clarify the earlier passages and show that they formed a mere stage in the developing understanding of the people of God. For instance, Paul's discussion of the ethics of the servant-master in Ephesians 6:5-9 or Colossians 3:22 should not be used to "prove" the validity of the institution of slavery. Rather, the principle of equality in Galatians 3:28 or Philemon 16 as well as the fact that slavery was strictly controlled for the Hebrew (according to Ex 21:2 or Lev 25:47-55 the Hebrew could be indentured but had to be freed at the Sabbath or Jubilee years) eventually eroded the system.

Expository Preaching

It is my contention that the final goal of hermeneutics is not systematic theology but the sermon. The actual purpose of Scripture is not explanation but exposition, not description but proclamation. God's Word speaks to every generation, and the relationship between meaning and significance summarizes the hermeneutical task. It is not enough to recreate the original intended meaning of a passage. We must elucidate its significance for our day.

Walter Liefeld (1984:6-7) says that an expository message has hermeneutical integrity (faithfully reproduces the text), cohesion (a sense of the whole), movement and direction (noting the purpose or goal of a passage) and application (noting the contemporary relevance of the passage). Without each of these qualities, a sermon is not truly expository. Some have a false concept of exposition as a mere explanation of the meaning of a passage. Complex overhead transparencies and presentation of the Hebrew or Greek details highlight such sermons. Unfortunately, although the people go away impressed by the learning demonstrated, their lives often remain untouched. The "horizon" of the listeners must be fused with the "horizon" of the text in true expository preaching (see the discussion of Gadamer in appendix one). The preacher must ask how the biblical writer would have applied the theological truths of the passage if he were addressing them to the modern congregation.

Robinson defines expository preaching as "the communication of a biblical concept, derived from and transmitted through a historical, grammatical, literary study of a passage in its context, which the Holy Spirit first applies to the personality of the preacher, then through him to his hearers" (1980:30). This is an excellent definition and touches upon several issues discussed above. Modern expositors must first encounter the text in its original situation and then the significance of that original meaning for themselves. They then transmit this to the audience, who should be led first into the biblical context and then into its relevance for their personal needs. Too often preachers stress one side or the other, so that the sermon becomes either dry exposition or dynamic entertainment. Both spheres, the original meaning of the text and the modern significance for our context, are critical in expository preaching, the true goal of the hermeneutical enterprise.

Conclusion

The process of interpretation consists of ten stages, all of which are taken up in turn in this book (see figure 0.2). Exegetical research can be subdivided into inductive study (in which we interact with the text directly to form our own conclusions) and deductive study (in which we interact with other scholars' conclusions and rework our findings). The inductive study of the Bible takes place primarily in the charting of the book and

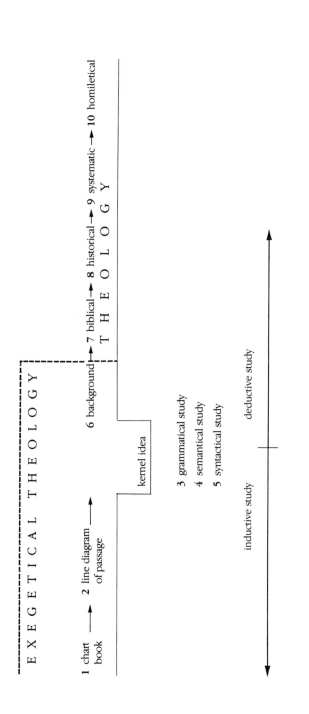

Fig. 0.2. The Ten Stages of Interpretation.

paragraphs in order to determine the structural development of the writer's message at both the macro (book) and micro (paragraph) levels. The result is a preliminary idea regarding the meaning and thought development of the text. This is important so that we interact with exegetical tools (commentaries and so forth) critically rather than uncritically, merely parroting the views of others (an all too common problem in term papers).

Deductive study utilizes stages 3-6 together as separate but interdependent aspects of exegetical research. Here all the tools—grammars, lexicons, dictionaries, word studies, atlases, background studies, periodical articles, commentaries—are consulted in order to deepen our knowledge base regarding the passage and to unlock the in-depth message under the surface of the text. The preliminary understanding derived from the inductive study and the in-depth understanding unlocked through research interact and correct one another as we make final decisions regarding the original intended message of the text.

One major purpose of deductive study is to take us away from the contemporary meaning of the word-symbols in the text, which, because of our preunderstanding and personal experiences, we cannot help but read back into the text. Our effort then is to get back to the meaning the ancient author intended to convey. We could not do this without exegetical tools, for without help we know too little about that ancient period. Therefore we must use the inductive and deductive sides together to understand the "meaning" of the text.

Finally, the contextual or theological research completes the task of interpretation, moving us from the textual meaning (what the Bible meant) to the contextual meaning (what the Bible means for us today). The "hermeneutical spiral" takes place not only at the level of original intended meaning, as our understanding spirals upward (via the interaction of inductive and deductive research) to the intended meaning of the passage, but also at the level of contextualization, as our application spirals upward (via the movement from biblical to systematic to homiletical theology) to a proper understanding of the significance of the passage for Christian life today. Biblical theology collates the partial theologies of individual passages and books into an archetypal "theology" of Israel and the early church (thus integrating the Testaments). Historical theology studies the way the church throughout history has contextualized biblical theology to meet the challenges and needs of the church at various stages of its historical development. Systematic theology recontextualizes biblical theology to address current problems and to summarize theological truth for the current generation. Finally, homiletical theology (so-called to stress that the sermon preparation is part of the hermeneutical task) applies the results of each of these steps to the practical needs of Christians today.

The figure itself is adapted from Nida and Taber's study of the process of translation (1974). The theory is based on the belief that the crosscultural communication of ideas is never a straight-line continuum, for no two languages or cultures are linked that closely. A "literal" or unitary approach always lead to miscommunication. Instead, each communication unit must be broken up into "kernel ideas," or basic statements, and then reformulated along the lines of the corresponding idioms and thought patterns of the receptor culture. This is necessary not only at the basic level of translation but also at the broader level of interpretation as a whole. It is the exegetical aspect (grammar, semantics, syntax) which uncovers the kernel ideas, and the process of contextualization which reformulates them so that they speak with the same voice to our culture today.

Readers will note that I have placed the discussion of the biblical genres not at the end of the book (many hermeneutical texts place this last as "special hermeneutics") but after the presentation of the general hermeneutical principles. Since the genres are concerned primarily with "what it meant" (the original intended meaning of the text), the discussion logically belongs at that point. Moreover, each genre provides a "case study," reapplying the exegetical principles to each separate type of biblical literature.

Readers will also note that I have used transliterated Greek and Hebrew throughout most of the text, with the exception of chapter two on grammar. My editors and I have thought that this would allow those who do not regularly use Greek and Hebrew to follow the discussion and perhaps observe some matters regarding vocabulary. The technical matters in chapter two require that readers be able to use the original languages; therefore, it seemed easier there to simply make use of Greek and Hebrew script.

Part 1
*G*eneral Hermeneutics

1
*C*ontext

T HE FIRST STAGE IN SERIOUS BIBLE STUDY IS TO CONSIDER THE LARGER CONTEXT WITHIN which a passage is found. Unless we can grasp the whole before attempting to dissect the parts, interpretation is doomed from the start. Statements simply have no meaning apart from their context. If I say, "Give it all you've got," you would rightly query, "What do you mean by 'it'?" and "How do I do so?" Without a situation to give the command content, it becomes meaningless. In Scripture the context provides the situation behind the text.

Two areas must be considered at the beginning of Bible study: the historical context and the logical context. Under the first category we study introductory material on the biblical book in order to determine the situation to which the book was addressed. Under the second category we use an inductive approach in order to trace the thought development of a book. Both aspects are necessary before we begin a detailed analysis of a particular passage. The historical and logical contexts provide the scaffolding upon which we can build the in-depth meaning of a passage. Without a strong scaffolding, the edifice of interpretation is bound to collapse.

The Historical Context
Information on the historical background of a book is available from several sources. Perhaps the best single source is the introduction to the better commentaries. Many contain quite detailed, up-to-date summaries of the issues. It is important to consult recent, well-researched works because of the explosion of information uncovered in the last few decades. Older works will not have information on the exciting archeological discoveries or the theories coming out of the recent application of background material to a biblical book. Old or New Testament introductions are also a tremendous help, since they interact more broadly than a commentary normally does. A third source would be dictionaries and encyclopedias, with separate articles not only on books but on authors, themes and background issues. Archeological works and atlases enable us to grasp the topography behind a book. With books like Joshua or Judges, indeed all historical narrative, this is a critical consideration. Books on Old or New Testament theology (such as Ladd) often aid one in discovering the theology of individual books. Finally, books

on customs and culture in the biblical period are invaluable sources to help us grasp the historical background behind particular emphases in the text.

At this stage we are using secondary sources to learn preliminary data for interpreting a text (we will use them later when we begin the exegetical study). The information we gather from them is not final truth but rather becomes a blueprint, a basic plan that we can alter later when the edifice of interpretation is actually being erected. These ideas are held by someone else, and our later detailed study may lead us to change many of the ideas. The value of this preliminary reading is that it draws us out of our twentieth-century perspective and makes us aware of the ancient situation behind the text. We need to consider several aspects here.

1. In one sense the *authorship* is more important for historical-critical research than for grammatical-historical exegesis. However, this aspect still helps us to place a book historically. For example, when studying the minor prophets, we need to know when and to whom Amos or Zechariah ministered so that we can be aware of the situation behind their actual statements. It is also helpful to know what kind of ministry they had and what their background was. A good introduction will recreate the historical era within which a book was written. This is an invaluable interpretive tool, since the words of the text were addressed to that original culture and cannot be understood properly apart from that culture.

2. The *date* when a particular work was written also gives the reader an interpretive set of tools for unlocking the meaning of a text. Daniel would mean something quite different if it were written during the period of the Maccabees. First Timothy would take on a different hue if it were written in the latter part of the first century by a disciple of Paul. James would be interpreted differently if it were addressed to a diasporate community of A.D. 110 (as Dibelius theorizes). I would argue for the traditional view in all three cases, and it makes a difference in the way I approach the text. Also, if I place the book of Revelation at the time of Nero (A.D. 60s) or Domitian (A.D. 90s), I will see different backgrounds for many of the symbols.

3. The group to which a work is *addressed* plays a major role in the meaning of a passage. Their circumstances determine the content of the book. Of course, this is more a problem in the New Testament, since the Old Testament works were always addressed to Israel. Nevertheless, the situation behind the prophetic books (such as the state of the nation in Isaiah's day) is critical for understanding the message of those works. It does make a difference whether the Epistle to the Hebrews was addressed to a Jewish, Gentile or mixed church. In actual fact, the latter is the most likely, although the problem was Jewish. A few years ago a fellow delivered a paper on 1 Peter to the Evangelical Theological Society, assuming that the Epistle was addressed to a Jewish church. When he was asked what would be the implications for his paper if the addressees were both Jewish and Gentile, he had to admit that it would radically alter his thesis. In actual fact, 1 Peter was indeed written to a mixed congregation.

4. The *purpose* and *themes* are probably the most important of the four areas as an aid to interpretation. We should not study any passage without a basic knowledge of the problems and situation addressed in the book and the themes with which the writer

addressed those problems. Without realizing that John was fighting an incipient Gnosticism in his first epistle, one could easily misread the polemical tone of 1:8-10. Only recently have commentaries begun to discuss the biblical theology of individual books. Yet such is immensely helpful as an interpretive tool. By noting the broader perspective of a book, we can more easily interpret correctly the details of particular statements. To realize that Luke centers upon salvation (history) while stressing other themes like the Holy Spirit, worship and social concern helps greatly when we try to understand parables like the rich man and Lazarus (chap. 16).

The information we glean from the sources becomes a filter through which the individual passages may be passed. This preliminary material is open to later correction during the detailed exegesis or study of the passage. Its purpose is to narrow down the interpretive laws so that we might ask the proper questions, forcing us back to the times and culture of the original writer and the situation behind the text. We will therefore have a control against reading twentieth-century meaning back into first-century language. Such an approach leads to the proper type of preunderstanding, linked as it is to the text and its background. At the same time, this information too must be placed in front of the text rather than behind it; that is, it must be open to correction as we study individual passages in detail. This data must never be allowed to force the text in its own direction, for it is secondary rather than primary knowledge until we have studied the text itself.

The Logical Context

In a very real sense, the logical context is the most basic factor in interpretation. I tell my classes that if anyone is half asleep and does not hear a question that I ask, there is a fifty per cent chance of being correct if he or she answers "context." The term itself covers a vast array of influences upon a text. These can best be diagrammed as a series of concentric circles moving outward from the passage itself (see figure 1.1).

As we move nearer the center, the influence upon the meaning of the passage increases. Genre, for instance, identifies the type of literature and helps the interpreter to identify parallels, but these are not as influential as the rest of Scripture is on the passage. We can, for example, identify the book of Revelation as apocalyptic; yet although intertestamental and Hellenistic apocalyptic provide important parallels, most of the symbols are taken from the Old Testament. At the other end of the scale, the immediate context is the final arbiter for all decisions regarding the meaning of a term or concept. There is no guarantee that Paul uses a term the same way in Philippians 1 as he does in Philippians 2. Language simply does not work that way, for every word has many meanings and a writer's use depends upon the present context rather than his use of it in previous contexts. A good example would be the use of *aphiemi* in John 14:27, "Peace I *leave* with you," and in 16:28, "I am *leaving* the world again." We would hardly interpret the one by the other, for their use is exactly opposite. In the first Jesus gives something to the disciples, in the second he takes something (himself!) away from them. Even less would we read into the term its common use (as in 1 Jn 1:9) for "forgiveness." The other passages help us to determine the semantic range (the different things the word might mean), but only the immediate context can narrow the possibilities to the actual meaning.

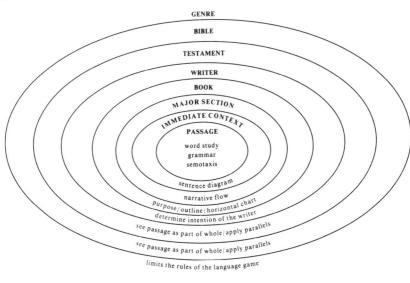

Fig. 1.1. The Logical Context.

Figure 1.1 also describes the succeeding chapters. Two aspects comprise what is often called "inductive Bible study"; namely, charting the whole of a book and diagramming the paragraph. An inductive approach normally means an intensive, personal study of a text without recourse to other study aids or tools like commentaries. I move immediately from the text and make my own conclusions about its meaning rather than use someone else's conclusions to understand it. This critical control protects me from being overly influenced by the commentaries and other sources as I study the text more deeply. I must first form my own opinions before I can interact with other people's conclusions. Otherwise, I will simply parrot these other ideas. The introductory material draws me into the stancient situation behind the biblical passage, and my inductive study gives me preliminary data with which I can critically assess the commentaries.[1]

1. Studying the Whole: Charting a Book. An invaluable service for biblical scholarship has been provided by literary criticism in the last decade. Unfortunately, through the influence of form criticism, the emphasis to date has been upon isolated parts rather than upon the whole of a section, and scholars have dissected books into separate and independent units before analyzing their meaning. Commentaries have furthered this unbalanced approach due to an overemphasis upon word studies that have been strung together with little or no cohesion. Literary critics have pointed out, however, that the parts have no meaning apart from the whole. Only when the message of the whole passage is considered can the parts be studied for details of this central message. In reality, the hermeneutical process can be summarized in this way: first, we chart the whole of a book to analyze its flow of thought in preliminary fashion; next, we study each part intensively in order to detect the detailed argumentation; finally, we rework the thought-development of the whole in relation to the parts.

Adler and Van Doren in their classic *How to Read a Book* (1972:16-20) discuss four levels of reading: (1) elementary reading, which centers upon the identity of individual terms and sentences; (2) inspectional reading, which skims a book to discover its basic structure and major ideas; (3) analytical reading, which studies the book in-depth in order to understand its message as completely as possible; (4) syntopical reading, which compares the message with other books of a similar nature in order to construct a detailed and original analysis of the subject matter. The first two levels are inductive, the latter two are research-oriented, involving secondary literature (interpretations of the book or subject by others) as well as primary literature (the text itself).

Adler and Van Doren develop inspectional reading, the subject of this section, in two ways (1972:32-44). First, a prereading examines the introductory sections (preface, table of contents, index) and then skims key chapters and paragraphs in order to ascertain the basic progress and general thread of the work. In a biblical book this would entail the introduction and section headings (if using a study Bible) plus a perusal of particular chapters (such as Rom 1; 3; 6; 9; 12). Second, a superficial reading plows right through the book without pausing to ponder individual paragraphs or difficult concepts. This enables us to chronicle and understand the major ideas before we get lost in the particular details.

I would like to expand this inspectional reading to cover structural development and call this method a "book chart" (Osborne and Woodward 1979:29-32). Here it is critical to use a good paragraph Bible. We must remember that verse and chapter divisions were never inspired. In fact, the Bible was never versified until 1551, when a Parisian publisher, Stephanus, divided the whole Bible into verses over a six-month period as he publicized his latest Greek version. Tradition says Stephanus did it while riding his horse, and the subsequent divisions were the result of the horse jostling his pen! Stephanus's version became so popular that no one dared tamper with the results, and his divisions have continued to this day. The problem is that Stephanus often chose both verse and chapter divisions poorly, yet people tend to assume that his decisions were correct and interpret verses and chapters apart from the context around them. Therefore, we should never depend on verse divisions for meaning. The paragraph is the key to the thought-development of biblical books.[2]

When teaching Bible study method seminars to church groups, I have discovered that the most difficult thing for the novice to learn is how to skim each paragraph and summarize its main point. People get bogged down in details and never seem to surface for air. We need an overview here, and the student should try to write a six- to eight-word summary for each paragraph. When we read the paragraph in too detailed a way, the summary statement often reflects only the first couple of sentences early in the paragraph rather than the paragraph as a whole. Such an error can skew the results of the entire study. In figures 1.2 and 1.3, I use Jonah[3] and Philippians as examples to demonstrate how the process can work in both testaments.

As the Jonah chart shows, each paragraph is encapsulated briefly in turn, and by

Chap. 1	Chap. 2	Chap. 3	Chap. 4
1-3 Command to preach; rebellion and flight 4-12 God's storm, the sailor's fear 13-16 Sailors obey, throw Jonah overboard 17 Wall-to-wall whale	1-5 Prayer: Jonah's distress 6-9 Prayer: Jonah's faith 10 Jonah expelled	1-3a Command repeated; Jonah obeys 3b-9 Preaching and Nineveh's repentence 10 God's forgiveness	1-4 Jonah resents; God questions 5-8 God's lesson 1: vine withers, Jonah resents 9-11 God's lesson 2: divine compassion

Fig. 1.2. Chart of Jonah.

Chap. 1	Chap. 2	Chap. 3	Chap. 4
1-2 Salutation 3-8 Thanksgiving for fellowship and sharing 9-11 Prayer for their love and discernment 12-14 His imprisonment advances the gospel 15-18a Rejoices when his opponents preach 18b-26 Will rejoice whether freed or executed 27-30 Unity in spite of persecution	1-4 Unity and humility rather than conceit 5-11 Christ's example in humiliation and exaltation 12-13 Responsibility and empowering from God 14-18 Witness rather than complain and fight 19-24 Timothy commended for his genuine interest 25-30 Epaphroditus commended for risking his life	1-4a Warning against the Judaizers 4b-6 Paul's greater credentials 7-11 All loss to gain Christ 12-14 Striving for more of Christ 15-16 Call to heed 17-21 Contrast between true and false teachers	1 Stand firm 2-3 Plea for harmony 4-7 Exhortations to rejoice, be gentle, and pray for anxieties 8-9 Think and do the right things 10-13 Joy and contentment in their sharing and Christ's provision 14-19 Joy and contentment explained further 20-23 Doxology and closing greetings

Fig. 1.3. Chart of Philippians.

perusing the summaries we can gain a very real feel for the flow of thought. Moreover, by looking across the chart the basic contours of the book become visible. For instance, we can see easily that chapter 3 gives the results of the original purpose of chapter 1, namely, the mission to Nineveh and the people's repentance. Thus there are two parallel sections, chapters 1 and 3 and chapters 2 and 4. Further, the emphasis is on the latter pair, so that Jonah is not so much about mission as about Jonah's (and Israel's) attitudes toward God and those upon whom God shows compassion. Chapter 4 contains the actual "moral of the story," a lesson about divine compassion.

If we were to label chapter 4 "Jonah's anger" or "anger answered," we would miss the crucial point that Jonah learned the meaning of divine forgiveness. Therefore, each heading must catch the essence of the paragraph. However, we must remember also that this is a preliminary overview and will be subject to correction if the detailed exegesis so warrants. This sort of overview of a book the length of Jonah or Philippians should take forty to forty-five minutes.[4]

Let us now go more deeply into the process and explore the stages by which the chart approach proceeds.

a. The most efficient way to skim the paragraphs is with pen in hand. I try to summarize as I read. This helps enormously with my concentration. The major problem when skimming a text (or reading more carefully, for that matter) is a wandering mind. I often discover after reading a paragraph that my mind has shifted to a current problem or the events of the day, with the result that I must repeat the process (sometimes several times!). If I take notes as I go, stressing first impressions, I am able to concentrate far better. Also, I attempt to catch the progression of thought in a section (for instance, in the series of exhortations in Phil 4:4-7; see chart), whenever a single summary is not possible. Again, taking notes as I skim helps tremendously. The value of the process is that the chart becomes a map tracing the flow of the entire book. When studying individual passages more deeply later, I can at a glance determine the progression of thought surrounding that statement.

b. After charting the book, it is time to return and look for patterns of thought in the progression of the book's paragraphs. As we detect breaks of thought between paragraphs, we should indicate them with a single line (see the chart above). Paragraphs with similar material form major sections of the book and greater precision results. Some breaks of thought are quite easy to detect, such as the switch from Paul's personal comments (1:12-26) to the Philippian situation (1:27-28) or the further switch from the Philippians to Paul's commendation of Timothy and Epaphroditus (2:19-30). Other changes are not so easy to detect, such as the slight alteration from humility (2:1-11) to warning (2:12-18), or placing 4:1 with 3:17-21 rather than 4:2-9. In the latter case, the reader can make only an educated guess at this stage and should wait for later clarification as he or she exegetes the book in detail.

This is why I include both Jonah and Philippians here. Jonah is one of the few biblical books whose outline follows the chapter divisions, thus providing a relatively simple example. The only question in Jonah is whether 1:17 is the conclusion of chapter 1 or the introduction to chapter 2. Philippians is far more complex and demands more careful thought. It is an example of didactic or teaching material rather than narrative or story (like Jonah). As such the breaks are more discontinuous (such as between 2:25-30 and 3:1-6) and the progression of the book as a whole is not so easy to ascertain. Nevertheless, the process in both cases will help the student to understand the thought-progression of the book as a whole.

Another difficulty is the method for noting major pattern breaks. While every biblical passage has a meaningful organization, the pattern of thought often is not easy to detect. Stuart states: "Try to identify the patterns, looking especially for key features such as developments, resumptions, unique forms of phrase, central or pivotal words, parallelisms, chiasms, inclusions, and other repetitions or progressive patterns. The keys to patterns are most often *repetition* and *progression*"(1980:36; italics his). Kaiser provides greater detail, listing eight "clues" for discovering such "seams" between units of thought (1981:71-72):

1. A repeated term, phrase, clause or sentence may act as the heading to introduce each part or as the colophon (tailpiece) to conclude each individual section.

2. Often there may be grammatical clues such as transitional conjunctions or adverbs; for example, "then, therefore, wherefore, but, nevertheless, meanwhile," and the Greek words *oun, de, kai, tote, dio.*

3. A rhetorical question could signal a switch to a new theme and section. It may be that there also will be a series of such questions which carries forward the argument or plan of a whole section.

4. A change in the time, location or setting is a frequent device, especially in narrative contexts, to indicate a new theme and section.

5. A vocative form of address deliberately showing a shift of attention from one group to another constitutes one of the most important devices. It is often used in the epistolary type of literature.

6. A change in the tense, mood or aspect of the verb perhaps even with a change in the subject or object may be another clue that a new section is beginning.

7. Repetition of the same key word, proposition or concept might also indicate the boundaries of a section.

8. In a few cases, the theme of each section will be announced as a heading to that section. In those unusual cases, the interpreter need only make sure that all of the contents of the section are judged in light of the stated purpose of the author.

These basic types of breaks will aid us as we skim the paragraphs and summarize the contents. By being aware of the possibilities, we often can determine a break of thought even while preparing the chart. Even more, these breaks will be of service as we begin the more detailed exegesis.

c. The final step is to subdivide the sections further into major units by virtue of double lines. This will be especially valuable in didactic books like Philippians. The process is the same as the previous stage but now involves larger thought units than paragraphs, building upon the results of stage two. After completing the process, it would be helpful to compare the results with the commentaries and introductions we have gathered for the exegetical study. We might even indicate the results on the chart (for example, put the names of commentators like Ralph Martin [Tyndale series on Philippians] or Gerald Hawthorne [Word series on Philippians] beside the places where they see major section breaks) for comparison's sake in order to guide our thoughts in future study. However, it is crucial not to check the secondary sources until we have done our own work inductively at the beginning. Otherwise, we are too easily controlled by another person's opinions. The inductive study provides an important check against blindly following commentaries so that every reader seeks always his or her own interpretation rather than merely parrots this or that scholar's observations.

This method, however, will not work with Psalms and Proverbs. (It will work with individual psalms but not the collection as a whole.) Although many have attempted to group the psalms in various ways, a topical organizational pattern is superior. The same is true with Proverbs: those portions which have linear development (such as chaps. 1—9 or 31) can be charted, but the collection of proverbs cannot be studied easily as a connected whole (see chaps. seven and eight below).

In addition, we might validly ask whether the method will work for longer books like Isaiah or Jeremiah. While it is more difficult, I earnestly believe that it is quite helpful. Let me illustrate with not only a longer work but one of the most difficult portions of Scripture, the book of Revelation. Rather than take the space for a full-length chart (which I recommend for the reader), I will discuss the structural implications (steps two and three). As we look for patterns in the text, it becomes obvious that the Apocalypse is organized in cyclical fashion along spatial lines. A glance at the chart will demonstrate that chapters 1, 4—5, 7 (10), 14—15 and 19:1-10 take place in heaven while chapters 2—3, 6, 8—9, 11—13 and 16—18 occur on earth. The concluding section (19:11—22:2) unites heaven and earth. Moreover, within this alternating pattern, the heavenly scenes are dominated by praise and worship while the earthly scenes are increasingly characterized by chaos, agony and divine judgment. The best proof of this pattern is the relationship between the seals, trumpets and bowls. By using the inductive chart we can see that their organizational pattern is the same. Therefore, the seals, trumpets and bowls are organized in cycles and are characterized by a progressive intensification of judgment and doom (in 6:8 a quarter of the earth is affected, in 7:7-8 a third of the earth, and in 16:3-4 all the earth). The contrast between the heaven and earth scenes points to the unifying theme of the book, divine sovereignty (the vertical dimension), and leads to the horizontal dimension, which asks the church to put its trust in God in spite of present and future sufferings.[5]

Again, I must stress that this is a preliminary rather than a final outline. It represents the reader's viewpoint and not necessarily the original author's (which must await further study). Meyer and Rice (1982:155-92) demonstrate how differing reader strategies produce different organizational charts for a text, though they admit that "the reader's task . . . is to construct a cognitive representation of the text which is similar to that intended by the writer" (p. 156). The control group studied a text on railroads to ascertain how the individual strategies affected their view of the structure of the text. Needless to say, their varied expectations led to their seeing quite different organizations in the text. We must recognize the ease with which our own presuppositions affect our view of the text. The reader plays a crucial role in the inductive process, and deeper study is necessary before one can arrive at the writer's intended plan. However, the inductive method still is invaluable for providing perspective in the process of interpretation.

2. Studying the Parts: Diagramming the Paragraph. When we try to chart the smaller unit (the paragraph) in similar fashion to the larger unit (the book), a vertical chart is better than the horizontal chart used previously, since the unit is smaller. For this type of study I recommend the New American Standard Bible (NASB) for those not familiar with the languages. Though not as fluent as other versions, its literal nature makes the NASB the closest approximation to the Hebrew or Greek. Thus the student can see more closely the original patterns of the biblical authors. Several possible diagramming models are available (we will use Eph 1:5-7 as our control). Many Greek exegesis courses use a complicated diagramming procedure (see figure 1.4) in which each term is placed under

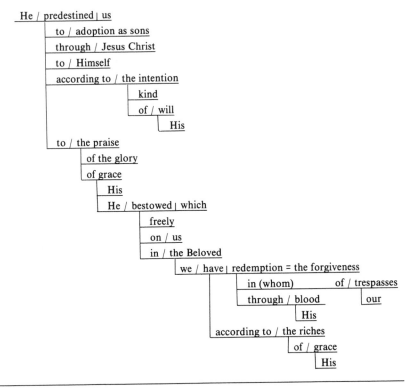

Fig. 1.4. Grammatical Diagram of Ephesians 1:5-7.

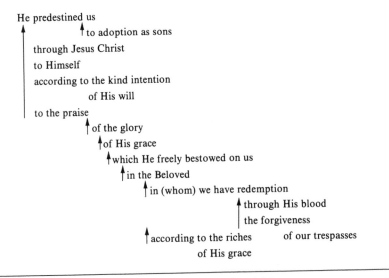

Fig. 1.5. Phrase or Sentence Flow Diagram of Ephesians 1:5-7.

He predestined us to adoption as sons through Jesus Christ to Himself,
    according to the kind intention of His will,
    | to the praise of the glory of His grace
        which He freely bestowed on us in the Beloved,
          in (whom) we have | redemption through His blood
                          | the forgiveness of our trespasses
          | according to the riches of His grace[6]

Fig. 1.6. Block or Line Diagram of Ephesians 1:5-7.

the word it modifies and the relationship is explained (see Grassmick). Gordon Fee (1983:60-76) suggests a sentence flow diagram (figure 1.5) that is similar to, but not as complicated as, the grammatical chart method. Both place the subject, predicate and object at the top left-hand corner of the page and indent the subordinate terms under the words or phrases that they modify. Fee suggests annotations to explain grammatical decisions and color-coding for repeated words or themes.

I prefer the simpler block diagram (figure 1.6) to word or phrase diagrams (figures 1.4 and 1.5), for it functions at the clause level and provides a better overview. The other two methods diagram every word or phrase, while the block diagram charts only major and minor clauses (or lengthy phrases). These are larger building blocks of speech, and so the three charts function at increasingly broader levels—word, phrase or clause. The block method does have some disadvantages; for instance, it does not demonstrate as many details as the other two. However, three advantages outweigh this weakness: (1) it is simpler and takes less time, thus encouraging the busy pastor or layperson to continue using it;[7] (2) most of the other relationships (such as adjectives, modifying nouns, adverbs or prepositional phrases modifying verbs) are fairly self-evident from the clause structure; (3) the purpose of the sentence diagram is to visualize as simply as possible the thought-flow of a paragraph rather than to decide grammatical details. The other two methods introduce too many visual complexities to do this well. Grammatical details become more evident during the exegetical study (chaps. 2-5), but at this early stage such details may hurt more than help. Grammar is best left for a later stage in the process. Moreover, at the later exegetical stage diagramming is not as important because we want to clarify details within the sentence rather than to visualize thought-flow. Therefore, the sentence diagram will serve our purpose better than the detailed grammatical diagram.

The first thing to do in the sentence diagram is to distinguish between major and minor clauses. It is amazing how little of this is done in our educational system. I normally ask my Greek classes when they last had grammar or diagramming, and the majority have had nothing since junior high; several English majors have had nothing in their university courses! Therefore, it is not surprising when we admit that we know little about such things.

Clauses are those portions of the sentence which contain a subject and a predicate, for instance, "I saw the boy" (main clause) or "because I saw the boy" (subordinate or minor clause). The difference between the two is that the first can stand alone as a sentence while the second cannot. When reading through a biblical sentence for the first time, I find the best way to distinguish is to read each clause out loud to myself to see which ones form incomplete sentences and which can indeed stand by themselves.

For instance, let us consider Philippians 2:6 (diagrammed below). Again I prefer a literal version like the New American Standard, since it is closer to the original Greek and Hebrew and so is a better study Bible (of course, those who know Greek or Hebrew will use them). Philippians 2:6 reads, "who, although He existed in the form of God, did not regard equality with God a thing to be grasped." Here the "who" introduces the marvelous incarnational hymn of 2:6-11 and so should be considered a noun ("Christ Jesus" in v. 5). When we read the verse orally, it becomes evident that "although He existed in the form of God" cannot exist by itself as a sentence and so is subordinate to the main clause, "He . . . did not regard equality with God a thing to be grasped." For the diagram, we indent minor clauses one-half inch or so and indicate the clause they modify with an arrow.

     ↓ although He existed in the form of God

who . . . did not regard equality with God a thing to be grasped.

Many like to indent each clause under the term it modifies. While this provides a good visual aid, I find it unwieldy. Many subordinate clauses will modify the last word in a clause, and this takes an inordinate amount of space. Moreover, Paul is famous for his convoluted sentences. For instance, Ephesians 1:3-14 is a single, impossibly complex sentence. To diagram it in this fashion would take a horizontal scroll eight feet wide rather than a sheet of paper! I find it better to indent a half inch and place the arrow under the clause that it modifies.

There are several aspects to note in a block diagram (figure 7). First, the arrows should point to the term modified, while the subordinate clauses or phrases are indented a half inch past the clause they modify. Second, there is often a series of indented clauses, as minor clauses modify other minor clauses. This is one of the major values of a sentence diagram, for it will visualize such complicated relationships and simplify greatly our understanding of the thought-flow. Third, parallel clauses or phrases are linked together either by an arrow (if they are subordinate like the two prepositional phrases of Eph 1:5-6 above) or by a bar (if they are not subordinate like the two nouns of v. 7). What we find in Ephesians 1:5-7 is a flow of four successive subordinate relationships. If we were to string these out, it would take a great deal of space. It is simpler and more efficient to employ arrows to do the work for us. Arrows also enable us to follow the order of the text and therefore to avoid confusion.[8] Minor clauses that come first have arrows pointing down (see diagram of Phil 2:6 below) and those which come after have arrows pointing up (such as Eph 1:5-7 above).

Perhaps the best means for detecting clauses in the biblical text is to study the connecting words. This is especially true for biblical study because of the frequent employment of conjunctions in both Hebrew and Greek. We must ask whether it is a coordinating conjunction (and, but, yet, both—and, not only—but also, either—or, therefore, for, so)[9] that indicates a parallel or main clause, or a subordinating conjunction (unless, before, after, while, when, since, because, that, if, although, though, so that, in order that, except, as, then, where) that indicates a modifying clause.

We can also state the basic type of subordinating relationship by developing a series of codes for the various syntactical relationships (such as *T* for temporal, *Ca* for causal, *Cn* for concessive, *Cd* for conditional, *R* for result, *Rel* for relative, *P* for purpose, *Me* for means, *Ma* for manner, *I* for instrumental). These codes can be written beside the arrow so that a glance can show the pattern of subordinate clauses in the paragraph. Let me demonstrate by diagramming the entire incarnational hymn of Philippians 2:6-11 (see figure 1.7).

Although He existed in the form of God
    C ↓
who . . . did not regard equality with God a thing to be grasped
(but) emptied Himself
Me ↑
  | taking the form of a bond-servant
  | and being made in the likeness of men
Me |
  ↓ and being found in appearance as a man
He humbled Himself
  Me ↑ by becoming obedient to the point to death,
        even death on a cross.
Therefore also God | highly exalted Him
       | and bestowed on Him the name
             ↑ *Rel*
      which is above every name
  ↑ that at the name of Jesus every knee should bow
  | | those who are in heaven
P | | and on earth, and
  | | under the earth[10]
  | and that every tongue should confess . . . to the glory of God the Father
                     |
    that Jesus Christ is Lord.

Fig. 1.7. Diagram of Philippians 2:6-11 with Syntactical Codes.

This shows at a glance that the two major sections are Jesus' actions and God's actions. Under the former fall three basic ideas: Jesus' subordination, his emptying and his humility. Under the latter there is one major idea—God's act of exaltation—and two subordinate ideas—all knees bowing and all tongues confessing. As we can note immediately, this is the sermon outline in a nutshell. In fact, the block diagram leads directly to a preliminary sermon or Bible study outline. When we look at the pattern of clauses in the diagram, major and minor points suggest themselves immediately (as we saw in Phil 2:6-11).

However, there are two caveats: first, the outline, like the diagram, must remain preliminary, subject to revision as the detailed exegesis unfolds. Second, while the syntactical relationships help greatly to determine major segments of thought, they do not determine them automatically. Often, the clauses are parallel (emptying and humbling in vv. 7-8 or bowing and confessing in vv. 10-11) and should be combined into a single point. Just as important, what is subordinate grammatically at times can have equal or greater stress than the main clause in the writer's actual thought development. Paul is especially known for this. If the subordinate idea is given extensive clarification, it is a sign that the writer considers it to be a major stress. For example, Philippians 2:2 says, "Make my joy complete by being of the same mind, maintaining the same love, united in spirit, intent on one purpose." Obviously, the primary emphasis is not the completion of Paul's joy but the harmony of the Philippian church, developed in four successive subordinate phrases telling the means for bringing Paul greater joy. In the sermon outline the point would be harmony, not joy. Likewise, in the Philippians hymn the fact that Paul uses two subordinate clauses to modify emptying (v. 7) and humbling (v. 8) shows that Paul actually is emphasizing the incarnational aspects ("made in the likeness of man").

The preacher should develop the preliminary sermon outline from the line diagram. The best way is to place it alongside the diagram and line up the points. At this stage the sermon outline resembles a Bible study. But as I will argue in chapter fifteen, the text should dictate the organization of an expository sermon. If we manipulate the text to fit our preconceived message, it will no longer be the Word of God proclaimed but rather our ideas shared. Of course, there are times for such messages (topical sermons) but such is not truly expository preaching. Therefore, the outline will fit the organization of the text:

I. State of Humiliation, 2:6-8
  A. State of mind, v. 6
    1. his essence
    2. his decision
  B. State of being, vv. 7-8
    1. his incarnation, v. 7
      a. his essence
      b. his likeness
    2. his humiliation, v. 8
      a. his appearance
      b. his obedience
II. State of Exaltation, 2:9-11
  A. Exaltation by God, v. 9
    1. his new estate
    2. his great name
  B. Exaltation by man and creation, vv. 10-11

  1. exaltation via submission, v. 10
  2. exaltation via confession, v. 11
     a. universality of it
     b. contents of it
     c. result of it

Again, this is a preliminary outline, awaiting the final reworking after the completion of the exegesis. At that stage the passage can be transformed into a dynamic sermon model (see chap. sixteen; Liefeld 1984:115-20). However, as a future Bible study or sermon outline, the potential message provided by our study of Philippians 2:6-11 thus far is certainly meaningful. Only John 1:1-18 contains similar depth of theological reflection on the incarnation[11] and exaltation of Christ exhibited in this passage. The moment of incarnation is described in all three of the main clauses in the first half (vv. 6-8). It is described first negatively, as Jesus refuses the prerogatives and glory of deity (v. 6), and then positively as an emptying and a humbling, as Jesus adds to his divine nature ("form of God," v. 6) his human nature ("form of a bond-servant," v. 7, compare v. 8). This servanthood Christology forms the model or paradigm for Christian attitudes (note v. 5), which makes the exaltation passage (vv. 9-11) all the more exciting. As with Christ, we who "humble ourselves" (compare v. 3) will be exalted by God and share the glory of Christ. Of course, we do not have "the name which is above every name." However, here a parallel passage from John 17:22 will help: "The glory you have given me I have given them." When we share Jesus' attitude of humility, we will share his exaltation.

Let me also demonstrate this method with an Old Testament passage, Isaiah 40:27-31. First, we need to know the background of the passage in its larger context. Chapter 40 begins the second major section of Isaiah (chaps. 40—55), which centers upon the "servant songs" and God's universal salvific love for the nations. This opening chapter is a marvelous hymn to the omnipotence and redemptive love of God. The second half (vv. 18-31) features a series of rhetorical questions chiding Israel for her lack of faith. God is incomparable (vv. 18-20), infinitely greater than earthly or heavenly glories (vv. 21-26), and at work on behalf of his people (vv. 27-31).

Why do you say, O Jacob
      and assert, O Israel,
  My way is hidden from the Lord
  And the justice due me escapes the notice of my God?
Do you not know?
Have you not heard?
The everlasting God, the Lord, the Creator of the ends of the earth
  does not become weary or tired.
His understanding is inscrutable.
He gives strength to the weary,
And to him who lacks might He increases power.
      Though youths grow weary and tired,
  Cn And vigorous young men stumble badly,
Yet those who wait for the Lord will gain new strength;

They will mount up with wings like eagles,

They will run and not get tired,

They will walk and not become weary.

The first thing we notice about Old Testament passages is the lack of subordinate clauses. Diagramming is not nearly as helpful as in the New Testament because Hebrew does not employ as many conjunctions. Poetic passages like this one primarily contain main clauses. In prose the main conjunction or "and" clause predominates. Therefore, we must look for rhetorical patterns and see where the ideas themselves change. At this point a line diagram is still helpful, as it places the sentences side by side. In this passage the first thing we notice is that the thoughts come in pairs. Each idea is repeated to give it emphasis. Also, there is an ABA pattern after the introductory question. The first set of pairs is God-centered, telling who God is (v. 28b) and then what he gives to the needy (v. 29). The swing pair (v. 30) contrasts God's people to the vigorous warriors whose strength fails, and the final set of pairs (v. 31) shows the result of waiting on the Lord. A preliminary study outline would look like this:

Introduction—the Question of Theodicy (vv. 27-28a)

I. The God Who Acts (vv. 28b-29)

    A. Who he is (v. 28b)

    B. What he does (v. 29)

II. Receiving His Power (vv. 30-31)

    A. Those who do not (v. 30)

    B. Those who do (v. 31)

Another option would be to make verse 30 the second major point and verse 31 the third. As we study the pattern of ideas, one thing strikes us immediately: all three sections center upon athletic or military imagery, specifically upon the connection between running and weariness. God never tires, young athletes do, but the one who trusts God partakes of his strength and gains a miraculous endurance. The applicability of such a message to our present life is obvious.

3. Arcing. Dan Fuller has developed a new method for diagramming the interrelationships of a paragraph (or book), which he calls the "arcing" method (chap. four of his unpublished hermeneutics syllabus at Fuller Seminary). This is based upon the same premise as the block diagram but is horizontal rather than vertical, and in many ways is an even better visual aid for thought development (see figure 1.8). The clauses related to one another are arced together and the relationship labeled, then the larger whole is arced and labeled. From this we could easily detect main points and subpoints within the larger whole, and be able to pinpoint the exact relationships between the parts.

It is best to develop one's own list of relationships and keys; however, in addition to the previous list (see above), I would suggest the following for coordinating clauses: *Adv* for adversative, *Pr* for progression, *S* for series, *Co* for comparison, *Wh-Pts* for wholeparts, *Id-Int* for idea-interpretation, *Qs-As* for question-answer. For subordinating rela-

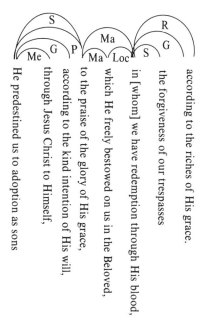

Fig. 1.8. Arcing Diagram of Ephesians 1:5-7 (NASB).

tionships, use *Inf* for inference, *Loc* for locative ("in"), *G* for ground or basis. The value of these codes is the ability to visualize at a glance the precise development of thought. My personal recommendation is to use the block diagram on the complex sentences of Paul (and several other New Testament writers), which may visualize better in terms of a vertical model, and to use arcing for the parallel clauses of the Old Testament where the block diagram will have little value. In fact, the use of Ephesians 1:5-7 itself shows one problem with using the arcing method for Paul. There is no easy way to arc a passage like verse 5, in which the three prepositional phrases all modify the major clause but not each other. With arcing it seems as if all modify one another when in reality they modify only the primary clause. Nevertheless, this visualization model is extremely helpful.

Rhetorical or Compositional Patterns

When diagramming the structural development of ideas in a paragraph, one often comes into contact with rhetorical techniques, that is, stylistic methods for getting across a message. This provides the third and final level of the context within which an idea is found; namely, the macro level of the organizational pattern in the book as a whole and the intermediate levels of the paragraph and the compositional techniques used within those paragraphs. The micro level (the detailed structure of the words themselves) is the subject of the next four chapters.

We may accept as a working hypothesis Aristotle's classic definition of rhetoric as "the art of discovering the best possible means of persuasion in regard to any subject whatever" (Kessler 1982:2). Rhetorical studies often have confused the formal (genre) and the functional (organizational techniques) aspects.[12] The four classical divisions of rhetoric as expounded by Cicero were invention, arrangement, style and memory techniques. Genre is peripheral to this, for rhetorical criticism by definition primarily is concerned with the communication process per se, that is, with the techniques and organizational patterns by which the author's arguments are presented. Kessler (1982:13-14) argues that the synchronic side—namely, that side dealing with the text itself—should predominate in rhetorical analysis. I am using this approach in this section, as we look to the structural dimensions of the text and detect the stylistic techniques by which the biblical writers (and others) link their arguments (see the excursus in chapter four for the other types of rhetorical criticism).

Literally scores of different types of relationships exist between ideas or thoughts. Classifying these types, however, has been difficult. I have chosen to combine the efforts of Meyer and Rice and of Nida et al.[13] Such a classification is important because it will guide our study of individual structures in the Bible; a basic understanding of these types will prove immensely helpful as we study various passages. Therefore, I will illustrate each rhetorical type with examples from Scripture.

1. *Collection relations* (Nida, "repetition"; Liefeld, "continuity") connect ideas or events on the basis of some common point of agreement. This was a common type of rhetorical feature in the ancient world. The rabbis called it "pearl-stringing" and would often collect messianic texts together. This explains the connected series of proof-texts in Hebrews 1:4-14, taken respectively from Psalm 2:7; 2 Samuel 7:17; Psalms 97:7; 104:4; 45:6-7; 102:25-27 and 110:1.[14] Similar collections are found in the five discourses of Matthew's Gospel; for instance, in the apocalyptic section of the mission discourse (compare Mt 10:16-22 with Mk 13:9-13). Often catchwords will link a seemingly disorganized series. Such is the case in Mark 9:33-50, a collection of sayings on reward and punishment. The section is organized around "in my name" (vv. 37-41), "offend" (vv. 42-47), "salt" and "fire" (vv. 48-50).

Repetition can be organized around either sound or idea. As Nida shows, Hebrews 1:1 contains five Greek terms beginning with *p,* five occurrences of *l,* and two adverbs ending in *-os.* This was a memory technique that also added emphasis to the statement. Similar patterns can be found in the Beatitudes (Mt 5:1-13), the explanation of John's purpose in writing (1 Jn 2:12-14) and the letters to the seven churches (virtually "form letters") in Revelation 2—3. Repetition of idea is much more predominant. While we will discuss Hebrew poetic parallelism more in chapter seven, it is helpful to note here the predominance of parallelism in prose as well as in poetry, in the New Testament as well as in the Old. It is certainly the most frequent rhetorical pattern in the Bible. A basic error of many exegetes is to emphasize the differences of meaning between synonymous terms found in a list; for instance, the terms for "love" in John 20:15-17, the types of sacrifice in Hebrews 10:8 or the terms for prayer in Philippians 4:6. We must at all times be aware of the possibility that the reason for the employment of different terms or phrases may be stylistic rather than theological; repetition may have been used for emphasis, and the differences between the terms should not be stressed.

2. *Cause-effect* and *problem-solution* relations contain an antecedent action and a

resultant consequence.[15] We can choose from numerous illustrations. The denunciation of Israel by the prophets often takes a cause-effect form. For instance, Amos 2:6-16 begins with the cause ("for three transgressions of Israel and for four," v. 6), proceeds to an enumeration of those sins (vv. 6b-13) and then concludes with the judgment (or effects, vv. 14-16). The entire book of Amos centers upon the social injustice and rampant materialism of Israel (for example, 4:1 condemns the "cows of Bashan . . . who oppress the poor, who crush the needy") as the basis for divine judgment (4:2, "the days are coming . . . when they will take you away with meat hooks"). The messianic promises of the prophets provide examples of problem-solution. The problem was that the righteous remnant of Israel would suffer alongside the apostates. For them God provided a solution: he promised that he would "not totally destroy the house of Jacob" (Amos 9:8). While the sinners would die (9:10), God himself would "raise up the fallen booth of David" (v. 11, using imagery drawn from the Feast of Tabernacles).

Similar to this is a *question-answer* format, used frequently by Paul as well as by the prophets (note Is 40:28-31 above). This is especially true in the Epistle to the Romans, where Paul frequently employs a rhetorical question (which presents the views of his opponents) then proceeds to answer that erroneous perspective. A series of such dominates Romans 3, beginning with the justice of God in light of Jewish unbelief (3:1-4), then proceeding to the righteousness of God in light of Jewish unrighteousness (vv. 5-8) and then to the equality of Jew and Gentile under sin (vv. 9-26), the impossibility of boasting in light of the necessity of faith (vv. 27-28), God as the God of the Gentiles as well as of the Jews (vv. 29-30) and faith as establishing rather than nullifying the law (v. 31). In each unit Paul begins with a rhetorical question and proceeds to give his answer. Similar questions introduce the discussions of justification by faith (4:1-2), the defeat of sin by union with Christ (6:1-2), the problem of the law and sin (7:1-2, 13), God's salvific intent (8:31-32), and the justification of God (9:19-24, 11:1-2).

Under this rubric too we could include *purpose* and *result* or *substantiation*. These also answer the question Why? Purpose reverses the order and tells the intended result rather than the result itself. The two (purpose and result) are frequently quite difficult to differentiate, but as Liefeld states, "Often, considering the providence of God, the distinction is not important" (1984:69). Whether we translate "in order that" (future oriented) or "so that" (past oriented), the emphasis is upon God's sovereign control of the situation. Liefeld mentions 1 Corinthians 2:1-5, where Paul explains that his preaching lacked eloquence "so that your faith might not rest upon men's wisdom but upon God's power" (see also 1:29, 31). Purpose and result blend together in such instances. The conjunction "for" often leads into a similar substantiation of a theological statement. For instance, Romans 8:29-31 tells why we can know that "all things work together for good" (v. 28): God has foreknown, predestined, called, justified and glorified his people. In other words, God is in control and we can place our trust in him.

3. *Comparison* demonstrates similarities or contrasts between ideas. A famous example is the Adam-Christ contrast of Romans 5:12-21; both figures are corporately identified (note "the one and the many," v. 15) with sinful humankind and the Christian, respectively. We might also note the debated relationship between Romans 7:7-13 (past tense)

and 7:14-25 (present tense). One must decide whether the two sections move from the unregenerate to the regenerate state or from Israel in the past to Israel in the present (Moo 1986). Another well-known contrast is the Johannine antithesis between light and darkness in John 1:5; 3:19 and especially 8:12—9:41. The setting is that of a cosmic war in which darkness cannot "overcome"[16] the light (1:5) and then the continuing skirmish between the two as we encounter Christ, the "light of the world" (8:12-13). Proverbs employs numerous examples in the wise-foolish contrasts of 1:7; 15:5 and similar patterns (see chap. seven on interpreting Proverbs).

Several scholars have a separate discussion of *interchange,* but in reality this is simply a variation of comparison. Instead of straightforward comparison, interchange alternates persons, events or categories in order to produce thematic comparison. A good example is John's alternating of Peter's denial (18:15-18, 25-27) with Jesus' steadfast courage before Annas (vv. 19-23) and Pilate (vv. 28-40). The contrast between Peter's cowardice and Jesus' courage is obvious. Mark uses a similar technique when he inserts one scene into another in order that the one can be interpreted by the other. This is exemplified in Jesus' rejection by his family (3:20-21, 31-35) and the scribes (3:22-30); in the juxtaposition of the healing of Jairus' daughter (5:21-24, 35-43) and the woman with the hemorrhage (5:25-34), both dealing with laws of cleanliness; and in the cursing of the fig tree (11:12-14, 20-25) illustrating the judgment of Jerusalem behind the cleansing of the temple (11:15-19). We can also find alternating categories in the Adam-Christ contrast (Rom 5:12-21) mentioned above.

4. *Description* is a broad category entailing clarification of a topic, event or person by means of further information. This might be called *continuation* (see Osborne and Woodward 1979:70-71) and is differentiated from *repetition* in that it "extends" rather than "repeats" the discussion. The technique can be demonstrated in the elaboration of Jonah's flight (1:3) in 1:4-17 or in the further description of the divine blessing of Abraham (Gen 13:14-18) in 14:1-18. Christ's use of two parables in Luke 14:28-32 to clarify the importance of "counting the cost" in discipleship (vv. 26-27, 33) is another example. The message is that no one dare enter the process of discipleship until he or she realizes what it entails. The parables provide a graphic description of one who wants to be a disciple without "bearing his cross" (v. 27). Christ demands unconditional surrender of all ties with the world (v. 33).

The principle of *summation* might be placed under this category, for it usually comes at the end of a lengthy descriptive piece in order to tie the ends together and show the basic theme or result. Needless to say, detecting such a technique is rather helpful in determining the basic thrust of a passage. At times such a summary comes at the beginning and end of the passage, as in Joshua 12:7, 24, "Now these are the kings of the land whom Joshua and the sons of Israel defeated . . . in all, thirty-one kings." Most of the time, it occurs at the end. In historical books such summaries or "seams" help to link material and themes. For instance, the summary sections of Acts contain one of Luke's primary theological emphases, how the Spirit of God triumphs over the church's troubles. Each summary centers upon the "increase" of the "word" (a technical term referring both to the proclamation of the gospel and to the successful results in the growth of the church) in spite of internal dissension (6:1-6 with v. 7), the persecution of the church (8:1—9:30 with v. 31), persecution by a tyrant (12:1-23 with v. 24), and the occult (19:13-19 with v. 20).

Similar to summation is the Jewish practice of *inclusio,* a technique in which the author at the end of a discussion returns to the point he made at the beginning. Thus he reiterates the basic point he has been developing and ties together the whole description. One of the best examples is John 1:18, which concludes the Johannine prologue and repeats the themes of 1:1, such as Jesus as the revealer of God and as always with the Father. Raymond E. Brown also notes inclusion in John with respect to the Cana miracles in 2:11 and 4:46, 56; to the Transjordan in 1:28 and 10:40; and to the paschal lamb in 1:29 and 19:36 (1966:cxxxv).

Another Jewish technique that highlights major themes is *chiasm,* which reverses words or events in successive parallel clauses or sections. It is found frequently in the Old Testament, of course, as in the ABC:CBA organization of Isaiah 6:10 (NASB):

A   Render the hearts of this people insensitive
B   Their ears dull,
C   And their eyes dim
C   Lest they see with their eyes
B   Hear with their ears
A   Understand with their hearts

Chiasm is also found frequently in the New Testament. Lund sees it in passages like 1 Corinthians 5:2-6; 9:19-22; 11:8-12 and many others (1942). Raymond E. Brown makes a cogent argument for chiasm in John 6:36-40 and 18:28—19:16 (1966:276; 1970:858-59).

5. *Shifts in expectancy* includes many compositional types. As Nida says, "They depend for their significance on the fact that the reader recognizes the unusual word order, syntactic structure, or meaning of a word, phrase, or complete sentence" (1983:36). In some ways this category is too broad, as it could include such other categories as rhetorical questions, inclusio or chiasm. Moreover, it clearly overlaps with *figures of speech,* which we will discuss in chapter four. However, the rhetorical devices transcend such figures as anacoloutha (mentioned by Nida here). Nevertheless, such shifts are keys to structural emphases so must be included here as well. Jesus' Farewell Speech (Jn 14—16) contains many such shifts, so many in fact that some scholars see no unity in the section but rather a series of overlapping traditions haphazardly strung together. This results in theories of a Johannine "circle" or series of editors who imposed an artificial unity on the Fourth Gospel, resulting in *aporias,* or structural inconsistencies. In an important recent article, however, Edwin C. Webster argues that "the Gospel, as a literary whole, is meticulously constructed on the basis of symmetrical design and balanced units" (1982:230). Webster notes two concentric sections in chapters 13 to 16, each with three divisions (pp. 243-45).

I. Jesus and the Disciples	II. Disciples and the World
A. Jesus washes their feet;	A. Metaphor of vine and branches;
his example, 13:1-20	example of his love, 15:1-16
B. Judas' departure, 13:21-32	B. The world's hatred, 15:17-27

C. Dialogue on Jesus' departure,   C. Dialogue on Jesus' departure,
     13:33—14:31   16:1-33

Webster argues for a chiastic relationship between the critical sections of chapters 14 and 16, which could explain the repetitive themes. This type of shift is difficult for the modern reader but easily detectable and understandable in the ancient world. The difficulties disappear when we understand the structural development. In other words, there are no clumsy inconsistencies or repetitions but rather a carefully crafted discourse.

Climax and *cruciality* also belong under this rubric. The former is found in narrative and the latter in epistles, but both have a similar function in that they designate the pivotal or turning point of the writer's basic argument. In the healing of the demon-possessed child (Mk 9:14-29) the climax does not occur with the miracle itself but with the cry of the father, "I believe; help my unbelief." That is a pivotal point in Mark's discipleship theme as a whole and provides an antidote to the disciple's failure in verses 18-19 as well as a precursor to the necessity of faith-prayer in verse 29. Liefeld (1984:63) provides an excellent example of climax in the different order of the temptations in Matthew 4:1-10 and Luke 4:1-12. By having his story climax with the temptation regarding the kingdoms of the world, Matthew concluded with an emphasis appropriate to his royal messianic theme. By climaxing with the pinnacle of the temple, Luke on the other hand centers upon the temple and in particular upon the Jewish origins of Christianity, one of the major themes in his Gospel. In both cases the climax is a key to the basic theological stress. Similarly, Romans 9—11 is the crucial turning point of that book. Most scholars today believe that it is not an excursis but rather is the discussion Paul had been preparing for since his argument that Jew and Gentile alike are under sin and condemnation (1:18—3:20).

Finally, I would include here Nida's discussion of *omission* (1983:33-36). When an author deliberately omits a point that the reader is expecting, it provides a "shift in expectancy" that is startling and emphatic. Usually such passages omit particular words (such as *kai* in 1 Cor 13:4-7 or the introductory formula of Heb 1:5, 8, 10). At times, however, the crucial omissions were understandable to the original readers but cause unbelievable difficulties for the modern interpreter; for instance, the deliberate omission of any explanation/identification of the "restrainer" (2 Thess 2:6-7) or of "666" (Rev 13:18). Hundreds of theories have been propounded for the two, and it is likely that we will not know the true meaning for certain until the Lord himself returns.

2
Grammar

E XEGESIS MEANS TO "DRAW OUT OF" A TEXT WHAT IT MEANS, IN CONTRAST TO EISEGESIS, to "read into" a text what one wants it to mean. The process is complex and forms the heart of hermeneutical theory, which seeks first to determine the author's intended meaning (see appendices one and two for the possibility of doing so) and then to apply it to one's life. This is a single task, and the two aspects—meaning and significance—cannot be separated, since the determination of meaning (what it meant) is already done from the standpoint of modern perspectives or significance (what it means). Nevertheless these are still differing aspects of the larger hermeneutical whole, so we will devote chapters two to five to general hermeneutics (that is, meaning—what the biblical text "meant") and chapters thirteen to sixteen to applied hermeneutics (that is, significance—what Scripture "means" to us today). Werner Jeanrond calls these different reading perspectives, that is, different purposes or goals that are not mutually exclusive but work together to produce understanding (1988:126-28).[1] Exegesis proper could be subdivided into linguistic and cultural aspects. The former is concerned with the alignment of terms or concepts that together form the propositional statements. The latter relates to the historical and sociological background behind those statements.

The next three chapters discuss the three aspects of linguistic study. Grammar, the subject of this chapter, denotes the basic laws of language behind the relationship between the terms in the surface structure. Semantics (chap. three) looks at the meaning of individual words as each functions in the sentence. Syntax studies the configuration of the sentence units and the way the message as a whole can speak in differing cultural contexts (chap. four). In other words, syntax concerns "transformational grammar" (according to Chomsky, the way the developing context transforms the communication process). All three aspects are interdependent and cannot truly exist apart from the others. Nevertheless, we must consider them separately, for the linguistic rules differ for each. The interpreter, however, will consider all three at the same time when studying the surface structure (the sentences) in order to delineate the original intended meaning.

Naturally, the person who does not know the original languages will have a perceptibly greater difficulty in dealing with grammar and syntax. Most of the material below will assume a basic knowledge of Hebrew and Greek. However, the task is not completely hopeless for those who have never studied the languages. The problem is that they must then depend upon secondary sources, mainly translations and the better commentaries. My suggestion is to use the information below to test the commentaries. Many older or less informed works will make basic errors in the conclusions they draw regarding the significance of tense, mood and so forth. The grammatical information in this chapter can become resource material when commentators argue particular points. Another suggestion is to memorize the Hebrew and Greek alphabets and then purchase an interlinear version that has the Hebrew or Greek side by side with one or more English versions (normally also with the corresponding English word under each Hebrew or Greek term). Hayes and Holladay (1982:58) suggest a good use of analytical concordances like Strong or Young, which give the Hebrew or Greek words behind the English terms and key them to appendices or even lexicons that explain the original language. Finally, one can compare several English versions to see how different committees have translated the passages. All in all, it is hoped that the ensuing chapter will aid those with little linguistic background as well as those with more training.

The Preliminary Task: Establishing the Text

Before we can begin serious exegesis of a scriptural passage, we must establish the text itself. Many different manuscripts of both Old and New Testaments exist, at times having quite dissimilar readings. Two processes enable us to establish the original reading: first, text criticism compares the various readings and decides which one was probably the basis of the others. Second, decisions are made as to whether letters or phrases belong with the previous or following term (more so in Old Testament study). In the ancient world there was neither punctuation nor spaces between words. In addition, Hebrew writing used no vowels. In many instances a letter can be either a suffix of the previous word or a prefix of the succeeding word. Also, phrases like "in love" can belong either with a previous clause (Eph 1:4-5 KJV) or a following clause (Eph 1:4-5 NIV).

Text criticism is necessary when we note wide disparities between the versions on individual passages. For instance, the "longer" ending of Mark is present in the King James Version but missing in recent versions like the Revised Standard, New American Standard and the New International. Determining the correct reading is often an almost impossible task. We must remember that the class of professional scribes did not develop until quite late within both Judaism and the early church. In the New Testament era text copyists were amateurs and made all the errors one would expect in a text.[2] They added or subtracted words, substituted alternate readings, and smoothed out rough grammar. There were sight errors, reversed letters, and deliberate changes to add significant theological points or to harmonize seeming contradictions. Indeed, all the errors that modern proofreaders are supposed to find and eliminate in manuscripts are present in the ancient recensions of the Bible.

Moreover, text criticism is certainly an inexact science. Old Testament study before 1947 delineated three major textual traditions:[3] the Masoretic Text (MT) compiled by the Masoretes, a group of Jewish scholars who added the vowel points and codified the oral tradition, from the sixth to the ninth centuries A.D.; the Septuagint (LXX), the

Greek Old Testament translated from the third to the first centuries B.C.; and the Samaritan Pentateuch (SP), the official Bible of the Samaritan sect at Shechem. Readings from the Targums (Aramaic paraphrases, see chap. one above), the Peshitta (the Syriac version) and the Vulgate (Jerome's Latin version) have been regarded as secondary and as reflecting one of the other traditions (see Klein 1974:59-61). At first the discovery of the Qumran scrolls was thought to strengthen the importance of the Septuagint, since several "LXX readings" were found in the Qumran material. Therefore, there was little shift in the alignment of the evidence. However, several recent challenges to the traditional view have made it necessary to reopen the question of textual "types."

Emanuel Tov (1980:45-67; 1982a:11-27) has shown that the relationship between the scrolls and the Septuagint is not nearly as persuasive as hitherto thought, since differences in many cases outweigh similarities and there are diverse text types in the readings common to the scrolls and the Septuagint. Tov (1981:272-751; 1982b:429-34) argues that these represent not text types but simple texts, and that one must study the external evidence individually passage by passage rather than via external criteria (see further below). However, he admits, "On the whole, the readings of the MT do deserve more respect than readings found in other sources" (1981:287).[4] Moreover, Tov also agrees that the Qumran scrolls do indeed support the Septuagint in many instances. Therefore, Tov goes too far when he states that "there exist *no relevant external considerations* that can be applied to the evaluation of readings," and that "internal criteria are the *only valid criteria* for evaluating retroverted variants" (1981:286, 288; italics his). He has probably succeeded in showing the tentative nature of the tripartite division into text types, but he has not disproved the basic validity of external criteria, so long as we recognize the tentative nature of such conclusions.

Textual criticism of the New Testament is usually regarded as much more stable, due to the greater number of manuscripts (over 5,000) and the vast amount of work accomplished by scholars such as Westcott and Hort at the end of the last century, or Aland and Metzger in more recent times. The manuscripts likewise have been subdivided into text families or types, based upon the style of changes but even more upon the geographical distributions: Alexandrian, Caesarean and Byzantine. However, while it may seem to have greater stability, several challenges to the eclectic method developed by Westcott and Hart have made it necessary to temper the conclusions. First, proponents of the "majority text" (such as Pickering and Hodges) have argued that the vast majority of the manuscripts are in agreement behind the Textus Receptus (TR) of Erasmus, the version used in the Authorized Version, and that the text-family approach ignores the presence of TR readings in many of the church fathers. Although this challenge must be respected and taken seriously, I would agree with Carson (1979) and Fee (1978) that a much stronger case can be made for the eclectic method. Second, many scholars agree that the entire methodological apparatus of text criticism is overdue for an overhaul and that the evidence for the text types is particularly suspect. Most today recognize the tentative and subjective nature of most decisions.[5] We must use the evidence with great care and sophistication.

There are great similarities between the criteria for text-critical decisions in the Old and

New Testaments. Therefore, I will present one set of criteria and use examples from both testaments. The main thing to remember is that no reading is proven by any single criterion. Rather, all the variants must be evaluated on the basis of all the criteria, and the most probable reading will be the one that best fits the whole.

1. External Criteria. External criteria are those rules which relate to the documents themselves. These weigh the distribution of the variant readings, judge the relative merits of the manuscripts within which the readings are found, and detect "biases" (tendencies) in the transmission habits of the texts. Many, like Tov, believe these have less merit because of the secondary nature of such judgments, based as they are upon prior decisions regarding the date and geographical nature of the various manuscripts. Certainly there is some truth to this, especially in light of the great disparity of patterns in the changes in any given manuscript. Nevertheless, those who have done primary research on manuscripts state that it is indeed possible to give a basic "grade" to the quality of individual readings, so long as one realizes the subjective nature of such decisions.[6] When we study various possibilities for the original text of a particular passage, it is advisable to use the following procedure.

a. *Determine the relative dates of the textual sources.* This is more easily done for the New Testament but still has value for the Old. For instance, the Targumim for the Writings portion of the Old Testament stem from a later period, and there is a considerable amount of text-critical work to be done on the Septuagint itself before it can be compared to other recensions. Würthwein (1979:114; compare 12-27) and Tov (1982b:438) relate the major exception to this rule: the Masoretic Text is the most recent of the major versions of the Old Testament, yet at the same time it is the most trustworthy, that is, it contains the oldest traditions. Many of the oldest extant copies at Qumran (such as 1 Qp Hab) have undergone extensive revision due to the theological proclivities of the community, while others (such as 1 Q Isᵃ) are very accurate. In other words, transmission procedures have precedence over age (this is true for both testaments). Dating for New Testament manuscripts is a fairly exact science, and several manuscripts are dated fairly close to the first century. For instance, Bodmer Papyrus II (P66), containing portions of John 14—21, can be dated around A.D. 200, close to the actual writing of that Gospel. The earlier manuscripts are not automatically superior to older ones, as we have seen; nevertheless, they are immensely helpful.

b. *Determine the temporal and geographical distribution of the manuscripts behind each of the variants.* If a reading is found in major manuscripts from several sectors of the early church, it is more likely to be original. Of course, this must be combined with the first criterion. For instance, the longer ending of Mark (16:9-20) is omitted in Alexandrian readings (Codices Sinaiticus, Vaticanus), in the Old Latin codex Bobiensis (itᵏ), several Armenian manuscripts, as well as in Origen and Eusebius. It is found primarily in the "wilder" (expanded or longer) Codex Bezae or Byzantine (Ephraemi, Alexandrinus) readings. Therefore, most scholars doubt its authenticity (as part of Mark's original Gospel).

c. *Determine the genealogical relationship of the manuscripts behind each reading.* This, as I said above, is the most tenuous of the criteria, based as it is on theories of text type.

Theoretically, a reading found in several text families is superior to one from a single family. In Old Testament research Würthwein (1979:114) states that the Masoretic Text should be given greater weight, and decisions against a Masoretic Text reading should be made with great care.[7] Tov (1982b:435) takes the opposite pole, stating that no one version should have greater status than another. On the whole a mediating position is best. We should recognize the general weight of the manuscript evidence but not make it the only deciding factor. If the Masoretic Text itself contains a possible reason for a change (such as theological preference or smoothing out a "rough reading"), we will go with the Septuagint or the Samaritan Pentateuch. In some cases it will be fairly conclusive. For instance, all the important ancient New Testament versions omit the story of the woman caught in adultery from John 7:53—8:12; only Codex Bezae and later sources (such as the Byzantine texts) include it. All three of the above criteria strongly support the omission of the story.

d. *Note the relative quality of the manuscripts.* Again, we are forced to make a subjective decision. However, by stressing "relative quality," this criterion does have limited value. We look for the degree of divergence in a text or text family, that is, which ones generally contain shorter readings, fewer theological additions and common errors. We have already noted the general consensus that the Masoretic Text is superior to the others. The same could be said for Codex Vaticanus (B) in the New Testament. This is not conclusive by any means, and we would not go quite so far as Klein or Würthwein in supporting the Masoretic Text unless forced to do otherwise. However, if all other criteria are equal, the presence of the Masoretic Text or B behind a reading is at least a solid point in its favor.

2. Internal Criteria. Internal criteria are rules that relate to the construction and inner clarity of the text itself. These, of course, also are subjective, depending as they do upon the reader's apprehension of the text and what "must" be the case in it. Yet as Hayes and Holladay state, "In spite of their complexity they are commonly sensible, for they are primarily attempts to reverse the process of composition and transmission" (1982:35). When we are aware of the types of changes that occur, it makes sense to erect criteria that aid in detecting such changes.

a. *The more difficult reading is more likely.* It makes sense to think that later scribes would smooth out difficulties rather than add them. Of course, this too cannot stand by itself, for there are many ways an error could be made in a text, and "smoothing" difficult passages is only one of them. Nevertheless, when one is aware of the ways a scribe could write the wrong form or term in a text (see Metzger 1964:186-206; Klein 1974:76-84) this rule can be helpful. In fact, many have made it the primary criterion for text-critical decisions. For instance, later scribes noted the clumsy wording of Philippians 3:16 (lit., "only unto what we have attained, let us walk in the same") and added "by the same rule, think the same thing" to smooth out the staccato phrase. The clumsier reading is definitely more likely for this verse; it is highly improbable that later scribes would omit the last half of the verse and produce so clumsy a reading.

b. *The shorter reading is preferred.* It was far more common to add material to a text than to reduce it. Therefore, if all else is equal the shorter text has greater likelihood of being correct. Scribes would clarify the subject or explain difficult terms. Often they would harmonize one text with another in order to avoid a seeming contradiction. One of the most common additions occurred when one scribe added a comment in the margin and the next scribe, thinking he had accidentally deleted part of the text, included it. For instance, Codex Bezae on the book of Acts is one-tenth longer than other manuscripts; nearly all of that is added material that certainly is not part of the original text. Of course, in cases of haplography (see below) the longer passage is preferred, and the rule is hardly absolute. Nevertheless, it is a valuable signifier helping the student to note the likely Urtext (original reading).

c. *The reading that best fits the author's style, and especially the immediate context, is more probable.* This is often called the criterion of intrinsic probability (the first two are the criteria of transcriptional probability). Tov considers this the one pertinent criterion (1981:288). Yet it too remains problematic, and Fee calls it "the most subjective of all the criteria" (1983:57). An author's "style" is difficult to identify, for the type of statistics scholars often use (e.g., taking the number of times a word is used as an index to an author's preferred choice of terms) seldom applies to works as short as the biblical books. Writers are just not that predictable. Therefore, scholars differ in their evaluation of and use of style as a text-critical criterion. The immediate context is more valuable, but again few readings are settled easily by such considerations. Scribes often would change a reading so it would better fit their ideas regarding the context.

Moreover, this criterion often clashes with the "more difficult reading" criterion, since context often guided the choice or changes by later scribes as well. In virtually every example Tov gives (such as Is 45:1-2; Deut 31:1; 32:8; 1 Sam 17:8; Jon 1:9; see 1981:289-92) the more difficult reading favored one reading while the context favored the other. However, as Fee notes, intrinsic probability still has some limited value, for it can eliminate one or two of the possibilities and strengthen some of the other criteria (1983:57).

Added to the external evidence for the longer ending of Mark (see above), this criterion points to a strong probability against Markan origin. As Metzger points out, the vocabulary and style of 16:9-20 are too unlike the Second Gospel (1971:124-26). Moreover, the immediate context makes it unlikely, because the break is too clumsy, with a change of subject between verses 8 and 9 and the complete neglect of the other women besides Mary in verses 9-10. In short, a later editor probably compiled traditions on the resurrection appearances and the life of the early church to form a better conclusion to Mark's Gospel than that afforded by verse 8.

In conclusion, we must study the various possibilities on the basis of a grid determined by the criteria listed above. The reading that most coherently meets these rules is the probable original reading. The New Testament scholar will use the Nestle-Aland text and study in depth both external and internal criteria, utilizing the extensive apparatus (Aland 1987:228-56 provides an excellent discussion). The nonexpert should use the UBS text, which grades the readings, study closely the explanations provided by Metzger (1971), then use the information above and work with, rather than accept wholesale, the arguments of Metzger or the commentators. To be sure, the busy pastor often has little time for text-critical decisions but needs to be aware of the issues and to ascertain the text with as great a precision as possible in the limited time available. I would recommend that those in the pulpit ministry heed Liefeld's caution (although one must interact more deeply in biblical study):

> Unless the Bible used by those in the congregation has a different reading from that used by the preacher, or has a footnote indicating that there is a textual variant, it is probably

best not to mention the uncertainty. If it seems necessary to introduce the matter, I would encourage that the preacher affirm every time this happens, that this does not affect the integrity of the original and that no doctrine would be left unsupported if a favorite reading must be abandoned because of a more valid variant. This does not mean, as one sometimes hears, that no doctrine is affected by textual variants. That would not be true. Rather, any doctrinal statements in the Scriptures that are affected by textual variants are adequately supported by other passages. (1984:143)

Grammatical Analysis of the Text

The first stage of determining the inner cohesion of the text is to analyze the relationships between the individual units or terms in the text. It is interesting to contrast the emphasis upon Hebrew or Greek grammar in seminary exegesis courses with the space actually given to grammar in hermeneutics texts or in commentaries. In recent works like those of Kaiser, Liefeld or McQuilkin, grammar is not even discussed in any depth (happily, Mickelsen has an excellent discussion)! Hayes and Holladay have a chapter on grammar but never go beyond syntax and semantics in their discussion. I see three reasons for this absence: first, the busy pastor and layperson have little time for such depth and so it is perceived best to give tools that they can and will use; second, grammar is perceived as less important than syntax and so is subsumed under the larger category; third, publishers have space limitations and for the first two reasons grammar is one of the areas omitted.[8]

However, I would argue against these reasons. When one has a good working knowledge of Greek and some fine tools like the Greek reference grammars by Blass-Debrunner-Funk, Turner, Moule or Zerwick,[9] it does not take an inordinate amount of time to make grammatical decisions. Further, one does not have to study every single grammatical construction but can note the critical points of the passage and study them. The second point contains a degree of truth but not enough to justify the neglect grammar receives.[10] Syntax is rightfully coming to the forefront of exegetical discussions. However, individual grammatical decisions will always provide the foundation for syntactical study. I will never be able to determine the thought-flow of Philippians 2:6-7 until I decide whether ὑπάρχων is a concessive ("although he was"), circumstantial ("being") or temporal ("when he was") participle. Nor can I decide the theology of Romans 5:12-13 until I determine whether ἐφ᾽ ᾧ is causal ("because all sinned") or sequential ("in that all sinned").

I will not attempt to discuss the details of grammar here. Such would be impossible. However, I will summarize the broad contours and select some critical examples in order to illustrate areas where grammar is often misused. Moreover, I will again discuss Hebrew and Greek side by side, for the areas of necessity overlap and a comparison will prove educational.

1. The Historical Development. Understanding the historical development of the languages is critical for a proper understanding of grammar. A failure to understand the diachronic or historical dimensions of Hebrew and Greek has led to a misuse of grammar time and again. As Carson says, "It is important to remember that the principle of entropy operates in living languages as well as in physics. Languages 'break down' with time: the syntax becomes less structured, the number of exceptions increases, the morphology is simplified, and so forth" (1984:68). Further, the influences of the surrounding languages are formative in their development. Both biblical Hebrew and Greek demonstrate this. Therefore, a basic understanding of these phenomena will prove indispensable.

a. Biblical Hebrew is part of the Northwest Semitic language group, composed of ancient Amoritic (of the Mari texts) and the Canaanite dialects: Ugaritic (seen in the Ras Shamra tablets), Phoenician (from which all these dialects derived their alphabet), Moabite (found primarily on the Mesha Stone) and Aramaic (seen in Jer 10:11; Dan 2:46—7:28; Ezra 4:8—6:18; 7:12-26). Also important is East Semitic, spoken in ancient Mesopotamia and the main language of the Near Eastern world from 1700—700 B.C. This group is composed of Akkadian, the lingua franca of the region in the second millennium; Babylonian, the language of the Code of Hammurabi (Old Babylonian) and of Nebuchadnezzar (New Babylonian); and Assyrian. Due to the political and economic domination of this language group throughout much of the biblical period, it has particular importance. These all share certain linguistic features such as the noun and verb root of one to three consonants utilizing prefixes, suffixes or stem changes to indicate usage in the sentence. The case and tense systems are also quite similar (see Moscati 1969). We should also include Egyptian, traces of which often can be found in the Old Testament.

Therefore, one of the most important tools for serious exegesis of the Old Testament is comparative linguistics. Much work needs to be done, and great care must be taken in using the results. Since the study is still in the formative stages, many have overdone the parallels. One of the best examples of overkill is Michel Dahood's three-volume commentary on the Psalms (Anchor Bible), which found Ugaritic parallels in virtually every verse. Yet this ground-breaking work did demonstrate the potential inherent in a comparative approach (see his index in the back of the commentary). Utilizing the sister language can uncover the potential background and meaning of many obscure Hebrew words and syntactical arrangements. Further, many phrases or terms seem to have been directly borrowed from the surrounding religions, so such an approach becomes doubly valuable. In doing so, however, we must be careful to search *all* the potential parallels and select the one that *best* answers the problem rather than settle for any possible parallel (too often the one that best suits our purpose!). This principle will recur several times in our survey of hermeneutics, for it is also a problem of semantic research and the use of parallel passages.

The major problem in developing a Hebrew grammar is that our understanding in some ways is still in its infancy. Scholars are still trying to unlock the developmental stages of the language from the Pentateuch to Chronicles and into the New Testament period. This in fact is the primary reason why no major grammar (at the level of Blass-Debrunner for biblical Greek) has appeared; most feel that it is too difficult to discover rules that can cover the various levels of Hebrew grammar at the different stages of its development. Nevertheless, it is possible to supply basic rules for interpretation that cover most instances, and I will attempt to summarize those here.

b. The Greek of the New Testament has been very heavily debated. In the last century many believed that the New Testament contained a "Holy Spirit" Greek due to the obvious differences between the New Testament and classical Greek writings. However, Adolf Deissmann, in his monumental study of the papyri (1908), proved that the Greek of the New Testament was actually the common, colloquial (Koine) Greek of the marketplace. Several have challenged this thesis, primarily Nigel Turner, who argues that the New Testament is a unique combination of Greek and Semitic sources (1963:9). However, a nuanced form of Deissmann's theory still best fits the evidence (see Silva 1980:198-219).

The Koine period began with Alexander's conquests. Prior to Alexander several dialects competed in Greece, with Attic Greek (the dialect of Athens with its poets and philosophers) the language of diplomacy. Alexander made Attic the universal language, though traces of the others, especially Ionic, appear in later Koine Greek. This classical dialect was characterized by great subtlety of expression and a sophisticated but rigid system of particles and prepositions, each of which had a specialized meaning. The vast array of tenses and moods were used with an almost scientific accuracy. However, the masses of conquered peoples had trouble learning all the subtle nuances, and the language gradually lost its precision. Minute differences between prepositions, cases and tenses began to disappear. The movement was away from the sophisticated, synthetic mode of the classical to an analytic style capable of greater emotional expression. To be sure, a movement back to a stylized classical form, called "Atticism" and characterized by the rigid rules of the older period, did occur, but it was restricted to the intelligentsia.

The New Testament writers followed popular writing styles. Of course there were differences of style. The best Greek is that of Luke, James and the author of the Epistle to the Hebrews. At times Paul can approach elegance, and 1 Peter exhibits quite good Koine style. The roughest Greek occurs in 2 Peter, Revelation and the Gospel of John.

Of course, we cannot properly understand the language of the New Testament until we note the influence of Semitic grammar and septuagintal Greek upon the writers. It is impossible to discuss this difficult subject in depth, but no survey would be complete without acknowledging the presence of both. The writers for the most part were Jews for whom Greek was the second language, and at times grammar and word usage reflects this. Also, in the Gospels and Acts the use of primitive traditions may reflect a strong Semitic origin (see Black 1967). Also, many translation Semitisms reflect either Semitic originals or the Septuagint. The latter especially would influence the style, as in the hymns of Luke 1:46-55, 68-79 (see Blass-Debrunner 1963:3). On the whole, it is important to recognize such influences and avoid a misuse of grammar (see Zerwick 1963:63-64).

2. The Verb System.
a. Hebrew, unlike many other Indo-European languages, preferred kind of action to time sense. There are two tenses: the perfect, stressing completed action; and the imperfect, emphasizing incompleted action. An exception to this is with verbs denoting state of being or mind (such as "I am clean," "I love"), where the perfect is used for the present state. With regular verbs, however, only context can tell whether it should be translated a past ("I did"), perfect ("I have done"), pluperfect ("I had done") or future perfect ("I will have done"). Also, only context can tell whether the imperfect should denote a future

("I will do"), repeated or habitual action in the past ("I used to do"), present ("I do") or conditional ("if I do"). Again, there is no time sense in the verb; such must be inferred from the context.

The verbal system centers upon the seven "stems," which are named to signify the perfect tense, third person masculine singular form of the verb *pl* in the various stems, such as *niphal* due to the prefix *n-* and *piel* due to the doubling of the middle consonant. Briefly, the grammatical use of each stem indicates the following syntactical functions (taken from Lambdin 1971; Williams 1967). The *Qal* is the basic or simple stem, used for both transitive ("I do") or stative ("I am old") statements. The *Niphal* is more often passive ("I am helped") but at times reflexive ("I help myself"). The *Piel* (active) or *Pual* (passive) stems change intransitive or stative verbs into transitive verbs (for example, "to be holy"—→ "to sanctify"; "to learn" —→ "to teach"), and are also used with verbs whose roots are nouns (such as "word" —→ "to speak" or "blessing" —→ "to bless"). Seldom if ever do they intensify (the traditional distinction). The *Hithpael* adds a reflexive ("sanctify oneself") or reciprocal ("bless one another") force. Finally, the *Hiphil* (active) or *Hophal* (passive) stems are causative ("to make righteous"), at times permissive ("see" —→ "allow to see") or intransitive ("to be old" —→ "to grow old").

Mood in Hebrew is fairly complex. The imperative is similar in form and function to the imperfect. It is used to designate a simple command (such as "do it" or "love God") while the imperfect is used for strong injunctions ("you must do it" or "you shall love the Lord your God"). The jussive and cohortative resemble the imperfect and imperative in form and function. The jussive is the third person imperative ("let him do it") and the cohortative is the first person imperative ("let us do it"). When two imperatives (or imperative followed by jussive or cohortative) are found together, often there will be a sense of condition ("If this occurs, you will do . . ."; see Is 36:16) or purpose/result ("Do this so that I may . . ."; see 2 Kings 5:10).

Infinitives and participles are verbal nouns and adjectives, respectively. There are two infinitive forms. The infinitive construct often functions like the English gerund, standing as the subject ("helping the child is good," compare Gen 2:18) or object ("I enjoyed helping the child," compare Deut 10:10). Most frequently, it is found with prepositions used with לְ for purpose or result ("I worked so that I might feed my family"), with כְּ or בְּ in a temporal clause ("when he worked . . ."), with מִן, בַּל or בְּלִי in a causal clause ("because he worked . . .") or with בַּל or כְּ in a concessive construction ("although he worked . . ."). The infinitive absolute functions as an adverb. Frequently, it is used emphatically to repeat and stress the verbal idea ("killing he will kill," meaning "he will surely kill," compare Gen 2:17; Amos 9:8). The infinitive absolute is sometimes employed to complement the verb and give attendant action ("He heard and *followed* . . .") and can even stand for the main verb itself, often as an imperative (Is 14:31) but also as a finite verb (Num 4:24, "consuming fire") or a noun ("shepherd," "seer"). With an article it can function as a relative clause (see Gen 26:11, "he who touches") but often also stands by itself as a main verb (such as 1 Kings 3:3, "he sacrificed and burnt incense") with the accent upon durative or continuous action.

b. The Greek verbal system is similar to Hebrew in some respects. Greek too is characterized by inflection more than by word order or helping verbs. Like Hebrew, tense does not have time sense but rather stresses kind of action. Time sense is found only in the indicative mood. Two tenses (imperfect and future) have primarily a temporal aspect and as a result by the late Koine period were restricted almost entirely to the indicative mood. The following kinds of action can be distinguished: (1) continuous or durative force, utilizing the present ("I am doing"), imperfect ("I was doing") or future ("I will be doing") tenses; (2) iterative or repeated action again with the present ("I do often"), imperfect ("I used to do") or future ("I will do") tenses; (3) punctiliar force, perceived either as a single act, utilizing the aoristic, or simple, present ("I do") and aorist ("I did") tenses, or action perceived as a whole, using the global aorist ("the temple was built in forty years"); and (4) action viewed as complete, with the results seen either as existing (perfect tense, "he has done") or complete (pluperfect tense, "he had done").[11]

Tense is very misused, and the student must be extremely careful not to read too much rigidity into its use in the New Testament, such as seeing the aorist as a "once-for-all" tense. As Frank Stagg has noted, the aorist never means "once for all" and often has no sense of completed action (1972:222-23). For instance, Paul uses aorists in Philippians 2:12, "as you have always obeyed," and in Philippians 4:11, "for I have learned to be content in whatever circumstances I find myself"; in both cases these are culminative, stressing present consequences. In the next verse (4:12) Paul follows with present tenses to clarify ("I know . . . I know"). Obviously, here—as elsewhere—the aorist tense overlaps the perfect. In the other moods this absence of a strong punctiliar force is even more obvious. An aorist is the common form in the imperative, infinitive or participle and often has no force whatsoever. If the present tense is used in these three moods, the stress will be on the progressive nature of the action. However, with the aorist there is often no tense emphasis.

Therefore, it is wrong to read the aorist infinitive "to present your bodies" in Romans 12:1 as a crisis act, and the same is true of the aorist subjunctive "that we might walk in newness of life" in Romans 6:4. In other moods like the imperative, it is commonly thought that an ingressive force often is indicated. However, while such is true on occasion (such as Jas 4:9; Rom 13:13), it usually occurs in an exhortation passage and by no means is the normal case (see Blass-Debrunner 1961:173-74). Luke 9:23, for instance, adds "daily" to the aorist imperative "take up your cross." The iterative force is obvious.

Voice is equally problematic. No longer can it be said that the middle voice is mainly reflexive. More often than not, the force is more indirect, involving the subject in the results of the action as well as in the process. At times the reflexive idea is strong (such as Mt 27:5, "he hung himself") but at other times the middle voice is virtually equivalent to an active (such as Acts 12:4, where Herod "put [Peter] in prison"). Zerwick (1963:72-75) shows how the middle voice was losing ground to the passive voice (in deponent verbs) and to the active voice (with reflexive pronouns). Thus it is wrong, for instance, to read "tongues . . . will cease" (1 Cor 13:8) as a strong middle, that is, "cease in and of themselves" (see Carson 1984:77-79). Consulting a lexicon, we would find it readily apparent that παύομαι often appears in the middle with active force (such as Lk 8:24, "the waves . . . ceased"). In short, it is best to conclude with Moule, "as a rule, it is far from easy to come down from the fence with much decisiveness on either side in an exegetical problem if it depends on the voice" (1959:24).

An adequate discussion of the various moods is impossible given the space restraints of this chapter. Nevertheless, I will mention a few highlights in addition to the discussion above of tense use in the oblique (nonindicative) moods. In both form and function the subjunctive is related to the future. This is true in ἵνα clauses (most frequently = future purpose) and in deliberative questions, where the stress is upon potentiality (see Mk 12:4). Yet this must be tempered in conditional sentences. According to Zerwick (1963:109), the so-called third-class condition with ἐάν plus the subjunctive is "eventual" or "probable"; he adds that at times it is used in an ironic context to state an impossible situation (such as Mt 21:3). However, James Boyer has challenged this view, showing that this condition relates only to a future event with no assumption of probability or improbability (1983:164-75; compare Carson 1983:81-82). A similar caution must be made against the assumption that a first-class condition with εἰ is virtually causal (Turner 1963:115) and should be translated "since." As Zerwick shows, the degree of reality must be inferred from the context (1963:103). The reality of the hypothesis is assumed for the sake of argument, but not the truth of it. The context can give the clause virtually a causal force (for example, Phil 2:1) but often the statement is in fact untrue (as in Mt 12:26-27 or Mk 3:24-25).

Participles are extraordinarily difficult to interpret. This is true partly because of the encroachment of Semitic influence. Periphrastics (participle + verb "to be"), for instance, are much more common, especially in Semitic portions like Acts 1—12 (seventeen of the twenty-four occurrences in Acts). Here, however, I will restrict my comments to the most difficult type, the adverbial participle. Only the context can tell us whether the participle is circumstantial, causal, resultative, temporal or some such. The decision is often very problematic; it is possible that more than one might fit. I find it helpful to group the possibilities syntactically. For instance, we can group circumstantial (attendant circumstance), modal (manner), instrumental (means) and causal; these proceed from the weakest to the strongest and are all found quite frequently in the New Testament. Temporal participles are also plentiful, although they were in the process of being replaced by subordinate clauses like a ὅτε clause or by infinitival clauses (ἐν τῷ, μετὰ τό). Concessive participles are found infrequently (for example, Mt 7:11; Acts 19:37), as are conditional (such as Lk 9:25; Heb 11:32). Purpose and result clauses are also interrelated, and often we cannot differentiate between them clearly (see Lk 7:6; Acts 8:27; for an excellent discussion, see Turner 1963:153-57). Fee cautions against "overexegeting" here (1983:82). Since the basic purpose of a participle is attendant circumstance, and since there were many unambiguous ways of indicating purpose, condition and so forth, the context must indicate fairly clearly if one of the other adverbial usages should be used.

The infinitive is not quite so difficult, for like Hebrew it is a verbal noun and often functions like the English gerund. The one problematic area occurs when the infinitive is linked to the Greek article and functions adverbially like a subordinate clause. Once the basic concept is understood, however, it becomes simple to detect and translate. The causal function is introduced by διὰ τό plus the infinitive (Phil 1:7; Lk 2:4); purpose by τοῦ, πρὸς τό, or εἰς τό (Acts 7:19; Jas 1:18); result by ὥστε (Lk 4:29; 20:20); temporal by ἐν τῷ ("while," Mt 13:4, 25), μετὰ τό ("after," Mk 1:14; 14:28) or πρὸ τοῦ ("before," Jn 1:49; 13:19). I encourage students to consider these particles vocabulary words and memorize them. Once you understand the basic concept, these infinitive functions are not difficult (see Blass-DeBrunner 1963:205-8).

3. The Noun System.

a. The Hebrew noun is simpler than its Greek counterpart. The case endings (found in Akkadian, Ugaritic and others) disappeared around 1000 B.C. Subject and object are differentiated by word order, context or, most often, by the presence of אֶת before the object. The genitive is determined by a "construct" or bound relationship between two or more nouns. The second or final noun carries the article for both and has an "of" relationship with the former (for example, "the wife of the son of the king"). As a general rule the Hebrew construct carries most of the Greek genitival functions plus some of the dative (such as result, means; see Williams 1967:12-13). Dative functions for the most part are expressed by prepositional phrases.

Adjectives are found with the nouns they modify and agree with their antecedent, although the predicate adjective is normally anarthrous (without an article). Comparative adjectives utilize מִן before the noun ("than," compare Gen 36:7); superlatives are designated by the articular adjective (Gen 9:24), a construct relation (2 Chron 21:17) or a suffixed ם. (Micah 7:4). A type of comparison also is seen in the so-called plural of majesty or respect (as in the אֱלֹהִים of Gen 1:1 or the אֲדֹנִים of Is 19:4), often found with singular adjectives.

Articles and pronouns are also much simpler than their Greek counterparts. Pronouns function similarly to those in English, although the possessive pronouns take the form of a suffix rather than a separate word. Personal pronouns, however, add more emphasis than in English because the verbs themselves carry person and number; thus the pronouns are redundant. The two demonstratives point to something about to be mentioned (זֶה) or a thing already discussed (הוּא). Interrogative and relative pronouns function as they do in English, but there are no true reflexive or reciprocal pronouns in Hebrew; instead it uses either suffixes (or נֶפֶשׁ for the reflexive) or the verb stems (see above) for "themselves" or "one another."

The article also functions in some ways comparable to its use in English. It often refers to someone or something known or previously mentioned, although at times it retains some of its demonstrative force ("that") and can even function in place of the possessive pronoun (see 1 Sam 16:23). With a participle (as in Greek) the article is equivalent to a relative clause, and it can be used generically to refer to a class of items (such as "a dog," Judg 7:5; "a raven," Gen 8:7) or with adjectives to indicate a superlative (2 Kings 10:3). However, it is a mistake to assume that the absence of the article means that the noun is indefinite, for Hebrew omits the article in the first member of a construct, and in other instances. Context alone will tell us whether or not we should have the article in the English translation. For instance, we would translate "a dog" and "a raven" in the generic use of the article above (see Williams 1967:19-21).

b. The Greek noun system is more complex. Unlike Hebrew, inflection determines all case usages in a sentence, and there are three declensions, with the third containing a myriad of separate endings. The case system can be quite confusing. Scholars vigorously debate the proper number of cases. Some, following the historical development of Greek grammar, argue for an eight-case system (nominative, vocative, accusative, genitive, ablative, dative, locative, instrumental); others, following the actual forms themselves, opt for a five-case system by combining the ablative with the genitive and the locative and instrumental with the dative (since in both situations they employ the same endings).

I myself was trained under the eight-case system and employed it for several years. However, through studying the more recent grammars I became convinced that morphology demanded five cases, and so for a time I became a "modified five-case grammarian," seeing the ablative, instrumental, and locative as major subsets of the genitive and dative cases (like Mickelsen 1963:142). Yet, after several more years of teaching Greek grammar, I am now convinced that even this is not quite correct, for many categories placed under the three subsets do not belong there (such as means under the ablative, manner with the instrumental). Therefore, I was forced to conclude that in reality these three are simply other types of the genitive and dative cases, that is, minor rather than major subsets. I would summarize the case uses by the following chart:

I. Nominative Case—identify or designate
    A. Subject ("The *Father* loves the Son"—Jn 3:35)
    B. Predicate nominative ("You are *witnesses*"—1 Thess 2:10)
    C. Appellation ("the mountain [called] *Olivet*"—Lk 19:29)
    D. Apposition ("the king [who is] Herod"— Mt 2:3)
    E. Exclamation (replaces the vocative)
II. Vocative—direct address
III. Genitive—define or describe
    A. Possession ("the boat which was *Simon's*"—Lk 5:3)
    B. Description ("mammon *of unrighteousness*"—Lk 16:9)
    C. Epexegetical—apposition ("the temple [which is] his body"—Jn 2:21)
    D. With verbal nouns—action implied
        1. Subjective genitive—performs the action implied ("the lust of the flesh" ["the flesh desires"]—1 Jn 2:16)
        2. Objective genitive—receives the action implied ("the blasphemy of the Spirit" ["they blaspheme the Spirit"]—Mt 12:31)
    E. Comparison ("greater [than] his Lord"—Jn 13:16)
    F. Ablatival—separation ("alienation *from* the commonwealth of Israel"—Eph 2:12)
    G. Source ("power *from* God"—2 Cor 4:7)
    H. Means or agent ("spoken *by* the shepherds"—Lk 2:18)
    I. Partitive ("half *of* my kingdom"—Mk 6:23)
    J. Adverbial genitive
        1. Time ("he came *during* the night"—Jn 3:2)
        2. Place ("dip his finger *in* the water"—Lk 16:24)

       3.   Reference ("heart evil *with reference to* unbelief"—Heb 3:12)

  K.   Content ("fill you *with* all joy and peace"—Rom 15:13)

IV. Dative—person or thing more remotely concerned

  A.   Indirect object ("I will give *to* you all things"—Mt 18:26)

  B.   Advantage/disadvantage ("treasure *for* yourselves"—Mt 6:19, or "bear witness *against* yourselves"—Mt 23:31)

  C.   Possession ("no child was *theirs*"—Lk 1:7)

  D.   Adverbial dative

       1.   Reference ("we died *with reference to* sin"—Rom 6:2)

       2.   Cause ("in bondage *because of* fear of death"—Heb 2:15)

       3.   Association ("he pleads *with* God"—Rom 11:1)

       4.   Locative—limits "in" which action occurs

          a.   Place ("they came *in* the boat"—Jn 21:8)

          b.   Sphere ("strong *in* faith"—Rom 4:20)

          c.   Time ("*on* the third day he will be raised"—Mt 20:19)

       5.   Instrumental—means "by" which action occurs

          a.   Means or agency ("cast out the spirits *with* [by means of] a word"—Mt 8:16)

          b.   Manner ("prophesying *with* the head unveiled"—1 Cor 11:5)

       6.   Cognate ("judged *with the judgment* you judge"—Mt 7:2)

V. Accusative—direction or extent of the action

  A.   Direct object ("I speak *the truth*"—Jn 8:46)

  B.   Subject of infinitive ("It is necessary *for* the Son of Man to be lifted up"—Jn 3:14)

  C.   Adverbial accusative

       1.   Measure—how long ("separated *about* a stone's throw"—Lk 22:41)

       2.   Manner—how ("*freely* you received, *freely* give"—Mt 10:8)

       3.   Reference ("labored *with reference to* many things"—Rom 16:6)

  D.   Cognate ("fought the good *fight*"—2 Tim 4:7)

  E.   Double accusative ("teach *them many things*"—Mk 6:34)

I have decided to provide a much more detailed chart than usual in order to illustrate a further hermeneutical error often made. I call it "slide-rule exegesis," that is, the belief that one must always identify exactly the one type of grammatical construction for each syntactical unit and then combine the units to yield the meaning of the passage. Koine grammar cannot yield such information. The major point I have been trying to make in the discussion thus far is the absence of precision in Koine as opposed to classical Greek grammar.

This is nowhere more true than with respect to the cases. First, many case usages were being replaced by prepositional phrases whose basic purpose was to make the syntactical thrust more explicit, such as ablative genitive by ἀπό or ἐκ (see Turner 1963:235) or locatival dative by ἐν. Second, when the case is used there is sometimes a deliberate ambiguity. This can be illustrated with one of the more difficult expressions, the subjective or objective genitive. Sometimes neither is fully satisfactory and, as Zerwick says, to choose one over the other is to "sacrifice to clarity of meaning part of the fullness of the meaning" (1963:13). For example, "the love of Christ" which "constrains us" (2 Cor 5:14) and "the patience of Christ" (2 Thess 3:5) include both aspects.[12] Therefore Zerwick argues for a "general genitive" that deliberately bridges the objective and subjective sides. It is both Christ's love for us and our love for him that compels us. In short, the student of the Word must always realize the state of flux in the Koine and avoid too many rigid conclusions on the basis of grammar. When the context indicates, we may indeed stress a particular kind of case usage; but often precision is missing and we must stress the whole context over a single isolated part.

Adjectives and pronouns are fairly straightforward in Greek, and we do not need to spend a great deal of time on them. Moreover, since we are centering on syntactical function rather than on morphology, there is no need to depict the various ways we can find the comparative or superlative in the Koine. Rather, we would notice that here as elsewhere the categories slide together. The simple can be used for the comparative (Mt 18:8-9, καλός, "better") or for the superlative (Mt 22:36, μεγάλη, "greatest"); the comparative can have simple (Jn 13:27, τάχιον, "quickly") or superlative (Mk 9:34, μείζων, "greatest") meaning, and the superlative, which is normally elative ("very" or "quite," see Mt 11:20; Acts 19:32), can have a comparative thrust (Mt 27:64, πρῶτος, "former" and ἔσχατος, "latter") (see Turner 1963:29-32). The near (οὗτος) and far (ἐκεῖνος) demonstratives normally maintain their distinction but can be used in a weakened sense as virtually equivalent to the personal pronoun as subject of a sentence (see Jn 10:6). Greek has an abundance of pronouns of every type (see Mickelsen 1963:145), and so interpretation is seldom difficult.

The definite article, however, is another story. Primarily, the presence or absence of the article does *not* correspond to the English "the" or "a." Rather, the articular (with the article) noun emphasizes the concrete aspect of the noun (for example, ἡ πίστις in Eph 4:13 is translated "the Christian faith") while the anarthrous (with the article) noun stresses the abstract or theological aspect (πίστις, "faith [as trusting God] is being sure of what we hope for," Heb 11:1). This becomes important, for instance, in John 1:1, where the Jehovah's Witnesses read, "The Word was *a* God" on the grounds of the anarthrous form in θεὸς ἦν ὁ λόγος. Two rules explain the absence of the article. According to "Colwell's rule," a predicate noun coming before the verb "to be" lacks the article (θεός) in order to distinguish it from the subject (ὁ λόγος). Furthermore, even if the order were reversed the article would be missing, for ὁ θεός would refer to God the Father, and θεός as it is looks to the "quality" of divinity. In other words, John is saying, "The Word was divine." On the whole the presence or absence of the article is an important interpretive device.

4. Prepositions, Particles and Clauses.

a. Hebrew has fewer prepositions (fifteen in Williams) than Greek. However, those it does include have an impressive array of uses. According to Williams, the preposition בְּ has fifteen different functions and לְ nineteen. The Brown, Driver, Briggs lexicon has over three pages on בְּ alone. This makes the exegetical task quite difficult, for we must consider an amazing number of possibilities when prepositions are involved. There are no shortcuts, and we can only try all the options and see which fits best. Prepositional phrases are very important in Hebrew. With very few adverbs, prepositional phrases or adverbial accusatives often take their place. For instance, לֶאֱמֶת (Is 42:3) describes the servant of Yahweh as "faithfully" causing justice, and בְּצֶדֶק (Lev 19:15) demands that the Israelite judge his neighbor "fairly." Context usually narrows the possibilities, and if the student keeps in mind the basic meaning of each (בְּ, "in"; לְ, "to"; כְּ, "like"; עַל, "upon" and so on), the meaning will not be too difficult to ascertain. For instance, אֶל־ indicates motion toward an object. It is similar to the Greek dative (the Septuagint often translates it with a dative) and likewise can be used for advantage or disadvantage, indirect object, accompaniment or locative. Yet all these functions are related to its basic force above.

The paucity of conjunctions in Hebrew is related to the basic construction of the language. As it does with prepositions and adverbs, Hebrew relies on flexibility rather than on precision of language to make its meaning known. Every term has a multiplicity of purposes, and context must tell the reader the intended meaning of the words, phrases and clauses. Hebrew is dominated by coordinate constructions, especially by the *waw* conjunction, which simply means "and," yet can introduce purpose, cause, adversative or any other type of coordinate or subordinate clause (see Gesenius-Kautzsch 1910: par. 154). This causes great consternation for the beginning student but for the ancient Hebrew added a richness of meaning to the statements. The only simple conjunctions in Hebrew are אוֹ, which always means "or," and פֶּן, which usually means "lest" and leads into the reason for a warning or precaution. כִּי and עִם are multicausal but can also be concessive, recitative, conditional, temporal or resultative. The latter normally is conditional but also can be concessive, optative, privative or pleonastic. לֹא is either conditional or optative and אֲשֶׁר, while usually relative, also can lead into result, purpose, causal, recitative, substantival or conditional clauses. As we can see, conjunctions are multipurpose at the core.

As a result, clause construction can be difficult, since one has to decide whether the conjunctions are coordinate or subordinate. Only the logical development of the context can tell the reader which is correct. It is always helpful to compare versions and consult commentaries or grammars, but in the final analysis we must come to a somewhat subjective decision. It is not my purpose to describe all the different types of clauses (for a good basic discussion, see Mickelsen 1963:153-57). Mickelsen describes two basic types: the noun or verbless clause, emphasizing a state of being; and the verbal clause with both subject and predicate, stressing movement and action. Each clause is grammatically independent or coordinate and only logically subordinate.

Lambdin (1971:279-81) describes three types of clause sequences: (1) the present-future narrative, which contains a series of *waw*-conversives that build upon a leading clause and refine its ideas; (2) a conjunctive nonconverting sequence, which has clauses that do not build upon one another grammatically but simply add further information, for instance two imperatival clauses with the second supplying the purpose or result (1 Kings 1:12 is translated with consecutive imperatives in NASB but in NIV reads, "Now, then, let me advise you how you can save your life and the life of your son Solomon"); (3)

punctual, habitual sequences, which contain temporally prior action that is disjunctive but leads into a resumption of the narrative (such as 1 Sam 17:34-35, with two such temporal subordinations: "when a lion or bear came" and "when [the lion] turned on me"). These are all *waw* or coordinating sequences. When the text utilizes the other conjunctions, we must translate accordingly.

b. Greek particles are more numerous but just as complex as those in Hebrew. The tendency to misuse them in exegesis is greater, again because of false feedback from classical Greek. Prepositions, for instance, originally were adverbs added to the cases for more specific expression. By the Koine period they were grammatical units in their own right. Five aspects summarize the change from the classical to the Hellenistic periods: (1) In increasingly frequent instances, prepositions were replacing the cases as part of the general tendency toward greater explicitness. (2) On the other hand, the number of prepositions was decreasing as part of the historical development from nineteen in the classical period to seven in the modern period; in the New Testament period ὡς and ἀμοί have disappeared, while ἀνά and ἀντί are used much less frequently. (3) The use of several cases with prepositions was being curtailed. The dative was in process of disappearing with all except ἐν, and only ἐπί, παρά and πρός (only once with the genitive) still take all three cases (genitive, dative, accusative). In modern Greek only the accusative is used with prepositions. (4) The use of adverbs or nouns for prepositions was increasing, and they tend to replace the older prepositions for greater richness and expression, such as ἔμπροσθέν for πρὸ or ἐπάνω for ἐπί. At times an adverb is added to a preposition to give it greater force, such as ἀπό τότε or μεχεὶ ὅτε. (5) The classical distinctions between prepositions was becoming blurred, with ἀπό for instance encroaching upon ἐκ, παρά and ὑπό, εἰς being confused with ἐν and πρός, ὑπέρ overlapping ἀντί and περί (see Zerwick 1963:27-37; Blass-DeBrunner 1961:110; and for numerous examples, see Turner 1963:249-57).

As Moule correctly observes, "it is a mistake to build exegetical conclusions on the notion that classical accuracy in the use of prepositions was maintained in the *Koine* period" (1959:49). Yet this is just what many of the older commentators do. The student of the Word must be careful to check the accuracy of such conclusions, for prepositions are exceedingly important exegetical tools with far-reaching theological implications.[13] I might mention one other caveat: while many of the distinctions were becoming blurred, this is not universally true. Certain authors tended to maintain classical precision from time to time, and we should use the better grammars and such works as Turner on the style of the various authors. A good example would be baptizing εἰς τὸ ὄνομα (Mt 28:19). Due to the tendency to confuse the εἰς and ἐν in the Koine period, some scholars have argued that "in the name of" is actually a formula for baptism. On the other hand, Matthew tends to observe the distinction between the two prepositions (see Zerwick 1963:35), and it is more likely that εἰς should maintain its full theological force here. In other words, baptism results in a new relationship, as one becomes the possession of and is brought "into the fellowship of" the entire Godhead (see Osborne 1984:93). Context and the writer's own proclivities must be considered before reading too much or too little into a preposition.

Hellenistic Greek also employs many more particles and conjunctions than Hebrew but fewer than in the classical period. Each of the particles has a very wide use, and only context can tell us exactly how a particular preposition or conjunction is used. I discussed the conditionals above; we should now note that εἰ and ἐάν at times are confused (Mt 5:29; compare Mk 9:43-44), and εἰ can be used for an emphatic negative oath ("certainly not") as a Semitism in Septuagintal style (Mk 8:12; compare Ps 7:4-5 LXX). Likewise, ἵνα has expanded its thrust, found not only with its normal force of purpose but also replacing the infinitive in a recitative sense (in modern Greek the infinitive as object has been completely replaced by ἵνα) as the object of verbs of asking (Mt 7:12, "wish that"; 26:4, "plotted to") or even as subject (Jn 16:7, "that I depart is better for you") or appositive (Jn 17:3, "this is eternal life, that they know you"). It is unnecessary to list all the other uses of these particles; my purpose is to provide a "feel" for Hellenistic Greek, to enable the reader to understand better its flexibility.

Interrogative particles are fairly straightforward, especially expecting an affirmative response. However, μή (or μήτι) can be difficult, for while it normally presupposes a negative answer, it also can be employed to indicate strong doubt. Such is certainly the case in John 4:29, where the Samaritan woman could hardly be saying, "This is not the Christ, is it?" In the context the statement provides a bridge to the virtual evangelization of the town. Therefore it is certainly indicative of doubt, and the New International translation is correct, "Could this be the Christ?"

In a very real sense most of this chapter relates to clause construction, for all the verb moods (such as participles, conditionals) apply to the clause as well. Greek clauses are easier to distinguish than are their Hebrew counterparts, due to the greater variety and specificity of conjunctions and particles. Certain writers (Mark, Luke at times) follow the Semitic habit of overusing the coordinating conjunction "and" (καί), so that the reader has to supply subordination from the logical context. Paul, on the other hand, often subordinates in so complex a fashion that it becomes almost impossible to understand his train of thought (for example, Eph 1:3-14, a single sentence). It is not my purpose to discuss each type of clause (see Mickelsen 1963:149-53 for a good discussion), for a basic understanding is sufficient and the differences between coordinating and subordinating conjunctions are fairly simple to learn.

In many grammars a discussion of sentence and clause construction includes figures of speech, but that is a subject for the chapter on syntax. Here I will note two grammatical peculiarities: asyndeton and parenthesis. *Asyndeton* occurs when the conjunction joining two phrases or clauses is omitted. It often occurs when a list is being enumerated (1 Pet 4:3; 2 Tim 3:2) but also can be found in subordinate clauses, as in the absence of ἵνα after an imperative (Mt 5:24; 8:4), and even between coordinate clauses (Jn 1:23, 26, 29 and so forth). In the Gospels asyndeton can be used as a rhetorical device to add solemnity to a statement (such as in Mt 5:3-17). A *parenthesis* is a digression on an important theme; it usually interrupts the train of thought and clarifies a certain aspect (much like the modern footnote). Paul is especially adept at this and his use of it can be confusing at times. Translations often help by placing such asides in parentheses or marking off the portion by dashes; for instance, the long excursis on the Gentiles and the Law in

Romans 2:14-15 or the shorter parentheses on grace and faith in Ephesians 2:5b, 8b.

One final aspect that should be discussed is the order of clauses in the Greek New Testament. Often the organization of clauses does not quite fit our modern thinking, and misunderstanding can result. Beekman and Callow discuss three major problems (1974:222-28), arguing that "the order of the original must not be slavishly followed (in the translation) for it may not convey the original message faithfully in the RL" (the Receptor Language; for instance, English). The first problem occurs when the linguistic order (the actual order of the clauses or sentences in the text) does not fit the chrono-logical order (the way it is worked out in experience). This is found often in a "flashback" scene like the imprisonment of John the Baptist (Mk 6:17-18), where the final events are first. If a culture does not understand flashbacks, it can be misleading, even to the extent of seeming to say it was John who had the immoral relations with Herod's wife. Another example would be Hebrews 10:21, "let us draw near to God with a sincere heart in full assurance of faith having our hearts sprinkled to cleanse us from a guilty conscience and having our bodies washed with pure water." In actual experience the order is reversed and each statement depends upon the one following. First, we experience the washing and cleansing; then as a result have the full assurance that only faith provides that God is near. Only then can we go before the throne with a sincere heart. This descending series is seen frequently in the New Testament and must be recognized to be understood.

A second problem occurs when the linguistic order does not follow the logical order. Such a distinction is seen often in passages where a reason is given for an action, such as Mark 6:31. The New American Standard Version translates it in the literal order of the Greek: "And He said to them, 'Come away by yourselves to a lonely place and rest awhile.' For there were many people coming and going, and they did not even have time to eat." The New International Version, however, places it in its proper logical order: "Then, because so many people were coming and going that they did not even have a chance to eat, he said to them, 'Come with me by yourselves to a quiet place and get some rest.'" The "by this" passages of 1 John are a special problem, for the commentators are divided as to whether "this" refers backwards (2:5; 3:19; 4:6) or forwards (2:3; 3:16, 24; 4:2-3, 13; 5:2). In each instance context must decide. In the latter instance, however, there is a logical disorder, for the "this" clause (2:3a, "By this we know that we have known him") is the logical result and follows the experience of the "if" or "when" clause (2:3b, "if we keep his commands"). Beekman and Callow (1974:225) call this a "grounds-conclusion" relationship; the conclusion that we are assured we have known him is based upon the grounds that we have obeyed his commands. We could (and must in certain cultures) rewrite the sentence, "when we obey God's commands, we realize that we really have known him."

A third type of clause structure could be called "negative-affirmative statements." Often the negative element of a pair is first in the text, and this too can cause difficulty in some cultures. For instance, some may find misleading "not to do my will but the will of him who sent me" (Jn 6:38) or the Gethsemane cry, "not my will but yours" (Mk 14:36). The interpreter must be aware of such ancient idioms. Other Semitic types of clause structure (such as chiasm, inclusio) were discussed in the last chapter. Here I would add only that in some cases the preacher (or translator) may need to take them out of the textual order for the sake of clarity. In many instances a detailed explanation of the Semitic style may be counterproductive. The level of the audience and the purpose of the message will be the deciding factors.

In conclusion, it has been common in the past to link grammatical structure with the basic make-up of the society. Boman (1960) and others concluded that the following differences characterized the two languages (see the excellent summary in Barr 1961:10-13):

a. *Dynamic vs. static.* The Hebrews were action oriented and stressed God's acts in linear history; the Greeks emphasized contemplation and the true, unchanging ideal behind movement, that is, the world of appearances.

b. *Concrete vs. abstract.* Hebraic thought stressed the reality of the object perceived while Greek philosophy abstracted it, separating the object from the subject and thinking through to the idea behind it.

c. *Concept of the human.* Greek anthropology teaches a dualism with the immortal soul imprisoned in a mortal body; Hebraic concepts stress the unity between the outward, visible manifestation and the soul within. Also, the Greeks stressed the individual while the Hebrews emphasized the corporate group.

These scholars taught that Greek forms an analytical thought-pattern that makes distinctions between being and becoming, reality and appearance, time and eternity, body and soul, spirit and manner, group and individual. Hebrew is a "totality type" of language and refuses to note such differences.

Barr proceeds to criticize severely the linguistic basis for these distinctions (1961: chap. three). At the outset, he argues that it is an artificial comparison, since two linguistic groups are isolated from the broad spectrum of ancient languages without considering the others. More important, their semantic method is faulty, for these scholars use circular reasoning to determine the differences and then read the data accordingly. The true issue is to determine the interrelationship between philosophy and language in a culture. In other words, which has influenced the other? The two, he believes, cannot be brought together so easily. The problem is the lack of a proper linguistic approach. The relative absence of abstract nouns in Hebrew, for instance, does not demand a stress on concreteness, nor does the presence of two Greek words for "body" (Hebrew has only one) mean that Hellenists saw greater distinctions. Such differences relate only to the development of the language and have no bearing upon the ways the two groups perceived reality.[14]

At first glance Hebrew grammar does not seem to offer as much as does Greek grammar for exegesis, since it is not as developed a language as is Greek. As a result, it appears to be more subjective. Certainly Hebrew needs a grammar of the depth of Blass-Debrunner. Gesenius-Kautzsch centers more upon morphology than upon syntax, and Williams is an intermediate rather than a detailed work. However, a glance at the secondary literature and the number of dissertations convinces us that such is indeed on the horizon. It will certainly be welcome to all serious students. However, Hebrew grammar is still an invaluable tool, and an awareness of the way minor clauses function or the construct works helps immensely when one seeks to make sense of the text. Greek grammar is actually more difficult to use, since many of us have to rework previous misconceptions before we may begin to employ it correctly.

Roy Harris provides an excellent synopsis of the difficulties of modern grammar in his *The Language Myth* (1981:54-85). He argues that the entire process has defaulted because of its faulty methodology, restricting itself to categories derived from Latin and removing itself from morphology, syntax and lexicology. The result is a series of "fixed codes" that rigidly define parameters of speech without consulting the ways people are actually speaking. It is an artificial, unrealistic system that forces older categories upon correct usage. This is exactly what is done often in biblical exegesis, transferring classical categories into Koine passages. Moreover, it ignores the major truth: the immediate context alone can decide how we define a grammatical relationship. The grammatical list or examples from elsewhere in the book or testament can provide nothing more than possibilities, and the reader must be as flexible as the text. Harris calls for an "internalised linguistic knowledge" that allows the dynamic "use" of language by its speakers (in other words, the synchronic or current rather than diochronic or historical use) to provide the key to the development of grammatical "rules" (p. 75). This is quite important, for it allows the individual authors of Scripture the right to pursue their own grammatical modes. It is no longer adequate to say that in the book of Revelation John "broke grammatical rules" or that it was the "least literary of the NT books" (Zerwick 1963:6). Rather, the book of Revelation deliberately employed the grammar of apocalyptic literature (see chap. ten below), which was completely valid within its own context. In every case the reader must allow the context to make the final grammatical decision.

Exegetical Procedures

I recommend a "study sheet" for exegesis, divided into five or six columns. In the first will go the text itself, with the words flowing as they are discussed in the other columns. In the second will be a grammatical identification (for example: pres. act. impr. 3s of λέγω, "I say") and in the third the grammatical-syntactical information (such as: stress on the durative, "keep on saying"). The fourth column should be reserved for lexical study and the fifth for historical-cultural backgrounds. A final column may be used for application (see chap. sixteen). As you proceed through the text, it is important to highlight certain key points for special study. While you need to be aware of the whole text, only a few require specific, in-depth analysis (see Fee 1983:77-78 for a more detailed list of the types of things to include). On these points you will wish to consult grammars and commentaries, working through the types of possibilities mentioned above. Fee mentions four steps in making grammatical decisions: (a) be aware of the options; (b) consult the grammars; (c) check out the author's usage elsewhere (use a concordance); (d) determine which option makes best sense in the context (1984:82). I would add a fifth: (e) keep your emphasis upon the total syntactical development and never isolate grammatical units.

At all times it is necessary to keep in mind the total syntactical context. In fact, this demonstrates the artificial nature of our discussion. We cannot make grammatical decisions without syntax or make syntactical decisions without the results of grammar. I have separated grammar, semantics and syntax into distinct chapters not because they are unrelated but because each has distinct problems and criteria. In the exegetical spiral there will be an interdependent circularity as the reader studies them simultaneously, continuing to work upward to the whole of the statement. These are three aspects of a larger whole: first, we note the particular use of the tense, voice and mood of the verbs and place them in their total syntactical context. Next, we study the function of the cases and of prepositions and other particles within the sentence as a whole. Finally, we put the sentence together, noting emphases on the basis of word order, and trace the interrelationship of the parts for the total meaning of the sentence within its paragraph. For instance, in terms of the Greek tense, present and aorist provide the greatest problems; and in terms of case, genitive and dative yield the greatest difficulties. In Hebrew the construct and *waw*-conversives are the most complex.

3
Semantics

MEANING IS AT THE HEART OF COMMUNICATION. WORDS PROVIDE THE BUILDING BLOCKS of meaning, grammar and syntax the design. However, until recently semantics (determining word meaning) was more an art than a science. Louw (1982:1-4) says that it is only in the last twenty-five years that the study of words and their meaning has come to the forefront of academic concerns. Moreover, only in this century has it been truly recognized as a linguistic science in its own right. James Barr's epochal work *The Semantics of Biblical Language* (1961) first applied linguistic principles scientifically to biblical study. The results were startling, to say the least. Previously, scholars thought that the meaning of a word could be found in its historical development (the thesis of the first volume on semantics ever published, by M. Breal in 1897). We now know how much more complex is the true discovery of word meaning. Silva mentions the frustration of attempting to cover this field, "a task that cannot be executed in one volume without oversimplifying the material" (1983:9). How much more difficult is it to cover the issue in a single chapter?!

Word studies have certainly become the most popular aspect of exegesis. A glance at the standard commentaries, with their structure organized as a word-by-word walk through the text, will demonstrate this. So will the average college or seminary classroom, where exegesis courses often spend an inordinate amount of time on word studies. This is especially true of many Old Testament courses, where the seeming lack of a strong return from Hebrew grammar leads the professor to center upon word studies as the most important factor in exegesis. Of course, as I stated in the last chapter, grammar can contribute a great deal, and I would argue here that we cannot actually separate the two. Without grammatical relationships with other words, there is no meaning. If I utter the term *counter,* the hearer has no idea what I mean. Without a context in a grammatical sentence, a word is meaningless. Only as I say "Look on the counter" or "Counter his argument" does the term have a connotation.

Most modern linguists recognize the centrality of the literary and historical context, that is, the linguistic and extralinguistic dimensions, to the whole issue of meaning (see Thiselton 1977:75). In other words, the semantic analysis of a concept involves not only syntax but also the historical-cultural background behind the statements. Analysis is part of and yet presupposes the total hermeneutical package. One does not perform these steps one at a time upon a passage. Rather, there is a constant spiraling action as one aspect (such as grammar or backgrounds) informs another aspect (such as semantics) and then itself is transformed by the result.

Yet as critical as an understanding of semantics actually is, it is amazing how little emphasis has been given to the subject. Carson presents basic linguistic fallacies of many contemporary works (1984:25-66), and Silva laments,

> How does one . . . explain the fact that even reputable scholars have attempted to shed light on the biblical languages while working in isolation from the results of contemporary linguistics? One could just as easily try to describe Jewish sects in the first century without a knowledge of the Dead Sea Scrolls. (1983:10)

The problem of course is that we have been taught several erroneous assumptions. That is the subject of the first section of this chapter.

I want to make clear at the outset that I am not merely trying to establish "rules" for semantic analysis. W. P. Alston (1974:17-48) demonstrates the error of what he calls "the rule theory of linguistic meaning." Alston argues that such rules should meet four require-ments: (1) distinctiveness, with conditions specified for the correctness or inadequacy of an utterance; (2) a translinguistic connection, relating to the referential content behind an utterance; (3) noncircularity, going beyond definitions to determine the valid structure within which meaning can be incorporated; and (4) scope, covering all types of speech behavior (such as assertions, questions, promises) and not just the meaning of particular terms. Thus any such rule at the outset must be *descriptive* (stating how speech functions, that is, what "is") rather than *prescriptive* (determining artificial standards for what "must be").

Following J. L. Austin, Alston calls for an "illocutionary act" approach, that is, the determination of the actual conditions that communicate meaning. These conditions must be culture-specific; they must be aligned with the way the individual culture com-municates. This means that at every stage of biblical study the speech patterns of the ancient culture (biblical Hebrew or Greek) must determine the semantic principles (notice I deliberately say *principles* rather than *rules*). In this chapter I will then discuss previous-ly held ideas that do not work and then elucidate several that I trust will enable the reader to determine the probable meaning of the utterances (not just the terms) in a given context.

Semantic Fallacies

In this section I will not merely discuss semantic errors but try to work through the topics to a proper delineation of principles under each category that will enable the reader to use the tool correctly. In other words, the discussion will provide a topical bridge to the more systematic presentation of methodology in the second half of the chapter. Naturally, I cannot be exhaustive in my coverage. However, the more important problems will, I trust, be considered.

1. The Lexical Fallacy. It has become common, especially since the appearance of Kittel's

Theological Dictionary of the New Testament (TDNT, 1932—1977) and to a lesser extent its Old Testament counterpart (1970—) to assume that word studies can settle theological arguments. For instance, some seem to assume that a decision as to whether κεφαλή means "source" or "authority" in 1 Corinthians 11:2b or Ephesians 5:23-24 will solve the issue of the woman's role in church and home. While none will state it quite so starkly, an inordinate amount of time is spent tracing the term(s) through extant Greek literature and too little time is spent in noting the context. This is not to argue against establishing the semantic field but rather for recognizing the centrality of the immediate context. This error can occur in works of the highest quality. Silva (1983:23) notes the overemphasis upon word studies in George Knight's *The Faithful Sayings in the Pastoral Letters* (1968), citing A. T. Hanson's review that "in his scrupulous examination of the lexicography of the sayings, Mr. Knight has all too often missed the wood for the trees" (in *JTS* 1969:719).

This overemphasis upon words to the detriment of context leads to one of the most serious of Barr's criticisms, "illegitimate totality transfer" (1961:218). After going to so much trouble to find multitudinous meanings and uses for a word, it is hard for the scholar to select just one for the passage. The tendency is to read all or most of them (that is, to transfer the "totality" of the meanings) into the single passage. Such is "illegitimate," for no one ever has in mind all or even several of the possible meanings for a term when using it in a particular context. Consider the term *grill*. We hardly think of the connotation "grill a hamburger" when speaking of a fence "grill," let alone the idea of "grilling," or questioning, a person. These are rather obvious examples but at times similar errors can be made when interpreting a language with which we are not so familiar, like biblical Hebrew or Greek. This in fact leads to Barr's criticisms of Kittel. In seeking the theological concept behind the terms, the articles repeatedly stress breadth over specifics. Barr especially notes (1961:218) the article on *ekklēsia* ("church"). While the term may be interpreted variously as an "assembly," as "the body of Christ," as "the community of the Kingdom" or as "the bride of Christ," these constitute possible meanings of *ekklēsia* but not *the* meaning of the term in Matthew 16:18.

Thiselton (1978:84) notes Nida's contention that "the correct meaning of a term is that which contributes least to the total context" (1972:86). Nida means that the narrowest possible meaning is usually correct in individual contexts. The defining terms surrounding it limit the usage quite radically. Thiselton uses the term *greenhouse* as an example. The various meanings of "green" and "house" hardly have much bearing upon the combination of the two either in "green house" (itself open to differing meanings in various contexts) or in "greenhouse." The same must be true of *ekklēsia* in Matthew 16:18; Acts 7:38 or Ephesians 1:22-23.

2. The Root Fallacy. This common error assumes that the root of a term and its cognates carries a basic meaning that is reflected in every subordinate use of the word(s).

It seems to be commonly believed that in Hebrew there is a 'root meaning' which is effective throughout all the variations given to the root by affixes and formative elements, and that therefore the 'root meaning' can confidently be taken to be part of the actual semantic value of any word or form which can be assigned to an identifiable root; and likewise that any word may be taken to give some kind of suggestion of other words formed from the same root. (Barr 1961:100)

This fallacy is closely related to etymology, and many scholars in fact equate the two. However, it has two aspects that I would like to separate: the belief that a basic root meaning is to be found in all subsets (root fallacy); and the belief that the historical development of a term determines its current meaning (lexical fallacy). "Etymology" would be a cover term that encompasses both aspects.

Gibson notes the misuse of comparative philology in Old Testament research (1981:20-34). On the basis of similar roots scholars cross time lines and apply a particular meaning to a difficult term or concept from a document belonging to a related language but from a different era. One example he mentions (pp. 24-28) is equating *lotan* in the Baal texts (Ugaritic) with "leviathan" *(lwytn)* in Isaiah 27:1, although little evidence connects the Ugaritic texts of the late second millennium with the Hebrew of Isaiah's time. Barr provides an even better example: "bread" *(leḥem)* and "war" *(milḥāmâh);* they obviously come from the same root but could hardly have a shared meaning, "as if battles were fought for bread or bread a necessary provision for battles" (1961:102; for further Old Testament examples, see Kedar 1981:82-98). The problem is to define exactly what constitutes a universal meaning that can be transferred across time and language barriers. Most doubt whether any such universal aspect exists in semantic domains. However, many of the older lexicons (such as Thayer's Greek lexicon) and word study books (such as Vincent, Vine or Wuest) assumed such. This can lead to many misinterpretations. Thiselton notes the linguistic connection between "hussy" and "housewife" and asks whether one would wish to equate the two (1977:81).

Similarly, it is erroneous to take a compound word, break it into its component parts, and read the resultant meanings in that light. Louw states unequivocally, "It is a basic principle of modern semantic theory that we cannot progress from the form of a word to its meaning" (1982:29). Two well-known examples may help: *ekklēsia* and *paraklētos.* The first is often said to mean "the called out" believers, while in reality nowhere in extant Greek literature does *ekklēsia* have this connotation. The other is the major title for the Holy Spirit in John 14—16 and contains the roots *para* ("beside") and *kaleō* ("call"). At one time the term did have a meaning similar to its root, "one called alongside to help," and was used in Hellenistic circles for a "helper" or "advocate." However, this is inadequate for John 14:16, 26; 15:26; and 16:7-8, 13 because that sense is never used in the context. Moreover, the semantic field does not build upon that root. Brown (1970:1136-37) distinguishes two forensic or legal meanings (advocate, mediator) and two nonforensic meanings (comforter, exhorter). However, he finds none of them adequate for John and posits that the major thrust is continuity of person and ministry. The Spirit as "another Paraclete" is "another Jesus," that is, continuing his ministry.

The main point is that the root meaning, although closer to the semantic range of the term, is not a "universal meaning" that permeates the whole. All who have studied Greek are aware that a prepositional prefix can affect a stem in three ways (see Wenham 1965:55): (1) The force of both preposition and verb continues *(epagō,* "I lead away"; *ekballō,* "I throw out"); (2) the preposition intensifies the thrust of the verb *(luō,* "I loose";

apoluō, "I release"); (3) the preposition changes the meaning of the verb *(ginōskō,* "I know"; *anaginōskō,* "I read"). The student can never assume that a prepositional prefix affects a compound in any one of the three ways. Only the context and word usage can decide.

Most students assume that the root or basic meaning of a term is the definition memorized as vocabulary in the basic language course. However, what they memorize is the usual or normal meaning rather than the root of a word. For instance, *ballein* means to "throw," but the standard lexicon (Bauer-Arndt-Gingrich-Danker) also defines it as to "put," "place" or "bring." These obviously do not derive from "throw" but are other linguistic usages. Similarly, *praxis* means "act" or "deed" but can also be translated "undertaking," "business," "state" or "situation," depending on the context.

For this reason the basic tool for serious word study is not a theological word book but a lexicon. The best for Old Testament study is Brown-Driver-Briggs (BDB) and for New Testament study is Bauer-Arndt-Gingrich-Danker (BAGD). Both can function as concordances as well, for many terms have all their occurrences listed. For more serious students there is also Liddell and Scott for classical Greek, Moulton and Milligan for the papyri. In addition are the excellent concordances, Mandelkern or Lisowsky for the Old Testament, Moulton and Geden or Aland's computer concordance for the New Testament, Hatch and Redpath for the Septuagint, Rengstorf for Josephus. Those engaged in detailed research have no end of tools to guide their study. Similar works on the intertestamental literature and the rabbis are currently in progress. For the student without knowledge of the languages, Strong's, Young's or Cruden's concordances are available.

At times a study of roots can be highly illuminating. As I already mentioned, some compounds do maintain their root meaning. In 1 John 2:1, *paraklētos* does follow its root meaning of "advocate": "If anyone sins, we have an advocate with the Father, Jesus Christ the righteous." On these occasions, the root meaning adds richness to the exegesis. The point I made above is that we dare not assume any type of universal meaning for a root. Louw discusses the general or most common meaning of a word (see above) and points out that while it never yields a universal meaning, it does have linguistic value in what is called "unmarked meaning" (1982:33-37). He defines this as "that meaning which would be readily applied in a minimum context where there is little or nothing to help the receptor in determining the meaning" (p. 34). For instance, farmers and stockbrokers would interpret the sentence "They had a large amount of stock" in different ways. However, add specifics like "The stock died" or "The stock averages fell" and all would understand the sentences. In a minimum context (with few modifiers) each one understands on the basis of his or her most common meaning. As an example, Louw refers to L. Goppelt's article on *trapeza* ("table") in TDNT (vol. 8), where Goppelt has divided his discussion into "General Use" (including etymology) and specific uses like "Dining Table," "Moneychanger's Table" and such like.

Finally, I might mention Gibson's extensive discussion of roots in a Semitic context (1981:176-206). He shows that no "common sense—bearing" transfer takes place between an original root and its later descendants. However, at a lesser level, there is semantic transfer between cognate languages and so a limited value to comparative linguistics at the semantic level. Louw describes this as the "functional referent." There is no "genetic" relationship between roots, but if obvious parallels exist between terms in two languages, then there is semantic overlap between the two terms. Silva (1983:42-43; compare Kedar 1981:98-105) points out that this is especially valuable in Old Testament study, since there are 1,300 hapax legomena (once-only words) and 500 others that occur only twice (out of a total vocabulary of 8,000!). While many can be known from other sources, several hundred obscure terms have no Hebrew cognates and are not found in extrabiblical literature. In these instances root transfer, although it can yield only possible meaning, is invaluable. For instance, Silva points to Job 40:12, "Look on every proud man [and] humble him, and *hadok* the wicked where they stand." The Arabic *hadaka* "conforms to the established phonological correspondences between Arabic and Hebrew, and its meaning 'tear down' fits the context perfectly" (p. 43). The key is linguistic and functional parallels between the terms.

3. Misuse of Etymology. Actually, this category includes the first two as subsets, but for convenience I have separated them. Etymology per se is the study of the history of a term. Louw traces the problem back to the ancient Greek belief that the meaning of a word stemmed from its very nature rather than from convention (1982:23-25). Thus until recently scholars believed that the key to a word's meaning lay in its origin and history. This assumption of linear development lay behind the misuse of etymology, wherein any past use of a word could be read into its current meaning.

Ferdinand de Saussure, in his *Course in General Linguistics* (1915), pioneered the distinction between "diachrony" (the history of a term) and "synchrony" (the current use of a term). He argued radically that "the linguist who wishes to understand a state must discard all knowledge of everything that produced it and ignore diachrony . . . by suppressing the past. The intervention of history can only falsify his judgment" (1915:81, in Silva 1983:36). Of course, Saussure did not deny the validity of etymology altogether; rather, he restricted it to its proper sphere, the history of words. Therefore, current usage rather than history alone could define a word's meaning. The example that appears most frequently in the literature is the word *nice,* which stems from the Latin *nescius,* "ignorant." Thus, it is not the background or evolution of a term but its present usage that has relevance for its meaning.

Scholars have long been guilty of errors in this area. An oft-cited example is the misunderstanding with respect to *hypērētēs* ("servant"). Barclay followed Trench in arguing that the concept derived from the Homeric *eressē,* "to row," then went further and said the *hypo* added the idea of "under," therefore designating "a rower on the lower bank of a trireme." *Hyperetēs* thereby became a "lowly servant." This derivation combines root fallacy with etymology fallacy, for according to Louw this meaning cannot be found in Greek literature current to the New Testament. It is highly dubious at best. The problem is that it makes great preaching and so is difficult to resist. Yet if it is not *true,* dare we risk the danger?

Silva notes the frequent danger of equating Greek words in the New Testament with their Hebrew counterparts (1983:56-73). Since Edwin Hatch in the last century, many have assumed that the Septuagint had such an enormous impact on New Testament lexicography that much of its language was transformed into a type of semitized Greek. Some have taken this to the extent that terms in biblical Greek often are assigned the same meaning as the Hebrew word they translate (Turner 1980 is criticized for this error). To do so, however, is to misunderstand the true state of New Testament Greek. As I noted in the last chapter, the consensus is that the New Testament is written in colloquial Greek. Therefore, the link between the Masoretic Text, the Septuagint and the New Testament is complex rather than simple. We dare not assume that any particular word is influenced primarily by its Hebrew counterpart. To be sure, there may be influence; but the degree of continuity can be established only after detailed study. As Silva points out (p. 72) this is true of the Septuagint itself; how much more true of the New Testament, a further step removed from the Masoretic Text.

Thiselton discusses the further danger of "dead metaphor" (1977:81). This occurs when the imagery behind a word in its past no longer has meaning. For instance, *splanchni-zomai* ("to show compassion") is given the connotation of involving one's innermost being, due to the presence of *splanchna* ("internal organs"). However, this metaphorical thrust was no longer present in the first century. One should never refer to the use of a term in Homer or Aristotle to "prove" or "demonstrate" a meaning in New Testament times. This error can become anachronistic, for example, reading *dynamis* ("power") as "dynamite." As Carson explains, dynamite blows things up and destroys while the Word makes whole and heals (1984:33). More important, a modern metaphor can never be used to define but only to illustrate.

Perhaps the best statement of the problem is that of J. Vendryes's *Language: A Linguistic Introduction to History* (in Barr 1961:109; Silva 1983:46-47):

> Etymology, however, gives a false idea of the nature of a vocabulary for it is concerned only in showing how a vocabulary has been formed. Words are not used according to their historical value. The mind forgets—assuming that it ever knew—the semantic evolutions through which the words have passed. Words always have a *current* value, that is to say, limited to the moment when they are employed, and a *particular* value relative to the momentary use made of them. (Italics his)

This does not mean, however, that etymology has no place in word studies, only that it must be employed with care. The key is to discover whether or not there is a conscious allusion to background meaning in the text. One example would be the use of *pararymen* ("drift away") in Hebrews 2:1. Two metaphors are possible, both attested to in current Greek literature of the day: (1) A ring that "slips off" the finger and is lost (Plutarch); or (2) a ship that slips downstream past the point of safety. Since the author used a nautical metaphor in the similar context of 6:19 ("anchor of the soul"), the second becomes somewhat more likely. The important point is that both synchronic or current usage and the context itself have made the etymological metaphor possible.

Another word that also has been under much discussion is *hamartanō*, one of the basic words for "sin." Louw points out the inadequacy of utilizing the Homeric idea of "miss the mark" or "purpose" as the "hidden meaning" of the term (1982:29-30), but Silva correctly points out that this may indeed be the connotation in a specific text, Romans 3:23, with the idea of sin "as a failing to obtain God's glory" (1983:50). We cannot make a general assumption based on this, but an individual instance can draw upon an etymological distinction. This is especially true of biblical puns or plays upon words (see Gibson 1981:180-81), as in the preceding example.

At all times the synchronic dimension has priority, and diachronic considerations are utilized only if current usage makes such possible and if the context itself makes historical allusions probable. This is often the case in the biblical writings due to the importance of tradition and canon. The prophetic works of the Old Testament contain many deliberate allusions to the Torah, and the New Testament often uses a term in the sense of its Old Testament or Septuagint background. This is the basis of Leon Morris's argument for the forensic use of the passive *dikaiousthai* in Romans 3:24 (and elsewhere) for "justify" rather than "make righteous" (1956:233-35, 259-60). He grounds his position partly on the direct influence of the Septuagint on Paul's technical language. The context makes it probable that Morris is correct. Of course, this is even more true of direct quotes or allusions to Septuagint passages. As we will see later, the best clue to the symbolism of the book of Revelation lies in its background (much of it from the Old Testament).

In studying the history of a word we must consider the strong possibility of semantic change, when a word alters its meaning over the course of years. This is a basic fact of language. The New King James Version was necessitated because the average layperson no longer understood many of the terms in the 1611 version. As Sawyer states, "What is quite inadmissable . . . is the assumption that because a word has a particular meaning in one context, it automatically has the same meaning in another quite different context a couple of thousand years earlier" (or later! 1972:9).

In fact, semantic change has a very real value in word study, for it acts as a control against an overly zealous delineation of the semantic field to include archaic meanings. The most comprehensive coverage of such is found in Silva (1983:53-97), who notes how difficult it is to trace semantic change in the Old Testament (due to the paucity of extrabiblical material and the difficulty of dating the texts) and primarily studies semantic change from the Septuagint to the New Testament. At times the semantic field can expand (such as the use of *artos*, "bread," for "food" in general); at other times it can contract (such as the use of *ho pistis*, "faith" for the Christian faith). In many cases virtual substitution has occurred, as in the use of *angelos* for the Hebrew *mal'āk*, "angel." The great influence of the Hebrew Bible has resulted in a great deal of semantic borrowing, as in cases of loan words *(abba,* "father") or structural considerations (the centrality of *kardia,* "heart," for the mind due to the influence of the Hebrew *lēb*). We must be aware of such possibilities if we are to read the evidence correctly. I will discuss many details from this category (such as polysemy, homonymy, ellipsis) in the next chapter.

4. Misuse of Subsequent Meaning. The opposite problem from etymology occurs when we read later meanings back into the biblical material. This occurs, for instance, when *martys* ("witness") is interpreted in terms of its second-century meaning of "martyrdom," or when the "fish" of John 21:11-14 is made a symbol of the Eucharist because of its presence in the sacrament in the later church. Kaiser coined the phrase "the analogy of antecedent Scripture" to cover the process of interpreting the theology behind a text (1981:134-40). This means that we must interpret a theological term not on the basis of what it came to mean later but rather on the basis of what it meant in the past, especially as that past meaning affected the current use of the term. While that is broader than the topic here, Kaiser applies it first to "the use of certain terms which have already acquired a special meaning in the history of salvation and have begun to take on a technical status (e.g. 'seed,' 'servant,' 'rest,' 'inheritance')" (p. 137).

This principle is even more applicable to word study. One of the basic problems of modern popular interpretation is the tendency to read twentieth-century meanings into the ancient terms of Scripture. All of us have attended Sunday-school classes where great theological points were drawn from Webster's Dictionary or from particular phrases in the Amplified Bible. A similar problem is the tendency to read New Testament meaning into Old Testament concepts like salvation, grace, mercy and truth. At all times current usage and the context must determine the meaning. Future meaning does have a place, of course. Canon criticism (such as Child's commentary on Exodus) has demonstrated the value of an awareness of later interpretation on a text. However, it dare not influence the meaning of the current text but only can show how a text or term was later applied to the life of God's people.

5. The One-Meaning Fallacy. At times we encounter the view that every appearance of a Hebrew or Greek term should be translated by the same English word. This of course is closely related to the root fallacy described above. The Concordant Version has attempted this with disastrous results. The problem is a distorted view of language. The average person has, say, a vocabulary of 20,000 words; yet linguists have shown that in that person's lifetime he or she will express four to five million different ideas. Simple mathematics demands that the words must be used in many different combinations with many different meanings in order to meet the need. Naturally, some highly technical terms (such as those in the sciences) will approximate a single meaning; but not words in everyday language. This is complicated even further when one crosses language barriers to communicate, as is the case when studying the Bible. No two languages express themselves or use words the same way. To say a simple phrase such as "I will get it" in German, for instance, one must ask which of the many possible German words for "get" will express that particular idea. Cassells' *Wörterbuch* has two columns with scores of word combinations for the simple English word "get."

The same is true when translating from the Hebrew or the Greek. Louw uses the excellent example of *sarx,* "flesh," a word often translated literally in the versions (1982:39-40). However, note the following widely different semantic uses: Matthew 24:12, "no flesh will be saved" (no person); John 1:14, "the Word made flesh" (became a human being); Romans 9:8, "children of the flesh" (children of natural birth); Hebrews 5:7, "days of his flesh" (his earthly life); Romans 8:13, "live according to the flesh" (sinful nature); Jude 7, "go after strange flesh" (sexual immorality). The point is obvious: the English term *flesh* cannot adequately express all these divergent connotations, and a translation would be wrong to use "flesh" in all these instances. As Louw concludes, "one can never say what *sarx* means, but only what it means in this or that context" (pp. 39-40).

Below I will discuss the linguistic concept of "primary" and "secondary" meanings, but this is a quite different phenomenon from "one meaning." The "primary" meaning relates to the "thread of meaning" that ties together the semantic field of a word (Beekman and Callow 1974:96-97). However, even that definition is debated and most linguists agree that many associated meanings are related only peripherally (see below). The technical term for the multiple senses an individual word can have is "polysemy," literally "multiple meaning." This is an extremely important linguistic principle, for it forces us once again to the semantic field and the context as the two factors in determining the meaning of a term.

6. Misuse of Parallels. This provides another of the most frequent sources of error. An excellent article by Robert Kysar (1970:250-55) shows that Rudolf Bultmann and C. H. Dodd in their commentaries on John (specifically the prologue) used entirely different sources of evidence to "prove" their respective theories. Rarely did either consider the parallels adduced by the other. In other words, they chose only those parallels which would support their preconceived notions. This happens all too often in scholarly circles. Instead of a comprehensive study of all possible parallels in order to discover which *best* fits the context, scholars will select only those most favorable to the thesis and ignore the others. Further, they will often accumulate numerous examples in order to overwhelm the reader with volume. Carson calls this "verbal parallellomania, . . . the listing of verbal parallels in some body of literature as if those bare phenomena demonstrate conceptual links or even dependency" (1984:43-44). Such occurs frequently with some practitioners in the History of Religions school. In their desire to show the Hellenistic rather than Jewish origin of a concept or term, they virtually ignore evidence from Jewish circles. Martin Hengel in his many writings has done a brilliant job of overturning many of the invalid assumptions of this school.

It is critical to recognize the relative value of parallels. For instance, when studying Paul's use of *dikaiousthai* ("justify") in Romans 3:24, we must consider several levels. First, the passive voice verb rather than the noun or adjective is truly relevant. Second, Paul's use elsewhere *in Romans* is more important than his use elsewhere. Third, the use of *dikaioun* and cognates elsewhere in the New Testament does not tell us how it is used in Romans. All the latter can do is expand the semantic field and provide possible meanings from the use of the term in the early church. Fourth, we must ask whether there is a direct allusion or indirect influence from the Septuagint or the Old Testament. Fifth, we must study extant Greek literature for other possible semantic parallels.

Most important, we must search for true parallels rather than be satisfied with seeming or potential parallels. The difference is not always so simple to detect. We must consider the whole semantic range and compare the contexts behind the possible parallels before deciding. Then we must chart each occurrence and see which uses of the term elsewhere have the greatest degree of overlap with the use of the term in the particular context we are studying. Any individual occurence is no more than a possible parallel until it has been shown to have a higher degree of semantic overlap (that is, it corresponds to the biblical term at several levels) than the other possibilities, even if the parallel is found elsewhere in the same book or section. We need to remember that we often use the same word with slightly different nuances only a couple sentences apart and think nothing of it. Paul, for example, uses *nomos* ("law") in several different ways in Romans 5—7 (see the chart in Moo 1983:76). It is not the nearest parallel but the best one that counts, and the immediate context is the final arbiter in deciding the proper parallel.

7. The Disjunctive Fallacy. Often two options are presented as either-or, forcing the reader to make a choice when one is not necessitated. Carson connects this with "a prejudicial use of evidence," which presents the data in such a way that the reader is influenced in a direction not actually demanded by the evidence (1984:54-56). We have already seen this in the previous chapter with grammar, for instance, when one is asked to choose between an objective and subjective genitive when a general genitive is indicated. This error is often made with word studies as well. One example would be the use of institutional language by proponents of Early Catholicism, which assumes that the early church was charismatic and free and only at the last part of the first century developed church government. Therefore, all mention of "elders" or "bishops" (such as Acts 14:23; Phil 1:1) had to be late, while language of Spirit-led activity (for example, 1 Cor 14:26-28) stems from the primitive church. This is an unwarranted disjunction, however, for charismatic freedom and institutionalism are not dichotomous. A good parallel was the Jewish synagogue, which had freedom and yet regimen within its programs.

8. The Word Fallacy. Another major problem is a failure to consider the concept as well as the word, that is, the other ways the biblical writers could say the same thing. This naturally includes synonyms; one of the purposes of the *New International Dictionary of New Testament Theology* (NIDNTT) was to correct that basic error in TDNT. However, as Moises Silva has said, even in NIDNTT "the grouping of semantically related terms does not really evince sensitivity to linguistic theory; it appears to be only a matter of convenience. Cf. my review in *WTJ* 43 (1980-81), 395-99" (1983:21n). We dare never study only occurrences of the particular term if our purpose is to trace the theology behind a word or phrase. Such will help in determining the semantic range of that particular term but will not recapitulate the range of the author's thought or of biblical teaching.

None of us ever uses the exact same words to describe our thoughts. Rather, we use synonyms and other phrases to depict our ideas. Therefore, a truly complete picture must cluster semantically related terms and phrases. The methodology for this will be discussed in the next section; at this stage I want to note the danger of neglecting the procedure. For example, to discuss the spiritual realm and center only upon *pneuma* is fraught with danger. Thiselton (1977:91) charts the concept and notes the related terms under wind (such as *anemos, lailaps)*, spirit *(sōma, sarx, psycho)*, seat of emotion or insight *(kardia, etarachthō)*, the whole person *(to emon, me)* and several other categories. We would do an injustice to the topic by ignoring passages dealing with the same theme but using other related terms. Here a semantic field approach (see below) is needed to determine all the terms and phrases which express a concept.

9. Ignoring the Context. In one sense this is the basic error that encompasses the others and makes them possible. For instance, etymology is misused as formative of meaning when the diachronic history of a term is given priority over the context. I have already noted that context and the current semantic range of a word are the two aspects of the synchronic dimension. The failure to note context may be the most frequently occurring error, since the majority of commentaries are organized around a word-by-word approach that usually isolates each word from the other terms surrounding it and as a result fails to put the message of the text together as a coherent whole.

For instance, in Philippians 2:7 *heauton ekenōsen* ("emptied himself") has become the focus of widespread debate centering upon the kenotic theory, namely whether Christ "emptied himself" of his deity. The traditional evangelical approach has been to respond that Christ emptied himself of the prerogatives and glory of deity but not of his divine nature (compare v. 6; see Lightfoot). However, as Hawthorne has noted, this ignores the context (1983:25-86). There is no (genitive of) content given for the "emptying," and it is better in this light to recognize the intransitive nature of the verb. In the semantic range another use fits the context better, to "pour out" or "make himself nothing." This fits the transition from "did not consider equality a thing to be grasped" to "took on the form of a servant" as well as the parallelism with "humbled" in verse 8. A proper regard for context removes the necessity of debating the kenotic school on their own grounds.

Basic Semantic Theory

1. Meaning. In a very real sense this chapter is the heart of the entire book. Everyone who studies this work has one basic question: What procedure can I follow to discover more precisely what the Bible means? Yet there are several issues involved, as we have already seen. For one thing, what is "meaning"? Earlier we distinguished between the author's intended meaning, which is singular in essence, and what the text "means" for each of us, which is multiple, depending upon its significance for us at given times. Yet we still have not defined "meaning." One major area of agreement on the part of semanticists is that meaning is not an inherent property of words. Contrary to popular assumptions, terms really do not carry meaning by themselves. It is true that some terms do produce a word picture in the mind, like "apple" or "house." However, they confer this meaning as part of sentences or "speech-acts," and often they do not carry that particular meaning at all, as the term "pineapple" or the sentence "His suggestion housed several different ideas" illustrates.

Thus, there is no inherent meaning in a word. As Ullmann has noted, dictionaries give us the impression that words carry abstract content by their very nature (1964:39). Yet in reality words are arbitrary symbols that have meaning only in a context. They function on the basis of convention and practical use in any language system, and they must be studied descriptively (how they are actually employed) rather than prescriptively (according to preconceived rules). Nida provides a working definition of meaning as "a set of relations for which a verbal symbol is a sign" and adds that a word should be understood as "a token or a symbol for this or that meaning" (1975:14). Similarly, Kedar begins his discussion by noting that speech is primarily a "symbol system" (1981:9). In other words, the individual term is not the basic unit of meaning. "As Saussure has shown decisively in one way, and Wittgenstein decisively in another, the meaning of a word depends not on what it is in itself but on its relation to other words and to other sentences which form its context" (Thiselton 1977:78-79).

This theory of meaning can be illustrated in many ways. Note the use of *peirasmos* in James 1:2 and 1:12-13. In itself the word has no single meaning but only meaning potential. It is a symbol waiting for a context, when its meaning will be decided by interaction in a sentence. In these three passages there is a definite shift of meaning. In 1:2 *peirasmos* clearly means a "trial," defined further as a "test of faith" (v. 3) that comes in a myriad of forms (v. 2). After the discussion of prayer and doubting (vv. 5-8) and poverty and wealth (vv. 9-10), James returns to his topic in verse 12, specifically renewing the idea of "enduring trials" (compare vv. 3-4). In verse 13, however, the meaning changes to another aspect of the semantic range, that of "temptation." This subtle shift is necessitated by the statement "I am tempted by God" and leads into a discussion of the source and progress of temptation-sin-death (vv. 14-15). Meaning was not inherent in *peirasmos* but was given to it by its context; without a context the term has only meaning potential.

2. Sense and Reference. Most of us have grown up with some form of the reference theory of meaning.[1] This theory posits a direct relationship between a word as symbol and the thing to which it refers. But the problem is that words do not always "name" the reality behind them. As Gilbert Ryle has said,

> If every single word were a name, then a sentence composed of five words, say "three is a prime number" should be a list of five objects named by those five words. But a list like "Plato, Aristotle, Aquinas, Locke, Berkeley" is not a sentence. . . . What a sentence means is not decomposable into the set of things which the word in it stands for, if they do stand for things. So the notion of "having meaning" is at least partly different from the notion of "standing for." (1963:133; in Silva 1983:106)

Silva modified this functional view of language by noting the fact that some words do indeed have a direct link with physical entities (or in the case of biblical study, with theological concepts). This is true of proper names, as Ryle suggests, and is sometimes true of technical or semitechnical terms like *nomos* (law) or *hamartia* (sin). However, we have already noted the flexibility of *nomos*. W. Günther points out that in the Septuagint "two words, *hamartia* and *adikia,* represent between them almost the whole range of Hebrew words for guilt and sin" and that in the New Testament the term and its cognates are used "as the most comprehensive expression of everything opposed to God" (1978:577, 579). In short, even these semitechnical expressions have a certain flexibility in their use. Silva correctly notes that we must distinguish between technical and nontechnical terms, but I must add one caveat: there is no absolute or clear-cut distinction.[2] Semitechnical terms like *nomos* can be used in a nonreferential way, for example as "legal principles" in general. Silva's diagram (1983:107) is helpful (see figure 3.1).

fully referential	mostly referential	partly referential	non- referential
(Plato)	(law)	(cold)	(beautiful)

Fig. 3.1. Silva's Diagram of Degrees of Reference.

We can study a term that is completely or mostly referential by what linguists call the "word and thing" approach (as utilized in TDNT). This method assumes the identity between the word and the "thing" to which it refers and proceeds to define the referent in exact terms. However, not many words can be studied this way, and the method is open to many pitfalls. Carson, for instance, cautions against "false assumptions about technical meaning," in which a person presupposes the content of a technical term like "sanctification" without letting the text define it (1984:45-48). In the case of "sanctification," passages like Romans 6 or 1 Corinthians 1:2 equate it with the moment of justification rather than with the process of spiritual growth. In other words, even with technical terms the context has priority.

The well-known triangle of Ogden and Richards (1923:11; in Silva 1983:103) illustrates the basic distinctions in defining words (see figure 3.2).

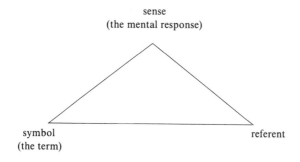

sense
(the mental response)

symbol   referent
(the term)

Fig. 3.2. Ogden and Richards Triangle.

It is not easy to establish the link between a symbol and its referent, as we have already discussed. The major point is to note the difference between the sense of a word and its reference. The latter is an extralinguistic factor, the specific object denoted by the statement. The "sense" is the picture built in the mind by the term, that image which is connoted. For instance, if we say "The ship is at the docks," we have a symbol (ship), a sense (a large boat) and a referent (the Queen Mary). Let us consider Peter's confession at Philippi, "You are the Christ" (Mk 8:29). The symbol, "Christ," actually refers to Jesus (as we know from the context) but its sense is that of the Jewish expectation of the Messiah. In most other cases we must deal with sense more than reference. Abstract terms like "faith," "hope," "love" fit only this former category. In tracing salvific terms in the Old Testament (see Sawyer 1972), we are dealing with sense relations. Therefore, I will center upon sense in the ensuing discussions.

3. Structural Linguistics. The sense of a term depends upon its function in the larger linguistic unit, the sentence. This realization is at the heart of a structural (not structuralist; see chap. six) view of language. Saussure also grounded his system in the difference between syntagmatic and paradigmatic relations. The former is linear and defines a word's relationship with the other terms that surround it in the speech-act, such as the interrelationship of concepts in "God is love." A paradigmatic relation is vertical or associative, noting other terms that could replace it, such as words that are synonymous. Rather than "love" one could say "kind," "merciful" or "gracious." Both aspects are connected to the key exegetical question, Why? Why did the writer choose this series of relationships by which to express his thoughts? This leads to a series of "what" questions: What limiting relationships do the series of terms develop with one another? What other terms could have been chosen to describe the writer's thoughts? What is the larger semantic domain (range of meanings) of which these terms are a part, and what does it add to the thought? In biblical study this takes us straight into the theological domain.

Both aspects must be considered in a proper word study. For instance, "love of God" in Romans 8:39 is part of a much larger structure, the statement of the inseparability of the child of God from his love (vv. 38-39). We cannot understand it without considering the whole statement of which it is a part. Further, we must note that it stands in deliberate parallel with "love of Christ" in verse 35. Here we see the syntagmatic combined with the paradigmatic, as the entire Godhead (compare vv. 26-27) is involved in our security. On the concept of love, we would want to study parallel concepts like *ḥesed* (lovingkindness) and omnipotence (due to the stress on inseparability). These latter are sister concepts that will both inform and place in bold relief the concept elucidated here. More on this later.

My purpose here is to note that the terms have meaning only as part of the larger structure. Naturally, "love of God" does have meaning as a technical phrase; however, a better label is "meaning-potential." Remember our use of this very concept in our discussion of the genitive in the previous chapter. It *could* mean many things—"God loves me"; "I love God"; "God is love" and so forth. I can only know what it *does* mean when I see it as part of a larger context like Romans 8:39. Moreover, the meaning of a statement is not the sum of the meanings of its individual words (the impression given by many commentaries) but the total message produced by the words in relation to one another. Consider the difference between "I help the boy" and "The boy helps me." There is never an accumulation of separate meanings but only a single message. Each term is a part of a whole, and to change any term or its relationship to other terms is to change the whole.

4. Context. I have stressed this throughout the book; I want here to explore its relationship to semantics. Silva summarizes the universally accepted axiom regarding its importance when he assigns "a *determinative* function to context; that is, the context does not merely help us understand meaning; it virtually *makes* meaning" (1983:139; italics his).

In chapter one we used two aspects of context—the historical and the logical—to describe the prolegomena to serious Bible study. Here we note a similar breakdown and, following linguistic convention, will label them literary and situational.

Sawyer calls the literary context the "linguistic environment" that relates semantics to several concerns that will be covered later, such as syntax and genre (1972:10-28). In his study Sawyer centers upon stylistics, that is, upon grouping semantic units on the basis of similar types of expression. This is indeed a critical area of linguistic investigation, for it recognizes that every writer (as well as every genre—see chaps. six through twelve) uses language differently. At the same time every language has certain stylistic preferences (idioms, ways of saying things) that often determine word selection. These two forces work in opposite directions: individual style produces variety of expression, cultural norms produce conformity of expression. The student of the Word must be aware of both and ask what stylistic factors are at work in the context.

This is especially valuable in studying the question of synonyms (see below). Without presupposing the data to follow, consider Paul's use of *ginōskein* and *eidenai,* the two basic words for "to know." Burdick examines the Pauline occurrences and believes that in the majority of cases (90 of 103 for *eidenai* and 32 of 50 for *ginōskein*) Paul follows the classical distinction between *eidenai* as denoting knowledge already possessed (characterized by assurance) and *ginōskein* as the process of gaining knowledge (1974:344-56). Silva, however, challenges the results, arguing that *eidenai hoti* is conventional language and should not be pressed (1983:164-69). Paul's usage is dictated more by stylistic concerns (Silva 1980 calls this "lexical choice") than by classical distinctions, and therefore the two are often synonyms in Paul's letters.

Hirsch (1976:50-73) challenges the importance of style and syntax for meaning, arguing that synonymous ideas can be stated in varying stylistic forms, such as active ("I hit the ball") or passive ("The ball was hit by me"). However, his arguments are not conclusive for two reasons. First, he has carefully selected an example that might prove his point, but in reality linguists have taken that into consideration. We must consider the context and ask whether the passive gives greater stress to the "ball" and the active to the act of hitting. However, in other stylistic choices, the influence of style is more direct, as we have seen. Second, Hirsch is attacking a deterministic view that assumes that style is the creative force in meaning. I am saying that style is *a* key rather than *the* key to meaning, one among many factors that one must consider when investigating the contribution of a word within a sentence structure. Therefore, Hirsch's objection is a valuable caution against an exaggerated view of the importance of style but not applicable to a more nuanced understanding.

The situational context is more difficult to determine, for it involves the reconstruction of the historical situation behind the surface context of the passage. This looks forward to the discussion of historical-cultural exegesis (chap. five) but needs also to be addressed in relation to semantic research. I will discuss the difficulty of understanding something uttered in the past (see appendices one and two), but linguists at least do not consider this to be an impossible task. Historical documents help recreate not only the meaning of words but also the events and situations behind most ancient documents. Moreover, these situations themselves are determinative of meaning. For instance, the command to "confess your sins" in 1 John 1:9 is surrounded by three statements addressed to John's audience: "If we claim to have fellowship with him but walk in darkness" (v. 6); "If we claim to be without sin" (v. 8); and "If we claim we have not sinned" (v. 10 NIV). There have been many interpretations of this discourse, but the best stems from the realization that John is addressing his opponents, a group of perfectionist proto-Gnostics whose "knowledge" in their opinion has lifted them above sin. John commands his readers to recognize their sinfulness, to confess it, and to return to the "light" (v. 5). Thiselton correctly observes, "To try to cut loose 'propositions' in the New Testament [or Old Testament!] from the specific situation in which they were uttered and to try thereby to treat them 'timelessly' is not only bad theology; it is also bad linguistics. For it leads to a distortion of what the text *means*" (1977:79; italics his).

5. Deep Structure. Louw speaks of the surface and deep levels of an utterance (1982:75-89). By this he does not identify with the psychologistic approach of the structuralists but rather speaks purely from the linguistic perspective. The surface structure deals with the basic grammatical and semantic relationships of a sentence. It is akin to a modern translation like the New International Version, pariphrastic when it needs to but faithfully reproducing the original. The deep structure, however, looks to the underlying message behind the words. For biblical study this is the theological truth embedded in the statement. This is based upon the transformational grammar of Noam Chomsky, a topic I will explore further in the next chapter. Yet it has implications for semantics, and I wish to explore these. Chomsky taught that behind the surface grammar of every statement lay linguistic transformations, that is, the deeper message of the utterance. There is a very real danger to this, for some, like the structuralists, have been led to denigrate and virtually ignore the surface text. Many semanticists, however, have recognized this pitfall and rightly seen that the surface grammar controls the transformations. The two are interdependent parts of a larger whole.

Louw uses Ephesians 1:7 as an example (1982:75-76). The surface statement is "by whom we have redemption through his blood." The deep structure says "God sets us free because Christ died for us." This considers not only syntax but also deep-level semantics. Both halves, "redemption" and "blood," are analyzed in terms of syntagm and paradigm, then transformed into their underlying theological statements. Behind this there must also be serious exegetical study. One by-product of the method is the elimination of ambiguities (Thiselton 1977:96). We must work through the interpretive options before we can identify the deeper message.

This works at grammatical as well as at semantic levels. For instance, "God loves us" and "we love God" are two possible deep structures (in the next chapter I will call these "kernel sentences") for the surface statement "the love of God." In semantic investigation let us consider *parakaleite* in Hebrews 3:13. Most translate it "encourage one another daily," partly on the basis of its parallel in 10:25, "encourage one another, especially since you see the day drawing near." However, as I stated earlier in this chapter, we must use parallels carefully, examining whether the contexts match sufficiently. There are two possible deep meanings for *parakaleite* in this context, the positive "encourage" and the negative "admonish." In this case the context (different from the positive context of 10:24-25) "lest any of you be hardened by the deceitfulness of sin" makes the latter definite. The deep structure would be, "It is necessary to keep examining one another for sin, because if you don't, it will deceive and then harden you."

6. Syntax and Semantics. Nida and Taber discuss the two basic factors that influence meaning (1969:56-63), and this will provide a good summary for the first half of the discussion of structural semantics. It is amazing that with the millions of idea possibilities and our limited vocabulary, ambiguity is not a constant result. Yet a remarkable degree of precision is achieved through the wide range of meanings and uses attached to words in different contexts. The first factor that leads to meaning is syntax, the subject of the next chapter. Whether a word is used as a noun, a verb or an adjective makes a great deal of difference. Consider: "he threw the stones"; "he was stoned" (with several possible meanings depending on context); "he had a stony countenance." The meaning can change radically with each syntactical usage. The same is often true of biblical words. We must always ask what the term contributes to the meaning of the whole statement, not just inquire as to what it "means" in the context. Thiselton uses Wittgenstein's concept of the "language game" (1977:1130-32; 1980:373-79) to express this truth. Each word used in an utterance is not an entity in itself but is part of a larger activity grounded in everyday life. Thus speech-acts have no uniform pattern; hermeneutical rules above all must be flexible enough to allow the syntax to speak for itself, to allow the language to play its own game.

"Semotaxis" is the second factor and refers to the influence of the surrounding words. This of course can be exceedingly complex, since all the given elements in a surface structure interact with each other. One of the critical aspects concerns the modifiers (adjectives, subordinate clauses and so forth). As modifiers increase, the specificity of the statement increases proportionately, for example, "his father," "the father of the blond fellow," "the father of the blond fellow standing there." Yet in many cases ambiguity abounds. Louw provides an excellent illustration by diagramming the two semotactic ways of understanding Romans 1:17 (1982:75)—see figure 3.3.

These two interpretations are quite different but each is based on viable semotactic relationships. On the basis of the larger context the interpreter must choose, but the principle of semotaxis helps us to realize that we are dealing with whole statements and not just individual phrases.

7. Semantic Range. As we turn from the structural aspects of language to the actual tools of semantics, we must begin with the basic task of establishing the parameters of word meaning in individual cases. The semantic range of a word is the result of the synchronic study, a list of the ways the word was used in the era when the work was written. For Old Testament study, apart from comparative linguistics (such as Ugaritic or Akkadian texts) the terms can be traced in Jewish inscriptions and rabbinic literature. Lexicons (Koehler-Baumgartner, Holladay, Brown-Driver-Briggs) and concordances (Mandel-

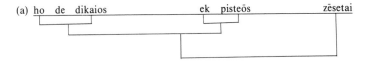

= "he who through faith is righteous shall live" (RSV)

= "he who is put right with God through faith shall live" (GNB)

= "the just (righteous) shall live by faith" (KJV, NKJV, NASB, NIV)

= "the upright man finds life through faith" (JB)

Fig. 3.3. Louw's Diagrams of Romans 1:17.

kern, Lisowsky, Wikgram) are the primary source for such statistics. The person doing frontline semantic research will trace the occurrences, note the distribution (such as special uses in wisdom or prophetic literature), check syntactical groupings (such as preference for a certain preposition) and organize the data into primary, secondary, and metaphorical meanings. Above all, we must study each context in detail, for many have made mistakes by assuming a primary meaning in a passage that actually favors one of the secondary uses of the term. Extrabiblical sources must be employed with care, since the use of the cognate languages can easily lead to the etymological fallacy (see above) but parallels properly adduced can be highly illuminating (see Stuart 1980:120-26; Kedar, 1981:70-82).

In New Testament word study we need to trace the word carefully in both Graeco-Roman and Jewish contexts, noting its use in Philo and Josephus as well as in the papyri. Again for serious research we will want to consult the primary sources and both trace and collate the usages of the word in different contexts. Next we will do the same in the New Testament (using a concordance like Moulton-Geden or Aland's computer concordances), noting the proclivities of certain authors (for instance, John's preference for the verb form of "believe" and "know"). Etymology, as I noted above, can be very helpful since many passages deliberately allude to Septuagint or Old Testament meanings. Moreover, some Greek words are more transparent, continuing the past uses of the term.

The major lexicon, Bauer-Arndt-Gingrich-Danker (BAGD, 1979), is a valuable tool because it traces the origins and distribution of the term as well as its basic semantic range. However, it is important to remember that BAGD is descriptive and interpretive. When it places a passage behind a certain meaning it is an opinion and not an established fact. Fee notes the handling of *archontes* (rulers) in 1 Corinthians 2:6-8 (1983:87-89).

BAGD places it under the rubric of the evil spirits. However, a closer look at the evidence yields several interesting facts: only the singular is used in the New Testament for Satan; the plural always refers to human rulers; the first use of the plural for demonic forces in Greek literature appears in the second century. While the demonic remains a possible interpretation, I personally follow those who favor human rulers as the meaning of *archontes* here. My point is that we should not assume BAGD's decisions to be irrefutable.

Beekman and Callow discuss the "multiple senses" of a word from the standpoint of translation procedures (1974:94-103). They recommend that the student consider three levels of word meaning. The primary level is the common meaning that the word carries when it stands without a context and in most cognate terms. For example, the primary meanings of *lutroun* would be to "free" or "ransom."

Secondary meanings are specific meanings that often share an aspect of the primary sense but occur only in some contexts. Beekman and Callow speak of a "thread of meaning," but such is not always true. A good example of the latter is *rûaḥ/pneuma*, which can mean "wind" or "spirit" or "breath" or the person (see above). The various uses cover a broad band of semantic categories and cannot be restricted to a common thread (see above on the root fallacy). Therefore these meanings are used infrequently. For *lutroun* these would be the idea of a ransom payment, redemption, the liberation of a prisoner of war or the manumission of a slave. The first two of course are found frequently in the New Testament, but still the context must decide whether or not a ransom payment ("blood") is stressed.

Finally, figurative meanings are based upon "associative relations with the primary sense" (p. 94). (I will consider this in the next chapter under "figures of speech.") Under this category the term is used metaphorically to depict a word picture. For *lutroun* BAGD lists its use in prayer ("save me from . . .") as a figurative sense. These categories will prove helpful in organizing the data one has collected on the semantic range of a term.

The majority of us will never be engaged in the type of detailed research described herein. We will not have the time to retrace each use in its original context and reorganize the results on the basis of recent semantic theory (as did Barr, Sawyer or Kedar). We will have to be satisfied with secondary sources like BDB or BAGD. However, we can still use them knowledgeably, and when commentaries or monographs employ semantic research and argumentation, we can be aware of the level of sophistication with which the data is utilized. Certainly those of us who are pastors, missionaries and scholars in related fields will not have the time to do primary research. Yet if we know the theory we can use the secondary tools with far greater understanding and awareness. This chapter will be used on many different levels by its readers, from serious devotional reading to writing major monographs. I do not want to give the impression that this is only for serious scholars. If we know what is involved in developing a semantic range, we can properly use those semantic studies which have been developed for us. We can also avoid misusing tools like TDNT, TDOT or NIDNTT, which have not been intended for detailed lexical study. They are certainly invaluable exegetical resources but are not exhaustive on semantic range (TDOT comes the closest) since they deal more with theological usage.

8. Connotative Meaning. Nida and Taber (1969:37-39) present the four basic components of the dynamic employment of words in a context: the object element (O), the event connoted (E), the abstract nature acquired (A) and a relationship implied (R). Wycliffe translators as well as others use this OEAR complex to identify more precisely the exact way a particular word is used in its context, and to provide a guide to select a dynamic equivalence term or phrase in the receptor language into which the passage is being translated. This does add time to the exegetical task, but on key words that deserve detailed word study it is a worthy tool that will enable the student to think through the surface structure of a text much more carefully.

For instance, "justify" has an E-A complex of meanings ("declare righteous"), "justifier" an O-E-A thrust (the object "declares righteous") and "reconcile" an E-R emphasis (a new relationship is mediated). An "object" or "thing" word constitutes an animate entity and emphasizes the person or thing concerned in a statement. An "event" word connotes action and stresses the movement aspect of a statement. An "abstract" term is theoretical in essence and centers on the qualitative aspect of the word. A "relational" term looks at the concept in its association with other people or ideas and emphasizes the correlation between the terms. In Romans 1:17 ("The just shall live by faith," see above), "just" or "righteous" is an O-A-R term because the person is seen in "right" relationship with God. "Live" is an E-A term because it is the action word in the sentence and a key idea for the new life with God in the Epistle to the Romans (see 2:7; 4:17; 5:17-18 among others). "Faith" is also an E-A term because it is the basis of right "living" and stresses the abstract aspect of "faith" in God.

9. Paradigmatic Research: Synonymity, Antonymity and Componential Analysis. This section concerns the semantic field of a concept, not just the various meanings the term itself might have in different contexts but other terms that relate to it. This paradigmatic approach increasingly is recognized as having great value in serious word study. The technical term for the former is polysemy (a term with more than one meaning) and the term for the latter is polymorphy (several symbols with the same meaning), or synonymy. Nida (1972:85-86) calls this paradigmatic method "field semantics" and goes so far as to say that "critical studies of meaning must be based primarily upon the analysis of related meanings of different words not upon the different meanings of single words" (p. 85). Certainly this is an overstatement, but it is true that synonyms are very neglected in semantic investigation and can be quite helpful in broadening the thrust of the actual term chosen in the syntagmatic or surface structure. The difficulty of course is avoiding over-exegesis of the actual term found; for instance, overstating the differences between the word and its synonyms on the one hand or illegitimately reading the others into it on the other hand. A nuanced use of the method will nevertheless enrich the meaning of the passage, leading to the biblical theology behind the concept embedded in the term.

Silva notes three types of synonyms (1983:120-29).[3] The predominant category is that of overlapping relations, so called because synonyms meet at the level of sense rather than reference. This means that some of the various senses of the terms overlap or cohere. There are few if any absolute synonyms, terms that agree with one another at every level. However, we can say that terms are synonymous in particular contexts, such as *pneuma* ("spirit") and *psychē* ("soul") in 1 Thessalonians 5:23 or *agapaō* and *phileō* ("love") in John 21:15-17.

There are two uses of synonyms in Bible study. If we are looking to the larger theological pattern behind the use of a certain term, we will study similar terms for the same concept in order to find the larger semantic field, which can enrich a particular study. For instance, in a study of *proseuchomai* ("pray") in 1 Thessalonians 1:17, we could look up similar terms for prayer like *aiteō, deomai, eucharistia, enteuxis* and *iketoria* and see how they expand and clarify the biblical concept.

Second, we can study synonyms used in the same passage and ask the extent to which they overlap. This is often quite difficult. To use as an illustration the prayer language just noted, four of the terms occur in Philippians 4:6, "Stop worrying about anything, but in every case by prayer and supplication with thanksgiving let your requests be made known to God." Most likely Paul is deliberately stockpiling prayer terms synonymously in order to present prayer in its most comprehensive form rather than speaking of different aspects of prayer. In other situations, however, the language is more akin to step parallelism (see chap. seven on poetry), that is, the accent is more on the development of ideas. Gibson gives two examples of pseudo-synonymy, a false claim of synonymity (1981:199-206): (1) Lindar's assumption (1968:117-26) that terms for the law in Deuteronomy ("judgments," "statutes," "commandments") are synonymous; (2) Bultmann's statement that "see the Kingdom of God" and "enter the Kingdom of God" (Jn 3:3, 5) are synonymous. Neither assumption is proven, and the latter is based on theology rather than on language. It is likely that neither example is synonymous. Nida and Taber illustrate the method of overlapping relations by comparing repentance, remorse and conversion (1974:66)—see figure 3.4.

repentance	remorse	conversion
1. bad behavior	1. bad behavior	1. bad behavior
2. sorrow	2. sorrow	2. _____
3. change of behavior	3. _____	3. change of behavior

Fig. 3.4. Nida and Taber's Illustration of Overlapping Relations.

Silva calls the second type of synonym "contiguous relations," or "improper synonymy." These terms share some similarity of reference but could never be interchanged. For instance, the "upper garment" *(himation)* and the "under garment" *(chitōn)* obviously are quite similar but they could never be true synonyms. The same is true of "man" and "woman," "boy" and "girl." The key question is whether the two could replace one another in a statement without changing the meaning.

The third category is labeled "inclusive relations" and is technically called "hyponymy," or "semantic domain." This relates to a hierarchical relationship between words (see Nida and Taber 1974: 68-70) from the generic to the specific; for instance, creature-animal-mammal-dog-terrier-"Bozo." Semantic domains are seldom used with accuracy; people frequently use "that dog" to refer to a specific pet. Since individuals do not use the components of a domain in the same way, it is critical to note the particular speaker's or author's use and not to read greater specificity into a term than is there. The context is the final arbiter. Further, substitution is not as simple in hyponymy. As Silva states, " 'Flower' can take the place of 'rose' in many sentences, . . . whereas 'rose' can take the place of 'flower' only in sentences where another type of flower is not meant" (p. 127).

Mistakes in this category are quite similar to Barr's warning against "illegitimate totality transfer" (noted above). Scholars are constantly reading the whole of a doctrine into isolated statements. This is especially true of theologically loaded passages like John 6:37-40, where many scholars see the full-fledged doctrine of predestination, or Acts 2:38, where others read a developed view of baptismal regeneration. We must remember that the biblical authors normally stressed one aspect of a larger dogma to fit individual situations. Doctrines must be based on an accumulation of all biblical passages on a topic. Individual terms or passages relate only to aspects of the larger whole.

Finally, let us note Nida's diagram of the three types of synonyms (from Silva)—see figure 3.5.

Overlapping   Contiguity   Hyponymy

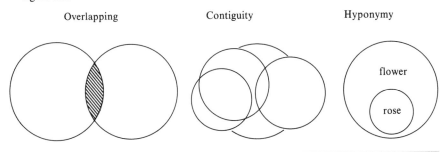

Figure 3.5. Nida's Diagram of Three Types of Synonyms.

Antonyms belong to the semantic category of opposition. This is also quite common in biblical language and is similar to the Hebrew poetic pattern of antithetical parallelism. Scholars are quite divided on subcategories of opposition, but we might note three types (combining Lyons 1977:1:322ff.; Thiselton 1977:90-92; Silva 1983:129-32). The strongest type is the binary opposite, a black-and-white structure in which the assertion of the one entails the denial of the other. To be single is not to be married, to receive is not to give. Paul establishes such a contrast in Romans 11:6 and Ephesians 2:8-9, *tē chariti* ("by grace") . . . *ouk ex ergōn* ("not of works"). The hymn of 1 Peter 3:18 has a similar twofold contrast: *thanatōtheis men sarki* ("died in the flesh"), *zōopoiētheis de pneumati* ("made alive in the spirit"). Another example is the so-called dualism of the Gospel of John, seen in light-darkness, ascend-descend, above-below and so forth.

Less stark in its contrast is relative or gradable antonymy, a hierarchical opposition that compares but does not establish mutual exclusion. Such examples as tall-short, happy-sad, good-bad are comparative: "George is taller/happier/better than John." Thiselton mentions Paul's use of spirit-flesh, which at times is a binary opposite (Rom 8:9, 12) and at other times is not. "On the one hand, whilst the Corinthian believers are in some sense men of the Spirit (1 Cor 2:6-16; 12-14) in another sense Paul refuses to accept their inference that therefore they are 'not fleshly' (3:1-4)" (1977:92).

A third opposition is converse. For instance, "buy" is the converse of "sell." To say the one is to imply the other; if George buys from John, obviously John sells to George. German sometimes indicates this with the prefix *ver-*: "buy" is *kaufen*; "sell" is *verkaufen*. This can also be a matter of perspective; from one viewpoint you "go" to the house, from the other you "come" to the house.

The whole process of paradigmatic analysis is complex and those who have the time to compile such statistics would do well to chart the results by means of what Nida (1974) and others call "componential analysis." The purpose is to compare synonyms and antonyms by a chart of what semanticists call the "components of meaning," the various categories that define the content of the terms. We used such a chart above to compare repentance, remorse and conversion. Another frequently used example is found in figure 3.6.

	man	woman	boy	girl
human	+	+	+	+
adult	+	+	-	-
male	+	-	+	-

Figure 3.6. Chart of Components of Meaning.

The vertical columns relate to members of the semantic field, the horizontal categories are the components by which they are graded. However, this method has some basic problems (see Carson 1984:50-51; Silva 1983:134-35). Nida himself admits that the method is restricted primarily to referential or extralinguistic categories. This limits its use for it does not apply to structural meanings and demands an encyclopedic listing of categories. Further, it is open to subjective misuse, and indeed scholars using the method have come up with widely differing conclusions. In other words, it is not as "scientific" as it appears on paper, for it demands exhaustive coverage to be precise. Nevertheless, it is a helpful way to visualize the results of one's study and to use the tools with greater precision.

10. Ambiguity and Double Meaning. In studying both syntagmatic and paradigmatic aspects of words (see above), it is important to note the many types of vagueness, at times intended and at other times seemingly accidental, probably due to the fact that we do not have enough data to interpret the author's meaning. It is important to recognize this and not to read into the text greater precision than it has, a problem especially apt to occur in overexegeting synonymity or antonymity (overstating the similarities or differences). At all times the context must tell us the extent to which terms cohere or differ. As mentioned earlier, "context" is broader than the immediate context and refers also to the writer's emphases and style elsewhere. Earlier I alluded to the synonymous use of *agapan* and *philein* in John 21:15-17. What makes this interpretation conclusive is the congruence of the immediate context (the two words for "know," the two words for "tend" and "sheep" also used synonymously) and the wider context (John's tendency to use terms synonymously and the extensive number of times he does so with *agapan* and *philein* in his Gospel).

Ambiguity is the most difficult aspect of exegesis. Often the phenomenon occurs with *hapax legomena* or obscure, infrequent aspects of the semantic range. The interpreter is mystified because none of the usual meanings works or, even worse, more than one makes sense in the context. Ambiguity is the reason why many Old Testament scholars so frequently suggest emendations in the text, often without any textual evidence. On the surface the Masoretic Text does not make good sense in the context. In reality very few emendations are actually needed, and with new knowledge from the cognate languages the trend is away from such drastic and subjective measures. Nevertheless the problem of ambiguity is greater in the Old Testament.

The semanticist Martin Joos has formulated an important principle in such situations: when faced with a *hapax legomenon* or problem of multiple meanings, "The best meaning is the least meaning. . . . He [the lexicographer] defines it in such fashion as to make it contribute least to the total message derivable from the passage where it is at home" (1972:257; in Silva 1983:153-54). While this is expressed negatively it is meant positively: the meaning that is most likely is that one which causes the least change in the context. Silva applies this to the difficult use of *paschō* ("suffer") in Galatians 3:4, "Did you suffer so many things in vain?" Everywhere else in the New Testament the verb has its normal meaning, but a variant use, attested infrequently elsewhere, is "experience"; thus the text would read "Did you experience so much [that is, blessings from the Spirit] in vain?" The context in many ways favors the latter, for persecution is never mentioned in the epistle; however, the vastly predominant New Testament usage favors the former. Using Joos' principle, Silva argues that "the neutral sense 'experience' creates less disturbance in the passage than does 'suffer' because the former is more redundant—it is more supportive of, and more clearly supported by, the context" (p. 155). Clearly this principle is a valuable exegetical tool supportive of the structural approach already taken in this chapter.

A good example of deliberate ambiguity in Scripture is the oft-discussed phenomenon of "double meaning." These expressions are notoriously difficult to interpret, for the contextual framework itself is often ambiguous. The famous word-play on wind/spirit in Genesis 1:2 is a fairly simple example, but others are not so easy. The Gospel of John is justly famed for its widespread use of double meaning. Note for instance *anōthen gennēthēnai*, "born from above/again" in John 3:3, 7; *hydōr zōn*, "living/flowing water" in 4:10-11; and *hypsōthō*, "lifted up (to the cross/the Father)" in 12:32. However, should we read double meaning into the interchange between Jesus and the disciples in 1:38-39, specifically in *menō*, which occurs three times in these verses and may mean "live" on the physical plane but "remain" on the spiritual plane? The theological use of the term (which occurs forty times in the Gospel and twenty-seven times in the Johannine Epistles but only twelve times total in the Synoptics) in John, where it binds together Father-Son-believer in mutual cohabitation (compare 15:4-10), would favor the possibility, but the context itself gives no actual hint of such. However, John's preference for dramatic development along salvific lines (compare 1:35-51 with 3:1-15; 4:1-42; 9:1-34) may favor a soteriological double meaning. On the whole, it is a difficult decision, but I cautiously do find double meaning in 1:38-39.

Conclusion: A Methodology for Lexical Study

When scholars write about method, they too easily climb their ivory towers and speak only to each other. I don't wish to do this; therefore, at the outset I want to make it clear that the methodology will be developed on several levels. At the top level, of course, is the scholar who deals with the primary evidence, takes nothing for granted and works intensively, dealing with every occurrence of the term in order to derive its range of meaning and its particular meaning in the context. However, few readers of this book will be working on such a level, which would require as much as several weeks of steady research for key terms. Most of us will be working on a much lower level. The busy pastor cannot spend more than an hour on any individual word-study and for the most part will be forced to spend less time than that. The average layperson, as well as the pastor or missionary, will certainly depend upon the secondary tools (commentaries, word-study books and the like) and will want to be aware of the ensuing methodology even though they will hardly ever pursue these various steps.

Nevertheless, the knowledge of a proper methodology is critical because the student of the Word will want to note whether or not the commentator has indeed done a proper word study or only a cursory background study before coming to any conclusions. It is crucial to understand at all levels of Bible study how to determine the semantic range of a word and to narrow that range down to the probable meaning of that particular term in an individual context. Therefore, those working with the secondary tools can note whether or not the commentator has done his homework; if not, they can use lexicons and other word-study books to delineate the true meaning of the word in that context. Above all, the methodology that follows will provide a perspective for understanding how one determines word meaning in individual cases and therefore will be a valuable corrective to a misuse of words in sermons and Bible studies.

1. *Determine the key words in the context.* As we work at the structure of the passage (see chap. one above) we should note those terms which stand out in the context as demanding extra study. Naturally, it is not always simple to discover which words deserve

extra work. Most of us would make those decisions on the basis of personal preference; Adler and Van Doren state that "the most important words are those that give you trouble" (1972:102). To an extent this is true. We would wish to study more deeply those aspects that we ourselves do not quite perceive. However, in studying Scripture we certainly want to probe more deeply and choose the significant words in the passage. Fee gives us four valuable steps in isolating the key words (1983:84-85):

a. Note those terms in the context which are "theologically loaded." If you see terms that state basic New Testament truths (such as "grace," "Lord" or "salvation"), these terms will certainly deserve extra study. It is quite common to read too much meaning into them in individual context on the basis of their use elsewhere. Therefore, it is particularly important to locate precisely the way they are used in the individual context.

b. Note those terms which are crucial to the meaning of the passage but may be ambiguous in their context. Fee notes the use of "virgins" in 1 Corinthians 7:25-38 and of "vessel" in 1 Thessalonians 4:4 as examples. Many more could be mentioned. When a term is critical to the meaning of a passage but is unclear, the passage will hinge upon your interpretation. Therefore, that particular term will become an important clue to the meaning of the whole, and must be studied more deeply.

c. Those words which are repeated in a context or become themes within the paragraph must be investigated. A good example would be the use of "rejoice" in Philippians 1:18. In the first half of the verse Paul uses "because of this I rejoice" to conclude the paragraph. The last portion of the verse, "Yes and I will continue to rejoice," begins the new paragraph of verses 19-26. Paul's emphasis upon rejoicing in the midst of the two trials in the succeeding paragraphs makes it worthy of special attention. Another example where "joy" becomes the key theme for the context would be James 1:2-4. In both cases the concept of joy demands extra study.

d. We must look for those terms which may be more critical to the context than might seem to be at first glance. Naturally, this can be done only after more detailed research. However, we must always be aware that our research will uncover other terms that will be far more worthy of research than we had at first suspected. Fee notes the use of *ataktos* in 2 Thessalonians 3:6, which might mean "lazy" in a passive sense or "disorderly" in an active sense. Also in this category are words used in a semitechnical sense but not appearing to be so at first. For instance, at first glance one might pass across "faith" in Ephesians 4:13 when reading "unity in the faith." However, "faith" is probably used in a semitechnical sense for the Christian faith and is critical for understanding the whole statement. During detailed exegesis these types of things will need to be uncovered and probed.

2. *Study carefully the context in which the word occurs.* It is very important to keep the context firmly in mind at every stage because the time-consuming process of gathering the semantic range causes one to become so immersed in the word itself that illegitimate totality transfer becomes quite easy. It is difficult to spend a great amount of time gathering material and then use it only briefly in the context. In order to control this tendency, context must at all times be uppermost in the process of data gathering. Note how the word fits into the total statement of the passage and try to elucidate the influence of the surrounding terms upon it.

3. *Determine the semantic range of the term.* As I have already argued, this means the synchronic more than the diachronic dimension of meaning. That is, the student will want to investigate how the word was used at the time of writing rather than how the word had developed in earlier times. This does not mean that etymology has no value, for if the context indicates, one might discover that a past meaning was consciously in the mind of the author at the time of writing. This occurs especially with an allusion to an Old Testament passage or when the word is "transparent" and still carries its past meaning. Therefore, etymology has limited value but on occasion can add a great deal to the context. As we gather the various uses of the word we will want to collate and organize the meanings into related sets, always keeping in mind the various contexts in which the word was used. This is important because we will want to select that meaning which is used in a context similar to the passage we are studying. We must try to be as complete as possible in gathering the semantic range because even an obsolete or rare meaning of a term is a possibility for the use of that term in the biblical context. It is also critical to remember that the use of the term in the New Testament is as important as its use in parallel literature. Many New Testament words had a semitechnical force that derived its meaning from the life of the early church as much as from Hellenistic usage. In those cases we must at all times be aware of the Christian meaning inherent in terms like "love" or "faith."

4. *Note whether the word is used primarily in terms of sense or reference.* This combines the previous categories of context and semantic range. Silva makes this the first step, stating that a semitechnical or referential term is not susceptible to structural analysis but rather needs a conceptual approach similar to that of TDNT (1983:176). While this is true, few words in the New Testament are used so technically that the semantic range becomes an invalid tool. I believe that a conceptual approach must still consider the semantic range and that the latter is essential to word meaning in terms of both sense and reference. Therefore, this will determine *how* one uses the semantic range rather than whether or not one utilizes it.

5. *If the term is referential, study it conceptually.* This will involve the further collection of synonyms and antonyms in order to derive the theological deep structure underneath the use of the particular term. Of course, we must avoid reading more into the term than the context will allow but this is controlled by the previous decision as to the extent to which the word is used referentially in the context. The theological background behind the word becomes an important factor in determining the overall message of the passage, and a referential term is elevated automatically to a position of extreme importance in the context. Therefore, we must be extremely careful in determining exactly the extent to which the technical or theological sense is being stressed. The methodology of biblical theology will be paramount in this approach (see chap. thirteen) and will guide the student in his or her study. Above all, we must consider the theology of the individual book and then of the writer before broadening it to the New Testament as a whole. Here we must recognize the danger of misusing parallels (see above), for scholars frequently read more into the passage than is warranted.

6. *If the word is used in terms of sense, study it structurally in its environment.* We

will utilize the paradigmatic dimension here differently than we would for a referential term. In this case we will want to study synonyms and antonyms in order to determine the exact parameters for the use of the term that the author actually chose. Again, we must proceed with extreme caution, for similarity and opposition to related terms can be subjectively misused to read more into the passage than the context will allow. Therefore, the syntagmatic or contextual investigation will at all times have priority over the paradigmatic.

7. *Rework the semantic range in terms of the writer's proclivity and immediate context.* On the basis of related context choose that aspect from the semantic range which most closely parallels the use of the term in the passage you are studying. Note the connotative aspect, whether the term is used in terms of object, event, abstract meaning or relationship. This will help you to see dynamically exactly how the term relates to its context and will enable you to choose more precisely the set of meanings from the semantic range that most closely parallels its use in the passage. Above all, as Mickelsen cautions, be aware at all times of the tendency on the part of both you and your listeners or readers to read modern meanings into ancient meanings (1963:128-29). It is the author's intended meaning that is paramount at this stage. We cannot transform the context crossculturally until we have determined first of all its meaning in its original context. This becomes the basis for the dynamic transference of that meaning into our modern context. Good expository preaching will always blend what it meant with what it means and will seek to unite the hearer with the message of God in the text.

4
$ yntax

HE SEMANTIC RANGE OF THE TERM *SYNTAX* HAS BOTH A NARROW AND A BROAD CONNO-
tation. In its narrow sense it refers to the relationship between the words of a
sentence and is virtually equivalent to grammar. Some grammars (such as Williams) include "syntax" in their title. In its broad sense syntax refers to all the interrelationships within the sentence as a means of determining the meaning of the unit as a
whole. In this broader sense, syntax includes compositional patterns, grammar and semantics, and so forms a valid conclusion to the previous three chapters.

I am using syntax in this broader sense and therefore want to describe in this chapter
how these three aspects of exegesis (structure, grammar, lexical study) can be used together rather than separately. Rhetorical patterns deal with the relationship between
sentence units and so provide the foundation for syntactical study. Grammar is concerned
with the relationship between individual terms and phrases and therefore provides the
second stage of syntactical analysis. Semantics investigates the semotactic relationships
between the meanings of the terms in the larger surface structure and thus provides the
final building block of syntactical analysis. A common thread in all of these aspects of
exegesis has been structure. In the study of compositional techniques I noted the fact that
they form a pattern that weaves together the larger whole of the paragraph. Individual
grammatical decisions likewise are based upon the structural development of the whole
statement. Finally, we took a structural approach to semantics, noting that words have
meaning only as part of the larger context.[1]

Therefore, syntax is structural at the core. None of the elements of the surface structure
dare become an end in itself. We are not looking primarily for chiasm or climax. We are
not searching only for subjective genitives or circumstantial participles. We do not wish
to center upon word studies of individual terms as if the meaning of the whole paragraph
could be narrowed down to a particular key term. Rather we want to elucidate the
thought development and meaning of the whole statement. In communication none of
us ever isolates words or particular statements as the meaning of the whole. We seldom
dwell upon one portion of a sentence or paragraph and neglect the rest. Rather we intend
for meaning to be communicated primarily by the entire utterance taken as a whole.

Recent investigation into communication theory has dealt with the problem of information interference, those aspects of communication which conceal rather than aid the transference of meaning. Ambiguous or unknown terms, grammatical errors, or hidden agendas within the communication process often restrict rather than aid meaning. This is why human beings so very often fail to communicate with one another. They define terms differently, unintentionally (or intentionally) mislead or simply speak from a perspective completely different from that of the hearer or reader. The task of exegesis is to uncover such communication lapses in a text and to try to recover the original intended meaning of the author. Syntax puts together the various aspects of the hermeneutical task and enables us to search deeply into the biblical text in an effort to recover the God-given message.

Biblical Transformations

Many have attempted to apply transformational techniques to biblical study (see the excursus in this chapter). The structuralists go to extremes when they virtually replace the surface structure (the text) with the deep structure (ideas underlying the text). Gerhardt Güttgemanns has developed "generative poetics," which uses "poetics" in its broadest sense to consider a text both as a historical production of meaning and in terms of contemporary interpretation (1976:1-21). However, he defines *history* not in its normal sense but rather by means of transformational rules; for Güttgemanns the meaning of a historical statement is found not in its sociocultural background but in the deep structure underlying the surface statement. Perhaps the most helpful aspect of his theory is his restructuring of transformational rules along the lines of Wittgenstein's game theory. Güttgemanns visualizes the deep structure as a "game tree," a range of functional alternatives for the grammatical basis of the surface text. When one recognizes these possible choices, it becomes much easier to allow the structural context to determine the best choice (pp. 8-11). For instance, when we see the phrase "the faith of Christ" we must posit several possible transformations, such as "faith in Christ," "the faith which Christ gives," "the faithfulness of Christ." Individual context then decides which is the best alternative. Güttgemann's application of his method to specific texts is closer to structuralist exegesis than I would like, but it is a healthy step in the right direction (pp. 127-74).

Much better for our definition of *syntax* is the work of Eugene Nida and Charles Taber (1969), who develop a three-stage system of translation from the original language (OL: Hebrew or Greek) to the receptor language (RL: English, for example). The first step is analysis, in which the surface structure is studied in terms of its grammatical relationships and word meaning. This would conform to our use of syntax or exegetical methodology. The second step, transfer, mediates from the original to the receptor language. That is, the results of the analysis are transferred to the receptor language. Finally, the material is restructured to be completely understandable to the new language. In other words, we seek to rephrase the idioms and surface grammar of the biblical text so that the resultant meaning will be understandable in the modern context. These latter two steps primarily refer to the process of contextualization and therefore will be covered in later chapters.

More important, Nida and Taber integrate grammatical and semantic components in the larger syntactical task. I have already noted in the previous chapter the importance of the context in determining which of the possible meanings from the semantic range is intended in a particular statement. Indeed, grammar and semantics are completely interdependent, for meaning depends upon the play between these two aspects. This is where Nida and Taber find the true value of transformational rules. As figure 4.1 indicates, the more complex surface structure is broken down into "kernel sentences" by means of "back-transformation." Nida and Taber theorize that all language is made up of six to twelve basic structures that are "transformed" into more complex "surface structures." All languages are similar at the "kernel level," where the transference of meaning can occur. This is an overstatement of the reality (see below), however, for it is debatable whether such universal meanings can indeed be transferred automatically from language to language. Nevertheless, the concept of "kernel sentences" is immensely helpful in enabling the interpreter to break down the statements of a text into explicit and implicit propositions.

Fig. 4.1. Surface Structures and Kernel Sentences.

The kernel sentence denotes the basic individual affirmations of the sentence. Sentences can be broken up into simple and complex types; the simple sentence contains only one basic affirmation (such as "the ball is hit") while a complex sentence contains more than one affirmation ("the ball belonging to the boy is hit"). The latter sentence has two kernels, "the ball belongs to the boy" and "the ball is hit." The back transformation of a complex sentence involves the determination of each individual affirmation within the larger surface structure. Nida and Taber illustrate this (1969:53-54) by eluding to Ephesians 2:8-9, "For it is by grace you have been saved, through faith . . . and this not from yourselves, it is the gift of God . . . not by works, so that no one can boast" (NIV). They reduce this surface statement to seven kernel sentences: (1) God showed you grace; (2) God saved you; (3) You believed; (4) You did not save yourselves; (5) God gave salvation; (6) You did not work for it; (7) This is done so that no man may boast. This differs from Chomsky's deep grammar in its combination of grammar and lexical meaning, yet makes it all the more relevant for our purposes.

Indeed back transformation involves the deepest level of semantic investigation. Louw provides a transformational translation of Ephesians 1:5-7:

> Because God had already decided to make us his children through Jesus Christ. He did this because He wanted to and it gave him pleasure to do so. Let us praise the wonderful favor He gave us. This favor was that He gave us His son, whom He loved. Yes, it is because Jesus died for us that God set us free. With this I mean that God forgives our sins. How abundant is the favor He showed us. (1982:87-88)

Louw notes eight transformations in the passage: (1) "adoption" (E) = "God makes us His children"; (2) "good pleasure" (E) = "God is glad about it"; (3) "good pleasure of His will" (E + E) = "God wants to do it and therefore is glad about it"; (4) "to the praise" (R + E) = "It serves as praise"; (5) "glory of His grace" (A + E) = "The favor He gives is wonderful"; (6) "redemption" (E) = "God redeems us"; (7) "through His blood" (R + E) = "Because Christ died for us"; (8) "forgiveness of sins" (E + E) = "God forgives us our sins/sins we commit"; (9) "riches of His grace" (A + E) = "He gives an abundant favor." This excellent example of connotative meaning (see p. 84) demonstrates the definite value of detailed word study for syntactical exegesis.

Sawyer provides a different example, this time of paradigmatic (semantic field, see pp. 84-87) research in syntactical study (1972:62-63). He studied related transformations dealing with Old Testament language for salvation and notes four sentences that proceed from the same basic kernel: "The Lord saved His anointed" (Ps 20:7); "Save me" (Jer 17:14); "I shall be saved" (2 Sam 22:4); "You have let your servant win this great victory" (Judg 15:18b). The first three are similar since they deal basically with the idea of Yahweh saving. The fourth example contains a "nominalization." This occurs when the verbal element ("save") is replaced by a noun phrase ("great victory"). Sawyer notes that such a transformation usually involves the deletion of the subject (Yahweh) or object (Israel) as well as the absence of the tense marker (compare "the chastisement of our peace" in Is 53:5, which could be past, present or future). Often more than one kernel lies under the surface, for instance, "You have helped your servant win," "your servant has won," and "the victory is great" in Judges 15:18b above. When comparing the verbs for "salvation" that describe the underlying kernel, we find nuances of meaning that occur in differing contexts and can thereby determine with greater precision and depth both individual meanings and the broader theological overtones.

The second stage of syntactical investigation is forward transformation (see figure 15), as the individual kernels are collated in order to determine the inner connections between the statements. Of course, here we utilize the same rhetorical techniques discussed in chapter three, but now the decisions are finalized. In inductive study a preliminary chart is developed and functions as a control and guide for the detailed exegesis, where the parts are intensely studied grammatically and semantically. This results in kernel sentences, that are now recombined on the basis of compositional patterns into a final delineation of the thought development of the whole passage or paragraph.[2] Beekman and Callow provide an excellent display of the propositions in Philemon 4-7.

Propositional Display of Philemon 4-7

Philemon 4-7: "I was moved because you love all the saints."

4a	I always thank God	
b	whom I (worship)	COMMENT about God in 4a
c	when I pray for you	TIME of 4a
5a	because I hear	5a-c give the REASON (objective) for 4a
b	that you love all the saints	CONTENT of *hear* in 5a

c	and that you believe/trust the Lord Jesus	CONTENT of *hear* in 5a
6a	(I pray)	implied from 4c
b	that (you may) fellowship more and more fully (with those)	6b-f give the CONTENT of *pray* in 6a
c	who also believe/trust (the Lord Jesus) with you	IDENTIFICATION of those in 6b
d	by means of (your) coming to know all the good (things)	MEANS of 6b
e	which we (incl.) (can do)	COMMENT about things in 6d
f	in order that Christ may be honored by us (incl.).	PURPOSE of 6e
7a	Moreover, I rejoiced greatly	
b	and I was greatly encouraged/comforted	
c	because you love (the saints)	REASON (objective) for 7a-b
d	specifically, because you are the one who refreshed the saints in spirit, brother.	SPECIFIC restatement of 7c

Of course, when one has isolated the kernels, the display becomes even more exact. For instance, let us note Philippians 2:6.

(Though) He partook of the divine essence	concession
He was equal with God	comparison
He did not demand equality	concession-contraexpectation
He did not have to seize equality	clarification

Beekman and Callow then summarize the relations between propositions that can supplement the discussion of compositional techniques in chapter three above (1974:287-312):

Additional Relations (those which develop the idea)
    1. Chronological sequence (such as Mk 4:28, "first the blade then the head then the kernel")
    2. Simultaneity (such as Mt 24:29, "The sun shall be darkened and the moon shall not shine and the stars shall fall")
    3. Alternation (such as Mt 6:31, "What shall one eat . . . or drink or how shall we be clothed")
    4. Conversational exchanges or dialogue (such as Jn 3)
    5. Matched support (such as Gal 3:29, "If you are Christ's then you are Abraham's seed and heirs according to the promise")
Associative Relations (those which support or clarify the idea)

1. Support by distinct clarification

   a. Manner (how the event occurs, such as Phil 2:8, "found in appearance as a man, he humbled himself")

   b. Comparison (such as Jas 1:6, "he who doubts is like a wave of the sea")

   c. Contrast (such as Mt 10:28, "fear not those . . . but him")

2. Support by similar clarification (overlapping content)

   a. Equivalence (such as Rom 12:19, "Vengeance is mine, I will repay")

   b. Generic-specific (from the class to a particular instance, such as Mk 6:48, "he came . . . walking on the sea")

   c. Amplification-contraction (summary or rhetorical question, such as the summaries in Acts 6:7; 9:31; 12:24; Rom 6:12; "should we continue to sin? God forbid . . .")

3. Support by argument (cause-effect propositions)

   a. Reason-result (such as Jas 4:2, "You have not because you ask not")

   b. Means-result (such as Phil 2:7, 'he made himself low by taking the form of a servant")

   c. Means-purpose (the desired result might not take place, such as Mk 14:38, "Watch and pray, that you might not enter into temptation")

   d. Condition-consequence (such as Jn 3:3, "If one is not born again, he cannot see the Kingdom of God")

   e. Concession-contraexpectation (a reversal of expectancy, such as Phil 2:6 above)

   f. Grounds-conclusion (either in argument form [such as Rom 5:9, "being justified . . . we shall be saved"] or imperative [such as Mt 9:37-38, "The harvest is great, the laborers few; pray therefore . . ."])

4. Support by orientation (background or setting)

   a. Time (such as Mk 1:32, "when the sun set, they brought . . .")

   b. Location (such as Mk 1:30, "He went throughout Galilee, preaching . . .")

   c. Circumstance (attendant action [such as Jn 19:5, "Jesus came out wearing the crown of thorns"])

Performative and Emotive Language

The discussion thus far has primarily centered upon descriptive or cognitive propositions, statements whose purpose is to argue or to provide information. However, this by no means exhausts the type of utterances found in speech-acts. Frequently in Scripture the language does not merely convey observations or increase knowledge but also performs an act. J. L. Austin labels this "performative language" because it describes what actually happens rather than what should or should not be the case (1962). When Paul says "I am sending [Tychicus] to you" (Col 4:8), he is telling the Colossians what he is actually in process of doing. When Pharaoh gave Joseph control over Egypt (Gen 41:41), that authority descended upon Joseph. As Caird observes, "Performatives commit the speaker to stand by his words" (1980:21). When Jephthah vowed to sacrifice whatever came out of his house as a burnt offering to Yahweh on behalf of his victory over the Ammonites (Judg 11:30-31), he had to do so even though that sacrifice turned out to be his only child (11:34-39). When Ananias and Sapphira tried to renege on a vow to God, Peter became

Yahweh's avenging angel in striking them down (Acts 5:1-11). John differs from Paul in making such terms as "believe" or "love" performatives by using only the verb (Paul prefers the noun). Indeed, words throughout Scripture are viewed as living organisms that bind the speaker to act upon them. This is why there are constant admonitions against careless language (such as Eph 5:29).

Two other aspects of performative language must be understood. Austin argues strongly that any performative utterance depends upon the presence of a commonly accepted or true environment (1962:45). Today one could not state, "I will sacrifice two turtle doves in the temple" because such is no longer possible. In the same way, the test of a prophet is simple: if the prophecy comes to pass it is of the Lord (Deut 18:21-22). Thiselton uses this to accuse the New Hermeneutic of what is near to "word magic," since its adherents make biblical language a word event in itself when in actuality Scripture's effectiveness depends upon the reader's acceptance of a wide range of dogmatic assertions (1980:337, 354-55). This has critical repercussions for hermeneutics in general, for behind many performative statements in Scripture lies a deep structure of theological affirmations that must be understood before the surface contents can be properly exegeted. In other words, part of the exegetical task is to recover the biblical theology (what I call the "deep structure"; see chap. thirteen) behind biblical statements. For instance, when Mark begins his Gospel with a combined citation from Exodus 23:20; Malachi 3:1; and Isaiah 40:3 (Mk 1:2-3), several concepts form major themes in his Gospel—the messenger/herald, the way, the Lord, the wilderness. Each must be seen in light of his entire work in order for his purpose and message to be understood in its fullness.

Austin also differentiates between illocutionary and perlocutionary force (1962:99-131). Illocutionary language asks for a response, but perlocutionary speech actually causes the effect it seeks to produce. There is no guaranteed result with the former. For instance, the Hebrew imperative is illocutionary, asking for action, but the prophetic future (imperfect) is perlocutionary, since the "Thou shalt" is accompanied by blessings (if it is kept) or cursings (if it is not). Caird provides an interesting addendum when he connects the latter with the biblical doctrine of predestination but notes that this never descends to determinism because response is always essential to the divine call (1980:23-24). For instance, while Paul alludes to Jeremiah's call when he describes himself as "set apart from birth" (Gal 1:15-16; compare Jer 1:5), it is clear that the commission was not actualized until he later decided to accept that call.

In addition to performative language we must also recognize the important place of emotive or expressive speech in the Bible. Certainly the emotional feeling within an epistle is an important aspect of its total meaning. In fact, it could be argued that the true meaning is lost without the portrayal of the emotions to guide the interpreter. There is no depth without the personal element, no grasp or feel for a passage without the underlying tone. This is especially essential for the preacher, who wants to lead first himself and then the congregation into the intensity of the text, to awaken those slumbering passions for God and his will that were so essential to early Christian experience but often have been set aside by the pressures of modern life.

The determination of emotional patterns is easy when the author uses highly emotive language, as Paul does when he argues that the Corinthian women's refusal to have their heads covered was "dishonor" (1 Cor 11:5), "a disgrace" (11:6), improper (11:13), and unnatural (11:15), and concludes that no church anywhere follows such a practice (11:16). Paul's deep-felt emotions rise to the surface in such a passage. In many others, however, it is not so easy to detect. Nida speaks technically: "Emotive meanings consist of polar contrasts separated by a graded series with a high percentage of usages for most words clustering around the neutral position" (1964:113). He means that most words are part of a larger matrix between poles like good-bad, beautiful-ugly, love-hate, rejoicing-miserable or desired-rejected. Most of us choose terms in the middle, and it is helpful to note where on the line between those poles an author's choice of language falls. The closer to the poles a writer comes, the more emotion-laden his message is.

The interpreter must perform a paradigmatic and a syntagmatic study of emotional coloring. Paradigmatically, he must investigate where the word fits in such a graded scale. For instance, "happy" is less than "overjoyed" but clearly more than "calm," which itself is above "sad" and "miserable." Of course, there is no automatic scale and writers do not always use such language with precision. One writer may use "happy" in a very positive sense while for another it could have an almost neutral tone. Therefore we must always see how a writer tends to use language. Jeremiah and Paul, for instance, are very emotional writers and wear their feelings on the surface. One can expect highly charged terms from them. They tend to choose words at the top and bottom ends of the scale.

The final arbiter is always the total context of the passage. For instance, while *makarios* in the Beatitudes (Mt 5:1-13) can be translated "happy," the eschatological tone of the context makes it unlikely that this is the actual meaning. More likely, it refers to the outpouring of divine "blessing" upon those who sacrifice for the kingdom. The delineation of those very blessings in each beatitude makes this the likely meaning. Nevertheless, an emotional tone exists under the surface, for those who experience such blessings will indeed know joy. In many contexts the presence of emotionally charged language colors the whole. This is especially true in the prophetic works. One cannot read very far in Amos before encountering "The Lord roars from Zion and thunders from Jerusalem. . . . I will not turn back my wrath" (1:2-3 NIV). Every paragraph is filled with such language, and it is impossible not to feel the terrible anger of Yahweh against social injustice. The formula of judgment ("for three sins, even for four, I will not turn back my wrath," 1:3, 9, 11, 13; 2:1, 4) is first addressed to the surrounding nations, and Israel may well have felt secure, even smug, at God's wrath kindled against her traditional enemies. How much more devastating then when in 2:6 the awesome eyes of Yahweh blaze against Israel herself. The emotional language at that time becomes all the more powerful.

Figures of Speech

Figurative expressions traditionally have been discussed in a topical section labeled "special hermeneutics," which included such diverse topics as language (metaphor, simile), genre (prophecy, parable) and theology. I believe, however, that this is artificial and prefer to deal with these linguistic elements logically in accordance with the developing structure of hermeneutical criteria. Figures of speech contain both grammatical and semantic aspects (as we will see) and so are properly discussed as a specific section of syntactical analysis.

As already noted (p. 83), figures of speech form the third level of the "multiple senses" of meaning, following the primary or most common meaning and the secondary or less common uses of the semantic range. Figurative expressions associate a concept with a pictorial or analogous representation of its meaning in order to add richness to the statement. Literal meaning comprises the first two levels and identifies the basic thrust of a term. A "roof," for instance, is the cover over a house or other structure. A figure of speech concerns an associative relation between senses, such as the "roof" of one's mouth.

The Bible constantly employs colorful imagery drawn from a multitude of experiences. Business terminology is used to depict discipleship ("steward," "servant," "husbandman"), and domestic affairs describe the relationship between God and his people ("groom-bride," "father-child").[3] In fact, a knowledge of customs and culture (see chap. five) is necessary in order to understand many of the images adduced. For instance, the "scroll written on both sides, sealed with seven seals" (Rev 5:1) is built upon either the Roman last will and testament (which was sealed with seven seals) containing the inheritance of the saints or the Roman doubly inscribed contract deed containing blessings and curses (my preference). Either will fit the word picture, but the modern reader could not possibly know the options without a knowledge of ancient customs. Yet the symbolism behind Revelation 5—6 is greatly enhanced by uncovering such background information.

Beekman and Callow describe two major groups of figurative or associative senses (1974:97-101). Contiguous relationships between words are built upon proximity or nearness of meaning. This group has three types: (1) In temporal associations, a time-note replaces an event, as in the technical "day of the Lord," which refers not just to the parousia itself but to all the events of the "last days." In another sense Jesus said "Abraham rejoiced to see my day" (Jn 8:56), referring to the Incarnation. (2) Spatial relations utilize local ideas, as when "heaven" is used for God (Mt 21:25, "was the baptism of John from heaven or men?"). In Ephesians (1:3, 20; 2:6; 3:10; 6:12) "the heavenlies" speaks of the spiritual realm where the cosmic conflict is fought.[4] (3) Logical or cause-effect relations substitute the cause for the effect or vice versa. For instance, the "hand of the Lord" (cause) refers to judgment and the "sword" to persecution and division (Mt 10:34), to discipline (Rom 13:4) or to conviction (Heb 4:12).

There are also three types of part-whole associations: (1) In member-class relations, a specific member stands for the generic whole. One of the best-known examples is "Give us this day our daily bread" (Mt 6:11), where the "bread" refers to all the believer's needs, physical and spiritual. The beatitude on those who "hunger and thirst after righteousness" (Mt 5:45) represents the class of intense desires by the single metaphor of hunger-thirst. (2) In constituent-whole relations, a single part of a larger structure stands for the whole, such as "roof" for house (Mt 8:8) or "three thousand souls" for people converted to Christianity (Acts 2:41). (3) Attribute-whole relations occur when the traits or purposes of a thing are used for the thing itself. An interesting example is "serpent," which is used negatively in "You serpents, you generation of vipers" (Mt 23:33) but positively in "wise like serpents" (Mt 10:16). Two different traits associated with snakes are obviously intended in the disparate passages.

The major difficulty in interpreting figures of speech is that languages develop their associative relations independently; therefore, metaphorical language in Hebrew or Greek often does not correspond at all to English expressions. Of course this is similar to differences between modern languages (see Beekman and Callow 1974:104-7). It is a problem in semantics and must be investigated at that level (see chap. three).

When the original language employs an idiom or figurative expression, it can be translated in three possible ways: (1) If the figure of speech is paralleled in the receptor language, we can translate directly. This situation occurs more frequently in Western languages due to the impact of Christianity upon our culture and thus upon the development of our languages (for example, the influence of Luther's translation of the Bible upon modern German). Expressions like "the Lord saves his anointed" (Ps 20:6) or "they began to speak in other tongues" (Acts 2:4) are easily understood (though in many other languages this may not be true). (2) If the transfer of meaning is not automatic, but there is still a slight correspondence, the term itself may be retained but a clarification added to clear up any ambiguity. At times Scripture itself does this, such as "dead in their trespasses and sins" (Eph 2:1; compare Rom 6:11, "dead to sin"). However, we will often have to add the clarification ourselves, such as "the hour is at hand" (Mt 26:45) = "the time when I must die is near." (3) If there is no correspondence at all between the original and the receptor language, the figure of speech will be replaced by a corresponding idiom. Beekman and Callow specifically mention euphemistic expressions for death, sex, God and the Gentiles here. An obvious example would be the frequent use of "he knew his wife," which must be translated "he had sexual relations with his wife." This idiom in Matthew 1:25 is translated "did not know her" in the New King James and "he had no union with his wife" in the New International Version.

The solution is to back transform the biblical figure of speech into the appropriate "kernel" and then to forward transform it into the proper equivalent in the receptor language, allowing the needs of the audience to decide which of the three is best in a given situation. Indeed, this is why there cannot be any final or universal translation of the Scriptures into English or any other language. Not only does the language change from year to year; it differs radically from locality to locality. In England or Germany a person's home can be pinpointed to the very village or town by the dialect spoken. Every hamlet favors its own set of idiomatic expressions. The preacher must be sensitive to translate the Word afresh for each audience.

There is enormous tensive power in figurative language to evoke fresh images in the mind of the learner. Ricoeur's discussion of metaphor (which includes all figures of speech) is helpful here.[5] He argues that figurative expressions operate not so much at the level of semantics but in the broader sphere of discourse or communication. A metaphor sets up a state of tension between the literal and figurative meanings of the word, which causes the former to "self-destruct" "in a significant contradiction" (1976:50). Ricoeur means that a figurative expression is a deliberate choice on the part of an author who uses it to force the readers into a new awareness of the message. At first, the readers are jarred by the incongruity of the thought, for normal literal meanings do not fit. They are led to a new word picture of reality and forced to rethink the categories of the proposition stated (1975a:83-84). A new world of discourse is fashioned, and the reader is drawn into it.

Of course, the value of this new vision of reality depends entirely upon a correspondence between the author's and the reader's worlds of experience. This could not be assumed even in biblical times. Paul was frequently misunderstood and himself made cultural gaffes (the Lycaonians in Acts 14:8-18). The problem becomes even greater with the passing of the centuries; if metaphors are as central to the process of speech communication as Ricoeur argues, the necessity of translating them properly for our audiences becomes even greater. This sense of the importance of our topic will guide our discussion in the ensuing pages.

While some have attempted a new linguistic organization of the various figures of speech (see Nida et al. 1983:172-87), I feel that the traditional pattern (Bullinger, Mickelsen, Kaiser and others) still makes the best sense. There are six basic types—comparison, addition, incompleteness, contrast, personal figures and association or relation. It is helpful to note the specific type of figurative expression used in a context because that will provide important hermeneutical data for interpreting the statement more precisely. Many passages remain obscure until the figurative language is isolated and understood.

1. Figures of Comparison. Two figures, metaphor and simile, deal with direct comparisons between items. A simile establishes a formal comparison employing connective terms such as "like" or "as." Similes are used often in Proverbs; for instance, "When calamity overtakes you like a storm, when disaster sweeps over you like a whirlwind" (1:27) or "Free yourself, like a gazelle from the hand of a hunter, like a bird from the snares of the fowler" (6:5). Jesus also used similes constantly, and they function in much the same way as his parables, which have rightfully been called extended similes ("the Kingdom of God is like . . .") or metaphors. They add poignant meaning to his statements, as in "How often I wanted to gather together your children as a hen gathers under her wings her chicks, but you refused" (Mt 23:27). The interpreter should not hurry past such vivid images, for they are built upon the very patterns of life experienced in ancient times and had great power in their original settings. Jesus could hardly have conveyed better the contrast between his living concern and Jewish obduracy than in the Matthew 23:27 simile.

A metaphor is an implied, but in many ways even more direct, comparison because the reader is expected to identify the comparison without the "like" or "as"; for instance, "You are a shield around me, O Lord" (Ps 3:3). There are two types of comparison (see Beekman and Callow:1974:124-26). A full or complete comparison states both items and the similarity between them. The two may be contrasted directly ("I am weak but he is strong") or by degree ("he is stronger than I"). The resemblance may be relative ("I am strong and so is he") or absolute ("I am as strong as he"). An abbreviated comparison leaves the similarity implicit and the reader has to supply it, as in "You are the salt of the earth" (Mt 5:13, metaphor) or "His eyes were like a flame of fire" (Rev 1:14, simile). At other times the object of the image is unstated, as in "his sheep will be scattered" (Mk 14:27).

A metaphor or simile has three parts: the topic or item illustrated by the image, the image itself and the point of similarity or comparison (the actual meaning of the metaphor or simile in the passage). Often all three are present in a comparison; for example, "The heavens [topic] shall vanish [point of comparison] like smoke [image]" (Is 51:6) or "Go rather to the lost (point of comparison) sheep (image) of the house of Israel (topic)" (Mt 10:6). As Beekman and Callow point out, one or more of these can be missing and therefore must be supplied by the interpreter (1974:128-31). The topic may be implied, as in "sheep among wolves" (Lk 10:3), where the "wolves" are the persecutors of the disciples. The point of similarity may be unstated, such as "and he is the head of the body, the Church" (Col 1:18), where the ruling function of Christ (the head) and the directed function of the church (the body) are assumed. Further, both topic and point of similarity may be omitted; for instance, in "beware the leaven of the Pharisees," which implies both the topic (their teachings) and the point of similarity (their permeating effect). Finally, the image and point of similarity can be missing, as in "it is hard for you to struggle against the goads," which assumes the ox and the point of similarity, namely the struggle against guidance and control. The reader must be alert enough in such instances to supply the missing information; this demands a knowledge of the cultural background.

Above all, we must be careful not to overexegete figures of speech. Unlike modern metaphors, ancient figures of speech were inexact. They overlapped only at one point, and the modern reader often has trouble understanding that point. Caird provides an informative example:

> When the psalmist tells us that a united family is like oil dripping down Aaron's beard on to the skirts of his robe, he is not trying to persuade us that family unity is messy, greasy or volatile; he is thinking of the all-pervasive fragrance which has so deeply impressed itself on his memory at the anointing of the high priest (Ps. 133:2). (1980:145)

We need help in unlocking such language, and for this the nonspecialist must turn to the better commentaries and background books. This is especially true when the biblical writers pile image upon image, as in Psalm 92:10 (combining the "glory" of the strength of the ox with that of anointing the head) or Ephesians 4:14 (from infants to a helpless boat to a helpless bird to cheating at dice). Mixed metaphors were highly prized in ancient literature; rather than stress the ambiguity of the resultant statement (as we do today), classical writers emphasized the richness of the literary expression. We today must work behind the imagery to uncover the exact point accented in the compilation of metaphors. Often the image behind a metaphor is unknown. Numerous articles have been written on the "whitewashed sepulchre" of Matthew 23:27 or the "restrainer" of 2 Thessalonians 2:6-7. The actual thrust may never be known for certain before we get to heaven itself. The image also can be ambiguous, as in the many possible meanings of the "water" metaphor in John 3:5.

Finally, we should note the presence of live and dead metaphors in the biblical text.

In a dead metaphor the image has become an idiom, understood directly by the hearer without producing a word-picture in the mind. A live metaphor is constructed on the occasion to teach a fresh point and force the hearer to recall both primary and associative meanings in order to understand the image. This distinction is critical because the interpreter can read too much into a dead metaphor by erroneously stressing its picture value.

The difficulty is that we have not grown up in the ancient culture and cannot easily identify such differences. Two criteria will help us understand the distinction. Etymologically, if the figurative thrust has been in existence for some time, it could well be a dead metaphor. According to BAGD, *sarx* ("flesh") was already used figuratively in the time of Epicurus, three centuries before Christ. When Paul contrasts "flesh" and "spirit" he is not trying to build a picture as an illustration of a truth but to use a semitechnical concept for the natural person. The same is true of *karpos* ("fruit"), also present in the time of Epicurus (BAGD). In passages on the "fruit of the Spirit" (Gal 5:22-23) or "the fruit of lips which confess his name" (Heb 13:15), the term has become an idiom and should simply be interpreted as "result." However, if the metaphor is elaborated in a series of pictures or its fresh image stressed in the context, it is more likely a live metaphor. This is true of *karpos* in several passages: Matthew 7:16-20, where "you will know them by their fruit" is expanded by successive images regarding grapes and thorns, figs and thistles, trees and the fire; John 15:1-8, where *karpos* is part of the vine-and-branches parable (a very live metaphor) and leads into the teaching on bearing fruit (vv. 4, 8); Jude 17, where it is part of the larger figure of "autumn trees—without fruit and uprooted—twice dead" (NIV). The context is the final arbiter in all such decisions.

2. Figures of Addition or Fullness of Expression.

a. *Pleonasm* refers to the redundant addition of synonyms to emphasize a point. This was a favorite stylistic trait of ancient writers for clarification or emphasis, similar to the poetic device of synonymous parallelism. A major example is the constant use of "he answered and said" in the Gospels; others include "he did not remember but forgot" (Gen 40:23), "the earthly house of this tent" (2 Cor 5:1) and "the household master of the house" (Lk 22:11). The tendency of modern translations is to omit such phrases as in the New International Version on Luke 22:11, "the owner of the house." The reader must be careful not to read too much into such repetitive phrases; they are usually stylistic.

b. *Paronomasia* refers to words that are similar in sound and placed side-by-side in the text for emphasis. Often words are chosen to catch the original readers' attention and drive home the point. For instance, *tōhû wābōhû* ("waste and void"; Gen 1:2) or *panti pantote pasan* ("all sufficiency in all things"; 2 Cor 9:8) have a dramatic flair. Many times important theology is presented by means of paronomasia. Beitzel argues cogently that paronomasia was often used in the ancient Near East for solemn pronouncements and often in terms of divine names (1980:5-20). Rather than link *yhwh* (KJV "Jehovah"; Hebrew "Yahweh") with the verb "to be" *(hyh)*, Beitzel argues that it is linked with the use of *yw* in Ugaritic, *yahwe/yiha* in Egyptian and *Ieuw* in Babylonian, all three instances of divine names. Therefore, *Yahweh* is connected with those and as a term has an "unknown lexicographic and ethnic origin" (p. 19). It derives its meaning not from etymology but from its paronomastic relation with *hayah* in Exodus 3:14, thus "He who causes to be [what is]" or "The Performer of the Promise."

c. *Epizeuxis* or *Epanadiplosis* occurs when a crucial word is repeated for emphasis. John tends to employ this with the *amēn* ("truly, truly") formula; the Synoptic writers use only one. The use of the *amēn* formula has enormous implications for Christology, for it replaced the prophetic formula "thus says the Lord" and became a divine self-authentication by which Jesus was taking upon himself the authority of Yahweh. By using epizeuxis John (1:51; 3:3, 5; twenty-five times in all) gives this solemn aspect special stress. Similar would be the threefold "holy, holy, holy" in Isaiah 6:3 and Revelation 4:8 to highlight the holiness of God.

d. *Hyperbole* is a conscious exaggeration or overstatement in order to drive home a truth. Jesus adopted this rabbinic ploy as one of his main teaching methods. Understanding it is critical to a proper interpretation of the Sermon on the Mount (Mt 5:29, "If your right eye offends you, pluck it out"). Many serious errors have been made by interpreting literally such statements as "turn the other cheek" or "if he asks your tunic, give him your cloak as well" (Mt 5:39-40), as if those teachings defined the limits of a servant attitude. Jesus was talking generally of forgiveness and service rather than specifically, using these as hyperbolic examples. Similarly, when Jesus said the mustard seed was "the smallest seed" (Mk 4:31), he was not making a scientific statement but using a hyperbolic contrast (smallest-greatest); the mustard seed was the smallest seed that produced such a large plant (v. 32).

e. *Hendiadys* occurs when two or three terms are added to one another to express the same thing, such as "fire and brimstone" (Gen 19:24), "blessed hope and glorious appearing" (Tit 2:13) or "kingdom and glory" (1 Thess 2:12). The difficulty is deciding when there is one thought and when they express different aspects. For instance, "full of grace and truth" in John 1:17 may be hendiadys but more likely reflects the Jewish concepts of *ḥeseḏ* (covenant love) and *'ᵉmeṯ* (covenant faithfulness). The context and background of the terms must determine in individual cases.

3. Incomplete Figures of Speech. This reverses the previous category, considering figures of speech that involve omission rather than addition.

a. *Ellipsis* is a grammatically incomplete expression requiring the reader to add concepts in order to finish the thought. Mickelsen mentions two types (1963:189-90). In repetitional ellipsis the idea to be supplied is expressed earlier in the context or is clearly related to that which has been explicitly discussed; for example, "Does God give you his Spirit and work miracles among you because of the works of the law or . . ." (Gal 3:5). The reader supplies the idea, "Did he do it?" (see also Rom 11:22). In nonrepetitional ellipsis the concept to be supplied is not in the larger context. This is the more difficult, for the reader must speculate from the total message of the context. For instance, "Do we not have the right to eat and drink?" (1 Cor 9:4). Nothing has been mentioned previously and only later statements about the apostle's right to be supported by the congregation help us to understand it. In Acts 18:6 "Your blood upon your head" could be "Your blood *be* upon your heads" (the traditional interpretation) or "May your blood *come* upon your head" (BDF par. 480[5]).

b. *Zeugma* is a special form of ellipsis in which two terms are combined that do not belong together and have to be separated by an added verb, as in 1 Timothy 4:3, "who forbid marriage [and order people] to abstain from certain foods." The statement has been abbreviated in order to give it greater effect, and the reader must catch the intervening idea.

c. *Aposiopesis* occurs when a portion of the sentence is consciously omitted for reasons of emphasis. In John 1:22 the Jewish delegation to the Baptist queries, "Who are you? [We ask] so that we may give an answer to those who sent us." Mickelsen (1963:191) mentions an interesting example from the parable of the fig tree (Lk 13:9). The caretaker, trying to save the tree, pleas for one more chance: "If indeed it bears fruit for the future [it should be allowed to grow]. Otherwise [if it does not produce fruit] then cut it down." Both clauses omit information for rhetorical effect.

4. Figures Involving Contrast or Understatement.

a. *Irony* is an important rhetorical device that consists of stating one thing while meaning the direct opposite. It is most frequently employed in polemical contexts and is accompanied by sarcasm or ridicule, as in Michal's retort to David, "How the King of Israel has distinguished himself today" (2 Sam 6:20), with open contempt for his dancing before the ark. Matthew 23 is filled with irony, as in Jesus' blistering denunciation of the Pharisees, "You fill up the measure of your fathers," referring to the murder of the prophets (v. 31). Many also see irony in the statement "The teachers of the law and the Pharisees sit in Moses' seat. So obey them and do what they tell you" (23:1-2). In such cases irony becomes biting sarcasm.

b. *Litotes* are phrases that understate or lessen one thing in order to magnify another. As Caird notes, the Old Testament contains few examples because Hebrew did not develop the form of understatement (1980:134). Two examples would be Genesis 18:22, "I am but dust and ashes" to demonstrate God's overwhelming greatness or "a drop of water" in Genesis 18:4 to wash the feet of the angels. More are found in the New Testament due to Hellenistic influence, such as Acts 21:39 ("a citizen of no ordinary city") or 1 Peter 2:10 ("those who are no people").

c. *Euphemism* substitutes a cultured or less offensive term for a harsh one. This is especially true with taboo or sexual items. For instance Judges 3:24 (compare 1 Sam 24:3) has "surely he covers his feet," a euphemism for "goes to the bathroom." Several euphemisms describe sexual intercourse, such as "to know" and "to uncover nakedness." To "come near" is to entice sexually. Further, in Acts 2:39 "all who are afar off" refers to the Gentiles.

d. *Antithesis* is a direct contrast in which two sets of figures are set in opposition to one another. We see this in the Adam-Christ antithesis of Romans 5:12-21 and in the flesh/law versus Spirit opposition of Romans 7—8. In fact Jesus' teachings about the differences between the "laws" of the new kingdom and of the Torah in Matthew 5:21-48 have been labeled "the Antitheses." The so-called dualism of the Gospel of John (light-darkness, above-below, death-life) also belongs to this category. We must interpret such oppositions carefully, for many have read later Gnostic teaching into John or Paul by overstating the contrasts. In actual fact the Johannine dualism is not Gnostic, for it is built upon Jewish-Christian rather than Gnostic patterns.

5. Figures Centering upon Association or Relation.

a. *Metonymy* occurs when one noun is substituted for another that is closely associated with it. Modern examples include Jell-o for gelatin, saltines for crackers, the White House for the presidency, or the bottle for drunkenness. In the Old Testament "throne" (1 Chron 17:12) stood for the kingship, "sword" (Is 51:19) for judgment or war and "key" (Is 22:22) for authority. In the New Testament "principalities and powers" (Eph 3:10; 6:12) refers to the demonic realm (some would say the demonic in government), "circumcision" (Gal 2:7-9) to the Jews, and "Moses" (Lk 16:29) to the Torah.

b. *Synecdoche* is a figure of speech in which a part is substituted for the whole or vice versa. Since I have already dealt with this in some detail above on part-whole relations, I will simply mention it here for the sake of completeness.

6. Figures Stressing the Personal Dimension.

a. *Personification* occurs when a thing or idea is represented as a person.[6] The most widely recognized example is "wisdom" in Proverbs, personified as a herald (1:20-21; 8:1-2), a creative force (3:19-20) and a hostess (9:1-2). In 9:13-18 wisdom is contrasted with "folly," itself personified as a hostess of a house of ill repute. We could note also *logos* ("word") in John 1:1-18. Similarly, the book of Revelation contains many personified symbols like the eagle (8:13), the locusts (9:3-11), the dragon (12:3-17) and the two beasts (13:1-17).

b. *Apostrophe* is a rhetorical device in which a statement is addressed to an imaginary object or person for effect; for instance, "Why gaze with envy, O rugged mountains, at the mountain where God chooses to reign" (Ps 68:16) or "Sing, O barren woman . . . [for] your descendants will conquer nations" (Is 54:1-3). In Psalm 114:5-6 the seas, the mountains and the hills are successively addressed. As we can see, most instances also involve personification, and the final result is a powerful and poignant message to God's people.

Conclusion

Figures of speech are especially rich sources of imagery. While the discussion primarily has centered on the hermeneutical aspects, I want to note also their value for the sermon. It is my contention that some of the best illustrations come not just from cute stories or clever repartee but from the text itself and specifically from the background behind figurative language. Ricoeur's view of the world-referential value of metaphor (see above) is helpful in reminding us that our task is to immerse the audience not merely in entertaining anecdotes but in the Word itself. We are to help our congregation to live anew the message God has revealed in the text and to feel its power to change their situation as well. The startling reverberations of meaning inherent in the Bible's figurative language is the best place to start, for it is alive with powerful, colorful ideas. In recapturing the vitality and forceful presentation of the language, we will help our listeners to place themselves in the shoes of the original hearers and both to relive and to apply anew that eternal message.

Biblical Examples

In order to illustrate the exegetical methodology of the previous chapters we will study two passages, one from each testament. It is necessary to point out once more that the steps of structure, grammar, semantics and syntax are not exclusive, to be done one at a time, but are interdependent, to be done together. We first study a text inductively, taking a preliminary look at the passage in order to provide a control against a naive dependence upon others' opinions. Then we use the tools (lexicons, commentaries, word study volumes and the like) to study the passage in depth, asking grammatical, semantic and syntactical questions as they arise in the text. In using the tools, the most valuable thing is not the conclusions that the authors make but the evidence they utilize. As France says, "no serious exegete should be content merely to follow where some revered commentary or version leads. He should satisfy himself whether the job has been properly done" (1978:253). This is the mistake of many term papers, which become little more than glorified lists of other peoples' opinions. When I study a text, I want to consider the material discovered by other scholars but come to my own opinion as to the original meaning of the text. The conclusions of the commentaries are not as important as the data and information they contain. Only after assembling the data and considering the options on the basis of the immediate context (which best fits the passage itself) do I make up my mind. Then it becomes *my* interpretation.

The two examples cited below are chosen deliberately. They are quite different in style and format in order to provide a broader demonstration of the techniques. I am assuming the inductive and preliminary notes in order to provide a more polished sample; the reader must be aware that the original notes will not have this look.

Zephaniah 3:14-17

Zephaniah prophecied just prior to the reform of Josiah (621 B.C.). His strong denunciation of the pagan practices of Baal worship and child sacrifice (1:4-9, 11-12; 3:1-4) that typified the previous reign of Manasseh helped prepare for the Josianic reform. After proclaiming judgment on the world and on Judah (1:2-6), the book prophecies the imminent coming of the Day of Yahweh (1:7—2:3) and the outpouring of wrath against the nations (2:4-15; 3:6-8) as well as against Judah herself (3:1-5). However, God's mercy would be experienced by the righteous remnant, who would inherit the land of their enemies (2:7, 9) and bask humbly in the worship of their God (3:9-13). The section we consider here forms a fitting conclusion to the book, as it details what Yahweh will do and why.

1. The Joyful Response of Israel (vv. 14-15).[7] The three commands of this verse provide the perfect conclusion to the enumerated blessings of verses 9-13 above. The worship scene of verses 9-10 is now explicated fully. The three successive verbal units, *rānni* ("sing"), *hāri'û* ("shout"), *śimḥî w^e'olzî* ("rejoice and exult") are used synonymously here to describe this worship. All have strong emotive content. The accumulation of such terms is a common device in Semitic poetry to stress the extent of the jubilation experienced when Yahweh's saving presence is felt. We see the worshipers singing then erupting into shouts of joy as they feel the renewal of God's covenant with his people.

Many scholars have called this an enthronement hymn due to the presence of such common themes as the call to singing, victory over enemies and Yahweh as King (see R. L. Smith 1984:144). However, I believe it more likely that Zephaniah uses an enthronement pattern because it fits the prophetic call to rejoicing rather than this being an enthronement hymn. Once again Yahweh sits on his throne vindicating his people. The prophetic rejoicing is paramount.

The titles used to designate the remnant are also important. We must remember that the apostate nation symbolized in her holy city (3:1-5) had forfeited the right to be called God's children. The proud and the haughty had been removed (3:11) and only the righteous remained. Therefore the covenant names—"Zion," "Israel," the figurative "daughter of Jerusalem"—are reinstated in this passage. The name "Jerusalem" was carefully omitted in 3:1-5, and only the description (with "prophets" and "priests," v. 4) showed her identity. Only with the remnant is the name worthy to be uttered, and the significance would not be lost on the original readers.

The reason for the rejoicing (syntactically v. 15 is related causally to v. 14) is twofold, external and internal. At the outset it is difficult to know the progression of thought. In the first line *mišpāṭayik* could mean "adversaries" (NEB, taking it as a piel participle) rather than "judgments," thus producing synonymous parallelism in the first two lines. However, the more common meaning of "ordinance" or "judgment" fits the context, and step parallelism would sum up the previous emphases of the book. The "judgments" against Israel (3:1-5) have been removed, and the "enemies" of Israel (those listed in chap. 2: Philistia, Moab, Ammon, Cush, Assyria) turned back. This makes more sense here. Internally, the remnant is promised that they need never again fear danger because "Yahweh, King of Israel, is in your midst." It would be helpful to note the kernel sentences of verse 15b:

The King of Israel is Yahweh *(melek yiśrā'ēl* is first for emphasis)
Yahweh is in your midst
You will not experience evil *(rā'āh,* "see," as an idiom for "experience")
Evil will never appear again (emphatic use of *lō'* "never . . . again")

Each of these ideas is an essential element of the others. Their covenant God has once more become their King and sits again on the throne. In fact, all four elements (Yahweh on the throne, divine presence, protection, eternal promise) are essential components of the message. Yahweh functions as Israel's protector and shields them with finality from their oppressors. So many Old Testament themes coalesce around this promise that it becomes impossible to discuss them all (such as the exodus motif, Yahweh as Savior of Israel, messianic promises of vindication). Moreover, in the highly eschatological atmosphere of prophecy it is not "illegitimate totality transfer" (see p. 66) to note such themes, for the reader is supposed to recall these covenant motifs in the atmosphere of this powerful prophetic promise.

2. The Message of Hope (vv. 16-17). The third plural "they will say" interrupts the train of thought and undoubtedly refers to the surrounding nations. All who observe Israel will be forced to note her strange fearlessness, made all the more startling in light of her complete domination by her enemies.[8] For nearly a century Israel had had little control over her own destiny, and this must have been devastating to her self-image and concept of God. In the ancient world when a nation was conquered its gods were also conquered and shown to be ineffective. This undoubtedly played a part in the prevalence of apostasy in Israel and Judah. The promise here would be doubly startling because it is based upon the premise that God was on the throne all along. The "day" of course is the Day of Yahweh, already proclaimed as that coming of Yahweh in apocalyptic judgment against his enemies (1:7, 10, especially 1:14—2:3). Here the positive side of the "Day" is stressed, the vindication of the remnant, entailing the final removal of any grounds for fear.

The message of verse 16 builds upon the tone of verses 14-15. There is a chiastic effect in the passage, with the AB:BA pattern stressing the new relationship between Yahweh and his people (A: vv. 14, 17) and its result, the cessation of fear (B: vv. 15-16). This compositional pattern places great stress on both elements. In this verse, the absence of fear is seen in the colorful imagery of the last clause, "Do not let your hands fall limp." In the ancient world the metaphor pictured the depths of numbing despair and terror (compare Is 13:7; Jer 6:24). God's chosen will never again experience the paralyzing grip of terrible anguish. He will vindicate them against their enemies.

The high point of the book is verse 17, and indeed it is one of the truly exciting passages of Scripture. Few biblical statements approach the depths of its imagery or the evocative force of its presentation of Yahweh's love and redemptive power on behalf of his people. It begins by repeating the critical premise of verse 15b, "Yahweh is in your midst," but adds a further title, *yhwh 'elōhayîk* ("Lord your God"), with the emphasis upon the relational "your." The contrast between this new relationship and the angry tone of the denunciation against Judah in 1:4-13 would have been obvious to the ancient reader. Indeed, the relational tone accented in the title provides the basic atmosphere for the whole statement in verse 17.

Yahweh is further described as the warrior-hero who delivers *(gibbôr yôšia')*. Each term is important. In 1:14 the "warrior" cries bitterly because the Day of Yahweh has wrought his utter defeat. Here the effect is completely the opposite. Yahweh is the warrior, and he "saves" his people from their enemies. In this context "hero" is an E-R term, with the semotactic aura of the passage making it an event-word (E) that pictures Yahweh fighting on behalf of his elect and establishing a new relationship (R) as the "deliverer" of true Israel. The picture of God as "warrior" is important to the Old Testament (especially crucial to the prophets) and is emphasized in the New Testament (see Longman 1982:290-307). The strong overtones of Yahweh in conflict with the enemies of his people justifies our noting them as opposed to the weaker translation "hero who helps." The mixture of military metaphor ("warrior") with exodus imagery ("delivers") is particularly meaningful.

Further, this hero-warrior returns after his victory to claim his bride. While we cannot identify this extended metaphor with certainty, the picture of love described in the last half of verse 17 may be best paralleled by other passages depicting Yahweh as the groom of Israel (such as Is 49:18; 61:10; 62:5). Few statements in all of Scripture so powerfully depict the divine love. Three successive clauses give the impression of the inability of human language to plumb its depth adequately. We can graph the progression of these clauses in three possible ways: (1) They could be synonymous, expressing the same basic idea of Yahweh loving his people; this is unlikely because the second ("be quiet") does not overlap sufficiently the other two. (2) The first could establish the basic theme (exultation) and the others express the two concomitant aspects (silence, rejoicing). This is a viable possibility, but the question is whether the first verb is sufficiently broad to encompass the other two. (3) There could be an ABA pattern, with the two verbs, *yāśîś* and *yāḡîl,* synonymous. The decision depends upon the degree of synonymity between the two verbs. A perusal of the lexicons demonstrates that indeed a strong semantic overlap exists between the verbs, and the context here favors the synonymity of the first and third, that they speak of the "joyful exultation" of a deeply felt love. Thus the third option is the more likely rhetorical pattern.

The second verb *(yaḥªrîš)* is the most debated. Many have objected to the translation "be quiet" since it could hint that Yahweh is overlooking their sin. The actual term has a wide range of meaning, from "plow" to "engrave" to "be silent" (see BDB, Smith). Some even propose emendations (RSV, "to renew," from *ḥāḏāš)* or reverse the flow of thought (NIV, "he will quiet you with his love," based upon parallelism with the "over you" of the other two clauses). Yet neither of these other options is necessary. The stress is upon the extent of the divine love, and the contrast pictures the two sides of love, in the second clause denoting "love deeply felt, which is absorbed in its object with thoughtfulness and admiration" (Keil and Delitsch 1971:161) and in the first and third clauses having to break out with "shouts of joy" (one meaning of *yāḡîl).*

The final three verses of the book (vv. 18-20 again in an ABA pattern) summarize the two emphases: Yahweh's vindication (v. 18) and restoration (v. 20) of his people as well as his judgment of their oppressors (v. 19). The conclusion of Zephaniah is another of those marvelous promises to the righteous remnant that set the stage for the New Covenant age of grace and prepared for the eschaton.[9]

Ephesians 3:16-19

Paul has given us two intercessory prayers in his circular letter to the Ephesians, 1:17-19 and this one. Recent studies of Paul's intercessory prayers have demonstrated that they are essential to the message of the epistle and usually encapsulate its basic purpose. This is certainly true of these two prayers, for they incorporate key terms central to the basic thrust of the epistle, as we shall see. The prayer of chapter 3 concludes the doctrinal section of the epistle and prepares for the practical or ethical section of chapters 4—6. It forms an inclusio with the prayer of 1:17-19, which itself introduces the section on the unity of the church (1:15—2:22). In the immediately preceding context (3:1-13) Paul uses his own apostolic commission as an example of the centrality of the Gentile mission in the church. Indeed the unity of Jew and Gentile in the church is part of the mystery revealed by God (v. 6) and a bold witness to the demonic realm regarding the divine wisdom (v. 10).

The prayer of verses 14-21 petitions God to cement this unity by sharing his very presence and power with the Ephesian saints. Paul introduces the prayer with an uncharacteristically lengthy address to the Father as the one "by whom every family in heaven and on earth is named." This stresses the authority of God over all his creation. As in Genesis 2:19-20 (the naming of the animals by Adam) the act of "naming" implies dominion or authority. Here God is the one naming, so the authority is absolute: every earthly and heavenly "family" derives its identity from God. Especially in mind would be the Jewish-Gentile conflict of chapters 1-3. Since both groups have been "named" by God, they are equal before him. The prayer applies the relationship between God and his people to the Ephesian situation. Three *hina* ("that") clauses provide the organizational pattern for verses 16-19. These are the three petitions of the prayer introduced in verse 14 ("I bow my knees [i.e., pray] . . . that . . .").

1. Prayer for Power (vv. 16-17a). The basis of the first petition is "the wealth of his glory." Both terms are major emphases in Ephesians, with *ploutos* occurring five times.[10] In each instance (1:7, 18; 2:7; 3:8, 16) it refers to God's unfathomable bounty as he shares his gifts and blessings with his people. The emphasis is always on realized eschatology: these gifts belong to us *now*. Interestingly the other place where "riches of glory" occurs is in the prayer of 1:17-19, where it refers to that future "glory" which God will share as our "inheritance" (literally, "his glorious inheritance among the saints"). Here that "glory" could be descriptive ("his glorious riches," NIV) but more likely is a Hebraism, "rich as he is in glory" (Barth 1974:368). The whole emphasis is upon the character of God poured out upon his church.

The "gift" for which Paul petitions the God of glory is "power." The word Paul chooses is the basic word for power or strength, *dynamis*. While it can at times refer to "ability," "meaning," "miracle," "resources" or a personal supernatural being (BAGD), it here almost certainly has its basic thrust of "might" or "strength." In 1:19 Paul sets it alongside its sister terms *energeia* ("working"), *kratos* ("strength"), *ischys* ("might") in order to describe the omnipotence of God available to his people. It would be erroneous to stress the differences between the terms in that context; Paul is piling synonyms one upon another to describe God's marvelous strength because human language is inadequate to express it properly. A similar compilation of terms surrounding *dynamis* occurs in the striking use of superlatives in the doxology of 3:20-21, "Now unto him who has the power *[dynamai]* to do incomparably more than we can ask or think on the basis of that power *[dynamis]* which is operative *[energeō]* in us. . . ." Both passages are encapsulated in Paul's prayer for "power" here. In the context this divine "power" is now bestowed upon the believer. It is an A-E term because the emphasis is upon the qualitative "power" given to the saints so that they might exercise it (the "event" aspect) in order to gain spiritual "strength."

This empowering activity has two specific purposes or results (seen in the infinitive of vv. 16b and 17). First, the believer receives power "in order to be strengthened *[krataithēnai,* an E term; compare the noun in 1:19] through his Spirit in the inner being." In 1:18-19 Paul had prayed that the Ephesians might "know . . . his incomparably great power," obviously a reference to experiential and not merely intellectual knowledge. Here that earlier prayer is repeated and clarified. The same power operative in the resurrection and exaltation of Christ (1:20-21) has been given to the believer (see 2:6-7 building upon 1:20), and here both the means (the active side) and the operative sphere (the passive side) are explicated. The first kernel sentence would be "may the Spirit empower you" and the second "may your inner being be empowered."

Throughout his writings (Rom 8:1-27; 1 Cor 2:9-16; 12:1-26) Paul stresses the Spirit as the operative power behind spiritual growth and gifts. The presence of the Spirit has been implicit in the earlier passages (compare 1:13-14 with vv. 15-23) and here is explicitly the force of the triune Godhead behind the scenes of spiritual development. The sphere within which he works is the "inner being." Only Paul uses the concept (Rom 7:22; 2 Cor 4:16) and it cannot be understood without a paradigmatic (concept study, involving the semantic field) comparison with such other Pauline terms as *nous* or *dianoia* ("mind"), *kardia* ("heart") or *kainos anthrōpos* ("new self"). While the use of "inner being" in Romans 7:22 and 2 Corinthians 4:16 clearly overlaps the first two, the concept here includes also that of the "new self," which has been created in the believer as a result of the death of the "old self" (Eph 4:22-24; compare Col 3:9-10; 2 Cor 5:17). There are also parallels with the "transformation of the mind" *(noos,* Eph 4:23; compare Rom 12:2). "The heart" is explicitly mentioned in the next clause (v. 17). In other words, Paul is praying that God's power might be abundantly poured out so that it might transform the understanding of every Ephesian Christian through the inner activity of the Holy Spirit.

The second purpose for the divine power is the indwelling of Christ. The two ideas in verses 16b-17 are interdependent: we receive strength when Christ indwells our hearts. The organization of the two clauses is remarkably similar. The Spirit is paralleled by "faith" (both introduced by *dia)* and the "inner man" by "heart" *(eis = en).* The figurative use of "inhabit" for the indwelling presence of Christ does not occur elsewhere in Paul (compare Col 1:19; 2:9, in which Christ indwells with "all the fullness of God"), although it is paralleled by the "in Christ" theme so predominant in the prison epistles. The means by which we put this presence to work "in our hearts" or lives is "faith." It is clear both in 2:8 and in this passage that "faith" is God's (here the Spirit's) gift and that only the divine "grace" (2:8) makes faith possible. Yet that personal trust in God still is the force within that allows us to discover the empowering presence of the Spirit and to depend on his strength in our daily struggles. It does not function automatically or guarantee spiritual victory (if it did Paul would not have needed to petition God for this power on behalf of the Ephesians!). Faith is an appropriating mechanism within us, the means by which our "hearts" can know his indwelling presence.

"In love" may be taken with the following ("rooted and grounded in love") as indeed in most modern versions (AV, NKJV, RSV, NASB, NIV), but I agree with Robinson (1904:85, 175) that it is better with the preceding "that Christ may dwell in your hearts through faith in love" (compare 1:4; 4:2, 16). "Faith" thus is the vertical dimension and "love" the horizontal dimension of the indwelling presence of Christ. As believers learn to put into practice the empowering work of the Spirit through faith, that strength will bind together all factions (here Jew and Gentile) in a spirit of "love." There are two kernel sentences in this concept. First, "faith appropriates the indwelling presence of Christ"; second, "love is the sphere within which Christ's presence works in the church."

2. Prayer for Insight (3:17b-19a). "Rooted and grounded" could be either a nominative absolute detailing the results of the indwelling presence of Christ or an anacolouthon modifying the understood "you" in the following clause. The strange placement of the participles before the *hina* clause makes it likely that these participles provide a transition from the first to the second prayer requests and as such function in both ways. The result of Christ's presence is a strong spiritual foundation, which makes it possible to grow in spiritual insight. The two verbs combine agricultural ("rooted") and construction ("grounded") metaphors and function synonymously to emphasize the strong foundation that Christ provides for one's life. Here they are not intended to add separate meanings to the context but work synonymously to emphasize the importance of Christ as the foundation stone of spiritual growth. The believer must at all times remain aware of the true basis of spiritual knowledge. We can spend hours immersed in the academic pursuit of exegetical knowledge and yet fail to truly "know," because knowledge rather than Christ is on the throne of our lives.

Therefore, Paul goes on to pray that the Ephesians might "have power to grasp" spiritual truth. Both terms used here connote the depths of Paul's desire. The first means "to have sufficient strength" to attain an ideal. It is a military or athletic term used often of power exerted to attain a goal. The second term is also military and often is used of "overtaking" and "seizing" an objective; here it is metaphorical and means to "comprehend" or "grasp" a truth. In this passage both aspects are present; the prayer is for "strength" to grasp actively the truths of Christ. This "power" is not achieved by one's self but is a corporate act attained "with all the saints." We cannot assimilate the "mystery" (3:9) or "manifold wisdom" (3:10) or "unfathomable riches" (3:6, 8) apart from our brothers and sisters in Christ. The importance of the church as a whole in spiritual growth is stressed throughout the Epistle (1:12, 15; 2:18; 4:3) and too often is ignored in the church today. Indeed Ephesians has with good reason been called the "body life" epistle, for the vertical aspect of the spiritual life is inseparable from horizontal fellowship. As we study the Word, we must continually dialogue with our fellow saints in order to come to grips with its implications. In a very real sense hermeneutics demands this, for the community of believers (both in the church and via commentaries) challenges and at times corrects our understanding.

The goal of community study is "the width and length and height and depth" of "the love of Christ." Literally scores of interpretations of these nouns have been made throughout church history (see Barth 1974:395-97), from a delineation of the mystery of God (Chrysostom) to the extent of Christ's love (Origen). The latter is more correct, although in itself the fourfold idea is used in Jewish wisdom writings to emphasize the incomprehensibility of divine wisdom. The four aspects are not separate but form a hendiadys (meant to be taken together) to indicate that one can never plumb the true depths of divine love exemplified in Christ. Paul is asking God to give the Ephesian

Christians strength to begin the lifelong process of delving into the unfathomable depths (Barth: the "four dimensions") of divine truth.

Not only are they to "grasp" the depths of divine realities; they also need power to "know the love of Christ which surpasses knowledge." Again the idea is to know the unknowable. As the mysteries of God are unfathomable in the preceding phrase (the first infinitive object of "have power") so the love of Christ is beyond comprehension here (the second infinitival complement). Obviously Paul wants his readers to understand the human impossibility of comprehending spiritual truths apart from the indwelling presence of Christ and the Spirit. In one sense Paul is asking the impossible; we can never understand the things of the Spirit. Yet with God all things are possible, and Paul is aware that divine strength is available to attain the unattainable. As God infuses the saints with his strength, the believers together begin the spiritual odyssey of growing in knowledge. The goal of that knowledge is not cognitive learning (such as theology) but experiential, to "know the love of Christ." In verse 17 Paul prays for the "love" of the Ephesian saints; here the basis of that love, the love of Christ, is the focus of the prayer. The Ephesians had not experienced unity because the depths of the divine love had not been realized by the saints. They lacked the spiritual power to "seize" or "grasp" that understanding. "Love" here is an E term, emphasizing the act of loving; the genitive "of Christ" is probably not objective, "our love of Christ," but subjective, "his love for us." As we begin to understand the depths of his love, that fact begins to transform our love for one another.

3. Prayer for Fullness (3:19b). Paul climaxes his prayer by summarizing the earlier requests in his petition that the Ephesians might experience "all the fullness of God." The use of the cognates "filled . . . unto fullness" (a pleonasm) builds upon the concept of divine fullness already stressed in 1:23, the church as "his body, the fullness of him who fills all in all" (NASB, NKJV). The meaning of *plērōma* ("fullness") is strongly debated. The word can have active force ("that which fills," "contents," as in 1 Cor 10:16, "the earth and all in it"), passive force ("that which is filled or completed," as in Rom 15:29, "the fullness of Christ's blessing") or stative force ("the state of being full," as in Gal 4:4, "fullness of time"). It also can be used in a fulfillment sense (Rom 13:10, "love is the fulfillment of the law"). In Gnostic circles the term was used of the total number of manifestations emanating from God and also of the spiritual force uniting God and humanity. While some see Gnostic ideas in Ephesians (primarily on the basis of the use in Col 1:19; 2:9; Eph 4:13), I would argue that there is a closer connection to Old Testament and wisdom ideas where it speaks of the Shekinah or Spirit of God that fills (such as Prov 15:4 LXX; Wisdom 1:7; Ps 72:19).

In Ephesians 1:23 the church is "being filled" (passive thrust of the noun) by God who "fills" (active force of the verb) all things completely (idiomatic thrust of "all in all"). In the context of the prayer the thrust in 3:19b is similar. The church is "filled" with the "fullness" of God. With the preposition *eis,* the "fullness of God" is the perfect goal for which we strive and in which each believer becomes a Christlike individual (compare 4:13, "the measure of the stature of the fullness of Christ"), filled totally by the presence of

God so that God alone is seen in the person. The divine "fullness" is that completeness, that experience of the totality of God, toward which the church strives. It is both individual (as each saint grows in him) and corporate (the church grows together in him). The goal toward which we strive is nothing more than the fulfillment of all that God has set aside for his people, and to attain that goal the church must open herself to the complete presence of the divine Godhead.

Conclusion

As is the case with grammatical and semantic analysis, syntactical research will occur at several levels. The researcher producing a major monograph or commentary on a biblical text will take a great deal of time working through the primary materials and charting the syntactical development of the ideas. Each unit of the surface structure will be analyzed in detail, tracing themes through all the extant parallel passages and noting the deep structure underlying it with its effect upon the total message of the surface structure. The result will be a continuous spiral upward toward the intended meaning of the text in terms of both the parts and the whole. The separate units can be understood only from the standpoint of the immediate context, for the possible interpretations of a unit like "warrior who delivers"/"hero who helps" (Zeph 3:17) will be narrowed down only on the basis of semotaxis, the influence of the surrounding ideas. Therefore, there is a continuing spiral as the interpreter moves in a circular motion from the parts to the whole and back to the parts, then in a spiral upward to the most likely interpretation—not just of the "warrior" imagery but of the entire message unit in Zephaniah 3:14-17.

The pastor does not have the unlimited time necessary for such detailed research. The scholar can take years, if necessary, to prepare a commentary. The average Ph.D. dissertation takes three years of solid research on a single project. Ernest Best, former professor at the University of Glasgow, several years ago was given the opportunity to do the new I.C.C. commentaries on both Ephesians and Mark but demurred, saying he would not live long enough to do both. Pastors do not have this kind of time to do a monograph on the binding of Isaac in Genesis 22 or the hymn in Philippians 2:6-11. They preach such passages in one to two Sundays with approximately seven to ten hours of preparation time (if they preach or teach two to three times each week). Of course there are exceptions. Some who pastor large congregations have staffs to handle the daily work of the church and opt to spend as much as thirty to forty hours per week in the study. However, the majority of these pastors opt to spend much of that time on packaging rather than research, that is, on the homiletical rather than the exegetical side.

The sermon is much more complex than the commentary, for it must blend exegesis with contextualization (see chap. sixteen). A pragmatic approach to hermeneutics must recognize this practical problem and seek solutions. One solution is the decision of some (Donald Grey Barnhouse, Martin Lloyd-Jones, James Montgomery Boice) to take many years preaching through smaller segments of Scripture like Romans (Barnhouse), the Sermon on the Mount (Lloyd-Jones) or John (Boice). I must admit that this would not be my personal choice, for I would rather bring my congregation through more of Scripture. However, I prefer this to the commonly accepted theory on the other side that one should never preach a series longer than six to eight weeks. Most congregations will enjoy a series of a year or more on a major book like Genesis or Matthew.

Nevertheless, the pastor must work on a "lower" exegetical level than will the scholar. This does not mean that the contents of this chapter do not apply, for there are two ways this material will be useful. The pastor who is acquainted with the techniques can utilize the secondary tools with greater expertise (commentaries, background books, lexicons and so forth), noting when the commentator has done his homework or has made a shallow decision. Also, on the critical portions of the text, when a key word study or syntactical unit demands more detailed study, the pastor can take the time for a more intense investigation, using some of the syntactical techniques elucidated in this chapter (and books like TDNT, NIDNTT, encyclopedias). Key figures of speech, for instance, provide exciting illustrations and cross over into homiletics. The potential rewards for the sermon in such instances justify a deeper study, for biblical metaphors are sermon illustrations in embryo and will save immense time in the search for good examples.

Those doing a devotional study of a passage will probably spend more time on the inductive side, working through the text themselves. Yet there are several levels of devotional study, and I recommend all be utilized from time to time to maintain variety and freshness. Sometimes we will read through large chunks of Scripture to get a sense of the whole, as in the "Read through the Bible in one year" programs. At other times we may read more carefully a paragraph (or chapter) at a time, following inductive Bible study methods. Or we may read a devotional book (such as Swindoll) or use a devotional guide (such as *Daily Bread*). In this case we can still keep basic exegetical procedures in mind to make as certain as we can that the passages are not misinterpreted or manipulated. Finally (and I must admit this is my favorite method), we can go through the text with one or two commentaries but with a devotional goal in mind (what does it say to me?).[11] The problem with many devotional commentaries is that they at times play fast and loose with the text, so we need hermeneutical rules to help us see when they are worth using.[12] In this latter type of devotional experience I recommend note-taking (for future reference) with three columns: one for the text, a second for the insights we garner (as we interact with the text and commentary) and a third for prayer thoughts coming out of the study. This can guide our prayer time as well.

Excursus on Transformational Grammar

Although transformational grammar is analogous to structuralism, the actual theory and techniques were developed by Noam Chomsky, particularly in his *Syntactic Structures* (1957) and *Aspects of the Theory of Syntax* (1965). The basic concept of transformational syntax is part of a larger theory that Chomsky developed by watching the startling ability of children to integrate syntactical rules into their own speech patterns. Chomsky named his comprehensive theory for the structure of language "generative grammar." Lyons calls this movement "the Chomskyan Revolution," asserting that it is "the most influential theory of syntax so far developed in any period of linguistics, ancient or modern" (1981:108). Certainly this can be called an overstatement, especially by Saussure's followers. However, Chomsky's ideas have certainly had a profound effect upon all linguistic theoreticians in the last thirty years.

It is important at the outset to realize that Chomsky is a rationalist (one who believes that knowledge is derived through reason) rather than an empiricist (one who believes that knowledge is derived through the senses). Like other rationalists (such as Descartes or Leibniz), Chomsky believes that the mind is not a "tabula rasa" but rather has an *innate* ability to learn. The importance of this for generative grammar can best be exemplified in the 1975 colloquium in which Jean Piaget and Chomsky discussed the differences between Piaget's developmental views of learning and Chomsky's theory of a preprogrammed native mind (see Piattelli-Palmarini 1980). As the debate developed between what could arguably be called the two most influential systems of cognitive learning today, the discussion again and again returned to the subject of a child's development. Chomsky argued that a child learns on the basis of genetically endowed linguistic categories that enable the child to learn abstractly in spite of very inadequate learning opportunities. With respect to the debate whether genetics or environment shapes human learning and personality, Chomsky clearly sides with the former.

On the basis of his view of innate knowledge, Chomsky developed his foundational theory regarding language as competence and as performance. Competence refers to the set of linguistic categories in the mind that makes possible the infinite series of linguistic utterances which constitute speech. In other words, generative grammar refers to a system of grammatical rules that generates actual speech and that according to Chomsky is based upon one's genetic capacity for language learning. A child very quickly learns how to speak in complex sentences, and Chomsky believes that this could not be merely the product of environment but must depend upon an inner capacity for language acquisition that is inherent in the mind itself. Performance, on the other hand, refers to the actual speech patterns as they develop. These, of course, are influenced by the linguistic environment, by the cultural idiosyncrasies and linguistic habits that surround the individual. A child thus already contains a mental store of grammatical rules (competence); these are universal laws common to all human beings. The individual child fills in these categories with the actual speech patterns of the culture within which he or she develops (performance). In other words, every human being has the capacity to understand the relationship between the subject, the verb and the object but the actual way these are presented in individual languages will differ from group to group. The competence is the same for everyone, but the performance, the actual surface grammar of an individual language, will differ markedly from culture to culture. The syntactical competence is universal and innate, but the actual performance is infinitely varied and arbitrary.

Nevertheless, the infinite arbitrariness of individual syntactical utterances is still, for Chomsky, a rule-governed activity. Here we are at the very heart of generative grammar. Again, Chomsky draws much of his evidence from the speech patterns of children. He asks how it is possible that the syntactically correct statements of small children could merely have been acquired by parroting adult speech. Rather, Chomsky argues that an inherent ability must have guided their competence patterns. The creative use of language by children could not have been merely the product of environmental stimuli; instead this creativity is controlled by underlying syntactical laws that are a part of a child's mental capacity.

Generative grammar seeks to determine these linguistic universal laws that govern language acquisition. Chomsky wants to go behind individual language syntax to those universal rules that govern all speech and are common to all language systems. In actuality, Chomsky finds several levels of grammar. It is not my purpose to go into detail on this point, but it is important to understand exactly what Chomsky is saying. He believes that each level has greater influence than the one before in terms of generating surface statements. For instance, he argues that finite-state grammar leads to phrase-structure grammar and then finally to transformational grammar. Finite-state grammar deals with individual surface grammars that work in some languages but not all. Phrase-structure grammar deals with underlying matrices or rules that govern a group of languages. Transformational grammar, on the other hand, deals with the universal laws that underlie all linguistic performance. Transformational grammar, therefore, is the final goal of generative grammar, because it deals with the deeper structure that determines the individual statement.

Chomsky's recent *Rules and Representations* (1980) refines many of the generative rules but demonstrates clearly that the underlying assumptions above have not been changed in recent years. The first three chapters deal successively with the mind, the capacities for learning and the innate knowledge of grammar. This leads into his updated discussion of transformational grammar. There he argues that two distinct types of rules are in operation: the base rules that determine the abstract representations of the surface structure; and transformational rules that determine the basic arrangement of those structures.

Transformations convert the deep (D-) structures into surface (S-) structures by means of the generative rules. Here it is important to understand that Chomsky is not asserting that the deep structure contains the actual meaning and that the surface structure is irrelevant (as many structuralists do). Rather, he is saying that the deep structure generates the surface structure and therefore contains the basic meaning.

Chomsky, in fact, in this recent work, argues that the surface structure more than the deep structure is relevant for semantic interpretation, because it is the surface structure that determines the syntactical relationships that produce meaning. He illustrates this by comparing two sentences: "I didn't have a good time in France or England" (which means in neither place) and "In France or England, I didn't have a good time" (which connotes the idea "I do not recall"). The deep surface of the two is the same but the surface structure actually yields two separate meanings. Chomsky explains, "Properties of surface structure . . . determine the interaction of negation and disjunction" (1980:156). In short, the deep structure embodies the rules that transform the meaning into the representations of surface structure (pp. 141-81).

Generative grammar has important repercussions for biblical research (as we saw under "Biblical Transformations"). It is important to realize that Chomsky is speaking primarily at the linguistic level. In fact, his basic theory deals far more with syntax than with semantics and has great promise for syntactical interpretation.[13] However, several cautions must be lodged.

First, it is far from clear the extent to which the underlying theory of universal grammar is valid. I already noted in the last chapter that theories of universal semantic meaning are invalid. The extent to which this is also true for syntax is currently heavily debated. Thiselton points out the similarities between universal grammar and Wittgenstein's notions about elementary propositions in his *Tractatus,* which he later rejected in favor of language-game theory (1978:98). Certainly one could argue that Chomsky's theories would fit language-game theory. However, it is not so clear that the notion of a universal grammar can avoid these criticisms. Lyons points out that the actual transformational rules since the mid 1950s have been progressively modified and restricted in the three decades following and states that "the future of transformational grammar as such (though not of generative grammar) is currently in doubt" (1980:128). In other words, while we can discover deep structural syntax underneath a surface statement, it is not at all clear that this provides a universal meaning that automatically crosses between language systems. We must be exceedingly cautious about such generalizations.

Second, as Thiselton states, there is a very real danger in placing the cognitive element above the emotive, cultural or religious deep structures that also underlie a surface statement (1978:98). Indeed, deep structure properly considered certainly goes beyond the categories Chomsky elucidated. For biblical study it demands a recognition of the many areas of nonlinguistic realities behind the actual statements of a passage.

Third, Piaget is certainly correct in stating that Chomsky overlooks the important factor of empirical development on the part of the child. As Gardner's forward intimates, Chomsky and Piaget were speaking somewhat at cross-purposes, since both dealt with different aspects of the larger question of learning (Piatelli-Palmarini 1980:xxx-xxxiv). Indeed, Chomsky's stress upon native intelligence must be balanced by Piaget's stress upon the actual stages of learning. For the process of exegeting a text this means that we dare not neglect any of the factors that have led from the deep structure to the surface structure. Therefore, generative grammar provides a matrix for deepening our understanding of biblical statements but dares never degenerate into an end in itself. Syntactical research must recognize that it is only a part of the larger whole, and that only in looking at every aspect of meaning in an utterance can we discover its relevance for our time.

Excursus on Rhetorical Criticism

An introduction to rhetoric in terms of style has already been given in chapter one, and indeed this has been the general approach to rhetoric since Augustine first introduced biblical studies to it in Book IV of his *On Christian Doctrine* (Augustine had taught rhetoric before his conversion and applied that knowledge to a delineation of rhetorical or stylistic patterns in Scripture). Yet over the centuries there were only a few works published on biblical rhetoric, and these were primarily studies of figures of speech or tropes (e.g., the Venerable Bede, Bullinger, Norden) and chapters in the major grammars (e.g., Blass-DeBrunner-Funk, Turner, Moule). Rhetorical criticism as a discipline did not really develop until after the 1968 Society of Biblical Literature presidential address by James Muilenberg, "Form Criticism and Beyond" (1969). In it Muilenberg challenged scholars to move beyond form criticism by noting the aesthetic dimensions of literary style and structural patterns. He labeled this "rhetorical criticism," and his address led to an avalanche of articles and books exploring this discipline, primarily in Old Testament studies (the focus of Muilenberg's remarks). The New Testament counterpart developed more under the influence of Amos Wilder's *Early Christian Rhetoric* (1964). Both of these movements centered on stylistic and poetic dimensions of texts.

Yet there is another aspect of rhetorical analysis, rhetoric as the study of persuasion or the means of argumentation. This has been the primary function in literary studies since the time of Aristotle and is the focus of this excursus. Rhetoric developed in ancient Greece[14] in the fifth century when Corax of Syracuse produced a treatise called "The Art of Rhetoric" to help property owners engaged in legal disputes over land. When his pupil Tisias introduced this to mainland Greece, a class of rhetorical teachers called sophists arose. These were itinerant, professional teachers who offended the Greeks by charging for their services. Plato (427-347 B.C.) himself was opposed to the sophists for stressing technique over art and persuasive speech over truth. His pupil Aristotle (384-322 B.C.), however, did not reject the discipline of rhetoric. Rather, he grounded it in philosophy and logic, producing his master work, "The Art of Rhetoric."

For Aristotle rhetoric was primarily the art of persuasion, and he sought to wed it with philosophical reasoning by classifying rhetoric in terms of its various facets. He noted three types of speech—judicial (legal), deliberative (political or religious debates) and epideictic (praise or blame)[15]—and developed eight aims or values for proper speech—that which is right, lawful, advantageous, honorable, pleasant, easy, feasible and necessary. Also, Aristotle and the classical handbooks (e.g., Cicero's *De inventione)* developed the five "canons," or laws, of rhetorical persuasion: *invention,* delineating the topic and developing the argumentation; *arrangement,* organizing the material into an outline and determining the best sequence for the argumentation; *style,* selecting the proper words and figures of speech to achieve clarity and heighten the argument; *memory,* seeking a natural and forceful presentation; and *delivery,* adding vocal inflection, gestures and facial features.

Finally, for Aristotle the concept of "judgment" *(krisis)* is predominant. Rhetoric in this sense centers on the development of "proofs," or arguments, which are convincing enough to persuade. He found three types of proofs—*ethos,* the authority or credibility which a speaker or writer develops in the work; *pathos,* the emotions stirred in the audience by the speech; and *logos,* the logical arguments produced in behalf of the thesis. In each of these areas Aristotle set the tone for subsequent rhetorical study.

It is difficult to know whether or not most (or any) of the New Testament writers were trained in ancient rhetoric. As Kennedy points out (1984:8-10), rhetoric was universally a part of Hellenistic training at "the level of high school education today and was, indeed, the exclusive subject of secondary education" (p. 9). Several ancient rhetoricians came from Palestine, like Theodorus of Gadara (the teacher of the emperor Tiberias), or were of Jewish descent, like the Sicilian Jew Caecilius or Hermogenes of Tarsus. Whether or not there was formal training involved in the case of Jesus, Paul or Luke, their works certainly demonstrate a good knowledge of rhetorical technique, and a rhetorical approach to the patterns of persuasion in New Testament works is justified.[16]

Classical Rhetorical Patterns. It will be helpful to establish the ancient patterns of rhetorical argumentation (discussed in Cicero and Quintillian), for these form a control with which one can compare the patterns of New Testament writings. This in fact is the method employed by recent works like Betz's study of Galatians or Watson's study of Jude and 2 Peter.[17] It was debated (see Quintillian *Institutio Oratoria* 3.9.1-5) whether there were four (the method presented in Mack) or six (the method presented in Kennedy) parts in a proper speech. The outline itself originated in judicial rhetoric but was employed in the other types as well. I will provide the more complete list and leave the debate to others, for all six are helpful for New Testament study.

1. The *exordium* is the introduction which establishes rapport between the speaker and audience and creates interest and goodwill toward the subject matter.

2. The *narratio* states the proposition being discussed and provides background information and a rationale or reason for the point to be made. Often, for the sake of effect, the proposition would be given in figurative language and the reason would restate it in straightforward language.

3. The *partitio* (often made a part of the *narratio*) is the enumeration of the particular points to be made, often in the form of the opponent's arguments as well as one's own.

4. The *probatio*, or *confirmatio*, is the presentation of the logical arguments for the case. The speaker would marshal the evidence on behalf of the proposition, quoting authorities and citing parallels which enhanced the case being made. Proofs would take two forms, an analogy or comparison with something the audience found favorable and an example which demonstrated the value of the speaker's position.

5. The *refutatio* (often made a part of the *probatio*) seeks to disprove opposing views, usually by similar means to the *probatio*. In a judicial speech this would involve the refutation of an opponent. In declarative speech this would involve a rhetorical presentation of the opposite perspective so as to enhance the argument. At times this could include a digression (often seen in Paul) which provided added information.

6. The *peroratio*, or *conclusio*, is the conclusion which would summarize the major points and appeal to both reason and the emotions on behalf of the thesis.

This of course was only the basic outline, and practitioners were encouraged to be creative in the arrangement and composition of the actual speech or treatise. The task for the rhetorical critic is to study the ancient unit (e.g., a particular speech of Jesus or an epistle) and to trace the developing argument in order to determine the patterns of persuasion. This will be a valuable addendum to the exegetical task, for it enables the student to note more accurately the formal type of passage being investigated.

In the Sermon on the Mount,[18] for instance, the Beatitudes (Mt 5:1-13) are the *enconium* and establish the ethical parameters for the speech as well as draw the audience into the topic. The *narratio* begins with the proposition in 5:17-20, which states the relationship of both Jesus (fulfills the law) and his hearers (their righteousness must surpass that of the scribes and Pharisees) to the law. The reasons are then enunciated in the antitheses of 5:21-48, which demonstrates Jesus' own view of our relation to the law. The *partitio* is 6:1-18, which applies the thesis (note the presence of *dikaiosyne* in 5:20 and 6:1) and addresses the three specific practices of almsgiving, prayer and fasting.

These are more than examples; they relate to the false "piety"/"righteousness" of many of Jesus' hearers.[19] The Lord's Prayer (vv. 9-15) is the centerpiece of this section and possesses great rhetorical power, forming as it does an early climax to the sermon.

The *probatio* consists of 6:19—7:20 and forms a series of commandments addressing specific issues (material possessions, anxiety, judging others, giving holy things to unworthy people, asking and receiving, the narrow and the wide gates, false prophets).[20] Here Jesus uses analogies and examples which anchor the theme of the radical ethic required of Jesus' followers.[21] The *conclusio* is 7:21-27, with vv. 21-23 recapitulating the theme in a new way (anchoring "entering the kingdom" in "doing the will of the Father") and vv. 24-27 demanding immediate action from the hearers ("hearing" must lead to "doing"). As stated above, these formed the two parts (recapitulation and the appeal to the emotions) of a good conclusion. Again, this does not mean that Jesus and Matthew were trained in Hellenistic rhetoric; rather, they are using a pattern found throughout the Mediterranean world of that day.

Of course, all such delineations are simple deductions and will seldom satisfy everyone. However, as each one studies the pattern of reasoning, the meaning of the whole as well as the parts will become more clear. The many studies of the rhetorical pattern in Galatians will demonstrate how widespread the disagreement can be. Betz in his commentary (1979) argues that Galatians is a judicial or apologetic letter centering on justification by faith rather than the works of the law. Kennedy on the other hand (1984:144-52) believes it is a deliberative work urging the Galatians to endure in the Christian faith rather than to turn to Judaism. Mack (1990:66-73) believes that both are too narrow and argues that Galatians is too complex an epistle to be classified by any one rhetorical type. Rather, four issues (refuting the "other gospel," showing that his simple gospel was enough without circumcision, etc., establishing his credentials, and urging the Galatians not to give away their faith or their unity) are forged together in a passionate and powerful letter. Mack's thesis is certainly closer to the truth and demonstrates how carefully rhetorical study must proceed. As one might guess, the corresponding outlines of the three scholars differ markedly as well. This demonstrates one important fact: rhetorical criticism is no more precise than any other hermeneutical tool. It still depends upon the subjective decisions of the interpreter. Nevertheless, when done in concert with the other exegetical tools, it will help deepen one's understanding of the forces at play in a particular passsage (the micro level) or book (the macro level).

A Method for Rhetorical Criticism. In any method, the goal is to minimize the dangers and maximize the potential of the critical tool. The dangers must be recognized—subjectivism (reading one's own theories into the text); the application of the wrong tool (for instance, reading Greek patterns into Jewish rhetoric, as possibly in the Sermon on the Mount above); reductionism (overly simplifying a complex pattern, as Kennedy did with Galatians above); delusions of grandeur (thinking we know more about ancient rhetoric than we do); and a further erosion of the propositional aspect of biblical truth.[22] When dealing with the outline of a book, it is a simple fact that there are nearly as many outlines as there are scholars.[23] Therefore, rhetorical studies must be aware of their own finiteness and must be done with extreme care.

The best method for accomplishing this has been developed by Kennedy (1984:33-38) and Watson (1988:8-28). As will be demonstrated below, these build on all the exegetical steps enumerated in chapters two through four (hence the placement of this excursus here). However, this does not mean that rhetorical criticism is the final step of the process, for the rhetorical strategy decided upon will have hermeneutical implications for the interpretation of the passage. For instance, if the predestinarian passages of Romans 9 are part of a diatribe against Jewish-Christian misunderstandings regarding the nature of God (due to the divine judgment against Israel), this may mean that the statements regarding divine election there do not comprise dogmatic assertions regarding the process by which God saves people (the traditional Calvinist interpretation) but may instead comprise metaphors describing one aspect of the process (that is, God's sovereign choice [the emphasis in Romans 9] working with the individual's decision [the emphasis else-where]). Paul would be stressing one aspect of a larger whole to make his point. In short, rhetorical criticism must be utilized as part of the holistic process of exegesis rather than as an end in itself.

1. Determine the rhetorical unit. This is based upon the final outline rather than the pre-liminary one discussed in chapter two. It can only be determined with extreme care, for it is important to decide whether a transitional passage belongs with the preceding or fol-lowing section. Such decisions can radically alter the final product and therefore demand exegetical depth. The rhetorical unit has an introduction, a developed point and a con-clusion. Wuellner (1987:455) calls this "a text unit as an argumentative unit affecting the reader's reasoning or the reader's imagination . . . either a convincing or a persuasive unit." It may be a macro-unit (major section [for instance, Matthew 5—7 or Romans 9—11] or book) or a micro-unit (single pericope, for instance Matthew 6:1-18 or Romans 9:6-18). If the latter, it will be studied first in itself and then as part of a larger rhetorical strategy.

2. Analyze the rhetorical situation. This is akin to determining the purpose (or with form criticism, the *Sitz im Leben)* of the passage/book. It is objective when that situation is described in the passage itself (usually in the introduction). It is subjective and debat-able if it is simply surmised from the themes themselves. For example, there have been several articles examining the social situation behind Luke's Gospel, often seeing an upper-class audience due to the emphasis on social concern. This is far too subjective to be likely. Nevertheless, to the extent that the social situation can be determined, it is extremely helpful. In fact, in literary theory, the identification of the original situation is an essential component, for that situation dictated the rhetorical strategy employed. The determination of the audience's situation adds hermeneutical precision to the task of interpretation. Watson (1988:9) speaks of three constituents of the rhetorical situation: the problem or obstacle which needs to be corrected, the audience to which the rhetorical solution is directed, and the constraints brought by the speaker's/writer's analysis of the situation. Each aspect should be investigated as part of the critical process.

3. Determine the type of rhetoric employed and the question behind it. Above we discussed the three major types—judicial, deliberative and epideictic. Judicial passages render judgment on a past situation; deliberative passages offer advice regarding potential situations in the near future; and epideictic passages either celebrate or condemn someone in order to seek assent from the audience regarding a particular value. Speakers or writers would often interweave such patterns into their larger work. Philippians could be called primarily a judicial work in that it castigates many arrogant individuals in the church (2:1-18; 4:2-3) and the Judaizers (3:1—4:1), but it contains epideictic material in 2:19-30 and deliberative passages in 1:27-30 and 4:4-9.

The question is not simply the situation or problem behind the passage. It is the rhetorical statement of that issue and controls the development of the text. Watson (1988:11-13) speaks of "stasis theory" (stemming from Quintillian) as the means of defining the question more closely. There are three stases: fact (whether a thing is), definition (what a thing is) and quality (what kind of thing it is). One must determine how many questions are addressed in a passage and what type of questions are involved. In the case of the Judaizers of Philippians 3:1—4:1, the student will note Paul's queries regarding the fact of their teaching and its quality (that it constituted false teaching).

4. Analyze arrangement, technique and style. The arrangement of the material in the macro structure is the next important aspect. How do the various rhetorical segments achieve their desired effect? What persuasive purpose is seen as the writer creatively weaves the various parts together? The task is not only to determine the structural configuration of the text but also the writer's strategy behind that configuration. The rhetorical effect is created not only by the proofs utilized but by the way they are arranged. This is an essential component of the techniques used by the author. The basics of arrangement have already been discussed, and here the goal is to see what creative patterns have been used and what intended effect is envisaged. Style refers to the artistic arrangement of linguistic devices in order to enhance the intended effect. The goal of style is to induce pleasure, attract interest and persuade the reader. This includes not only the literary devices in chapter one, or the figures of speech in chapter four, but also the disposition of these in the whole structure of the developing argument. The choice of words, the metaphors and syllogisms artfully arranged, the examples and allusions presented, all figure in the style of the author. It is the task of the rhetorical critic to determine not only the what but the why of the individual style of a passage, not only what is said but why it is said, that is, the goal of the whole.

5. Evaluate rhetorical effectiveness. This does not mean simply to judge whether the argument was good or bad. Kennedy (1984:38) means by this that the critic must re-examine each step of the process and see if the critical study properly evaluated the audience, the problem and the rhetorical means used by the author in accomplishing his goal. Note how the author moved from the statement of the problem to the rhetorical solution. What implications did the passage have for the author and the audience? What is the overall impact of the passage not only upon the original readers but also upon the modern reader? In this latter sense one moves from meaning to significance, for rhetoric has a timeless quality which speaks crossculturally in many different situations.[24]

5

Historical & Cultural Backgrounds

H ISTORICAL-CULTURAL EXEGESIS DIFFERS FROM HISTORICO-CRITICAL STUDY IN THAT IT
applies background data to a passage in order to understand better its meaning,
but does not use it in order to determine the authenticity or editorial expansion
of that text. Since Christianity is a historical religion, the interpreter must recognize that
an understanding of the history and culture within which the passage was produced is
an indispensable tool for uncovering the meaning of that passage. "History" is the diachronic aspect, relating to the milieu within which the sacred writers produced their
works; it refers to the events and times within which God's sacred revelation is couched.
"Culture" is the synchronic aspect, referring to the manners, customs, institutions and
principles that characterize any particular age and form the environment within which
people conduct their lives.[1]

Biblical literature has two dimensions: historical intentionality, in which the author
assumes certain shared information with the original readers; and literary intentionality,
in which he encodes a message in his text. Authors either address (prophetic and epistolary literature with a present historical thrust) or describe (historical narrative with a
past historical thrust) background situations. In both of these cases there are "shared
assumptions" between the author and the original readers, information not found in the
text, data that they knew but we do not. While semantic research and syntactical analysis
can unlock the literary dimension, background study is necessary in order to uncover that
deeper level of meaning behind the text as well as within it.

The primary tool for uncovering this data is archaeology. However, its relevance for
hermeneutics has been debated. It is quite common to use it primarily for apologetic
purposes to "prove" the authenticity of the biblical account. Indeed, there is some value
in the use of archaeology for confirming the veracity of the biblical record. The classic
example is of W. M. Ramsay *(St. Paul the Traveller and Roman Citizen)*, the great
historian and agnostic whose study of the archaeological evidence behind Luke-Acts led
to his conversion. For instance, recently acquired knowledge of the history of the second
millennium B.C. and of seminomadic movements in the ancient Near East has lent greater
authenticity to the patriarchal narratives. LaSor, Hubbard and Bush (1982:102-7) summarize the evidence: (1) the names of the patriarchs fit the late second millennium but

not the first millennium; (2) Abraham's journey from Ur to Haran to Canaan fits the geographical and political conditions of the period; (3) the pastoral nomadic lifestyle of the patriarchs fits the cultural and topographical features of the period; (4) social and legal customs described in the biblical text accurately reflect the period in which the Bible sets them; (5) the portrait of patriarchal religion is authentic, especially the relationship between the patriarchs and local shrines and the portrayal of God as the personal God of the clan and not just as the God of the sanctuaries (as among the Canaanites). Nevertheless, there is great danger in using archaeology for apologetics. It is a two-edged sword. Jericho provides an excellent example. On the basis of John Garstang's excavations of 1930-36 evangelicals have argued that archaeological evidence indicates that the walls did indeed fall outward. Yet some today seem still unaware that Kathleen Kenyon's work of 1952-58 demonstrated that Garstang's fortifications actually stemmed from an earlier period, namely an early Bronze Age city destroyed by an earthquake and fire about 2300 B.C. (rather than the 1400 B.C. date of Garstang). To date, there is an absence of evidence for the biblical story regarding the walls of Jericho. This does not disprove the biblical data (see Dumbrell 1985:130-39) but does provide serious problems for an apologetic use of archaeology. We dare not reach too hasty conclusions as to the relevance of archaeological discoveries. Often the problems outweigh the solutions, and it is dishonest to use a tool only when it supports us and to neglect it when it does not.

Yamauchi discusses the "fragmentary nature" of archaeological evidence (1972:146-58). In a series of descending spirals, he studies the extent of the evidence that is available to us.

1. Only a very small fraction of what was made or written has survived, due to the erosion of the material by natural forces (wind, rain, soil) and the destructive nature of humans. In addition, site after site has been denuded when inhabitants have stolen priceless artifacts.

2. Only a fraction of available sites have been surveyed. Mound upon mound lies unnoticed in Greece or Syria. For instance, in Palestine alone the number of sites rose from 300 in 1944 to 5,000 in 1963 to 7,000 by 1970.

3. Of those surveyed only a fraction have been excavated. Of the 5,000 in Palestine in 1963 only 150 had been excavated in part and only 26 had become major sites.

4. Only a fraction of an excavated site is ever examined, due to the unbelievable costs involved and the amount of time required. Yadin estimated it would take 800 years to clear Hazor, a site of 175 acres. Some cities are small (Jericho comprises 7 acres and Megiddo 13) but many others are quite large. Babylon, with 2,500 acres, would take 8,000 years to excavate entirely! This can lead to skewed results. For instance, from 1894 to 1963 there was no evidence for a Bronze Age existence at Ephesus. Then in 1963 Turkish engineers building a parking lot found a Mycenaean burial ground. Few archaeologists are willing to make categorical judgments on the basis of an absence of data.

5. Only a fraction of the discovered material has been published. Important finds may languish in the basement of a museum for 50 to 75 years. For instance, 25,000 cuneiforms have been unearthed at Mari but to date only 3,500 to 4,000 have been published. Too many scholars have rushed new discoveries into print only to be embarrassed when later

studies have proved them wrong. Caution is the watchword!

Yamauchi estimates that being supremely optimistic we could have 1/10 of the material in existence, 6/10 of that surveyed, 1/50 of that excavated, 1/10 of that examined, and 1/2 of that published. This means that we have only .006 per cent of the evidence. One could become extremely pessimistic about the value of archaeology were it not for several compensating factors. We do not need complete evidence when studying customs. The more evidence we have, the more certain the conclusions, but even a few pottery shards depicting, for instance, the dress of the Egyptians will suffice to demonstrate such domestic customs. Yamauchi gives us a helpful discussion on methodology (1972:158). He divides evidence into three categories: traditions (written or oral evidence from Herodotus, Homer, the Old Testament and other sources), material remains (pottery, debris and so forth) and inscriptional evidence. Conclusions are stronger when there is overlapping evidence from more than one source (see figure 5.1).

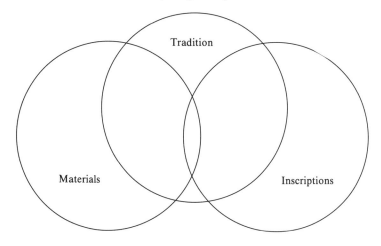

Fig. 5.1. Overlapping Sources of Archaeological Evidence.

This also means that the primary value of archaeology is descriptive (providing background material) rather than polemical (apologetics). It is too uncertain in its results to be used primarily in the latter. Certainly I do not mean that it is useless in apologetics, for it can affirm the basic veracity of John's or Luke's historical and geographical references. However, its major contribution is in providing sociological information so that the modern reader can better understand the milieu within which the biblical passage or event developed.

Areas for Research

1. Geography. The movements of peoples and topography of the land can add marvelous insights to the study of a passage. As Beitzel points out, "history itself in many respects is inseparably bound by and subject to the limitations of geography. Geography is an impelling force that both initiates and limits the nature and extent of political history, what we might call geopolitics" (1985:2). Beitzel mentions two biblical examples (pp. 102, 170).

First, an analysis of the conquest of Canaan shows that all the cities overrun lay in the highlands, while the plains and valleys, where Canaanite chariots could turn the tide of any battle, remained outside her control. Interestingly, in the 1967 Six-Day War Israel reconquered almost exactly the same territory (see the map on p. 103, which visualizes and traces the modern conquest in 1967 alongside the ancient conquest under Joshua). Even with the millennia in between and immense technological changes, geography still dictates military conquest. Second, Jesus' choice of Capernaum for his Galilean headquarters may well have been due partly to geographical factors. The city lay on the "Great Trunk Road," or major trade artery, that linked Egypt and Mesopotamia. The cosmopolitan nature and international flavor of Capernaum made it a natural center for Jesus' forays into Galilee and Trans-Jordan as well as a place of preparation for the universal mission.

2. Politics. It is very helpful when studying the historical accounts (such as the history of Israel or the life of Jesus) to know something of the political developments behind the accounts. For instance, the prophets wrote within the context of the larger political arena, and much of what they said can be understood better when interpreted in light of those developments. The fact that Israel was a buffer state between the Assyrians, Babylonians and then the Persians created many of the religious and social problems. For instance, Ahab followed Solomon's practice of syncretism and political treaties and under him Israel adopted many of the practices of the pagan nations. The governmental structure had increasingly changed to a semifeudal system, and by the time of Ahab the monarchy had been replaced by an absolutistic dictatorship. Under this system the social justice of the Torah and the early years of Israel had disappeared, and the upper classes exploited the poor.

3. Economics. Every culture may be defined somewhat on the basis of its socioeconomic situation. There are several difficulties, however, in tracing the economic background of any given era. One must study long periods of time and generalize when specific practices probably differed slightly from period to period. It is too easy to apply practices seen at Mari or Ugarit, for instance, to Israel or Canaan. Moreover, it is quite difficult to make a qualitative analysis of the trade situation during the time of Solomon or of Christ when one does not possess specific quantitative data on the movement of materials or artifacts. Since the evidence (wood, textiles, dyes, spices) did not survive and since few accounts have been found (Yamauchi estimates there were twenty-four *million* meters of papyri used for temple records but only twenty-five meters have survived), this is very difficult to trace. However, the evidence we do possess is highly illuminating.

The development from the seminomadic economy of the patriarchs to the agrarian economy of early Israel to the mercantile economy of Solomon and the cosmopolitan situation during the Graeco-Roman period helps us to understand details in the text. For instance, Beitzel theorizes that Egypt did not intervene while Israel was conquering the highlands of Canaan because her trade routes through the Canaanite plains were never threatened (1985:102). As a further example, Elliott argues that the recipients of 1 Peter were resident "aliens" (1:17; 2:11) who were not allowed to own land and were restricted to tilling the land or working in local trades (1981:677-73). Rome's urbanization program had failed in Asia Minor, and the province was predominantly rural. This was an economically depressed area, and the economic factors probably contributed to the oppression of the saints, the focal point of the Epistle. Since their conversion had forced a further break with previous alliances, the situation of the Christians was doubly difficult. While I would question the extent to which *paroikos* ("alien") and *parepidēmos* ("stranger," 1:1) are intended to be socioeconomic descriptions rather than spiritual metaphors (for those who are spiritually alienated from society), the material Elliott provides adds depth to an understanding of 1 Peter.

4. Military and War. The term *war* is found over three hundred times in the Old Testament alone, and a good part of the imagery dealing with divine succor (God as our "refuge," "strength" or "present help") stems from military metaphors. Palestine's position as the sole land-bridge between Africa and Eurasia meant that for reasons of trade routes and strategic military position it was essential for powerful nations to control it. No other portion of real estate in the world has been so embattled.

It is interesting to trace the history of Israel from a military standpoint. For instance, Abraham's defeat of the four kings with only 318 men (Gen 14) has been called impossible from a military standpoint. However, Abraham chose to fight in the canyons of Mount Hermon near Damascus ("Dan" in 14:14 is probably the Dan-Jaan of 2 Sam 24:6 in northern Peraea), and in the narrow confines of the gorges a small but well-trained and mobile force has a distinct advantage. Another interesting fact is that Israel did not become a technically competent military force until Solomon. When David defeated a sizable Syrian force with a thousand chariots (2 Sam 10:17-21) he did not keep the chariots, probably because he felt they would do his forces little good. This is startling in light of the fact that for centuries chariots had been the prime military weapon. However, it was not until Solomon that chariots became common in Israel (1 Kings 10:26). Israel still controlled the highlands rather than the plains and this dictated their strategy. They won victories on the basis of superior tactics and primarily through divine intervention.

5. Cultural Practices.

a. *Family customs,* such as marriage ritual or educational practices, are critical. For instance, Israel practiced "endogamy," with marriage to non-Israelites excluded. This was true even in the patriarchal period (Gen 24:4; 28:1-2). Great stress was placed upon ancestry, for it became crucial to ensure the purity of family lines. Also, ancient education was geared to preserving the scribal and ruling classes, with the emphasis upon rote memory and imitation. For the Hebrews, however, this was a religious duty required of all and the daily life of the family was conceived as an instrument of religious education. Parents gave their children religious, moral and vocational training. The home was the focus until the postexilic period when synagogues took on an educational function. Elementary schools began in the first century B.C., with children (that is, sons) beginning between the ages of five and seven.

b. *Material customs* (homes, dress) can also provide valuable information. For instance, Israelite villages throughout the Old Testament period were constructed of inferior materials and workmanship. The architectural masterpieces of Solomon, Omri or Ahab were all constructed by Phoenicians. Otherwise, a rough rural architecture predominated. Most homes were simple one-story affairs, small rectangular or square buildings with dirt floors and with mud-brick walls sealed by layers of mortar and whitewash. They were restricted to a size of about ten-feet square because they had not learned to "vault" (laying stones side by side in a diagonal direction); the ability of the Canaanites to do this intimidated the spies in Numbers 13:28. They had few lamps; since oil was expensive the average family would have one, usually set in a niche in the wall or on a "bushel" or grain-measure turned upside-down to use as a table (see Mt 5:15). Roofs consisted of beams over which were laid branches or reeds, then packed dirt. Grass often grew upon it (Ps 129:6; Is 37:27). Wealthier homes had Hellenistic tile roofs (Lk 5:19) and, since they were flat, families would often rest there or entertain friends there.

c. *Everyday customs* affect far more passages in Scripture than one would think. Even daily hygiene was more a religious custom than a personal one. As described in Mark 7:3-4 the Jews would dip their hands if remaining home but immerse and wash them thoroughly if they had been to the marketplace (where they could have come in contact with Gentiles). While the Romans were clean-shaven, the Jews let their beards grow but had to keep them trimmed. Young men liked to wear them long and curled, with special pride in thick, abundant hair (Song 5:11; 2 Sam 14:25-26). In fact the cry to Elisha, "Go up, bald head" (2 Kings 2:23), may have been a curse rather than just mockery, since baldness led to suspicion of leprosy.

d. *Athletics and recreation* form an important part of the leisure time of any people, and this is true in biblical times as well. Athletic prowess in the ancient world was closely tied to the military. The "mighty men" of Israel were famed for their swiftness (1 Chron 12:8) and strength (Samson). While there are no Old Testament references to games, archaeology has uncovered several; for instance, a game with pegs and a board similar to cribbage (one such with fifty-eight holes has been found at Megiddo). A game with dice played at Sumer has actually been reproduced and sold in stores under that name. Paul is the sacred writer who uses the imagery most consistently. In 1 Corinthians 9:24-27 he juxtaposes two events, the foot race with an emphasis on the goal and prize (vv. 24-26a) and boxing with a defensive emphasis upon avoiding blows (vv. 26b-27a). Paul demands rigorous discipline and training so as to win the laurel wreath (v. 25) and avoid defeat (v. 27b).

e. *Music and art* are among the noblest of human endeavors, expressing the deep sensibilities of the soul. It is obvious why worship became one of the primary functions of music. However, this is one of the more difficult aspects to trace, for musical scores have not survived the ravages of time (indeed, music was taught orally without actual "scores"), and we have to divine from bas-reliefs and lyrics the actual melodies used.

Werner mentions four types of music in the ancient world: social merrymaking (Gen 31:27), military (Judg 7:18-20), magical incantation (pagan) and worship (1962:457-58). I would add a fifth—work or harvest songs (Num 21:17; Is 16:10). The flute and horn existed early in seminomadic tribes, and tambourines were used at the song of Miriam upon crossing the Red Sea (Ex 15:20). In 1 Samuel 10:15 the prophetic band ministered with harps, tambourines, lyres and flutes. With David's influence a great choral and orchestral tradition soon developed (2 Sam 6:5, 10), which predominated throughout Israel's history.

Many have called Israel a "nation without art" due to the prohibition of Exodus 20:4 (Deut 5:8), "You shall not make for yourself any idol in the form of anything in heaven above or on the earth beneath or in the waters below." However, this censured idolatrous art and a genuine artistic tradition did develop, centered upon the tabernacle and the temple. To be sure, foreign artisans did most of the work on the temple (1 Kings 7:13-14), but the tradition was Israel's. The sculptured panels of wood inlaid with gold; the pomegranates, grapes, gourds, lilies and palm trees embroidered on curtains (but note that there were no animals); and the cherubim sculptured in the Holy of Holies demonstrate a love for religious art that rivals that of the surrounding nations. In the New Testament period Herod was famed for his artistic and architectural achievements, not only in terms of the temple; he also erected many structures employing Hellenistic style and statues—gymnasiums, theaters, amphitheaters and the entire city of Caesarea Philippi. The Hillel school apparently allowed such buildings and art work so long as they were not used for religious purposes. Gamaliel himself wore a signet ring engraved with a human head to demonstrate this attitude of tolerance.

6. Religious Customs. This area controlled every aspect of the daily life of the people. Every activity carried religious overtones, and the modern dichotomy between religious and secular simply did not exist. As Daniel-Rops says, "Since the civil authority identified itself with the religious authority, secular law was merely the application of the law of God" (1962:341). What people wore, how they spent their free time and related to one another, even the very type of home they lived in had an essentially spiritual dimension. Many passages cannot be understood without relating the religious situation behind them. For instance, tracing the pagan-Jewish syncretism in the Lycus Valley is quite helpful when studying the heresy addressed in Colossians. Moreover, knowing the actual purpose behind the oral tradition and the Pharisaic injunctions is necessary before studying the encounters on the part of Jesus and Paul in the New Testament.

A brief perusal of prayer practices may demonstrate the value of this. In the first century the Jews prayed three times a day and recited the Shema (Deut 6:4, 5-9; 11:13-21; Num 15:37-4) in the morning and evening. Jews normally prayed standing and knelt or prostrated themselves only at solemn times. It was common to pray aloud with upraised hands (1 Tim 2:8; folding the hands did not originate until the fifth century A.D.) and downcast eyes (Lk 18:13). It was also customary to don the prayer shawl (the *tallith)* and the phylacteries or amulets (the *tefillin).* The prayer *(tefillah)* consisted of a series of liturgical blessings, codified by the end of the first century in the "Eighteen Benedictions." After this liturgical portion the individual would present personal petitions to God. Jesus participated in this (Mk 1:35, morning prayer; Mk 6:46, evening prayer) but transcended it by beginning often "a long time before daybreak" (Mk 1:35) and praying at times through the night (Lk 6:12). Luke especially stresses Jesus' prayer life (see 5:16; 6:12; 9:18, 28). Jesus transformed earlier prayer teaching in his "Abba" theology, which introduced a new intimacy into the communion between the person and God (see Jeremias 1967 contra Barr).

7. Summary. Mickelsen follows Eugene Nida *(Message and Mission)* in noting the influence of cultural diversity on communication (1963:170-72). Any communication takes place when a "source" gives a "message" to a "receptor." God, the ultimate source, speaks through the human writers of Scripture (the immediate source) within the diverse cultures of their day. The receptors, or recipients, of that message interpret it from within other cultures. Therefore, the task of the receptor in the modern cultural framework is to recapture the total framework within which the sacred writer communicated and to transfer that message to our own day. The cultural aspects presupposed in the passage help interpreters get behind the words to the underlying message, understood by the original readers but hidden to the modern reader. This becomes a necessary prelude to the application of the text to current situations (see figure 5.2).

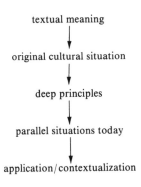

textual meaning

↓

original cultural situation

↓

deep principles

↓

parallel situations today

↓

application / contextualization

Figure 5.2. Steps from Original Text to Contemporary Application.

The cultural background not only deepens our understanding of the original text but also provides a bridge to the current significance of the text (see chap. fifteen). A delineation of the customs presupposed or addressed in the text enable us to separate the underlying principles (the doctrines used to address the original context) from the surface commands (the contextualization of the deeper principles from the original situation). Next, we can identify similar situations today and allow those deep principles to address us anew.

Specific Sources for Background Material
1. Old Testament Allusions. As noted earlier, there are more Old Testament allusions

than outright quotes. Yet most books on the use of the Old Testament in the New focus upon the quotes. As Moo states, the allusions may actually have had greater emphasis because the writer was presupposing his readers' knowledge (1983:169). This means that the source and significance of these allusions must be discovered if the original meaning of the passage is to be recaptured. I would note five principles for finding and evaluating allusions:

a. Does the wording and the style point to an Old Testament passage? This could well demonstrate a deliberate allusion. Style, however, is difficult to evaluate. There are "Semitisms" (Hebrew or Aramaic style rather than Greek) and Septuagintalisms (due to the influence of the Septuagint, the Greek Old Testament), but they may be unconscious rather than conscious reflections of the Old Testament. Without any linguistic similarity the possibility of an allusion should not be pressed.

b. Consider the individual writer's traits. First Peter, Hebrews and the Apocalypse, for instance, have a very high incidence of allusions. In the cases of these books a potential allusion has greater probability.

c. Does the reflection of an Old Testament background make sense in the context? If it is out of keeping with the thought- development of the passage it is less likely. However, if the context is favorable the allusion will add richness to the meaning of the passage. For instance, the use of Isaiah 53:10, 12 in Mark 10:45 (Mt 20:28) adds the nuance of the Servant of Yahweh who atones "for the sins of many" (Is 53:12). Several scholars (such as Hooker 1959:140-47) argue that (i) the language ("servant," "for") is not used in Isaiah 53 (principle "a" above); (ii) the paucity of allusions to Isaiah 53 in the Gospels makes any allusion here doubtful (principle "b" above); and (iii) atonement imagery does not fit the context (principle "c"). However, Moo responds that while the linguistic parallels are not exact the conceptual meaning of Mark 10:45 is so close to Isaiah 53 that an allusion is highly probable (1983:122-27). Further, while the Gospels do not contain many direct allusions to Isaiah 53, there are many indirect reflections (see the chart in Moo 1983:163-64) and these may well have greater force (as noted above). Finally, as Carson points out (1984:432-33), it is common in Jesus' teaching to begin with the disciples' death to self (Mk 10:43-44) and to illustrate this with the example of Jesus' atoning death (10:45). In short, the use of Isaiah 53 in Mark 10:45 is probable and becomes a powerful illustration of the servanthood attitude enjoined of the disciples.

d. Dodd argues that an allusion or quote often presupposes the original Old Testament context behind the allusion and not just the allusion itself (1952:126-33). This is an important point. Of course, the extent to which it is true depends upon the immediate New Testament context. For instance, some think that the cry of dereliction in Mark 15:34 ("My God, my God, why have you abandoned me?") should be understood in light of the whole psalm (Ps 22, see vv. 22-31) as a faith statement placing trust in the God who will vindicate (see Trudinger 1974:235-38). Yet this ignores the obvious thrust of the context, for it occurs on the cross and the sense of abandonment is paramount. The lament is stressed here, although the whole psalm may still be in the larger context. The thanksgiving may be proleptic in the cry, anticipating the later joy of the resurrection.

e. Do not overexegete. It is common especially for Old Testament scholars to read all their detailed exegesis of the Old Testament passage into the New Testament setting. Rather, we should seek to determine (on the basis of the interaction between the Old and New Testament contexts) both the aspect of meaning highlighted in the New Testament setting and the way in which the New Testament writer understood the Old Testament passage. For instance, Hebrews 2:12-13 provides an interesting juxtaposition of three passages, Psalm 22:22 (v. 12), Isaiah 8:17b (v. 13a) and Isaiah 8:18a (v. 13b). At first glance, the Old Testament passages seem unrelated and clumsy, but when we look at their meaning in the Old Testament context and compare that with the development of Hebrews 2, the whole begins to make sense. The three briefly summarized speak of overlapping themes—victory in the midst of suffering (v. 12), trust in the midst of judgment (v. 13a) and promise in the midst of judgment (v. 13b). The latter two passages are concurrent in the Hebrew text but are treated separately in this Epistle. In the midst of God's judgment (Is 8) the remnant place their trust in him (v. 17b) and become his children (v. 18a).

2. Intertestamental Allusions. The actual quotes from intertestamental literature are sparse, but the ideas generated during the period between the testaments are crucial for understanding New Testament doctrine. Many of the Jewish parties in the time of Christ (Pharisees, Sadducees, Essenes) developed during this period, so New Testament customs and culture have their antecedents here. In addition, the oral tradition has its origin during this time and doctrines such as belief in the resurrection of the dead or baptism have strong roots here. Wisdom and apocalyptic literature flourished and are important sources for passages like the Sermon on the Mount, the Olivet Discourse, or the Gospel of John. Since apocryphal and pseudepigraphical literature are similar to the documents of Qumran, I will discuss principles for using this material in the ensuing subsection.

3. Qumran Parallels. In the early 1950s, as a result of the idealistic fervor following the discovery and publication of the Dead Sea Scrolls, scholars made rash decisions regarding the influence of Qumran on the New Testament. For instance, John the Baptist was seen as an Essene, Jesus was considered to be modeled after the Teacher of Righteousness (the "founder" of the sect), the church was said to be the Christian equivalent of the Qumran community, the Gospel of John and the Epistle to the Hebrews were declared to be Essenic documents and many practices (such as baptism) and beliefs (such as pneumatology, eschatology) were thought to be dependent upon Qumran. However, upon later reflection, many of these points have been strongly modified (of these points only Hebrews is still thought by some to be strongly influenced by Qumran).

LaSor summarizes the current scholarly opinion when he states that the two groups (Qumran and the Christians) differ in their essential historical perspectives but are similar in their religious perspectives (1972:247-54). Historically they arise from different periods, and Qumran cannot confirm or disprove New Testament data. They are independent movements that developed differently, and Qumran cannot be an antecedent of Christian ideas. However, Qumran and Christianity were both sectarian Jewish sects with similar eschatological expectations, so Qumran provides a valuable parallel for Jewish ideas. The key is a proper methodology for utilizing Qumran (and intertestamental) backgrounds:

a. Use a good translation. Millar Burrows is especially good but lacks versification. Geza Vermes is also good, but for a one-volume translation Dupont-Sommer is probably the best. A good translation will keep the interpreter from misunderstanding and therefore misusing the text. Of course, using the original Hebrew is even better, but this is not always feasible.

b. For word study use the concordance by K. G. Kuhn (1960) and its supplement in *Revue de Qumran* 4 (1963): 163-234. These are critical for tracing ideas through the Essenic literature.

c. Before alluding to a parallel, study the exact theological nuances of the Qumran or intertestamental passage before applying it to a New Testament passage. Here secondary sources are helpful, and there is a growing literature exploring intertestamental books in depth (such as in the Anchor Bible series). Since opinions vary widely it will be helpful to check more than one source. Best of all, trace parallel passages and work out the meaning for yourself before applying it to the New Testament.

d. Before using the intertestamental passage to interpret the New Testament passage, make certain that the former is a true parallel and not merely a seeming parallel. As stated above, the key is to note the degree to which the thrusts of the two passages in their respective contexts overlap. Also, one should compare the extent of the overlap with other potential parallels and determine which possibilities are the closest to the New Testament passage. Only then will it be possible to call the intertestamental passage a valid parallel.

4. Rabbinic Parallels. The major problem is the dating of the Talmudic traditions. While this problem is somewhat overcome by the care with which the rabbis preserved the material, there are many debates as to which material actually fits the situation before A.D. 70. When the temple was destroyed in A.D. 70 by the Romans, Judaism was forced to redefine the essence of her worship and ritual. Things were never again the same, and many customs written down in the later Talmud have their origin in Judaism after A.D. 70.

Longenecker lists four strands of Talmudic traditions that are relevant: (a) practices and rules deemed by Rabbi Johanan ben Zakkai to be very ancient, introduced by "our rabbis taught" or such like; (b) teachings of rabbis who lived before A.D. 70 or had roots in that period (such as Pirke Aboth 1-2); (c) passages that are not a reaction to either religious oppositions (mainly Christianity) or political oppression and do not stem from a later debate or situation; (d) ancient liturgies, confessions and prayers such as the Shema or Eighteen Benedictions (1975:75).

However, many dispute even this list. Jacob Neusner, for example, argues that we cannot assume the validity of the Talmudic dating but must question even those which claim to be early (1983:105). Neusner argues for form-critical techniques in the use of rabbinic material.[2] I agree with the three cautions of Sanders (1977:60-61) and add a fourth:

a. We cannot assume that rabbinic discussions automatically continued Pharisaic views. While the majority of scholars hold to the basic continuity of the two groups, all agree that individual rabbinic quotes cannot be assumed to be representative of Pharisaism. This is the problem with the massive work of Strack-Billerbeck (1961-65), which places quotes from third- and fourth-century rabbis alongside New Testament passages without asking whether these actually reflect first-century Pharisaism.

b. We cannot assume that the early material is authentic, that it actually represents the period claimed. The ancient rabbis may have edited and re-created many of the sayings. However, I believe we can be more optimistic than Sanders allows. As with the sayings of Jesus there is more reliability in the collection of rabbinic quotes than many scholars concede. The burden of proof is upon the skeptic to disprove their reliability.

c. We cannot assume that the material is united in its views. It is varied and very eclectic. Many of the sections in fact involve rabbinic dialogue giving both sides of the question. A common pattern of religion binds the whole together but does not give a united perspective on isolated issues. For instance, several famous quotes demonstrate a misogynist strain within Judaism (such as j. Sot. 19a, "Sooner let the words of the Law be burnt than delivered to a woman"). These are often presented as *the* Jewish position, but this was only one strain of Judaism. The rights of women were often upheld (divorce was the husband's prerogative but the woman was given the right to petition the court to force him to divorce her) and on occasion women filled positions of leadership (see Stagg 1978:51-53).

d. We should consider the possibility that the New Testament and the rabbis borrowed from a common Jewish tradition. Vermes posits this as a solution to the problem when a Jewish source seems to lie behind a passage but cannot be shown to be before A.D. 70 (1982:373). He would like to consider the New Testament to be a valid witness to first-century Jewish beliefs and as such to study it as part of the line of development from Targum to midrash. When considered from this perspective rabbinic (and Targumic) material takes on a new relevance. We must still be careful not to misuse this by ignoring the historical dimension (points a-c above). However, as a further possibility this can be extremely helpful.

5. Hellenistic Parallels. Since Hellenistic backgrounds have been so misused by the History of Religions schools, many have virtually denied the relevance of Greek ideas in favor of Jewish ideas as proper backgrounds for New Testament study. Unfortunately, this has developed into an adversarial relationship. However, since the work of Martin Hengel (1980:110-26) scholars have recognized that Hellenistic ideas had permeated Judaism by the Maccabean period and on into the Christian era. With the onset of the universal mission this influence had increased, and we must consider Greek as well as Jewish parallels to all New Testament literature. Here of course I want to repeat the cautions on using Hellenistic material mentioned in chapter two as well as the principles for interpretation in the summary following. Hellenistic backgrounds can be extremely helpful for understanding those epistles addressed to gentile churches and many individual customs mentioned—for instance, Graeco-Roman attitudes toward women in 1 Corinthians 11:2-16 or 1 Timothy 2:8-15. Also, they help to clarify details regarding the missionary journeys, such as divination practices behind Simon Magus (Acts 8) or the possessed slave girl (Acts 16). Aune provides an excellent example of Hellenistic back-grounds (1983:5-26), convincingly pointing out that the throne room scene of Revelation 4—5 is built upon the imagery of Roman imperial court ceremony. This fits the emphasis throughout the book opposing the imperial cult and provides excellent illustrations for sermons today dealing with the problem of church and state.

6. Summary. Since I have discussed other sources of parallels (Philo, Josephus, the Targums) in chapter three, I will not cover these here but will summarize this section with a general discussion of criteria. (1) We must be certain that the evidence comes from the same period as the passage being studied; shoddy use of period data (third-century gnostic practices read into first-century Christian concepts) has led many to false theories. (2) We must ascertain the reliability of the evidence; often Talmudic parallels have been casually introduced as background to New Testament events like the trial of Jesus with-out ascertaining their reliability for first-century Judaism. (3) We dare not be selective in the evidence gathered; if we do not search widely enough we may miss the true parallel, such as Graeco-Roman customs as well as Jewish in the passages on slavery. (4) Work not only on the current situation but on the historical development behind it; often the factors that led to a state of affairs are as important as the predicament itself. For instance, the development of the oral tradition in Judaism is crucial for understanding many of the conflict situations between Jesus and Judaism. (5) Remember that the biblical accounts also provide historical data. Scholars often neglect the text itself and assume all the data must come from outside sources. This is often unnecessary, for the explanation is present either in the passage being studied or in parallel passages.

Sociology as a Tool for Interpreting Scripture

It has become increasingly popular to employ modern sociological methods in order to study more deeply the influence of society and customs on the biblical text. This has resulted in part from a feeling that the historical-critical method has produced a vacuum in actually understanding Scripture. Many have declared the labor of the last forty years "bankrupt," stating that as a result "the biblical-theological study of the Church seems to have stood still" (Edwards 1983:431). Scholars are searching for a new perspective that will enable the Bible to come alive in its original setting, that will re-create the dynamic of biblical texts for the original hearers. The feeling is that the dry academic exegesis of the past has stiltified the true power of the text. As T. F. Best says, form (and redaction) criticism, even with an emphasis on the "life-setting" of texts, failed to describe the historical or social situation behind the literary and theological dimension; "even Paul, who springs virtually to life in his letters, was reduced inexorably to a propagator of ideas" (1983:182). The desire is to reproduce not just the thoughts but the thought-world of the biblical text.

Sociology as a discipline studies the human relationships and the social changes that shape a society. As Gager has said, most would differentiate between "social description" and "sociological interpretation" (1982:259).[3] The former deals with the "what" of the text, trying to uncover background that will help us to identify the social factors, laws and so forth behind a particular statement. For instance, we could study first-century customs regarding proper hairstyle behind the "headcovering" in 1 Corinthians 11:2-16 (see Hurley 1981). Richter names three types of descriptive studies (1984:78-81). The most frequent is the study of the social environment within which Israel or the church developed, such as Jeremias's monumental portrayal of the economic, social and racial background behind first-century Jerusalem (1967). Also important is the delineation of the social history of a group in terms of movements and events, such as Malherbe's work on the social environment behind Paul's Epistles and the house church movement (1983). Finally, analytical studies trace the sociohistorical development of a class or sect, such as the debate over the social level of the early Christians, whether they penetrated society from the top down (the wealthy, so Judge and Malherbe) or the bottom up (the poor, so Gager and Theissen).

"Sociological interpretation" studies the "why" behind the text and uses current sociological theory not just to understand the meaning of a text but to re-create the social dynamics that led to the production of the text. Sociological study most frequently employs current sociological theories to explain aspects of Jewish or Christian history. For instance, Gottwald uses a "peasant-revolt" model taken somewhat from Weber but primarily from Marx to argue that the conquest of Canaan took place not via invasion from outside but rather via a revolt of the dissatisfied lower class in Canaan itself (1979). Gager's study (1975) first describes the early church as a millenarian movement by comparing it to Melanesian cargo cults (which also had charismatic leaders and a following from the outcast groups). Gager then uses the theory of "cognitive dissonance" (L. Festinger) to explain how Christianity as a millenarian movement survived. According to this theory the church adapted to the failure of its prophetic expectations by reworking its eschatology and instituting the universal mission. In both these cases various theories and anthropological models are applied to biblical history in order to determine "what really happened."

The modern movement of sociological analysis had its precursor in the University of Chicago school, particularly in the work of Shailer Matthews *(The Social Teachings of Jesus,* 1897) and Shirley Jackson Case *(The Social Origins of Christianity,* 1923). The theoretical basis, however, was not strong and the school was short-lived. More important is the continuing interest in social backgrounds expressed by such scholars as Deissmann and Troeltsch as well as by proponents of the History of Religions school. The modern movement began in the 1970s with such Old Testament scholars as Gottwald and such New Testament scholars as Gager and Theissen. Interest is growing to this day, and the school is rapidly taking a place in the forefront of biblical scholarship.

Just as important for us is the history of modern sociological theory. As Yamauchi explains, the "father of sociology" was Auguste Comte (1798-1857), who pioneered a "scientific" study of societal development from simple to complex forms (1984:176). Herbert Spencer (1820-1903) applied Darwin's evolutionary theories to societal change, and Karl Marx (1818-1883) wedded Hegel's dialectical theory to Feuerbach's materialism in centering upon economics as the primary cause of societal disruption. Max Weber

(1864-1920) introduced the modern era; he theorized that value systems rather than economics provide the grist for the mill of sociological development. In his study of Israel (1952) Weber theorized that its concept of the covenant led Israel to unity, and the charismatic leaders during the time of the Judges molded it into a cohesive force. The second major figure was Emile Durkheim (1858-1917), who was the first to see society as an organic whole containing many interrelated parts. This functional view had a lasting impact upon sociological method. In recent decades this functional approach has been quite influential, especially in biblical studies.

Malina describes three major models (1982:233-37). The structuralist-functional approach believes that society consists of certain expected patterns of interaction (structures) that are controlled by shared purposes or concerns (functions). In contrast to form criticism, which isolates competing traditions in Israel or the church, functionalism views both as integrated wholes and seeks to determine the larger factors that generated those movements. As also seen in literary criticism, this tendency to recognize the unity of the biblical text is a valuable corrective to historical-critical excesses. The second is the conflict model, which studies society in terms of the disagreements and power politics between the various interest groups that are represented in the larger structure. The tracing of the changes that these pressures force upon a society is the task of this approach. Finally, the symbolic model studies society in terms of its deeper value system, what persons, things and events mean within the societal structure. The shared aspirations and expectations of a society determine its structure.

With respect to the church, for instance, the first approach would study how its component parts (apostles, elders, local churches, men and women as individuals) related both within the Christian society and within the larger Jewish and Graeco-Roman societies surrounding the church. The conflict model would note tensions in the church (Jewish vs. Hellenistic, tradition vs. false teaching and others) and in the larger realm (Christian vs. Jew vs. Greek) and use these to understand the development of the church. The symbolic model would research particular symbols like power or authority (Holmberg 1978) or ritual purity (Malina 1981) as keys for understanding the early church.

Problems in the Sociological Approach

Many criticisms can be leveled against the validity of this new school of research, and I will summarize them briefly here.

1. Misuse of the Models. It is easy to read historical situations in the light of modern theories without asking whether or not these current models actually fit the ancient data. The old "Life of Jesus" scholars recast him in the mold of the then-current liberal teacher. Many sociological researchers are doing the same with Israel or the church. Gager, for instance, has been accused of ignoring aspects of early Christianity that did not fit his millenarian model. This problem is noted often in academic circles, and it is not different among proponents of this method. Scholars often choose only those groups which fit the model they wish to impose on the data and then select those aspects from Israel or the church which fit their theory. They then studiously omit aspects in both the external model and the biblical material that are not parallel. Best labels this "the problem of personal bias" and calls for "a fundamental stock-taking by those who want to employ" later models to demonstrate biblical theories (1983:189).

In many cases sociology is an ideological tool for proving a thesis rather than an instrument for studying a movement. Gottwald (1979) is often accused of forcing his liberation theory upon the data. He theorizes that egalitarianism rather than monotheism was primary in Israel's "socio-economic revolution" against the Canaanites. Yahweh was the symbol of the revolution, not the reason for it. Therefore, the conquest of Canaan was socioeconomic rather than religious at the core. As Long states, "The model for contemporary analysis is an ancient revolutionary society of which religious expression was but a part. Biblical theology seems to have become a kind of liberation socio-theology" (1982:255). In a more negative vein, Yamauchi says, "Despite his massive erudition, Gottwald reads into the OT his ideological biases in his imaginative reconstruction that disregards both the Biblical and the archeological data" (1984:183).

2. Revisionism. Critical scholars often seem to have a preconceived notion that the biblical history is wrong as it stands and needs to be revised. This is not a problem with the sociological method per se, since by nature this approach tends to take the biblical data more seriously than previous schools. However, many work with the results of the historical-critical method and assume the validity of those conclusions. This is the case with Gottwald. Theissen discusses the problem of history for sociological research (1982:175-79). The historian is "entirely dependent on chance sources which have survived" (p. 175), and none of those documents are framed as sociographic statements. All too often theological assertions are treated as social statements. The problem of affirming the reliability of hypotheses is immense. How does one test a case that is built on such obscure evidence? My answer is to treat the biblical text seriously as a historical record in its own right.

3. Tendency to Generalize. The problem with the structuralist-functional model is that it centers upon a cross-section of society and has no place for individual contributions. Theissen lumps together Jesus and the apostles as "wandering charismatics" and gives little place to differences between them (1978). The creative genius of Jesus and Paul are replaced by social forces that shaped their contributions. This makes little sense, for true genius (Galileo, Shakespeare, Newton, Einstein) transcends the society in which it appears. By failing to take account of individual contributions and by overstating the place of social pressures, one's results are usually skewed. Best decries the "tendency in sociological theory to regularize the data in favor of interpretive theories" in light of "the extraordinary diversity of social structures" in the church (1983:192). We dare not force unity upon diversity.

4. The Paucity of the Data. Modern sociological conclusions are not made without extensive data collected over long periods of time. In comparison the biblical data is sparse indeed and that which we have is not couched in sociological language. It is erroneous to read theological statements as sociological evidence, and we must exercise great caution in trying to do so. For instance, Elliott has to argue that "stranger" and "alien" (in 1 Pet 1:1, 17; 2:1) are used as technical terms for the dispossessed rather than as theological metaphors for the Christian as an "alien" in the world (1981:24-48). I am not convinced that he is correct exegetically and for all the sociological depth of the book it founders at this crucial point.

Malina responds that the task of modern study is predictive and so needs a large data base (1982:238). Since the use of the social sciences in Scripture "is oriented toward efficient causality" (reproducing the past), the amount of evidence needed is not so great. However, this is disputable because modern sociology is descriptive as well as predictive. Scroggs says that "the researcher must work with the utmost caution and strictness, with adequate guard against overenthusiasm" (1983:340).

5. Tendency to Debunk the Systems. Sociologists claim that theirs is an objective or value-neutral discipline, but this is in reality a façade. Yamauchi points to Peter Berger as especially stressing this aspect (1984:181, 189-90). Yet it is inherent in such an empirical system as sociology to place religious phenomena in the end within the human sphere. The spiritual experience surrounding Israel and the church is read as the product of internal factors (such as societal) rather than external (such as supernatural). As Berger himself states *(The Sacred Canopy,* p. 180), "Sociological theory must, by its own logic, view religion as a human projection."

6. Reductionism. The tendency to explain all given aspects on the basis of societal factors is reductionist at the core. To be sure, many argue that modern approaches have surmounted this obstacle. Malina (1982:237) claims that the use of models to explain sets of data is not reductionist, but he does not quite explain how to avoid subsuming broad aspects of Israel and the church under general models, whether or not the data actually fits. The more sophisticated do avoid this error to a large extent. However, it is quite common to fail here. For instance, Edwards (1983:444) critiques Elliott (1981) for his assumption that all the inhabitants of Asia Minor can be assigned the status of resident alien or that Asia Minor was primarily a rural area. Elliott has overly simplified the evidence and overstated his case. As one general observation on the more complex situation behind 1 Peter, Elliott provides very useful material. However, on the broader plane he has failed to prove his hypothesis. Even Theissen, although he avoids reductionism in his study of Corinth (1982), falls into this pitfall in his study of the disciples (1978). Theissen has artificially elevated the class of "wandering charismatic" missionaries and given the settled leaders of churches (such as Philip, Timothy, Titus) a secondary and subsidiary role. As Richter says, "Theissen never really gets beyond marshalling the relevant data. He fails to offer any adequate models that begin to explain the data satisfactorily" (1984:80).

7. Theoretical Disarray. There are a tremendous number of sociological theories, some more valid than others, but the practitioners often fail to recognize the difficulties in applying them to biblical material. As Yamauchi points out, this is generally true of the whole field of academic sociology (1984:179-80). He quotes Gareth Steadman Jones (from *British Journal of Sociology* 27 [1976]: 300):

> The vague and shifting character of its object, the inconstancy of its definitions, the non-cumulative character of much of its knowledge, its proneness to passing theoretical fashions and the triteness of some of its "laws" suggest that its theoretical foundations are contestable and insecure.

This very lack of correlation between specific data and general theory or model is the problem at the level of application to biblical material. Practitioners are guilty of the abstraction fallacy, which tries to capture the dynamic of the ancient situations in abstract modern concepts that often remove the life and breath from the original situations. Scroggs suggests two ways of overcoming this tendency: (1) understand the methods completely and be clear of the extent to which they apply to the data; (2) be aware of the theoretical presuppositions when explicating the ancient situation (1983:339). I would add a third: allow the data to control and alter the models as the situation warrants.

8. Determinism. Since the social sciences center upon human behavior, the possibility of divine activity is almost ruled out by definition. To be sure, the biblical practitioners are very aware of this tendency and take care to leave room for the noumenal as well as the phenomenal realms. However, since the entire task involves searching out the societal factors behind the text, the divine element is still too often neglected. In the study of Paul as a charismatic leader, for instance, the social phenomenon is highlighted and the biblical emphasis upon divine commissioning at times seems replaced by the needs of the community (see Holmberg). Moreover, society gains absolute control of all human behavior, as every contingency is explained by these societal factors. This overstatement of the influence of society is deterministic, since events in Scripture that are attributed to God are placed under the aegis of society.

9. Tendency to Disjunctive Theories. To support a certain theory writers often make an "either-or" out of a "both-and." This is true of the attempts to argue that the early church centered upon the lower class (Gager, Theissen) or on the upper class (Judge, Malherbe). Gager himself points out that there were some converts from both sides, but he argues that the focus of the church was upon the disadvantaged (1982:262). However, R. H. Smith provides an interesting analysis of Matthew and his congregation that points to a middle-class background (1983:441-57). Meeks, in the most far-reaching study I have seen, proves that the strata of society reached was mixed and ambiguous, ranging from Caesar's household (Phil 4:22) and the proconsul Sergius Paulus (Acts 13:7) to slaves and the disenfranchised (1983:51-73). Meeks concludes that Paul's congregations represented "a fair cross-section of urban society" (p. 73). However, I doubt Meeks's further disjunction between urban and rural society. Although Elliott overstates his thesis, he shows that the locus of 1 Peter and the first missionary journey of Paul was quite rural in its make-up.

Evaluation and Methodology

One is tempted to be as negative toward the potential of sociological research as is C. S.

Rodd, who states:

> It appears to me that the difficulties posed by the nature of the evidence and the differences in culture, are greater than the exponents of sociological interpretation of biblical societies recognize, despite the qualifications which they insert into their writings . . . . I would claim that the attempt to apply sociological theories to biblical documents is not likely to be fruitful. (1981:103-4)

Rodd would use such theories only heuristically to suggest further lines of research. The theorist must rigidly control conclusions, noting that such general theories never can deal adequately with the contingencies of history. Since the researcher never can "test" his conclusions as in a living society, all results will be tentative at best.

To some extent I agree with Rodd's assessment. The problems enumerated above are indeed difficult to surmount, and most of the attempts to do so have not been particularly convincing to date. Nevertheless, we must recognize the fact that the discipline as applied to biblical studies is still in its infancy. It needs time to mature and integrate its methodology with the other tools of historical research. In particular, sociological approaches to Scripture must begin to explore the ways in which this discipline can fit into a "field" approach to hermeneutics, that is, an integration of all the tools into a comprehensive whole. To date the exponents of sociological methodology have treated it as an end in itself, resulting in overstatement and confusion of issues. I must admit that in my opinion the more important aspect is "social description," for "sociological research" (see above regarding the distinction) is too reductionistic and cavalier in its results. However, the latter does have heuristic value if the resultant models are treated as approximations rather than as established truths.

Therefore, I would suggest the following hermeneutical guidelines for background studies, moving from the particular (social background) to the general (sociological models). This will function as a conclusion to the whole chapter, for sociological methodology is placed within the larger context of background studies as a whole. This is the only way in which the sociological approach can have validity, when it is placed within the larger framework of the other exegetical tools as one method among many to determine the meaning of the text.

1. Make certain the passage has been studied thoroughly along grammatical-semantic-syntactical lines. The results of detailed exegesis will form the control for determining the proper background parallels to adduce in deepening the meaning of the text. For instance, I cannot decide whether Galatians or 1 Corinthians 1—3 should be paralleled by Jewish or Hellenistic background until I have studied the language and concepts Paul employed.

2. Be comprehensive in the collection of data. At times the passage itself will indicate the background material, as in the use of Old Testament quotes and allusions. In such instances one will not need to search more widely. Also, when the narrative itself builds upon Jewish customs, as in the Gospels, the source is relatively simple to define. However, many passages are ambiguous. The background to Genesis is notoriously difficult to define, and in many cases scholars despair at finding the correct parallel. For example, the ceremony of walking between the parts in Genesis 15:7-21 can have several possible

meanings (see Hasel 1981:61-78). It could signify mystical union, the transferral of life, a self-curse or self-obligation or (in Hasel's opinion) covenantal promise. In this case similar practices in the Mari letters, Assyrian treaties and vassal ceremonies all point to the covenantal aspect. This convergence of evidence is an important pointer to the meaning of the ceremony. Also, most of Paul's letters draw upon Jewish and Hellenistic sources. The interpreter must discover all possibilities in order to study the passage properly.

3. Study the contexts of the biblical and nonbiblical passages and see which converge most closely. We desire true parallels rather than seeming parallels, and only when all the possibilities have been exhausted can we decide which is the best one. Those parallels which overlap the biblical passage to the greatest extent are the most likely. If this is true with respect to social customs it is more so in the case of sociological research when one is applying models drawn from current theories. Wilson notes six guidelines (1984:28-29): (1) be thoroughly familiar with the approaches and their limits; (2) center upon the results of competent social scientists; (3) understand the theories completely in the modern context before applying them to ancient contexts; (4) survey a wide range of societies that parallel the phenomenon being studied; (5) note interpretive schemata used to study the data and avoid them unless they are actually useful; (6) allow the text itself to provide the controlling factor, so that the hypothesis will be tested by the biblical data.

4. Do not read nonbiblical parallels into the text any further than the data allows. In other words, do not force the data to fit the theory. Instead modify the theory to fit the data. Most important, rework only those aspects which are truly clarified further by the background material. Do not exaggerate the importance of the sociological aspects to the denigration of the individual or spiritual dimensions. Remember that the text must control the background data and *not* vice versa!

5. Go into the passage with a large volume of potential theories and allow the text to select the theory that best fits. Often sociologists, like biblical theologians, take a paradigm approach in which they artificially select a single model and then force the evidence to fit their theory, ignoring any disparate data. There is no reason why Jewish and Hellenistic backgrounds cannot converge upon a passage or why cognitive dissonance, conflict and structuralist-functional models cannot explain different aspects of the church's development. In modern society a sociologist works from the bottom up, from the actual social situation of a group to a model that is constructed to fit rather than is forced upon the data. The same should be true of using the social sciences to understand the Bible more deeply.

6. The text is primary and not the background material. We must remember that historical-cultural exegesis is a supplement to the text and not an end in itself. Therefore, we must apply the "event" behind the text only to the extent to which it will aid in understanding the message in the text. Too many background studies end up replacing the text rather than supplementing it and deepening our understanding of it. Some passages, such as theological or credal material, will need very little. Others, such as historical narrative, will benefit greatly; however, even here we should use cultural data only to the extent that the text allows.

7. When we move from the text to the sermon, background information has a further value. By immersing the audience in the original situation behind the text we help them to place themselves into the world of the text and see how it was speaking to the original audience. At that time we can then help the hearers to discover situations parallel to the text in their own life and to contextualize the principle behind the text for their current situations.

Part 2
Genre Analysis

The basic hermeneutical task outlined in chapters one to five must now be applied to specific *genres,* or types of literature. This functions on several levels, the larger literary unit (such as the book of Revelation as "apocalyptic" literature), the smaller section (such as Lk 15 as a series of parables within the larger Gospel) or the individual saying (such as Acts 1:9-11 as "apocalyptic" imagery in Jesus' statement). I will adopt the classical working definition of genre by Wellek and Warren: "Genre should be conceived, we think, as a grouping of literary works based, theoretically, upon both outer form (specific meter or structure) and also upon inner form (attitude, tone, purpose—more crudely, subject and audience)" (1956:219). I will expand this below as we consider how to detect the genre to which a passage belongs.

The current debate over genre is whether or not it can function as a classification device. Many argue that generic categories shift from epoch to epoch depending upon literary interests and that every text differs in its use of generic forms. Therefore, they conclude, no criteria for classifying works under specific genres can be established. As I have argued elsewhere, however, these arguments are not conclusive (Osborne 1983:1-27). My primary purpose here is to enable the reader to note the characteristics of the ancient genres as a key to interpreting biblical texts. Modern categories when imposed on the biblical framework (such as modern biography or fiction as a device for understanding the Gospels) are misleading and even inimical to actual understanding. However, the application of ancient characteristics (and of those modern devices that supplement and uncover the historical approach) is a necessary hermeneutical technique.

Moreover, arguments regarding the "mixing" of genres and the difference between individual texts belonging to a particular genre do not militate against the classification function of genre. The very fact that we can identify "differences" and even classify them (such as wisdom portions of prophetic books) presupposes a larger unity. Novels do contain plot, characterization, climax and so on. Poetry does employ meter, rhythm, symmetry, parallelism and so on. Certainly novels differ radically in particular expression (such as the French "new novel"), and some poetry employs rhyming while other stresses a free form (T. S. Eliot's *The Waste Land*). However, these very distinctions occur within a larger framework. Daniel contains apocalyptic sections within the larger framework of prophecy; the Gospels utilize narrative, parables, proverbs, teaching and apocalyptic but still function overall as Gospels. Yet the very possibility of detecting the smaller generic units within the larger supports the possibility and even the importance of classifying texts along generic lines. Longman states correctly,

> While it is true that the individuality of many compositions must be maintained, the similarities between the form and content of texts must not be denied. That there are similarities between texts which can serve as a rationale for studying them as a group is especially true for ancient literature where literary innovations were not valued highly as they are today. (1983:3-4)

Genre functions as a valuable link between the text and the reader. As I have noted in previous chapters, we cannot neglect the reader in the process of interpretation. Every interpreter comes to a text with certain expectations based in part upon his or her genre understanding. If a reader expects the Gospels to contain fiction rather than history (such as understanding the story of Lazarus and the rich man in Luke as parable, not an actual event), the interpretation will differ quite radically. Hirsch speaks of "intrinsic genre," meaning that every text is part of a larger group of generically related texts (1967:69-71). As readers study a particular text, their expectations are increasingly defined as they narrow the possibilities to identify the proper genre to which the text belongs. The process proceeds by trial and error, as the text progressively revises the reader's identification. By applying to the text the potential extrinsic genre-types (those imposed on the text from outside) the interpreter eventually determines the intrinsic, originally intended genre and thereby is able to utilize the correct "rules" for understanding that text. For one studying an ancient text this process cannot take place automatically. The modern reader needs help in understanding how those ancient genres functioned, and that is the purpose of these chapters.

Yet we must ask how one determines the genre of a particular book or passage.[1] As Wellek and Warren's definition makes clear, there are external and internal considerations. The external aspects concern the overall structural pattern, the form (meter, rhythm, narration), style, interrelationships and content. Internal factors include the cohesive plot, action, narrative voice, setting and language. The characteristics of works that show similarities are studied both synchronically (within the same period) and diachronically (the development of the forms). Only when we understand the historical patterns can we avoid the oft-repeated tendency to draw generic parallels from the wrong period (see also p. 139). For instance, we would have been spared Bultmann's use of Mandaean literature to interpret John if he had realized that gnostic literature came from a much later period and could not parallel John. The parallels must not only be sufficient to justify the inclusion of the text in the particular class, they must also be drawn from the correct period.

Genre analysis represents both large portions of Scripture (entire books) and smaller units. As noted previously, poetry can be found in the Psalms, but it is also a subgenre found in both wisdom and prophetic literature. This is also true in the New Testament. Apocalyptic is not only the genre of the book of Revelation (often called "The Apocalypse"), but it constitutes a major portion of 2 Peter, Jude and 2 Thessalonians as well as minor portions of the Synoptic Gospels, 1 Thessalonians and the epistles to the Corinthians. Parable is a subgenre only, but it is so critical to the teaching of Jesus that we must treat it separately. Most readers hardly consider the epistle a genre, but I will attempt to demonstrate how helpful it is to understand ancient epistolary customs when interpreting this crucial body of literature. As Hartmann says, genre represents a set of literary conventions shared by readers and authors: authors accept it, more or less faithfully, and shape their texts in adherence to it; readers' expectations and attitudes when approaching texts are colored by it, and it affects their understanding of texts (1983:332). This is to say that discussing genre means discussing something that has to do with communication.

I would go one step further and state that genre provides a set of rules that further refine the general exegetical principles elucidated in chapter one through five and allow the interpreter greater precision in uncovering the author's intended meaning.

6
Narrative

HE CURRENT INTEREST IN LITERARY CRITICISM IN BIBLICAL STUDIES WAS SPAWNED IN large part by the failure of form and redaction criticism to interpret the text. The tendency to break the text into isolated units is widely perceived as counterproductive, and so scholars turned to the much more literarily aware field of narrative criticism to breach the gap (see the excellent summary in Petersen 1978:9-23). Narrative studies recognize that meaning is found in a text as a whole rather than in isolated segments, and so narrative criticism has become "the new kid on the block." Yet like all fads it has its dangers, such as the tendency to ignore or even reject the historical element in the text and a philosophical stress on the reader as the agent in producing meaning (see appendices one and two). Therefore narrative criticism as developed below should never be done by itself but should be combined with source and redaction criticism, which will act as a corrective to its ahistorical tendencies and to the excesses of its stress on the text as a final product rather than as a developing unit (see further the conclusion to this chapter). Nevertheless, it is an invaluable aid in the task of interpreting a text and is one of the more positive "schools" of criticism to have appeared in recent years.

The major premise of narrative criticism is that biblical narrative is "art" or "poetry," thus centering upon the literary artistry of the author. While many would not deny the presence of a historical nucleus, the tendency is to treat the biblical stories as "fiction" (with Sternberg being a notable exception). It is certainly true that there is little difference (at the genre level) between historical narrative and fiction, since both utilize the same methods to tell the story: plot, characters, dialogue, dramatic tension. In fact there is nothing inherently antihistorical in taking a "fictive" approach to biblical narrative.[1] Rather, such a perspective simply wants to recognize the presence of the "story" genre in biblical history.

As many have noted,[2] the biblical narratives contain both history and theology, and I would add that these are brought together via a "story" format. The historical basis for the stories is crucial, but the representation of that story in the text is the actual object of interpretation. Adele Berlin somewhat overstates the case when she says, "Abraham in Genesis is not a real person any more than a painting of an apple is a real fruit. This is not a judgment on the existence of a historical Abraham any more than it is a statement about the existence of apples. It is just that we should not confuse a historical individual with his narrative representation."[3] Yet there is a great deal of truth in this, for we are studying a text and not re-creating an event. Berlin is not judging the existence of the historical Abraham but is concentrating upon the biblical texts about Abraham. While I believe that background is critical in biblical study, it must be controlled by the text and not vice versa (see chap. five above). Our task is to decipher the meaning of the historical-theological text in biblical narrative, not to reconstruct the original event.

The Methodology of Narrative Criticism

The basic method by which we are to study biblical narratives is simple: we are asked to READ them! Most of us have grown up with the Gospels or Old Testament history as isolated stories. We have seldom sat down and simply read them through to catch the drama and power of the stories as they fit together to form a holistic panorama. Literary critics have developed techniques that will aid us greatly to perform a "close reading" of the text and to note such features as plot and character tension, point of view, dialogue, narrative time and settings, all of which will enable the reader to detect the flow of the text and therefore to see the hand of God as he has inspired the biblical author to develop his story. Evangelical hermeneutics has somehow stressed the author's intention for every book of the Bible except the narrative portions. We forget that each Gospel is developed differently and must be studied by itself as a single whole in order to understand its inspired message.

Since Krieger[4] the common metaphors for these dimensions of the text have been those of pictures, windows and mirrors. The literary aspects guide the reader to the text as a picture or portrait of the narrative world presented in the story. The historical nature of the Bible leads one to treat the story as a window to the event behind the text. Finally, since the Bible is supremely relevant for today, the text is a mirror in which meaning is "locked up" so that readers see only themselves as part of the believing community for whom the text was intended.[5] The thesis here is that all three elements are part of a biblically valid interpretation; to neglect any factor is to do an injustice to the text.

The interpretation of narrative has two aspects: poetics, which studies the artistic dimension or the way the text is constructed by the author; and meaning, which re-creates the message that the author is communicating.[6] The "how" (poetics) leads to the "what" (meaning). Sternberg calls narrative "a functional structure, a means to a communicative end, a transaction between the narrator and the audience on whom he wishes to produce a certain effect by way of certain strategies" (1985:1). To diagram these "strategies" let me develop those of Seymour Chapman (1978:6) and Alan Culpepper (1983:6)—see figure 6.1.

The purpose of this schematic is to demonstrate how an author communicates a message to a reader. Each of the categories below will explain an element within this diagram.

1. Implied Author and Narrator. No reader sees the real author in a text. Rather, as Juhl points out, we know the author only to the extent that he reveals himself in the text (1978). This perspective helps us to overcome the tendency to psychologize the text in

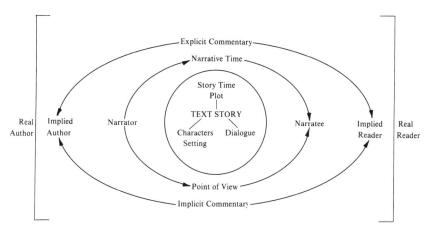

Fig. 6.1. Aspects of Narrative Criticism.

order to discover the author in a manner similar to that of Schleiermacher and Dilthey. The author is not present but has created a persona of himself in the text (the implied author), and we study the text, not the author. There we see those concerns, values and theological perspectives which the original author has chosen to highlight in this particular text. Furthermore, this will keep us from reading one text into another, even if from the same author, such as Deuteronomy into Exodus. Nevertheless, the presence of the author is critical in order to tie us to the historicality of the story, to keep central the original intended meaning of the text.

In some stories it is necessary to separate the implied author from the narrator; for instance, when there is a specific narrator in the story. However, this is rare in the Bible (an exception may be the "we" sections in Acts) and so I combine the two here. The narrator is the invisible speaker in the text, audible especially in the editorial sections. The narrator tells us the story and at times interprets its significance. For instance, in Acts the narrator continually tells us of the success of the gospel through the Spirit's work in the church, in spite of the many problems and opposition the people of God encountered (see 2:47; 6:7; 9:31; 12:24). It is also the narrator who intones the marvelous poetic prologue to John's Gospel (1:1-18).

The biblical narrator has many important characteristics, but most importantly we must agree with Sternberg that he is often indistinguishable from God who inspires him. "The very choice to devise an omniscient narrator serves the purpose of staging and glorifying an omniscient God"[7] (see further below on "point of view").

The value of the stress on implied author and narrator is that it forces the reader to look at the seams and editorial asides of the text as important indicators of its meaning.[8] For instance, the decision of most commentators following Tenney (1960:350-64) that John 3:16-21 is an editorial comment rather than the words of Jesus provides an important clue to the narrative function of that critical text. It becomes John's commentary on the significance of the difficult dialogue between Jesus and Nicodemus in verses 1-15.

2. Point of View, Ideology and Narrative World. The point of view is the perspective taken by various characters or aspects in the narrative. Most frequently it is connected to the narrator, who interacts with the action within the story in various ways and so produces the effect that the story is to have on the reader. In other words the point of view points to the force or significance of the story. Every author has a certain message that she wishes to get across to the reader, and this is true also of biblical narrative. This point of view guides the reader to the significance of the story and determines the actual "shape" that the author gives to the narrative. In fact, as Berlin points out, a story usually has multiple perspectives as the biblical narrator like a movie camera zeros in on one aspect then another in the developing plot, thereby guiding the reader in several meaning directions at the same time (1983:43-55). Scholars have identified five areas where point of view operates.[9]

a. The *psychological dimension* studies how the narrator provides "inside" information as to the thoughts and feelings of the characters. In this respect biblical narrative is "omniscient"; it gives the reader knowledge no one could possibly know.[10] The Gospels are the most obvious examples. Luke describes the inner thoughts and feelings of characters like Simeon and Anna as they recognize the Messiah in the baby Jesus (2:29, 38) and relates Felix's desire for a bribe from Paul (Acts 24:26). John tells us Jesus' intentions (1:43) as well as the extent of his knowledge (2:23; 4:1). However, when the point of view is that of the characters within the story, the perspective is finite and often wrong. One of the clues to the Samson story is the carnal, mistaken perspective of Samson (Judg 13—16) contrasted to the omniscient comments of the narrator. As a result the reader experiences in a poignant way the tensions within the story.

b. The *evaluative,* or *ideological,* point of view denotes the concepts of right and wrong that prevail in the narrative. The actors in the drama are often at odds with one another and with the narrator as to the judgment of their deeds. In both Matthew and Mark the measuring rod of valid reasoning is "thinking the things of God" vs. "thinking the things of men." This is the criterion for true discipleship (see Petersen 1978:107-8; Rhoads and Michie 1982:44; Kingsbury 1986:33). John has three levels, depending upon the faith-response of the individual to Jesus. The ideological mentality of the leaders of Israel leads them to reject Jesus; the point of view of the crowds often draws them to Jesus but more because of his signs than due to true faith (2:23-25; compare 6:60-66); and the faith of the disciples leads them to follow Jesus in spite of the price (6:67-71). The reader must choose between these three perspectives.

c. The *spatial perspective* of biblical narrators is "omnipresent"; that is, they have the ability to move from place to place freely and to relate the story from various vantage points. In the walking-on-the-water miracle the narrator is with the disciples in the boat and with Jesus on the water simultaneously (Mk 6:48; note "he was intending to pass them by"). The result is an ability to lead the reader more deeply into the story than would otherwise be possible. In the story of finding a wife for Isaac (Gen 24) the reader is moved from the place of ignorance (Canaan) to the place of testing (Abraham's former home), where a startling act of hospitality leads the servant to Rebekah. The reader is expectant throughout the narrative as the geographical movement of the story unfolds.

d. Closely connected is the *temporal perspective,* which can consider the action from within the story (from a present point of view) or from the future. John especially is well known for narrating from a postresurrection viewpoint. While Luke carefully saves the concept of Jesus' "glory" for the resurrection narrative, John stresses the fact that Jesus' glory was observable all along to the eye of faith (1:14; 2:11; compare 1:51). Similarly, at the call of Jeremiah (1:4-19) the voice of God reaches into past (v. 5) and future (vv. 7-10) in prophesying Jeremiah's significance for the divine plan. On the other hand, the book of Nehemiah is written in a first-person style and shows a finite knowledge of events and the future. When the news comes of Jerusalem's desolation Nehemiah weeps (1:2-4). Thus the reader is made a part of the story and feels the drama in a different way than when a more divine perspective is taken.

e. The *phraseological* point of view relates to the dialogue or speeches in a narrative. Here again we see the omnicompetence of the author. The reader is able to listen in to dialogue one would never hear in the normal world, for instance, the personal conversation between Haman and his wife and friends (Esther 5:12-14) or the private dialogue between Festus and Agrippa regarding Paul's innocence (Acts 26:31-32). In such cases these interactions become the high points of the narrative, and the reader is given valuable inside information that leads to the dramatic and theological lessons. As Kingsbury points out, the use of Old Testament formula quotations in the speeches of Matthew links both the narrator and Jesus with God's point of view and adds authority to the Gospel as a whole (1986:34).

These elements of point of view form the perspective of the "narrative world" of a book. As I said above, the historical books of the Bible present a realistic world. Walhout notes an important distinction between fictional and historical texts:

> The assertive stance of the historian embraces an interpretation and evaluation of certain data as well as a narrative or descriptive account of the data. . . . The historian claims—asserts—that the projected world (the story) of the text together with the authorial point of view counts as a story and an interpretation of events as they actually occurred.[11]

Nevertheless, the portrayal is restricted to the limited horizons of the text itself. Thus the author is able to communicate to the reader. As Keegan states, "At the end of the narration the implied reader will have a reasonably clear picture of this well defined, circumscribed, narrative world" (1985:102). The writer is not limited to the constraints of the real world but can provide vistas of perspective that the normal person cannot know. Thus the reader is given a sense of the presence of God behind the story and this divine authority permeates the whole.

3. Narrative and Story Time. This refers to the order of the events within the story and the way they are related to one another. Narrative time is distinct from chronology because it has to do with literary arrangement rather than with historical sequence. The concept is very important when studying ancient history because sequential order was not as important as dramatic portrayal to chroniclers then. This can be demonstrated best by comparing the four Gospels. The Synoptics (Matthew, Mark, Luke) give the impression that Jesus engaged in a one-year ministry, while John details a two-year ministry. The reason is that John tells of three Passovers (2:13; 6:4; 11:55) while the Synoptic Gospels mention only the Passover at the crucifixion. Clearly no attempt was made to be chronological, and the Evangelists were more concerned to relate the significance of Jesus' life and ministry (who he was as well as his impact upon the disciples, the crowds and the religious leaders) than merely to give details regarding his life. Even in Matthew, Mark and Luke the sequence of events is startlingly different (as a perusal of any Gospel harmony will prove).

Sternberg speaks of "temporal discontinuity" or suspense as a means of heightening reader involvement in the drama (1985:265-70). The author will cause a "gap" in the story by shifting events and will create suspense by providing incomplete knowledge of the future. This occurs in the binding-of-Isaac story, since the reader feels that Isaac will be spared but is kept in suspense until the last minute. However, as Sternberg points out, the Bible tends to curtail suspense due to the divine control of the world order: since God is supreme there cannot be undue stress on uncertainty. The narrator controls the drama or temporal displacement by foreshadowing or shaping the narrative future through analogy (applying the lessons of the past, such as the increasing number of younger brothers elevated over their elders, from Jacob to Joseph to Moses to David), paradigm cases (establishing a divine law of logic, as in the cycle from sin to judgment to repentance to reinstatement in Judges, see 2:11-19), or dramatic forecast (as in the prophetic period).

The space given to narrative events will vary depending on the writer's purposes. Genesis 1—11 is a kaleidoscopic dash through a bewildering sequence of events, linked together largely by the narrative or theological purposes of the text. The patriarchal narratives of the rest of Genesis, however, slow down considerably and take us on a lengthy stroll through a series of interconnected details. Similarly, the Gospels have at times been called a passion story with an extended introduction due to the disproportionate length of the passion events compared to the other scenes in Jesus' ministry. Culpepper says that for John "the scenes can be fitted into about two months of the two-and-a-half-year period covered by the narrative" (1983:72). This will be helpful when studying the selective process of the author in developing his plot and emphases. For the evangelists the question was not what to include but what to omit (see Jn 21:25).

4. Plot. Seymour Chatman speaks of plot, characters and setting as comprising the story itself (1978:19-27; see also Kingsbury 1986:2-3). The plot encompasses the united sequence of events that follow a cause-effect order; these build to a climax and involve the reader in the narrative world of the story. The basic element of plot is conflict, and every biblical narrative centers upon such—God vs. Satan, good vs. evil, discipleship vs. rebellion. Plot can function at either the macro (the whole book) or micro (a single section) level. For instance, at the micro level John 9 contains an amazing drama contrasting the man born blind (who begins blind but progresses toward spiritual as well as physical sight) with the Pharisees (who claim spiritual insight but end up blind).[12] These conflicts often are amazingly complex, since they can be external as well as internal in the narrative. This is the key to the Samson story. Supposedly his is an external battle with the

Philistines, but in reality it is an internal conflict between his calling to be a judge and the self-centeredness and sensuality he increasingly exemplifies. This leads to a conflict with God and ultimately to his downfall.

At the macro level the Gospels each have a different plot, even though they are relating essentially the same story. For instance, both Matthew and Mark center upon Jesus' encounter with the secular authorities, the crowds and the disciples. Yet they do so in quite different ways. Mark stresses the so-called Messianic Secret, showing how Jesus' messianic nature was rejected by and hidden from the leaders, misunderstood by the crowds and disciples, and acknowledged by the demons. Matthew recognizes this but heightens the contrast by showing a growing understanding on the part of the disciples (compare Mt 14:33 with Mk 6:52). Also, Mark emphasizes discipleship failure while Matthew notes the difference that the presence of Jesus made as the disciples were enabled to overcome their ignorance and failures. The narrative world inhabited by both is the same—the in-breaking of the kingdom or reign of God into history. However, the plot and thereby the detailed emphases of each differ considerably. Luke has even greater divergence of plot, as a comparison of the sayings of Jesus common to Matthew and Luke (commonly called "Q") will show. The same or similar sayings appear in radically different contexts and lead to a unique set of theological thrusts, such as God's grace extended to outcasts and a major accent on social concern in Luke.

The reader must study carefully the plot and miniplots within narrative books in order to determine the developing themes and characterizations of the author. This is the best indicator of the basic message(s) of a literary work. The interplay of opponents and the interaction between major and minor characters are the clearest possible guidelines to the meaning of a passage. The unity and lines of causality within the dramatic sequence of the story first draw the reader into the narrative world and then help the reader to relive its point and understand its purpose. In this way theology may be better served by narrative material than by didactic. We not only learn the truth but see it enacted in living relationships.

5. Characterization. The success of a story depends in large part upon its success in developing interesting, real people with whom the readers can identify. Culpepper notes Aristotle's dictum that characters should have four qualities: they should be morally good, suitable, lifelike and consistent.[13] In many ancient works characters remain undeveloped with few of these qualities. However, biblical narrative is replete with realistic figures seen in all their human frailty. Literary scholars have long noted the amazing transparency of biblical portraits. Samson's carnality, David's lust, Solomon's political and religious compromise or Elijah's cowardice in running from Jezebel are all presented with remarkable forthrightness. As a result they are all the more appealing and applicable to the reader. There was no attempt to hide the human frailty of biblical heroes. When Abraham tried to talk his wife into posing as his sister and would have allowed her to become part of Pharaoh's harem, Genesis (12:14-29) recorded the incident intact. Yet the important point is not that discreditable facts are recorded of biblical characters but that this characterization is carried out with a depth and subtlety that makes them very realistic and thus applicable to those with similar problems in every age.

Sternberg speaks of the contrast between the character of God, which is immutable or unchanging, and the characters of the individuals with whom God works; the latter continually change in the text (1985:322-25). The constant alterations within God's actions are not due to changes in his character but rather to the ever-changing developments in the people within the stories. These developments are in five overlapping types of characterization, which Sternberg illustrates with the description of David in 1 Samuel 16:18 (p. 326): physical ("a man of good presence"); social ("a son of Jesse the Bethlehemite"); singular or concretizing ("skillful in playing"); moral and ideological ("the Lord is with him"); and psychological in a broad sense ("able in deed, a man of war, wise in counsel"). In every case, the depictions are not hyperbolic or extensive but serve to stress the power of God; God, not the biblical heroes, is magnified throughout. This is nowhere better demonstrated than in the book of Judges. Every victory wrought is a triumph of God and of the faith of those who place their trust in him. Those who trust in themselves (like Samson) are doomed to failure.

The narrator uses many techniques to portray the characters and to lead the readers to a proper understanding of their roles.[14] The most common is through description. David's bravery and Saul's jealousy are stated directly then further anchored in the drama enacted between them. Thus inference is added to description. Moreover, irony is added to inference, for Saul's actions undermine his initial description and promise, which is carried out by David rather than by him! There is one difference between the Gospels and the Old Testament narratives in this regard. In the Gospels traits are simpler, and both the rulers and the disciples can be lumped together as displaying basic characteristics. For instance, the Pharisees, Sadducees and Herodians (normally competing ideologies) together form the opposition to Jesus' messiahship. Peter and the other disciples differ somewhat but on the whole exhibit together the qualities of ignorance and burgeoning faith. In the Old Testament the major characters (Moses, David, Solomon, Elijah) are more dynamic and at times change drastically. David vacillates from bravery and faith to self-centeredness, and Elijah from power to fear. In every case the reader's perception changes with the characters as the narration and dialogue expand the reader's horizons.

6. Setting. The setting of the story, Chatman's third level of narrative technique, can be geographical, temporal, social or historical; it will provide the basic context within which plot and characters develop. As Rhoads and Michie state, the setting serves many functions: "generating atmosphere, determining conflict, revealing traits in the characters who must deal with problems or threats caused by the settings, offering commentary (sometimes ironic) on the action, and evoking associations and nuances of meaning present in the culture of the readers" (1982:63). An example of the use of a geographical setting is the Emmaus Road journey of Luke 24. The entire story is set in a framework of geography, with the two disciples leaving Jerusalem in defeat, meeting the Risen Lord in Emmaus, then returning to Jerusalem in victory.

In a very real sense the Galilee-Jerusalem contrast is a controlling factor in the resurrection narratives of all four Gospels. Traditionally scholars have made Jerusalem the place of rejection and Galilee the place of acceptance. However, it is closer to the narrative development to see Jerusalem as the place of the passion and Galilee as the place of witness and understanding.[15] In Mark and Matthew Galilee becomes the place of revelation, where Jesus will make himself known to the disciples as the Risen One.

Temporal settings are equally important. The three Passovers in John (2:13; 6:4; 11:55) form a temporal framework for the entire ministry of Jesus. In a broad sense the salvation-historical nexus of all the Gospels is a temporal setting. There is the time of Israel, the time of Jesus, and the time of the church. Jesus anchors his new revelation, the Torah of the Messiah, to the past revelation of God to Israel; he preaches the time of fulfillment in the in-breaking of the kingdom in the present; and he prepares for the ongoing salvific plan of God for the church in the future.

Social settings also can communicate a strong message. Consider the Lukan theme of table fellowship. An amazing number of scenes occur in banquet settings, with three different aspects: soteriology, symbolizing God's forgiveness and acceptance of sinners (5:27-32; 15:1-32; 19:1-18); social, with the message of God invading the social arena and bathing it in God's wondrous light (14:7-24; 22:31-32); and mission instruction, as Jesus uses the setting to teach his followers regarding his true purpose and mission (9:10-17; 22:24-30; 24:36-49). Each of these builds upon the Jewish notion of table fellowship, which assumes that the practice of sharing a meal involves sharing a life (Osborne 1984:123-24).

Finally, the historical setting provides a helpful interpretive tool. This is true in two directions. The historical setting behind the text (such as the dating of Isaiah or Amos) tells us what historical period we apply to them. We can identify the exact set of problems that Amos was addressing and thereby understand the text far better. Second, the historical setting behind the writing of the biblical books also makes a difference. It is important to know whether Matthew was writing within a Jewish or Gentile context (a greatly debated topic), since issues like Matthew's supposed anti-Semitism are greatly affected by the decision.

7. Implicit Commentary. In the diagram at the beginning of this section implicit commentary refers to the rhetorical techniques whereby the author tells his story. By utilizing irony, comedy, symbolism and other literary devices the writer guides the reader through the drama of his story. In this section I will center upon those literary devices specifically used in narrative but not covered in detail in the earlier sections (pp. 35-40; 100-108). The problem for the reader is identifying and interpreting properly the underlying message behind these techniques. However, identifying them and understanding how they function are the first steps.

One of the more frequently seen methods is repetition. This is so important that Alter has devoted an entire chapter to it (1981:88-113, especially 95-96; see also Longman 1987:95-96). Alter identifies five types: (1) the *Leitwort*, or word-root, in which cognates of a root word are repeated for effect ("go" and "return" in the book of Ruth); (2) motif, the repetition of a concrete image used symbolically (fire in the Samson story or water in the Moses cycle); (3) theme, in which a certain idea or value becomes the focus (obedience vs. rebellion in the wilderness wanderings); (4) a sequence of actions, often in a threefold pattern (the three captains and their companies warned of fiery destruction in 2 Kings 1); and (5) the type-scene, a key event in the life of a hero that is repeated more than once (the feedings of the 5,000 and the 4,000 or the three commissions of Paul to the Gentiles in Acts 22:21; 23:11; 26:17-18).

Some literary critics assert that these are purely literary devices while many evangelicals counter that the doublets are present because they simply happened. However, this is disjunctive thinking. There is no reason why history and literary artistry cannot exist side-by-side. There is no good argument apart from form-critical presuppositions for denying the historical authenticity of these multiple events, but the sacred authors included them not merely for historical reasons (they omitted far more than they included) but to make a point. Berlin states that repetition is often utilized to show a story from more than one point of view; for instance 2 Samuel 18 describes David's grief over Absalom from three vantage points—his own as well as that of Joab and all the people. In this way the intensity of his grief is magnified (1983:73-79).

Another major technique is that of "gaps" in the narration. These are bits of information deliberately omitted by the writer in order to force the reader to get involved in the drama. As Sternberg points out, the text controls the gap-filling process by means of previous information, the development of the plot and its characters, and the cultural conventions behind the story.[16] In this way the search for meaning is both a quest and a process on the part of readers, who are forced to immerse themselves more deeply into the narrative world.

Sternberg uses the David and Bathsheba story (2 Sam 11) as a test case (1985:190-219). The writer does not label David's sins or tell how much Uriah realized, and the reader is forced to speculate and fill in the missing information. The writer also intentionally refrains from saying why David summons Uriah (vv. 6-13), so that the reader thinks the best until the terrible plot is revealed (vv. 14-15). This makes doubly ironic the seemingly inadvertent comment on Uriah's part, "How could I go to my house to eat and drink and lie with my wife? As surely as you live, I will not do such a thing!" (v. 11). The reader does not know whether Uriah is merely expressing loyalty to David or stating bluntly that he is not going to get David out of his dilemma by sleeping with his wife. Through the gaps in the narrative the suspense is heightened and the reader feels the emotions of the text in ever more powerful ways.

8. The Implied Reader. At first glance this seems another example of academic trivia, useful only to dry scholars holed up in dusty rooms. However, it is one of the most practical of the tools for the average reader. This theory is grounded in the supposition that every book has a group of readers in mind. These original readers are no longer available to the "real reader" (the person actually reading it today), and so the text yields only an "implied reader" behind the intended message.[17] The actual reader is called upon by the text to read it from the standpoint of these "implied readers" and to identify with the problems and message intended for them. This process will help the actual readers to associate with the feelings and responses indicated by the text rather than with the meanings that they might read into the text.[18]

While the possibility of discovering the original intended message is widely denied by literary critics, I believe that the implied reader is a figure that enables a person to detect the original intended message of a text rather than an elusive entity that allows one to play with multiple meanings in the text.[19] Culpepper says, "As the reader adopts the perspectives thrust on him or her by the text, experiences it sequentially, has expectations frustrated or modified, relates one part of the text to another, and imagines and works out all the text leaves for the reader to do, its meaning is gradually actualized."[20] In other words the text guides readers to its intended meaning via devices like the "implied reader" that force them to enter the textual world and relive it.

While exegesis and biblical theology enable the interpreter to work out the propositional or theological meaning of the text, the implied reader helps us to discover the commissive or relational meaning of the narrative.[21] I call this step "reader identification," asking what the text is demanding of its intended or implied reader and then "identifying" with that purpose. In other words, in the act of reading a text I allow the text to determine my response by submitting to its internal dynamics and reordering my own life accordingly (note the diagram on contextualization on p. 337). In this way the real readers discover the significance or application of the story for themselves. This is a critical tool for preaching biblical narrative.

For instance, the story of the wedding feast at Cana often has been used to teach persistence in prayer: if we like Mary insist that Jesus meet our needs (Jn 2:3-5), he will do it. However, this is not the stress of the context. It is clear from its setting in chapters 1—2 and from the editorial explanation of 2:11 ("He thus revealed his glory, and his disciples put their faith in him") that the message is christological, centering upon Jesus' "glory" rather than oriented to prayer. Mary's request is part of the emphasis on Jesus' messianic office (it meant the beginning of his public ministry) and is not a paradigm for discipleship. The implied reader is called to faith, and we recognize Jesus' "glory" with Mary.

Similarly, a close reading of the Elijah-Elisha chronicles (1 Kings 17—2 Kings 13) shows many deliberate parallels with Moses and Egypt. The miracles of 1-2 Kings have two purposes in this regard: to demonstrate Yahweh's power over Baal (as the plagues showed the powerlessness of the Egyptian gods) and to portray God's judgment on idolatrous Israel. Throughout these narratives the implied reader is being asked to trust God alone and to reject the overtures of secularism. The modern reader will not seek to duplicate the miracles so much as to relive the faith-commitment of these stories.

9. Conclusion. The process described in the preceding pages is both simple and complex. The terms and concepts seem beyond the average reader, and yet the methods they describe are based upon a commonsense reading of the text. These are not separate aspects of reading but provide a perspective by which we can achieve a "close reading" of the text. By keeping all of these in mind while reading the text several times, the reader will gain a "feel" for the dramatic flow. The various dimensions of the story (plot, characters, setting) and of the discourse (the way it is told—implied author, point of view, implicit commentary, implied reader) will become elements of the reading process done simultaneously as the text dictates. In other words, we will look carefully at the literary artistry of the biblical author as he creates the narrative world within which we will discover the meaning and significance of the story.

The Weaknesses of Narrative Criticism

Like all schools of thought, literary criticism is a many-faceted discipline, and we cannot lump its adherents together under a single category. The problems mentioned below do not apply to all, but generally they can be exemplified in the movement. When a person becomes enamored with a new toy, even an academic one, it is often the case that caution is thrown to the wind and the individual uses the tool uncritically, not knowing when it will hurt. The list below is not intended as a denigration or a rejection of narrative criticism but rather is a set of warnings against its excesses. I hope that the student will utilize the techniques in the first section in such a way as to avoid the dangers of this section.

1. A Dehistoricizing Tendency. As noted in the quote from Collins (fn. 1), many literary critics radically deny any historical element in reading a text. The radical autonomy of the text (see appendix one) means that it is removed not only from the original author but also from the historical framework within which it was originally written.

For some this involves a repudiation of the historical-critical method, and indeed there is some validity in this. Form and redaction criticism in their traditional garb have ignored the final form of the text. In fact I have long felt that the very success of narrative criticism in showing the unity of the biblical stories has removed the very basis for the more negative forms of tradition and source criticism, since decisions about "later additions" to the text are always based upon the seeming incongruity of the flow of the text as it is. Narrative studies have shown the viability of seeing Genesis as a united text, and the aporias or clumsy literary connections are seen to make perfect sense as they are.[22]

Nevertheless, many others also have denied the historical background behind the text. Indeed, the Bible has been cast adrift from its moorings and left to float on a sea of modern relativity. The "play" of meanings in the stories is seen to be openended, and modern readers must construct their own interpretation. Rhoads and Michie thus call Mark "a literary creation with an autonomous integrity" existing independently from any resemblance to the actual person and life of Jesus. It is a "closed and self-sufficient world," and its portrayals, "rather than being a representation of historical events, refer to people, places and events *in the story"* (1982:3-4; italics theirs).[23]

The classic presentation of this view is given by Hans Frei, who calls for a departure from the preoccupation with history on the part of modern critical scholars and for a return to a precritical "realistic" reading of biblical narrative, or cognizance of its "history-like" character (1974:10-35). However, he separates this from any connection with the originating historical event; for Frei the narrative *is* its meaning; there should be no search for the event behind the text but only a close reading of the text itself. Yet this fails to do justice to the texts themselves. As Sternberg remarks, "It is a pity indeed . . .

that enthusiasts about the 'literary' approach to the Bible should preach as historical
doctrines whose brief heyday has long passed and which were never quite literally meant,
let alone practiced, even by their New Critical originators."[24]

In reality the literary and historical exist side-by-side and are interdependent. As a
literal representation of event and its significance, both text and its background are
essential components of meaning. This is especially true in light of the shared assumptions
between the author and his contemporary readers, data that should be recovered in order
to understand the text in its fullness. In short, two aspects of history are important to
biblical narrative, the historical events behind the narratives and the background material
that helps to elucidate the intended meaning of the text.[25]

2. Setting Aside the Author. Reader-response criticism is the final stage of a lengthy
movement away from the author in the author-text-reader schema, which is at the heart
of the hermeneutical debate (see appendix one). Most proponents of this school accept
some form of the autonomy theory, that a text becomes autonomous from its author as
soon as it is written down. Therefore, delineation of a text's meaning stems from the
present reader rather than from the "past" author or text.[26] Yet this dichotomy is unnecessary. As Thiselton puts it,

> valid insights about the role of the reader in literary and philosophical hermeneutics
> are sometimes pressed in such a way as to imply an infinite relativism on the part of
> the text or its author. Questions about meaning are reduced entirely to questions
> about language-effect in the modern world. (Lundin, Thiselton, Walhout 1985:81)

Such a skepticism and reductionism are unwarranted. The reader uses hermeneutical
techniques to understand and identify with the intended meaning of a text. There is no
need to banish the biblical author from his work.

3. A Denial of Intended or Referential Meaning. This is also the subject of the two
appendices to this book, so it is unnecessary to go into detail here. Since for radical critics
the implied author replaces the real author behind the text, and fiction replaces history,
the words as well as the text as a whole become autonomous from their original reference
or meaning, and the readers produce their own meanings in the text. Many literary critics
reject the possibility of detecting the "referential" meaning of an utterance, that is, the
original reality behind the words of the text. In each case this is an unnecessary and
dangerous step, leading potentially to a radical relativism in which every person's "meaning" is as correct as another's and validation of "truth" becomes an impossibility. As Scot
McKnight states,

> literary theorists may stand in awe of the ice "floating on" the water and they may
> describe its aesthetic shape and its evocative powers, but sooner or later their ship will
> awaken to a crashing "Titanic-like" revelation of the fact that what they were staring
> at was in fact an iceberg, with much more below the surface than above. (1988:128)

4. Reductionistic and Disjunctive Thinking. To reduce meaning to intertextual factors like
plot or setting is not only unnecessary but patently false. At one level literary criticism

performs a needed service in reminding us that meaning resides in the text as a unity and not in isolated segments. However, half-truths can become falsehoods when elevated to the whole of truth. This is the case here. Without the broader horizons provided by exegetical and historical-cultural research we simply cannot arrive at the intended meaning of the text. Of course, this has been the debate all along, and in a very real sense we are at an impasse. The radical literary critic does not believe we either can or should arrive at the author's original meaning, while one of the purposes of this chapter is to dispel that very notion.

The two sides—exegetical research and a close reading of the text—are not an either-or but a both-and. Semantic research (as I have argued on pp. 75, 78) is counterproductive without the control of the text itself and leads to "illegitimate totality transfer" of meaning. Also, research into the event or background behind the text often results in revisionist history and speculative sociological theories (see p. 142) unless the text controls what is done. At the same time literary analysis descends into subjectivism without exegetical controls. If it is impossible to detect the author's meaning, the radical literary critics are correct, and we will have to live with our subjective encounters with the text. But such is not the case, so we must judge the efforts to center upon "the text and only the text" misguided at best and dangerous in the extreme.

5. The Imposition of Modern Literary Categories upon Ancient Genres. Many modern theorists derive their approaches from a perusal of modern fiction. Even Adele Berlin, who attempts a "poetics of biblical narrative," falls into this error when she defends "closing off the world of the text from the real world" on the supposition that "literary works should be analyzed according to the principles of literary science" (1983:16). We could agree with her larger point that literature rather than archaeology or psychology determines the rules of the language game. However, the problem is that usually modern literature rather than ancient genres supply the theories.

Berlin herself (along with Sternberg and Alter) is a healthy exception, but perhaps the best corrective is supplied by David Aune, whose *The New Testament in Its Literary Environment* deliberately seeks to redress the balance by considering each genre in light of its Jewish and Graeco-Roman parallels. For instance, he carefully compares the Gospels with both Jewish and Graeco-Roman biographical literature in order to determine how the Evangelists chose the form they did and in order to deepen the hermeneutical guidelines for interpreting them according to their own generic rules (1987:17-76). He responds to current methods by asserting that "the literary styles and structures associated with fiction by modern scholars cannot exclude the use of narrative art in ancient cultures to mediate a historical view of reality" (p. 111; see also Sternberg 1985:23-24). In other words the fictive genre was often employed in the ancient world (and at times is today as well) to depict what actually happened. It is erroneous to presuppose an ahistorical stance on the part of the biblical historians.

6. A Preoccupation with Obscure Theories. Tremper Longman notes the proliferation of technical phrases and jargonistic explanations on the part of advocates (1987:47-50). Reading some of the reader-response or deconstructionist literature is tantamount to learning a foreign language. The difference is that a foreign language deals with practical concepts and the literary textbooks with philosophical concepts that one would swear were beyond even the scholars who propounded them! Terms like "actantial," "aporia," "narratee," and "implied reader" are bewildering to all but the inner circle.

Furthermore, many of the theories themselves contradict one another. Longman notes the time lag between the latest avant-garde school of thought and its appearance in biblical studies. The current fad is a preoccupation with the social sciences, and as a result works begin appearing in biblical studies about a decade after they have become popular in the social sciences (such as deconstruction; see appendix one). Everyone wants to be a part of the latest movement; we are repeating the error of the Athenians who "spent their time doing nothing but talking about and listening to the latest ideas" (Acts 17:21). Here let me add a caveat: there is nothing wrong with "new ideas," and every field—like medicine or engineering—has its own jargon (have you ever tried to make sense of a TV commentary on a sport with which you were not familiar?). However, when a field of thought claims to offer a pragmatic method that will be useful to the average person, it must avoid overly technical language and must unify its theories. In actuality this is one major purpose of this chapter: to simplify the bewildering array of technical approaches and to present a technique that unifies the disparate theories.

7. Ignoring the Understanding of the Early Church. While the hermeneutic of the early church cannot be determinative for modern methods, since we are hardly bound to their modes of thinking, it is still worthwhile to note that the earliest exegetes universally considered the biblical stories to be historical. As McKnight states, "I know of no early church writings which treat the Gospels as literary masterpieces, no extensive comments which prove that the interpreters were interested in such things as plot, technique, character development and the like" (1988:146). This does not prove that a literary approach to the texts is wrong, only that it is new.[27] Yet it also shows that those who were closest to the actual events did not conceive that they could be purely literary creations. Since a referential approach was utilized from the beginning, we would need far better evidence than has heretofore been presented before we would jettison it.

8. A Rejection of the Sources behind the Books. As noted above, narrative critics have rightly rejected the negative results of form and redaction scholars, who have too facilely separated the stories into authentic and inauthentic portions (those which go back to the original event and those added by later communities). However, literary criticism has ignored the positive contributions as well.

While the isolation of sources is very speculative in many biblical books, it is not so in the case of Kings-Chronicles or of the Gospels. While many debate over which was the first Gospel, there is virtual consensus that they are interdependent. As I will try to demonstrate below, this plays a critical role in interpreting any individual Gospel because the evangelists were deliberately working with their sources. If the source-critical problem can be solved in any sense (and I believe it can; see the next section of this chapter) then it will play a critical part in determining the author's intended meaning. Any method that deliberately avoids this aspect can hardly claim to have found this intended meaning. While we are not creating a pre-Gospel or artificially reconstructing the events behind the text, it is another thing to ignore the external dimension altogether. We must consider both internal and external factors in order to understand a text.

9. Conclusion. There are obviously both pros and cons to the value of a literary study of biblical narrative. The problems are very real, and some are skeptical about any abiding value in the movement. McKnight goes so far as to say that "much of the good in literary criticism has already been exposed through redaction criticism in its 'composition criticism' emphases" (1988:50). He would subordinate literary criticism under the tradition-critical process. I would not go so far. Meaning is found more in the final form of the text than in the traditioning process, so if anything I would subordinate source criticism under the larger rubric of literary analysis. In fact, however, there need be no "subordination"; all aspects (historical-critical, grammatical-historical, literary) function together and inform one another in the hermeneutical process of discovering the meaning of a narrative text. All that remains is to provide hermeneutical principles for accomplishing this task and blending the components together in such a way that the narratives produce their intended goal in the life of the reader.

Methodological Principles for Studying Narrative Texts

Narrative criticism, as we have seen, has a rightful place in the pantheon of critical methodologies within the hermeneutical temple. The various factors that produce meaning in a story and that draw a reader into the narrative world within that story are clearly elucidated in this discipline. Furthermore, they have proven themselves to be valuable components of a close reading of a text; in short, they work! Yet if cut off from historical and referential meaning, they become arbitrary and subjective. Therefore, any proper methodology must blend the two (literary and historical) in such a way that they modify one another, magnifying the strengths and avoiding the weaknesses of each. I will follow the basic outline established in the section on general hermeneutics, introducing literary elements as they fall into the larger pattern.

1. Structural Analysis. We begin with a study or close reading of the text itself, looking for narrative flow and getting a preliminary idea of plot. First, this is done at the macro level, noting the development of the work as a whole. Then we analyze the micro structure of individual pericopes, or stories. Each story is broken up into its "actantial" units, its individual elements or actions. These are charted to determine how the characters interact and how the conflict ebbs and flows within both the single story and the larger narrative of which it is a part. Next, we study the effect of the setting (geographical, temporal or social) upon the plot line, and put the whole story back together in terms of its structural development.

The resurrection in Matthew (27:66-28:20) is a good example. A competent reader will note that the whole is structured along the lines of a series of encounters with Jesus' opponents. When broken into its basic units, we will note the following progression: the efforts of the priests to secure the tomb and thereby to thwart the plan of God (27:62-66) is parallelled by the misbegotten trip to the tomb on the part of the women (who expected to anoint Jesus' corpse rather than to celebrate his resurrection, 28:1). Both are overturned by the miraculous intervention of God in raising Jesus from the dead (vv. 2-4; note that Matthew favors supernatural scenes, 27:51-53) and in the angels' message to the women (vv. 5-7) and by the first appearance to the women (vv. 8-10). The second attempt to thwart God's plan occurs when the priests bribe the guards to lie about the resurrection (vv. 11-15), and this is parallelled by the disciples' doubt (v. 17). Both of these are overturned by the Great Commission (vv. 18-20). Note the contrasts between the guards (who faint for fear, v. 4) and the women (who are told not to fear, v. 5) and between the priests (who commission a lie, vv. 11-15) and Jesus (who commissions the mission, vv. 18-20). The setting is both temporal (the time notes in 27:62; 28:1) and geographical (with all the meaning of Jerusalem-Galilee noted above under "setting").

2. Stylistic Analysis. The exegete must identify the various literary devices used to present the material, then see how these techniques deepen the plot structure and highlight certain aspects within the narrative. We must look for chiasm or inclusio (framing techniques), repetition, gaps, antitheses, symbol, irony and other literary traits. Each will add a different nuance to the passage. We should also study the individual stylistic tendencies of the author and see which of those are at work in the individual pericope.

In Matthew 28 several of the basic devices are used. For instance, there is a gap in that Matthew fails to provide a description of the resurrection but allows the reader to infer it from the context. The suspense builds as the priests do everything humanly possible to stymie the plan of God, yet the marvelous contrasting scene with the power of God causing the hard-bitten soldiers to quake and faint out of fear is drama at its best. A scene of great irony occurs when the priests in their frustration are forced to bribe the guards to propound the very lie that they had begged Pilate to prevent in 27:62-66 (that Jesus' body had been stolen). The dialogue scenes lead the reader to feel this conflict between God and humanity—the manipulating machinations of the priests, the implicit rebuke by the angels, the unbelievable promises of the Risen Lord. As Kingsbury says, the central element in Matthew's plot is conflict,[28] and that is certainly true of his resurrection narrative. In fact, there is inclusio with the infancy narrative, which also centers upon the conflict between God's plan and a Jewish leader's plot (Herod's) to frustrate the divine will.

3. Redactional Analysis. For Kings-Chronicles and for the Gospels especially a source-critical and redactional study is invaluable as a supplement to the structural and stylistic studies in order to determine the distinctive emphases. At both the narrative and the theological levels redactional techniques provide a control against subjective interpretation. There are two types of approaches, and both depend upon the use of a synopsis that places the Gospels line by line next to each other. The first is more technical—a composition analysis that looks for the ways the writer used his sources. This demands a word-for-word comparison and the use of word statistics in order to determine what vocabulary was distinctly Markan or Matthean. Moreover, its results depend upon a developed theory of Gospel origins. While there is a general consensus that Mark and a collection of Jesus' sayings (called "Q") were used by Matthew and Luke, this is challenged by some. I am reasonably confident that it is correct, but still encourage readers to proceed cautiously.

The second type of redactional analysis is more useful to the nonspecialist. A comparison between the Gospels will help us to detect basic differences and to identify additions, omissions and expansions that greatly aid in determining major emphases in the text. This comparison has both external and internal criteria.[29]

Externally, the reader will look for the specific changes introduced into the text, namely the way the writer has altered his sources. The "seams" that introduce sections and provide transitions to further material in the story point to distinctive linguistic and thematic emphases, because it is at the seams that we see the writer's hand most clearly. Summary statements (such as Mt 4:23-25 and 9:35, which point to Jesus' preaching activity and frame a major section in the Gospel) provide helpful clues as to the purpose of a section. Editorial asides and explanatory additions can identify an author's distinct theology. For instance, Matthew's "formula quotations" (such as 2:5-6, 15, 17-18) are the key to his concept of fulfillment and to his messianic thrust. Thus the alterations between the Gospels or Kings-Chronicles are critical clues to the distinct purposes and stylistic characteristics of an author.

Internally, the scholar looks for the "threads" or recurring patterns and characteristic expressions that the writer uses to carry his message to the reader. The structure as a developing whole (rather than the traditions employed by the author) is now the focus of attention. The interplay of the subgenres in a section (parable, didactic material, apocalyptic in the Olivet Discourse of Mark)[30] are helpful pointers to the artistic construction of the whole. Logical points of tension and particular uncertainties in the narrative also guide the reader further into the story world of the text. For instance, the use of misunderstanding in John's Gospel has often been noted.[31] Throughout the Gospel Jesus continually refuses to answer questions directly but seems to speak over the person's head (such as Nicodemus in chap. 3). We do not read very far before realizing this is a deliberate narrative ploy, part of the above/below structure of the entire Gospel. Jesus deliberately speaks from a heavenly point of view, while his hearers respond from an earthly perspective. In this way the reader is forced to recognize the difference and make a choice. In other words the text uses this technique to encounter the reader with the demands of God in Jesus.

In summation, the interpreter studies the way the writer has arranged his materials, noting how he has utilized his sources as a control to see more clearly the specific message of the whole narrative. In other words, we combine source and redaction techniques with narrative criticism, allowing these (sometimes disparate) methods to interact and correct one another in order to understand the author's intended story and theological message.

4. Exegetical Analysis. After a detailed examination of the author's redactional choices, the scholar will next take a grammatical-historical approach to the passage, using the methods discussed under general hermeneutics above. The grammar will enable one to determine with greater precision the exact relationship of the words and therefore of the flow of the story, and semantic research will give clarity to the nuances of meaning intended. Of course, this is not necessarily done *after* steps one to three; in actuality these methods are utilized together. For instance, grammar and word studies are aspects of stylistic analysis; they are interdependent. Also, redaction-critical analysis is part of the exegetical tools utilized in studying narrative literature. Exegesis functions in some ways as a summary of the others; in other ways it provides a control, for many narrative studies have neglected serious exegesis, and the results have been less than satisfactory.

Background data is also exceedingly critical for narrative research. These stories are written within a culture that is no longer known to us; without these details we can recover only the surface plot but never the deeper significances. Of course, these aspects are not done separately from the redactional study above; rather, these are part of a holistic study of the narrative, including the narrative techniques, the writer's use of his sources and the grammatical-historical configuration of the text.

5. Theological Analysis. The scholar must separate the detailed emphases within a single passage from the major theological threads that link them to the major section and the book as a whole. These will yield the major and the minor points of the passage. Both dramatic and theological aspects are found within stories; the theological dimension relates to the propositional component and the dramatic to the dynamic or commissive (related to praxis) component of meaning.

The interpreter must relate to both aspects of the passage. As we are drawn into the narrative world of the story, the drama forces us to interact with the plot and characters and to align with the implied reader. At the same time the theological lessons penetrate through the drama, and we learn even as we react to the story. These two elements of interpretation are interdependent and should not be separated. Theology without praxis is sterile, and praxis without theology is contentless. For instance, Matthew's resurrection narrative (see points 1 and 2 above) centers upon Christology, teaching that Jesus is the Risen Lord and finalizing Matthew's major stress on Jesus as the divine Son of God who has the authority of Yahweh (v. 18) and is omnipresent (v. 20). At the same time it teaches the futility of opposing God's plan and the privilege of discipleship. Finally, the Great Commission (28:18-20) culminates the First Gospel's emphasis on the universal mission "to all nations" (v. 19).

6. Contextualization. This step is the core of biblical narrative, which asks the reader to apply the lessons to one's own situation. Narrative at the heart is a contextualization of the significance of the life of Israel (Old Testament), of Jesus (the Gospels) or of the early church (Acts) for the later community of God. For the Gospels there is the *Sitz im Leben Jesu* (the situation in the life of Jesus) and the *Sitz im Leben Kirche* (the situation in the life of the church community for which each Gospel was written). The latter aspect was the evangelist's inspired contextualization of the life of Jesus for his church. This makes it natural to apply it to our own needs today. In every sense biblical narrative is theology seen in living relationships and enacted in story form.

At the same time, narrative demands a reaction to the drama itself. Therefore, we cannot read it without reliving and applying the conflicts and lessons. Like the disciples we stand in awe and worship Jesus. With Jesus we submit to the Father; for us too discipleship means to "take up the cross," even if like many of them "the cross" involves our own martyrdom. I discussed the method in the section on the "implied reader" above. Our task is to "identify" with the intended "reader" of the text and allow the story to guide our response. Many (e.g., Robinson 1980:123-24) believe that narrative preaching should employ indirect rather than direct contextualization. There is some truth in this for the original Gospels seldom spelled out their points explicitly. However, if we become too indirect, the intended message becomes lost in a sea of subjectivity. I prefer to "suggest ways and means" (see pp. 349-52) and to guide the congregation's involvement with the significance of the story for themselves.

7. Use a Narrative Form for the Sermon. Contextualization means to move from exegesis to sermon (chaps. fifteen and sixteen). For biblical stories this involves what Greidanus calls "the narrative form."[32] Instead of a "three-point" sermon constructed logically around the main points of the text, this form of sermon follows the contours of the biblical story itself, retelling the drama and helping the congregation to relive the drama and tension of the unfolding narrative. Here the background information becomes a sermonic tool, drawing the audience into the original setting and thereby enabling them to experience anew its message. Many practitioners of the "story sermon" argue strongly against the use of sermon "points" here (Buttrick renames them "moves") on the grounds that this replaces the emotional power of the text with cognitive data. Yet this is disjunctive thinking. If there are two or three parts (or "moves") of the story in the text, it would be natural to construct the sermon around them.

Moreover, I also oppose the current tendency to deny the theological dimension on the grounds that narrative is indirect rather than direct. This ignores the results of redaction criticism, which has demonstrated that biblical narrative is indeed theological at the core and seeks to guide the reader to relive the truth encapsulated in the story. Narrative is not as direct as didactic material, but it does have a theological point and expects the reader to interact with that message. My argument is that biblical narrative is in some ways even better than the teaching applied to similar situations in the lives of the people.

Biblical narratives contain theology, and as stated above there are principles or themes that are intended for the reader. At the same time, however, they are still primarily stories and therefore should be proclaimed as such. If the task of the preacher is always to enable the hearers to be drawn into the world of the text and to feel its evocative power, this is doubly true of narrative, for which this is its primary purpose. The key to the narrative sermon is that the plot line of the story controls its outline. In this way the "actantial" units become the "points" of the sermon, although it is better to think of "movements" (the "acts" of a play) rather than points (which are better for a didactic sermon).[33]

After completing the six steps above, the preacher will try to incorporate the elements (plot development, dialogue, theological emphases, reader identification) into a dramatic sermon that recreates the original contextualized message for today. Using background, preachers will want to retell the story in such a way that the congregation will re-experience, even relive, it and also see the relevance that its message has for their contemporary needs. As the story is retold, application (or reader identification) will suggest itself in natural ways within the story. As in parable preaching, it is important to separate local color (those aspects which are part of the story) from theological emphases (those aspects which should be recontextualized for our day). The former will help the hearers to be drawn into the story and feel its power, and the latter will help them to see its relevance for their needs. There is little need for illustrations from modern life. The story form is filled with illustrations from within itself, and they lead naturally into application. That is why narrative preaching has even greater potential for motivating and persuading than does didactic preaching; the latter describes Christian truths while narrative preaching acts out these truths in "life situations."

7
*P*oetry

I T WAS NOT UNTIL THE REVISED STANDARD VERSION OF 1952 THAT THE ENGLISH READER was made aware of the true place of Hebrew poetry in the sacred canon. Previous versions had put only the Psalms into poetic format, but the Revised Standard did so with all biblical poetry. There are many songs in narrative books (Gen 49; Ex 15:1-18; Deut 32; 33; Judg 5; 1 Sam 2:1-10; 2 Sam 1:19-27; 1 Kings 12:16; 2 Kings 19:21-34) and poetry comprises entire prophetic books (Hosea, Joel, Amos, Obadiah, Micah, Nahum, Habakkuk, Zephaniah) as well as extensive portions of others (Isaiah, Jeremiah, Jonah, Zechariah). Much more of the Old Testament is poetry than just the more widely known books like Psalms, Proverbs, Lamentations, Song of Songs or Job. Poetry is therefore a device that cuts across other genres, being a major rhetorical technique in wisdom and prophetic literature.

The meaning and theology of the Psalms are very disputed today. The tendency for much of this century has been to place each psalm within the larger *Sitz im Leben* (historical situation) of ancient Israel's cultic life (such as Albright, Freedman). This diachronic approach uses the poetic works to reconstruct the patterns and thinking of Israel's developing worship. Others, however, following the new literary criticism (see appendix one), consider each psalm a separate unit and seek only its individual artistic world (Alonso-Schökel 1960). However, the majority of scholars refuse to separate the corporate (the psalm as part of Israel's cultic worship) and the individual (the psalm as the product of a particular author) aspects. They are interdependent and should be studied together (see Gerstenberger 1985:424-25 and Brueggemann 1988:ix-x). In fact, Gerstenberger distinguished several stages from the individual to the family or tribe to national religious identity centering upon the temple (1988:33-34). There are individual as well as corporate psalms, and each plays a somewhat different role in the religious formation of Israel's hymnody.

It is crucial to understand how Hebrew poetry functions. It has rightly been pointed out that no portion of Scripture is more widely read than the psalms. In pocket versions of the New Testament the psalms are often appended, and in most worship services they are still sung or chanted regularly. The extent to which the psalter is quoted in the New Testament shows its importance in the life of the early church. Yet the psalms are not easily understood. The parallelism and metrical patterns are often difficult to unlock, and the unwary reader can read far more into the parallel statements than the context actually warrants. Moreover, many (like lament or imprecatory psalms) seem to be inapplicable at first glance. In addition, scholars and pastors often overexegete the imagery or metaphors in Hebrew poetry and give it more theological weight than they should. It is necessary to understand something of the form and function of Semitic poetic patterns in order to make sense of them.

The Form of Hebrew Poetry

1. Metrical Patterns. Poetry can be identified both by metrics or rhythm and by parallelism of grammar and language. The former is useful primarily to specialists and does little to aid preachers, so I will not spend undue time on it. Yet a basic knowledge of metrics is important in order to enable the reader to gain some feel for Hebrew poetry. No one has yet discovered a formula for unlocking the secret of Semitic rhythm. As Freedman notes, every poem seems to bear different marks (1977:10-12). Scholars are divided as to whether to grade the structures via stress or syllable counts. Both depend upon a knowledge of Hebrew and of phonetics. Stressed units refer to the oral side of poetry and divide a line on the basis of the syllables the Hebrew reader stressed as he recited a verse. For instance, Psalm 103:10 divides along the following stresses:

Not on the basis of our sins/ does he deal/ with us,

Nor on the basis of our iniquities/ does he make payment/ against us.

Syllables are the basic units of speech, and many like Freedman believe they provide a more accurate and identifiable basis for structuring a poem. For instance, Psalm 113 has fourteen-syllable lines divided 7:7 and on occasion 8:6.

Yet not all poems are so easy to demarcate on the basis of either plan. There is simply too much variation and each poem in Scripture must be studied on its own merits. The most we can say is that rhythm is one of the major identifying marks of Hebrew poetry. Using stress lines, scholars have divided psalms into 2:2, 3:2, 2:3 and many other patterns. Dividing by syllables has produced any number of patterns, with ten- or twelve- or fourteen-syllable lines. Moreover, strophes or verses are made up of two (as Ps 103:10 above) to five lines of parallel ideas. Within these there can be a myriad of forms, as the metric pattern and the parallelism are intertwined. In fact, many scholars believe that the two systems may represent stages in the development of Hebrew poetry. While this remains speculative and unverifiable, the fact remains that the poet's choice of language depended to an extent upon metrical considerations. At the same time, sound (including not only metrics but oral reading, alliteration, onomatopoeia and such like) was often determinative in the choice and clustering of words in the strophes of the poem (Gerstenberger 1985:413-16).

In short, the interpreter dare not assign more meaning to individual terms than the whole psalm will allow. Word studies are not as determinative in the Psalms as they are in the New Testament Epistles, and meaning is derived more by the whole than by the parts. For all these reasons we must focus our attention more on parallelism than on metrics.

2. Parallelism. In 1750 Bishop Robert Lowth developed the position generally advocated in modern times, of three basic types of parallelism: synonymous, synthetic and antithetical. Most still follow this today (such as Gerstenberger, Murphy, Gray). However, a growing number of scholars (such as Kugel, Alter, Longman) are challenging this theory, arguing that it virtually reduces poetry to prose by "flattening out the poetic line" (Longman). They assert that the second line always adds meaning; in some fashion it clarifies the first. This latter approach is not only gaining ground of late; it is approaching consensus among younger scholars. One could say that it is "winning by a landslide." Yet I have an uneasy feeling that twenty years from now scholarship may have come back to a middle position. The truth might indeed lie somewhere between the two.

As in so many areas there are not simply two types—synonymous (where the terms mean the same idea) and synthetic (where the second adds a new idea) but many gradations between the two. Some passages exhibit virtually identical meanings (see below), but in some the second adds a slight nuance and in others a great deal of meaning is added to the first. I will seek to demonstrate this below. The many studies pointing to word-pairs (a fixed stock of synonyms that were used regularly) mitigates against the view that there is always development between lines (for a good survey, see LaSor, Hubbard, Bush 1982:314-15). Pairs like earth/dust, enemy/foe, Jacob/Israel, voice/speech, people/nation and similar combinations point toward synonymous parallelism on occasion. Context as always must decide each case.

a. *Synonymous parallelism* occurs when the second line repeats the first with little or no added meaning. Often this includes grammatical parallels, as the second line matches the first grammatically (such as prepositional phrase, subject, verb, object) and possibly also matches in meaning. The interpreter in some instances should not read too much into the semantic variation between the two lines, for that could be intended more as a stylistic change for effect. On the other hand, there is frequently an added point, and this leads Alter, Berlin et al. to challenge the traditional approach. For instance, many point to Psalm 2:2-4 as an example of synonymity. Let us consider each pair at a time. Psalm 2:2a states,

> The kings of the earth take their stand
> and the rulers gather together

While the subjects ("kings of the earth"/"rulers") are probably synonymous, there is development between "take their stand" and "gather together," for the second implies the treaty that follows the "stand." The same is true with verse 3,

> "Let us break their chains," they say,
> "and throw off their fetters."

Certainly "chains" and "fetters" mean the same thing, but there is progression from "break" to "throw off." It is unlikely that these are merely stylistic differences.

On the other hand, consider Isaiah 53:5:

> But he was pierced for our transgressions,
> he was crushed for our iniquities;
> the punishment that brought us peace was upon him,
> and by his wounds we are healed.

The first two lines more likely exhibit synonymous parallelism, for the word pairs "pierced/crushed" and "transgressions/iniquities" do not exhibit significant variation in meaning. Proponents of the synthetic approach argue that the second line intensifies the first and so is not purely synonymous. Yet there is no new idea added; so it could still be labeled "synonymous parallelism." The latter two lines are clearly synthetic. Line three speaks of the means and line four the result. More difficult is the parallel idea in Psalm 103:3.

who forgives all your sins
and heals all your diseases.

Some interpret the second line as physical healing. Certainly the Bible sees a connection between spiritual and physical healing; the two are combined often in Jesus' healing miracles (such as Lk 5:20). Yet we must be careful not to overexegete poetic parallelism in this light. While such is certainly possible, in Psalm 103 it is debatable. The two word pairs—forgives/heals and sins/diseases—often are synonymous in Scripture and in this context I would argue that one should not add physical to spiritual healing. The parallelism may be too strong, with the verb therefore referring to spiritual healing. The recent tendency, however, is to see the second line as a reference to physical healing.

b. *Step parallelism* is also called "synthetic parallelism" and refers to a development of thought in which the second line adds ideas to the first. Some doubt the validity of this category because the further meaning destroys the "parallelism." Yet it is a poetic form and should be noted. In fact, it is far more common than synonymous parallelism. A well-known example is Psalm 1:3,

He is like a tree planted by rivers of water,
which yields its fruit in its season
and its leaf does not wither.
Whatever he does prospers.

There are three "steps" here, from planting (line 1) to fruitfulness (line 2), to endurance (line 3), to a bountiful harvest (line 4, which drops the metaphor). Often the development is so stark that many think there is no parallelism at all. For instance, Jeremiah 50:19b reads:

But I will bring Israel back to his own pasture,
and he will graze on Carmel and Bashan;
his appetite will be satisfied
on the hills of Ephraim and Gilead.

There is some development in the first two lines (some would call it synonymous, but the thought moves from returning to the peaceful grazing awaiting Israel). The second pair may repeat the idea of line two, with the parallelism due to metrics rather than meaning. However, there the movement is from the act of grazing to the results (appetites satisfied). Yet consider also Psalm 139:4,

Before a word is on my tongue
you know it completely, O Lord.

There is no parallelism here, for the second line completes the idea of the first.

In conclusion, the reader must always let the lines themselves dictate where they lie on the scale from synonymous to synthetic to nonparallelism (metrical). I must admit that my own studies have convinced me that Berlin and Longman are mostly correct when they say that the tendency in Hebrew poetry is to add further nuances in the second line. Nearly every so-called example of synonymity I have seen in my studies (such as Ps 19:1; 103:7, 11-13) has turned out to exhibit some degree of synthetic development. Alter summarizes this school of thought when he asserts that "an argument for dynamic movement from one verset to the next - [sic] would be much closer to the truth, much closer to the way the biblical poets expected audiences to attend to their words" (1985:10). Yet while this is indeed "closer to the truth," it may well be that the new school is also guilty of excess when it states that there is "always" movement.

Let us consider Proverbs 3:13-20, another text commonly used as an example of synonymous parallelism. Nearly every pair actually exemplifies step parallelism, as verse 16,

> Long life is in her right hand,
> in her left hand are riches and honor.

or v. 17,

> Her ways are pleasant ways,
> and all her paths are peace.

Yet v. 14 is virtually synonymous,

> for she is more profitable than silver
> and yields better returns than gold.

One could argue that the second line makes the first more vivid (the same could be said of Is 53:5), but that is hardly a difference in meaning. In short, I would conclude that in some instances (such as Is 53:5; Prov 3:14) there is no further clarification and therefore they would fit the normal meaning of "synonymous parallelism." Though some nuance (vividness or concreteness) may be added, there is still synonymity. When there is added meaning the extent of synthetic (or formal) development will differ from case to case; exegetical study will be needed to decide.

c. *Climactic parallelism* is a type of step parallelism, but here several units build the thought to a climax. For instance, consider Psalm 8:3-4 (vv. 4-5 are quoted in Heb 2:6b-8a):

> When I consider your heavens,
> the work of your fingers,
> the moon and the stars,
> which you set in place,
> What is man
> that you think of him,
> and the son of man
> that you care for him?

The first four lines build upon one another in a sense of steps to the climactic denouement in the parallel lines of verse 4. Otto Kaiser speaks of a particular kind of climactic parallelism in which the second line repeats the key word of the first then adds the climactic thought (1975:322). For example, Psalm 29:1,

Ascribe to the Lord, O mighty ones,
ascribe to the Lord glory and strength.
Ascribe to the Lord the glory due his name
worship the Lord in the splendor of his holiness.

d. *Antithetical parallelism* reverses the stress of the others and is the third of the major types (with synonymous and synthetic). Instead of building upon an idea, the second line is contrasted to the first. However, it still constitutes parallelism, for the second line restates the idea of the first by asserting the opposite. For instance, Proverbs 3:1 says,

My son, do not forget my teaching,
    but keep my commands in your heart.

Both units state the same idea but in opposite ways. However, in other cases the antithesis has elements of synthetic parallelism in which the second adds further clarification; for instance, Psalm 20:7 says,

Some trust in chariots and some in horses,
But we trust in the name of the Lord our God.

The first line tells what not to trust and the second what to trust. Note also Proverbs 1:7:

The fear of the Lord is the beginning of knowledge,
but fools despise wisdom and instruction.

The wise and the foolish provide the major contrast in the book, but there is clear development from "fear of the Lord" (line one) to "wisdom" (line two). This is paralleled by the upright vs. wicked contrast, as in 3:33,

The Lord curses the home of the wicked,
but blesses the home of the righteous.

e. *Introverted parallelism* is a particular type of antithetical parallelism, in which two lines are contrasted with two others. Often it is presented in chiastic fashion, where the external pairs are contrasted with the internal pairs (AB BA), as in Psalm 30:8-10 from the Masoretic Text (Mickelsen 1963:326):

Unto thee, O Jehovah, I was crying
Unto the Lord I was imploring favor.
    What is the profit in my blood?
        in my going down into the pit?
    Will the dust praise thee?
    Will it make known thy truth?
Hear, O Jehovah, and be gracious to me
Be a helper for me.

f. *Incomplete parallelism* occurs when one element from the first line is omitted in the second; this normally occurs in synonymous lines, as in Psalm 24:1, where the predicate is missing:

The earth is the Lord's
    and everything in it
The world and all who live in it.

g. The *ballast variant* occurs when the second line compensates for the missing element by adding a further thought (Kaiser 1981:220, from Cyrus Gordon). This occurs more frequently than the pure incomplete form, as in Psalm 18:17:

He rescued me from my powerful enemy,
From my foes, who were too strong for me.

3. Poetic Language and Imagery. The psalmists used many of the rhetorical techniques discussed in previous chapters, such as synonymity, climax and chiasm. In addition, they used paronomasia (play on words), alliteration (where the lines begin with the same letter of the alphabet), acrostics (each line beginning with a successive letter of the alphabet) and assonance (similar sounding words). Paronomasia is exemplified in Isaiah 5:7, "He looked for justice *[mišpāṭ]* but there was only bloodshed *[mispāḥ],* for righteousness *[ṣᵉḏāqâh]* but there was only weeping *[ṣᵉᶜāqâh].*" Psalm 119 provides a good illustration of both alliteration and acrostics. The strophes of this magnificent hymn, which celebrates the Word of God, begin with successive letters of the alphabet and within each strophe the lines all begin with the same letter (for other acrostic poems, see Ps 25; 34; 37; 111; 112; Lam 3). Assonance is seen in Jeremiah 1:11-12, where God shows Jeremiah an "almond branch" *(šāqēḏ)* and connects this with the promise that he is "watching over" *(šōqēḏ)* his people. Kaiser seeks an English equivalent: "God showed Jeremiah a 'pussy-willow branch' and said, 'This is what I *will-a-do* to my people if they do not repent' " (1981:227; italics his).

The use of figurative imagery in poetry is particularly rich. The poets constantly reach into the everyday experiences of the people to illustrate the spiritual truths they are espousing. In Psalm 1:3-4 the psalmist contrasts the righteous, who are "like a tree planted by streams of water, which yields its fruit in season" with the wicked, who are like "chaff that the wind blows away." Such similes are found throughout poetry (Job 30:8; Ps 31:12; Prov 11:12; Is 1:30).

Metaphors are even more frequent. In an especially suitable metaphor, Amos 4:1 addresses the "cows of Bashan . . . who oppress the poor . . . and say to your husbands, 'Bring us some drinks.' " In Psalm 19:1-2 creation is personified as a herald ("The heavens declare the glory of God, the skies proclaim the works of his hands") and as a foreign emissary ("There is no speech or language where their voice is not heard"). Metaphors to depict God naturally are particularly apt. God is pictured as an enthroned king, a shepherd, a warrior, a charioteer, a father, a shepherd, a rock, a refreshing pool and much, much more.

Such imagery draws the readers into the text and forces them to picture the truth in a new way. When God is asked to "take up shield and buckler; arise and come to my aid" (Ps 35:2) the idea of God as the victorious warrior who fights alongside his people adds rich meaning to this psalm, which asks God's help against David's former friends who are slandering him. The potential of such imagery for preaching is great indeed! Every instance is an illustration waiting to be uncovered.

In conclusion, identifying the type of parallelism is a critical aid to interpretation. This will help us to avoid reading too much into successive lines and to identify the key elements of the passage. When the structural patterns are combined with the imagery employed within them, a rich devotional as well as preaching experience results. Yet the richness added by metaphors has a corresponding problem—lack of specificity and accuracy. As Gerstenberger says, "Poetic language breaks through the confines of rationalistic world views, intuitively approaching the essence of things. Therefore, the use of comparative, inductive, indirect language is imperative for the poet" (1985:416-17). In such cases one does not seek "literal" meaning but rather "intended" meaning, that is, the meaning intended in the context of the poem. For instance, Psalm 44:19 states, "But you crushed us and made us a haunt for jackals," which means a desolate uninhabitable area. The psalm itself talks about a crushing military defeat (see vv. 9-16) and this recapitulates that defeat in a section protesting Israel's innocence before God (vv. 17-22). While the defeat was indeed serious, metaphors such as "a haunt for jackals" and "sheep to be slaughtered" (v. 22) constitute poetic license describing the unremitting enmity and suffering Israel experienced from her hostile neighbors.

Types of Poetry
Semitic poetry had its origin in the religious life of the people, both corporate and individual. Prose was inadequate to express the deep yearnings of the soul, and poetry as an emotional, deep expression of faith and worship became a necessity. The many types of religious need called for different types of hymns. Hebrew poetry was not recreational but was functional in the life of the nation and its relationship with Yahweh. Poetry had a worship function in mediating between the people and God and a sermonic function in reminding the people of their responsibilities before God. The Psalms, for instance, were not peripheral as hymns often are today but were a focal point of the service both in temple and in synagogue. It is not without reason that prophetic utterances from God were so frequently given in poetic form. Not only were they more easily remembered, but they were also more emotive and powerful in their message.

1. War Songs. War songs were one of the earliest forms of poetry. The call to arms of Exodus 17:16, the war cry of Judges 7:18, 20 (and perhaps of Num 10:35-36), according to many, have poetic overtones. The best-known are the victory songs of Moses (Ex 15:1-18) and Deborah (Judg 5); note also the song of victory over the Moabites in Numbers 21:27-30 and the shorter cry regarding David's military prowess in 1 Samuel 18:7; 21:11; and 29:5 ("Saul has slain his thousands, David his tens of thousands"). While in the latter case the dependence upon God was not stressed, most others dwell rapturously upon the hand of God stretched out against the enemies of Israel. The glory belongs to Yahweh, who shares the spoils and the honor with his people.

2. Love Songs. Love songs constitute a second category of poetry. The Song of Songs, which has mystified scholars for centuries, comes immediately to mind. Childs notes five different ways the book has been interpreted throughout history (1979:571-73): (a) Judaism and the early church (as well as Watchman Nee, among others, in modern times) allegorized it as picturing the mystical love of God or Christ for his people; (b) some modern scholars have seen it as a postexilic midrash on divine love (similar to the first option); (c) a common view sees it as drama, either of a maiden with her lover (the traditional view) or with three characters (as the king seeks to entice the maiden away from her lover); (d) most modern critics see no structural development but believe it is a collection of secular love songs, perhaps modeled on praise hymns; and (e) a few believe the book uses love imagery for purposes of cultic ritual and was used in the festivals of Israel.

Of these the third and fourth have the greatest likelihood; my personal preference is to see it as a lyric poem describing the love relationship between the beautiful maiden and her lover, described both as a rustic shepherd and as a king. Since both pictures relate to David and by extension to his son Solomon, I see no reason to follow the more complex (and difficult) three-figure drama. Nor do I see the structure as so loose that it represents a mere collection of poems. The central feature is certainly the love between the two. The poem has only a slight plot structure, and the love relationship is as strong at the beginning as at the end. Therefore it is pre-eminently a love song,[1] and would be excellent in a marriage seminar.[2]

3. Lament. The lament is the most common type of psalm. More than sixty laments are found in the psalter. These include both individual (such as Ps 3; 5—7; 13; 17; 22; 25—28; 31; 38—40; 42—43; 51; 54—57; 69—71; 120; 139; 142) and corporate (such as Ps 9; 12; 44; 58; 60; 74; 79—80; 94; 137) laments in which the person or nation cries out its anguish to God. David uttered two outside the psalms, for Saul and Jonathan (2 Sam 1:17-27) and for Abner (2 Sam 3:33-34). Such hymns both agonize over the situation and petition God for help.

Hayes notes seven common themes in the structure of lament psalms (1976:58-59): (a) address to God (such as the cry of dereliction taken up in Ps 22:1, "My God, my God, why have you forsaken me?") often with a confession of faith (71:1, "In you, O Yahweh, I have taken refuge; may I never be put to shame"); (b) description of distress, often highly figurative (57:4, "I am in the midst of lions . . . whose teeth are spears and arrows"), at times presented as concern regarding himself (69:2, "I sink in the miry depths") or even as a complaint against God (44:9, "Yet you have rejected and humiliated us"); (c) plea for redemption, both for deliverance (3:7a, "Arise, O LORD! Deliver me, O my God!") and the defeat of his enemies (3:7b, "For you have struck all my enemies on the jaw; you have broken the teeth of the wicked"); (d) statement of confidence or trust in Yahweh (12:7, "O Yahweh, you will preserve us; you will protect us from this generation forever"); (e) confession of sin (25:11b, "Pardon my guilt, for it is great") or affirmation of innocence (17:3-5, "You have tested me and found nothing. . . . I have avoided the paths of the violent . . . my feet have not slipped"); (f) a vow or pledge to do certain things if God grants the request (56:12, "I must present vows to you, O God; I will render thank offerings to you"), often involving a reminder to God of his covenant commitments (74:18, "Remember this, O Lord"); (g) conclusion, which may be in the form of praise (57:11, "Be exalted, O God, above the heavens; let your glory be over all the earth") or restatement of the request (80:19, "Restore us, O Lord God Almighty; make your face shine upon us, that we may be saved"). Few psalms contain all these elements. Nevertheless, these do constitute the basic lament.

The value of such psalms for every believer is obvious. Whether one is ill (Ps 6; 13; 31; 38; 39; 88; 102), beset by enemies (3; 9; 10; 13; 35; 52—57; 62; 69; 86; 109; 120; 139) or aware of sin (25; 38; 39; 41; 51), the lament psalms offer not only encouragement but models for prayer. Many have claimed that one should pray them directly; I agree but prefer to meditate, contextualize and then pray these psalms as they reflect upon my own situation.

4. Hymns or Praise Songs. Hymns or praise songs are the nearest to pure worship of any type of biblical poetry. They are not the product of sorrow or need but directly celebrate the joy of worshiping Yahweh. This is an important reminder of the true purpose of the Christian life as expressed in the Westminster Confession, which says that the goal of man is to "glorify God and enjoy him forever." Nearly all hymns contain the same structure: calling upon Yahweh (139:1, "O Lord, you have searched me and you know me"); a call to worship (111:1, "I will extol the Lord will all my heart"); a motivation clause praising Yahweh and giving the reasons for worship, often centering upon God's attributes and deeds (111:2, "Glorious and majestic are his deeds"); and a conclusion repeating the call to praise, often including a series of blessings (111:10, "to him belongs eternal praise").

Fee and Stuart note three specific types of hymns (1981:176-77): Yahweh is praised as Creator (Ps 8; 19; 104; 148), as protector and benefactor of Israel (66; 100; 111; 114; 149) and as Lord of history (33; 103; 113; 117; 145—47). Several hymns go into detail regarding God as in control of history by recapitulating the great salvation events in the life of Israel (78; 105—106; 135—136). These recapitulate Israel's failures and contrast them to God's faithfulness, calling upon the nation to renew its covenant pledge. Such hymns were sung at harvest celebrations and festivals, at pilgrimages to the temple (84; 87; 122; 132), after military triumphs (Ps 68; 1 Macc 4—5) and at special occasions for joy. The Hallel psalms (113—118) formed a special part of the Passover celebration and were also a regular part of the synagogue service. The development of these psalms from the divine compassion for the oppressed (113) to his redemptive power (114) and help to Israel (115) to Israel's praise and thanks to Yahweh (116—118) provides as fresh and meaningful a worship experience today as it did when originally written and sung.

5. Thanksgiving Hymns. More specific than hymn or praise songs, thanksgiving hymns thank God for his answers to specific prayers. We could almost say they form the "before" and "after" of religious trust, with the lament placing the problem before God and the thanksgiving praising him for his response. Like the laments, thanksgiving hymns divide into individual (Ps 18; 30; 32; 34; 40; 66; 92; 103; 116; 118; 138) and corporate (65; 67; 75; 107; 124; 136) expressions. In the life of the people they would be sung after God had delivered them from the calamity that led to the lament. Such is the form of Jonah's prayer from the belly of the great fish (2:2-9), expressed as a thanksgiving that re-enacts the crisis (vv. 2-5) and the repentance (vv. 6-7), then vows to sacrifice to Yahweh and repay the debt (v. 9). In addition to thanking God for his deliverance, such psalms regularly pledge future fidelity and worship to God (18:49, "Therefore I will praise you among the nations, O Yahweh") and specifically give the glory to Yahweh for the defeat of the psalmist's enemies (18:39, "You gave me strength for battle; you subdued my adversaries") or his recovery from illness (30:3, "O Lord, you raised my soul from Sheol; you rescued me from those who descend into the grave").

There are six structural elements in thanksgiving songs (Gerstenberger 1988:15; see also LaSor, Hubbard, Bush 1985:519-20):

Invitation to give thanks or to praise Yahweh (Ps 30:2, 5 [RSV 1, 4]; 34:2-4 [RSV 1-3]; 118:1-4)

Account of trouble and salvation (Ps 18:4-20 [RSV 3-19]; 32:3-5; 40:2-4 [RSV 1-3]; 41:5-10 [RSV 4-9]; 116:3-4; 118:10-14)

Praises of Yahweh, acknowledgment of his saving work (Ps 18:47-49 [RSV 46-48]; 30:2-4, 12-13 [RSV 1-3,11-12]; 40:6 [RSV 5]; 92:5-6 [RSV 4-5]; 118:14, 28-29)

Offertory formula at the presentation of sacrifice (Ps 118:21; 130:2; 138:1-2; Is 12:1)

Blessings over participants in the ceremony (Ps 22:27 [RSV 26]; 40:5 [RSV 4]; 41:2 [RSV 1]; 118:8-9)

Exhortation (Ps 32:8-9; 34:10, 12-15; 40:5; 118:8-9)

Several psalms (11; 16; 23; 25; 27; 62; 91; 111; 125; 131) praise God for his beneficent protection and invoke faith in his loving care. These hymns are very meaningful in stressful situations and provide valuable parallels to New Testament teaching on trust in God (such as 1 Pet 5:7).

6. Songs of Celebration and Affirmation. Songs of celebration and affirmation encompass several types of hymns that celebrate God's covenant relationship with the king and the nation (Fee and Stuart 1981:176-77). These hymns were at the heart of Israel's sense of self-identity and so can rightly be placed under a single rubric, even though most scholars separate them. At the heart are the psalms of covenant renewal (50; 81) probably sung at the annual covenant ceremonies and valuable for a sense of spiritual renewal today. The Davidic covenant psalms (89; 132) celebrate God's choice of David's lineage and have messianic implications. As such these psalms affirm the election and calling of Israel to be God's special people.

The royal psalms contain several types. The coronation psalms (2; 72; 101; 110) and enthronement psalms (24; 29; 47; 93; 95—99) were written to depict the implications of the accession to the throne, with its ritual crowning, swearing in before Yahweh, anointing with oil and receiving the homage of the people. The enthronement psalms may have gone beyond the single coronation to encompass an annual ceremony celebrating the kingship. The view of some scholars that they also teach the enthronement of Yahweh over Israel is based on slim evidence and is not as likely. The obvious messianic implications of these psalms often have overshadowed the deep theological significance of each within the life of the nation. We must seek to understand their historical meaning before plumbing their eschatological features. Other types of royal psalms are the lament (89; 144), thanksgiving for victory (18; 118), war preparation (20; 27) and royal wedding (45). In each case the king is central.

Another type of psalm, Songs of Zion, praises God for his gift of Jerusalem, the Holy

City. The history of Jerusalem, from its connection to Abraham and Moses to its choice by David as the new capital is sung and its sacred name, Zion, is central. Hayes elaborates the themes (1976:42-52). The annual pilgrimage required by the Torah, a sacred and joyous occasion, is central in Psalms 84 and 122. The entrance into the sanctuary after the pilgrimage is celebrated in Psalms 15 and 24. The Songs of Zion per se (46; 48; 76; 87; 125) proclaim God's election, his protection of the sacred city and temple, and the security of the city against its enemies. Therefore, the pilgrims and indeed the nation are bidden to behold God's works there.

7. Wisdom and Didactic Psalms. Wisdom and didactic psalms (1; 36; 37; 49; 73; 119; 127; 128; 133) parallel Proverbs in the celebration of wisdom as God's great gift to his people and its connection to the inscripturated Word and Torah. The people are called to a new awareness of their privilege and responsibility to heed the divine wisdom via spiritual purity and obedience. As in Proverbs, the way of the righteous is contrasted with that of the wicked (Ps 1; 49; 73) and the prosperity of the faithful is promised (1; 112; 119; 127—128). The high ethical quality of these songs makes them directly accessible to the modern Christian.

8. Imprecatory Psalms. Imprecatory psalms (12; 35; 52; 57—59; 69; 70; 83; 109; 137; 140) are usually lament psalms where the writer's bitterness and desire for vindication are especially predominant. This leads to such statements as Psalm 137:8-9, "Happy is . . . he who seizes your infants and dashes them against the rocks." Such statements are shocking to modern sensitivities and cause many to wonder at the ethical standards of the biblical writers. However, several points must be made. The writer is actually pouring out his complaint to God regarding the exile, as in Psalm 137. Also, he is heeding the divine command of Deuteronomy 32:35 (Rom 12:19), "Vengeance is mine, I will repay." Finally, as Fee and Stuart note, the author is calling for judgment on the basis of the covenant curses (Deut 28:53-57; 32:25), which make provision for the complete annihilation of the transgressors, even family members (1981:183). The hyperbolic language as noted above is common in such emotional passages.

In short, these do not really contradict the New Testament teaching to love one's enemies. When one can pour out one's animosity to God, that very act opens the door to acts of kindness akin to Romans 12:20 (Prov 25:21-22). In fact, meditation upon and application of these psalms could be therapeutic to those who have suffered traumatic hurt (such as child abuse). By pouring out one's natural bitterness to God, the victim could be freed to "love the unlovely." We must remember that the same David who penned all the above except for Psalms 83 and 137 showed great mercy and love to Saul.

Poetry in the New Testament

While the presence of hymns and poetic passages is not nearly so predominant in the New Testament, it is clearly present and plays an important role. Gaebelein notes five kinds of poetic passages (1975:813-14): (1) quotations from ancient poets (Acts 17:28, from Epimenides in the Mars Hill address; 1 Cor 15:33, the aphorism of Menander of Athens);

(2) fragments of hymns (1 Tim 3:16; Phil 2:6-11); (3) poetic passages following Hebraic forms (the hymns of Lk 1—2); (4) passages lacking meter but containing the exalted expressions of poetry (the Beatitudes of Mt 5:3-12 or the Johannine prologue, 1:1-18); (5) apocalyptic imagery containing hymnic portions (Rev 4:8, 11; 5:9-10, 12-13). Of these the two most important for our purposes are the hymns of Luke 1—2 and the creeds and hymns of the Epistles.

It is clear that New Testament poetry has close affinities with Old Testament patterns. Most of the characteristics described above can be demonstrated in the New Testament. The Magnificat alone has

(1) synonymous parallelism

My soul glorifies the Lord

and my spirit rejoices in God my Savior (Lk 1:46-47)

(2) synthetic parallelism

He has performed mighty deeds with his army

he has scattered those who are proud in their inmost thoughts (Lk 1:5)

and (3) antithetical parallelism

He has brought down rulers from their thrones

but has lifted up the humble (Lk 1:52)

In the New Testament, especially in the Epistles, the hymns demonstrate the highest level of theological expression. The creeds and hymns utilize poetic format to present cardinal New Testament doctrines, especially christological truth, often centering upon the humiliation and exaltation of Christ (Phil 2:6-11; 1 Tim 3:16; 1 Pet 3:18, 22; see also Eph 2:14-18; 5:14; 1 Cor 13:1-13; Heb 1:3-4; and possibly Jn 1:1-18). These hymns provide excellent evidence for the possibility of blending the poetic format and the highest possible theological message in biblical times.

Theology in the Psalms

Many modern critics, stressing the "poetry" and "art" of the Psalms, argue against theological content and prefer to think of the "world" portrayed in the Psalms. Yet it is also true that biblical poetry expressed the deepest dimensions of the faith of ancient Israel, especially the view of God. In fact, theology is central to biblical poetry. Israel's cultic hymnody is so vast that any attempt to systematize it will never be able to capture its grandeur and depth. Yet those themes which are central to the Psalms are certainly worthy of such a pursuit. Primarily, the Psalms center upon worship and prayer; they demonstrate better than any other biblical genre Israel's God-consciousness. They make no actual theological statements, but their very God-centeredness is highly theological. Every area of life is related to God, and he is seen as sovereign over all. As Craigie points out, the framework for this is provided by the covenant concept: "Their knowledge of God is rooted in covenant; they respond to God in prayer, in praise, or in particular life situations because of an existing covenant relationship which makes such response possible" (1983:40). Primarily, the covenant God is portrayed in intimate relationship to his people, and in this sense the psalms reflect popular religion, for they reflect the life of faith essential to every child of God, from the king to the common person.

The first step in determining the theology of the psalms as a whole as well as of individual psalms is to consider genre. Each type has a distinctive message. The lament centers upon suffering and trials, the royal psalm upon king (and Messiah at times) and imprecatory psalms upon relating to one's enemies. In every case, however, divine sovereignty and covenant promise are central. Secondarily, the Psalms celebrate the ethical responsibility of God's people as they relate to him in faith and apply that to everyday life. "Righteousness" in the psalms is life-related, depicting the moral life practiced by those who have experienced God's mercy. It is primarily a relationship with God and then the life of faith that results.

The second key is holistic exegesis. Due to the highly poetic nature of the Psalms and the constant metaphors, the interpreter must read the parts in light of the whole. Hyperbole (in the imprecatory psalms) is frequent, and so archetypal themes must be developed by looking at the psalm as a whole and by noting the theological thread that links various psalms with similar themes.

Third, all the controls mentioned with respect to wisdom writings apply to the Psalms as well. The reader dare not interpret individual statements like the all-encompassing promise of prosperity to the righteous in Psalm 1 apart from the larger context of the Psalms as a whole. Some psalms (such as Ps 1) stress the positive side of the life of faith; others (such as Ps 39) center upon the negative side, the transitoriness of existence. As Ridderbos and Craigie state, "The Psalms as a whole reflect a fully rounded wisdom on the nature of human life in relation to God, whereas the individual Psalms may contain only a part of the larger picture" (1986:1038).

Finally, every aspect must relate in some way to Israel's cultus, its ritual worship system. Even the wisdom orientation reflected primarily Israel's celebration of her life and walk before God. In this sense the Psalms are a celebration of life, stressing the fact that existence has no meaning without the divine presence and imprimatur. Most scholars agree that every psalm was utilized in Israel's worship. Corporate laments and thanksgivings most directly reflect this orientation, but even individual psalms were secondarily related to the cultus. Interpretation must recognize this formal setting, for the theology is derived from this purpose.

Hermeneutical Principles

While each of these categorical descriptions of biblical poetry has been helpful, they have not clearly told us how to approach and interpret properly the poetic passages.

1. Note the strophic (stanza) patterns of the poem or hymn. As mentioned earlier, structure is the first step of exegesis. The primary element of Hebrew poetry is the pattern of parallel lines and strophes. The newer translations aid the reader by placing the lines side-by-side, indenting the parallelism, and leaving a space between the strophes. The most important criterion for discovering a break between strophes is thought-development. For instance, in Psalm 31 the first strophe (vv. 1-5) is David's plea for help, the second (vv. 6-8) contains his statement of trust and the third (vv. 9-13) has his complaint. Stylistic changes also indicate new strophes. In Psalm 30 the first stanza (vv. 1-3) addresses God, the second the saints (vv. 4-5), the third returns to the relationship between

the psalmist and the Lord (vv. 6-7), the fourth (vv. 8-10) is a direct prayer and the fifth (vv. 11-12) describes the results. Furthermore, chiasm or alliteration distinguish strophic divisions. In Psalm 119 the acrostic outline is quite clear, with eight lines in each stanza and each stanza beginning with successive letters of the alphabet. The effect of *Selah* is more debated, since no consensus has been reached as to its meaning. Kaiser correctly calls for caution, due to the use of the term in awkward places (such as in titles or in the middle of strophes) but tentatively accepts its use in some cases to distinguish strophes (Ps 46 but not in Ps 57; 67—68).[3]

2. Group parallel lines. The poet is expressing his thought in whole units using very emotive, colorful language. As stated above, the interpreter must walk a fine line between reading too much into individual lines and assuming synonymity whenever the thoughts are similar. Dahood mentions a thousand word-pairs or synonymous terms that are used in both Ugaritic and Hebrew poetry (1976:669). The reader must avoid the temptation to see too great a difference in meaning in such situations. Yet at the same time the context must indicate whether or not the clauses are totally synonymous. For instance, the three lines of Psalm 23:2-3a form a single unit and should be interpreted together:

He makes me lie down in green pastures;

He leads me beside the quiet waters.

He restores my soul.

David is not speaking chronologically. The restoration of the soul in line three states the basic meaning of the imagery presented in the first two lines. Further, it is important to note the type of parallelism. We do not have purely synonymous parallelism. As Craigie notes (1983:207), the "meadows" may recall the "holy pasture" (Ex 15:13) that was the goal of the exodus from Egypt, and the "quiet waters" may echo the "resting place" associated with the ark in the wilderness wanderings (Num 10:33). Therefore, the imagery adds a sense of divine guidance and protection from the exodus and the wilderness wanderings to David's current experience. The basic idea is similar, but the second line adds a nuance to the first.

3. Study the metaphorical language. In poetry the figurative language is more predominant and at times more difficult to understand than it is in prose. Psalm 19 with the "heavens" declaring the glory of God is not meant to teach Hebrew cosmology, nor does Psalm 121:1 ("I will lift up my eyes to the hills") mean God lives there. Yet the background to such imagery adds richness and depth to the understanding of the psalm. One can hardly overstate the beauty of Psalms 23 or 121, seen in the evocative symbolism of the shepherd and Sinai metaphors. Yet the imagery of the imprecatory psalms (see above) must be studied carefully from the standpoint of the covenant curse. Theology rarely stems from the metaphor itself but rather from the whole context of which it is a part. Here structural considerations will tell the reader how the metaphor fits into the whole message. Determining whether climactic parallelism, chiasm, inclusio or repetition controls the psalm is the first step to deciding how the metaphors interact to produce the psalm's message.

4. If possible, note the historical background to the psalm. In many cases the traditional title of the psalm will provide this. While these titles were added later and are not

part of the canonical Scriptures, they are generally reliable traditions, although scholars differ as to how reliable they are. They contain five different kinds of data: the author or person(s) connected to the psalm, historical background, musical notations, liturgical comments and the type of psalm (for example, Ps 120, "A song of ascents"). What interests us here are the historical notes, found in the titles of fourteen psalms (3; 7; 18; 30; 34; 51; 52; 54; 56; 57; 59; 60; 63; 142), all connected to David's life. Many doubt the authenticity of the titles, arguing that they were added at a later stage of the tradition; namely, when they were added to the canon, citing the fact that by the time of Christ (as evidenced in the Septuagint) most of the psalms have titles (see Childs 1971:137-50). Others give the titles canonical force and argue for their full authenticity on the grounds that there is no evidence these psalms ever existed without the titles (see Archer 1964:428-33).

However, it is probably best to take an optimistic but cautious approach to the titles (see Longman 1988:40-42 and Ridderbos and Craigie 1986:1031). On the whole, there is little reason to doubt the basic trustworthiness of the titles; such information has been discovered on similar ancient psalms, and it was likely a common ancient practice. Yet at the same time we cannot assume that the Masoretic traditions were always accurate, and we must check the historical note by the context. In most cases the title fits quite well. In some instances, however, there are difficulties. For instance, Psalm 30 is a hymn of thanksgiving for deliverance from a serious illness, yet the title calls it "For the dedication of the temple" (or house). On the basis of the title some link this psalm with 1 Chronicles 21—22, specifically with God's lifting the plague in 21:14-30, leading to the preparations for building the temple in chapter 22. Yet others (such as Craigie and Longman) doubt this since it is an individual psalm and contains little that would relate directly to temple liturgy and worship. On the whole, it is best to be cautious in such instances.

Commentaries will help the reader to deal with these issues psalm by psalm. The content of the psalm itself helps even more. To add the historical material from the biblical records makes the message of the psalm come alive. For instance, the title tells us that David wrote the penitential Psalm 51 after Nathan had confronted him with the sin of his liaison with Bathsheba (2 Sam 12). The depth of his spiritual agony and of his repentance are given added meaning in light of its historical occasion. Counselors would do well to make this psalm required reading for others who fall prey to sexual temptation and sin! An excellent sermon series would be to preach several of the Davidic psalms chronologically (on the basis of superscriptions) as they relate to incidents in David's life.

5. Study the psalm in terms of its type and basic stance. Each category of psalm elucidated above (lament, praises, royal) must be studied differently. Some overlap (such as the royal lament) and should be interpreted accordingly. The statements about God and his relationship to his people differ markedly from type to type, and the applicability to present circumstances also changes. Those who wish to worship God will prefer a praise psalm to a lament, while those who are depressed about God's seeming absence from their lives clearly need the latter.

6. Study the messianic psalms in terms of their historical purpose before noting their

eschatological import. Psalms 2; 8; 16; 22; 40; 45; 69; 72; 89; 102; 109; 110 and 132 have in part or in whole been seen as messianic. Yet they also have historical dimensions primarily in terms of David's situations. Both dimensions must be noted and combined to catch the full meaning of the text. The interpreter must first exegete the psalm to determine the author's intended meaning. Many of the "messianic psalms" may not have been intended messianically but may have been understood as such in a typological sense (see Osborne 1988:930-31). In such cases we would see the psalm primarily in its original sense and secondarily in its canonical/messianic sense. Of course a detailed discussion is not possible here but this general caution may prove helpful (see also Payne 1975:940-44).

7. Study the psalm as a whole before drawing conclusions. The thought flow of the psalm is critical to its meaning. This also follows general hermeneutical guidelines as elucidated in chapters one through five. After noting the basic structure of a passage and exegeting the details it is necessary to return and rework the whole before elucidating its meaning. The Psalms intend to be understood as literary units, for they were written individually on single occasions. Therefore, it is even more true of poetry (than of prose) that the whole is the key to the parts.

8. New Testament poetry must be studied on two levels. Since the creeds and hymns are often being quoted, they may have had a liturgical meaning in the life of the church before their incorporation into the particular New Testament passage. Moreover, each had a "canonical" status, and so that meaning has importance for us as well. The first level is the original theological meaning, and the second level is the use of the creed or hymn in the individual context. Philippians 2:6-11, for example, must be understood first as an incarnation hymn (its original meaning) and second as a model for Christian attitudes (its use in the context of Phil 2:1-11).

8
Wisdom

O NE OF THE LEAST-KNOWN OF THE BIBLICAL GENRES IS WISDOM LITERATURE. THE OLD TESTA-
ment books placed under this rubric are Job, Proverbs and Ecclesiastes. In addition I would add the apocryphal books Sirach (Ecclesiasticus) and the Wisdom of
Solomon. Few people know quite what to make of these works, and even fewer sermons
are preached from this body of literature. When they are preached, however, they are
frequently misused to support an almost secular lifestyle. The reason is their subject
matter. Preachers often have defined wisdom as "the practical use of the knowledge that
God gives." Yet Georg Fohrer defines it as "prudent, considered, experienced and competent action to subjugate the world and to master the various problems of life and life
itself" (1971:476). Its goal is to use properly God's creation and to enjoy life in the present
under his care. Since wisdom writings deal so constantly with the pragmatic side of life,
it is easy to misuse them to support an earth-centered lifestyle.

Yet this very aspect makes wisdom literature so valuable for the modern Christian who
seeks a relevant religion. Jesus and the early church recognized this, and the New Testament contains numerous wisdom themes (see below). All ancient religions had to cope
with life's problems, and as a result all developed wisdom teachings. Egypt and the entire
region of Mesopotamia had wisdom traditions, and it is likely that the Israelites took
these traditions and reworked them on the basis of their Yahwist theology. Central to
all these traditions is the concept of the "wise man"; not as one who escapes the world
but as one who learns to live in the world with God's guidance and help. There is no
body of literature as practically ordered as wisdom, and this alone makes its value
immense.

Characteristics of Wisdom
Scholars continue to debate whether wisdom is primarily a perspective on life, hence a
theological construct, or a body of literature (note the similarities to the debate on
apocalyptic). I believe that wisdom is first a way of life and then a genre. Primarily
wisdom is a theological pattern of thinking that applies the "wisdom" of God to practical
issues of life. This attitude results in wisdom sayings and then in larger bodies of literature
that collect such sayings (such as Proverbs, Sirach) or discuss wisdom themes (such as

Job, Ecclesiastes). I will deal with the generic aspects below. Those characteristic patterns which define a "sapiential understanding of reality" (von Rad, Sheppard, Murphy) are the subject of this section. Before we can exegete wisdom sayings properly, it is important to understand how they function within the life and mindset of Israel.

1. A Practical Orientation. A practical orientation is the basic characteristic of wisdom thinking. The proverbs and sayings help the young initiate take his proper place in society. The "wisdom" of the past is handed down to the young in order that the societal order and mores might continue unabated. Therefore, the collected sayings center upon proper etiquette and speech (Prov 29:20, "Do you see a man who speaks in haste? There is more hope for a fool than for him"), self-control (25:28, "Like a city whose walls are broken down is a man who lacks self-control"), family relationships (10:1, "A wise son brings joy to his father, but a foolish son grief to his mother"), material wealth (11:4, "Wealth is worthless in the day of wrath, but righteousness delivers from death"; but compare 10:22, "The blessing of the Lord brings wealth, and he adds no trouble to it"), as well as topics like why the righteous suffer (the book of Job) and the evil prosper (Ps 49; 73). Kidner lists the following subjects discussed in Proverbs: God and man, wisdom, the fool, the sluggard, the friend, words, the family, life and death (1964:31-56). These topics provide the best possible evidence for the pragmatic nature of wisdom literature. The value of this for Christian life today is also obvious; few portions of Scripture are more directly applicable to the modern age.

However, it is critical to heed the strong caution of Fee and Stuart in this regard (1981:188). They note three ways wisdom books are misused. First, people tend to take the sayings out of context and misapply them in literalistic fashion. For instance, Proverbs 10:22 (on God blessing one with wealth) is preached as God's wanting all believers to prosper materially, while in reality it is part of the larger contrast between the righteous and the wicked in chapter 10 and must be tempered by other passages on the place of poverty (see 17:5; 18:23) in God's plan. Second, many Christians fail to define properly wisdom terms like *fool* in Proverbs 14:7 ("Stay away from a foolish man, for you will not find knowledge on his lips"). *Fool* refers to the unbelieving pagan who ignores God and follows self; it cannot be applied to the uneducated or to other believers regarded as "fools" because of theological differences. Third, people do not note the line or argument in a text and apply what the biblical text shows is actually wrong. For instance, Job 15:20-22 ("All his days the wicked man . . . despairs of escaping the darkness") is often preached as meaning that unbelievers are actually unhappy. However, Job denies (17:1-16) this speech by Eliphaz, and practical experience (as well as Calvin's doctrine of common grace) shows the erroneous nature of such a statement.

When applying practical wisdom teaching, it is crucial to use the exegetical tools at one's disposal in order to ascertain what the text meant originally before applying it to the modern situation. It is a dangerous practice to apply wisdom statements casually without noting what they do not say as well as what they say. When the author's intended meaning speaks directly to Christians today, however, it yields a rich treasure. Not only should there be more sermons from this portion of Scripture, but wisdom sayings should also be utilized much more frequently as secondary texts to anchor the application of other Scriptural texts.

2. Dependence on God. Dependence on God is the other major theme of wisdom literature. In the past scholars often have said that this genre was originally secular and became religious only at a later stage of development. However, few today make this claim for the Mesopotamians or Egyptians (see below), let alone for the Hebrews. As Morgan says, "The evidence available confirms the view of those who maintain that Israelite wisdom, as it has been passed down to us in wisdom and non-wisdom literature, was thoroughly Yahwistic" (1981:145). The many variables and paradoxes faced in life forced the wise person to recognize his limitations and depend upon God as the true source of wisdom. Proverbs 9:10 (compare 2:5) shows this: "The fear of the Lord is the beginning of wisdom, and knowledge of the Holy One is understanding." God is seen as sovereign (Prov 16:4, 9; 19:21; Job 38—42), omnipotent (Job 38:31-33; Wisdom of Solomon 6:7; 8:3), omniscient (Prov 15:3; 21:2) and as both Creator (Prov 14:31; Job 28:23-27; 38:4-14) and Judge (Prov 15:11; 16:2).

Crenshaw notes three aspects of the religious dimensions (1976:24-25). Although he believes they are successive stages of "theologization," I prefer to think of them as parallel constituents of wisdom thinking. First, wisdom links daily experiences with the centrality of God's covenant. Since Yahweh alone rewards virtue and punishes vice, the faithful must place every aspect of experience, domestic and social as well as religious, in his care. Second, the divine presence transcends the prophetic, sacrificial or priestly spheres. The divine presence also is felt in the practical life of God's people; divine Wisdom dwells in their midst. Third, wisdom is especially identified with Torah. While Crenshaw sees this as a late development found primarily in Jesus Ben Sira, the Torah link is identifiable in several places, such as the connection between the "commandments" and wisdom in Proverbs 3:1-12 and 4:4-5. In short, the connection between Torah and wisdom had its foundation in the earlier period, though its explicit expression came later.

I would add a fourth characteristic of wisdom, the tendency to personify wisdom as an extension of God himself, seen in one sense as a "craftsman" standing alongside of and aiding the God of creation (Prov 8:29-30), as a female teacher inviting students to learn from her at the gates of the city (Prov 1:20-21; 8:1-36) and as a hostess inviting people to her banquet (9:1-12). Wisdom is contrasted with the adulteress (2:16-19; 7:6-27) and with the foolish hostess (9:13-18).

Central to wisdom is the overriding concept of the "fear of the Lord," combined in Job 1:1; 28:28 as well as Proverbs 3:7; 8:13; and 16:6 with the ethical maxim, "turn away from evil." These are two sides of the same coin. Nel discusses the combination of the ethical ("fear" as denoting a prior relationship with God) and the cultic ("fear" as denoting obedience to the Torah and the religious cult) in Israel and its wisdom literature (1982:97-101). The "fear of the Lord" is the milieu or sphere within which true wisdom is attainable. Therefore, wisdom does not connote the acquisition of cognitive knowledge but rather is lived as an ethical concept. It comes from "listening" to the Lord[1] and obeying his precepts (Prov 1:5, 8; 2:2). The other side of this is an active opposition to evil. The "wicked" are the antithesis of the wise (Job 27:13-23; Ps 1:1-6; Prov 1:20-33) and will inexorably move toward their own destruction (Prov 5:23; 10:21). Evil is pictured as a wanton woman luring the foolish down the path to death (Prov 2:16; 5:1-14; 9:13-18). The wise both avoid and oppose evil (Prov 14:16; 16:6). Again we see that one cannot discuss the religious orientation without discussing the practical ethical overtones. The two go hand in glove.

3. Indirect Authority. In the past many argued that there was an absence of authority, and that wisdom derived its influence from tradition or from its practical value (from the fact that it worked). This view has been drastically revised, primarily due to the realization that the Yahwistic perspective behind wisdom thinking is paramount. However, the name of Yahweh never becomes the source of the wisdom tradition itself (unlike prophecy), nor do we find explicit formulas of the type used by the prophets, such as "Thus says the Lord." Therefore, divine authority is presupposed but not explicitly enunciated. Others argue that the family or the educational system provided the authority. This is extremely unlikely. While family and school may have played important roles in the development of wisdom thinking (see below), neither is ever mentioned as the force behind the movement itself.

Nel is closer to the truth when he notes that each wisdom admonition draws its authority from within, particularly from the motivating clause attached to it (1982:90-92). It is the "intrinsic truth" embedded in the saying that demands obedience. Therefore, in a sense all three of those mentioned above (God, tradition, experience) played a role in the indirect authority of the wisdom promulgations. For instance, Proverbs 2 demands that the reader adhere to wisdom and centers its motivation upon the fact that God is the source of wisdom (vv. 6-8), that wisdom will please the soul (vv. 10-11), that evil (the "strange woman"; compare vv. 12-17) destroys (vv. 18-19) and that the righteous inherit the land (vv. 21-22). God is behind the whole but the practical benefits are stressed and the reader is expected to adhere to the admonitions for all these reasons.

4. Creation Theology. An emphasis on creation is part of the basic fabric of Old Testament wisdom thinking (see Zimmerli 1976:175-99 and Hermisson 1978:118-34). Here it closely parallels Egyptian wisdom, which centered upon the "order" of life. This of course is at the heart of the theodicy of Job. The argument is that God created the world in the way that he saw fit and humans should not question the divinely appointed order. All wisdom literature, not just Job, develops this theme. Human beings must take their proper place in the cosmos, find their appointed life and make the most of it. Since the Lord has made both "ears that hear and eyes that see" (Prov 20:12), a person must use all the senses under the rules God has established.

We should note two aspects of this theology. First, the principle of retribution governs the universe. The same God who created the universe remains in control; the actions of the righteous and the wicked in the final analysis must answer to him alone. Since God is ruler as well as judge of the world, he will reward the pious and punish the wicked, as in Proverbs 11:21, "Be sure of this: the wicked will not go unpunished, but those who are righteous will go free" (also Prov 10:27; 12:21; 13:25). Of course common experience often challenged this, and the writers had to deal with the problem of the wicked person's prosperity. They did so by declaring that such is only illusory and will end in folly when God's inevitable judgment comes (Ps 73:18-20, 27). Death, the great equalizer, will show the fleeting nature of their so-called glory (Ps 49:14-20). The wise therefore want to discover and then submit to the will of God (Prov 16:1-3).

Closely connected is the second aspect of creation theology, the polemic defending the concept of divine justice. Crenshaw notes the union of creation theology and theodicy in Job and Qoheleth (Ecclesiastes) (1976:28-32). Both books deal with what could be called a crisis in wisdom theology, namely the twin problems of evil and the suffering of the innocent. Both books provide the same answer, our inability to comprehend the divine order. God's justice transcends human frailty, and our duty is to await his answers. Rather than assume the right to determine the laws of God's created order (Crenshaw calls this "Titanism"), we must humbly submit to God's greater wisdom.

The Forms of Wisdom Literature

We can identify several subgenres within this body of literature, each with its own distinctive traits and rules for identification. It is important for us to delineate these characteristics in order to develop a proper hermeneutic for wisdom sayings.

1. The Proverb. The basic and most prominent wisdom form, a "proverb" (Heb. *mashal)* may be defined as a brief statement of universally accepted truth formulated in such a way as to be memorable. As noted above, proverbs are found in Scripture other than just in the book of Proverbs (such as in Gen 10:9; 1 Sam 24:14). There are many different types of sayings, and several of the genres described below are called *meshallim* in the Old Testament, such as allegory (Ezek 17:1-10), aphorisms (Eccles 9:17—10:20), popular sayings (Jer 23:28), discourse (Num 23:7, 18) or similitudes (1 Sam 10:11). There are also several types of proverbs per se, such as the instruction (Prov 22:17—24:22), the wisdom saying or speech (9:1-6), admonition or prohibition (8:24-31, 33), the hortatory proverb or counsel (22:28), the numerical proverb (6:16-19), synonymous (22:22-27) or antithetical (11:1-31) proverbs and factual or experiential statements (17:27).

Most important, we dare not read more into the proverbial statement than is there. By their very nature they are generalized statements, intended to give advice rather than to establish rigid codes by which God works. As Hubbard states, ancient wisdom "tends to emphasize the success and well-being of the individual," unlike "the prophets' marked emphasis on national and corporate religious life" (LaSor, Hubbard, Bush 1982:545). For instance, Proverbs 16:3 states "commit to the Lord whatever you do, and your plans will succeed." This seems to promise an unlimited bounty of plenty, but as Fee and Stuart point out it is hardly meant to include any ill-conceived plan dedicated to God: "A hasty marriage, a rash business decision, an ill-thought out vocational decision—all can be dedicated to God but can eventually result in misery" (1982:198). As in Joshua 1:8 or Psalm 1:3 the meaning of "success" or "prosperity" must be understood first in terms of the divine will and only second in a materialistic sense. What is successful in God's eyes may appear quite opposite to worldly standards. The interpreter must recognize the general nature of the sayings and apply them via the analogy of Scripture, that is in keeping with other biblical teaching that fills out the truth being elucidated.

2. The Saying. Although sayings include proverbs (see Murphy 1982:4-5), I chose to discuss proverbs separately since they are so basic to wisdom literature. The saying is not quite as developed a form and has not attained the universal "stature" of the proverb. Sayings are often local, connected to a particular setting in the life of the people (such as Gen 35:17; 1 Sam 4:20), and are didactic in purpose. Murphy notes two types. First, the experiential saying describes actual situations, but remains open to clarification. These are observations but not fixed rules. For instance, Proverbs 11:24 ("One man gives freely, yet gains even more; another withholds unduly, but comes to poverty") does not give advice but merely states what occasionally happens. Proverbs 17:28 ("Even a fool is thought wise if he keeps silent, and discerning if he holds his tongue") describes what sometimes is the case but is not even a general rule. Second, the didactic saying is less general and intends to inculcate a particular value, such as Proverbs 14:31, "He who oppresses the poor shows contempt for their Maker, but whoever is kind to the needy honors God." The behavior expected is obvious; this type of saying is closer to the proverb, for it has more literary polish.

Often these sayings are collected into a general discussion or instruction on a topic. This is especially true of Proverbs 1—9, which discusses extensively the wise man versus the fool and righteousness versus evil. We could also place the wisdom psalms and Ecclesiastes under this rubric. The instruction often concludes with a pithy statement that Childs calls a "summary-appraisal" (1967:129-36). He finds this specifically in Isaiah 14:26-27; 17:14b; and 28:29, and finds wisdom parallels in Psalm 49:13; Job 5:27; 8:13; 18:21; 20:29; 27:13; Ecclesiastes 4:8; Proverbs 1:19; and 6:29. Proverbs 1:19 summarizes the discussion of the way of evil (vv. 10-18) by saying, "Such is the end of all who go after ill-gotten gain; it takes away the lives of those who get it."

3. The Riddle. Riddles are found in their pure form only in Judges 14:10-18 (the riddle Sampson gave the Philistines about the honey and the lion). This of course is not wisdom literature in itself, but the strong use of riddles in the ancient Near East has led many scholars to propose a riddle form behind such numerical proverbs as Proverbs 6:16-19 (six things the Lord detests) and 30:15-31 (vv. 15-17, four things never satisfied; vv. 18-20, four things not understood; vv. 21-23, four things under which the world trembles; vv. 24-28, four things small yet wise; vv. 29-31, four things with a stately bearing).

4. The Admonition. Nel has shown that the admonition is another basic wisdom form (1982). In its regular pattern the admonition is followed by a motivation clause that tells the hearers why they should adhere to the command, as in the parallel statements of Proverbs 9:9:

Admonition	Motivation
Instruct a wise man	and he will be wiser still
teach a righteous man	and he will add to his learning

The admonition can be positive (a command) or negative (a prohibition, such as Prov 22:24-25), while the motivation clause in both instances relates the practical consequences of the action entailed. Obviously, the whole statement is intended to convince the hearer of the wisdom of following the injunction. At times the motivation clause may not be stated (Prov 20:18)[2] or may be implicit (Prov 24:17-18; 25:21-22), but at all times commands are meant to stimulate response and obedience.

5. The Allegory. Although it is found often in Mesopotamian and Egyptian wisdom, the allegory can be demonstrated explicitly only twice in the Old Testament: in the series of figurative statements on the evils of adultery and blessings of marriage in Proverbs 5:15-23 and in the extended metaphor on old age and death in Ecclesiastes 12:1-7. In passages using highly figurative language (see chap. seven), it is important to divine the imagery and try to determine the reality pictured behind it. The images of Ecclesiastes 12:1-7 are quite difficult; for instance, in verse 5 does the "almond tree" signify gray hair and the "grasshopper" the brittle limbs of the elderly, or are they more literal images depicting an advanced time of life? Either way, the picture of advanced age leading to death is certainly the meaning of verses 5-6.[3]

6. Hymns and Prayers. Hymns and prayers abound in all ancient wisdom literature (see Crenshaw 1974:47-53). This is not only true in the case of the wisdom psalms but also occurs in the many poetic sections in the wisdom books (Job 5:9-16; 9:5-12; 12:13-25; 26:5-14; 28; Prov 8; Sirach 24:1-22; Wisdom of Solomon 6:12-20; 7:22—8:21; 11:21—12:22). The two major themes of wisdom hymns are the glorification of wisdom and thanksgiving to God as Creator and Redeemer. Wisdom allows us to participate in the creative power of God and to experience his deliverance. Wisdom prayers are based upon the prose prayers of Solomon (at his dedicating the Temple, I Kings 8:23-53), Ezra (Ezra 9:6-15) and Daniel (Dan 9:4-19). Its developed form is restricted to extracanonical literature (such as Sirach 22:27—23:6; 36:1-17; 51:1-12; Wisdom of Solomon 9:1-18).

7. The Dialogue. While several forms are found within the book of Job (such as the lament, the courtroom drama, the confession), the dialogue is the primary subgenre in Job. The book is organized around a series of dialogues between Job, his friends and God. Crenshaw links this form with the "imagined speech" in which the thoughts of an adversary are rhetorically presented and then refuted.[4] Such is utilized also in Proverbs 1:11-14, 22-23; 5:12-14; 7:14-20; 8:4-36 and Wisdom of Solomon 2:1-20; 5:3-13.

8. The Confession. The confession is autobiographical and employs the problems experienced by the sage as an example for others. Qoheleth (Ecclesiastes) would certainly rank as an example; there Solomon frankly confesses his struggle with the presence of God and meaning in a vain, secular world. This is especially exemplified in 1:12—2:26, which on the basis of Egyptian parallels has been called a "royal confession" because it shows the emptiness of life that often surrounds the throne. On occasion Job pours out his heart before his friends and God (29—31; 40:4-5; 42:1-6). Finally, Proverbs 4:3-9 (from the time he was a child Solomon was told to seek wisdom) and 24:30-34 (a personal glimpse of the dangers of laziness) rank as confessions. In each of these the personal experiences of the sage are used to drive home the truthfulness of the argument.

9. Onomastica. Wisdom lists, or onomastica, have been recognized since the work of von Rad (1955:267-77). He showed that the series of questions posed by God in Job 38 is paralleled by the Egyptian wisdom work, the Onomasticon of Amenemope. In both cases the cosmic creative acts of gods are enumerated. Von Rad correctly refused to posit a direct relationship between them but rather argued that the genre was common to the two cultures. He finds parallels in Psalm 148 as well as Sirach 43. Crenshaw adds Job 28; 36:27-37, 40—41; Psalm 104 and other apocryphal parallels (1974:258-59). These branch out from creation to other fields like psychology and even the trades (Sirach 28:24—29:11) or to a standard curriculum of the wise man (Wisdom of Solomon 7:17-20).

10. Beatitudes. Found frequently, beatitudes add a distinctly theological tone. One of the best known is Psalm 1:1, "Blessed is he who does not walk in the counsel of the wicked," and explicitly religious are Psalm 112:1, "Blessed is the man who fears the Lord" and Proverbs 28:14, "Blessed is the man who always fears the Lord" (see also Eccles 10:17; Prov 3:13; 8:32-34; 14:21; 16:20; 20:7; 28:14; 19:18). These others are more general, shading over perhaps into motivation statements, promises of a happy and prosperous life, of God's blessings to follow.

Wisdom in the New Testament
A current fad labels much of the New Testament "wisdom," considers Jesus a "teacher of wisdom" and labels entire books (such as Hebrews or James) wisdom literature. While certainly there is some exaggeration in claims that Jesus primarily taught within the wisdom tradition, there is also a certain amount of truth. The definition of wisdom as ethical instructions or maxims demonstrating the centrality of God in the daily affairs of life fits much New Testament teaching. Aspects of the Sermon on the Mount (such as the Antitheses, Mt 5:21-48) and the emphasis upon holy conduct parallel Jewish wisdom. Practical exhortations like Romans 12; James 1—3; the paraenetic portions of Hebrews (3:12-19; 4:11-13; 6:1-12), social codes (Eph 5:22—6:9; 1 Pet 2:11—3:7), vice or virtue lists (Gal 5:19-23; Col 3:5-17) all partake of wisdom influence. In addition, 1 Corinthians 1—3 centers upon the problem of worldly versus divine wisdom (with the cross as the centerpiece of divine wisdom), and 1 Corinthians 13 is a wisdomlike paean to love. As with poetry, New Testament wisdom is similar to Old Testament wisdom and should be interpreted with the same hermeneutical criteria.

Hermeneutical Principles
As we have seen, wisdom literature can be difficult to interpret and apply. A basic hermeneutical error today is the tendency to take biblical statements out of context. General statements become absolute commands when interpreters fail to note the strong

clarification added when they consider the whole of Scripture on a particular issue. For instance, many today take Proverbs 1:8 ("Heed, my son, your father's instruction and do not forsake your mother's teaching"; compare 6:20) as enjoining children to obey their parents no matter what and to trust the Lord to make right any erroneous teaching or commands on the parent's part. Some say that if a parent tells a child to quit attending church or taking part in Christian activities, the child must obey. Yet this is to extend the passage beyond its intended meaning and to ignore the many proverbs enjoining the parents to responsibility (such as 4:1-9; 22:6). Moreover, it fails to consider the example of the disciples (Acts 4:19; 5:29), who, when faced with the command from the Sanhedrin to refrain from their Christian duty, said, "We must obey God rather than men."[5] It is ironic that those who demand absolute obedience to parents never tell the children that they must heed parental teaching on humanism or sexual freedom; yet these parables deal more with teaching than with commands! In light of this and other interpretive problems let us note some basic hermeneutical guidelines.

1. Note the form of the wisdom saying. Is it a proverb or longer didactic saying? Is it allegorical? If it is a dialogue or imagined speech, is it presented as a correct or incorrect saying? As I have shown above, each subgenre has its own rules for interpretation, and noting the type of saying is essential for understanding. For instance, when Proverbs 15:25 says, "The Lord tears down the proud man's house, but he keeps the widow's boundaries intact," the reader must note the metaphor behind the statement. It is erroneous to take it literally. "It is a miniature parable, designed by the Holy Spirit to point beyond the 'house' and the 'widow' to the general principle that God will *eventually* right this world's wrongs, abasing the arrogant and compensating those who have righteously suffered (cf. Matt. 5:3, 4)" (Fee and Stuart 1981:200).

2. Ask whether the context is important. Proverbs 1—9 and 30—31 each have a lengthy discourse style, and context is important. The rest of the book is primarily a collected series of proverbs, and context becomes less relevant. I would interpret Proverbs 10—29 on the basis of each proverb's parallelism (the lines interpret each other) and collate similar proverbs, interpreting them together. While context is often important, it is helpful to collect the various proverbs into topical or subject lists, then to note the cross-referential influence of similar sayings upon one another (Kidner's commentary on Proverbs is a good example of what I mean).

This is critical in perhaps the most widely misused statement in Proverbs, "He who spares the rod spoils the child" (13:24). First, "spoil" is not quite correct; the verse should say, "He who spares the rod hates his son." Second, the context adds a clarifying statement, "But he who loves his child disciplines him with care." This does not enjoin the type of heavy-handed beatings administered by several sects recently; in fact, just the opposite. It calls for careful, gentle punishment. Third, this is one of the places in chapters 10—29 where context is important; the saying is placed within a completely positive context in chapter 13, with the wise son following the father's discipline (v. 1). The whole emphasis is on the way of righteousness. Therefore, corporal punishment is only one part of a larger pattern of positive discipline, as one seeks to raise a child "in the discipline and instruction of the Lord" (Eph 6:4).

Context is equally important when interpreting Job and Qoheleth. We discussed Job above, so here I will turn to Ecclesiastes. The entire book until the conclusion is a lengthy, at times almost rambling, discourse on the meaninglessness and futility of life (compare "vanity" in 1:2; 12:8, which most interpret as "meaningless" or "futile").

At key intervals the discussion is sprinkled with more positive statements, but on the whole the specter of death leads the preacher almost to decry the validity of a pious life (compare 2:15; 3:19; 5:16; 8:14). Some have seen hints of a positive outlook,[6] and the writer is hardly denying the presence and power of God or the place of happiness in life. However, Solomon writes as one who takes a predominantly secular view of life. His advice on living life to the full (5:11-15; 8:15; 11:8-10; 12:1-8) exemplifies this approach, and he adds that death removes the final value of it all (compare 2:16; 9:5-10; 11:8). Indeed, there seems at first glance to be an almost schizophrenic outlook on life, as the writer in one passage affirms the importance of reverence and dependence on God, then in another passage elucidates a pessimistic hedonism.

Yet this need not be. The key is the epilogue (12:9-14), written in the third person as a "theological commentary" on the rest of the book (Sheppard 1977:182-89). The book ends with "Fear God, and keep his commandments; for this is the whole duty of man" (12:13).[7] Verse 13 shows that the book throughout was written for a similar purpose as Romans 7—8, namely to show the emptiness of a life lived apart from God and the wisdom of living in the fear of God. We must understand the negative verses in light of the larger context, specifically the positive statements and especially the concluding epilogue. Sermons on Ecclesiastes could draw on current critiques of society (such as Henry Fairlie, *The Seven Deadly Sins Today,* or Christopher Lasch, *The Culture of Narcissism*) and produce a highly relevant series of messages.

3. Determine whether hyperbole is present. Many statements deliberately exaggerate or generalize the truth presented, and we must detect such situations. For instance, Proverbs 3:9-10 argues, "Honor the Lord with your wealth . . . then your barns will be filled to overflowing." This could be taken as a guarantee that the Christian farmer or businessman will be blessed with plenty in terms of this world's goods. Yet the very next verse commands one not to "despise the Lord's discipline," and 23:4-5 says, "Do not wear yourself out to get rich. . . . Cast but a glance at riches, and they are gone." The earlier passage is saying simply that God will repay all that one sacrifices for him. Fee and Stuart point out that such proverbs are not "legal guarantees from God," nor are they meant to be followed absolutely (1981:198-99). Rather, they are general maxims centering on a command with a promise given in hyperbolic language.

Wisdom sayings are written in order to be remembered, and so they tend to be pithy statements that prefer rhetorical skill to accuracy. "Proverbs tries to impart knowledge which can be retained rather than philosophy which can impress a critic" (Fee and Stuart 1981:201). The reader must go behind the surface structure to the deeper truth that is embodied. For instance, Proverbs 22:26-27 seems to deny the right to take out a mortgage on one's home: "Do not be a man who strikes hands in pledge, or puts up security for debts; if you lack the means to pay, your very bed will be snatched from under you." However, the prevalent use of debts and bartering in Israelite life showed that this was not taken literally. Rather, the proverb cautions care in incurring debts, since one can lose everything in the process.

4. Obscure passages must be crossculturally applied to analogous situations today. Many of the wisdom sayings depend on ancient customs and cannot be understood from a modern perspective. The timeless principles embodied in such sayings must be extracted and reapplied to current situations. Of course, this is true of all wisdom passages, indeed all of Scripture (see chap. fifteen below). Yet, since the "wisdom" of the ancients, by the very nature of its practicality, was particularly tied to that long-dead culture, we must be careful in handling and applying the material.

For instance, Proverbs 11:1 ("The Lord abhors dishonest scales, but accurate weights are his delight") depends upon the use of scales to determine the value of goods and is for today a call to honest business practices. Similarly, when Proverbs 25:24 says that it is "better to live on a corner of the roof than share a house with a quarrelsome wife," it is describing the flat-bed roof of biblical times, a place where families would often share a meal. We would say "better to live in the attic." When Proverbs 26:8 says "Like tying a stone in a sling is the giving of honor to a fool," it refers to the use of slings as weapons. It means that such honor will be thrown away like a stone. We could translate, "Honoring a fool is like putting a bullet in a gun; it will soon go off and disappear." The crucial thing is to choose analogous situations so that the deeper truth comes through.

Excursus: The History of Wisdom Teaching

No one knows the exact origin of wisdom as a movement. Macedonian, Sumerian and Akkadian archives contained many works such as proverbs or ethical teaching intended to enable the individual to deal successfully with life. These forms were developed further by the Assyrians and the Babylonians, and an extensive literature appeared.

As Murphy points out, Macedonian wisdom literature was more diversified than its Hebrew counterpart, utilizing proverbs, folk tales, essays, riddles, dialogues, precepts, fables, parables and many other forms (1981:9). The Sumerians and Babylonians had a professional class of scribes or wise men who collected and transcribed the sayings. Similarities exist between works like the Counsel of Wisdom and Proverbs, and the Babylonian Theodicy and Job. However, the extent of literary influence is debated. The class of "wise men" or teachers of wisdom is a more certain parallel. In Jeremiah 18:18 (compare 1 Sam 14:27) they are mentioned alongside priest and prophet as leading figures of Israeli society, apparently functioning as royal counselors and officials. Later they added the scribal role. Throughout the ancient world such teachers exercised a moral influence on society. However, Israel was somewhat unique in the centrality of the religious dimension. While Macedonian wisdom was closely linked with the gods, the teachers themselves were secular figures, and their interest was intensely practical. Only in Israel was the major goal to please God (Prov 3:7) more than to live successfully in society.

Egypt had an ancient and flourishing wisdom tradition. The key concept was *maat*, "order" or "truth," the prerequisite for living in harmony with the divine "order" of things. One noteworthy aspect is the lack of emphasis on personal experience and the stress on complete submission to the way of the gods. The Egyptians developed a technical term for the wise man who followed the proper course—"the silent man," one who is in complete control of himself and avoids excess by yielding completely to *maat*. In contrast the "passionate man" throws himself at life and has no "order." Scholars thought at first that Egyptian wisdom was completely secular and had little religious content, since so many of the instructions are completely utilitarian and seem designed to teach youths how to make their way in the world. However, recent studies have shown decisively the underlying religious presuppositions (see Würthwein 1976:116-20). However, this *maat* or order is not given by divine revelation but is passed on by tradition from those teachers who have discussed it pragmatically. Success in this life and reward in the next life awaits the one who submits.

The extent of the influence of Egyptian and Mesopotamian wisdom on Israel is very debated. With the continuous interaction between ancient peoples (military, political and trade) some influence is certainly warranted. This is especially true in Solomonic times; Solomon married princesses from Egypt, Mesopotamia and many other lands, and his court teemed with foreign influences. However, it is wrong to say that Israel had no tradition of its own and simply borrowed it wholesale from her pagan neighbors. Recent research provides evidence that Israelite wisdom predated Solomon and that he was actually the most distinguished of a long line of wisdom teachers (1 Sam 24:14 shows "wisdom" was in existence at least as early as the beginning of the monarchy).

Moreover, in spite of the parallels, the differences between the emphases of Israel and of her neighbors are striking. For instance, Israel had no technical use of the "silent one," and stressed personal experience as well as submission to Yahweh (the two in fact work together to make one "wise"). It appears that wisdom categories in the ancient world developed somewhat independently, with a certain crossover of themes but not wholesale borrowing of entire traditions. Yet there was at times strong influence from other wisdom traditions, as in Egyptian themes behind Proverbs 22:17—24:22, as well as parallels with metaphors like God weighing the heart, righteousness as the foundation of the throne and the garland of honor (Crenshaw 1975:7). There is also some evidence that the Hebrews considered themselves part of an international wisdom movement, as in their recognition of the "sages," or wise men, in Egypt and other nations (Gen 41:8; 2 Kings 4:30; Is 19:11-15). Many believe that the riddles by which the Queen of Sheba tested Solomon (1 Kings 10) were linked to his reputation as a teacher of wisdom. In Jeremiah 18:18, the sage is placed alongside the priest and the prophet as a leader in Israel (see Sheppard 1988:1076-77).

One possible source of evidence for the premonarchical origin of wisdom stems from the presence of family or clan wisdom in the ancient Near East. Although such an origin can only be surmised rather than proven, the educational process in ancient Israel depended first on the father and then on the tribe or clan in developing the child into a responsible adult. This process centered primarily on the Torah but also included practical advice for living. The authority structure of the family and the clan is obvious in the patriarchal and Mosaic periods and provided an important source for the development of pragmatic wisdom. While many scholars take this too far and virtually equate wisdom and Torah at the earliest stage (see Morgan 1981:39-41), several factors do point to family and clan as a locus of the wisdom tradition. Of course, this does not mean it was a flourishing movement at the earliest stages. Nevertheless, the use of the "father-son" metaphor in Egyptian as well as in Jewish proverbs and the centrality of the family in all ancient Near Eastern wisdom literature would support this thesis.

More difficult to assess is the belief that the Israelite school provided an early locus for wisdom teaching. There are several problems with this view, such as the question as to whether schools existed at an early date in Israel.[8] The strongest argument is from historical parallels, namely influence from the Egyptian and Mesopotamian educational systems. However, few are willing to read this into the period before the monarchy. This problem parallels the previous discussion of family or clan wisdom: any solution can only be surmised; there is no direct evidence. It would seem logical that an authoritative passing on of wisdom traditions would center on the school (if such was in existence) as well as on the family, and certainly the "high literary quality of the sayings" could well point to "origins, or at least culturation, among a scribal class that had some expertise with words or ideas" (Murphy 1981:8). However, we can go no further than note the possibility of such an early source as a school system, with possible educational sessions also in the temple and court life from the Solomonic era on (see Crenshaw 1974:228-29). Such are possibilities but no more. I agree with Sheppard that the data as we know it favors the presence of some type of public instruction, yet it is probable that no formal school system existed. Education occurred primarily through the home and sporadically via appointed sages who "taught the people" (2 Chron 17:7-9; Eccles 12:9). The earliest recorded "school" is that of Ben Sira in the second century B.C. (Sirach 51:23). Before that the synagogue was probably the center of Hebrew education.[9]

An important topic is the possible wisdom influence on early nonwisdom literature like the historical books. The major difficulty is the criteria for assessing such sayings. As Sheppard notes, "The present wisdom influence labors under a lack of sufficient historical information and control" (1980:12). This is especially true with reference to the relationship between form and function. A saying may have the form of a proverb and yet not function as a wisdom saying. A well-known example is Exodus 23:8 (compare Prov 16:19), "A bribe blinds the officials and subverts the cause of those who are in the right." This has the form of a proverb, but it is speculative to assume that it is a wisdom saying, for the setting is legal rather than popular wisdom.

Many proverbs have been noted in the historical books (such as Gen 10:9; Judg 8:21; 15:16; 1 Sam 16:7; 24:13), but these cannot be automatically identified as early wisdom. Most today argue that the proverb is the basic wisdom form, but it is a subgenre in its own right and can be used in many different traditions. Crenshaw tries to rectify the situation by developing a methodology (1969:129-42). He begins by differentiating types of wisdom thinking: family wisdom, legal wisdom (a possible basis for Ex 23:8 above), court wisdom, scribal and didactic wisdom. However, in the remainder of his essay he critiques the methodologies of others rather than develops a precise set of positive criteria. Two basic problems with current methodologies are circular reasoning (reading a wisdom function back into possible wisdom forms) and a failure to reckon with the possibility of a "common linguistic stock" (such as the proverb) that crossed genre boundaries (see Crenshaw 1975:9-10). This has hermeneutical importance for more than wisdom literature, as these two common errors appear frequently in all genre decisions.

Several features may point to a wisdom saying. One basic type, as already stated, is the proverb. Other stylistic traits would be personification ("Wisdom" as a living entity), antithesis (strong contrast between two paths or forces, like wise-foolish), earthy metaphors (such as the foolish path pictured as a seducing prostitute in Prov 9:13-18) and above all the pragmatic nature of the teaching. The latter shades over into function, and indeed these two aspects (form and function) must merge together in identifying a particular saying as wisdom in essence.

On the whole the proverbial sayings above may represent nascent wisdom, although many (such as 1 Sam 10:12, "Therefore it became a proverb, 'Is Saul also among the prophets?' " or Gen 10:9, "Therefore it is said, 'Like Nimrod, a mighty hunter before the Lord' ") are local sayings rather than wisdom. Judges 8:21 ("As a man is, so is his strength") and 1 Samuel 24:13 ("As the proverb of the ancients states, 'Out of the wicked flows wickedness' ") both have the form and function of wisdom sayings and could well constitute evidence for an early tradition.

In conclusion, it is best to say with Nel that wisdom was present in Israel at an early date but that it became a fixed tradition only with the establishment of the monarchy (1982:1-2). It could hardly have been otherwise; in the earlier period Israel focused all its energy on survival and hardly had time to develop such an intellectual movement.

Two areas are of interest for hermeneutical purposes. First, the recent fad of finding wisdom themes in nearly every book of both testaments utilizes dubious criteria and produces very doubtful results. Such attempts should be treated with extreme caution and subjected to rigorous scrutiny. Second, wisdom themes nevertheless played an important role in the ancient world, and we need to pay greater attention to this extremely fruitful body of literature. Most likely the wisdom movement began early in Israel's history, although with David (note the wisdom psalms mentioned in the previous section) and Solomon it entered its greatest era.

9
Prophecy

PROPHECY HAS BECOME ALMOST A FAD TODAY, THE SUBJECT OF INNUMERABLE SERMONS, books and even entire ministries (such as Jack van Impe and Hal Lindsay). Unfortunately there is widespread misunderstanding about the nature and purpose of biblical prophecy; my purpose here is not just to correct these erroneous views but to enhance the value and power of biblical prophecy for today. Prophecy was predominant not only in the latter part of the Old Testament period but in the New Testament age as well. It is interesting that the writing prophets ministered for only three centuries (from the eighth to the fifth centuries B.C.) and yet spawned some of the most powerful works in Scripture. Only the New Testament age (just one century long!) can rival it for intensity and dynamic production—and that latter age also rightly can be called "prophetic."

Mickelsen has recognized the difficulty of the hermeneutical task regarding prophecy, calling for "an approach that will read nothing into prophecy that is not there, that will make clear all that the prophet said or wrote to his own people, and that will make the correctly interpreted message of the prophet relevant to our own times. That is no small task" (1963:280). There are many issues to be considered in fulfilling this task, such as the nature of the prophetic office, the origin and forms of the prophetic message, the types of prophetic literature and principles for interpreting prophecy.

The Nature of the Prophetic Role

Before we can interpret prophetic passages we must understand how and why a prophet functioned as he did. Each prophetic message grew out of the call and role of the prophet in the society of his day. As all recognize today, the prophet was a "forth-teller" before he was a "foreteller," and the true purpose of the latter was to assist and strengthen the former.

1. The Call of a Prophet. The prophet's call may come via a supernatural revelatory experience, as in the cases of Isaiah (6:1-13) or Jeremiah (1:2-10); it may also occur by natural means, as when Elijah threw his mantle over Elisha (1 Kings 19:19-21), signifying the transfer of authority and power, and may involve anointing (1 Kings 19:16). Unlike the priest or the king, the prophet never took his "office" indirectly through inheritance but always directly as a result of the divine will. The significance of the call is always the same: The prophet is no longer in control of his own destiny but belongs completely to Yahweh. He does not speak for himself and may not even want to utter the message (see Jer 20:7-18), but he is under the constraint of Yahweh, called to deliver the divine message to the people.

God often used a symbolic action to drive home this truth to the prophet. Isaiah was given a burning coal to place on his lips, which signified the purifying of his message (Is 6:7), and Ezekiel was told to eat a scroll that tasted "like honey in its sweetness" (Ezek 3:3), signifying the joy of delivering God's words. The major stress, however, is the direct involvement of God and the revelatory nature of the prophet's message. Two Old Testament genres depend upon a sense of direct divine revelation: the Torah (the Law or legal portions of the Pentateuch) and the prophets. These are the only Old Testament genres with so direct a sense of authority. The issue of authority is an important one in hermeneutics (see p. 12), and the prophets provide the crucial interpretation for such discussions. The prophet was "filled with the Spirit of God" (Joel 2:28; Is 61:1; 2 Chron 15:1; 20:14; 24:20; Ezek 2:2). This sense of divine inspiration was the basis of prophetic authority.[1]

2. The Complex Role of the Prophet. The prophet's role was complex and multifaceted. Primarily he was a messenger from God sent to call the people back to their covenant relationship with Yahweh. Petersen challenges the designations "office" and "charisma" for the role of a prophet (1981:9-15). The two concepts often have been contrasted, as if an office is institutional and charisma is anti-institutional. Petersen argues that the prophets played a role rather than filled an office. He is essentially correct, for we have little evidence for institutionalization among Israel's prophets (unlike her neighbors, such as the Philistines). Jewish prophets were individualists like Elijah or Jeremiah; they were called by God directly and belonged to no "institution." In one sense they were "charismatic," for they were filled by the Spirit of God—the impetus came from God rather than from them. They had no control over their role but simply followed God's directions.

Some scholars have posited prophetic guilds, based upon the common meal of the prophets in 2 Kings 4:38-41 and the references to groups of prophets ("sons of the prophets," found seven times between 1 Kings 20 and 2 Kings 9).[2] Others have even theorized a prophetic "school," based somewhat upon the erroneous translation of "the second quarter" of Jerusalem as "college" in the King James Version (2 Kings 22:14; 2 Chron 34:22). However, there is too little evidence for either a guild or a school. Certainly, prophets could associate themselves with such groups on occasion (as Samuel in 1 Sam 10; 19 or Elisha in 2 Kings 4—6), but these were temporary rather than permanent. The groups of prophets do not play a major role in the biblical text; they were probably pious men who wanted to serve Yahweh and aid the prophets. They were assistants rather than fellow members of a guild. We have no evidence that the actual prophets belonged to such or even came from such groups.

The terminology for prophet is varied, ranging from "seer" *(rō'eh)* to "prophet" *(nābî'* or *ḥôzeh)* or "man of God" *(ʾîšʾᵉlōhîm).* These are not used to distinguish separate aspects of the prophetic role but rather are terms used at different periods or in different places. All refer to the central function of the prophet as God's mouthpiece. Petersen (1981) distinguishes several roles, centering upon two specific aspects: the "peripheral prophet," an itinerant holy man who stands outside the societal structures and proclaims Yahweh (such as Elijah, Elisha); and the "central morality prophet" who legitimates and strengthens the basic mores of Yahwistic society as he calls the people back to God (Isaiah, Amos). However, this is too reductionistic and I personally doubt if we can make such a distinction between the ministries of Elijah and Amos, for instance. Many others have differentiated between oral and writing prophets, but the latter certainly had an oral ministry, and Amos's denunciation of corporate injustice in Israel does not differ radically from Elijah's condemnation of Ahab's court.

As Clements says, "We can discern recognizable similarities between the very earliest prophets mentioned in the Old Testament, such as Balaam, as well as those who appear in connection with Saul and David, and the later canonical prophets both in their activity and in the characteristics of their preaching" (1975:3). It is better, I believe, to see differences of ministry or message as dependent not on *types* of prophet but rather upon the exigencies of the moment, that is upon the religious-social sins of the particular society. Therefore, we will discuss the roles of the prophets as a single class rather than artificially divide them into different types of prophet.

a. *Receiving and communicating revelation from God* was their major purpose. Here we can differentiate oral from writing prophets. Grudem (1982:9-10) believes that the prophetic message had two aspects of authority: an authority of actual words (in which the prophet claims to be revealing the actual words of God) and an authority of general content (in which the prophet claimed that the ideas were from God but not the actual words). Both prophetic ministries were revelatory and Yahweh was equally involved in both. At the same time the writing prophets had a canonical function not seen in the latter. We must remember that of the scores of prophets chosen by God, only sixteen were led to collect and publish their proclamations in written form. The oral prophets are known more for their deeds than for their actual messages. Of course, some of the writing prophets (such as Daniel, Jonah) also are known for their deeds as well as their words. However, many of the writing prophets (such as Obadiah) chronicle their preaching rather than place their message in a historical setting. For these books, the modern reader has the difficult task of understanding the message without the historical situation behind it. We will return to this later.

It is popular in many circles today to make the prophets revolutionaries or at least urban social reformers. This is not the case, however. While they decried the social sins of their contemporaries, they did not do so as an end in itself but rather as particular instances of their true message, the religious apostasy of the nation. They were not social workers but primarily were preachers, God's ambassadors representing him before a nation that had turned from his ways. They delivered not their own messages but Yahweh's, and their introductory formulas ("Thus says the Lord," "The Lord said to me") demonstrate their consciousness that they were entirely vehicles for the divine message.

b. *Reformation rather than innovation* defines the basic purpose of the prophets (see Wood 1979:73-74). It was common in the past (Wellhausen, Scott, Whitley) to view the prophets as playing a formative role in the evolution of Israel's religion, in fact to make them the formulators of ethical monotheism. Most recent scholars, however, recognize the paucity of evidence for such a view. The prophets did not develop a new message but rather applied the truths of the past to the nation's current situation. Theirs was a ministry of confrontation rather than of creation. They were not innovative theologians but rather revivalists, seeking to bring the people back to Yahweh and the traditional truths of the Jewish faith. For instance, the prophets did not construct the doctrine of messianic hope; that was already present from Mosaic times (Deut 18:18). They elaborated it, adding further details, but hardly created messianism ex nihilo.

c. *The preservation of tradition* was therefore an important concomitant in the prophetic ministry. We can see this not only in the prophetic cry for Israel to return to her ancestral worship of Yahweh but also in the literary dependence of later prophets upon the accepted statements of the Torah and of earlier prophets, such as Ezekiel's use of Jeremiah, Jeremiah's use of Isaiah, and Hosea or Isaiah's use of Amos (see the discussion in Fishbane 1985:292-317). Part of their task was to "pass on" the "received" tradition (compare 1 Cor 15:3; 2 Tim 2:2).

I am not ignoring the individual contribution of the prophetic movement to the Hebrew religion. Rather, I am redressing the exaggerated emphasis upon this contribution on the part of many critical scholars. The call of Israel to a new awareness of temple and cult (ritual worship) in Ezekiel was not a new message, but it introduced a new era in postexilic Israel. Clements demonstrates the interaction between traditional or cultic elements and individualistic or dynamic features in the most personal of the prophetic experiences, the call of God.[3] Studies of the calls of Isaiah (chap. 6) and Jeremiah (chap. 1) have shown that both scenes had recognizable cultic traits. In other words, the distinctive calls were set in a traditional background that linked the prophetic role with the past and not just with the present and future.

The connection of the prophets to the cultic religion of Israel has been widely debated (see the excellent summary in Smith 1986b:992-93). In the past, critical scholars (such as Wellhausen) posited a radical opposition between prophet and priest on the basis of such passages as Isaiah 1:10-15; Jeremiah 6:20; 7:22-23; Amos 5:21-25; Hosea 6:6; Micah 6:6-8. Yet this ignored the many passages that showed a connection between prophet and tabernacle or temple (such as 1 Sam 3:1-21; 9:6-24; 2 Sam 7:4-17; Amos 7:10-17; Jer 2:26; 5:31; 8:10), and as a result others (such as Mowinckel) went to the other extreme and viewed the prophets as temple officials. Most today fall between these two, recognizing that the prophets acknowledged the centrality of temple and cultus but called for reform. The prophets functioned within the established religion but sought to excise the irreligious and unethical practices that predominated, to call both the people and the priests back to the ancient truths.

The basic message is elucidated in 2 Kings 17:13-14, which explains why the northern kingdom was sent into exile:

The Lord warned Israel and Judah through all his prophets and seers: "Turn from your evil ways. Observe my commands and decrees, in accordance with the entire Law that I commanded your fathers to obey and that I delivered to you through my servants the prophets." But they would not listen and were as stiff-necked as their fathers, who did not trust in the Lord their God.

The stress on the ancestral religion as well as the designation of Moses and leaders of the past as "prophets" illustrates the place of tradition in the prophetic message.

d. We must also note the *centrality of the covenant and Torah*. Fee and Stuart (1981:151-52) call the prophets "covenant enforcement mediators,"[4] which refers to the presence in the prophets of blessings (positive enforcement; compare Lev 26:1-13; Deut 4:32-40; 28:1-14) and curses or judgment (negative enforcement; compare Lev 26:14-39; Deut 4:15-28; 28:15—32:42) attached to the covenant and Torah from the times of Abraham and Moses. Following the model of Sinai, the prophets warned the people of the dangers attached to neglecting the commandments.

Fee and Stuart summarize the biblical material into six general categories of blessings (life, health, prosperity, agricultural abundance, respect and safety), and ten types of punishment (death, disease, drought, dearth, danger, destruction, defeat, deportation, destitution and disgrace). The prophetic proclamation centered upon these categories and would accent one or another depending upon the situation. The "messianic" promise of such passages as Amos 9:11-15 centers upon prosperity (vv. 11-12), agricultural abundance (v. 14) and safety (v. 15); and the curses of Nahum 3:1-7 relate danger (v. 2), destruction and death (v. 3), disgrace and destitution (vv. 5-7). The specific stress on the covenant is seen first in Hosea 6:7; 8:1, which condemned Israel for "transgressing the covenant." Jeremiah elaborated this into a full-fledged covenant theology, beginning with its strict requirements (11:6-7), which Judah had broken (11:8-10). Since the covenant was necessary as a guarantor of Yahweh's mercy (14:21) and since the old covenant was inadequate (31:32), Yahweh would establish a new and better covenant (31:31-34).

The place of Torah and cult is more difficult. There are seeming contradictory emphases: some passages seem to make ritual worship a necessary element of the prophetic religion (the prophets at the high place in 1 Sam 10, the centrality of the altar in the Mount Carmel battle between Elijah and the priests of Baal in 1 Kings 18). Samuel was reared and called by God to his prophetic ministry at Shiloh (1 Sam 3), and Nathan was consulted when David wished to build the Temple (2 Sam 7). Yet at the same time several passages deride sacrificial worship, stating that Yahweh would have no part in it (such as Hos 6:6; Amos 5:21-23; Mic 6:6-8; Is 1:11-14; Jer 6:20; 7:21-23). Amos, for example, cut himself off from the established religion of the priests (see 7:14).

Scholars have been found on both sides of the issue, some arguing that the prophets were merely extensions of the priestly order (Mowinckel, Eissfeldt), others that they were antisanctuary and anticult (most believe this is because in its early stages the prophetic movement followed Canaanite practices; see Robertson Smith). However, neither position is correct, and most today seek a more balanced perspective (Smith 1986b:992-93; Sawyer 1987:19-22). The prophets were not reacting against the Jewish system but rather rejected the apostasy and false religious practices of Israel and Judah. The prophets were protectors of Torah and cult and condemned Israel's worship because it was impure.

3. The Characteristics of False Prophets. Understanding the characteristics of false prophets provides a perspective for the true purposes of the prophetic "office." Further, the characteristics are hermeneutically relevant because they tell us what the true prophets rejected. The presence of conflict between prophetic groups is rarely disputed. At the earliest stage Micaiah inveighed against the 400 prophets for predicting success in battle (1 Kings 22:19-23), and Hosea derided the false prophets for causing the people to "stumble" (4:5). As might be expected, the presence of pseudoprophets increased as the divided kingdom moved toward the exile. Jeremiah has the strongest series of denunciations (6:13-14; 8:10-11; 14:14; 23:10-22) with Ezekiel close behind (2:14; 4:13; 13:1-23).

Many have spoken of "criteria" for identifying false prophets, but Crenshaw correctly challenges this, pointing out that too many questions are unanswered (1971:13-14). Does mere lack of fulfillment identify a prophet as false? Does an erroneous assessment of the situation turn a true prophet into a false one? Could a prophet move back and forth between true and false (see 1 Kings 13)? There was no actual criterion that could at all times distinguish true from false. However, there were "signs," or "marks," that pointed to a true or false prophet, and these could be applied in specific concrete situations to enable the people to distinguish them (see Crenshaw 1975:49-661; Tan 1974:78-82; Wood 1979:109-112; Smith 1986a:985-86).

a. *Divination* was often employed by false prophets (Jer 14:14; Mic 3:7; Ezek 12:24). This was expressly forbidden in Deuteronomy 18:9-14, but the techniques were impressive (passing through fire, interpreting omens, dealing with false spirits or the dead). Pagan prophets used them constantly.

b. *Fulfillment* of the prophecy is mentioned in Deuteronomy 18:22, and Micaiah uses this to test his message against his opponents (1 Kings 22:28). Isaiah (30:8), Jeremiah (28:9) and Ezekiel (33:33) stressed this criterion, and we cannot deny its importance in the biblical period. Of course, it is notoriously difficult to use, and is not applicable in the case of messianic or long-term prophecies, nor in terms of the conditional nature of many prophecies (see pp. 213-14). However, this is not quite valid as a criticism of the test, for the prophets only used it of concrete or short-term prophecies. While this test was limited, it still had validity in certain instances.

c. The *desire to please* clearly marked the false prophet. These individuals told the people what they wanted to hear rather than what Yahweh said. The true prophet, on the other hand, delivered God's message at the proper time and to the proper place, no matter what the consequences. Then as well as today the issue was whether one wished to be accepted by the people or to serve God. The true prophet was unswerving in his God-orientation, even if it meant his life! False prophets would say whatever could reap the greatest benefits for themselves. Jeremiah stated this most poignantly in the statement quoted in Lincoln's Gettysburg address ("saying, 'Peace, peace,' when there is no peace," 8:11; compare 14:13; 23:17; Ezek 13:10). Micah (3:5) charges his opponents with crying "peace" when paid sufficiently but prophesying "war" when given no remuneration. The false prophets were often guilty of practicing only for self-aggrandizement rather than out of a sense of ministry (Mic 3:11). Such men were not willing to suffer persecution for the truth of their message, as was Jeremiah (38:1-23) or Micaiah (1 Kings 22:27-28).

Rather, they desired popularity and the good life and so prophesied accordingly.

d. The *revelatory nature* of the prophecy was a crucial sign of its authenticity. The form (trance, vision, dream) was not as critical as the nature of the message. If the prophet drew people away from God to serve other gods (Deut 13:1-3) or failed to convict the people of their need for repentance, the message clearly did not come from God. The sense of a divine call was essential (see Amos 7:14-15; Mic 3:8); Jeremiah challenged Hananiah's call as an essential part of his denunciation of the latter (Jer 28:15).

e. *Continuity* between the message and the Torah or other true prophecies was another essential. If the prophecy contradicted the traditions it was unacceptable. On the other hand, if it was in keeping with such accepted truths it was valid. The elders of the land affirmed Jeremiah's prophecy of the fall of Jerusalem on the ground that it paralleled the prophecy of Micah, which led to the repentance of Hezekiah (Jer 26:17-19).

f. *Authentication* by a miracle was not a true criterion, for false prophets could duplicate acts of power (Ex 7:11-12, 22; compare Mk 13:22; 2 Thess 2:9). However, the prophets employed it as a sign at times. Elijah and Elisha, in particular, demonstrated this (for example, the Mount Carmel test between Elijah and the prophets of Baal, 1 Kings 18).

g. The *moral character* of the prophet was another sign of the validity of his message. False prophets are charged with lying (Jer 8:10; 14:14), drunkenness (Is 28:7), immorality (Jer 23:14), stealing prophetic oracles (Jer 23:16), treachery (Zeph 3:4) and even of persecuting other prophets (1 Kings 22:24; Jer 26:7-9). Of course this also was not a perfect test. As Smith points out, Hosea's marriage to a prostitute would have appeared questionable, and neither Jeremiah (38:14-28) nor Elisha (2 Kings 8:7-15) were always completely truthful (1986a:985). Nevertheless, this test was usually valid; even Jesus recognized its basic validity (Mt 7:17-20).

h. *Discernment* by Spirit-led men is seen in the incident where Jehoshaphat asks for a "prophet of the Lord" after the false prophets have spoken (1 Kings 22:7) and is emphasized especially in the New Testament (see Jn 10:4-5; 1 Cor 2:14). In 1 Corinthians 14:29, 32, the prophets will be judged by other prophets, for "the spirits of prophets are subject to prophets," and in 1 John 4:1 the believer is to "test the spirits to see if they come from God." In the final analysis all agree that only Spirit-led individuals can discern clearly whether a prophet or preacher is truly sent from God.

The Nature of the Prophetic Message

Much of what was said in the previous section applies also to the message of the prophets, for we cannot separate role from proclamation. However, several issues still need to be discussed, and these relate directly to the message itself. The basic misunderstanding regarding the prophetic literature of the Old Testament is that it relates primarily to the future. It is common to think that "prediction" is almost the definition of prophecy. Nothing could be further from the truth. Peisker notes that neither the Hebrew nor the Greek word lends itself to a future orientation (1978:74-84). *Nabi'* has both an active and a passive side: passively, the prophet is filled with the Spirit and receives God's message; actively, he interprets or proclaims God's message to others. The passive side may have predominated but both are present: a prophet is one inspired by Yahweh to preach his message to the people.

1. Present and Future Interact. While the message does not center upon the future, "prophecies" of future events occur frequently. Fee and Stuart argue that less than two per cent of Old Testament prophecy is messianic, less than five per cent relates to the New Covenant age and less than one per cent concerns events still future to us (1981:150). Of course, this figure depends largely upon exegetical decisions as to which so-called messianic prophecies were originally intended messianically. Nevertheless, the percentage either way would be relatively low. Most of the future prophecies related to the immediate future concerning Israel, Judah and the nations. Furthermore, the future prophecies were part of the larger pattern of proclamation, and their major purpose was therefore to call the nation back to God by reminding it that he was in control of the future.[5]

In short, the prophet was primarily a "forthteller" whose message was addressed to the people and situation of his day, and "foretelling" in reality was part of that larger purpose. Several issues must be discussed in this respect.

a. *Historical distance* makes interpretation difficult, for the prophetic books use analogies and language that stem from their contemporary periods. We have to re-create the historical background behind individual prophecies and often fail to understand them completely because we have not done so. Such prophets as Obadiah, Joel or Jonah provide no historical referents and a certain subjectivity enters the search for background information (though see 2 Kings 14:25, which dates Jonah with the reign of Jeroboam II at the start of the eighth century). Nevertheless, it helps to know that the invasion of Jerusalem and involvement of the Edomites, so central to Obadiah's short work, could have occurred during the reign of Jehoram (853-841 B.C.) when the Philistines and Arabs carried away the king's sons and a portion of the army (2 Chron 21:16-17); during the reign of Ahaz (743-715 B.C.) when Edom took part in a Philistine invasion (2 Chron 28:16-18); or during the final fall of Jerusalem under Nebuchadnezzar in 586 B.C. (2 Kings 25:1-21). The first is the only one to combine an invasion of Jerusalem with Edomite involvement and therefore is more likely. While we can catch the basic sense of the text without this data, it aids understanding greatly and avoids imprecision to regain the historical background as carefully as possible.

Fee and Stuart name three reasons why the prophets appeared at this particular juncture of history (1981:157): (1) unprecedented upheavals in the political, military, economic and social spheres led to a terrible crisis; (2) there was religious upheaval, as the divided kingdom progressively turned from Yahweh and his covenant to serve pagan gods; (3) shifts in population and national boundaries led to constantly unsettled conditions. Therefore, the divine message was needed anew, and God chose the prophetic medium to force Israel to realize that he was speaking. Understanding this historical situation is enormously helpful when the modern reader approaches the text. In individual instances one or another aspect of this historical background will be important, and the reader will have to study the passage carefully to determine which is predominant. The prophets addressed these issues, and their message is set against the backdrop of these historical problems.

b. The *question of fulfillment* is also quite difficult. We have already discussed this somewhat in chapter three, but here we might note the debate over the "double fulfillment" or "multiple fulfillment" of passages like Daniel 9:27; 11:31 and 12:11 (the "abomination which makes desolate"). The prophecy was originally fulfilled when Antiochus Epiphanes forced the Jews to sacrifice pigs on the altars and entered the Holy of Holies in 167 B.C. However, it was fulfilled again in the destruction of Jerusalem and will be fulfilled a final time in the end-time events (Mk 13:14 and parallels; compare Rev 13:14). The same is true of the Joel prophecy (2:28-32) alluded to in the Pentecost sermon (Acts 2:17-21). It too pointed beyond Pentecost to the eschaton.

I believe the answer is twofold. First, I prefer to use the term "analogous (or typological) fulfillment" to describe promise-fulfillment. The terms "double" or "multiplex" are unnecessary, for the New Testament writers would see analogous situations in salvation-history and link them prophetically. Second, the key is the Jewish concept of the telescoping of time. In God's acts within history a conceptual link would equate such analogous situations (2 Pet 3:8, "a thousand years was as a day," amalgamates past, present and future). Therefore, the New Testament could draw together Antiochus Epiphanes (past), the destruction of Jerusalem (present), and the eschaton (future).

Mickelsen discusses two related issues (1963:289-94). First, prophecy is not just history written either after (liberals) or before (evangelicals) the event. The first is the product of antisupernaturalism, the second of overstatement. Both flounder on the enigmatic character of prophecy that reveals certain details of the future event but leaves much of it in doubt. Both Old Testament and New Testament prophecy are ambiguous, and while pointing to actual historical events do not reveal them in their entirety. The interpreter must cautiously consider the issue of fulfillment, letting the text rather than current events determine the interpretation.[6]

The second issue is the progressive nature of prophecy. Later prophecies often add details to earlier ones, and the fulfillment is greater than the sum total of the preceding promises. Messianic prophecies in particular demonstrate this. Even with all the details predicted by successive prophets, the Jews were not ready for Jesus (note the constant misunderstandings of the disciples) and the reality far exceeded the expectations. The fact is that God gave the prophets only limited glimpses and never the entire picture. As Peter said, "The prophets . . . searched diligently and carefully to discover what person or time the Spirit of Christ within them meant" (1 Pet 1:10-12). In the same way, modern interpreters need humility rather than dogmatism as they try to understand the fulfillment of the end-time events. To borrow Pauline language (out of context), we too "see through a mirror dimly" when applying prophecy.

c. A *conditional aspect* is often seen, and some prophecies are dependent on the fulfillment of that condition. The destruction of Nineveh was clearly averted when the king and people repented, and the prophecy was nullified (Jon 3:4-10). The prophecy did not become unfulfilled, however, for it was conditional from the beginning. The principle is elucidated clearly in Jeremiah 18:7-10, which states that God would not fulfill doom pronouncements if the people repented, and he would remove promises if they departed from his ways. Many so-called unfulfilled prophecies (such as the prophecy of the total destruction of Damascus in Is 17:1 or the statement of Huldah that Josiah would die in peace in 2 Kings 22:18-20) can undoubtedly be explained along these lines.[7]

2. The Revelatory State Differed. The way the message was communicated to the prophet differed greatly depending upon the situation.

a. *Visions and dreams* were often the medium through which the message came. Critical scholars (Wellhausen, Holscher) have long argued that Israel's prophets learned the techniques of "ecstatic trances" and hallucinatory experiences from the Canaanites. This claim, however, is unnecessary. Wood examines the major passages (Num 11:25-29; 1 Sam 10:1-13; 18:10; 19:18-24; 1 Kings 18:29; 22:10-12; 2 Kings 9:1-16; Jer 29:26; Hos 9:7) and finds no support for such conclusions (1979:39-59). Saul's partial disrobing and stupor in 1 Samuel 19, for instance, can hardly prove such a thesis; Saul was not a prophet, and the others did not follow his example. The frenzy that accompanied an "ecstatic" experience was not really present. While pagan prophets did exemplify such frenzy (see 1 Kings 18:29), this is not seen of Israel's prophets. Lindblom allows ecstatic experiences for the early oral prophets but not for the later classical prophets (with the possible exception of Ezekiel; 1962:47-54, 122-23). The later prophets had visions but not ecstatic hallucinations. In fact, Petersen concludes that such behavior was not present at all in Israel's prophetic tradition (1981:29-30), and I concur with his assessment.

The difference is that the vision is a supernatural manifestation that corresponds to external reality while the hallucinatory, or "trance possession," is subjective and irrational. Numbers 12:6 states that God would indeed "speak" to his prophets via "vision" and "dream." At times, these visions were "night" visions (such as Job 4:13; 20:8; Is 29:7; Dan 7:2) but more frequently they occurred during the day. Such visions often contained esoteric imagery that crossed over into apocalyptic and had to be interpreted, such as the dry bones of Ezekiel 37 or the little horn of Daniel 8. Most important, the prophet was in a conscious state, and the vision was sent directly from God (Ezek 37 does not even mention the visionary medium; compare Ezek 1:1; 8:3).

Dreams differed from visions in that the prophet was not conscious. They were similar to the vision in that they too were sent from God. Nathan received such a dream regarding the Davidic kingdom (2 Sam 7:4-17), and Daniel received a dream regarding the four beasts (7:1-14), although the latter is also described as a vision (vv. 2, 15).

b. *Direct revelations* were the most common prophetic experience. Again and again Yahweh speaks audibly to his prophets. The formula "And the word of the Lord came to" (2 Kings 20:4; Jer 1:2; 2:1) led to the formulas "Hear the word of Yahweh" (2 Kings 20:16; Jer 2:4) or "Thus says the Lord" (2 Kings 20:5).[8] This of course is crucial for an understanding of prophetic authority as well as of inspiration. Often the revelation was linked to specific historical events, as when Nathan faced David with his sins over Bathsheba and Uriah (2 Sam 12:7-12) and when Jeremiah predicted disaster to Zedekiah as Nebuchadnezzar approached (21:3-14).

3. The Forms of Prophetic Proclamation Vary. This is important for hermeneutical study, for like the forms of wisdom literature each type must be interpreted differently.

a. The *judgment speech* is the basic form of the prophetic message. As Westermann has shown (1967:129-63), the prophecy of doom usually begins with an introductory section commissioning the prophet (Amos 7:15, "Go prophecy") followed by a section detailing the accusation or describing the situation that led to the judgment (7:16, "You say, 'Do not prophecy against Israel . . .' "). Then comes the messenger formula (7:17a, "Therefore thus says Yahweh") and the prediction of disaster (7:17b, "Your wife will be a harlot in the city, and your sons and daughters will die by the sword, and your land will be divided, and you yourself will die in an unclean land, and Israel will certainly go from this land into exile"). Of course this is only a basic formula. As Hayes states, the texts that actually follow this pattern may be "the exception rather than the rule" (1979:277). Nevertheless, these aspects are found in a great number of the texts and are helpful in understanding them.

b. The *prophecy of blessing or deliverance* (see Is 41:8-20; Jer 33:1-9) had much the same form as the first type, with the situation detailed, followed by the blessing itself.[9] The major emphasis in the salvation oracle is upon divine mercy. The prophets clearly state that the deliverance is due only to the intervention of God himself. Some (March 1974:163) separate the "oracle of salvation" (present deliverance) from the "proclamation of salvation" (future deliverance), but this is doubtful and the differences (such as the presence of "fear not" in the oracle and of the lament form in the proclamation) are due more to the situation addressed than to the form.

c. The *woe oracle* (Amos 5:18-20; Is 5:8-24; Mic 2:1-4; Hab 2:6-8) is a particular type of judgment prophecy that contains *hôy* followed by a series of participles detailing the subject, the transgression and the judgment. To the Israelite "woe" signified tragedy and imminent sorrow. It was a particularly powerful device for pronouncing doom, and the emphasis is more upon imminent judgment than upon the sorrow resulting (true also in the "woes" of Lk 6:24-26). There has been considerable study as to the origin of the "woe," some centering upon the "woe" as the negative counterpart to the beatitude, others upon the woe as a didactic device in popular teaching. The tendency today is to see their background in the funeral lament as a prophetic reaction to the inevitability of judgment to come (see Tucker 1985:339-40; Sawyer 1987:30).

d. *Symbolic actions* were also frequent in the prophetic period. These could be called "acted parables" and served as object lessons for the observers. Jeremiah and Ezekiel especially used this method. Jeremiah used a clay vessel to illustrate divine sovereignty (18:1-10; compare Rom 9:20-23), and Ezekiel (5:1-4) cut off a portion of his hair and burnt a third, struck a third with the sword, and scattered a third to signify the three types of judgment God would send upon Israel. Such actions were powerful illustrations of God's anger against his recalcitrant people.

e. *Legal* or *trial oracles* (Is 3:13-26; Hos 3:1-12; 4:1-19) contain a summons to the divine law court, a trial setting in which witnesses are called, leading to a stress upon both the guilt of Israel or the nations and the judgment or sentence due. Scholars debate whether the form originated from Hittite suzerainty treaties, the covenant or heavenly "lawsuit" *(rîb)*, current legal customs or the covenant renewal liturgy of Israel. Most likely we can never decide this type of detail with any precision, and the prophetic form reflected more general patterns related to many if not all of the above. March notes (1974:165-66) that this form is used to express Yahweh's judgment upon the gods of the nations (Is 41:1-5, 21-29; 43:8-15; 44:6-8) or upon Israel itself (Is 42:18-25; 43:22-28; 50:1-3). Again the exact form is not found in all, as one element or another is omitted.

For example, Isaiah 41:21-29 begins with the call of the pagan gods to trial, challenging them to assemble their evidence (vv. 21-23), followed by the charge that they are "nothing" (v. 24) and the witnesses who prove their guilt (vv. 25-28). Finally, the verdict is pronounced: they all are "false . . . worthless . . . wind and emptiness" (v. 29).

f. The *disputation speech* (Is 28:14-19; Jer 33:23-26; Ezek 18:1-20) has been examined in detail by Graffy (1984). It is used primarily to quote the people's own words against them and to use their own statements to show their error. It consists of three parts: an introductory formula ("the word of Yahweh came to me saying"), the quotation of the opponents in order to show their errors (often containing chiasm) and the refutation that points out the error in their reasoning and details God's intervention in the situation. Jeremiah 31:29-30 uses the disputation form as an introduction to the New Covenant prophecy of verses 31-34. The setting is the future ("in those days") and the quotation uses a local proverb on the collective punishment of the nation ("the fathers have eaten sour grapes, and the children's teeth are set on edge"). The refutation centers on the New Age, when punishment will be individual and the children will suffer for their own sins ("But everyone shall die for his own sin; each man eats sour grapes, his teeth shall be set on edge"). This prepares the way for the individualism of the New Covenant age in verse 34.

g. *Poetry* is used throughout the prophets. The ancient Near East was steeped in poetic expression. Poetry always had a more powerful voice since it was easily memorized and spoke more eloquently to the issue. Many of the devices discussed in chapter seven on Old Testament poetry will be helpful. Within the prophets there are laments (Jer 15:5-21; 20:7-18), thanksgiving songs (Jer 33:11), worship hymns (Is 33:1-24) and repentance hymns (Mic 7:1-12). One has only to glance through the prophetic books in a modern version to see how extensively they utilize poetry.

h. *Wisdom thinking* has long been allied with the prophetic movement (see Crenshaw and Clements), and several of the forms mentioned in chapter eight are also observable in prophetic literature. Proverbs are often used. In fact, one such asked, "Is Saul also among the prophets?" (1 Sam 10:11-12; see also Jer 31:29-30 [Ezek 18:1-2] as discussed in *f* above). Popular wisdom sayings are employed (Jer 23:28), and even allegories (particularly used by Ezekiel in chaps. 16, 20, 23).

i. *Apocalyptic* is found in later prophetic works like Ezekiel, Daniel and Zechariah. We will investigate this link further in the following chapter, but the form itself is restricted to exilic and postexilic prophetic works in the Old Testament.

Hermeneutical Principles

In light of the general information above, how can we approach prophetic literature so as to move accurately on the spiral from text to context? Kaiser provides an interesting discussion of four ways *not* to preach prophecy (1982:186-93): (1) In prophetic typology the contemporary situation controls the text rather than vice versa. This is especially observable in liberation theology, where passages decrying social injustice are used to support modern revolutionary movements. (2) Prophetic action preaching takes the individuals and episodes of a story and symbolizes them to speak to modern events. Again, the actual meaning of the text is ignored, and a contemporary grid is forced upon the surface of the text. For instance, the story of Ahab and Naboth's vineyard in 1 Kings 21 is used for the "little man" versus institutionalism or the state. (3) Prophetic motto preaching chooses one or two statements out of a larger context like 1 Kings 21 and constructs a message using these as a motto. For instance, verse 7 ("I [Jezebel] will give you the vineyard") is made a springboard for a sermon on women's liberation, even though in the context she is villain rather than hero. (4) Prophetic parable preaching constructs a modern parable on the analogy of the story line. The problem again is the surface parallels that are adduced without a deep understanding of the actual situation. Certainly there are many casual analogies, situations in which large corporations and so forth force people out of their homes, but again this ignores the prophetic component and the actual exegesis of the text.

I would add a fifth type of erroneous preaching, the "newspaper" approach of many so-called prophecy preachers today. This school assumes that the prophecies were not meant for the ancient setting but rather for the modern setting. Amazingly, that setting is often post-1948 (after Israel became a nation) America (see further pp. 227-30). Such preachers ignore the fact that God chose all the symbols and passages to speak to Israel and that modern people must understand them in their ancient context before applying them today. As we will see below, the modern interpreter must distinguish messianic prophecies from temporary (intended for the historical situation of ancient Israel) prophecies. "Newspaper" preachers instead take prophetic passages out of context and twist them to fit the modern situation. This is dangerous for it too easily leads to a subjective "eisegesis" (reading meaning into a text), which does anything one wants to the scriptural text. We need exegetical principles that can truly unlock the text and enable the modern Christian to hear the prophetic Word of God anew. The following seven steps are useful.

1. Determine the individual saying. As Fee and Stuart point out, we must learn to "think oracles," because many sections in the prophetic books are comprised of a collection of sayings, each addressed to different situations but without divisions indicated between them (1981:158-59). The reader cannot ascertain easily where one begins or ends, nor can one know for certain whether successive oracles were delivered to the same audience or situation. Naturally, the student needs help in doing this, and a good commentary is an essential aid. We do not want to misread successive oracles by taking them together and misusing the context of one to interpret the other. When the historical setting is provided, for instance in Jeremiah or Isaiah, the student is helped immensely. When it is missing and sayings are lumped together, the task is correspondingly more difficult. The servant songs of Isaiah 42—53 are placed in the context of a series of poems (Is 40—66) without historical referents. The interpreter must note each poem as a unit before running them together into whole sections (such as 40—55; 56—66).

2. Determine the type of oracle employed. As noted above, each subgenre has its own

language rules, and it is imperative to isolate the literary type of each oracle before interpreting it. It not only adds interest value to note that a saying is a "lawsuit" or "wisdom" oracle but enables the reader to look for a particular pattern or certain highlights depending on the type of saying employed. This has further value for the sermon. When preachers note a "lawsuit" oracle or "disputation" speech, they can choose illustrations that both highlight the text and make it more forceful and meaningful for the congregation.

3. Study the balance between the historical and the predictive. Ramm notes three questions in terms of the essence of a passage (1970:250): Is it predictive or didactic? (for example, Zech 1:1-6 is didactic and 7-21 predictive). Is it conditional or unconditional? Is it fulfilled or unfulfilled? In the latter case we must use caution because of the enigmatic nature of prophecy. First-century Jews thought Isaiah 53 was being fulfilled in the sufferings of the nation and did not realize it was messianic. We today also approach prophecy from a finite perspective and can very easily misunderstand the thrust of the promise. This demands a nuanced grammatical-historical exegesis of the passage. We must probe carefully the background not only of the words but of the larger issues before we can make any decisions. Many today leap too quickly into a futuristic interpretation of passages that were more likely meant to speak to the author's own day.

4. Determine the presence of literal meaning or symbol. There is an ongoing debate between adherents of a "literal" approach to prophecy and those who take a "symbolic" stance, centering somewhat upon the dispensational and amillennial schools of interpretation. While I will examine the biblical use of symbols in the next chapter, I must note the issue here. There are three possible approaches to this issue. With a completely literal approach, each symbol refers to a specific individual and a specific time. However, no one takes an absolutely literal approach, believing that there actually will be monster-horses with multicolored breastplates, heads like lions and breath like dragon-fire (Rev 9:17). Most pick and choose where to be literal, often without seeming criteria for doing so. In the recent Distant Thunder film series about the tribulation period, for instance, the Beast (Rev 13) was a distinguished-looking gentleman in a three-piece white suit while the locusts (Rev 9) were literal but as large as jet planes!

Second, the symbolic approach seeks the ideas behind the symbols, that is eternal truths without temporal or individual significance. Few take a completely spiritual approach, such as removing the referent from all prophetic passages so that they refer only to spiritual truths and not to events. For instance, even those (R. T. France) who interpret Mark 13:24 (the coming of the Son of man) as the destruction of Jerusalem rather than the parousia see an event behind the prophecy. Only the committed existentialist will see only spiritual meaning behind such texts.

The third approach seeks a "language of equivalents" that notes an analogous situation but refuses to overload the text in the direction of either literal or symbolic. When we study the Old Testament messianic texts, for instance, this is the best solution. They were not purely symbolic since they did point to coming events. Nor were they completely literal, for they contained historical correspondence as well as direct messianic prophecy. Passages like the prophecy of the thirty pieces of silver (Jer 32:6-9 [Zech 11:12-13] in Mt

27:9-10) are analogous rather than literal prophecies. This approach notes the future event predicted, for instance, in the locust plague of Revelation 9 but does not try to read too many details (the breastplates = tanks) into the text.

5. Carefully delineate christological emphases. Many (Vischer, Geisler) have seen the Old Testament as christocentric in essence. Certainly all of the canon in one sense pointed forward to Christ (Gal 3:19); yet it also spoke to its own day, and overly zealous Christian interpreters often negate the true canonical meaning of prophecy (as well as other Old Testament literature) by reading it in a christological rather than a historical direction. I argue throughout this book for the centrality of the "author's intended meaning," that thrust which God inspired the author to state. If we apply this to prophecy it means the interpreter is obligated to search for the original thrust of the passage.

Some passages are directly messianic (Mic 5:2 on the birth in Bethlehem; Mal 4:5 on Elijah as forerunner) while others are analogical (Hos 11:1 in Mt 2:15 on calling Jesus "out of Egypt"; Jer 31:15 in Mt 2:17-18 on the slaughter of the innocents). Still other prophecies are not messianic but had their fulfillment in their own day. Fee and Stuart mention Isaiah 49:23 (kings who will "bow down before you with their faces to the ground"), interpreted by some as a prophecy of the magi in Matthew 2 (1981:163-64). However, the context shows it refers to the restoration of Israel after the Babylonian exile, and both the intent and style of the passage demand it be interpreted of the nations' obeisance before Yahweh and his people.

While we must recognize the christological thrust of Scripture as a whole, we should interpret individual passages thus only if the text warrants it. We should never read more into a text than it allows. Nonchristological passages are part of the broader thrust of Scripture as it prepared for Christ but are not christocentric in themselves.

6. Do not impose your theological system upon the text. As stated throughout this book, one's theological system is an essential and valid component of the hermeneutical tool chest. Without a basic system of thinking a reader could not make sense out of any text let alone one as difficult as a prophetic passage. Yet at the same time a system that has become rigid can lead the interpreter to thrust the text in a direction it does not wish to go and thereby can seriously hamper the search for truth. On prophecy and apocalyptic, dispensationalists tend to be literalists, and nondispensationalists stress the symbolic more. Often the decision regarding a particular text can be made on dogmatic rather than exegetical grounds. Here dialogue is essential. We should use works from both schools in studying the background and meaning of the biblical text. This will force us to a more balanced approach that can allow the text itself to question a prioris and guide us to a correct understanding.

7. Seek analogous situations in the modern church. Since Old Testament prophecy was given to a culture long passed from the scene, many assume that it no longer speaks to our day. Nothing could be further from the truth. Kaiser points to 2 Chronicles 7:14, which says, "If my people, who are called by my name, will humble themselves and pray and seek my face and turn from their wicked way, then I will hear from heaven and forgive their sin and heal their land" (1981:194-95). The phrase "called by my name" would certainly include believing Gentiles and the promise would apply to the church

today. Indeed, a careful reading of the characteristics of prophecy above shows the applicability of these themes to our own day. The necessity of dwelling within God's New Covenant, the judgment warnings and salvation promises, all speak to the modern Christian with the same clarion voice they held for the Israelites. The condemnation of social injustice and immorality are as needed today as then.

10

Apocalyptic

OR MOST PEOPLE APOCALYPTIC LITERATURE REPRESENTS ONE OF THE MOST FASCINATING
and yet most mystifying portions of Scripture. When studying Daniel or Revelation readers feel they have been transported into a fairy-tale world of myths and
monsters, a Tolkien-type panorama of fantasy. The unreality of the symbols and the
constant shifting from one mysterious scene to another is greatly confusing. At the same
time, the text portrays the war in heaven and on earth, between good and evil, between
the children of God and the forces of Satan. The reader is caught between the literal and
the symbolic, not knowing quite how to approach these works. Once we know how to
handle the locusts and demonic hordes, the many-horned goats and fearsome beasts,
apocalyptic is a fascinating and pervasive vehicle for the presentation of theological truth.

Like narrative (chap. six), apocalyptic cuts across the testaments. In the Old Testament
we would note Daniel and Zechariah as well as the visions of Ezekiel (chaps. 37—39)
and perhaps Isaiah 24—27 or the locust plague of Joel. From the apocrypha and pseudepigrapha are 1 Enoch, Slavonic Enoch (2 Enoch), Hebrew Enoch (3 Enoch), Jubilees,
Assumption of Moses, the Ascension of Isaiah, 2 Baruch, 3 Baruch, 4 Ezra, Psalms of
Solomon, Testament of Abraham, Apocalypse of Abraham, portions of the Testament
of the Twelve Patriarchs (Levi, Naphtali, perhaps Joseph), Life of Adam and Eve (Apocalypse of Moses), Shepherd of Hermas, Sibylline Oracles (Books III-V) and several of
the Qumran scrolls (such as the War Scroll, An Angelic Liturgy, the Testament of
Amram). New Testament apocalyptic might include the Olivet Discourse (Mk 13 and
parallels); 1 Corinthians 15; 2 Thessalonians 2; 2 Peter 3; Jude and the book of Revelation. This material covers a period extending from the seventh century B.C. to the
second century A.D. The extracanonical literature is essential for a proper perspective
and control in studying the canonical material.

Formal Features and Characteristics

The term *apocalypse* was not used of this body of literature until it appeared in the book
of Revelation (1:1), and it was not until the second century that the term regularly
appeared for this genre. The word meant to "reveal" or uncover knowledge previously
hidden (see Smith 1983:9-20) and so was a natural term to employ. Apocalyptic has two

aspects: it is both a genre, or type, of literature and a set of concepts found in texts that belong to this genre.[1] Therefore, I will separate specific formal features related to the style and content of the texts and more general characteristics that describe the mindset that led to the production of those texts.

A preliminary definition (adapting those of Rowland, Collins and Aune) draws together these features and introduces an overall perspective on the apocalyptic genre:

> Apocalyptic entails the revelatory communication of heavenly secrets by an otherworldly being to a seer who presents the visions in a narrative framework; the visions guide readers into a transcendent reality that takes precedence over the current situation and encourages readers to persevere in the midst of their trials. The visions reverse normal experience by making the heavenly mysteries the real world and depicting the present crisis as a temporary, illusory situation. This is achieved via God's transforming this world for the faithful. (See Hanson 1983:25-26)

1. The Formal Features. Scholars have vigorously debated the formal features of the apocalyptic genre. Sanders sums up the current debate: (1) many of these features (symbols, cycles) also can be found in nonapocalyptic works; (2) many so-called apocalypses do not contain a majority of these traits; (3) many of the lists fail to contain other elements commonly found in apocalyptic works (1983:447-59). Recent scholars overcome this difficulty in two ways, first by separating "genre" (considering a work as a whole) and "form" (dealing with small discourse units within a work) and second by distinguishing apocalypticism (the sociological situation behind the movement), apocalyptic eschatology (the major theme of the movement) and apocalypse (the literary genre).

The most important of the distinctions is between form and genre. Few of the works listed above are entirely apocalyptic. Large portions of the biblical books, like Daniel or Zechariah, are prophetic, and the same is true of intertestamental literature like 1 Enoch (chaps. 91—104 are not) and Jubilees (it moves back and forth between general discourse and apocalyptic). The book of Revelation contains the letters to the seven churches (chaps. 2—3) in general epistolary style, and Ladd calls it "prophetic-apocalyptic" in tenor (1957:192-200).

It can be easily shown that there are almost as many variations in apocalyptic style as there are apocalyptic works. Yet this is hardly a new phenomenon. I have noted the problem in virtually every genre discussed above, and it is not a final deterrent to generic categories (see Osborne 1983). Therefore, I will concentrate more on "form" and note that the apocalyptic "genre" depends upon the accumulation of formal categories in small units within the larger whole. There is no such thing as a pure genre, and the attempt to elucidate such on the part of Sanders and others is doomed to failure.[2]

a. A *revelatory communication* is perhaps the most common trait. In the past it was often asserted that prophecy is characterized by a direct audition and apocalyptic by a vision or dream. While this is generally adequate it is not true in every instance. Zechariah 1—6 is a series of visions, while 9—14 comprises a series of oracles (see also Is 24—27; Joel 1—2). The calls of Isaiah (chap. 6) and Ezekiel (chap. 2) are in the form of visions and contain definite apocalyptic elements (compare 1 Enoch 15), as does Amos 7 on the locust plague (compare Joel 1—2, without a vision). Nevertheless, a revelatory situation is behind nearly every apocalyptic work, including the intertestamental ones. The major exceptions are New Testament passages like the Olivet Discourse (Mk 13 and parallels) and the epistolary material (2 Thess 2; 2 Pet 3), though their stature as apocalyptic is debated. These are narrative units that employ apocalyptic style and themes. Apocalypse per se employs visions (see the book of Revelation).

Another misconception is that apocalyptic literature had a secondary authority, since prophets had a direct communication from God while apocalyptists had only visions and normally needed an angelic interpreter. However, this ignores the fact that both vision and angel were directly from God and were part of a supernatural communication of the divine will.[3] In short, the vision is a basic trait but by itself cannot point to apocalyptic.

b. *Angelic mediation* is part of the revelatory medium. Given the symbolism employed in the vision, the writer is understandably confused about the meaning of the communication. Often an angelic guide conducts the seer on a "tour," as in Ezekiel 40 (the measurement of the temple; compare Rev 11:1-2), Zechariah 1 (the four horns), the Apocalypse of Abraham 10 (the angel Jaoel takes the patriarch to heaven) or Revelation 17 (the judgment of the great harlot). More frequently the angel interprets the vision or dream, as in the night visions of Zechariah 1—6, the visions of the four beasts and little horn in Daniel 7—8, the explanation of the heavenly Jerusalem in 4 Esdras 7, or the vision of the heavenly martyrs in Revelation 7.

Some late Jewish works like 1 Enoch, Jubilees and the Testaments of the Twelve Patriarchs also employ the medium of the "heavenly tablets," secret books given to the great figures of the past like Enoch, Jacob or Moses and now disclosed to the seer himself. These tablets record the divine plan for the ages and have a future orientation, preparing the faithful for what is to come. As Russell says, the divine revelations come via vision, angelic mediation or on "heavenly tablets" and disclose the long-hidden truths regarding past, present and future for the "last days" (1964:108-9). This disclosure was proof that indeed the End was near.[4]

c. *Discourse cycles* demonstrate the stylized literary form of apocalyptic (see Koch 1972:24). While the prophetic writings originally were spoken oracles, apocalyptic was literature from the start. The apocalyptist is told to "write" down his visions (compare Rev 1:19) and therefore the formal elements have even greater significance. In one sense this formal category encompasses the other traits, for the form is usually a series of dialogues within the visions between the seer and the angelic interpreter or God himself. Often there is an introductory formula such as "I looked and behold" (Dan 7:1; 8:2; Zech 1:18; 2:1; 5:17) followed by a series of questions asked by the mediator (Zech 4:2; 5:2) or by the seer (Dan 7:16; Zech 1:19; 5:6; Rev 17:6). The fear and turmoil of the seer is graphically described: "The recipient is beside himself; he falls to the ground, his trance sometimes being heightened to the point of unconsciousness" (Koch 1972:25; compare Dan 10:7-9; 2 Baruch 21:26; 4 Ezra 5:14; Rev 1:17; 4:2). God or the angel then calms the fears and explains the phenomena.

Scholars have too often neglected the literary effects and rhetorical techniques. While the actual structure varies from book to book, the literary communication of hidden truths in order to bring the reader into line with God's control of history is a uniform pattern. Hartman speaks of the importance of noting the place of the smaller units in the whole message of the work (1983:333-67). For instance, the appearance of the angelic mediator has the "illocutionary" function (a deeper message behind the surface) of linking heaven and earth and making the communication of divine realities possible. Moreover, the progression of visions has some importance, and they relate to one another in important literary ways. The book of Revelation is a carefully conceived work with a distinct structure and each element moves the reader forward in developing the basic apocalyptic thesis of God's sovereign control over history.

d. *Ethical discourse* often clarifies the purposes of the visions for the readers. Previously scholars often stated that apocalyptic was not interested in the present age and had a paucity of parenesis or exhortation. While the prophets warned and castigated Israel, the apocalyptists comforted and confirmed the saints (Morris 1972:58-61). While this distinction is basically correct, and while there are few condemnations of the saints (though see Testament of Benjamin 10:3; Rev 2—3), we dare not press this too far. There are constant ethical pronouncements, but they are more positive, calling the people of God to endurance and righteous living in light of the visions (compare Rev 16:15; 22:7). In fact, Charles could call apocalyptic "essentially ethical" in the sense that the saints were constantly called to an awareness of and faith in the God who controls present and future (1913:2:16). Charles has certainly overstated the case; Russell more correctly notes that "eschatology, not ethics, was their consuming interest" but that the two were not mutually exclusive (1964:101). "On the contrary they recognized the moral demands of God here and now. . . . Their one aim was to obey God and to carry out his commandments (cf. Dan 9:10f, 14, etc.)." In one sense the book of Revelation as a whole centers on the need of the saints to be "overcomers" (note the conclusion of each of the seven letters) rather than "cowardly" (21:8).

e. *Esoteric symbolism* is the most visible quality of apocalyptic literature. The source of these symbols also differs from the prophets and other biblical writers. The latter drew their symbols or metaphors from the experiential world, such as locusts, horses, salt, lamps. The apocalyptists would do so as well but added many symbols from the world of fantasy or myth, such as many-headed beasts, dragons, locusts with the tails of scorpions. However, these symbols were drawn from the times of the writers and many quickly became conventional; for example, animals stood for men, cosmic signs for supernatural phenomena and numbers for God's control of history.

The significance of numerology is particularly striking. In all apocalypses the numbers three, four, seven, ten, twelve and seventy predominate. For instance, the book of Revelation is dominated by the number seven and its multiples. At times this can be frustrating, such as in the mystifying use of 666 in Revelation 13:18 (for a survey of the possibilities see Mounce 1977:263-65). We will not know the meaning of that symbol for certain until we get to heaven, although it was probably well known to the readers. My own preference is to think that 666 refers to Nero Caesar—the letters of his name in Hebrew, if assigned numerical values, add up to 666.

The rich profusion of symbols leads to great confusion among interpreters and is the subject of the next section. The problem is that while many ancient apocalyptic works provide an interpretation, others do not. This is especially true in the book of Revelation, which contains only one angelic interpretation (chap. 17). The reader is increasingly bewildered as the images multiply. Morris provides a good example:

> Thus in I Enoch we read of stars falling from heaven and becoming bulls. They cohabit with cows and sire elephants, camels, and asses (I Enoch 86:1-4). Later we learn of a white bull that became a man (I Enoch 89:1) and of bulls which sired creatures as diverse as lions, tigers, wolves, squirrels, vultures and others (I Enoch 89:10). (1972:37)

We cannot begin to make sense of apocalyptic without coming to grips with the background and meaning of such symbols (see further below).

f. A *recital of history* is featured in many apocalyptic works, like Jubilees, that intertwine past and future. Several preoccupy themselves with the details of world history, especially that of Israel (Dan 2; 7—12; 1 Enoch 85—90; 4 Ezra 11—12; Apocalypse of Abraham 27—28). As Rowland points out (1982:136-39), this distinguishes these works from prophecy, which rarely recites historical facts (for example, Ezek 20 uses it only to chronicle Israel's sins). The purpose is to demonstrate the divine control over all history on behalf of the people of God. This can be past history (1 Enoch 85—90) or the immediate future (Dan 7—12); both come together to show the sovereignty of God. By reflecting upon God's control of the past, Israel or the church is asked to trust him in the present. The same God who was sovereign over past history is sovereign over present and future history. Israel need not fear the disasters of the present or the world empires of the future. Nothing takes place without the foreknowledge and consent of God. This has been proven in the past and will be reiterated in the future.

Often this recital takes the form of a calendrical reworking of the ages. Jubilees, for instance, divides history into "jubilee" periods of forty-nine years each, taking the reader from creation to the Passover and exodus from Egypt. All of this is seen as a direct revelation from God to Moses. The Apocalypse of Weeks in 1 Enoch 91:12-17 and 93:1-10 divides history into seven past "weeks" or periods and three future "weeks." The similarities to the seventy "weeks" of Daniel 9:24-27 are obvious. In 1 Enoch the seventh week is characterized by apostasy, while in Daniel it is the seventieth that is marked by "abominations."

g. *Pseudonymity* is the first characteristic mentioned by many, but it is certainly overstated, primarily because of the assumption that Daniel is a pseudonymous second-century work. This, however, is at the very least debatable and in my opinion is dubious.[5] However, even without Daniel we would have a difficult time proving pseudonymity for Ezekiel, Joel and Zechariah, and few try to do so for the book of Revelation. Yet pseudonymity is undeniably true of intertestamental works. In the ancient world a work had greater authority when it was linked to one of the great heroes of the past. The Apocalypse of Abraham, for instance, recalls details from the patriarch's life as providing the setting for visionary experiences. Similar attributions are made with respect to Enoch (1 Enoch), Moses (Assumption of Moses), Ezra (4 Ezra) and Baruch (2 Baruch, 3 Baruch).

Russell lists several factors behind this:[6] (1) On the basis of the corporate solidarity between the heroes of the faith and the nation, the choice of these figures showed the unity of God's people in all ages. (2) The idea of "contemporaneity" meant that all those within the tradition shared the same revelations from God and the same spiritual experiences as the great men of the past. (3) The "name" of a person bespeaks his character, and the choice of a name in a Jewish context linked the vision and the writer with the heroes of the past. Rowland argues that the first two notions have been recently challenged and are difficult to prove (1982:65-66). However, it is likely that such religious reasons approximate the reasons for such choices. The writers wished to deepen the impact of their visions by connecting them to the leaders of antiquity.

2. Characteristics. More difficult to delineate are characteristics that define the mindset of apocalyptists. Nevertheless, we can see clearly several aspects in a majority of the works.

a. *Pessimism toward the present age* may be the dominant characteristic. Most who attempt to isolate a *Sitz im Leben* (situation in the life of Israel that gave rise to the movement) believe that apocalypticism developed in a time of great crisis and peril for the nation. The situations were so desperate that there could be little hope for the present. All the child of God could do was await God's future intervention. Ladd believes that this is one basic difference between prophecy and apocalyptic (1957:198-99). The prophet argued that if Israel returned to God the condition would be met and the prophecy of doom avoided. The apocalyptist could offer no such optimistic forecast but could only comfort the reader that God in the future would bring contemporary history to a close and vindicate his people. In a very real sense one could say that the apocalyptists had a healthy respect for the depravity of humanity. They soundly rejected the falsely optimistic view of the progress of society and placed their trust not in man but in God. Morris calls this "the shaking of the foundations," for the whole Jewish perspective or world view was turned upside down (1972:41-43). No longer would things be right with the world, for not only did Judaism face troubles from without but troubles from within, a growing secularism and a clash of cultures with Babylonian, Persian and later Hellenistic values. Only God could bring order out of this chaos.

b. The *promise of salvation or restoration* is the other side of the same coin. Sanders believes this is so important that it is the one essential peculiarity of the movement.[7] While Sanders overstates the case, there is no denying the centrality of this characteristic. Throughout the visions of Daniel and Revelation the theme of restitution is predominant. In Revelation 6:9-11 and 8:3-5 the prayers of the saints for retribution are answered in the outpouring of the wrath of God, and the book moves throughout to its climax in the glory and joy of those martyred for Christ. In fact, the climax is prefigured throughout in the juxtaposition of wrath (chaps. 6; 8—9; 15—16) and glory (chaps. 1; 4—5; 7; 10; 19) passages.

c. A *view of transcendent reality* centering upon the presence and control of God is another major theme. Collins believes that this is in fact the primary distinguishing characteristic (1979:9-11). He finds two transcendent elements: the mediation of the revelation by a heavenly being; and a transcendent communication with a temporal axis (the coming eschatological salvation) and a spatial axis (the new order to be established by God on the earth). This divine transcendence relates to the futuristic eschatology of the apocalypses. The emphasis actually is not so much on the hopelessness of the present as upon the hopefulness of the future. Though it may have seemed as if God had disappeared from the scene, the apocalyptic writer is saying that this is illusory. In reality God still reigns over history, and he will bring it to a close in his own time.

However, this cataclysm would occur within history, and all humankind would see it. Descriptions of the event differ from writer to writer, and it was not until the time of Christ that their ideas were crystallized. Some stressed a messianic kingdom on this earth, others an otherworldly existence. For a time there was a two-Messiah doctrine that later coalesced into a single Messiah.[8] Many others had more interest in the messianic age than in the Messiah himself (the personal Messiah is missing in Tobit, 1 and 2 Maccabees, the Wisdom of Solomon, Sirach, Jubilees, the Assumption of Moses and 2 Enoch). However, all alike emphasize the intervention of God in catastrophic fashion (such as the seals, trumpets and bowls of Rev 6; 8—9; 16). This triumph would be absolute, visible to all, and would vindicate the faithful. Evil would be stamped out forever and righteousness prevail. Hartman delineates a fivefold pattern in the apocalyptic expectations: (1) cosmic catastrophes ending the sin and lawlessness; (2) divine intervention by God or a messianic figure; (3) judgment linked with retribution; (4) punishment of the wicked and (5) salvation of the faithful (1966:28-49).

d. A *determinism* was observable, in which God completely controlled all of history. A very strong predestinarian perspective prevailed, as God had already charted the future course of this world. In fact, apocalyptic could be labeled the "revelation" of this future history preordained by God. In the midst of the persecuted minority among Judaism and the church, this message held immense comfort. In the present they saw only the control and triumph of the wicked. The message that this was only temporary and that the future triumph of God and his people was assured was extremely meaningful.

e. A *modified dualism* is seen in the doctrine of the two ages, this age and the one to come. This age is characterized by total opposition between God and Satan, between the good and the wicked. An unceasing war is being waged between these opposing forces. The next age will be introduced by the complete victory of God and will be a new order. The poor and the dispossessed in the present order will experience exaltation at the hand of God, becoming like the angels or the heavenly stars (Dan 12:3; 1 Enoch 50:1).

The Interpretation of Symbols

Biblical symbolism is actually a special type of metaphor (see pp. 103-5 above) and therefore part of the multiple senses of the semantic range. The task of the interpreter is to determine which figurative sense the symbol has in the larger context. This means that the true meaning is not to be found in our present situation but rather in the use of that symbol in its ancient setting. This point can hardly be overemphasized in light of the misuse of biblical symbols in many circles today.

This does not mean that prophecy and apocalyptic should not be applied to the current situation nor that their "fulfillment" should not be sought. Rather, it means that the interpreter should seek first the "author's intended meaning" in the original context before delineating the way that the prophecies apply to our time. We should not look for the meaning of "666" (Rev 13:18) in things like the credit-card system or names of individuals in our current time but rather in the context of the first century (see Mounce 1977:263-65). At the same time the purpose of esoteric symbols in apocalyptic is to turn readers from the actual event to its theological meaning. In other words, readers are expected to see the hand of God in the future but are not supposed to know the exact sequence of events—that is, they are not given a description of what will actually happen. In short, we have no blueprint in Scripture for current events, but rather theological signs which tell us *in general* that God is going to draw history to a close. Symbols are literal in that they point to future events but not so literal that they tell us exactly how God is going to accomplish his purposes.

As Ramm points out, there are two elements in a symbol: the mental and conceptual idea and the image that represents it (1970:233). The problem is the cultural gap; both the symbol and the idea it represents stem from the ancient world and the biblical realities of that day. Symbols are actual objects (a boiling pot, a goat or ram, a chariot) often placed in strange combinations (a lion with an eagle's wings, Dan 7; a beast with ten horns and seven heads, Rev 13) to convey forcefully some religious truth. When the symbols are explained, as in Zechariah 6 (the chariots with red, black, white and dappled horses are heavenly spirits patrolling the four corners of the earth), the meaning is self-evident. When it is not the reader is tempted to give the symbols more specific meaning than is safe, for they are interpreted on the basis of current cultural meaning.

There are six types of symbols (see Mickelsen 1963:266-78; Ramm 1970:235-38; Sterrett:104-5): (1) external miraculous symbols (the burning bush, the pillar of cloud and fire, the ascension); (2) visions (the olive trees in Zech 4, the sheet filled with animals in Acts 10, the visions of the book of Revelation); (3) material symbols (blood = life, the cherubim on the mercy seat = holiness of God, the vine and branches = God's sustaining power); (4) emblematic numbers (seven and twelve in the book of Revelation), names (Isaiah's children in 7:3; 8:3), colors (the four horses of Zech 6 and Rev 6), metals (the hierarchical list from gold to clay in Dan 2) and jewels (the twelve foundation stones of the walls of the New Jerusalem in Rev 21); (5) emblematic actions (Ezekiel and John eating the scroll in Ezek 2 and Rev 10; Agabus binding himself with a belt in Acts 21); and (6) emblematic ordinances (the Jewish feasts celebrating harvest or the exodus and so forth, circumcision as a sign of the covenant, the eucharist as celebrating Jesus' sacrificial death).

In moving from the symbol to the reality it envisages, the reader should seek first the biblical background behind such symbols and then use this to interpret later allusions. For instance, the four beasts of Daniel 7 stand for the world empires and their leaders. The use of the beasts in Revelation 13 builds upon Daniel 7 and should be interpreted accordingly. It is debated whether the beast from the sea of Revelation 13 is a person (the Antichrist) or a world empire. In light of the presence of both in 2 Thessalonians 2 as well as in Daniel, it is doubtful whether such a distinction should be made: both are correct. The important thing is to allow the background behind the symbol to become a key to unlock its meaning.

One caveat is necessary: the past use of a symbol is a pointer to its meaning but is not determinative in itself. Symbols rarely became absolutely fixed or formalized in meaning. Therefore, we must check the total semantic field behind the associative senses of a term (see pp. 84-87), noting both similarities and differences in the uses elsewhere. For instance, the lion can be used for Judah, Christ or Satan in various contexts. At times the ferocity and predatory nature of the lion is stressed (1 Pet 5:8 of Satan); at other times his lordly nature is behind the image (Rev 5:5). In the latter in fact the lion is identified with the "lamb slain" (5:6), a marvelous juxtaposition of images! Natural qualities, such as salt used as a preservative or a seasoning (Mk 9:50), often provide a clue as well.

If the symbol is interpreted in the passage, that has important repercussions. Not only does the symbol lose its enigmatic character and become a known item, but it also becomes a control for other symbols in the immediate context and in the remainder of the book. We are given a critical clue to the mind of God in the particular vision, which aids us in tracking the progress of the visions elsewhere as they build upon and clarify the one known passage. Fee and Stuart list six interpreted images in the book of Revelation (1981:210): The one like a Son of man = Christ (1:17-18); the golden lampstands = the seven churches (1:20); the seven stars = the seven angels of the churches (1:20); the dragon = Satan (12:9); the seven heads = the seven hills on which the harlot sits (17:9; but what are the seven hills? Jerusalem or Rome?); the harlot = the great city (17:18, probably Rome, which was built on seven hills). These interpreted portions become keys for understanding the other visionary symbols.

Moreover, since Jewish and Christian apocalyptic did not exist in a vacuum, we must note the use of symbols in other cultures, such as Persian or Hellenistic. The Hellenistic background in the book of Revelation has been too long neglected. The readers came out of both Jewish and Greek circles, and God chose the symbols accordingly. The woman, dragon and child of Revelation 12 are an "international myth" (in a positive sense) with very close parallels in every ancient religion (such as Isis and Osiris, Marduk, Apollo). The symbol spoke eloquently to all backgrounds. Of course, Jewish background predominates, but this does not exclude Hellenism. For instance, Aune makes a very convincing case for a background from Caesar's court behind the throne-room scene of Revelation 4—5 (1983:5-26). This scene, following the central problem of the imperial cult in Revelation 2—3, shows where the true majesty and sovereign power exists and sets the stage for the use of Roman imagery throughout the remainder of the book.

Finally, note the total surface structure and on the basis of semotaxis (see p. 81) decide which of the possible meanings suggested by the diachronic (past background, for example, in Scripture) and synchronic (the current semantic range) analyses of the symbol best fits the immediate context. In this light the theological thrust of the whole passage is the key.

Let us consider the twelve foundation stones of Revelation 21:19-20 as an example. Many interpretations have been offered down through the ages. In the early centuries it was common to allegorize each jewel, for example, as the twelve tribes or twelve apostles.

However, this is only one among many options and is too subjective to be likely. The list parallels the jewels on the breastplate of the high priest in Exodus 28:17-20 and the similar royal list of jewels in Ezekiel 28:13. Philo and Josephus both believed that the high priest's jewels represented the twelve signs of the zodiac and from this Charles theorized that the list in Revelation reversed the order of the path of the sun through the zodiac (1920:2:165-69). However, there are too many discrepancies and this too is doubtful. Most likely, the jewels are not meant to be seen as individuals but rather suggest in a vague way the breastplate of the high priest and the magnificence of the New Jerusalem. While they may have had a more specific meaning, there is no evidence for such and we must be content with a more general interpretation.

Hermeneutical Principles

1. Note the type of literature. I pointed out above the differences between apocalyptic and prophecy. The fact is that none of the canonical books and few of the noncanonical are purely apocalyptic. Ladd has made a plea for the category "prophetic-apocalyptic" as better describing the biblical literature (1957). In many of the categories (such as pessimism vs. optimism, straightforward language vs. cryptic symbolism, prophetic figure vs. pseudonymity, no specification of time vs. the division of time into periods) the biblical works are mixed and in many portions are closer to the prophetic. The interpreter must be alert to these categories and work carefully with the smaller units within the larger whole. For instance, Zechariah 1—6 is primarily apocalyptic, but 7—14 is primarily prophetic. Daniel is an obvious blend of the two genres. Fee and Stuart argue that the book of Revelation is a composite of apocalyptic, prophetic and epistolary forms (1983:206-9). John does not merely await the eschaton but has a great interest in the current age primarily because the present is the Age of the Spirit (see 1:10-11) and because the book blends apocalyptic form with a prophetic perspective (see 1:3; 19:10; 22:18-19). Revelation speaks to the church of John's own day and to the church of every age. Further, John employs the epistolary form (see below; see 1:4-7; 22:21), addressing his readers in the customary "I-you" manner. This makes it even more important to recognize the extent to which many of the visions address current situations in John's church and blend the present with the future.

2. Note the perspective of the passage. While the first point centers upon the formal features of the work, this concerns more the characteristics discussed above. The interpreter must study the aspects emphasized and particularly the pattern by which they develop. For instance, Ezekiel 38—39 (Gog and Magog) follows a familiar pattern (noted by Hartman 1966:28-49) of chronicling the sins of the wicked followed by the cosmic catastrophe (38:19-20, 22) which publicly manifests the judgment of the wicked (38:23; 39:7, 21-23) and total destruction (39:9-20), magnifies God's holy name (39:7, 22) and, after demonstrating the iniquity of Israel (39:23-24), restores the remnant (39:25-29). Determinism is stressed, and the dualism is seen in the fact that a message of repentance is not present. The vision moves directly from the punishment of Israel for her sins (39:23-24) to the restoration of the nation after the exile (39:25-29).

3. Note the structure of the passage or book. No vision or detail functions by itself.

Critical scholars usually state that apocalyptic works are composite, that is, collections of isolated visions (Koch even makes it a formal feature). I have two responses: first, it is by no means proven that apocalyptic books are composite. I have already noted that apocalyptic is more literary than oral; if that is true the visions were never meant to be individual entities but rather were given as parts of larger wholes. I personally doubt the accuracy and validity of this assumption. Second, the canonical order is still critical. Even if we grant later redactors or collections (which I would argue against), most would agree that the structural development of the books is still crucial. Childs, for instance, grants a composite nature to Zechariah and accepts the view that each vision addresses a quite different historical circumstance (1979:474-76). However, he argues that the final shaping of the text has important theological implications for the meaning of the book.

This is not the place to argue the critical issues, but Childs's plea for the final canonical shape fits the recent trend toward literary exegesis rather than historico-critical restructuring and is essentially correct. The visions of Zechariah 1—6 provide an eschatological reinterpretation of the return from exile (539 B.C., twenty years prior to Zechariah's visions) in the direction of the final deliverance at the eschaton. There is a unified theological pattern and each one builds upon the other. The themes of chapters 9—14 (judgment and restoration), while quite different in form, expand and clarify the earlier chapters.

4. Note the function and meaning of the symbols. After noting the basic thrust of the whole, one must exegete the parts. Fee and Stuart make a special plea for the necessity of exegesis when studying the book of Revelation, primarily because it is so common to ignore historical factors when interpreting apocalyptic literature (1981:209-11). The prevalence of predictive elements causes the reader to forget the original situation and accent only the futuristic fulfillment (primarily in terms of the current age). Yet in every case the author's original meaning must predominate, for it is the key to the fulfillment.

Since I have already discussed hermeneutical principles with respect to symbols, a summary is sufficient here. We will want to ask first whether the symbol is interpreted in the immediate context or elsewhere in the book. If so, this will provide the control for the meaning of those symbols not directly interpreted. Next, we will study the synchronic (the use of the symbol in literature of the same period) and diachronic (the use of the symbol in the past) parallels. Especially important will be a direct allusion to a past text (such as the use of Ezekiel or Daniel in the book of Revelation). These provide specific helps to the meaning of the symbols, although the final arbiter is still the immediate context.

5. Stress the theological and note the predictive with humility. This does not mean that futuristic prophecy is not as important as the theological message to the writer's own day. Rather, the future even in apocalyptic texts was not an end in itself but a means to an end, namely to comfort and challenge the saints. I personally believe that one reason for the use of cryptic symbols was to keep the reader from giving the future fulfillment too great a place in the message of the book. The writer wanted to turn the reader toward God, not just toward future events. Therefore, the actual event prophesied was clouded in the mist of symbolism and the reader had to turn to the God who would bring it to pass.

This point is as relevant to the church today as it was to Judaism and the church in the past. We often forget how mistakenly Israel interpreted prophecies of the First Advent. We have no greater perspective from which to interpret prophecies of the Second Advent. We must remember that each era of the church through the ages has believed that Christ would return in its generation. Therefore, we need to stress the theological meaning of apocalyptic and hold to interpretations of fulfillment in our own day (such as those related to the reinstatement of Israel as a nation) with humility. Above all, we dare not preach such prophecies as absolute truth. Otherwise, when they fail to come to pass, people's faith can be hurt and the church made to look foolish. Such occurred recently with respect to some who gave too much credence to the pamphlet promising the Lord's return in 1988.

The implications of this for preaching are enormous. Apocalyptic contains a powerful theological message centering upon the ancient followers of God and their difficult situation. That same message has parallels with and repercussions for the saints of our own day. With unemployment on the rise, a greater amount of worldwide persecution today than ever before in history and vast uncertainty about the future economically and ecologically, the apocalyptic truths are more needed than ever before. Note the following recapitulation of the book of Revelation and ask the extent to which that historical situation applies today.

> The main themes are abundantly clear: the church and the state are on a collision course; and initial victory will appear to belong to the state. Thus he warns the church that suffering and death lie ahead; indeed, it will get far worse before it gets better (6:9-11). He is greatly concerned that they do not capitulate in times of duress (14:11-12; 21:7-8). But this prophetic word is also one of encouragement; for God is in control of all things. Christ holds the keys to history, and He holds the churches in His hands (1:17-20). Thus the church triumphs even through death (12:11). God will finally pour out His wrath upon those who caused that suffering and death and bring eternal rest to those who remain faithful. (Fee and Stuart 1981:212)

Even these passages primarily concerned with the future apply to the present. For instance, the Beast and his forces (the Antichrist of the future) depicted also Rome and the enemies of the church (the many antichrists) in John's day. The seals, trumpets and bowls are future outpourings of wrath but remind the unbeliever of the certainty of God's judgment and the believer of God's future vindication.

Above all, note the congruence of present and future throughout biblical apocalyptic literature. There is a very real "telescoping of time" throughout, which in the New Testament is built upon the tension between the "already" and the "not yet" in the eschatology of Jesus and the early church. The prophecies regarding the "not yet" are so closely tied to the "already" that the two can at times appear to be simultaneous. Therefore, we must avoid dogmatic pronouncements and contrive to address our present in light of the certainty of God's control over history and of his future vindication of his faithful followers and punishment of the wicked.

Excursus: The Origins of Apocalyptic

Many believe that apocalyptic developed primarily during the Maccabean period as a

Hasidic protest against the religious policies and persecution of the Seleucids and of Antiochus Epiphanes in particular (Rowley 1963:21-24; Russell 1978:2). Ezekiel, Zechariah and the other earlier works are considered to be prophetic precursors but not apocalyptic works (see the survey in Nickelsburg 1983:641-46). Certainly one could argue thus for Isaiah 24—27 and perhaps Joel. While themes of Jewish eschatology are present in the Isaiah passage (destruction of the earth, cosmic portents, heavenly banquet, Leviathan, the dragon), many of the signs of apocalyptic are not (the vision, the negation of the present in favor of the future, the dualism). The locust plague of Joel 1—2 does use symbolism but without the profusion of images, and it is more a prophetic call to the people to return to Yahweh.

However, when we look elsewhere there are clear signs of apocalyptic. Hanson (1971:463-68) finds the perspective of despair in the present and the direct intervention of God in several oracles of Isaiah 39—66 (such as 40; 43; 51). "This interlocking of primeval-past, historical-future . . . lends cosmic significance to the future event" (p. 465).[9] Such is even more true with respect to Ezekiel and Zechariah. Rowland (1982:199-200) notes the literary setting of Ezekiel 40, with its vision followed by interpretation, as a constant apocalyptic mode (compare Dan 8—10; Rev 17). Zechariah also employs an angelic interpreter (1:19; 3:1; 4:2). The use of cryptic symbols in the dream-visions and the themes of the visions demonstrate the presence of apocalyptic thinking.

Moreover, apocalyptic literature was present in the ancient Near East prior to the prophetic period. In Bergman's excellent article on Egyptian apocalyptic (1983:51-60) he discusses the Egyptian determinism and cyclical view of eternity, which in the opinion of some make any apocalyptic tradition in Egypt impossible. Bergman argues that this represents only one among many religious traditions in Egypt and in fact there was interest in the ages and in heavenly journeys. In the same volume Ringgren (1983:379-86), Widengren (1983:77-156) and Hultgard (1983:387-411) discuss the motifs in Akkadia and Persia respectively. Akkadia represents an early stage of developing apocalyptic ideas, but the Iranian texts on the role of Zoroaster as apocalyptic mediator, in spite of difficulties of dating, show a developed mode of thinking at an early period. On the basis of the divine names, S. Hartman (1983:71-73) argues that the basic Iranian traditions go back to the sixth century B.C. and that Iranian dualism as well as ideas of pre-existent wisdom and an eschatological redeemer were well known to Jewish thinkers. In short, there are parallels elsewhere in the period of the prophets. Naturally, the question of direct influence is subjective and difficult to detect. Rather, I would argue that there is little evidence to suggest that apocalyptic was a late development and every reason to conclude that it originated parallel to Iranian and Near Eastern ideas primarily in a prophetic milieu from the eighth to the sixth centuries B.C.

However, prophecy was not the only influence upon apocalyptic thinking. I have already mentioned the connection between wisdom and apocalyptic. Von Rad in fact argues that wisdom was the primary source for apocalyptic thought, since both movements stem from the quest for knowledge and human experience in this world (1972:280-81). Yet while a connection does exist, there are too many differences between the two traditions (such as the absence of an eschatological orientation and esoteric symbolism in wisdom thought) to posit direct influence (see Rowland 1982:203-8).

It is of course impossible to isolate any particular *Sitz im Leben* (situation in the life of Israel) for the rise of apocalyptic. It seems most likely that due to the pressures and exigencies of the exile, God added to his direct pronouncements through the prophets a series of visionary experiences relating his control of the future and the necessity of Israel's remnant trusting his direct intervention in the historical processes as the only answer to the situation. The mediums of vision and symbol became the best means for proclaiming these truths, and from Isaiah to Ezekiel to Daniel to Zechariah this method became increasingly predominant in the divine revelations. One thing is clear: the answer is not found only in sociological analysis. We must note the mind of God as the key to the process. Naturally the two are not mutually exclusive. God chose the mode that best fit the moment for the communication of his will.

A second and more developed apocalyptic movement took place in the second century B.C. In the post-Maccabean period the movement was linked with the Hasidim (the pious party that later gave rise to the Pharisees and the Essenes). Connections with both parties can be noted, but they are certainly more direct with the latter. Morris correctly notes that while some apocalyptic concerns can be found in Pharisaism (resurrection, the after life), on the whole the latter movement was opposed to such "enthusiastic" religious approaches (1972:14-16). At an earlier date a connection is likely, but the two groups went in different directions. Apocalyptic was not a political movement or party like the Pharisees or Sadducees. Like wisdom it was more a way of thinking, a mode of looking at life. It was first a divinely chosen means of revelation and then became an outlook on life that cut across the different Jewish sects and manifested itself at different times in all of them (with the exception of the Sadducees). Most important, it provided one of the most obvious links between Judaism and Christianity, far more direct than any single party.

11
$p$arable

PARABLES, ALONG WITH APOCALYPTIC, HAVE BEEN AMONG THE MOST WRITTEN ABOUT YET
hermeneutically abused portions of Scripture. This is understandable since the two
form at one and the same time the most dynamic and yet the most difficult to
comprehend of the biblical genres. The potential of the parable for communication is
enormous, since it creates a comparison or story based upon everyday experiences. However, that story itself is capable of many meanings, and the modern reader has as much
difficulty interpreting it as did the ancient hearers. Jesus himself gave the operating
principle, "The knowledge of the secrets of the kingdom of God has been given to you,
but to others I speak in parables, so that, 'though seeing, they may not see; though
hearing, they may not understand' " (Lk 8:10). Mary Ann Tolbert correctly states, "Judging by the varied opinions and continued controversies that mark the study of the parables of Jesus . . . it is undoubtedly true that most modern parable interpreters fall into
the category of the 'others' " (1979:13). The disciples had great difficulty understanding
the parables, and this is even more true in our day. If one were to read a cross-section
of works on the parables or hear a randomly selected cross-section of sermons, the
multiplicity of interpretations would be bewildering. Is the "author's intended meaning"
possible? And by "author" do we mean Jesus or the evangelist? These are only two of
the many issues we face when coming to grips with the parable genre.

The Meaning and Use of Parables
The importance of parables is evident when we realize that fully a third of Jesus' teaching
in the Synoptic Gospels comes in parabolic form. In modern terms, we think of a parable
as "an earthly story with a heavenly meaning." Yet what did it mean in the ancient world?
The Hebrew term is *māšāl,* which also is used for the "proverb" or "riddle" and has as
its basic meaning the idea of comparison. Indeed, the proverbial form often established
a comparison, such as Proverbs 18:11, "The wealth of the rich is their fortified city, like
a high wall in their imagination." As Peisker points out, *māšāl* developed from a popular
term for proverb to a technical term for wisdom teaching and finally to a broad term
used for prophetic proverbs, parables, riddles and symbolic actions (1978:744-45). Several
prophetic parables might be mentioned, such as Nathan's parable of the ewe lamb, which

dramatically demonstrated his own injustice to Uriah (2 Sam 12:1-2) or Isaiah's parable of the unfruitful vineyard, used to illustrate Israel's unfaithfulness and God's judgment upon the nation (5:1-7).

The background of the parable in wisdom and prophecy is crucial when considering Jesus' development of the parable form. It has long been recognized that Jesus was a teacher of eschatological wisdom and his parables demonstrate this quite well. Yet, as Perkins points out, there were significant differences (1981:37-39). Jesus was not a teacher of wisdom in the sense of helping the young learn to live as responsible members of society. Purely pragmatic issues like friendship, choosing a wife and future leadership in society are all missing. Rather, Jesus was preparing citizens of the kingdom, and he used the methods of wisdom to that end. This has important ramifications for the positive side of Jesus' use of parables to challenge the hearer to respond for the kingdom (see further below).

Like the many forms of the Jewish *māšāl*, the *parabolē* that Jesus used had a multiplicity of forms. There are proverbs (Lk 4:23, "Physician heal yourself"), metaphors (Mt 15:13, "Every plant not planted by my heavenly Father will be uprooted"), similes (Mt 10:16, "I send you out like sheep among wolves"), figurative sayings (Lk 5:36-38 on the new wine in old wineskins, which utilizes *parabolē*), similitudes or more developed similes (Mk 4:30-32, comparing the kingdom to a grain of mustard seed), story parables in which the comparison takes the form of fictional narrative (Mt 25:1-13, the ten virgins), illustrative or example stories in which the parable becomes a model for proper conduct (Lk 10:29-37, the good Samaritan) and allegorical parables in which several points of comparison are drawn (Mk 4:1-9, 13-20, the sower and the seed). The one common element is the use of everyday experiences to draw a comparison with kingdom truths. When most people think of "parable" they think of the story parables, but as we have seen the form is much broader. No wonder Mark could add, "And with many such parables Jesus spoke the word to [the crowds] . . . and without parables he did not speak to them" (4:33-34).

Let us delve a little more deeply into the similitude, parable and allegory. The first two have strong similarities, as each maintains a formal, literal comparison stressing a central idea. However, a similitude is a straightforward comparison with one or more verbs in the present tense, applying a common experience or typical habit to greater spiritual realities. Consider Mark 13:28-29: the everyday reality (the fig tree sprouting leaves as evidence that summer is near) demonstrates the kingdom truth (the events of 13:5-27 as harbingers of the return of Christ). A parable on the other hand is a narrative employing a particular event in the past tense without the direct and obvious comparison. It is indirect and demands that the hearer react. It does not appeal to the mind as much as to the whole person. As Linnemann says, the similitude finds its authority in the universality of the imagery, the parable in the "perspicuity" with which it is told, that is, in the power of the story to attract and hold one's attention.

The allegory paints a series of pictures in metaphorical form, all of which combine in parabolic fashion. It is common today to state that the major difference between a pure parable and an allegory is that in the latter all the details have symbolic significance with many thrusts rather than a single point. Yet this is debatable, as exemplified in Matthew

22:1-14 (parable of the royal wedding feast) in which the king refers to God, the servants to the prophets and the son to Christ.

The extent to which allegories are found in Jesus' teaching has been debated. Jeremias argues that allegorical details are later church embellishments or additions and must be removed to get back to Jesus' original parables, which have a single point (1972:66-89). However, as most now recognize, Jeremias was forced to employ circular reasoning to prove his case. From Jülicher (see below) he received his basic thesis that Jesus' parables had to make only one single point, and he then read this theory back into the evidence. The presence of allegory at the earliest stages of Jesus' teaching is strongly attested to in the Gospels. The very first parable narrated, the parable of the sower (Mk 4:3-9), provides one of the clearest cases of multiple thrusts; one could also mention the parables of the tares (Mt 13:24-30), the net (Mt 13:47-50) and the vine and the branches (Jn 15:1-8). However, only the context may decide which details provide local color without spiritual significance (part of the story world) or have individual theological meaning themselves (meant to be contextualized).

Craig Blomberg provides the strongest challenge yet to the "one-point only" school of Jülicher and Jeremias (1990:29-70, especially 36-47). He argues that the distinction between parable and allegory has been overstated, and that both Jesus and the evangelists intended the parables to be understood as having several points: (1) Both Old Testament and rabbinic parables show that the Jewish *māšāl* preferred a carefully controlled allegorical thrust. (2) There never was a distinction between allegorical and nonallegorical forms in the Greco-Roman world; most preferred mixed types in which some but not all the details had a "second level of meaning." (3) The form-critical assertion that the tendency in ancient times was to allegorize originally simple stories can be turned on its head; the tendency may well have been to abbreviate, not expand. (4) Even single-point parables are metaphorical and thus allegorical, since they involve further levels of meaning. (5) There is a difference between "allegory," a literary device in which the author draws the reader into a deeper and intended level of meaning; and "allegorizing," in which levels of meaning (never intended) are read into the text. The former is true of the Gospel parables, but not the latter. (6) So many details in the parables are indeed meant to be understood on the metaphorical level due to their extravagant nature (they go beyond the normal story line) that they cannot be mere added details; they must have spiritual significance.

The task is to distinguish between "local color" (details not meant to carry spiritual meaning) and theologically loaded details (those which do have allegorical significance).[1] This is determined on the basis of context, both macro (the larger context within which the parable is found) and micro (the parable itself), as well as the historical background of the details as seen in the story. In general, as Blomberg states, the main characters or symbols of a parable contain significance. For instance, in the parable of the sower, the four types of soil signify different types of receptivity to the gospel, the sower refers to God and the seed is the gospel. Here most of the details are allegorized. In the prodigal son parable (Lk 15:11-32), however, the characters have significance (the father = God, the prodigal son = tax collectors and sinners, the elder son = scribes and Pharisees; see

15:1) but the details (such as the famine, the pigs and the carob seeds) add vividness rather than spiritual meaning. In each case we must study the parable in terms of external (larger context) and internal (structural development) considerations before making any decisions.

The Purpose of Parables

One of the most difficult parable sections in the Gospels is the only one that clearly delineates their "purpose": Mark 4:10-12 (Mt 13:10-15; Lk 8:9-10), which gives a very negative perspective, "to those on the outside everything is spoken in parables so that, 'they may be ever seeing but never perceiving, and ever hearing but never understanding, otherwise they might turn and be forgiven' " (Mk 4:11-12). Modern interpreters have had a great deal of trouble accepting a statement that implies that Jesus used parables to hide the kingdom truths from unbelievers. Linnemann, for instance, argues that this could only have been added by a later church in absolute conflict with Jewish opponents (1966). Others argue that Mark created the story as part of his "messianic secret," his view that Jesus wished to conceal his true identity. This is convenient but hardly convincing. Kermode argues that this forms the very core of Jesus' enigmatic preaching, which both conceals and reveals (1979:25-47). The "mystery" of the gospel produced the enigma.

First, attempts to solve the question on the basis of the connectives are doomed to disappointment. We should not overly distinguish Mark's *hina* from Matthew's *hoti;* as Zerwick points out, both may be based upon the original Aramaic *di* and in this instance should not be set against each other (1963:146). Yet, at the same time, we should not remove all differences, as if the two were synonymous. The answer is found somewhere between the two poles. Furthermore, we cannot argue that *hina* in Mark 4:12 means result rather than purpose. While such is possible, the strong judgment context with its "those around/those outside" polarity makes result unlikely. The quote from Isaiah 6:9-10 is too strong for a resultative sense. The basic thrust of the Isaianic passage is divine rejection and judgment, and this is certainly Jesus' meaning as well. Finally, the interpretation of *mepote* as "unless" rather than "lest" is also possible[2] but unlikely, again because of the strong judgment context of the passage. This is hardly a promise of forgiveness in light of the rigid distinction between Jesus' followers (who obviously alone have forgiveness) and the outsiders. Thus Mark centers on Jesus' sovereign purpose ("so that") and Matthew on the reason ("because") for that judgment. They constitute two sides of the same coin.

In short, Mark 4:10-12 clearly indicates that Jesus chose the parable form to symbolize God's judgment upon his opponents. Jesus often used parables not from a desire to communicate truth but to hide the truth from unresponsive hearers. Parables confirmed unbelievers in their rejection. However, we must ask a further question: Was this *the* purpose of the parable form or *a* purpose? One of the keys to the determination of dogma from Scripture is to reject proof-texting (determining a doctrine from single statements rather than from the whole of Scripture). Two factors force us to seek other evidence: this quote is found within the conflict-and-rejection parables of Mark 4 and Matthew 13 and therefore occurs in a limited context; and parables are definitely used to challenge and instruct the disciples (such as the parable of the moneylender, Lk 7:40-43; the parables in the Olivet Discourse, Mt 24:32—25:46; those in the farewell discourse, Jn 14:2-3, 6; 15:1-8; 16:21-22) and also to challenge the crowds and even the Pharisees to respond (such as the parables on seeking the lost, Lk 15; the good Samaritan, Lk 10).

It seems clear that Jesus did indeed have a larger purpose in using the parable form. Parables are an "encounter mechanism" and function differently depending on the audience. In his controversies with the leaders and unbelieving Israel a large part of that purpose was to conceal the truth from them. This was a divine judgment on recalcitrant Israel that paralleled the judgment on Pharaoh and on the apostate nation of Isaiah's day. In response to their rejection of Jesus' message God will harden their hearts further via the parable. Yet this negative sign was part of a larger purpose that had its roots in the Old Testament wisdom use of parables to challenge and draw the people to response (such as Nathan's parable to David in 2 Sam 12). Indeed, here the "performative" language in the parables noted by the New Hermeneutic is valid (Funk 1966:193-96). The crowds are forced to make a decision for or against Jesus, and his disciples are challenged and taught by them. Each group (leaders, crowds, disciples) is encountered differently by the parables.

The parables encounter, interpret and invite the listener/reader to participate in Jesus' new world-vision of the kingdom. They are a "speech-event" that never allows us to remain neutral; they grasp our attention and force us to interact with the presence of the kingdom in Jesus, either positively (those "around" Jesus in Mk 4:10-12) or negatively (those "outside"). Scholars are beginning to agree that Matthew 16:19 and especially John 20:23 ("Whatever sins you forgive will be forgiven and whatever you retain will be retained") relate primarily to the proclamation of divine truths; the hearer must respond and this response leads to salvation or judgment. This is very applicable to the parable. For those who reject the presence of God in Jesus (the leaders of the Jews) the parable becomes a sign of sovereign judgment, further hardening their hearts. For those who are open (the crowds) the parable encounters and draws them to decision. For those who believe (the disciples) the parable teaches them further kingdom truths.

The Characteristics of Parables

1. Earthiness. Jesus borrowed pictures from home life (lost coin, leaven, prodigal son), nature (mustard seed, tares), the animal world (birds of the air, wolves in sheep's clothing), agriculture (sower, vineyard, lost sheep), commerce (talents, unjust steward, wicked tenants), royalty (royal wedding), hospitality (good Samaritan). To this extent Jesus followed in the tradition of the sages (wisdom teachers), who centered on the practical side of life. Yet Jesus also transcended the sages in that this was primarily the picture or image side of the metaphor and not the true thrust. At times there was an ethical message (such as the good Samaritan) but it formed a kingdom ethics.

At the same time the point of the parable can be skewed unless we understand the earthy details behind the image in the parable. For instance, explaining the topography of Palestine aids greatly in understanding and applying the parable of the sower. The seed "beside the road" is based upon the fact that roads run right through the middle of the fields and since farmers sowed seed liberally rather than scientifically some would naturally fall on the hard-packed road. The "rocky place" refers to the limestone shelf just a few inches below the soil in many parts of Palestine. This would hold in the water, allowing the plant to sprout quickly. However, the sun would dry it up just as swiftly and the crop would wither; there was insufficient soil for deep roots. The "thorns" were a type of weed that sunk roots more quickly and so "choked" the moisture and nutrition from the new stalks. Finally, in many parts of Palestine a hundredfold yield has actually been recorded, so Jesus' point is not just hyperbole.

2. Conciseness. The parables recorded in the Gospels are simple and uncomplicated. There are seldom more than two or three characters, and the plot line contains few subplots. Here we must correct earlier misunderstandings, however. From Jülicher and Jeremias, many have taught that parables have only a single perspective or plot. This is not quite true. The prodigal son does have a major plot (the profligacy of the son followed by repentance, forgiveness and reinstatement) but also has two other perspectives (the love of the father, the jealousy of the older brother), both of which have meaning in the parable and transcend mere "local color" (that is, are part of the story but have no theological significance). The parable itself must guide us into its complexities.

3. Major and Minor Points. This is the most debated aspect of parable research. Due to the tremendous influence of Jülicher still today, many demand a single major point and argue that minor points are "local color." However, I would modify this. I agree that the continuing tendency of many to allegorize parables subjectively must make the interpreter extremely cautious.[3] However, each parable must be interpreted individually, and the interpreter should be open to the possibility of minor points as the text dictates. There is in one sense a unified message; the individual details of the parable of the sower point to a basic truth, challenging the reader to identify which type of soil/response he or she will become/make. In the prodigal son parable, the forgiveness of the father is contrasted with the self-centeredness of the older brother. Yet in both parables (as stated above) the secondary elements do have significance.

We can speak of allegorical parables but not allegorizing per se. There is no license for interpreters to do whatever they wish with the details. There is a very tight control and the inner dynamics of the story tell us whether or not to see a theological point in a detail. For instance, the mustard seed and the great plant are the center of the Mark 4:30-32 parable, and it is unlikely that the birds in the branches should be allegorized;[4] their function in the parable is to emphasize the great size of the plant. Via says, "While the meaning of Jesus' parables cannot be restricted to one central point of comparison, that does not mean that they are allegories. . . . We must seek a non-allegorical approach to the parables other than the one-point approach" (1967:17). Yet I have noted many indications that the parables are indeed allegories, albeit tightly controlled by the author's intention. Blomberg (1990) in fact argues that there are as many points as there are characters in the parables and that they are indeed allegories. While this is somewhat overstated, it is nearer the truth than the "one point" approach.

4. Repetition. This is sometimes used to stress the climax or the major point of the parable, as in the twofold confession of the prodigal son (Lk 15:18-19, 21, "Father, I have sinned against heaven and against you; I am no longer worthy to be called your son") or the similar wording of the reward to the faithful servant (Mt 25:21, 23, "Well done, good and faithful servant. You were faithful in the few things. I will give you charge over many things"). Some parables are delivered in two settings, like the parable of the lost sheep, addressed to the disciples in Matthew 18:12-14 and to the Pharisees in Luke 15:1-7. Audience criticism will note slightly different emphases in such circumstances. In Matthew 18 Jesus teaches that the Father "is not willing that any of the little ones should be lost" (v. 14, with the stress on mission), and in Luke 15 the accent is upon the heavenly rejoicing "over one repentant sinner" (v. 7, with the emphasis upon conversion). This is often used as a prime example of the open-ended nature of parables, since the "evangelists" place them in different situations and give them slightly different thrusts. However, this ignores two things: (1) Jesus as an itinerant preacher would naturally use parables in more than one setting, so it could well be his own interpretations (this is my preference). (2) This does not give one license to remove parables from their historical settings and read multiple meanings into them; in fact, it argues just the opposite, for both Matthew 18 and Luke 15 are *textual* interpretations and not free renderings. Parables *can* be read in many ways, but if they are to be *Scripture* the context must decide!

5. Conclusion at the End. Jesus often uses a terse dictum to conclude a parable, such as "So is he who lays up treasures for himself" (Lk 12:21). Other times he may elicit the lesson from the listeners via a question such as the two debtors in Luke 7:42 ("Who will love him more?") or the good Samaritan in Luke 10:36 ("Who of the three was the neighbor?"). At times Jesus interprets the parable himself (Mt 13:18-23; 15:15-20). Of course this is a general rule rather than an ironclad law. The parable of the workers in the vineyard (Mt 20:1-16) ends with a statement on the reversal of roles (v. 16, "the last will be first and the first last") almost opposite to the thrust of the parable itself (vv. 1-15) on divine generosity to all alike. Yet these two aspects are not in conflict. While the concluding statement does not provide the main point of the parable, it does fit the situation. As Stein says, "If the *Sitz im Leben* of the parable is indeed Jesus' defense of his association with publicans and sinners and his offering to them of the kingdom of God, then there is a sense in which the parable does reveal that 'the last will be first and the first last' " (1981:128). In other words, the final saying (v. 16) does not interpret the parable but rather applies it to the broader situation (Jesus turning to the outcasts; note that this method parallels Mt 19:30 following the rich young ruler incident).

6. Listener-relatedness. This takes us to the heart of the parable form. Primarily Jesus intended to elicit a response from the listener, either positive or negative (see above on "purpose"). Crossan points out that this provides a basic difference between Jewish parables and those of Jesus (1973:19-21). Rabbinic stories are didactic, elaborating a specific text and illustrating a dogmatic proposition. Jesus' parables drive home a point and elicit a response. For instance, the question parables (see point 5 above) drew the audience into the action via dialogue and reached them in the midst of their situation. As Blomberg says, the centrality of the audience for interpreting the parables is coming more and more to the fore (1982:11-14). The parables were addressed to the actual historical situation in Jesus' dialogues with three concrete groups: the crowds, the scribes and Pharisees, and his disciples. In each situation Jesus challenged his audience, often emphasizing the urgency of repentance (Lk 12:16-21; 13:1-9) and demanding "decisive (Lk 16:1-8), radical (Mt 13:44-46), watchful (Mt 24:42—25:13) action because the kingdom is near" (Peisker 1978:749). I would add one clarification: the encounter related to the crowds and the disciples. For the religious leaders parables were intended only to confirm their rejection (see above on the purpose of parables).

Linnemann provides an excellent summary of the way parables accomplish this (1966:25-33). The parable is so structured as to "interlock" the hearer with the narrator's message. It does so by "conceding" a point to the hearer, by approaching the listener from his own world of experience. The parable then employs double meaning to switch from the listener's experience to the greater reality of the kingdom truths. It "claims one thing as another," drawing a comparison between the main point of the parabolic image and the reality the narrator (Jesus) wishes to convey. Thereby it becomes a "language event" in the proper sense as Jesus through it presents a new possibility to his hearers and moves them to the point of decision.[5]

7. Reversal of Expectation. The major way by which Jesus forced decision was to break conventional lines in his parables. Time and again a totally unexpected turn of events startled the hearers and forced them to consider the deeper implications of the parable. The normal way of things was shattered by the parable's reversal of norms, and the hearer was forced to consider the kingdom reality behind the image, for kingdom truths also run counter to the world's ways. At the same time the parables exhibit what Petzoldt calls an "antithetical structure," as Jesus' meaning clashed with the interpretation of his hearers and forced them out of their narrow religious framework (1984:24-30). God's call is never a comfortable one, and the parables are characterized by a discomfiting aspect as human expectations clash with the kingdom presence of God in Jesus.

Unfortunately, this reversal of expectations is often lost on modern readers because we no longer know the background. Perhaps no aspect of interpretation illustrates the importance of historical background information more than the parable. Consider the parable of the Pharisee and the tax collector (Lk 18:9-14), in which the Pharisee's self-centered prayer is rejected and the tax collector's plea for mercy was accepted. Most modern Christians accept this without question, having already accepted all Pharisees as self-righteous hypocrites. Yet this entirely misses the point. Thiselton quotes Walter Wink here: "The scholar, having finished his work lays down his pen, oblivious to the way in which he has *falsified the text* in accordance with unconscious tendencies; so much so that he has maimed its original intent until it has actually turned into its opposite" (1981:14, quoting Wink 1973:42; italics Wink's). While it is doubtful that the true scholar would make such a mistake, it is a common error to ignore the original situation. The Pharisee's prayer was perfectly acceptable to Jews of Jesus' day. The hearer would have been quite satisfied with the prayer and shocked to see the despised tax collector justified (see Jeremias 1972:140-41). Jesus' original purpose was to unsettle his audience, to reverse their value system and force them to rethink their religious priorities. Modern readers are confirmed in their assurance that they at least are not guilty of "Pharisaism," while partaking of the same errors.

This plot twist is quite common in the parables. The hated Samaritan, not the priest or Levite, is the one to bind the wounds of the robbery victim (Lk 10:30-37; normally the Samaritans were the muggers not the saviors!); the profligate son is the one given the banquet (Lk 15:11-32); the poor and the crippled sit at the great feast (Lk 14:15-24); the steward who alters the master's credit sheet is lauded (Lk 16:1-13). By doing so Jesus can force the hearer to take a new look at God's true kingdom realities. This also is part of the paradoxical purpose of parables already discussed. Only one with the proper key can unlock the mystery of the parable's meaning, and that key is the presence of the kingdom. Without the key the opponents of Jesus are confirmed in their rejection of his teaching. Only those who are open or have already accepted the "mystery" of the kingdom in Jesus can understand why God looks to the "sinners" and outcasts and rejects those the establishment considers "righteous."

8. Kingdom-centered Eschatology. The single theme that rebounds throughout the parables is the presence of the kingdom. This was Dodd's central contribution, although his misunderstanding of the parables as teaching a realized (present) eschatology had to be corrected by Jeremias. Yet they deal with more than the kingdom; the parables are christological at heart, focusing upon Jesus as the harbinger and content of the kingdom, which we will define as "God's rule."

God's rule is seen first as a present reality. In the parable of the new patch/wine and the old cloth/wineskins (Mk 2:21-22) the kingdom is seen as forcing a break with the past. The new era is here; as Jesus says in the debate over his exorcism, "The kingdom of God has come upon you" (Lk 11:20). In fact, the kingdom is now in the process of developing, as seen in the "growth parables," such as the mustard seed (Mk 4:30-32) or the leaven (Mt 13:33). While many believe these are futuristic and describe a final in-breaking of the kingdom, Marshall is correct in interpreting them in the light of inaugurated eschatology: the growth takes place in the present, although the full extent of the greatness of the kingdom will not be manifest until the eschaton (1963:27-29). In light of the kingdom's presence, several of the parables of growth demand radical response (the sower, the tares, the dragnet). Several other parables, especially in Luke, describe the course of the kingdom in this age as typified by discipleship and social concern (the rich man and Lazarus, counting the cost). Finally, a future crisis of judgment will consummate the presence of the kingdom. Several parables warn the hearers to be ready (the Olivet discourse parables, the great supper) and to work in light of that future reality (the talents) since it would judge their works (the wheat and the tares, the sheep and the goats).

9. Kingdom Ethics. The presence of the kingdom in Jesus demands a higher ethical stance on the part of his followers. This of course is developed especially in the Sermon on the

Mount and the parables in it. The disciple is the salt of the earth and the light of the world (Mt 5:13-16) and must at all times live as a citizen of heaven. Therefore, the follower of the kingdom must be characterized by a wholehearted devotion to heavenly rather than earthly treasures (6:19-24) and by an unwillingness to judge others (7:1-5). The believer takes the narrow way (7:13) and thereby builds a solid house that cannot be destroyed by the storms of life (7:24-27). These emphases are carried throughout Jesus' parabolic teaching. In fact, this is where Jesus comes the closest to the sages or teachers of wisdom; whatever the basis, the presence of the kingdom alters the grounds of the ethical conduct. The parables present a radical demand for a new approach to life involving absolute forgiveness (the unforgiving servant, the two debtors), reconciliation (the prodigal son), compassion (the good Samaritan), sharing (the friend at midnight), the wise use of money (the unjust steward) and resources (the talents).

Above all, the disciple is seen as living his life both in the world and before God. The one who is the "light of the world" must live kingdom ethics before the nonbelievers, yet primarily is responsible to God. In the parable of the sheep and goats (Mt 25:31-46) the judgment depends primarily upon deeds; acts of love performed to "the least of the brethren" are considered deeds done to God (v. 45).[6] Radical discipleship is the theme of several of the parables (the builders and king going to war, Lk 14:28-33; the hidden treasure and pearl of great price, Mt 13:44-46). The kingdom demands not partial but total, unswerving allegiance demonstrated before each other and God.

10. God and Salvation in the Parables. God appears in several guises in the parables as king, father, landowner, employer, father and judge. Throughout, the picture is of one who graciously and mercifully offers forgiveness but at the same time demands decision. In the prodigal son parable (Lk 15:11-31) the father forgives all as he welcomes back and restores fully the one who had so misused his privileges. In the parable of laborers in the vineyard (Mt 20:1-6) the employer graciously rewards all equally, even those who had not given as much. In the other parables of Luke 15 (the lost sheep, the lost son) the extent of God's yearning for the lost is seen. The parables illustrate the truth of 2 Peter 3:9, "The Lord . . . is patient, not willing that any should perish, but that all should come to repentance."

Salvation is present, and insistently demanding response. God's rule is typified by grace but that grace challenges the hearer to recognize the necessity of repentance. In the parable of the two sons (Mt 21:28-31) Jesus challenges the scribes to recognize the error of their own ways. The son who at first refuses to work in the vineyard then repents and does work obviously represents the "tax collectors and harlots" who inherit the kingdom, while the son who agrees to work then fails to do so represents the scribes and Pharisees. As Hunter says, "The story pops up and leaves [the scribes] flat" (1960:54-55). In the parable of the great banquet (Lk 14:16-24) the God of grace provides a double salvation invitation[7] and then sends his heralds into the highways and hedges after the original guests refuse. Clearly, salvation is a crisis invitation that demands response. The God of mercy is also the God of judgment who will bring history to a close and whose offer of salvation cannot be ignored, only accepted or refused.

Hermeneutical Principles

Three major approaches to the parables have been utilized throughout history (Hunter 1960:92-109). The first two have been widely rejected in our time and must be dismissed. Allegorizing, the method of the church fathers, can be utilized only if the text so indicates, and I have already noted that there is no subjective allegorizing in the Gospels. We must interpret those allegorical elements that are found in light of their Jewish background (such as the vineyard = Israel, the harvest = the Day of the Lord). Moralizing, the method of Jülicher and of nineteenth-century liberalism, is also dangerous, for it replaces the dynamic kingdom thrust of Jesus' preaching with pure humanism. Of course, many parables have a distinct ethical message (as noted above), but this is part of the larger picture of the kingdom presence in the lives of the community. The third method, the *Sitz im Leben* approach of Jeremias, also has its dangers. This "severely historical approach," as many call it, can denigrate the narrative dimensions of the parable and lead to a radical dichotomy between the "situation" in Jesus' life and the use of the parable by the individual evangelists. In our time a fourth has been added, an aesthetic or literary approach. However, it has been dominated by views of textual autonomy, and the parables often have been removed from their historical context. Therefore, none of these models is adequate and the interpreter must allow the text itself to control the process. The best approach will be a combination of the third and fourth methods, blending historical and literary interests.

However, we must consider another oft-repeated claim before we can develop a methodology. Some say that to interpret a parable is to destroy it as parable. They argue that the aesthetic dimension is lost when the parable is historicized, for the evocative power of the parable disappears. Therefore, the parable should be presented rather than explained. Teselle states it the most strongly when she says, "Metaphors cannot be 'interpreted'—a metaphor does not *have* a message, it *is* a message" (1975:71-72). Therefore, the reader does not interpret the parable but instead is interpreted by the parable. This is an obvious reflection of the New Hermeneutic and is subject to all the criticisms of that school. Via admits the problem but still argues for the necessity of interpretation, saying "aesthetic objects can be interpreted-translated to some degree, and the need for clarity justifies the effort" (1967:32-33). I would go a step further. *Without* interpretation the power of the parable is lost, for every parable must be understood before it can be applied. Its "evocative power" is best discerned when seen as Jesus intended it; that is, in terms of its first-century background and in its Gospel context. Nevertheless, we should not relegate it merely to a word-by-word analysis. It must remain parable lest its ability to startle and move the hearer be lost. Therefore, the form of the parable must remain intact. The following principles develop a basic methodology for accomplishing this goal.

1. Note the setting within which the parable is placed. This includes both the immediate context (the literary dimension) and the audience to which the parable is addressed (the historical dimension).[8] The specific group that Christ was addressing significantly alters the thrust of the parable (see the example of the parable of the lost sheep explained in point 4 above). The problem Christ was facing when he uttered the parable and the discussion that followed are also important background factors. For instance, the parable

of the two debtors (Lk 7:41-42) is addressed to Simon the Pharisee, who objected when Jesus allowed a prostitute to wash and perfume his feet. The cancellation of the debts of two individuals, one owing five hundred denarii and the other fifty, could be applied in several directions, such as the mercy of God or degrees of sin. In the immediate context Jesus takes it one direction (the sense of grateful love returned to the one who forgives debts or sins) and in the broader context another (Jesus' power to forgive sins). As many have noted, this parable is a simpler version of the parable of the unforgiving servant (Mt 18:23-35).

Most scholars stress here the distinction between the situation in Jesus' ministry and that in the Gospels. This does not have to mean the two are in conflict or that one is "historical" while the other is the product of the later church (see Stein 1981:75-79 for a good approach). The Evangelists highlighted certain aspects of the original situation for their own audiences. The situation in Jesus' day involves historical information; the situation in the Evangelists' day involves contextualization, as we note the themes that the various Gospels draw out of the individual parables. These two aspects are supplementary, not contradictory (see chap. six).

By comparing the Gospels we can detect an illuminating series of emphases. For instance, the parable of the pounds (Lk 19:12-17) or talents (Mt 25:14-30) is clearly the same basic parable told in two different settings with different emphases.[9] In Matthew it is part of the judgment parables on watchfulness in the Olivet Discourse and warns the disciples that failure to use their resources and to be ready for the parousia could result in exclusion from the kingdom. In Luke the setting is that of the crowd's expectation of the imminent in-breaking of the kingdom (19:11), and so the parable centers upon the delay of the king. In both parables stewardship is a major thrust, but the application of that theme to the needs of Matthew's and Luke's readers differs. Yet in both cases the thrust is also faithful to the original situation in Jesus' ministry. There is no reason to deny that Jesus himself had told the parable in those two settings.

2. Study the structure of the parable. The structural form of metaphor and similitude resembles those of wisdom literature already discussed, so I will center upon the story parables here. What was stated in the chapter on narrative applies even more to the parable, which is fictional at heart. Since the parable is indeed a literary phenomenon, the interpreter must apply compositional and rhetorical techniques (see chap. six) to discover its plot development and literary patterns. We must note chiasm or inclusio, repeated phrases and major divisions within the story. In Luke's version of the parable of the pounds, two plot lines are juxtaposed, one centering upon stewardship (Lk 19:12-13, 15b-26), the other upon rebellion against the king (vv. 14-15a, 27). The two interpret one another, illustrating the "hardness" of the king (v. 22) and the harsh justice by which he rules.

The following principles will aid the reader in delineating the structural development (see Bailey 1975:72-75; Tolbert 1979:74-83; Perkins 1981:50-58; Fee and Stuart 1981:127-28): (1) Note breaks in narrative style, such as the switch to direct discourse from third-person narrative in the prodigal son parable. (2) Study the changes in the focus and actions of the characters, such as the switch from the absentee landlord to the servants to the tenants in the parable of the wicked husbandmen. (3) Determine the points of reference, those items with which the hearer is to identify. The interaction of these referential aspects leads to the basic thrust. For instance, in the parable of the two debtors (Lk 7:41-43) we are to ask whether we are like the Pharisee (v. 39) or the sinful woman (vv. 37-38; compare vv. 44-47) in attitude. (4) Seek patterns in the outline and ask how they relate to one another. Bailey, for instance, notes step and inverted (chiastic) parallelism (see pp. 177-79) in Luke's parables. His chiastic outline in groups of three in the good Samaritan parable is illuminating (1975:72-73).[10] (5) Discover the climax of the story (such as the welcoming reaction of the father in the prodigal son parable), where the turning point occurs. (6) See how the action shifts before and after the turning point (such as the actions of the elder brother to the prodigal son).

3. Uncover the background of the earthly details. We must understand the historical context if the parable is to make sense. Yet this dare not become a mere recital of background details. Instead, the parable should be retold in light of this historical information. Here a good course in preaching techniques (see chap. sixteen) is essential, for the power of the story in all its drama and unexpected twists must come through for the audience. For instance, one must decide whether the parable of the unjust steward (Lk 16:1-13) stresses his dishonesty (so Bailey, Stein) or comes from the background of the laws of usury and commission (so Derrett, Fitzmyer, Marshall). When that decision has been made (I have tentatively sided with the latter view but may be in the process of changing my mind!) the story should be retold using that background to make it more forceful and understandable. Often it will be helpful to connect the story with modern parallels so the evocative power will be seen. Stein repeats the Cotton Patch version of the good Samaritan as a case in point:

A man was going from Atlanta to Albany and some gangsters held him up. When they had robbed him of his wallet and brand-new suit, they beat him up and drove off in his car, leaving him unconscious on the shoulder of the highway.

Now it just so happened that a white preacher was going down that same highway. When he saw the fellow, he stepped on the gas and went scooting by.

Shortly afterwards a white Gospel song leader came down the road, and when he saw what had happened, he too stepped on the gas.

Then a black man traveling that way came upon the fellow, and what he saw moved him to tears. He stopped and bound up his wounds as best as he could, drew some water from his water-jug to wipe away the blood and then laid him on the back seat. He drove on into Albany and took him to the hospital and said to the nurse, "You all take good care of this white man I found on the highway. Here's the only two dollars I got, but you all keep account of what he owes, and if he can't pay it, I'll settle up with you when I make a pay-day."[11]

4. Determine the main points of the parable. Often the clue comes in the context itself. At times it can come before the parable in the introduction (Lk 18:9; 19:11); at other times in an epilogue (Mt 15:13; Lk 16:9). Sometimes the indicator may be found via a question introducing the parable and an application afterward (Mt 18:21-35; 20:1-15; Lk 12:16-20). The larger context can help greatly in interpreting (such as Mk 4 and parallels; Lk 15—16).

Tolbert suggests clustering parables that exhibit similar traits or patterns.[12] We can do this either on the basis of thematic similarities (such as the servant parables) or structural similarities. She uses the parables of the unjust steward (Lk 16:1-8a) and wicked tenants (Mk 12:1-9 and parallels) as an example. Both have similar structures, with a setting (12:1 = 16:1a-b), a narrated wrongdoing of servants (12:2-5 = 16:1c), the decision of the master (12:6 = 16:2), an evaluation of the situation by the servants (12:7 = 16:3-4), the action of the servants 12:8 = 16:5-7) and the response of the master (12:9 = 16:8a). The quite different plot twists within the similar structures are highly illuminating. For instance, the wicked tenants parable ends with the destruction of the servants while the unjust steward parable closes with the commendation of the servant. In addition, the longest section of the former is that of the evil actions of the tenants (12:2-5), while the major section of the latter is the steward's evaluation and resultant action (16:3-7). Thereby we can note the major points of emphasis in each. Yet one caveat is necessary: the context within which each parable is found, not clusters of similar parables, is the final arbiter of meaning.

When a parable contains several points of emphasis, the decision is more complex. The parable of the sower (Mk 4:3-9, 13-20 and parallels) is one of the most debated. The traditional interpretation centers upon the sower or the seed and stresses the proclamation of the Word and the warning to "take heed how you hear." Another interpretation (Dodd, Jeremias) centers on the abundant harvest and stresses the eschatological triumph of the Word in spite of Satan's power. The key is the context in which the parable of the sower is found, namely the rejection of the Jews. Therefore, the parables of Mark 4 are called "controversy parables," and the place of the parable of the sower within this context is seen both in the purpose of the parables (vv. 10-12) and in Jesus' interpretation (vv. 13-20). Therefore, while there is an eschatological element (such as the end-time harvest), the major idea is the four types of soil.[13] The harvest relates only to the final soil-type and does not elevate it to central status. The hearers are challenged to identify themselves with one or another of the soil-types, and so the key meaning is one's response to the kingdom proclamation (the seed). Each type of soil relates to a different response and has equal importance to the parable's thrust. In other words, there are four main points and the harvest scene both concludes the final type or response and warns the hearer regarding the importance of reacting correctly to the Gospel.

5. Relate the point(s) to Jesus' kingdom teaching and to the basic message of the individual Gospel. Both of these points have been explored above so it is necessary only to relate them to the process of interpretation. After one has looked at the progress and message of the parable itself, it is important to place its message first within the larger context of Jesus' teaching and then within the emphases of the Gospel within which it is found. This will help the interpreter to avoid overstating or misinterpreting the points. For instance, the parables on constructing the tower and going to war (Lk 14:28-33) occur in a context of discipleship, and on the basis both of Jesus' teaching and Lukan emphases they center upon the radical demands of the kingdom for total commitment. Half-hearted discipleship will result in spiritual defeat. We must "count the cost" before entering into a spiritual contract with God, for he will hold us accountable.

6. Do not base doctrines upon the parables without checking corroborative details elsewhere. This is closely connected to the previous point, but because of widespread misuse of the parables in exactly this area I present it here as a separate point. For instance, the parable of the rich man and Lazarus (Lk 16:19-31) is often taken as proof of a compartmentalized Hades. However, such a doctrine is not found in Jesus' teaching in Luke, and indeed nowhere else in Scripture. Therefore, the setting of the parable in Hades is local color rather than dogma and cannot be pressed too far. Similarly, Calvinists and Arminians can use the parable of the vine and the branches (Jn 15:1-8) only with great caution, for its meaning depends upon the biblical theology on sovereignty and responsibility in John's Gospel as a whole.

Petzoldt has provided the most thorough treatment of the relationship between the parables and dogmatics. His basic thesis is that Jesus' parable preaching provides an indispensable supplement to Paul and provides the heart of dogmatic theology (1984:161-66). While Paul interprets Jesus, the latter interprets God with respect to God's interpretation of humanity. The opposition between the two, God's presence and the human's dilemma, is solved by the threefold schema of the parabolic form, "reception-interrogation-renewal." Petzoldt argues that this is the major contribution of the parables to dogmatic theology. While he stands firmly in the historical-critical tradition, his basic thesis is correct. We must recognize that the great themes of the parables carry theological weight, but we must exercise great care in delineating the theological core of each parable.

7. Apply the central truth(s) to similar situations in modern life. Via asserts that the aesthetic dimension of parables means they "are not as time-conditioned as other biblical texts, and the need for translation is not, therefore, as compelling" (1967:32-33). He believes the historical distance between the first century and our day is not as great in the case of parables. To an extent he is correct, although this does not remove the need to supply historical background, as noted above. The evocative power of the parable is as great today as it was in the first century. In fact, the great preachers of our century, like Spurgeon or Swindoll, are known for their parabolic style. The parables reach down to the deepest levels of the human psyche and grip the heart and will. Moreover, the themes noted above speak as clearly today as they did in Jesus' day. Forgiveness and compassion, jealousy and self-centeredness are certainly as meaningful in our day as in ancient times. The message of divine mercy and the radical demands of the presence of the kingdom should ring with a clarion call in the church today.

8. Preach the parable holistically. The tendency to fragment parables and to contextualize each element as it comes up tends to destroy the parable as story and to break its power to draw the hearer into its narrative world. Some parables may lend themselves to a point-by-point development (such as the parable of the sower), but on the whole it is best to dramatize the parable by retelling it via background information (to create a "you are there" atmosphere) and to allow its power to enthrall the hearer and then to draw out its significance.

Excursus: The History of Interpretation
As I have sought to demonstrate throughout this book, history provides the context, both

positive and negative, by which we approach Scripture. As we sift through the examples of exegetical technique and interpretive approaches, we must seek to learn from the successes and failures of the past. In the case of parable interpretation this will be helpful indeed, although we can do no more than summarize.

The basic approach during the patristic period and the Middle Ages was allegorical (see Hunter 1960:22-31; Stein 1981:42-48; Fee and Stuart 1981:23-25). Every element of a parable was reinterpreted and spiritualized to portray Christian truths. The only development was the extent of the allegorizing, as later writers went into more and more detail and in the Middle Ages utilized the "fourfold" sense method. For instance, in the parable of the good Samaritan the injured man became Adam who was headed for paradise (Jericho) but was waylaid by the temptations and pleasures of life (robbers), which led him into sin (wounds). Christ (the Samaritan) healed him (oil = comfort or compassion, wine = blood) and led him to the church (the inn). While the Reformers clearly rejected the allegorical method on behalf of a literal hermeneutic, they were inconsistent when interpreting the parables. Luther pretty much followed the patristic approach to the good Samaritan, but Calvin rejected it and regularly refused to spiritualize parables. However, Calvin's was a lone voice until the latter part of the nineteenth century. Trench's *Notes on the Parables of Our Lord* (1841), still on the shelves of many pastors, clearly follows in the train of Origen and Augustine.

The modern period of parable research began with Adolf Jülicher's *Die Gleichnisreden Jesu* (1888). Reacting to the domination of the allegorical method, he argued strongly that parables contain a single picture and teach a single point. Parables are not allegories and cannot be interpreted in that way. The influence of this work was remarkable. Works that followed built upon his thesis. C. H. Dodd's *The Parables of the Kingdom* (1966) went further and argued that the parables must be situated within the life and teaching of Jesus, primarily his preaching of the kingdom. Joachim Jeremias' *Die Gleichnisse Jesu* (1947) built upon both Jülicher and Dodd, systematically removing what he believed were later church additions (allegorical elements) to get back to Jesus' actual kingdom parables.

These seminal works are still highly influential today, and many (Linnemann, Crossan, Lambrecht) still accept Jülicher's basic premise. However, while most teach a modified form, there is a growing dissatisfaction with the rigidity of the "one-point" theory. We can note several weaknesses with this hypothesis (see Via 1967:3, 13-17; Stein 1981:54-56; Bailey 1976:16): (1) The single-point approach may overlook important elements in the parable and thus shift its actual meaning. (2) The rigid distinction between parable and allegory is arbitrary and is actually only a difference of degree, not kind; therefore, we cannot categorically deny the possibility that Jesus did use allegorical parables. (3) Many of Jesus' parables are indeed allegories. (4) Jülicher used Aristotelian categories and turned Jesus into a Hellenistic, rather than a Jewish, teacher; Jewish parables mixed allegory and similitude and therefore we cannot rule such out on a priori grounds. (5) Jülicher as a nineteenth-century liberal tended to moralize the parables and missed the central eschatological point. Therefore, a more modified approach is called for.

The redaction critics studied the parables individually in terms of their function within the various Gospels. Their use within a single chapter (Kingsbury on Matthew 13) or Gospel (Bailey on the Lukan parables or Carlston on the Synoptic parables) became a focus for research, and the evangelist's creative reworking of the parable came to the forefront of interest. This was an important shift from the situation in Jesus' teaching (Jülicher, Jeremias) to the situation in the evangelist's church (redaction critics).

However, in recent years a further shift of focus to the perspective of the modern reader has taken place. Two schools of thought have now centered upon the parables as prime examples of recent literary theory applied to biblical studies. The structuralists seek the "codes" of the text, establish grids and then delineate the "deeper structures" of meaning behind the surface parable. However, this school has many problems, as discussed below (see appendix one). As Lambrecht says, "One gets the impression that its lengthy descriptions tend to actually divert attention from the content of the text. Moreover, the method of structural analysis has been applied to the parables in rather divergent ways, and the results are disappointing" (1981:11).

More influential has been what Stein calls "aesthetic criticism," which applies literary paradigms from the ancient world, like tragedy or comedy, and tries to understand the communicative power of the parable. Following in the footsteps of the New Hermeneutic, these scholars view the parables as "language events" that compel the hearer to make a decision. Both structuralists and aesthetic critics stress the autonomous and polyvalent nature of the parables. Thus the original meaning of the parable is not a goal and in fact is perceived to be a detriment to the power of the parable to address us today in new and significant ways (see Via 1967:77-93; Wittig 1977:80-82; Crossan 1980; Tolbert 1979:15-50). However, this theory meets the same objection leveled in chapter one: there is no reason to ignore the original context and every reason to make it central to exegesis.

We can note several other problems (see Stein 1981:68-69; Boucher 1977:16-17): (1) When Jesus demanded that the listeners "hear" (Mk 4:9, 33-34), he referred to *his* message not the hearer's subjective understanding. Jesus' intended meaning was the only true meaning. (2) The parables are important not in their own right but because they are Jesus' parables; modern interpreters often seem to attribute deity to the parable rather than to Jesus! (3) When these critics lose sight of the original historical contexts of the parables, their interpretation invariably degenerates into allegory. (4) Poetry differs from rhetoric; while poetry is often autonomous, rhetoric can never be. Once rhetoric allows the aesthetic dimension to gain the ascendancy it loses its power to move the listener to decision. Since parables demonstrably belong in the camp of rhetoric rather than to aesthetics or poetry, they cannot be understood apart from their social context. Therefore, we argue for a contextual interpretation of each parable in its immediate Gospel setting.

12

*E*pistle

THIS IS THE MOST BASIC OF THE GENRE CATEGORIES, YET NO HERMENEUTICS TEXT TO MY knowledge has a section on epistles in the discussion of special hermeneutics. Yet many issues pertain particularly to the epistolary literature, and many mistakes in both interpretation and application are made due to a failure to understand the particular hermeneutical peculiarities of epistles.[1] Yet the principles discussed under "general hermeneutics" (chaps. one to five) might apply more directly to the Epistles than to any of the other genres. Part of this is due to the fact that we have been raised in the Epistles and our thinking (including hermeneutical principles) has been shaped by them. The Epistles do not contain such complicating factors as plot or characterization (narrative), esoteric symbolism (apocalyptic) or metaphorical subtleties (parable). However, they have several aspects with which we have not fully interacted and which we should explore. In order to do so, we will first consider letter-writing in antiquity and then note some of the crucial issues.

Letter-Writing in the Ancient World

At the earliest period messages were memorized and sent by courier. This had its natural limitations and by the third millennium B.C. messages were sent via wood or clay tablets, ostraca, wax surfaces upon wood or metal and then papyri sheets. In the ancient Near East many of the epistolary conventions (such as the opening address, the thanksgiving) were derived from the oral period and in many cases the messenger delivered the letter orally as well as by tablet.[2] As might be expected, the earliest type of correspondence was the official letter, which reported military or civic affairs to the king or other official. The "Ancient Epistolography Group" of the Society of Biblical Literature has identified ten types of ancient epistles: letters to the gods, edicts and proclamations, historical letters, military correspondence, administrative correspondence, scholarly letters (divination reports, astrological observations and so forth), letter prayers, letters to the dead, business letters and feminine correspondence. We can divide these into two major categories, the nonliterary letter centering upon personal correspondence and the literary epistle or treatise written for a general audience and intended for publication.

All ancient correspondence consisted of three sections: the opening, the body of the letter and the closing. While the opening and closing closely followed conventional patterns, the body of the letter differed widely depending on subject matter and thus cannot be so easily classified. The address often indicates relative status because ancient laws of etiquette were based upon social stratification (relating to those of higher, equal or lower status). The contents and style of the letter would differ depending on the relative status between sender and recipient (see Aune 1987:158-59). Knutson (1982:18) states that the superior's name always comes first in the Ras Shamra letters, while in Mesopotamian letters the addressee's name is first irrespective of rank ("To . . . say, 'Thus says. . .' ").

Salutations often would reflect social status as well, for instance in the "subordination formula" of the El-Amarna letters (for example, "I am the dust beneath your feet"). Letters between equals would include a more general blessing or wish for well-being. In the Neo-Babylonian period the salutations became more stylized and no longer reflected relative rank. However, Aramaic correspondence from the first millennium B.C. often used family names to indicate relative rank with "lord," "father" or "mother" used for superiors; "brother" or "sister" for equals; and "servant," "son" or "daughter" for inferiors. In the Aramaic correspondence the salutation normally involved some form of either "peace" *(šālôm)* or "blessing" *(bĕrak)* and often were highly religious, invoking Yahweh or the gods, although others employed more general wish statements. In Greek epistles the salutation was often brief: ". . . to . . . , greetings and good health." In many instances these are followed by a secondary greeting, either to be passed on to other relatives or friends or greetings sent from friends with the sender. The closing also embodies a formula with *šālôm;* Fitzmyer notes two types, "I have sent this letter for your peace (of mind)" and "Be (at) peace" (1982:36).

Practices related to the order of names also differed from period to period. As just mentioned, in ancient Mesopotamia the recipient's name was first ("To . . . , thus says . . .") while in Babylonian, Persian and Greek periods the order was reversed ("Tablet of . . . , to . . ."), except in the Ptolemaic period when correspondence from an inferior often mentioned the recipient first. Pardee applies this to Hebrew letters, including those in the Old Testament (1978:321-44; 1982:145-64). As would be expected, Old Testament Epistles omitted the opening and closing formulas and summarized the contents, since they were included in the larger narrative works of Scripture (2 Sam 11:15; 1 Kings 21:9-10; 2 Kings 5:6; 10:2-3, 6; 19:10-13 [= Is 37:10-13]; Jer 29:4-23, 26-28; Neh 6:6-7; 2 Chron 2:11-15; 21:12-15).

Interestingly, Aramaic canonical epistles have preserved the opening formulas, with the superior mentioned first: for example, Ezra 4:11, "To King Artaxerxes, your servants . . . the priest"; Daniel 4:1, "Nebuchadnezzar the king to all peoples." The normal Hebrew epistle placed the sender first if both were named but often only the recipient was mentioned ("To . . . , greeting"). Hebrew letters preferred *bĕrak,* "bless," to *šālôm* until the Bar Kokhba period (A.D. 132—135). Superior-inferior distinctions do not seem to be prevalent, and neither secondary greetings nor concluding formulas are found in pre-Christian Hebrew correspondence. One similarity with both Aramaic and biblical letters (in 2 Kings 5:6; 10:2; compare Neh 6:7; Jer 29:27; 2 Chron 2:12) is the use of *wᵉᶜattâh* ("and now") to provide the transition from the salutation to the body of the letter. The closest parallel to the New Testament is found in Hellenistic epistolary practices.[3] In the later Greek period letters became the accepted form not just for private correspondence but also for literary purposes. Cato, for instance, published his essays in the form of letters to his son, and many of Cicero's 931 letters were published in order to win public support. Evidence indicates that none were written specifically for publication and some were never meant to be published (indeed, they hurt Cicero's reputation with their criticism of Caesar). However, Cicero himself published several, and clearly his aim was to influence public opinion. Isocrates and Horace developed an exhortation epistle intended to instruct readers regarding various philosophical, historical or legal themes. Seneca's letters to Lucilius demonstrate a tractate type of epistle giving general moral advice. By the time of Jesus and Paul this literary epistle had become very popular. Students were taught epistolary style in the rhetorical schools, and several "handbooks" were produced to teach correct form. This tradition is important for the New Testament epistolary tradition, as we will see below.

Doty lists four basic types of letters in addition to personal correspondence (1966:102-23): the official letter (royal, military, legal correspondence); the public letter (see above); the "nonreal" letter (pseudonymous literature, the epistolary novel, heavenly letters); and the discursive letter (religious, scientific and moral parenesis, all designed to instruct). Stowers develops this typology in a different direction, taking a functional approach centering upon rhetorical conventions (1986:49-173): letters of friendship (see 2 Cor 1:16; 5:3; Phil 1:7-8; 1 Thess 3:6-10); family letters; letters of praise and blame (1 Cor 11; Rev 2—3); exhortatory or parenetic epistles (1 Thessalonians, the pastorals, Hebrews, James, 1 Peter); letters of mediation or recommendation on behalf of a person (Philemon, Phil 2:19-30); and juridical or forensic (accusing, apologetic, accounting) letters (1 Cor 9:3-12; 2 Cor 1:8—2:13; 7:5-16; 10—12).

The form utilized in these letters followed certain conventional patterns quite similar to those found in the ancient Near East. The opening began with the sender and recipient (". . . to . . ."), followed by a stereotyped greeting *(charein,* "grace" or "greetings") and sometimes a more developed thanksgiving or prayer for good health. The body of the text is then followed by a closing involving greetings sent to mutual friends and a final wish for good health and so forth. Letters were written primarily for the sake of "presence" or contact. As Longenecker says, for personal letters this took the form of maintaining a "friendly relationship," in pastoral letters of maintaining past contact and present authority, in public letters of conveying authority and in tractates or discursive letters of instructing the readers (1983:102).

New Testament Epistles

1. The Form. Deissmann believed that Paul's epistles were personal letters rather than literary epistles (1909:224-46). They were therefore occasional and circumstantial, the product of the moment rather than careful literary creations. According to Deissmann Paul's epistles were characterized by a dialectic between his powerful spiritual depth and the problems of the individual situations to which he wrote. However, as most now agree, this is too simplistic. For one thing, as noted above, there were far more patterns than

Deissmann suspected in Hellenistic and Jewish epistolary practices. The three that are most applicable are the private letter, the public epistle and the treatise. Of these the private letter is the least likely, for Paul and the other sacred writers wrote with a consciousness of apostolic authority and spoke to the whole church, intending that their epistles be read publicly in the assemblies (see 1 Thess 5:27; Col 4:16). Indeed the conclusion of each letter to the seven churches in Revelation 2—3 reads, "He who has an ear, let him hear what the Spirit says to the churches." To be sure, some individual epistles (Philemon, 2 and 3 John) could be placed in the personal category, but the others are clearly public in nature and some could be placed in the category of treatise.

Longenecker uses the categories "pastoral letter" and "tractate" to distinguish them (1983:102-6). The latter sometimes maintain the epistolary form (Hebrews lacks the opening, James, 2 Peter and Jude lack the concluding greetings and 1 John lacks both opening and closing formulas), but their content goes beyond local situations to speak to general concerns of the church as a whole. Letters that often are considered to be a treatise or tractate are Romans, Ephesians, Hebrews, James, 1 Peter and 1 John. Of course, several are debated, especially since all but 1 John maintain the epistolary form and 1 John seems to have a particular situation in mind (a protognostic group of false teachers). Many consider Romans to be addressed to Jewish-Gentile factions in Rome. Ephesians, Hebrews, James and 1 Peter are most commonly assigned to the tractate category. Ephesians centers upon the topics of Christ and church, 1 Peter may be a collection of Peter's sermons (though I personally doubt this) and Hebrews and James address problems within the Jewish-Christian community.

The epistles of Paul do not merely reproduce earlier patterns, and this is a clear departure from normal practice, which slavishly imitated established conventions. Paul's letters "are new in so far as form (introductory and closing formulae), content (variety and intensity of material in a single letter), or length (beyond the usual length even of the more literary-minded writers) is concerned" (Doty 1966:164-65). This is even more startling when we realize that the patristic writers returned to the stereotyped patterns. The New Testament Epistles therefore blend normal patterns with Christian innovations. For instance, the greeting combined the Greek *charis* with the Aramaic šālôm but added to both a theological depth hitherto missing. Moreover, the thanksgiving and prayer found in ancient epistolography is extended and avoids the cliché. Indeed, Schubert (1939:71-82) and O'Brien (1977:262-63) demonstrate that the thanksgivings and intercessory prayers embody in embryo the basic purpose or message of the individual epistles.[4]

The New Testament Epistles fall between the private letter and the treatise, having elements of both along with rhetorical features drawn from both Hellenistic and Jewish forms.[5] They speak to specific situations (even the more general letters like 2 Peter, James or 1 John) and yet are meant to be read again and again in the churches (such as Philem 2, showing that the epistle was also addressed "to the church in your house"). Moreover, nearly all the epistles (apart from pure letters like Philemon, 2 or 3 John) mix several forms and cannot be classified easily. For instance (as Roller correctly notes, 1933:87-88), the book of Revelation contains a hortatory section in somewhat epistolary style (chaps. 2—3) and, unique among ancient apocalyptic, is framed by an epistolary prescript and postscript (1:1-8; 22:10-21). Complex epistles like Romans or the Corinthian correspondence contain many of the rhetorical types and must be examined section by section.

The major point of hermeneutical significance is that the Epistles contain both occasional and supracultural elements. For our purpose here, we must be aware that many elements in the Epistles do not directly provide paradigms for the Christian life today. The extent to which a command is addressed to the particular situation of the readers is the extent to which the surface command does not apply today. While this is quite easy in some cases (such as the request that Titus come to Paul in Nicopolis in Tit 3:9), in others it is quite difficult to separate the cultural from the supracultural (for example, the passages on women in the church or on excommunication; see the excellent discussion in Aune 1987:226-49).

Fee and Stuart note other issues that stem from this problem (1983:45-46). The importance of identifying the problem behind some of the statements in the Epistles is critical but the task is difficult. "We have the answers, but we do not always know what the questions or problems were. . . . It is much like listening to one end of a telephone conversation and trying to figure out who is on the other end and what that unseen party is saying" (p. 46). Also, the reader must understand that the sacred writers were not producing a systematic presentation of their theology but rather were using theology to speak to specific situations. Therefore, we dare not read individual statements as finished dogma but rather must move from the individual statements to ascertain the biblical theology and then to develop a dogmatic or systematic theology (see chaps. thirteen and fourteen).

The opening and closing formulas in the Epistles follow ancient conventions and need to be understood properly. For instance, the emphasis upon "apostle" in Paul's correspondence (all except the Thessalonian Epistles) shows that these are official letters. In Galatians 1:1-2 the expanded form is due to the polemical nature of the epistle; since Paul's opponents challenged his authority he spent much of the first two chapters defending his status. Extensive thanksgivings and prayers were also common, as was the use of these to present the major themes of the epistle (Phil 1:9-11; Eph 1:15-19; 3:14-17). When the thanksgiving or prayer is missing (Galatians, 2 Corinthians, Hebrews, James, 2 Peter, 1 John, Jude) this is evidence of the extremely serious nature of the problems addressed. Finally, the closing greetings, benediction and farewell were also typical formulas in ancient letters (for fine discussions of this, see Stowers 1986:20-23; Aune 1987:183-87).

2. Authorship. Two issues are relevant here, the presence of a scribe or amanuensis (secretary) in the writing of several epistles, and the question of pseudonymity. Paul (Rom 16:22; compare 2 Thess 3:14) and Peter (1 Pet 5:12) both mention secretarial help. However, the extent of the involvement of the amanuensis in the production of the text is quite debated. A rudimentary form of shorthand was practiced in the first century; Plutarch credited Cicero with its invention. However, the degree of freedom exercised by the scribe varied widely, from word-for-word dictation to total freedom, with the master providing only the subject matter. Roller believes that Paul's amanuensis was given great freedom and that the styles of the epistles are mixed, with much left to the scribes to develop in their own way (1933:146-47). On the other hand, Kümmel argues that the breaks in the thought-flow of the epistles and the uniformity of the Pauline language would not occur if the secretaries had great freedom and that therefore Paul was dictating his letters (1975:251). The fact that Paul often added comments (presumably to a companion's writing) can hardly be doubted (in addition to the passages already named, see 1 Cor 16:21; Gal 6:11; Col 4:18; Philem 19). Thus we can hardly doubt the fact of secretarial activity.

Only the degree of freedom in writing is at issue. I would agree with Longenecker that "Paul's own practice probably varied with the circumstances encountered and the companions available" (1983:109). There is little evidence to suggest that the scribes had total freedom to produce the epistle, but in 1 Peter probably and the Pastorals possibly the style could well be due to the amanuensis. This in no way lessens the authority of these epistles, for the Holy Spirit could inspire the amanuensis as well as the author. The process of producing the canonical books was fully superintended by the Spirit, and there is no reason to believe that the sacred authors were not responsible for the content. In the ancient world the masters authenticated every word written under their direction. There were three general levels of scribal activity in the first century: the letters could be dictated (no scribal involvement), the contents could be told but the actual wording and style supplied by the secretary (moderate scribal involvement) or the topic could be told and the rest left up to the secretary (nearly total scribal involvement). There is no evidence for the third level but the first two can be found (1 Peter and the Pastorals at level two; many believe Luke was the amanuensis of the Pastorals due to the number of "Lukanisms" seen in them).

The possibility of pseudonymous (falsely attributed) writings in the New Testament is more the subject of an introduction than of a hermeneutics text, but if Ephesians, the Pastorals, 2 Thessalonians, James and the Petrine Epistles were actually the products of the later church, that would have hermeneutical implications, so the issue must at least be raised. It is common to argue that pseudonymous works were widely accepted in the ancient world, and that since the Holy Spirit was viewed as the true author of the Epistles the early church had no problem with pseudonymity (for example, Aland 1961:39-49; Mead 1986).

However, as Guthrie notes, while there were many pseudonymous works in the first century, there is too little evidence that they were accepted as authoritative (1970:282-94). The Jewish pseudonymous works were not included in the Hebrew canon, and it is doubtful that anyone believed they actually had been written by those under whose name they appeared. The question of pseudonymity must be decided on an individual basis, and I for one remain unconvinced regarding the late origin of works like Daniel, the Pastorals, James or 1 Peter. Anonymity is less of a problem, for this was common in the ancient world; in the case of Hebrews the letter carried its own authority (as Origen recognized). The historical situation is not really more difficult to ascertain, for the recipients and purpose are identifiable in the contents of the letter.

Hermeneutical Principles

We could simply recapitulate the process of hermeneutics elucidated in chapters one through five, namely structure-grammar-semantics-syntax-historical backgrounds. However, there are special issues that relate especially to the Epistles, and I will explore these while stressing that the reader should place them within the broader steps explained previously in this book.

1. Study the logical development of the argument. While this is not too difficult in some epistles (such as Corinthians, Hebrews), in others (such as James, 1 John) it is extremely difficult. Dibelius called James an artificially collected group of separate homilies (1976:34-38), and Marshall has despaired of making sense of 1 John (1978:22-26). He organizes the latter into separate sections. In neither case is the verdict wholly justified, but commentators have long struggled with the logical patterns of the two.

James, I believe, moves from an introductory discussion of trials and faith (1:1-18) to the first issue, practical Christianity (1:19—2:26). The latter section moves from the theme (1:19-26) to two specific aspects, partiality (2:1-13) and good works (2:14-26). The second major section then deals with teaching and the tongue (3:1—4:12), moving in rondo style from an introductory statement on teachers (3:1) to a general description of the dangers of the tongue (3:2-12), then back to the teacher's qualifications (3:13-18) and then to the problems stemming from a misuse of the tongue for fighting (4:1-10) and slander (4:11-12). There follows a series of problems in the church: self-reliance (4:13-17), the misuse of wealth to oppress the poor (5:1-11), oaths (5:12), prayer and healing (5:13-18). James concludes with a closing statement that sums up the ethical problems of the epistle and calls the church to bring the errant sinners back to Christ (5:19-20). There is a definite homogeneity to the epistle, as Davids recognizes (1982:22-27).

First John is more difficult but is written in rondo style around the three central "tests" of true Christianity, the moral test (obedience), the social test (love) and the doctrinal test (belief), as Stott notes (1964:55-56). The important point in each case is to relate the parts to the whole and to see each part as it relates to the author's developing argument.

2. Study the situation behind the statements. This is more important than at first sight appears, for it determines not only the background for the argument of a book but also the extent to which the passage applies to situations beyond the historical circumstances of the original readers. In narrative literature the situation is part of the context, but in the Epistles it is not always so easy to detect. There is a great deal of controversy behind the identification of Paul's opponents at Corinth, Colosse or Philippi, or John's opponents in 1 John. Yet the interpretation of key passages depends upon the decision. For this reason it is important to consult up-to-date commentaries and other tools. For instance, some argue that Paul was not fighting a particular heretical movement in Colosse but rather a general syncretism of Jewish and pagan ideas in a Christian setting (see Hooker 1973). Most scholars have not followed this line of reasoning, but if it were true the list of ritual and ethical characteristics of the cult in 2:16-23 would have to be rethought in terms of its true meaning. Paul would be providing a representative list rather than describing actual practices and beliefs.

Fee and Stuart discuss two related aspects, the problems of extended application and of particulars that are not comparable (1983:61-65). The key in their minds is to do our exegesis well enough to ascertain the specific life situations of the biblical times and to gain confidence that our situations are truly comparable with theirs. Extended application occurs when one applies a biblical text to a modern situation that is not genuinely comparable to the original meaning of the text. This is an extremely difficult task, because the interpreter must make a subjective decision as to when an application is extended too far. Yet the principle is important. For instance, 1 Corinthians 3:16-17 and 6:19-20 speaks of Christians as the "temple of God" and says negatively that God will "destroy" anyone who "destroys the temple of God" (3:17); further, Christians must "glorify God" in their bodies (6:20). This has been universally extended to refer to harmful foods, even though the original meaning had nothing of the sort in mind. Another example is 2 Corinthians 6:14, "Be not unequally yoked with unbelievers," applied to marriage between a Christian and non-Christian, although the context is more general, referring to participation in pagan practices. The first example is most likely erroneous because junk food, cigarettes and so forth are a different situation entirely, but the second is an adequate extension of the same principle, although unequal marriages should be preached as an implication of the text rather than its meaning.

The problem of noncomparable particulars deals with situations in the Epistles that no longer occur or are unlikely to occur today. An important example here would be the strong-weak passages of 1 Corinthians 8—10 and Romans 14—15. Since in the Western world we no longer have idolatrous temples or meat sacrificed to idols and then eaten in temple feasts or sold in the marketplace, we must seek first the underlying principle and then apply it to analogous situations. The basic principle is to do nothing that would prove to be a "stumbling block" to a weaker brother. However, this does not refer to that which offends legalistic Christians;[6] rather it means not to do that which can lead another into sin. Fee and Stuart note three commands: (1) they are forbidden to attend the idolatrous feasts, since that involves participation in the demonic; (2) Paul defends his right to financial support (9:14); (3) meat sacrificed to idols may be eaten, although one should avoid such when it might cause another to stumble. The first and third may apply in some Third World tribal settings today but have no parallel in the First World. Yet the issues to which they have been applied are legion (dress, length of hair, jewelry, cosmetics, movies, cards, gambling, drinking, smoking, to name but a few). Christians must be careful to maintain a balanced perspective, noting the complex situation caused by religious sensibilities and stumbling blocks to weaker Christians. It is wrong to flaunt one's freedom and thereby do disservice to the cause of Christ. At the same time, some of the issues mentioned above are allowable in private settings but should be avoided in public situations (a valid extension of the meat-sacrificed-to-idols principle).[7]

3. Note the different subgenres employed in the Epistles. Nearly every type of literature discussed in these two chapters is found in the Epistles, such as hymns and creeds, apocalyptic, proverbs. The reader must note these carefully and apply the particular principles of that genre when interpreting the epistle. For example, the cautions for interpreting apocalyptic will be invaluable when studying the man of lawlessness (2 Thess

2) or the destruction of the world (2 Pet 3). Rules for interpreting poetry will help one understand 1 Timothy 3:16 or 1 Peter 3:18, 22. In the case of the hymns this will lead to two levels of interpretation, the meaning of the hymn in its original form (such as the incarnational theology of Phil 2:6-8) and in its setting within the epistle itself (Phil 2:6-11 as a paradigm for humility).

Part 3

*A*pplied Hermeneutics

13

B iblical Theology

P REVIOUS CHAPTERS CENTERED UPON METHODOLOGY FOR DETERMINING THE ORIGINAL IN-
tended meaning of a text, a task that I identified in the introduction as the "third
person" approach, treating the text as an object to be studied in order to discover
the author's message. In this chapter we begin the switch from the text (meaning) to the
current context (significance). As noted in figure 13.1, biblical theology constitutes the
first step away from the exegesis of individual passages and toward the delineation of
their significance for the church today. At this level we collect and arrange the themes
that unite the passages and can be traced through a book or author as a whole. This is
done in three steps: first, we study the theological themes in terms of individual books,
then we explore the theology of an author, and finally we trace the progress of revelation
that unites a testament and even the Bible as a whole (that is, the historical development
of these themes throughout the biblical period). In this way biblical theology collates the
results of exegesis and provides the data for the systematic theologian to contextualize
in developing theological dogma for the church today.

Several scholars recently have described biblical theology as in "crisis" (see Childs 1970;
Reventlow 1986 for good introductions to this topic). The current emphasis on diversity
rather than unity (see pp. 14-15 above) has resulted in skepticism about the very possibility of discovering any "unified" theology. Moreover, the many works claiming to have
discovered the "central" theme of the Old or New Testament have not only failed to
establish a consensus; rarely do any two works even agree at all! Yet the task is not
hopeless, and several strands have begun to come together at the methodological level
as a way out of the impasse. This hermeneutical solution will be the subject of this
chapter.

We may define biblical theology as "that branch of theological inquiry concerned with
tracing themes through the diverse sections of the Bible (such as the wisdom writings or
the Epistles of Paul) and then with seeking the unifying themes that draw the Bible
together."[1] There are thus two types of inquiry: the search for unifying or central theme(s)
behind the testaments or Bible (the task of the scholar) and the attempt to trace a
particular theme (such as the Holy Spirit or perseverance) through the various stages of
the biblical period (the task of every Bible student). Therefore, while biblical theology

Biblical Theology

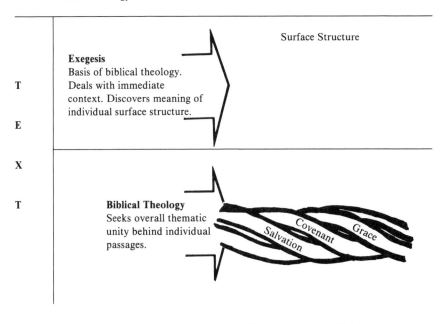

T

E

X

T

Exegesis
Basis of biblical theology.
Deals with immediate
context. Discovers meaning of
individual surface structure.

Surface Structure

Biblical Theology
Seeks overall thematic
unity behind individual
passages.

Salvation Covenant Grace

Fig. 13.1. The Task of Biblical Theology.

provides a bridge to systematic theology and the contextualization of Scripture, it remains primarily within the sphere of exegetical research because its major goal is to
discover the views of the biblical period.

Relationship to Other Disciplines

Figure 13.2 displays the relationships among the various theological disciplines. In the
next few pages we will look at biblical theology in relation to each of the other disciplines.

1. Biblical Theology and Exegesis. Gaffin asserts that "biblical theology is regulative of
exegesis" because "the historical framework of the revelation process itself" rather than
"literary relationships" determines the message of Scripture.[2] A continual tension exists
within the biblical theology movement between diversity and unity, between historical-
critical concerns and historical-grammatical exegesis.

Critical scholarship in this sense is often more "literalistic" than are conservative scholars in that it often assumes that any so-called contradiction or difference between biblical
writers removes the basis for a deeper theological unity between them. This is unnecessary, for writers use different terms or phrases for similar biblical concepts and stress one
side or another of a larger theological reality. For instance, divine sovereignty and human
free will are not contradictory aspects of the process of salvation but can be harmonized
at a deeper level. The same is true of faith (Paul) and works (James). While works cannot
save us (Eph 2:8-9), they are the necessary result of a true faith (Eph 2:10 = Jas 2:14-16).

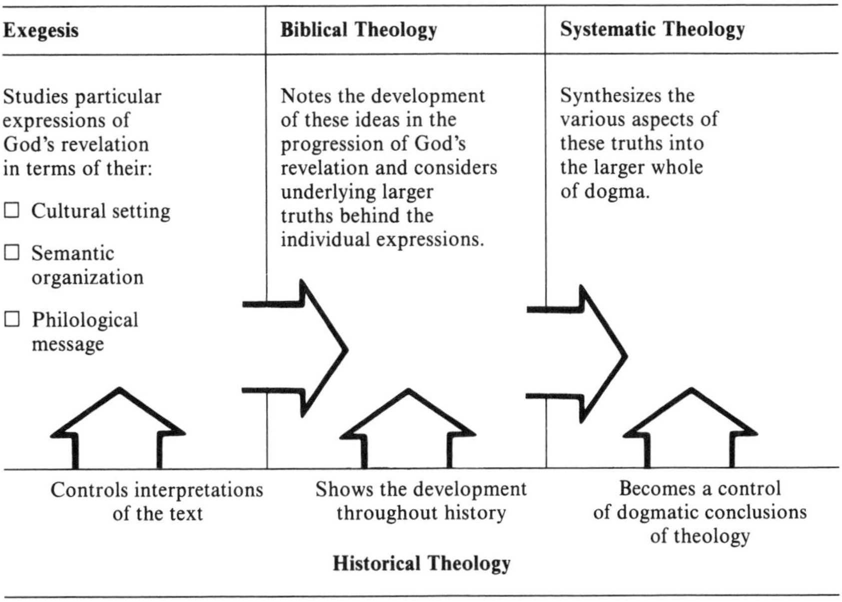

Exegesis	Biblical Theology	Systematic Theology
Studies particular expressions of God's revelation in terms of their: ☐ Cultural setting ☐ Semantic organization ☐ Philological message	Notes the development of these ideas in the progression of God's revelation and considers underlying larger truths behind the individual expressions.	Synthesizes the various aspects of these truths into the larger whole of dogma.
Controls interpretations of the text	Shows the development throughout history **Historical Theology**	Becomes a control of dogmatic conclusions of theology

Fig. 13.2. The Relationships among the Disciplines.

Yet this is only part of the picture. There is a two-way relationship between biblical theology and exegesis. The former provides the categories and overall scriptural unity behind one's interpretation of individual passages, while exegesis provides the data collated into a biblical theology. In other words, the two are interdependent. The exegete studies the author's meaning on the basis of literary considerations (grammar and thought-development) and historical background (socioeconomic), then the biblical theologian works with the results and compiles patterns of unity behind the individual statements.

In sum, the hermeneutical spiral is now extended to include theology in a dialogue between five compartments of the hermeneutical process:[3] exegesis, biblical theology, historical theology, systematic theology and practical theology. Within this scheme exegesis, biblical theology and systematic theology stand together in an ongoing trialogue.

2. Biblical Theology and Historical Theology. All scholars are part of a confessional community, and that community's tradition plays virtually a normative role over the individual scholar's interpretive processes and procedures. The history of dogma traces the development of these community traditions as well as of the doctrines that they hold. As such historical theology plays a critical part in the hermeneutical enterprise, though it is conspicuously absent in most commentaries or works of theology. Yet by emphasizing the background behind exegetical or theological decisions, the history of dogma is immeasurably valuable to the interpretive discipline. The importance of church history for hermeneutics is twofold: we can see how a doctrine has developed through the periods of the church, and we can trace the origins and belief structure behind our own confessional tradition.

Biblical theology, concerned as it is with the thought-patterns of the biblical period itself, seems removed from the debates and interpretations of later times. Yet this is idealistic, for our preunderstanding has been developed within these later debates, and this can obscure our attempt to determine a truly "biblical" theology. Historical theology provides an important check upon an overly exuberant tendency to read later ideas into the biblical period. The interpreter must at all times be aware of the fallacy of reading subsequent theological issues into the text. This has occurred often, for instance, in studies of the eucharist or baptism. A good knowledge of the developing practices between the first and second centuries will make us wary of reading New Testament passages in the light of later practices, like the use of fish in the second-century eucharistic celebration or complex baptismal liturgies of the later period.

Historical theology technically belongs between biblical and systematic theology. It studies the way later paradigm communities understood the biblical doctrines and enables us better to understand current theological debates by placing them in bold relief within the history of dogma. The process of revelation is seen in terms of inspiration (the data provided in the Bible) and illumination (the interpretation of that data throughout the history of the church).[4] In this way the theologian gains a critical hermeneutical tool for determining the validity and shape of dogma for the modern age.

At the same time historical theology provides a way out of the tension between biblical and systematic theology, namely a recognition of the proper place of tradition as preunderstanding in the interpretive task. Many have noted the positive value of community understanding (tradition) in providing categories for understanding (so Gadamer). Without traditional dogmas we would fail to catch the implications of biblical passages. Yet at the same time these preformed belief systems can play a negative role when they force biblical statements into preconceived dogmatic categories. The answer is a proper "hermeneutical circle" or spiral within which the text is reconstructed on the basis of our theological system, yet challenges our preunderstanding and leads to a reformation of our tradition-derived categories. The history of tradition greatly aids in this task by placing our theological prejudices in historical perspective and thereby making them more open to influence (and correction if necessary) from the text itself.

One of the major breakthroughs in hermeneutics is the place of "community exegesis" with its twofold thrust: dialogue with the past community of faith via the history of dogma, and dialogue with the present community via both recent theological works and debate between communities. The past aspect is our concern here. Church history helps us to avoid the facile assumption that the current community understanding is inviolate and enables us to forge an openness to the original world of the text, even if it conflicts with the community desires. Historical theology accomplishes this by enabling theologians to view the larger picture (the historical development of dogma) within which both the understanding of the text and the community's position might be placed.[5]

3. Biblical Theology and Systematic Theology. Piper mentions four limitations of biblical theology: the variety of ways in which the salvific events of the Bible were interpreted within Scripture; the diversity within the biblical kerygma, both in terms of form and function; the historical nature of biblical language, which forms a barrier between biblical theology and modern man; and the subjectivity of the exegetes, which causes them to shift the original meaning in subtle directions (1952:106-11).

I argue in this chapter that the dilemma can be solved via an integration between biblical and systematic theology, thereby bridging the gap between divine revelation and human understanding. These two disciplines both supplement and complement each other.[6]

The core of the issue is this: does the diversity within Scripture remove the possibility of discovering a biblical or systematic theology? The following discussion will attempt to demonstrate the underlying unity behind the diversity within the biblical traditions/ books. In fact, biblical and systematic theology are a critical component in the solution to the dilemma of modern hermeneutics. An overemphasis upon diversity has caused the liberal skepticism toward normative truth in biblical statements. The recovery of unity allows us to reaffirm the absolute nature of scriptural truth-claims and to renew the search for intended meaning.

Yet what is the exact relationship between biblical and systematic theology? In a very real sense they are inseparable and interdependent.[7] As stated above, all five aspects of the theologico-hermeneutical enterprise (exegesis, biblical theology, historical theology, systematic theology and practical theology) coexist in a conceptual unity. In one sense they flow in a straight line in the order presented here, as each forms the foundation for and flows into the next. In another sense the latter three provide the mental framework for exegetical and theological study (see figure 13.3). The theological preunderstanding established by one's confessional tradition is a necessary component for exegetical decisions.

In terms of method, however, each discipline also has a certain functional autonomy. This is why I discuss them in separate chapters. Biblical theology studies the individual themes behind the individual books and traditions within the Bible, seeking covering laws that integrate them into a holistic pattern. Systematic theology then contextualizes these into a logical and conceptual whole that reconstructs dogma for the modern period. As Nicole says, "Biblical theology is a foundation for systematic theology in that it provides the rich fruit of exegetical study conducted with a proper relation to the original context and the development of divine revelation" (1978:185; see 185-93). Yet many disagree at this point. Some (such as Guthrie in his *New Testament Theology)* believe that the organizing principles are derived ultimately from dogmatics. Others (such as Ladd in his *Theology of the New Testament)* take a descriptive approach, allowing the organizing principles to be derived from the text itself rather than from an external source like systematic theology. As Ward says, "The *structure,* or principle of *organization,* for a biblical theology should be determined by the literary units within the Old and New Testaments" (1977:383; italics his). I will develop this further below.

Let us consider Ladd and Guthrie as an example. One of Ladd's basic problems is a lack of synthesis (his failure to seek unifying themes that link the New Testament traditions) while Guthrie fails to allow the biblical documents themselves to determine the structure of his theology. Yet Guthrie's is the more serious error from the standpoint of biblical theology, for his is more of a systematic theology in the guise of a biblical theology.[8] Guthrie needs to allow the biblical authors themselves to dictate the theological categories and to determine the larger unity between themselves. The best approach would be to amalgamate the methods of Ladd and Guthrie, that is, to note the diverse expressions and themes of the various New Testament strata and then to compile these in order to forge a united core of theology within the first-century church. Ladd's analytical mode and Guthrie's synthetic mode can inform and correct each other.

In sum, biblical theology is descriptive, tracing the individual emphases of the sacred writers and then collating them into archetypal themes that unify the testaments; dogmatic theology collects the material generated by biblical theology and restates or reshapes it into a modern logical pattern, integrating these aspects into a confessional statement for the church today.[9] For instance, biblical theology begins with the realized eschatology of John (salvation/eternal life as a present possession of the believer) and the final eschatology of Hebrews or 1 Peter (salvation as a future attainment). Noting that these aspects are complementary and part of a larger truth (inaugurated eschatology, which recognizes that salvation begins in the present and is consummated in the future) the biblical theologian finds both security and responsibility in the Christian life. Systematic theology takes this result and places it within a more comprehensive doctrine integrating soteriology and eschatology.

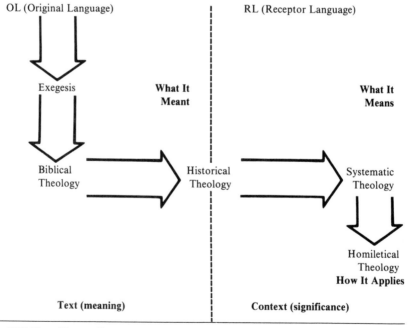

OL (Original Language)   RL (Receptor Language)

Exegesis   **What It Meant**   **What It Means**

Biblical Theology   Historical Theology   Systematic Theology

Homiletical Theology
How It Applies

Text (meaning)   **Context (significance)**

Fig. 13.3. From Text to Context.

Finally, systematic theology is the last step of the bridge between "what it meant" (the task of exegesis and biblical theology), "what it means" (the task of systematic theology) and "how it applies" (the task of homiletical theology)—see figure 13.3. Of course, this is not a totally satisfactory arrangement: biblical theologians object to being "dropped in some middle point between the text of the New Testament and modern reconstruction of the New Testament message" (Barrett 1981:5), and systematic theologians object to the denigration of their discipline into a contextual and philosophical study. In actuality any attempt to separate the tasks too greatly is artificial, for one cannot be done without the other: they are interdependent. Biblical theology must watch over the theologian to "check . . . when his enthusiasm runs away with him" (p. 7). In similar fashion the dogmatic preunderstanding of the biblical theologian interacts in a type of "hermeneutical circle" as each discipline informs and checks the other (see figure 13.4).

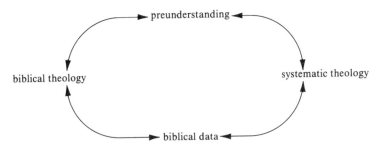

Fig. 13.4. The Interdependence of Theological Disciplines.

4. Biblical Theology and Homiletical Theology. All scholars recognize that biblical theology dare not merely describe the past thinking of the canonical authors but must demonstrate the relevance of those ideas for the modern context. Dunn stresses the "ecclesiastical level" of biblical theology, namely, the demarcation of the present implications of the canon for the church today (1982:26-27, 40-43).

Dunn argues that only this can carry influence for the modern church, since in fact every branch of the church builds more upon its own ecclesiastical tradition than upon the canon itself. While this is correct in a pragmatic sense, I would not wish to "canonize" diversity to this extent. One of the major purposes of this book is to provide methodological controls for avoiding just this error, so that interpreters can indeed allow the text to speak to their diverse theologies and thereby allow divergent traditions to interact and move together.[10] No person is *only* a biblical theologian or *only* a preacher. Everyone who reads a biblical text and seeks to discern its meaning (including what it *meant* and what it *means)* must of necessity blend the disciplines.

At the same time homiletics is further removed from biblical theology. The biblical data has been translated and interpreted by exegesis, collated by biblical theology, forward transformed into dogmatic theses by systematic theology, developed into the thought patterns of various church situations and traditions by historical theology, and now is applied to the current situation by homiletical theology. There is no single "hermeneutical circle" but rather a spiral of interlocking spheres of dialogue. The purpose is to allow what the text "meant" to address the church anew.

Specific Problem Areas

1. Unity and Diversity.   Here we are at the heart of the debate over the historical-critical method. Critical scholars doubt whether we can amalgamate individual scriptural statements into covering models of doctrine in light of the diverse streams of tradition in the biblical period.[11] Pokorny calls this an almost insurmountable problem for establishing continuity between biblical traditions. Since biblical material is circumstantial and linked to an irreversible historical development, Pokorny maintains, it becomes virtually impossible to derive a united theology (1981:1-3).

Certainly there is indeed tremendous diversity between the biblical books. The differing genres and purposes have originated from a plethora of situations and problems faced by Israel and the early church. Most of the New Testament books were written to defend apostolic Christianity against various aberrations, and there is a great variety of expressions and perspectives between the writers. Kelsey concludes that "there is no one, normative concept 'Scripture.' Instead, there seems to be a family of related but importantly different concepts of 'scripture' " (1975:14-15). Yet this skepticism is unwarranted. Diversity by no means connotes disunity, and a deeper level of unity can be discovered. Schnackenburg states, "Can we, then, really talk about a New Testament theology? We can and we must, precisely because the New Testament is a unity. . . at one in the confession of *one* Lord, *one* faith, *one* God and Father (Eph. 4, 5, 6)" (1963:22; italics his; see also Marshall 1976-77:5-14; Moule 1981:234).

Guthrie in his *Theology* does an excellent job of demonstrating the unity behind the diverse New Testament expressions, as do von Rad, Eichrodt and others in the Old Testament. The basic problem is linguistic, and therefore the difficulties will be solved at the semantic level, specifically via the semantic field behind theological concepts. Are we to see conflict between the Deuteronomic, Davidic and prophetic concepts of covenant or between the Matthean and Pauline concepts of law and grace? Here we must determine exactly how the terms (such as "fulfill" in Mt 5:17 and the language of Rom 4:13-15 or Gal 3:19—4:6) are used in the surface structure and message of the text and then delineate the underlying theological principles in the deeper structure. At this deeper level we often can promulgate unity.[12]

Many note the importance of the "social history of ideas" as an arbiter in deciding questions of meaning and authority (see Woodbridge 1982:26-27). We dare not assume unity or diversity without noting such factors as background, semantic field, community influence or the sociological development of Israel and the church. Carson's seven "positive reflections" provide a proper conclusion (1983:77-95): (1) Everyone manifests some type of "unified" theological system of beliefs. (2) The data base is the entire canon, which is open to the laws of logic; theology (or claims of diversity) must arise from the sacred text, not be imposed upon it. (3) Progressive revelation should be seriously considered but again must arise from the text. (4) Biblical differences often reflect "diverse pastoral concerns" rather than divergent confessional structures. (5) Diversity also often reflects the individual styles and interests of the writers themselves. (6) Theological harmonization is valid when the underlying statements are compatible. (7) The scholar must avoid prooftexting and allow each passage to determine its own meaning and theology.

2. Tradition History. Dunn and Sanders argue that the canon-consciousness of the communities depended on each stage of the development of traditions for their self-understanding; therefore, not only the final stage but the earlier stages constitute the Word of God, and the prehistory as well as the final codified form of the text is essential for a true biblical theology.[13] There are two ways to look at the traditioning process: via a radical reconstruction of the history of the text and of the nation along the lines of Martin Noth; or a dependence upon the text as canonically conceived without such a speculative revision of history. The former type makes a biblical theology virtually impossible since it tends to produce the kind of multiple interpretations that result in an extreme skepticism regarding the viability of any such enterprise. Therefore, most utilize the latter approach.

The scholar most commonly associated with a traditio-historical approach to biblical theology is Hartmut Gese, who takes a consciously canonical tack, arguing for a closed, united process of tradition that links both testaments. For Gese tradition history is not an artificial collection of fragmented and at times contradictory traditions but a lengthy process of development in which traditions were reinterpreted to meet new contingencies. For instance, there was more than one decalogue (Ten Commandments) as the Torah was reworked in differing situations. Yet there is continuity, and later interpretations built upon rather than displaced the classic laws.[14] Gese believes that only a tradition-critical process can unite the testaments; since texts develop out of the "life processes" of the communities, only a method that encompasses both redaction and composition criticism properly can assess the theological developments. Each stage is essential to the final product and yet dependent on that final goal. This means that for Gese the Old Testament is not fulfilled until the New Testament. Gese's program has come under a great deal of criticism.[15] He seems in many ways to replace the concept of a unifying center with his theory of a tradition or revelatory process; he ignores theology in favor of hermeneutics and history. Moreover, Gese's theory depends somewhat on his view of a late closure of the Hebrew canon (at the Council of Jamnia or even later), and this has come under some disrepute of late (especially with the growing consensus that Jamnia was not the turning point many have previously thought). All tradition-critical approaches depend upon speculative reconstructions of biblical history and so are dependent upon the shifting sands of historical opinion. In sum, the biblical theologian must be aware of the traditioning process in Israel and the early church, but it is one factor among many in the exegetical arsenal and not the key component in the formation of the history of dogma in the biblical period.

3. Theology and Canon. Closely linked to the issue of tradition is canon, and it is certainly a major issue of late, as witness the number of recent works on the issue. Taking a tradition-critical approach to the issue, Tate argues for a dynamic concept of canon that includes the stages of development as well as the final canonical product (1981:174-75). Therefore, there was no "intertestamental period" but a complex unity as the canon progressed to fulfillment. On the other hand, Childs considers canon to be a stance or perspective from which to view the Bible (1970:147). As such the canon relativizes the historical-critical method and challenges the scholar to consider the text as it is in terms of its function for the community. Therefore, "the canonical shaping . . . [forces] the interpreter . . . to confront the authoritative text of scripture in a continuing theological reflection" (Childs 1979:83).

The debate over canon and tradition in biblical theology has been both interesting and informative. Sanders objects to Childs's focus on a "final form," calling it a "canonical shape which few if any subsequent tradents heeded."[16] According to Sanders, the critic should consider not only the "freezing" of a tradition in the canonical text but also its prehistory and subsequent development. Since ancient communities read texts via tradition rather than via a "canonical" order, we must study the Bible not only synchronically (in its canonical shape, so Childs) but also diachronically (in its tradition-development). Childs responds that the results of tradition-critical research do not justify the emphasis placed upon that method, arguing that he includes the shaping process but that the final text must have priority: "The entire history of Israel's interaction with its traditions is reflected in the final text" (1980:54; see 52-60). Childs is attempting a constructive approach that will overcome the dilemma of critical scholarship and recognize the "theological role of canon."[17]

There is much to laud in the canonical methodology of Childs. His stress on the unity of the canon and the relationship of the whole of Scripture to each of the parts is similar to the "analogy of faith" of the Reformers (see below). In his Exodus commentary and monumental two-volume *Introduction to the Old Testament as Scripture* and *Introduction to the New Testament as Scripture,* Childs shows a brilliant awareness of canonical literature and indeed of the whole array of scholarship on the bewildering number of issues involved. He has indeed managed to blend critical scholarship with a canonical approach. In doing so, however, he has had to jettison interest in the historical "intended meaning" of the biblical author in favor of a canonical interpretation. To be certain, for Childs "intentionality" addresses mainly speculative reconstructions of historical background (such as attempts to rewrite the history of the conquest of Canaan or of the prophetic period) because they skew the canonical meaning of the text (1985:35-37). Yet at the same time all referential approaches to meaning (see appendix two) are rejected as inappropriate in favor of a canonical or literary tack.[18]

The centrality of the original community (Israel and the church) in Childs's system parallels the grammatical-historical method in biblical theology. We seek the theology of Israel or the early church as we collate the individual theological strands in the testaments. Yet as McComiskey points out,

> There is an important hermeneutical problem here. Canonical criticism forces us to
> derive our understanding of texts like the royal psalms from the community. Thus
> the narrower intent of the author is expanded. . . . Does not the community reflect

a hope fashioned more by historical circumstance than authoritative word? This dichotomy between author and community must be resolved.

From this vantage point let me address briefly the subtopic of a "canon within the canon." This controversial issue is related to the problem of preunderstanding and assumes the viability of choosing certain strands of biblical theology as more "canonical" or central than others. For instance, Käsemann freely admits that his Lutheran bias has led him to favor Pauline concepts of justification over other New Testament emphases as his "canon within a canon" (1964:95-107; see also Morgan 1973:60-61). Dunn goes a step further: "Whatever the theory of canonicity, the reality is that *all Christians have operated with a canon within the canon"* (italics his).[19] Whenever we place our theological system above the text and decide dogma on the basis of prooftexts rather than on the whole of Scripture, Dunn is correct.

Therefore, we must reject a "canon within a canon" approach to biblical theology. Hasel correctly notes that it is too speculative and reductionistic to provide any basis for deciding themes in biblical theology (1978:166-67). He quotes Hans Küng in labeling it "subjective arbitrariness" because it allows a person to choose any theme desired as the center of biblical theology. A "canon within a canon" cannot deal rightly with the totality of Scripture, because it is based on the principle of arbitrary selection, which itself leads to rampant subjectivity. To summarize, the canon must be taken as a whole; it demands a perspective on the unity of Scripture that allows neither community nor scholar to predominate over the canonical text itself.

4. The Analogia Fidei and Progressive Revelation. As stated in the introduction, the "analogy of faith" or (more properly) the principle of Scripture determining Scripture is a key concept in the determination of theological meaning. Yet its relevance for biblical theology is debated. The term that describes the danger of this tool (as well as the problem of the tradition-critical or "history of religions" approaches) is Sandmel's "parallelomaia," the tendency to apply any analogous passage (or religious situation) to define the meaning or origin of a biblical idea (1962:2-13). This also can lead to an overemphasis upon the unity of biblical texts, resulting in what Carson calls an "artificial conformity" that ignores the diversity of expression and emphasis between divergent statements in the Bible.[20] Ebeling goes so far as to claim that the *analogia fidei* actually undercuts a true biblical theology, since in the end "the faith" or the interpreter's preunderstanding takes precedence over Scripture itself.[21]

Certainly the danger of our "faith" rather than Scripture controlling our interpretation is very real; however, this does not mean that we must jettison the concept altogether. In fact, we could not do so if we wanted to. One's theological perspective is too deeply ingrained for that, and I would argue that it is an aid rather than an enemy in the task of discovering meaning. Rather, we should control our theological presuppositions in two ways: change the concept to the *analogia scriptura* (Scripture rather than our "faith" as the final arbiter), and allow "community exegesis" (dialogue with the past community via commentaries and so forth and with the present communities via constant interaction) to challenge our interpretation.

A further danger is shallow harmonization, the other side of "parallelomania." In biblical theology this is often seen, for instance, when canon criticism leads one to read later texts into earlier ones, as when one sees the Old Testament as a christological case book (see further below). Kaiser calls for "the analogy of antecedent Scripture" to combat this; namely, a "diachronically conscious" hermeneutic that allows a passage to stand by itself in light of its own prehistory rather than to read back into it the future development of the theological concept (1978a:18-19). In contrast, Childs argues that the totality of canonical revelation is applicable, indeed necessary, to any given part (1970:189-91). In my opinion, the truth lies between the two options. If we apply Kaiser's principle too woodenly, there could be no concept of the "progress of revelation," and we would become tradition critics, a position already seen to have serious problems for biblical theology. On the other hand, the canonical approach easily can lead to Barr's "illegitimate totality transfer," as the whole of the biblical witness is erroneously applied to a single biblical statement or theme. The answer is a proper use of parallels. They are not determinative of meaning but simply provide possibilities for reflection and yield parameters for the options. For instance, we do not choose Matthew 24:29-31 (posttribulation rapture), Revelation 3:10 (pretribulation rapture) or Revelation 20:1-10 (amillennial position) and then interpret the others on the basis of the preferred "prooftext." Rather, we set all three passages alongside one another and seek that position which best harmonizes them.

The hermeneutical principles by which we may do this are critical. Primarily, we must assess the relative value of each theological parallel, giving the most likely passages greater weight but giving due weight to all passages dealing with the theme. We need to differentiate true parallels from seeming parallels, but at the same time we must explore all ramifications of the larger issue and place them in their proper biblical framework (see Thomas 1980:45-53). I have already explored this at the level of semantics (chap. three), and the principles there can be applied also to theological parallels. The *analogia scriptura* is a key to a proper biblical theology and an essential ingredient in a canonical approach.

5. Authority. Critical scholars denigrate the authority of biblical theology since it is perceived as a purely descriptive science. Barr states flatly,

> It is less and less likely that biblical theology can be deemed to have said the last word about anything. . . . On the one side, the authority of the Bible can no longer be taken for granted, but must be *shown* on sufficient grounds. On the other side, biblical theology cannot work in isolation; involved in historical judgments on the one hand, it is linked with logical, philosophical, and finally, systematic-theological judgments on the other.[22]

The argument is that biblical theology, dealing only with "what it meant," is descriptive; systematic theology, telling "what it means," presents the normative element in Christian truth (and even here it is normative only for that particular community of faith). In this latter sense, Nineham goes so far as to assert that the Bible as poetry has spoken to each generation but that the "authority" question is culturally conditioned and caught up with the parallel authorities of church, conscience and reason.[23] He states, "What if God, taking history very seriously, actually wants the Church in the twentieth century to be engaged in dialogue with herself" (1976:271).

"What if" statements of course state mere possibilities rather than actualities, and invite response. I would answer that God indeed does want dialogue, but not in place of an authoritative text (as Nineham would have it). Naturally, Nineham and others can do as they wish, but even the simplest perusal of biblical claims demonstrates the fact that the Bible at least demands that it be the basis of that dialogue. This God-ordained "dialogue with herself" can never occur apart from biblical standards (Nineham) nor does it continue the process of God's inspired self-revelation (Achtemeier). The church dialogues at the level of interpretation but can have only one response: obedience to God's will as revealed in his authoritative Word (2 Tim 3:16-17).

Evangelicals recognize that the human element was present—in the stages of tradition and transmission, in the codification of the tradition in the canonical books and in the church's validation of the "inspired" books via the process of canonization. However, this in no way vitiates the divine element, which was central in each of these stages. While some conservatives are perhaps too docetic when they ignore the human side, many nonconservatives are too Arian when they ignore the divine side. In spite of all the historical problems enumerated above, we are continually brought back to the bottom line: God has spoken to humanity! The biblical revelation is not so relative or culturally conditioned as to be inaccessible to modern people. The science of hermeneutics enables us to get back to the intended meaning of the original propositions, and biblical theology is part of the process whereby we allow that authoritative message to address us today.

6. History and Theology. Barr notes four problematic aspects in any attempt to anchor revelation in history (1976:746-49): (1) ambiguity regarding the nature of the revelatory events and their connection with historical causation; (2) ambiguity about the sense of "history" in terms both of the accessibility of revelation to critical historians and of its being revelation if it is accessible; (3) ambiguity regarding the relation between revelation and history, as to whether they are equal or separate and whether any criteria can be adduced to prove it actually happened; (4) difficulties in the relation between revelation and the biblical text itself, since the latter shows no awareness of such. Barr argues that the tradition-history of Israel (or the church) is the true locus and that revelation per se played no part in the development of the canon.

The problem areas that Barr notes are valid, but his pessimism is unwarranted for several reasons. The history behind the Gospels, for instance, is quite accessible to the historian, as several recent works have argued.[24] There is no true dichotomy between theology (or revelation) and history in the Gospels or in the historical books of the Old Testament. While there is historical relativity in the Bible due to the circumstantial nature of the books, the cultural environment is not the controlling factor, at least not in the minds of the authors. Inspiration (and a concomitant sense of revelation) is frequently claimed, both in the prophets and in the apostolic authority behind New Testament literature. Lessing's "ugly broad ditch" between history and truth (his statement that "accidental truths of history can never become the proof of necessary truths of reason") was based upon the philosophical skepticism of the Enlightenment. However, the historical relativity of Scripture does not entail a relativism that destroys the uniqueness of the Christian faith. Rather, we should follow the lesson of church history and return to a "precritical" though critically informed view of the connection between history and truth in the Bible (see Hughes 1983:173-94 for an excellent discussion of this issue).

There is no reason why biblical theology must on the one hand divorce itself from the possibility of revelation in history (Barr's demand), or on the other hand demand a positivistic reconstruction of history as the basis for its work (the tradition-critical approach). Hermann calls for a "theology of history" based upon the biblical view of time and history as centered upon the interrelationship between human history and divine action.[25] While history itself betrays no revelatory aspect, God has made himself known in the midst of human history, especially via the dimension of promise-fulfillment. At the level of religious experience God's active presence in history is known. While I cannot agree with Hermann that history is ontologically incapable of being revelatory, he does provide a good basis for the union of history and theology. I would argue that since God has given his revelation in history the two are ontologically related.

Hayes and Prussner chronicle the reaction against the union of history and theology as opposed primarily to the "revelation in history" school of Wright and others (1985:241-44, 262-64). The current mode of thinking is to replace history with a view of the Bible as "story." In this way the question of historicity need not arise and the literary features of the narrative (in which the theology actually is found) can take precedence over the "event" itself. However, as stated in chapter six, the historical aspects of the biblical narrative are a part of the theology, and no such dichotomy should be made.

7. Language, Text and Meaning. Surprisingly, texts on biblical theology too seldom discuss the problem of language, except in the sense of descriptive (what it meant) vs. normative (what it means) tasks (such as Stendahl). However, the problem of language has moved to the forefront of discussion due to recent theories regarding language and hermeneutics. Henry discusses the preoccupation with this issue:

> They [scholars] have posed so starkly the "predicament" of "the modern person" to whom the meaning of the New Testament must be conveyed, they have drawn such a sharp contrast between the condition of persons today and their condition at any other time, that they have been compelled to concentrate almost all their efforts on the attempt to pry loose from the New Testament some word that is not tied to the particularity of Judaism or confused by partisan battles among the apostles. (1979:56-57)

The debate centers upon the interrelationship between the three aspects of meaning—author, text, reader. Tremendous problems occur at each link; what is the exact relationship between an author and the reader, and how does one get back to the theology of the biblical author in light of the great gap between the original setting and that of the current age? Yet I would argue that religious language is open to verification via hermeneutical criteria of adequacy and coherence. Since language contains both "dead" (static) and "live" (dynamic) metaphors, the Bible can be both propositional truth (static) and language event (dynamic). As such, a biblical theology is a vital element in the ongoing interaction between God and this world (see the appendices for a more detailed consideration of this essential issue).

8. Old Testament and New Testament. All agree that this is the central issue for any proper biblical theology. Once again the basic problem is unity and diversity: each testament must have its autonomous place within the larger unity of Scripture. Yet the balance between the two remains difficult to attain. Many have taught that Old and New Testaments should remain separate. Marcion was the first to demand a radical dichotomy, removing from the canon not only the Old Testament but also any New Testament works related to the Old Testament. In our time both Adolf von Harnack and Rudolf Bultmann have stressed discontinuity. For Bultmann and Baumgärtel this leads to a promissory approach to biblical theology. The Old Testament is the "presupposition" of the New, and the failure of the covenant hope of Israel led to a new religion centering upon the promissory hope of justification.[26]

However, this negative tone has not been influential. Westermann responds that the negativism of such scholars shatters the value of the Old Testament as religious history (1963:122-33). Moreover, New Testament background is also loosed from its historical moorings and flounders in a sea of mythical irrelevance. To remove "fulfillment" from "promise" is arbitrary and inadequate. In the final analysis it is impossible to separate the two testaments, and any truly biblical theology must begin with the recognition of unity and demonstrate such. The simple fact that there are at least 257 quotes and over 1,100 allusions (according to the Nestle-Aland Greek text) of the Old Testament in the New shows the extent to which the latter built upon the former. In terms of vocabulary, themes, religious emphases and worship the two depend upon one another. In terms of redemptive history a clear typological relationship of promise-fulfillment exists between the testaments, and any concept of the progress of revelation in history (the backbone of biblical theology) must build upon this deeper interdependence.[27]

Toward a Methodology

The second major area of disagreement (after a unifying center) is the methodology by which we develop a biblical theology. Scholars have never attained any consensus with respect to approach. Biblical scholars have tended to prefer an analytical or descriptive approach, and theologians have always preferred a synthetic method. For instance, Ladd in his New Testament theology utilizes an analytical method that takes each book as a distinct entity, while Guthrie follows a synthetic approach that proceeds theme by theme.

The solution is to examine the strengths and weaknesses of these and other proposed methods. Stuhlmacher suggests five criteria by which one can judge a viable biblical theology (1979:163): (1) It must correspond with the religious-historical as well as the churchly aspects of Scripture. (2) There should be historical and dogmatic coherence in defining the relationship between the testaments. (3) It must unite the strands of theology between the various books and traditions. (4) It should demonstrate the link between the biblical message of salvation and the church's attestation of faith in such a way as to reflect canonical history. (5) It should preserve scholarly expertise in the exegetical and hermeneutical disciplines. Of course, the way in which we will interpret these criteria will differ according to our own paradigm community; that is, according to the type of "critical" school to which we adhere. Nevertheless, this provides an excellent control in assessing the following methods. I would note three specifics: the method employed must be cognizant of the diversity of individual expressions; at the same time it must demonstrate the deeper unity behind those expressions; and it must trace the progression of the revelation/historical development of biblical dogma.

1. The Synthetic Method. In this method theological themes are traced through the biblical strata in relation to the various historical periods. Two different approaches are taken: some follow a history of religions approach that studies the sources and the changing theological situations (many Old Testament theologians), while others simply describe the differing theologies with little attempt to trace lines of continuity or development (many New Testament theologians). The strength of the synthetic method lies in its stress upon the unity of Scripture. It is often assumed that the themes elucidated draw together the various traditions behind the biblical writers. The thematic approach also graphically demonstrates the interconnections between the traditions. At the same time, however, the synthetic method can be artificial and subjective, since the categories can be easily imposed from outside (from theology) rather than arising naturally from within (from the text). Even when major concepts like covenant or kingdom are applied indiscriminately, the data itself can be ignored or twisted to fit the preconceived pattern.

Nevertheless, this approach has made a significant impact, for example, in Eichrodt's *Theology of the Old Testament,* in which a unifying theme (covenant) is traced by means of "cross-sections" of the canonical literature. Eichrodt wished to be true to history yet to retain the basic unity of Scripture. His selective process was intended to avoid the control of historicism on the one hand and of systematic theology on the other hand. However, while his method gained wide acceptance, his unifying theme did not. Using a similar approach, Vriezen (1970) argues for the communion concept, Kaiser (1978) for the promise theme, and Terrien (1978) for the presence of God as the central theme.

2. The Analytical Method. Stemming from the post-Enlightenment period, the descriptive or analytical method has always been central to the task of biblical theology. It studies the distinctive theological emphases of individual books and the developing traditions in order to discern the unique message of each. Theoretically it is opposed to harmonizing the individual messages into covering or unifying themes. Dulles notes several dangers this avoids: the tendency to exert a kind of tyranny over other approaches; a romantic tendency to "canonize" biblical thought patterns, as if the modern person should think like the ancient Hebrew; and an external control over biblical thought by contemporary philosophy and theology (1965:214-15).

At the same time there are clear dangers: the analytical method can result in a mere collage of individually diverse theologies without cohesion; while this could be correct, it is hardly how the Bible or the Jewish-Christian faith perceived itself. Moreover, it can easily degenerate into a history of religions approach, with concern only for genealogical origins rather than for the living faith that produced the documents. This in fact has been the most common form of the analytical method.

3. The History of Religions Method. As stated above, this has often been the analytical approach. Yet it is also a separate school and so deserves consideration, since it elucidates the development of religious ideas in the life of Israel and the early church. In its radical form it assumes that these ideas were borrowed from surrounding religions. In its more conservative form it traces the progress of revelation, that is the history of God's revelation in the canonical period. The key distinction is that this method centers upon history while the analytical approach centers upon theology.

The best-known proponent of this method, Bultmann, called the message of Jesus the "presupposition for the theology of the New Testament rather than a part of that theology itself" (1951:1:3). Theology therefore does not begin with the historical Jesus and his teaching but with the Christ of faith, which is the product of the preaching and teaching of the early church. Two aspects control Bultmann's thought—history of religions (the historical side) and existentialism (the interpretive side). For Bultmann the major stress is upon the latter, since biblical theology has meaning, "not as theoretical teachings, timeless general truths, but only as an expression of an understanding of human existence which for the man of today also is a possibility for his understanding of himself" (1951:2:251).

The basic error of Bultmann and his followers is what Hasel calls their "tunnel vision," which leads them to stress only those sections of Scripture which cohere with existentialist interpretation. As a result they often ignore works like Hebrews, James or Revelation (1978:101-2). Moreover, there are too few controls, so that their reconstruction of theology tends to leave the biblical data at the mercy of the critic. Finally, history of religion theorists often assume that any potential parallel is a precursor or source of New Testament ideas. More often than not, the parallels are analogical rather than sources of New Testament ideas. In conclusion, there is promise when the theorist sticks to the biblical data, tracing the historical development of biblical themes in light of the environment in which they developed (the progress of revelation). However, when the method steps outside the biblical framework and seeks a speculative revision of that data, it becomes too subjective to be useful.

4. Diachronic and Tradition-Critical Methods. I have already discussed the issue of tradition criticism (pp. 271-73), so I will concentrate here on the hermeneutical method used by this school. Gerhard von Rad's epochal Old Testament theology opposed a strictly historical-critical reconstruction of biblical theology on the grounds that it resulted in a negative approach. Instead he wedded history to kerygma, that is, a kerygmatic theology grounded in history. For von Rad history of tradition provides a positive key to the kerygmatic portrait of the biblical text; the developing confession of the community has greater theological relevance than a reconstructed history of that community. However, von Rad does not deny the viability of that reconstruction. Rather the developing creed has the place of primacy, and von Rad argues that the confessional formula rather than the originating event is the true task of biblical theology. He calls this "retelling" and believes that it bridges the gap between history and theology. Thereby the acts of God, or redemptive history, come to the fore. However, this very dichotomy between objective history and salvation history has occasioned most of the criticism directed against him (see Hayes and Prussner 1985:233-39 for a fine summary).

Although the developing community is important, I doubt whether it solves as many problems as it creates. Biblical theology should be erected upon a solid foundation, and the speculative theories of tradition or community development do not provide the necessary groundwork. I prefer a concept of the progress of revelation as exemplified in Vos (1948), which takes the text of Scripture at face value and does not try to impose a revisionist concept of tradition development upon it. The text itself, rather than historical-critical reconstruction, best determines the method. A book-by-book descriptive approach could be organized on the basis of the progress of revelation, and in this way a diachronic approach would be an important step forward methodologically. Here Childs's *Introduction to the Old Testament as Scripture* (and its New Testament counterpart) provides a good model.

5. The Christological Method. According to Vischer (1949) we must interpret every part of the Bible in light of the Christ event. The Old Testament tells us what Christ is and the New Testament who he is; thus we have a complete picture of Christ in the Old Testament. Hengstenberg, Barth and many modern Lutheran theologians show the popularity of the christological approach today. Indeed, the method has several advantages: it guards against an overly zealous historicizing tendency among many biblical theologians and recognizes the centrality of the Christian faith; for the Christian the whole Bible does indeed point to Jesus Christ. The analytic approach often produces an Old Testament theology that is virtually unaware of the New Testament or the prophetic purpose of the Old Testament.

However, on the whole there are greater dangers than strengths in this movement. Nearly all practitioners allegorize and spiritualize Old Testament texts to fit preconceived "types of Christ" or some such. The Old Testament as the history and record of God's salvific dealings with his covenant people Israel is lost. Subjective speculation and a reductionism reduce it to a series of prophetic acts. The intention of the text, the Old Testament as canon in its own right, and the validity of the religious experiences of the Hebrews as the chosen people of Yahweh are all sacrificed on the altar of "relevance." There must be a better way to demonstrate the continuity between the covenants.

Barr posits a "trinitarian approach" in which the Old Testament has historical priority and the New Testament christological authority, with both grounded in the unity of the Godhead—Father, Son and Spirit. When this is augmented with a promise-fulfillment perspective, the relationship between the testaments is given a much stronger foundation. The Old and New Testaments stand on their own as the record of God's covenant with his two peoples—Israel and the church—yet are united into a single Bible via the Christ-event.[28]

6. The Confessional Method. Practitioners of this approach consider the Bible to be a series of faith-statements that demand adherence and as such transcend history. Several scholars include this perspective in their systems (such as von Rad, Cullmann), but some make it the kingpin and radically oppose the analytic or historical approaches. Vriesen (1970) argues that a purely objective or neutral stance is impossible, and that only a theoretical stance like that of the original communities can understand biblical theology. Hasel mentions Otto Eissfeldt, G. A. F. Knight and Roland de Vaux as taking a similar stance (1975:40-41). The Old Testament must be understood as Christian Scripture, and theology as a science demands faith.

The major strength of this school is its cognizance of the centrality of creed and worship in biblical faith. Both testaments are certainly written by believing communities and demand assent on the part of all readers. As Jesus taught, kingdom truths are reserved for the faithful (Mk 4:10-12; Mt 13:10-17). Yet there are also distinct weaknesses. Hasel writes that Eissfeld's positions (accepted by all adherents) "are on the one hand dominated by a superseded historical positivism and on the other hand by an artificial and unsupportable separation of knowledge and faith" (1975:41-42). Like the christological method this approach reads more into the Old Testament than is actually there and tends to impose theological categories (such as Roman Catholic, Lutheran, Reformed) upon biblical statements in both testaments. The basic premise, that one should read the text from a similar faith stance to that of the originating community, is valid; but there needs to be strong controls upon the task. Moreover, both synthetic and analytic schools also recognize this point.

7. The Multiplex Method (see Hasel 1981:181-83). As stated above, each of the approaches has certain strengths, and by combining them and allowing the text to guide us, we can minimize the weaknesses. This method is my preference. Any such attempt to build a valid biblical theology has five criteria or controls upon it: (1) The data must reflect the individual theologies and genres of the biblical literature (such as wisdom, the theology of Ruth or Esther as well as of Mark or Matthew). (2) We must work with the final canonical form of the documents (lest we drown theology in the speculative reconstructions of historical critics) and seek the interrelationship between the themes of both writers and books. (3) The task is two-pronged, beginning with the diverse theologies of individual biblical works (the descriptive or analytic side) and then delineating the "longitudinal themes" as they emerge from the individual works and unite them with others (such as Paul with James). (4) The purpose is to trace the development of individual themes and then to discover the dynamic unity and multifaceted patterns that bind the parts together; in other words, there are two tasks: the study of individual themes and the discovery of unifying themes. (5) The final product must integrate the testaments, noting both the diversity and the unity between them.

At the outset the stance taken is a confessional one, accepting at face value the perspective of the biblical writers and identifying with it. However, this does not negate a descriptive approach. We seek a "biblical" theology not a dogmatic one. The study of the diverse "theologies" of the individual traditions combines two aspects that too often have been set in conflict with one another, a book-by-book and a historical-genetic approach. Each is valid but needs to be supplemented by the other. By itself the book-by-book approach can be artificial; for instance, does one follow the Hebrew canonical order or the early church's? Neither is completely satisfactory, for they do not yield true continuity of themes. Similarly the purely historical approach is usually dominated by alien historiographic presuppositions (such as tradition-critical or history of religions), which easily ignore the text and center upon theories of origin and development. The best solution is to combine them and allow each to correct excesses in the other. There is a basic tradition-critical unity within the books and yet a historical or chronological relationship between them.

At this point of the task the diversity of the data will dominate. Yet at the same time interlacing patterns will begin to emerge. The progress of revelation will become manifest as the individual themes begin to bridge to other works, first at the level of chronological similarity (such as the eighth-century prophets) and then between periods. As these interlocking themes appear, the relationship of the parts to the whole must always be in mind. The first task of the theologian is exegetical; the text must speak for itself. Individual statements should never be elevated to dogmatic status as assertions of the whole of dogma; instead, each should be seen in light of the context in which they appear and then collated with similar statements in the book or corpus (such as Pauline). Very seldom can a single statement be taken as indicative of the whole theological truth. Usually each relates a single aspect of the larger doctrine to particular situations and issues in the community addressed. For instance, one cannot "solve" the issue of election simply by appealing to Romans 9 or Ephesians 1. Rather, we must consult all passages dealing with God's "call" to salvation and our response. This is why exegesis and biblical theology are so interdependent. Each informs and at times controls excesses in the other. Exegesis provides the content, biblical theology the perspective for serious Bible study. As the patterns of dogma develop from the exegetical sphere, they begin to intersect with other streams in the historical development of the biblical documents. In this manner the themes appear inductively from within the scriptural data and are not imposed deductively from outside. This does not mean, however, that presuppositionless exegesis results. The very patterns detected are the result of interpretive choices and must be continuously clarified and if necessary corrected by the text itself and by competing interpretive communities. The value of challenge from opposing theories is that they drive us back to the text and allow it the final say.

8. The Problem of a Unifying Center.   The final stage in the development of a biblical theology is the identification of the archetypal concept(s) or unifying themes behind the diverse documents. As the interlocking principles between the strata of the biblical period become visible, the patterns coalesce around certain ideas that bridge the gaps between the individual witnesses. However, it is very uncertain whether any single theme or concept stands at the apex of biblical theology. Many believe that the complete lack of consensus demonstrates that a cluster of ideas, rather than a single theme, unites all the others. Walther suggests thirteen motifs at the core: captivity and deliverance, God and

Son of God, gift of Torah, covenant, people of God, cultus, kingship, creation, wisdom, Spirit of God, righteousness and justice, Day of the Lord, and promise/hope (1969:222-23). Yet we must wonder whether such complex ideas are not simply lists that easily could be unified further, such as God and Spirit or covenant and kingship.

Six criteria must be met in any search for a central motif (or motifs) that binds together the other themes: (1) The motif must express the nature/character of the Godhead. (2) The theme(s) should account for the people of God as they relate to God, their world and one another. (3) The concept(s) must include the world of humankind as the object of God's redemptive love. (4) The motif must explain the dialectical relationship between the testaments. (5) The motif must contain and sum up the individual emphases of the diverse parts of Scripture, such as wisdom as well as apocalyptic or epistolary portions. (6) The theme(s) should account for other potential unifying themes and must truly unite them under a single rubric. It should explain and balance the others and not merely be imposed upon them.

Most of those motifs proposed by various scholars fail to meet these qualifications. Eichrodt and Ridderbos propose "covenant" as the central theme, arguing that it expresses the binding relationship between God and his people and contains both the legal contract and eschatological hope or promise that results. However, too many portions of Scripture (such as wisdom) do not contain it, and it does not sum up the others below. Still others propose some form of the Godhead at the core—God and Christ (Hasel), Yahweh (Zimmerli), divine holiness (Sellin), lordship (Koehler), kingship (Klein), or divine presence (Terrien). Each of these variations, however, fails to account for the diverse aspects noted in the criteria above. Existential reality (Bultmann) or communion (Vriezen) considers the other side of the divine/human interaction but likewise fails to be broad enough.

Another motif often stressed is eschatological hope, either in the sense of "promise" (Kaiser) or "hope" (Moltmann, McComiskey). The strength of this proposal is the extent to which it unites the testaments, and it does in a sense unify the other themes above. However, several portions of Scripture (such as wisdom or the Johannine corpus) have no emphasis upon this, and in many ways it is one aspect rather than the whole of the redemptive plan.

More promise is found in various forms of a "salvation history" schema of von Rad, Cullmann, Goppelt or Ladd. This position recognizes God's/Christ's redemptive activity on behalf of humankind in terms of past, present and future communion. More than the others it subsumes into itself each of the categories normally mentioned. Yet there are major stumbling blocks here as well. It is more artificial than those above, which are supported by biblical language while this is a theoretical concept without linguistic support. Moreover, Scripture does not put a great deal of emphasis upon this concept. Only in Luke does it play a major theological role. Finally, the emphasis on the "God who acts" (Wright) often separated redemptive history from real history, making it a theological category bereft of real meaning (see Hayes and Prussner 1985:241-43).

For this reason most scholars today are positing a cluster of themes. Brueggemann believes that a "two-trajectory" track is emerging in Old Testament theology, variously defined as "visionary/pragmatic," "covenantal/sapiential" or "ethical/sapiential" (1984:5). He calls these "boundaries," or "parameters," around which a theology can be determined. Similarly, Knierim presents a twofold pattern: Yahweh's relationship to the world/its people and his relationship to reality (1984:44-45). These and other similar theories have not yet pointed the way to any consensus, but it is safe to say that most recognize that the Bible is too diverse in its interests and emphases to be summed up in a single theme.

Conclusion

The role of biblical theology in the hermeneutical task is twofold: internally it studies the diverse themes of individual books and of the testaments, organizes them into a holistic set of dogmas and then collates these into archetypal doctrines that reflect the progress of revelation; externally it provides a bridge from exegesis to systematic theology. In many ways biblical theology is the forgotten element in serious biblical research. Yet among those who have rejected the possibility of systematic theology it has also wrongfully been made the final stage of the hermeneutical process. I view biblical theology to be at the apex of the exegetical stage (discerning "what it meant") and as providing a transition to the contextualization stage (determining "what it means"). Biblical theology also provides the basis for systematic theology in that it tells us the systematic theology of Israel and of the early church. By collecting and collating the biblical material along the lines of the progress of revelation, biblical theology describes the emerging beliefs of the biblical period and theoretically organizes them in the patterns originally held by Israel and the church.

There are two types of study under the guise of biblical theology, one done by all Christians but the other pretty much restricted to the specialist. The former consists of tracing individual doctrines through the Word of God in order to determine exactly which theological statement actually fits all the data. Every church that has ever rewritten its constitution or gone through a doctrinal debate has had to do this. Issues like baptism, eternal security or the charismatic debate cannot be settled any other way. Yet churches inevitably fail to do the task adequately, for proponents seem to collect only those passages which support the position they prefer and fail to look at all the passages that bear upon the issue before formulating their statement of the doctrine. The answer is to trace the issue through each stage of Scripture and only then to organize the material and decide the issue. The key is to "bracket" our own beliefs and to allow the other side to challenge our preferred positions. This will drive us to examine the biblical data anew and to allow *all* passages on the topic to have equal weight.[29] I will examine this further in the following chapter on systematic theology.

The second type of biblical theology can be done at several levels, studying the theology of an individual book (such as Isaiah or Matthew), a corpus (Pauline theology), a testament (Old or New Testament theology) or of the Bible as a whole. Needless to say, this is a massive undertaking. The scholar must determine the individual theological emphases of each book and of each author, and then collate to determine the archetypal themes that tie together the testaments and unite them into a whole. I have discussed the viability of such a seemingly impossible goal several times in this chapter; I believe that it is not only possible but critical in order to understand both the diversity and the unity of Scripture. Most of all, the themes that unite the various tradition strata of Scripture must emerge from below and not be imposed from above; that is, they should be drawn out of the text rather than out of the theologian's imagination and should truly sum up the other major subthemes of Scripture.

14
$\int$ ystematic Theology

S YSTEMATIC THEOLOGY HAS DESERVEDLY BEEN CALLED "THE QUEEN OF THE BIBLICAL SCI-
ences." In essence every discipline and technique discussed thus far must be utilized
in constructing a systematic theology. One begins with the traditional views inherited from the chosen theological community (such as Methodist, Reformed or evangelical, liberal). This is the preunderstanding with which one begins. Then the theologian
traces a particular issue (such as atonement or eschatology) through Scripture inductively, determining which passages speak to the issue. At this stage exegetical study searches
for the exact nuances in each passage that addresses the doctrine and begins to organize
the passages in order to determine which aspect of the doctrine each passage teaches.
Biblical theology collates the results and determines the belief of Israel and the early
church on the issue. Next the theologian traces the issue through church history to see
how it was developed to meet different needs in different eras. This tells how the doctrine
was contextualized in the past and provides invaluable positive as well as negative clues
for the recontextualization of the doctrine for our own time.

In other words, systematic theology is the proper goal of biblical study and teaching.
Every hermeneutical aspect (including contextualization, discussed in the next chapter)
must be put into practice in constructing such a theology for our day.

In itself this process sounds complex enough. Indeed, each stage has enormous problems, and these difficulties as well as the process itself summarize the Gordian knot of
hermeneutics. In a nutshell the dilemma can be stated simply: each stage described in the
first paragraph is done by an interpreter who looks at the material through prejudiced
eyes, through an interpretive grid shaped by the believing community of which he or she
is a part as well as by experiences and personal proclivities that subtly shape the direction
of the study and the results. In other words, we all want to make certain that our side
wins! Hardly anyone at any time conducts a purely objective search for truth. These
biases, plus the unbelievable plethora of options available in our pluralistic world, make
it difficult if not impossible to determine which theological option is actually best, let
alone which of them is "true" (in the sense of final or absolute truth).

Yet these aspects of theological method—preunderstanding, community stance, experience, rational thinking—are not merely negative influences. Each contributes positively

to the process of constructing a personal and community theology. The problem is that in our complex world the ability to think critically—of one's own ideas as well as of other options—has been blunted, and it is increasingly difficult to make decisions on probability grounds. More and more critical scholars are replacing the concept of "truth" with a pluralistic openness to many possible "truths," even in theological matters. To some degree this is necessary, for the Bible itself is content to leave many issues open. Yet at the same time one dare not extend this openness to all issues. While the Bible may be somewhat ambiguous on issues like sovereignty and responsibility, the millennial question or church government (of course, many readers would respond that the Bible is quite clear on these questions too!), is it also unclear on the deity of Christ, his second coming or his substitutionary atonement? Any methodology for developing a systematic theology must answer these questions and tell how to decide between areas of pluralistic openness and absolute or cardinal dogma.

The purpose of this chapter is to provide a methodology for adjudicating between the numerous options and to discuss the many serious issues theologians too often ignore. In many ways this chapter provides a summary of the other chapters and will as such build on material presented elsewhere. The discussion of meaning and truth found in appendices one and two is especially critical in providing a rationale for the very possibility of discovering a systematic theology. The trend in higher-critical circles today is to replace the idea of *a* systematic theology with the possibility of *many* systematic theologies, each one "true" for a particular community of faith or a particular situation. This is part of the postmodern denial of any absolute truth and the affirmation of a plurality of possible truths. I believe that the problems in determining the best possible theological system as well as in constructing a particular doctrine are very real but not insurmountable. We will study these problems in the ensuing sections.

The Components of Theological Construction

Many factors intersect in theological decisions, and each plays an important role in the process. It is commonly assumed in evangelical circles that only the first—Scripture—is valid, and that the others are barriers rather than positive components of theological construction. Yet this is untrue. Each aspect is an important ingredient in the theological mix, and each one carries certain dangers that we must avoid.

1. **Scripture.** Many believe that dogma emerges automatically from Scripture. One need merely quote a few verses and the doctrine becomes clear. However, this ignores the fact that the *meaning* of those passages is far from clear, and that many have been debated for centuries. Moreover, these very debates account for the theological differences. As a result others go to the opposite extreme and posit an open-ended theology with a pluralistic core, that is, with many possible answers and no final dogma. Obviously we want to find a middle ground between the two extremes.

The first determining factor is one's view of biblical authority. Those like myself who believe that the Bible is the inspired, revealed Word of God accept it as the final arbiter of all doctrinal statements. Those who do not have this high view of biblical authority must take a different approach. The key is to recognize the centrality of one's conception of Scripture for theological construction. As van Huyssteen states it, this "fully determines the theologian's manner of problem solving and may function either as a considered, critically responsible model or uncritically as a submerged model serving as an invisible filter in the theologian's provisional and hence limited perspective on the Bible" (1989:179). In other words, we must carefully work through our view of Scripture in terms of both the Bible's authority and our own finite interpretations.

This tension produces the basic problem for theological study. Too often we assume that our interpretation is what the Bible says and fail to realize the many other factors that determine meaning. As a result doctrine is produced by a rabbinic type of "pearl-stringing" in which a connected list of favorite texts seemingly "proves" the viability of a particular dogmatic formulation. The difficulty is that opponents are providing their own set of proof-texts (often entirely different texts that address the same issue, with each side ignoring the other's proof-texts!), and the two sides speak around rather than to each other. For instance, many who argue for a pretribulation return of Christ center upon Daniel 9:24-27; Matthew 24:37-41; 1 Corinthians 15:51-52; 1 Thessalonians 4:13-18; 2 Thessalonians 2:6-7; and Revelation 3:10; 4:1, 4; the midtribulation position depends upon Matthew 24:21-22 and Revelation 11:15-19; and posttribulationists dwell upon Matthew 24:29-31; 1 Thessalonians 5:1-10 and 2 Thessalonians 2:1-3. Too seldom is there an honest dialogue or consideration of the other position's texts.[1]

Those who do theology from a liberal perspective argue that the Bible itself is the product of tradition and thus cannot be the ultimate source of theology. Gordon Kaufman argues that the gospel centers upon the liberation of the individual from all bondage, including that of religious traditions.[2] Theology therefore is always in a state of development and is subject to constant reformulation as the historical context changes. The pluralism of religious ideas and approaches caused by the constantly shifting circumstances and world views does not allow any final answer or theology. Tradition, even that of the Bible, is not ultimate but is subject to the changing needs of the community. Bible and creed, according to Kaufman, provide "truth" but must be restated and transformed for current needs.

In this regard Ogden (forthcoming) finds three "phases" in theological reflection: (1) the historical aspect, which traces the developing tradition beginning with the tradition behind the biblical statements (via tradition criticism) and moving to the changing perspectives within Scripture and then throughout church history; (2) the hermeneutical perspective, which studies the historical witness (step one above) as human witness to ultimate reality and then reinterprets that witness for the present situation (recognizing the pluralism inherent in both critical reflection and praxis); and (3) philosophical enquiry, which notes the centrality of the existential question, namely the meaning of ultimate reality for us. For Ogden human experience filtered through philosophical reflection determines the valid witness for our community.

For these scholars Scripture is a valuable witness to the power of God in the life of the community but not the final authority for theological formulation. Nonevangelical theologians believe that the original purpose of the biblical books was to attest to God's salvation-historical presence among his people rather than to provide an atomistic set of required doctrines. Farley and Hodgson call this latter perspective the "scripture principle" and believe it was the product of the early church, which due to pressure from rival Christian communities and the growing cosmopolitan and crosscultural nature of the Christian movement was forced to transform its view of the biblical writings into "a canon of officially recognized authoritative writings" that demanded "atomistic exegesis and proof-texting, and the establishment of revelation as the foundation of theology contained in human-historical deposits regarded as inspired and infallible" (1985:68). Due to the development of the historical-critical method and of modern theology, they argue, this view of infallible propositional authority has collapsed and been replaced by an understanding of Scripture as a symbolic expression of God's redemptive activity, which must be "redescribed" in functional terms for our day.[3]

In short, in this approach the Bible ceases to contain a revealed set of doctrines that must be believed but rather becomes a case-book that provides models to follow in constructing a modern Christianity. Moreover, the locus of theological construction shifts from an authoritative Scripture to the needs of the current community in much the same way as modern hermeneutics has shifted from the text to the reader as the locus for the construction of meaning (see appendix one). Following Tracy,[4] Sallie McFague defines scriptural authority as that of a "classic poetic text" in the sense that it speaks with power to all peoples of every age and is flexible, open to a wide diversity of interpretations (1982:59; see 54-65).

The Bible for McFague does not contain dogmatic assertions so much as it presents an alternative world that addresses and shapes Christian experiences in this and every age. Therefore, any consideration of the Bible as *the* Word of God is idolatry, since a human book (the Bible) is seen as the definitive portrait of God. Instead, the Bible addresses our concerns and provides answers that are relevant to our needs, and its authority is functional rather than absolute and dogmatic. Moreover, other Christian classics also address our concerns and are valid for contemporary restatements and redescriptions of religious truth. The Bible is the basis for Christian reflection and dogma but does not present ultimate truth. Rather, the theologian works with its metaphorical message and redirects that to the modern situation, changing what is no longer relevant.

Evangelical theologians dare not ignore this challenge, for there are many valid points in the liberal critique of conservative hermeneutics. It is indeed true that there is a plurality of interpretations and theological models. Every Christian tradition contains certain distinctive doctrines and beliefs, and at times these differ considerably from one another. It is also true that these religious traditions at the pragmatic level often have even more influence than Scripture in determining what a person believes (see further below). The actual process of sifting and interpreting the available data in constructing dogmatic theories is certainly far more complicated than has heretofore been said.

However, this does not mean that any hope of arriving at theological "truth" with Scripture as the foundation is groundless. As stated in appendix two below, there are indeed many "meanings" for which one may search, such as existential, contextual (which we call "significance") or theological. However, the author's intended meaning is another, and I believe it is the basis for the others. Every chapter of this book addresses the issue of the priority (and the possibility) of the intended meaning of a passage. While the reader's preunderstanding certainly makes it difficult to discover that meaning, and while there is always a plethora of possible interpretations to sift through, this does not make it impossible to make a probability decision as to the "meaning" that best fits the original context. Moreover, all the "possible meanings" are not equally valid, and there is no necessity to surrender and accept a multiplicity of possibilities. At times I have the feeling that a new "final authority" operates for many critical theologians, namely that of the contemporary context resulting in relativism and radical pluralism. The Bible itself demands that we understand it on the basis of the author's intended meaning. Therefore, we have a responsibility to seek that interpretation which best fits this goal.

Biblical theology allows the theologian to move from the individual text to the theological framework of which it is a part. It is common among liberal theologians to deny the validity of propositional theology. Scripture becomes a model of religious experience rather than a compendium of dogmatic statements. The problem with this is its disjunctive nature. The two—propositional and commissive—stand together. It is not an either-or but a both-and. Even narrative sections, as redaction criticism has shown, have a deposit of theological assertions that the author wished to communicate with his readers. Also, didactic sections contain a parenetic or commissive element that addresses action as well as belief. In other words, proposition and experience stand side-by-side in Scripture, and both are valid, indeed necessary, hermeneutical goals.

It is the task of biblical theology to collate passages into a coherent framework that describes the beliefs of Israel and the early church, and this in itself provides the strongest possible check upon the tendency to elevate individual passages to dogmatic covering laws and thereby to misinterpret both the passage and the doctrine. When the individual passage is re-examined in comparison with all other passages on the issue, the interpreter is forced to consider again its actual message.

Finally, Scripture itself claims to be the basis for belief and practice. Many today (such as Farley and Hodgson) separate Scripture from the "scripture principle." The Bible, they argue, was originally a record of the religious beliefs of the various traditions that existed alongside one another in Israel and the early church. Only later, under pressure from "heretical" opponents and the growing diversity within the church, did the "scripture principle" develop, that is, the belief that the Bible is the final arbiter for theological statements. However, this does too little justice to the fact that much of the New Testament was written to establish a set of doctrines that could guide the church's teaching. For instance, most of Paul's epistles correct misunderstandings and demand that false teachings be corrected. In other words, a good part of the New Testament was written to establish this "scripture principle." Therefore, we are correct in making the Bible the foundation and final arbiter for all doctrinal development.

2. Tradition. It is common to relegate the concept of "tradition" to the Roman Catholic "magisterium," but this is too simplistic. Every Protestant denomination also has its own magisterial "tradition," and in many ways these traditions are just as binding as Roman

Catholic dogma. In essence, "tradition" refers to that set of beliefs and practices which has developed throughout the history of a movement and which directs and shapes the current form of the group. To paraphrase an old gospel song, "How do I know? My church tells me so." When I approach Scripture I choose those passages which fit the dogma my church has taught me to believe. In one sense this is necessary, for this theological deposit provides the framework for developing a system of beliefs. The problem is that the church down the street has learned a different set of doctrines and a different set of proof-texts, and I too often fail to notice the radically diverse approaches we are taking to the same questions.

Here it is necessary to understand the history of dogma and to take a critically constructive approach to the sociocultural matrix that was at work in the formation of specific doctrines. The theologian must place his or her beliefs within the spectrum of historical interaction and understand where each aspect fits in the developing structure of church dogma. It is a humbling experience to realize that one's church tradition does not go back to the apostles themselves (no matter what creative reasoning may be behind the claim) and arose due to church conflict rather than to pure theological reasoning. This does not mean that all creeds and confessions are automatically suspect. Many are as valid today as they were when they were developed. However, we do not validate a belief simply by appeal to a tradition, for that is only a model which itself must be clarified and, if necessary, altered whenever one's study so dictates.

In other words, all traditions must be subject to the greater authority of Scripture. For instance, I can still say the Apostles' Creed but must omit one phrase, "descended into Hell," since my study of Ephesians 4:8-10 and 1 Peter 3:18-20 leads me away from the traditional belief that Christ descended into Hades (the nether world) after his resurrection. Instead, I believe that the 1 Peter passage indicates a proclamation of victory to the demonic spirits after the resurrection.[5] Therefore, I must leave that phrase out of the Apostles' Creed, though the rest of the creed still functions as a framework for theological affirmation.

The key is to recognize the interpretive nature of church traditions.[6] They do not possess intrinsic authority but are valid only in the extent to which they cohere to scriptural truth. Every confessional formulation has its origins in a concrete historical situation. As van Huyssteen states, "Since confessions claim to follow the Bible interpretively—and not to become a timeless Bible in themselves—every credo reflects the theological and nontheological climate of its time and is as such already a theological model, regardless of the authority it has in the course of time acquired in that tradition" (1989:184). As a model it must always be re-examined and if necessary corrected or restated on the basis of further biblical and sociohistorical reflection. Every tradition was not only a result of biblical research but was also a product of its time. As such each must be examined not only for scriptural reliability but also for sociohistorical aptness for our day. Many, such as the Nicaean or Athanasian creeds, are as apt today as they were originally. Nevertheless, we must often explain the language and rewrite the creed to be understood by the modern person.

Yet this is not meant to suggest that tradition plays primarily a negative role in theological formulation. That would be untrue. In fact, there could be no theological construction without tradition. Gadamer correctly notes that

> understanding is not to be thought of so much as an action of subjectivity, but as the placing of oneself within a process of tradition, in which past and present are constantly fused. This is what must be expressed in hermeneutical theory, which is far too dominated by the idea of a process, a method. (1975:258-59; italics his)

The interpreter does not directly or with complete objectivity apply the text of Scripture to a current issue. Rather, all theological understanding is consciously historical, as the biblical text is assimilated via tradition. Tradition not only informs but shapes our preunderstanding. As such it has a positive and often decisive role in every dogmatic decision.[7]

It is the task of church history to unlock the formative process of tradition development. Many critical theologians at this level refuse to separate Scripture and tradition, since both were part of the developing process by which the church defined itself. This means of course that the canon process in the first few centuries of the Christian era was a wrong-headed enterprise, since it effectively codified the Bible and placed it above critical scrutiny. These scholars would make Scripture and tradition part of an ongoing process of rediscovery as the church reaffirmed its identity in ever-new situations. However, as I have stated throughout, there is a distinctive difference between the Bible and the tradition that built upon it. Church history does not support a picture of theologians who constantly created new doctrines. Rather, it demonstrates that Christian leaders addressed new situations by applying scriptural truths to them. This is not creation but contextualization. Even in the Roman Catholic Church the magisterium was not a new set of doctrines created ex nihilo but was an authoritative set of "interpretations" of Scripture.

The task of church history then is to trace the development of dogma. It presupposes that all theological systems have their basis not only in Scripture but in the past and seeks to unlock the historical basis behind them. Moreover, it also assumes that every dogmatic formulation stems from a particular historico-cultural context and must be adapted to the present context. Here it has a critical function, asking whether the theological model taken from the past is truly adequate for the present community or whether it must be reformulated to speak to the present. Richard Muller states it well:

> It ought to be sobering in the mind of each and every systematic theologian that the moment his dogmatics is printed as a book, or at least very shortly thereafter, it ceases to be the latest doctrinal formulation on the "cutting edge" of Christian thought and becomes the property of historians whose task is to examine it as a socially and culturally conditioned document reflecting a particular moment in the ongoing life of the believing community. (Forthcoming)

The key is to realize that traditions, like confessions or even creeds, are contextualizations (or what Farley and Hodgson call interpretive "sedimentations") of biblical statements. In this way all current theological statements have their origin in history as well as in Scripture and to this extent are historically conditioned. The church today must examine traditions and creeds in two ways: their adequacy in restating the biblical truth and their ability to reflect the beliefs of the current community. These two aspects must ever be in tension. As Muller says, any attempt to be objective in theological reasoning does not stem from an unbiased, disinterested approach to the past but from a "methodologically controlled analysis of the materials of history." One must at all times be aware of the historical and cultural conditionedness of the data, of our community and indeed of ourselves and of all understanding. This realization will allow us to recontextualize biblical and traditional truths for our current needs.

Thus, Scripture provides the content and tradition recontextualizes the biblical models by developing new models whereby the present community of faith can reformulate dogma so as to speak with as clear a voice today as the biblical documents and traditional creeds did in their own time. Moreover, a consideration of historical issues provides positive and negative examples so that we can be aware of our own presuppositions and allow Scripture to have the final voice. It also helps us to place our church tradition within the spectrum of church history and thus provides a corrective to an arrogant assumption of the "inerrancy" of our own faith community.[8]

We need to discover the (often primarily political) historical origins of our tradition and thus gain a better appreciation for our theological opponents. For instance, we discover that the Reformed tradition has its roots in Augustine and even more so in Calvin, the Arminian groups in Arminius and Wesley, and dispensationalism in the Plymouth Brethren movement of the last century. None of these traditions go back to the first century. Even Catholicism has its true origin in the political skirmishes between Rome and Alexandria in the second and third centuries. I would argue that the resultant humility provides the best antidote against needless schism over noncardinal doctrines (see further pp. 312-14).

In short, tradition has both a negative and a positive impact on theological construction. Negatively, it too often has more formative influence than Scripture on our beliefs and can as such be a barrier to discovering truth. Positively, it guides and informs our task at every step and is a necessary aid to understanding.

3. Community. In one sense the faith community is part of the traditioning process, for as stated above one major value of tradition is the extent to which it guides the current community, and as soon as the present group defines its doctrine it becomes part of that historical process. Yet at the same time the faith community must be considered a separate topic, for it exercises control over tradition and re-evaluates the historical data in order to meet its needs. Reader-response theologians[9] go so far as to define theological "meaning" entirely on the basis of the faith community, which does not so much redefine past doctrine as re-create it. They argue that there is no way to reconstruct the meaning of past theological statements. Rather, the community simply "plays" with previous beliefs and formulates its own dogma entirely from the standpoint of present needs or theological "strategies." To such scholars both the Bible and church tradition merge into a set of dogmatic possibilities that the church community assimilates and reworks into a current belief-system. According to reader-response theory, the Bible, creeds and set of doctrines are not so much understood as transformed on the basis of the situation of the reading community. For these scholars there is no such thing as normative or static doctrine but only a dynamic and ever-changing development of beliefs.

This community and contextual orientation to theological construction achieves its ultimate statement in the various forms of liberation theology (Third World, black or feminist theologies). Liberation theology completely reverses the evangelical view of authority. The Bible is no longer the normative standard for faith and practice; instead the contextual situation becomes the norm. These theologians assert that the church must identify with oppressed communities and that doctrine is never final but is always culturally conditioned. Since the present age is dominated by the oppression of the poor and of minority groups, the only valid theology is one that seeks to liberate suffering. Both theory and praxis are dominated by the community situation, and the belief system is constructed accordingly.

Obviously these form the extremes of a community orientation to theology. However, they are very influential and must be considered. Moreover, it has long been my contention that liberation theologies have arisen because the church has neglected areas of biblical concern. Liberation theologians ask the right questions but arrive at the wrong answers. There is no doubt that community and context play a significant role in theological formulation. The issue is whether this aspect is formative or supplemental. I would argue that the community's situation influences but does not determine theological decisions. Actually, this statement must be slightly altered: the community's situation *should* not determine the choice. In actual fact there is no guarantee that the Bible is the final arbiter in the task of constructing theology. In practice many choices are made on the basis of situation and context. However, at the theoretical level the community should play a role—but not the decisive one. Context forms part of the complex "preunderstanding" (including tradition, community and experience) from which the biblical text is addressed in theological formulation. Moreover, the community's situation and cultural patterns guide both the wording and organization of individual theological constructions as well as of whole systems, thus recontextualizing traditional formulations for the modern age.

4. Experience. This forms the final third of the preunderstanding triumvirate (with tradition and community). The influence of each upon theological decisions narrows progressively, for tradition binds the church in every age, the community contextualizes those traditional beliefs for its own situation, and the individual reworks them on the basis of his or her own personal experiences. Yet each level has enormous potency to affect one's theological choices. "Experience" refers not only to that complex of events which shapes one's life but also to the world view that results. Of special importance here is religious experience, but secular experiences are critical too. The whole complex of circumstances that transpires in a person's life often determines that individual's view of God and religious experience as a whole.

Van Huyssteen makes this the core of the "nature" of theological statements: "The way the theologian, as a Christian believer, experiences his or her faith and the nature of religious language are mutually determinant of the status of theological statements, both in theology itself and in philosophy of science" (1989:128). Van Huyssteen believes that our religious experiences provide the basis for the theological language we employ and thus for the doctrine that results. Moreover, they are mutually interdependent, because our religious language is also critical in shaping our interpretation of what we experience. It is no longer valid to assume that objectivity is obtained only by standing outside our belief system. Most argue today that religious assent is vital to making rational decisions about theological truth. Truly cognitive components in theological statements must of necessity take account of a theologian's subjective beliefs, since the latter definitely affect the way we interpret the evidence. In other words, theological affirmations shape and in turn are shaped by religious commitment. The question is not whether the belief system influences the decision but whether or not one is aware of it (pp. 126-32).

Tracy calls this the "situation"; namely, contemporary sociocultural factors that condition the individual and must be analyzed in order to form a valid theology.[10] Yet this "situation" is always changing and the answers of yesterday cannot satisfy the present. For instance, the reply of existential theology (such as Tillich) to the alienation and meaninglessness of the modern age no longer addresses this postmodern society. According to Tracy such "classical" questions of the past must be reformulated for the contemporary situation, which centers upon conflict and pluralism. There is no longer any single answer but rather a babble of voices clamoring for attention, and the individual is suffering from overload. The theologian must establish a dialectic between the Christ-event and the complex situation at the macro (sociocultural influences upon all) and micro (the inner psyche of the individual) levels. A mutually critical correlation between normative Christian event and present human dilemma becomes for Tracy the only viable theology.

Certainly Tracy correctly perceives the enormous influence of the current situation or experience upon the theologian. However, he overstates its authority and understates the authority of the Word of God. Following Tracy, McFague demands a theology "for our time" that accepts no fixed, binding or absolute norm but recognizes the openness of religious truth (1987:21-28).

It is evident that fundamentalism does not accept the metaphorical character of religious and theological language, for its basic tenet is the identification of the Word of God with human words, notably those human words in the canonical scriptures of the church. The essence of metaphorical theology, however, is precisely the refusal to identify human constructions with divine reality. (p. 22)

McFague stresses the "is and is not" nature of all Christian theology, that doctrinal statements speak to the "is" of the current situation and yet in the end are partial and incomplete, needing constant revision or "redescription." Yet the evangelical rightly notes the twofold nature of a doctrine of inspiration, that the Bible was written by human authors but that they worked under divine impetus. Tracy and McFague correctly stress the importance of a "relevant" theology that addresses current issues, but they fail to give the Scriptures the normative place that they must have in a "true" as well as contemporary theology.

Moreover, this does not mean that all theological decisions are subjective at the core or that one can never arrive at truth (since all decisions have their origin in experience). The situation is a major component of preunderstanding but not the only or decisive one. One's experiences are interpreted on the basis of the community's teachings; both are heavily influenced by traditional beliefs; and all are informed by the Word of God. Let us say that a person goes through a financial crisis leading to bankruptcy. A process theologian might interpret the situation via chance societal factors and existential reality while a Calvinist might stress the sovereign hand of God and the necessity of faith. In each case the individual would struggle with both options but be influenced by the community of which he or she is a part. Most of all, each one should engage in a critical dialogue with the options and mediate between the choices by subjecting them to Scripture.

5. Philosophy. The theologian must truly be a renaissance person, for it is necessary to exegete the Scriptures, collate the theological threads via biblical theology, be aware of the development of dogma throughout church history, then contextualize all this for the modern situation; and at each stage philosophical reasoning plays a critical role. In a very real sense the theologian is asked to be an expert exegete, historian and philosopher. Vanhoozer follows Niebuhr in noting five possible approaches to the relationship between theology and philosophy (forthcoming; see also Erickson 1983:1:40-53): (1) Some (such as Kant, Hegel) have believed that only philosophy contains truth. (2) Others have taught that philosophy yields true knowledge of God and prepares the way for theology (such as Tillich's "correlation" between existentialism and theology or Tracy's concept of Christ as one of many "classics"). (3) Many argue that church and academy are autonomous but in dialogue (Schleiermacher's "absolute dependence" or Bultmann's dialogue between the cross and existentialism). (4) For many theology controls philosophy, and the theologian is free to borrow from many systems without obligation to any (Anselm, Barth, Frei, Lindbeck). (5) Finally, theology has at times repudiated philosophy. Tertullian believed that the Incarnation rendered human philosophy obsolete, and Luther often stated that philosophy was of the devil.

None of these positions alone is satisfactory. The best solution seems to be a combination of options three and four. Theology dare not be wholly tied to any single system but must be free to utilize any that make the biblical solutions relevant and clear. Most of all, philosophy helps the theologian to avoid subjective reasoning and to ground theological formulations in critical reasoning, coherence and rationality. Vanhoozer calls for three characteristics in such a balance: (1) individual integrity, as philosophy critically reflects upon the current situation and theology critically reflects on biblical truth; (2) relative autonomy, with each having a different starting point (world and Word) and serving a different community (academy and church) but mutually integrated at the level of world view, that is, the nature of reality and meaning of life; and (3) mutual accountability, as theology transforms the biblical world view into a coherent and relevant world view for the contemporary setting.

I would add that in the final analysis Scripture has the normative voice, and philosophy is a supplement to theology in helping the latter reformulate biblical truths rationally and coherently in order to address the current situation. They are not equal partners, for theology contains the ultimate truth, but philosophy forces the theologian to be both logical and open to new expressions/clarifications of the timeless truths.

Some have argued that biblical theology is historical and systematic theology logical (for instance, Murray 1978:18). In a general sense this distinction has some validity, but on the whole it is simplistic. The two are interdependent. Biblical theologians must logically consider the data in determining the unifying themes of Scripture, and systematic theology must note historical development in the formation of dogma, in terms of both the biblical period (see pp. 273-74 on the progress of revelation) and church history. The two build upon one another. Church history traces the developing contextualization of biblical theology in different eras of the church while systematic theology is the current contextualization building upon that inherited tradition. At each level philosophy provides the logical cast that determines the organization and development of dogma.

There are two basic approaches to theological reasoning: deduction, which proceeds from general assumptions or evidence to particular conclusions and involves a degree of probability as to the logic of the argument; and induction, which proceeds from particular or specific data to general conclusions and therefore arrives at possible rather than probable answers. It is common today to believe that evangelicals are deductive, beginning with a priori assumptions about God, truth and the Bible and then moving to absolutely certain conclusions about dogma. Nonevangelicals, on the other hand, are inductive, proceeding from the biblical evidence and allowing contradictions to stand, thereby coming to far fewer dogmatic conclusions. This too is simplistic, however, for there is a fundamentalism of the left (consider Bultmann's reaction to his "betrayal" by his student Käsemann) as well as of the right, and most evangelicals are more inductive than deductive.

Most theologians today argue that inductive and deductive methods must be integrated in constructing theological systems.[11] Pure deduction would lead to a univocal approach to the figurative metaphors in Scripture and would demand that the historical events themselves determine dogma. Moreover, pure deduction would ultimately demand a radical pluralism, since the many formulations of dogma would themselves be normative for each tradition. On the other hand induction by itself involves standing above the text and imposing a hierarchical system upon it. As Holmes says, induction demands an omniscient knowledge of Scripture on our part rather than an incomplete, analogical knowledge (1978:133-34).

In contrast, the theological enterprise centers upon a hermeneutical awareness of the preunderstandings we bring to the task, and this in itself calls for an interdependence between inductive and deductive reasoning (Holmes calls this *adduction*, Montgomery labels it *retroduction* and Feinberg uses the term *abduction*). The biblical material becomes the inductive basis for theological formulation; the data itself in the end provides the basis from which dogma is "adduced." Yet the formulation itself also proceeds from the deductive interpretation and collation of those texts as well as from the application of issues derived from the history of tradition. In short, these two aspects must remain in dynamic balance throughout the theological task[12] (see figure 14.1).[13]

The Adductive or Retroductive Approach

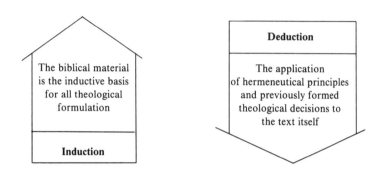

Balance and Interdependence Required

Fig. 14.1. The Integration of Philosophy with Exegesis.

Inductive reasoning utilizes the imagination to move from observations on the material (Scripture) to the theories or concepts that best explicate those truths for this day. Deductive reasoning utilizes logic to establish theological models that can be verified on the basis of the evidence. Moreover, as Montgomery states, there is a continuous cycle (I prefer to call it a spiral) from one to the other as the theologian continues to refine the model on the basis of an increased understanding of the data. The important thing to keep in mind is that there are not several norms (Scripture, experience, tradition, philosophical speculations) but only one final source of revelation, the Word of God. The others influence but should not in themselves determine doctrine. The Bible must at all times provide a logical control on the domination of divine truth by either existential subjectivism or theological abstractions.

Issues in Theological Construction

These five components—Scripture, tradition, community, experience, philosophy—together influence one's choices in the production of theological covering models that can explicate the divinely inspired truths of the Word of God for our day.[14] Yet we must face several issues before these can interact to produce a viable system or determine a particular doctrine. Each contains certain problems that make the process more difficult, yet at the same time each also contains certain provisions that enable the interpreter to ascertain more clearly how to make the resultant models more accurate and meaningful for our day.

1. Inspiration/Revelation. It is quite clear that the relationship between the five components above depends in large measure upon where one places the locus of revelation. If the theologian locates it in tradition as well as in Scripture (the classic Roman Catholic view), the resultant dogma will be dependent on the church's magisterial decisions. If one makes the current context (community and experience) revelatory (as in liberation theology), then the present situation will determine the shape and thrust of the theology. In other words, the issue of inspiration must be settled before we can begin forming a systematic theology.

The one position that has dominated since biblical times is that revelation inheres in Scripture, and that only the Bible contains the Word of God. Though it is common in many circles to argue that the Bible makes no internal "claims,"[15] I would agree with those who find a consistent atmosphere of divine inspiration behind such phenomena as the revelatory consciousness of the Old Testament, the prophetic emphasis on "Yahweh says," the New Testament's recognition that the Old Testament is God's Word, the growing credal and canonical consciousness within the New Testament period, the placement of the logia Jesu on a par with the Old Testament (such as 1 Tim 5:18) and the placement of Paul's letters on a par with the "other scriptures" (2 Pet 3:16).[16] Many nonevangelicals assume that the conservative position is outmoded and presuppositional, based on a deficient theory of language or truth and an uncritical acceptance of unproven assumptions. To say this, however, is to be unaware of the vast amount of literature on the issue within the evangelical camp.[17] Few evangelical scholars today are unaware of the hermeneutical issues involved. The very amount of literature addressing the problem demonstrates that the evangelical camp is not satisfied with past or trite answers but is continually searching for better definitions.

In short, if a theologian accepts the traditional view of inspiration, that God has revealed himself in Scripture, the Bible will provide the material upon which doctrine is based and the other components (tradition, community, experience) will be used to redescribe biblical truth for the modern situation. The formative factor, however, is Scripture, and the theologian's task is to interpret, collate and restate its teachings so that people today can understand and apply it.

2. The Question of Metaphor. Recent works on theology make this the central issue for developing a viable theory for theological formulation. It is an incredibly complex problem, especially as regards theology, because a case could be made that most theological statements are metaphorical at the core. Certainly this is true of Scripture. For instance, the titles of God (El Shaddai, Abba and so forth) are not simply literal terms that exactly denote God but are metaphors that we must interpret in their own context. To understand El Shaddai ("Almighty God," Ex 6:3), we must uncover the military roots of the metaphor and see the imagery of a God who defends and fights for his people. Abba is a similar metaphor and pictures God as a loving and protective "father."

In the same way theological concepts in Scripture are often presented via metaphors. Terms like *salvation* or *baptism* are clearly metaphorical, the first building upon the Exodus imagery of the "deliverance" and the second upon the cultic imagery of being "washed" or made pure before God. In fact, most theological concepts in Scripture are essentially metaphorical. This is because eternal truths cannot be expressed in human, temporal language with exactness. Metaphors are not only the best way to depict such concepts; they are the way God has chosen to express himself in Scripture. Moreover, it is not correct to intimate that metaphors by nature are vague or dispensable. The answer is a proper understanding of metaphor as a theological tool and a proper delineation of its referential nature.

There have been two different approaches to metaphor. Since Aristotle the "substitution" theory—that a metaphor is similar to literal or propositional language and can be replaced by a descriptive statement—has predominated. In recent years, however, the consensus has changed to a view of semantic opposition (Beardsley) or interaction (Black). A metaphor is now seen as an "odd" or tensive use of a term to clarify or describe a concept further. The two ideas are not simply compared, for the second term is not equivalent or analogous but dynamically changes the meaning of the first. There is interaction at two levels: interplay between the normal and figurative uses of the metaphor itself (such as "bear" in "The man is a bear," in which only certain aspects of a "bear" are connoted); and interaction between the subject and the metaphor that redescribes it. Moreover, the meaning is construed not at the level of the individual terms but at the level of the whole utterance or speech act. As Soskice points out, it is not so much that two distinct subjects interact (so Black) but that within the whole statement two sets of associations interrelate.[18]

An example would be the depiction of God as a "victorious warrior" in Zephaniah 3:17 (see pp. 111-12). In verses 15-17a God is seen as the heroic soldier who annihilates the enemy; in verse 17b he is described as one who is "quiet in his love" and "exults with joy" in Israel. Two metaphors (warrior and exulting love) stand side-by-side in the text and clash with each other in describing the two sides of the divine nature—his justice and love. Moreover, both do so by interacting separately with the idea of "Yahweh God" (also metaphorical titles) and then with one another. A certain semantic opposition is established, causing readers to redefine their view of God.

It is not similarity but dissimilarity that leads the reader to rethink definitions. As McFague points out (following Ricoeur), a new, extended understanding is "redescribed" or transformed via the unconventional interaction between subject and metaphor. There is a semantic clash between the traditional understanding of the subject (God) and the new qualities ascribed in the metaphors (in Zeph 3:17 the juxtaposition of warrior and love). Moreover, the resultant shift in meaning is more vital and apt.[19] Metaphors in this sense are seen as "rule-changing" and not just "rule-governed" aspects of language. They do not follow established conventions but break new ground in creating a dialectic between literal and figurative truth as one's perspective on "the way things are" (God and the world) is transformed.[20]

At this point a definition of metaphor is essential. Soskice correctly defines metaphor as "speaking about one thing in terms which are seen to be suggestive of another" (1985:49). In this way a metaphor creates its own meaning as it interacts with the subject that it clarifies. It does not need to be "translated" into literal language to be understood.

We must distinguish between literal and metaphorical language, yet we can detect the difference between them only at the level of the utterance or speech act as a whole. A statement like "she went off the deep end" is literal when used in the context of swimming and metaphorical when used of a mental breakdown. In essence, a statement is literal if the primary or conventional meanings of the terms are intended and metaphorical when associative meanings cause a semantic interplay between the terms that creates a dynamic new understanding of the subject.

Moreover, we cannot simply reduce a metaphor to a literal statement, as in theories of metaphor as analogy. In the past linguists have theorized that a metaphor can communicate only when translated into a direct utterance. However, metaphorical statements communicate on their own terms and are just as cognitively verifiable as are literal sentences. When reduced to literal communications, their actual meaning is significantly altered. "He is a ferocious fighter" does not mean quite the same thing as "he is a bear of a fighter." It is no longer valid to state that metaphors are noncognitive or have no referential value.

In fact, the current consensus is quite the opposite: metaphors speak directly and do not need to be translated into "literal" language to be understood.[21] Binkley points out that while the literal is behind metaphorical language (for without it the reader could not detect an "unconventional use" of a term in a metaphorical direction) there is no need to "translate" the figurative term (1981:142-45).[22] Indirect metaphorical meaning is accessible in and of itself. The context makes it clear, and the meaning is communicated on its own terms. "Although metaphors are not 'literally true,' there is no reason to suppose that truth has to be literal."[23]

In other words, metaphors communicate themselves indirectly but should not be unduly contrasted with literal language, as if an indirect relation to reality (metaphorical) is less meaningful than a direct relation to reality (literal). No term is either literal or metaphorical: context will tell us whether a word is used literally or metaphorically; the key point is that in both cases meaning is understood. In short the "truth" of an utterance does not depend upon its literal nature.[24] Soskice uses the distinction between "sense" and "reference" to argue for a referential theory of metaphor (1985:51-53). "Sense" is the dictionary definition of possible meanings, while "reference" denotes the actual meaning of a term in a particular context. In other words, metaphors impart referential meaning as part of a whole speech act. Moreover, they do so as metaphors and carry the same communication potential and truth value as literal statements, namely as part of a whole utterance.

We need not follow McFague and others who state that metaphors are indeed cognitive but in an uncertain and open-ended way. According to McFague theological metaphors refer to reality but do not do so in positivistic or ultimate fashion. The key to metaphorical truth is that it is apt or appropriate rather than binding.[25] As such, metaphors are attuned to particular situations and must yield to new and more vital metaphors when those situations change. For these scholars the great danger is assimilation, as the "shocking, powerful metaphor becomes trite and accepted"—that is, turns into a dead metaphor and is canonized into established dogma (McFague 1983:41). When this happens the metaphor loses both its tensive power and its ability to shape meaning. New generations fail to see the metaphor as "one interpretation among many" and thus it ceases to address the modern situation.[26]

If we accept this view of a "metaphorical theology," it means that there are no absolute norms except a theology "for our times." The contemporary situation, and not revealed or theological "truth," will control our language and beliefs. Alston provides one solution, asserting that while metaphors connote ideas on their own, they do not turn their back on literal meaning. Readers take the literal "model" and discover new resemblances that as contextual clues guide them to the correct choice. In fact, metaphorical truth-claims are able to be translated into literal language and thus can be verified.[27] However, Alston goes too far; this in actuality is another form of the substitution theory with which we disagreed above. Metaphorical communication can be verified on its own terms and need not be "translated." It differs in linguistic type but not in quality from literal communication, as if metaphor is partial and only literal truth can bridge the generation or situation gap. Both metaphor and literal communication impart cognitive information, albeit in their own distinctive ways.[28]

On this point I agree with McFague that metaphors impart meaning on their own terms and that this communication is dynamic and tensive. But I disagree with her that the meaning denoted is partial and nonauthoritative. Moreover, metaphors do not have to become "dead" with time, that is, cease to impart dynamic new meanings and turn into literal or static dogma. Theological metaphors like salvation or substitutionary atonement can be just as alive with meaning today as they were two thousand years ago. God does not become merely a Tillichian symbol that needs continuous redefinition to be known or understood. The theological metaphors of the Bible do indeed describe God as he is and are fully authoritative rather than replaceable codes or ciphers.

Nor is it correct to assert that all theological statements are by definition metaphorical. While evangelicals are guilty of ignoring the metaphorical component, liberals are guilty of ignoring the literal component. One example will suffice, and it is a critical one. Debates over the doctrine of election usually center upon the individual (Calvinist), corporate or foreknowledge (Arminian) options. Yet all fail to ask the extent to which the language is literal or metaphorical. There is no question that the New Testament writers primarily take up a term used by Israel to describe her special place before God. It is indeed possible that this figurative component (that we are God's chosen people) is the major message of election language in the New Testament, rather than the literal way the terms are often used; that is, to describe the actual process by which God saves people, namely by "electing" certain ones to be saved. It remains to be seen whether this obviates the (traditional view of a) literal use in some key passages like Romans 9—11[29] or John 6, but the metaphorical aspect must be considered more closely in future studies of election theology.

Terms have both a metaphorical and a literal aspect, and the two components interact in producing meaning, with specific linguistic markers in the context to indicate which is the communication strategy in a particular utterance. All terms and concepts (even theological ones) can be presented in literal or metaphorical fashion; the interpreter must decide which is being utilized on a given occasion. The meaning derived will be communicated on its own terms (as literal or metaphorical statement) and will contain its own inherent authority. Literal speech acts are not more "permanent" or binding than metaphorical ones, nor are they more easily understood. Both types of utterance speak and demand adherence on their own terms.

3. Theological Models. Models are by their very nature metaphorical since they are creative approximations intended to depict a particular theory or belief graphically. McFague defines a model as "a metaphor that has gained sufficient stability and scope so as to present a pattern for relatively comprehensive and coherent explanation."[30] However, this definition overstates the case. Barbour notes the presence of both literal and metaphorical models in science and religion (1974:45-48). The closer a theoretical model adheres to observable reality, the more literal it is. Soskice challenges the conflation of metaphor and model, pointing out that such an equation would reintroduce the comparison or substitution theory of metaphor, since a model is analogous to or a representative of the reality it envisages.[31] She prefers to think of the model itself as an analogous representation of a theory, while its linguistic presentation often takes the form of conceptual metaphors (such as the brain as a computer).

When we apply this to theoretical models in theology, the issues become even more complex. The Bible itself, as we have seen, tends to use metaphors to describe the reality of God and his relation to this world. Therefore, most biblical models are metaphorical at the core. Applying Soskice's distinction, we could state that while the linguistic presentation of biblical models in Scripture often is metaphorical, there is an analogous representation of the reality behind them. Yet this literal aspect recedes further into the background as we move away from the actual models of Scripture itself to biblical-theological models and then to systematic-theological models. Each level becomes more heuristic and metaphorical, as I shall develop below.

To distinguish further between metaphor and model, a theological metaphor is a temporary and figurative redescription of a concept intended to add a further nuance of meaning, while a model is a more permanent and comprehensive description that becomes a pattern for belief. For instance, the psalmist describes God via the metaphor "shield" (3:3) and then calls him by the titular model "Yahweh" (v. 7). A religious metaphor becomes a model when it attains permanent status in the credal confessions of the group.[32] It is one thing to call Jesus "master" but quite another to affirm him as "the Christ" (Messiah). Both are metaphorical, but the latter has become a model for christological reflection. Another way is to think of a metaphor as a literary device meant to heighten the meaning of a concept while a model is a theoretical device that provides theological scaffolding for our understanding.

A model is also a heuristic device that is used to organize and structure related ideas. It is at times a single notion (such as God as father) but at other times a representation or pattern that links together and systematically describes a set of ideas (such as the doctrine of God). This is best known in science where every discovery is conceived first in terms of a "map" of the theory, as in the DNA model that revitalized our understanding of heredity. Yet this is also true of religious models that not only depict the truth adhered to but also often determine the very theological structure of the group. Such models are essential in theology, and virtually every doctrine is expressed in terms of a model of the biblical teaching. The heuristic function is especially important for understanding the way in which models depict reality. Models do not observe reality (the positivistic approach) or relate exact descriptions (the naive realist approach) or provide dispensable approximations of a theory (the instrumentalist approach). Rather, models suggest and explore patterns that potentially depict the reality envisaged (the critical realist approach).[33]

Many, like McFague, posit that biblical or theological models do not so much teach truth as evoke response. This is closely connected to the existentialist theory propounded by the New Hermeneutic. Soskice discusses this in terms of the false notion that "the models of science are explanatory and those of religion affective" (1985:108; see 108-12). As she points out, this is a false dichotomy, the product of disjunctive thinking. Indeed, the cognitive function of metaphors and models, dependent as it is on "an explanatory grid between model source and model subject," makes the structural and explanatory function paramount (p. 109). In other words, theological models are primarily "reality depicting" in purpose and only secondarily evocative or action-guiding. For instance, to speak of God as "our father" is first of all to tell us who he is and on that basis to guide our response to him. Like metaphors, models have a referential function in and of themselves.

> As dominant metaphors, models emphasize the priorities of a particular religious tradition. As systematized organizational principles in the rich network of such a tradition's figurative language, religious models consistently lead us to systematic thought and theorizing; as comprehensive interpretive frameworks they also form the center of theological questions about their referential quality—and thus about truth and the depiction of reality. As metaphors, models control and regulate the way we reflect on God and humanity. (Van Huyssteen 1989:139)

Since theological models are in essence blueprints of a community's beliefs as well as representations of biblical truths, they also have a credal function and thereby shape as well as describe the belief system. As such they demand adherence and assent, forming the framework as well as the boundaries of the community's acceptable dogma.

The basic problem of theological models is the tendency of their adherents to give them an absolute or permanent status that often becomes more powerful than Scripture itself. This is demonstrated in the tendency of all traditions to interpret Scripture on the basis of their beliefs rather than to examine their systems and alter them as needed on the basis of the scriptural evidence. The answer is to utilize the basic hermeneutical metaphor of this book, that of the spiral. The systematic model forms the preunderstanding that we bring to the scriptural data when we interpret, collate and contextualize it, yet at the same time we must allow the text to challenge, clarify and if necessary change that very system. The continuous interaction between text and system forms a spiral upward to theological truth.

Scripture itself contains models that we identify via biblical theology. However, our very reconstruction of these models is done from the standpoint of our own preunderstanding and therefore must continually be re-examined. How do we know when the text has truly predominated over our theological proclivities? Our preunderstanding affects not only our interpretation but also our perspective and methods. The solution here is to welcome competing models as the best means for forcing us to re-examine the basis and structure of our dogma. It is difficult to question the systemic patterns of our faith since our commitment to them blinds us to their weaknesses. Our opponents keep us honest.

A primary issue here is the viability of this sense of permanent status attributed to theological models. Many scholars are utterly opposed to the idea of fixed or final dogma. Van Huyssteen speaks of "unchangeable and ageless icons, at the inevitable expense of all the provisional, referential, and open qualities of metaphors" (1989:140). There is undoubtedly some truth to this, for many groups do turn their founding fathers as well as their inherited traditions into virtually "inerrant" objects of veneration. However, van Huyssteen overstates the "provisional" and "open" nature of theological formulation/models. As stated above, metaphors (and models) communicate just as propositionally (albeit in different fashion) as literal statements. Therefore, we must be careful not to take his statement too far, as if there were no ultimate theological truth and every doctrine were valid only for a certain religious community.[34] A high view of biblical authority demands a corresponding search for a systematic theology that expresses those biblical truths in ways that are understandable and meaningful for the contemporary community. In this search we build upon the giants of the past and must both trust their insights and refine them.

Our constant goal is to develop the tradition in search of that theoretical model which best restates the eternal truths of Scripture. Rather than the completely open and changeable metaphorical theology of a McFague, I prefer to think of theological models as statements of doctrinal belief to which we give strong assent but that are still open to modification and even replacement if the biblical evidence so dictates. No model should have permanent status in and of itself, although those which have stood the test of time (such as the creeds) come close. Even these, however, are subject to further insight and restatement, as seen in the growing number of evangelical studies on cardinal doctrines like the Trinity or Christology.

Theological models are especially useful in helping us to structure and conceptualize whole systems, such as eschatology (premillennial vs. amillennial vs. postmillennial positions, or within premillennialism the pretribulation vs. midtribulation vs. posttribulation views) or soteriology. When competing models are placed side by side, it is much easier to understand and compare their differences. See figure 14.2 of the Calvinist vs. Arminian models within soteriology as an example.

Each model represents the way that position organizes and conceptualizes the biblical data on the basis of tradition, community and experience.[35] It is educational to compare the different ways in which the traditions understand and collate the same biblical material. Yet the question persists: Does this demand pluralism, the view that they are equally valid within their respective tradition-frameworks? It does demand a pluralistic or hum-

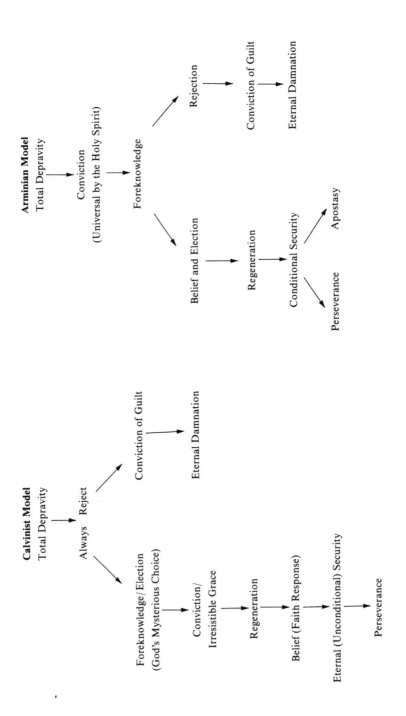

Fig. 14.2. Calvinist and Arminian Models of Soteriology.

ble attitude, for each side should recognize the possibility that the other might be right. Yet this need not lead to pluralism, for every person can examine the data and decide which of the options best fits the evidence. As stated above the best way to attain truth is to allow the opposing side to challenge our basic beliefs and then to seek to learn from it and be driven back to the text so that we might see anew what Scripture really teaches.

By comparing the models above we observe that both Calvinist and Arminian affirm total depravity (the view that sin so controls the individual that every person when confronted with the gospel rejects God's offer of salvation). For the Calvinist humankind is divided at this point into the elect and the nonelect. The elect are called or predestined on the basis of God's mysterious will and therefore are brought by his irresistible grace to faith-decision. For many Calvinists the extent of God's sovereignty is seen in the belief that God accomplishes his act of regeneration before the faith-response is made.[36] Once a person becomes a Christian God keeps him or her eternally secure. Perseverance is "final" or certain, for God oversees believers and protects them. On the other hand, the nonelect continue in their rejection of Christ, and the only "conviction" they experience is proof of their guilt before God (Jn 16:8-11). Their eternal damnation is certain but just, for they have continually refused the sufficient call of God (it is efficient only for the elect).

The Arminian model differs from this at several points. Both Arminius and Wesley affirmed God's sovereignty in the salvation process (unlike Pelagius) but argued that the individual makes a valid faith decision on the basis of free will. This is accomplished by the universal convicting power of the Holy Spirit, following God's desire that all be saved (universal salvific will). This Spirit-conviction allows the individual to overcome total depravity and make a "true" faith-decision. Divine election occurs simultaneously with this faith-decision (based on foreknowledge). The result is regeneration, which as in the Calvinist position is wrought by God rather than the individual (contra Pelagius).[37] Conversion for the Arminian leads to conditional security, which teaches that God keeps the believer secure but that the power to live the Christian life is only efficacious if the believer perseveres in God's enabling strength. If the believer does not do so apostasy (falling away from the Christian faith) might finally result.

4. Tentativeness and Authority of Theological Assertions. In the discussions above of both inspiration and models, the question of the staying power of theological statements has arisen. Since theological constructions are finite approximations that represent or redescribe biblical doctrines, how much authority do they have? When we consider the metaphorical core of theological concepts, it becomes clear that doctrinal statements are figurative representations of theoretical constructs, and the accuracy or "truth" of their portrayal is always a moot point. To this extent theological constructions tend to be tentative and provisional, and we must always determine the degree of adherence we should give individual dogmatic statements.

Moreover, all theological assertions have a historical dimension, for in every decision I am not only interpreting Scripture but am both reaffirming and interacting with a tradition. In Tracy's discussion of the "classic" (which includes not only the Bible but also great works like those of Calvin, Luther, Barth and so forth), he notes four stages in creating a theology: (1) theologians approach the task with a certain preunderstanding; (2) they react to the claims of the text with faith or recognition; (3) they engage in critical dialogue with not only the text but its history, effects and tradition-development; and (4) they employ all contemporary hermeneutical understandings to retrieve, examine and make public the claims of the tradition as they have reinterpreted them.[38] The total effect of this process will be a continual reassessment and refinement of theological schemata.

The basic difference between Tracy's approach and mine is the final authority I give the biblical text over all other "classics." Still, the process Tracy promulgates holds a great deal of truth. We do not simply move from the Bible to theological assertions, and those assertions are not automatic reproductions of biblical truths. Rather, all decisions are filtered through a network of tradition and preunderstanding, which itself exerts tremendous influence upon our interpretations and choices. To this extent each decision we make is provisional and we must establish a continual dialogue between tradition and biblical text in the spiral upward to truth.

In this sense the models above are themselves general rather than specific, for individual Calvinist and Arminian scholars would disagree with one or another aspect. For instance, Calvinists differ as to whether the "decrees" (such as election) came before the Fall (supralapsarian position) or after it (infralapsarian position). They also disagree regarding the predestination of the unbeliever to damnation (double predestination). Finally, Calvinists debate whether or not the atonement is limited to the elect. On the other hand, some Arminian scholars add the concepts of perfectionism or the second work of grace, and many define such doctrines as depravity or security differently than I have done here. Each of these is a refinement with which the burgeoning theologian must interact, and all are subject to debate and clarification.

We dare not assume any of these doctrines without an ongoing re-examination of the scriptural and historical evidence. Moreover, since T. S. Kuhn scholars have recognized the impact of the "paradigm community" upon all decisions—religious as well as scientific.[39] The influence from tradition and community cannot and should not be entirely rejected; on the other hand, theological formulations are seldom a pure reflection of scriptural truths, and the extent to which this is the case is the degree to which resulting dogmatic conclusions are tentative.

Yet dogmatic or credal statements are also models of scriptural teaching, and the more they cohere with the biblical data (attained by collating all the scriptural statements that address the issue)[40] the greater the authority they possess. It is simply erroneous to presuppose that the truths of God's revelation are always lost to us, and that therefore we must live with a plurality of metaphorical and temporary ideas. As I argue in appendix two, probability decisions are completely valid, in fact absolutely necessary, in drawing interpretive and theological conclusions from Scripture.[41]

We can even give such decisions a percentage value, so long as we recognize that any such is a personal estimate. For instance, I feel 99.99+ per cent certain that my views on the deity of Christ and substitutionary atonement are correct but only 90 per cent sure of my middle position on the charismatic issue (that tongues are used of God today but not meant for everyone) or my premillennial posttribulation belief. As for my moderate Arminian views or my openness to women's ordination I feel about 80 per cent certain.[42] Moreover, some of my colleagues disagree with me on many of these "models," some with nearly 100 per cent certainty! Still I preach and teach each with authority while seeking to instill an aura of humility into both my teaching and my students. At the same time I frequently debate these same positions with both colleagues and students, trying to demonstrate the superiority of the evidence for my position.

In short while there is a degree of tentativeness in theological models, this does not mean that we must be uncertain. Such degrees of certitude will be held by both the individual and the community. Moreover, some doctrines are more clearly taught in Scripture, and many of these are mandatory or cardinal doctrines. Such (the deity of Christ or justification by faith, for example) will necessarily have the highest possible authority, and to deny any of them is tantamount to biblical heresy. We identify these doctrines on the basis of the clarity of the biblical evidence as well as the combined agreement of most segments of the church. While they are open to further clarification they can never be replaced or rejected.

My point is that in every theological construction a natural tension exists between the tentative nature of all such conceptualizing and the final authority that they have in one's belief structure and in the community.[43] In fact this tension between provisionality and authority is a necessary component of any systematic theology. The verification process and the community itself give the theological model authority as it meets the test of time and answers challenges from competing schools. Yet this does not diminish the authority of the theological assertions confessed by individual and church. The process of reformulation, which includes comparison with Scripture and competing models as well as the fact of our faith in the tradition/system we have chosen, yields a high degree of authority. However, this is tempered by a humility and a continued search to make certain that our theological model is truly the best contextualization of scriptural teaching.

Finally, I would note three levels of authority: personal authority, denoting those formulations adhered to by me but contested by others within my tradition; community authority, referring to those beliefs that on the basis of accepted tradition control my denomination or group but are challenged by other Christian communities; and the authority of cardinal doctrines, which cross traditional and denominational boundaries as key beliefs of all Christians.[44]

5. Theology as Contextualization. Closely linked with the previous discussion is the concept that systematic theology is a contextualization of biblical theology, filtered through the history of dogma but recontextualized for the contemporary situation and both organized and expressed in current thought patterns. As stated in the previous chapter, biblical theology collates the biblical teachings and conceptualizes the theology of Israel and the early church. Church history studies the attempts of the church in differing social settings and with differing problems to redescribe or contextualize that data to meet specific problem situations in particular eras. Systematic theology continues that enterprise so that the Bible might speak as validly now as it has in the past. This means that the content of theological truth remains inviolate and is provided by the sacred Scriptures. However, the communication of that truth content does change, and the search to make certain that our tradition's formulation provides a superior model of that dogmatic core never ceases. The authority of our tradition depends upon the demonstration of its superiority over competing models and upon its ability to communicate those truths to the modern person.

This also means that the actual expression of theological truth will differ from culture to culture. For instance, the oriental culture should develop a more cyclical approach to theology in keeping with its patterns of logic, and many Third World cultures will place more stress upon story theology. Yet the content, namely basic theological truths, will not change (see chap. fifteen for further discussion of the methodology).

6. Verification or Validation of Theological Assertions. How does one assess the degree of tentativeness and authority of various theological constructions or the success of a particular dogmatic model? This of course has vexed scholars for centuries, especially in terms of debate with other paradigm communities (such as Luther and Zwingli's Marburg colloquy on the eucharist). Both sides believe that their doctrinal formulation is correct and neither will budge. Moreover the layperson is rightly confused, since both sound viable when taken separately. One of my advisees in seminary a few years ago went to a visiting Calvinist scholar (the student was a moderate Arminian) and asked, "What is the basic difference between my position and yours?" The professor answered (somewhat in jest), "Mine is biblical!" Yet how do we verify which is *more* biblical?

The method that I have chosen for verification is "critical realism."[45] The basic premise of this approach (which has been borrowed from a philosophy of science perspective) is that assertions, scientific or theological, are valid representations of the "way things are." At one time it was thought that religious statements could never claim to be "real," since they could not be verified. However, with the development of analytical philosophy (see appendix two) it was realized that religious or theological assertions could be verified, for there are several levels at which one can affirm "reality." This approach is also "critical" because it never assumes that theological constructions are *exact* depictions of revealed truth (unlike "naive realism"). Instead, dogma is an analogical model that approximates or *re*-presents truth. Thus critical realists never assume that they have achieved the "final" statement of theological truth; the process of validation and improvement never ceases, for there can be no facile assumption that they have "arrived," though of course one can verify that a particular statement is an accurate depiction of the biblical norm.

The process of validation within a critical realist approach is at once simple and complex. It is simple because the verification comes via criteria of coherence, comprehensiveness, adequacy and consistency. It is complex because each criterion must be applied hermeneutically to the many interpretations and organizing patterns of the competing systems. The most difficult (many would say impossible) aspect is to recognize one's own preunderstandings and to seek as objective an examination of the data as possible. This in fact is the most important contribution of critical realism, for it refuses to take itself too seriously and attempts to learn from competing schools of thought via an honest recognition that the others might be correct.

The first step in validating a theological construction is to see whether it fits the biblical data (criterion of coherence): Does it provide a better map of the biblical doctrine than do the other systems? This concerns the "explanatory success" (van Huyssteen 1989:152) of the model, whether it accurately portrays the scriptural teaching (tested by exegesis of the relevant texts) and has clarity, that is, makes the complex doctrine understandable.

The second step is to ascertain whether the dogmatic assertion is a true model of the biblical material taken as a whole (criterion of comprehensiveness): Does it account for all the statements of Scripture on that issue or does it merely arise from selected portions (a canon within the canon)? At this level too the theologian must compare the theological model with competing systems to see whether the others are in fact more comprehensive.

Third (the criterion of adequacy), does the formulation provide a better description of the doctrine than do those of competing schools?

Fourth (the criterion of consistency), does the system fit together and form a viable pattern? If some portions contradict others, this calls for re-examination and modification; if there is inconsistency throughout, the system may be fatally flawed.

The fifth step, the criterion of continuation or durability, asks: Does the theological construction have staying power? A scholar always writes a theological treatise with the hope that it will prove to be a major contribution to the field. At the same time one fears that the work will be heavily criticized by one's peers and prove to have no lasting power. In other words, the community over a long period of time helps to arbitrate the viability of a doctrinal statement. The creeds generally are ascribed more authority than other statements because the church down through the centuries has recognized their accuracy.

Sixth, have many differing schools of thought accepted the viability of the assertion (criterion of cross-fertilization)? If several traditions have recognized the truth of a theological construction, this demonstrates that it is not merely the logical outgrowth of a particular tradition but transcends regional interests. Such a phenomenon has a greater chance of success.

In the final analysis these criteria do not "prove" a doctrine or theological construction. Rather they help both the individual and the community to keep returning to Scripture in order to ascertain the actual teaching of the Word of God *as a whole* and the extent to which the modern redescription of the biblical teaching coheres with it. In addition a critical-realist approach will suggest ways in which the modern statement can be reworked so as to conform more closely to the biblical teaching.

7. The Politics of Theological Decision Making. Attempts to make changes in one's theological affirmations or to alter a traditional formulation of a doctrine are in some ways dangerous moves. Every decision made, every clarification pursued, every system in some sense altered has political ramifications within the traditional matrix or community and can result in the loss of one's job or ministry. This is not only the case in fundamentalist or evangelical circles. The number of university professors who have lost their posts due to a paradigm change in their position, the number of evangelical students whose theses have been rejected because of their conservative cast, all demonstrate the universality of the "politics of exegesis."

In any tradition there is a pressure to conform, a demand to affirm and not to question the basic beliefs of the group. Nor is this necessarily wrong. There must be controls against wild and dangerous speculations, especially in religious circles where the very life of the group is at stake. We must balance "academic freedom," the right to make certain that dogma truly does reflect scriptural teaching, with the harmony and homogeneity of the group. Clearly the Bible does demand a strong stance against false teaching. The problem is deciding what indeed constitutes heresy or false teaching. It is certain that some doctrines are essential to the core of biblical Christianity (the cardinal doctrines), while others are not clear in Scripture and were never intended by God to serve as controlling beliefs of the church. The difficulty is deciding whether a given teaching belongs to one group or the other (see figure 14.3; Osborne 1989a:152).

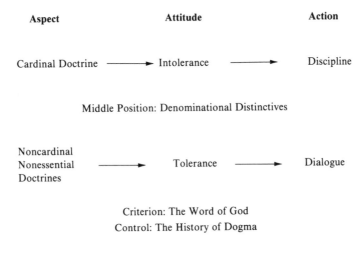

Fig. 14.3. A Perspective on Theological Debates.

It is important to exercise extreme care when a church encounters issues like eternal security, the charismatic debate or the status of women in the church. People tend to feel very strongly about such things, and every new pastor must learn at the outset of his or her ministry specifically which issues are the "hot button" ones (I pushed a hot button for many when I said "his or her ministry"; yet should anyone doubt this book because I remain open on this issue? See further below). What happens when differences of opinion arise in a church on such matters? In our age of mobility and cross-over between denominations, such debates are more likely than ever, as people from quite diverse backgrounds congregate together in the same church setting. When this occurs it is vital to know ahead of time how to deal with it.

At the outset the church or community must decide upon the proper attitude with which to approach the particular debate: tolerance, in which the group "agrees to disagree"; or intolerance, with the community refusing to allow the view to be promulgated. Each attitude leads to a corresponding action: tolerance produces dialogue on the issue, with each side trying to learn from the other and the opponents returning together to the Scriptures to rediscover the true biblical teaching. Intolerance produces discipline, as the offender is removed from a teaching role and perhaps brought before the church for censure. Yet we need some guidelines to help us know when dialogue is called for or when discipline is demanded.

There is only one basis for making this distinction: is the issue a cardinal or a non-cardinal doctrine? As already mentioned, a cardinal doctrine is a theological belief that is central to the Christian faith and clearly taught as such in Scripture (for instance, the return of Christ). A noncardinal (or nonessential) doctrine is one that is not clear in Scripture or is not presented as a mandatory belief of the church (such as the millennium or the tribulation positions). The latter are viable doctrines but have arisen more from the church's desire for comprehensive dogma than from biblical emphases. It is not that there is no warrant for such beliefs but that there is an absence of clarity and emphasis on them in Scripture. It is valid to pursue these issues (I tell my students that they owe it to the Bible, themselves, and their churches to determine such doctrines to the best of their abilities) but erroneous to make them tests of fellowship.

Yet it is extremely difficult in the final analysis to decide which are cardinal and which noncardinal doctrines. The single criterion is theoretically the Word of God, but as I have noted frequently the Bible is always filtered through tradition and personal proclivity (hobby horses) before it becomes dogma. In fact, in actual practice tradition more than Scripture often decides which are considered cardinal issues. In Reformed circles the Calvinist model is often seen as a cardinal doctrine, likewise the Arminian model within that tradition. Dispensational groups turn the pretribulation rapture into a "fundamental" doctrine.

We need a control to indicate when a doctrine that we consider essential in Scripture is actually a hobby horse on our part, in other words when it is our tradition rather than Scripture that is making the decision. Only then can we allow Scripture to determine the outcome. I propose that this control is the history of dogma. Whenever a theological debate arises, we subject the issue first to the light of church history. If the debate has been settled for centuries and agreed upon by all with a high view of biblical authority, that indicates the likelihood that this is a cardinal doctrine. If, on the other hand, the agreement is restricted only to our tradition, and other traditions have formed the opposite conclusion, then it is probably not a cardinal position. Issues that are not likely to be solved in the church before eternity arrives are not essentials.

There is, however, a middle position: many times in the historical development of a denomination an issue that Scripture does not designate an essential becomes a cardinal doctrine. Several examples can be given, like the Calvinist or Arminian dogma above within their respective denominations, or the charismatic and millennial debates. When this occurs, it is usually best for the individual to recognize the right of the denomination to determine its own distinctives but then to help the people within the movement to understand that it is not a cardinal doctrine and thus to respect members of other denominations who disagree. At times if one feels strongly enough about the matter (such as women in the church—see below), that person can try to encourage the community to remove it as a mandate and allow the other side to express its convictions.

Let me give examples of both cardinal and noncardinal issues. The debate over Christ's twofold nature was settled at the Council of Chalcedon; the church since has recognized that it is the best model of the biblical teaching on that doctrine. Therefore, there can be refinements in one's definition, but any teaching faithful to Scripture must reflect the unity of Christ's two natures, which is universally accepted as a cardinal doctrine. At the same time the most vociferous debate of this decade is over women in the church, and many on both sides treat it as a clear, cardinal issue. Yet many inerrantists, as well as those from other traditions, have accepted and continue to hold to the viability of women's ordination, and throughout the history of the church women have held positions of authority and prominence. Virtually every denomination has had women pastors and deacons in the recent past.[46] My point here is not to settle the debate but to argue on the basis of the figure above that women in the church is a noncardinal issue regarding which we need to exercise tolerance rather than intolerance. Both sides need to continue in dialogue with one another.

Finally, we cannot disregard the "political" repercussions whenever theological decisions are made. However, we can minimize the danger by considering carefully both the seriousness of the matter and the proper response to make. Many schisms over unnecessary issues can be avoided by determining the biblical importance of the doctrine. Even when the debate is central to the denomination or group we can encourage respect toward the other side (such as charismatics vs. noncharismatics). Our primary concern must be to safeguard biblical truth and preserve the "good deposit that was entrusted" to us (2 Tim 1:14) while, at the same time, guarding the biblical mandate regarding the unity of the church (Jn 17:20-23). Once more, a "hermeneutics of humility" must prevail.

Hermeneutical Principles

Theology is done at many levels, and it is difficult to develop criteria that can fit all the possibilities. At the lowest level all Christians make theological decisions while listening to sermons or even while thinking about their faith. Next comes the person teaching a lesson or Bible study on a particular doctrine. A pastor preaching a series of doctrinal sermons is called upon to do even more technical work. Then there is the person preparing an ordination paper or the seminary student doing a technical term paper. At the top are those writing theological treatises, but even here one finds several levels. A person producing a single-volume systematic theology will not work as deeply as one writing a multivolume systematics, and that person will not research as extensively as one doing a major work on a single topic, such as biblical anthropology. Finally there is the Ph.D. dissertation or magnum opus on a narrow subject, such as the perseverance of the saints or propitiation. Each level will probe more and more deeply into the subject matter and work more extensively in the various stages proposed below. All I can do is present the guidelines and provide general advice as to how these various concerns might be met.

In addition, two types of theological studies can be done, and each builds upon the other. The basic approach ponders a particular doctrine, traces it through Scripture and the history of dogma, then tries to formulate it accurately for today. This type of study is the one most commonly done. The systematic approach examines and reconstructs a model collating several doctrines in holistic fashion, such as pneumatology (including not only the doctrine of the Holy Spirit but also spiritual gifts and the charismatic debate). The principles below proceed from one to the other.

1. Consciously reconstruct our preunderstanding. If we desire an honest re-examination of the issue, we must define carefully where we and our tradition stand on the doctrine before beginning the study. This is accomplished at three levels—individual, church and denomination—for it is likely that subtle differences exist at each one. Unless these are brought to the surface they will dominate and skew the research, for it is natural to want the evidence to corroborate rather than challenge our presuppositions. Placing them in front of the biblical data will free us to use our preunderstanding positively to study the evidence rather than negatively to predetermine our conclusions.

2. Inductively collect all the passages relating to the issue. Using each of the tools available we must gather every biblical passage that addresses the doctrine. This cannot be done simply with a concordance; it is also necessary to examine books on the issue to see which passages they utilize. It is particularly crucial to note passages that seem to contradict the conclusion our tradition prefers (such as passages on security or on the necessity of perseverance). It is common for a tradition to interact only with those which favor its position and to explain the others away on the basis of the favored prooftexts. These two sets of passages should be placed beside each other so that the final formulation might be balanced.

3. Exegete all the passages in their context. This is one of the most difficult of the steps, for each major passage is a thesis in itself, and it is no wonder that few systematic theologies in our generation have provided an adequate study of the relevant texts. This aspect in fact will be done in depth only for a major study, for the time and space necessary would be immense. The pastor will nevertheless make this the core of the presentation. The critical part of this step is not only to "exegete" but to do so "in their context," for when the biblical statements are artificially placed side by side, the context can be ignored, with the result that the passages take on a life of their own and begin to interpret one another in ways that go beyond the author's intended meaning or theological emphasis. This leads to another form of "illegitimate totality transfer." The theologian needs to see which aspect of the issue the passage addresses *in its context* before considering the larger theological truth that emerges from all the passages placed together. Only then can the biblical data be collated into a coherent whole and decisions be made.

4. Collate the passages into a biblical theology. As stated in the previous chapter, the theologian organizes the texts in terms of both the history of redemption (the chronological or diachronic development of the doctrine in Scripture) and the beliefs of Israel and the church on the doctrine (the synchronic aspect). This is indeed a "systematic theology" of the early church, but it must be contextualized or reconstructed to speak to the contemporary church and its interests. As such it provides the primary content for

a modern theology, telling us "what the doctrine meant" to the biblical writers and thereby building a bridge to "what the doctrine means" for us. It also provides a crucial control against domination by any preconceived tradition, since it uncovers the belief pattern of the early church rather than of the history of dogma.

5. Trace the developing contextualization of the doctrine through church history. The changing models of the history of dogma exemplify the development and restatement of the issue through the differing eras and situations of the church. By considering carefully how the church reshaped and applied the dogmas to meet her changing needs, we are given negative (heresy) and positive (creeds and confessions) examples for our own contemporary contextualization. Most of the issues have already been discussed by the giants of the past, and careful consideration of them in a historical framework will greatly aid our task. Moreover, we should study the development of our own tradition to see where it fits into the history of dogma and what sociocultural factors led to its development. This will teach us humility as we assess the validity and contribution of our tradition to systematic theology as well as help us to go behind our tradition to the biblical text in reformulating the doctrine for today.

6. Study competing models of the doctrine. As stated above, metaphors and models are indeed "reality depicting" but do not provide exact replicas of biblical truth. The influence of tradition and community as well as experience can override Scripture in determining the shape of the theological model. The solution is a critical-realist approach to the data, in which the competing schools continually force us to rethink our approach. We cannot complete a redefinition of the doctrine until we have carefully considered and learned from our opponents. The way to a balanced statement is to allow the other systems to point out weaknesses in our models and then to return to the scriptural data to correct them. It is erroneous to think that any system has a lock on truth. All can be enhanced, and the constant appearance of new works on virtually every issue shows that improvements are always welcome. Today's magnum opus is often tomorrow's partial failure. Time uncovers logical inconsistencies and gaps that later works must clarify and fill. The best way to discover and plug these gaps is to allow our opponents to teach us, that is to point out biased interpretation of passages and inadequate argumentation. The result will be a stronger and more balanced model.

7. Reformulate or recontextualize the traditional model for the contemporary culture. The content of the doctrine (the extent to which it is based upon biblical teaching) is inviolate, but its expression or redescription changes as the thought processes of a culture change. Therefore, the way a systematic theology or individual doctrine will be expressed should alter from generation to generation and from culture to culture. In my opinion it is time for a new theological genius to rework the patterns of systematic theology, now that the Neo-Platonic and Aristotelian thinking behind Hodge and Warfield is no longer culturally necessary. The rigid demarcation of doctrines from bibliology to theology to Christology and so on to eschatology (last in order because it is the doctrine of "last things") no longer communicates as well as it used to.

This does not mean that the approach of the last century has no relevance at all; it is obvious that all of us who have been steeped in that method have found it adequate, and nearly all theology professors continue to use it with success. Yet there are serious drawbacks. Especially problematic is the failure to show the interdependence of doctrines; for instance, the necessity of eschatology (not only "last things" but the presence of the kingdom now) for understanding Christology (Jesus inaugurating the kingdom).

I do not know exactly what form this new theology will take,[47] but I believe that it will center upon a reorganization and restatement of traditional doctrines. The content will not change (except where the interpretation of texts has been logically weak and "unbiblical") but the form will; I also believe that there will be more balance between the competing systems, that is, they will move closer together.[48] A good example of one such attempt is the movement to "story theology," a narrative approach to theology that follows the models of the Gospels and centers upon the praxis element of theology rather than upon abstract reasoning. We must oppose those practitioners who use story theology to deny and replace propositional truth in Scripture, but Gabriel Fackre's *The Christian Story* (1984, 1987) is an excellent exception. He wishes to supplement other approaches by centering upon "community story," which he defines as "the Great Narrative of the deeds of God evolving from within the early kerygma through the Christian community's various expressions of it" (1987:185). It will be interesting to see how he works out this program in subsequent volumes.

8. After individual doctrines are reformulated, begin collating them and reworking the systemic models. The final stage is to redefine the systems themselves. Previous steps have dealt with individual issues like sovereignty vs. free will, election vs. faith decision, security vs. perseverance. After the theologian has finished restating these it is time to examine the larger pattern of which they are a part and to restructure the models like those presented in figure 14.2 (p. 306). We must first study and diagram the various traditional models (as well as the modifications suggested by past scholars) and then construct our own revised model to fit the patterns suggested by the conclusions arrived at earlier. The final step is to test the model by comparing it with the competing models and to ask at all times whether it fits (note the criteria on pp. 311-12) the biblical data and the lessons derived from the history of dogma better than do the others.

15

*H*omiletics I: Contextualization

T HE STUDY OF SCRIPTURE CAN NEVER BE COMPLETE UNTIL ONE HAS MOVED FROM TEXT TO context. The static study of the original meaning of a text dare never be an end in itself but must at all times have as its goal the dynamic application of the text to one's current needs and the sharing of that text with others via expository teaching and preaching. Scripture should not merely be learned. It must be believed and then proclaimed. This dynamic aspect of the Word is the task of contextualization and homiletical analysis.

As we move from the world of the text to its significance, we must wed those two aspects. We cannot finally separate exegesis from application, meaning from significance, because they are two aspects of the same hermeneutical act. To derive the "meaning" of a text is already to arrive at its significance, because the horizon of your preunderstanding has united with the horizon of the text, and exposition has become the beginning of significance. The preacher's task is to ensure that the Word speaks as clearly today as it did in ancient times. This does not occur easily and is often shallowly done. Even those who exercise great exegetical care in elucidating the original meaning of the text often fail on this point. For the most part this is because homileticians have failed to provide a strong hermeneutical foundation for application. When I began teaching a course on interpretation about ten years ago I looked in vain for a preaching text that discussed application from a hermeneutical standpoint. Several gave excellent presentations of practical methodology but none went deeper to the underlying theory behind it. The theory has now been provided by missiologists, and it is important to note that what they call "contextualization" is identical with what homileticians call "application."

Contextualization is "that dynamic process which interprets the significance of a religion or cultural norm for a group with a different (or developed) cultural heritage." At the heart it entails crosscultural communication, and while the theory is fairly recent, the process characterizes not only Christianity but every religion that has appeared on earth as each relates its theories to the "marketplace."

We must define the term "dynamic process" carefully, for as Hesselgrave and Rommen demonstrate, the priority of the text diminishes progressively as one moves away from a high view of scriptural authority.[1] The supracultural nature of biblical truth is replaced by the primacy of current cultural context. The result is what they call "syncretistic contextualization," in which the religious interests and cultural needs of the receptor audience provide content as well as focus. Liberation theologians, for instance, argue that the climate of economic oppression and deprivation controls the contextualization process, so "sin" is redefined as social injustice and "salvation" becomes the liberation of the poor. However, this is the antithesis of the approach taken here. God's revealed Word is the final arbiter of all truth and contextualization of necessity must recognize the inviolability of its truths. A plenary verbal, inerrantist approach to contextualization accepts the supracultural nature of all biblical truth and thereby the unchanging nature of these scriptural principles.

At the same time, an evangelical contextualization is aware of the transformational character of the current receptor context. While the *content* of biblical revelation is unchanging, the *form* in which it is presented is ever changing (see further below). These two aspects—form and content—provide the indispensable core of contextualization. The debate in hermeneutical circles relates to the relationship between form and content; in other words, how dynamic is the process? How free are we to translate a biblical concept into its corresponding idiom in the receptor culture and how do we do so? The fact that we must do so is inescapable. Perhaps the best way to demonstrate this is to note how often the biblical writers themselves had to contextualize previously revealed truths for their new situations.

Biblical Examples

The key issue is "relevance"; religious principles constantly must be adapted to meet new cultural challenges. This in fact is exactly the problem that led to the development of the "oral tradition" in Judaism during the intertestamental period. The Torah, developed for Israel during its wilderness and conquest periods, did not readily apply to the cosmopolitan culture of the Greco-Roman period. Therefore, the Jews developed an "oral Torah" to contextualize the laws for the new situation. Recent studies, like Martin Hengel's *Judaism and Hellenism,* have demonstrated how extensively Hellenistic ideas had permeated even into Palestine itself. This is seen, for instance, in the extent to which towns and even Jewish people bore Greek names in Palestine (see Mussies 1976:1040-64).

Yet this does not mean that the Jewish people Hellenized their religion. Within this contextualization there was still the unifying force of Torah and a strong nationalism. David Flusser argues that the Jews were quite tolerant of pagans in their midst and only reacted against religious encroachments among the Jewish people themselves (1976:1065-1100). Therefore, while much influence was seen on a cultural and linguistic level, the Jews "in Palestine and elsewhere were not attracted by paganism and remained faithful to their God and their distinctive way of life."

This is especially true of the diasporate communities, where we would have expected a great deal of "contextualization." Yet again the assimilation lay more in the externals, in form rather than in content. On the whole, the influence was quite similar to that which occurred in Palestine. The economic influence was very well defined; Applebaum shows the extensive military and trade involvements of diasporate Jews in Hellenistic society (1976:701-27). They often belonged to Greek societies, took part in the gymnasium education and in general contained families of both wealth and distinction. However, the extent of this is vigorously debated, and few doubt that diasporate Judaism as a whole stressed its separateness. Safrai states:

> The Judaism of the Hellenistic Diaspora was closely linked to Hellenistic culture. Not only was Greek the language . . . but even a Greek literature was produced, especially in Egypt. It was a literature which was closely identified with the rich culture of the Greeks, and with the mentality which dominated there. Various documents . . . show how closely the Jews were attached to institutions of Hellenistic law and to concepts tributary to this sphere. But the Jews of Egypt and the Hellenistic world . . . generally remained loyal to the Torah both in public and in private life. . . . It is clear from the sources that all the circles which departed from the spirit and practice of Jewish observance remained isolated. . . . There was no general tendency to assimilation with the environment and to the adoption of the cultural heritage of the Greeks. . . . Though the Jews of the Diaspora were part and parcel of Hellenistic culture and society, they regarded themselves essentially as Hebrews living abroad. (1976:184-85)

Philo, for instance, is best known as one who "contextualized" Judaism for the Greek way of life. However, he was an orthodox Jew who sought assiduously to keep the Torah. He was not trying to alter Jewish concepts but considered himself a student of Scripture who sought to show that Judaism was palatable with Hellenistic philosophy.

The early church followed the Jewish pattern. By studying Acts and the Epistles, we can determine the extent of contextualizing in the early church. There is no question that acculturation occurred; the movement of the church from a Jewish sect to a universal religion for "all nations" demands that. Norman R. Ericson provides several New Testament examples (1978:74-79): (1) The council at Jerusalem (Acts 15) ruled that Jewish cultic requirements, especially circumcision, could not be required of Gentiles; however, it asked Gentiles to respect Jewish customs. In short, cultural barriers were breached. (2) 1 Corinthians 8:1—10:22 shows that Paul accepted the basic cultural contingencies of Gentiles (especially 9:19-23) but asked that such freedom be waived for the sake of new believers. (3) 1 Corinthians 5:1-8 shows that Paul uses cultural regulations from society when they are conducive to Christian ethics. (4) Colossians 3:18—4:1 and the other social code passages illustrate situations when the church followed accepted social structures. Within this we note the tension reflected that the slave was at one and the same time to be "brother" of his master (Philem 16) and content with his situation (1 Cor 7:27). In other words, Paul refused to demand social change on the external scale but did demand an internal change on the relational level.

There is more than one aspect to this issue. First, we see relational changes in terms of interpersonal communication. This involves language, as demonstrated in the use of the Septuagint in Old Testament quotes, or in Latinisms, Aramaisms and so forth in the New Testament. It also involves cultural accommodation, as in the Jerusalem decree and letter above, and in the strong vs. weak in 1 Corinthians 8—10. Second, we note evangelistic contextualization, the cultural attempt to be "all things to all people" so as to "save some" (1 Cor 9:23). This is especially demonstrated in the preaching of Acts, with the very different approach to Jews (Acts 2:14-36; 3:12-26 and so forth) and to Gentiles (Acts 14:15-17; 17:22-31). In the Areopagus speech (Acts 17) Paul's utilization of Greek philosophers is an especially important example of contextualization, demonstrating what missiologists call "redemptive analogies."[2] Third, we would note polemical contextualization, in which the language of the church's opponents is used against them, as in Romans 3:5-9; 6:1-2, 15-16; 2 Corinthians 10—13; or Colossians 1:15-20.

This final category is especially crucial in showing the limits of contextualization. While the church borrowed the forms of their receptor cultures (1 Cor 9:19-23), it refused to compromise the content of its message.[3] This can best be illustrated in the two major heresies of the New Testament period (the Judaizers and Gnostics), both of which centered on a misguided contextualization. The Jewish Christians demanded that Gentiles accept Jewish culture and religious practices in order to be Christians. In Galatians and Romans especially, Paul told them that this would compromise the gospel; therefore, the church must refuse to do so. The incipient Gnostic movements at Colossae, Ephesus and so forth led to several epistles, notably Colossians, the Pastorals, 1 John and the letters to the seven churches (Rev 2—3). In each epistle the church was uncompromising against those groups which had allowed contextualization to produce another gospel. In other words, the early church looked upon contextualization as an evangelistic tool; to that extent, it influenced the form of the gospel presentation, but the content did not depart from the divinely revealed model.

Current Issues

Several important principles come out of this data. Most important, contextualization must occur at the level of form rather than of content. This corresponds to the discussion of surface and deep structures elsewhere (pp. 80-87). We must distinguish between the forms the gospel presentation took in the first century and the theological core that provided the core of the gospel message and its ethical ramifications. Biblical truths are absolute and must remain inviolate in any crosscultural communication. The recent missiological debate centers upon "dynamic equivalence" contextualization, which attempts to make the gospel and Christian theology meaningful and relevant in the diverse cultures of our modern world. Many approaches to contextualization have centered upon the contemporary context rather than the ancient text as the generating force. Charles R. Taber denies the possibility of an "absolutist" theology and argues that "failure to recognize the cultural relativity of theology" leads to confusing theology with God, a form of idolatry (1978:4-8). The "orthodoxy of verbal formulation" centering upon "abstract propositions to be believed" is the approach of the Western world and is no more valid than the Eastern symbolic framework (p. 7).

Charles Kraft takes a similar approach in his highly discussed *Christianity in Culture* (1979), where he calls the Bible a "divinely inspired casebook" rather than a theological textbook. As such it centers upon the subjective pole of communication (divine-human interactions) more than upon the objective pole of propositional dogma (see chap. ten).

Upon this theoretical foundation Kraft erects his superstructure (chaps. thirteen to seventeen). His major point is that the "translation" must be hearer-oriented rather than based upon "formal correspondence" or a literalistic model, which is grounded in an outmoded theory of language. Contemporary translations must achieve the same impact upon the receptor culture as was felt by the original readers.

Furthermore, Kraft argues that the form of the text must be changed in direct proportion to the distance between the source and the receptor cultures. The reason is that the supracultural truths of God were revealed in the culture-bound language of the human authors of the Bible. Therefore it must be contextualized.[4] Thus, while the translation is based upon reproducing the writer's intended meaning, we must "transculturate" that message for the receptor culture. This is done by reproducing the process of the original message and not merely the finished product. The interpreter must bridge the vast differences in perception among the cultures. In order to do so Kraft uses Kenneth Pike's famous distinction between "etic" and "emic" perspectives; that is, theology is communicated not from "outside" (etic) the culture by theoretical and comparative analysis, but from "within" (emic) the culture. An emic approach demands a new theological formulation and communicates (rather than merely produces) a *relevant* theology that avoids culture-bound perceptions. This may involve replacing the author's intent with God's higher intent, certainly within the range of interpretations yet expressed without Western theologizing.

In applying this theory Kraft finds three types of passages in Scripture (1979:139-43): (1) culture-specific commands, which are completely tied to the ancient culture and must be altered to fit the current situation (such as the head-covering on women, 1 Cor 11:2-17); (2) general principles, which apply ethical truths (such as "Thou shalt not covet," Ex 20:17) that transfer directly from culture to culture; and (3) human universals, which automatically transcend their own cultural context and are mandated in every age (such as love of God and neighbor, Mk 12:29-31). The latter two types of commands do not need to be contextualized, while the former does.

Certainly we applaud much of what Kraft is doing. His concern for the author's intention on the meaning level is laudatory and very close to our conclusions. However, the application of dynamic equivalence to the task of communicating theology needs to be considerably sharpened. There is too little left of the text when Kraft finishes, too little that is supracultural. The Bible as he sees it is too culture bound, with too little theological truth that carries over.[5] The separation of God's intention from the author's results in a canon within a canon and calls the interpreter to seek a "deeper structure" in some ways similar to that of structuralists (see pp. 371-74).

Again we come to the crux: Which is to be authoritative, the Bible or the receptor culture? All our evidence thus far is conclusive: we dare not neglect the supracultural content of the sacred Word. I certainly agree with the dynamic-equivalence school that we must go behind Western theologizing to the text itself. However, while I do not treat the creeds as inerrant, neither do I deny them. The text of Scripture must challenge the credal statements and if necessary alter them (such as removing *descensus ad inferno* ["descended into hades"] from the Apostles' Creed if one agrees with recent interpretation regarding 1 Pet 3:19-20), but meaning must never be negated in the name of contextualization. We do not rework the content, only the *presentation* of gospel truth. As we have seen, this is the model provided in the early church. In other words, we need much greater precision at the level of significance/application.

Kraft and other dynamic-equivalence contextualizers need a deeper appreciation of the dangers of relativism. James Barr argues that the Bible is a relativistic book that was written to a radically different culture with a message that cannot possibly be authoritative for the modern person because it is couched in terms that no longer relate to current problems and perspectives (1973:42-43). Barr typifies the relativism that is so pervasive among contemporary thinkers; there are no absolute truths, and modern readers must identify appropriate truths and transform the religious experience of the biblical writers for themselves. While Kraft himself would not accept Barr's radical relativism,[6] he does not provide a good methodology for separating form from content. The result is a relativizing of theology and a tendency to contextualize and alter even the supracultural elements of Scripture.

Relativism and syncretism are firmly in control of nonevangelical contextualization. Schoonhoven has studied nine major African journals and notes that African theologians blend Ricoeur and Wittgenstein (see appendix one) in calling for a purely African theology without Western hermeneutics (1980:9-18). Setiloane provides an example of this "purely African theology," which in his view should center upon African rather than Western religious images (1979:1-14). The individual is presented as a "participant in divinity" (a contextualization building upon animism), and the Christ-myth is expressed via the African *Bongaka,* or "witch doctor," who is possessed by divinity. Setiloane believes that the African concept of divinity is deeper than its Western counterpart, and goes so far as to say the "Christian orthodox trinitarian formula of divinity should be 'dismantled.' "

However, this is hardly justified. Ricoeur and especially Wittgenstein would never play so fast and loose with the content of Scripture. Only the most radical hermeneutic would treat the basic theological truths as pure symbol. Without controls that center upon the meaning of the text, one will contextualize to a religious expression that is no longer Christian. This is certainly the case with Setiloane. When cultural norms have ascendancy over the text itself, there is no longer *theo*logy but only a human-centered *anthropo*logy.

Of course, this does not mean that Western churches have the right to force their "forms" on Third World churches. African Christians should create an indigenous theology that re-expresses the normative biblical content in dogmatic symbols that communicate biblical truths to their own culture. Hiebert argues for a "transcultural theology" and religious system that is in essence a biblical theology in contextualized form (1985a:5-10; 1985b:12-18). While many in the dynamic-equivalence school locate meaning primarily in the reader/receiver, Hiebert proposes a "critical realism" that situates meaning in the text/sender and seeks to develop a contextualized model that fits the revealed truths. The key to critical realism is an openness to competing theories, a continual re-examination of conclusions by going back to the data. In other words, relativism is unnecessary, and the intended meaning of the text (meaning) must always be the norm that controls contextualization (significance).

The solution is to maintain the tension between meaning and significance as two aspects of a single whole. The intended meaning does have a life of its own as a legitimate hermeneutical goal. However, it is not complete until the significance of that data has been determined. Since I have already discussed the problem of preunderstanding for meaning, I will illustrate it with the hermeneutical spiral (see figure 15.1).

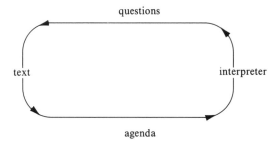

Fig. 15.1. The Hermeneutical Spiral.

The text itself sets the agenda and continually reforms the questions that the observer asks of it. The means by which this is accomplished is twofold: grammatical-syntactical exegesis and historical-cultural background. These interact to reshape the interpreter's preunderstanding and help to fuse the two horizons.[7] The actual contextualization then occurs as this process of fusion reaches out in another and broader hermeneutical spiral to encompass the interpreter's life and situation (see figure 15.2).

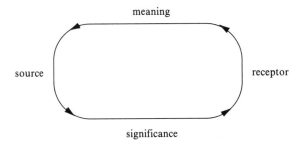

Fig. 15.2. A Broader Hermeneutical Spiral.

Here the receptor culture/interpreter goes to the source/Scripture to determine its meaning. This is the goal of the first spiral (figure 15.1). The source then yields not only meaning but significance. It is important that significance be grounded in the text's context. We certainly agree that communication is dynamic rather than static, yet these categories are too neat. The issue of abstract proposition and dynamic communication is not an either/or but a both/and. The Jews as well as the early church clearly perceived revelation to be propositional as well as relational (see appendix two). It is true that twentieth-century evangelical hermeneutics has emphasized only the propositional dimension; but we do not solve that by going to the opposite extreme. A biblical balance is required.

The key is to allow the dictates of Scripture to challenge and then to transform the receptor culture, yet in an emic rather than etic direction. Here I will follow David Hesselgrave's plan (1978:87-94). Missionaries first contextualize themselves to identify the text, thereby transforming their own perspectives. Then they further contextualize themselves to identify with the world view of the receptor culture. Only then can they contextualize or communicate crossculturally the biblical message. Most assume a two-way process, a source (Scripture) and a receptor audience. However, there is in any communication an intermediate step, the interpreter/proclaimer, and it is in the tension between these aspects that the dilemma of the preacher/missionary resides. Therefore, this "dynamic equivalence" model must be repeated, once for the preacher as interpreter, and again for the preacher/interpreter as proclaimer.[8] The second step fuses the interpreter and the text as the contextual communication takes place for the receptor culture (see figure 15.3).

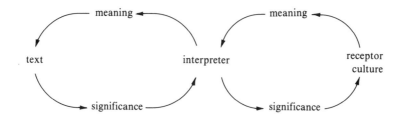

Fig. 15.3. The Preacher's Dual Role as Interpreter and Proclaimer.

It would be fairly simple to contextualize (apply) the two passages discussed in chapter four (Zeph 3:14-17; Eph 3:16-19). Neither passage is linked completely to culture. We would choose examples or illustrations from parallel situations in the life of the receptor culture. For instance, those elements in life which cause anxiety or fear, such as those which parallel the invading hordes of Assyria (cf. Zeph 3:15-16), would be used to demonstrate God's overcoming power. Naturally, the choice would depend on whether you were applying it to Ugandans or Japanese, to farmers or business executives. One would choose those areas which parallel the situation in the text and allow the underlying content to speak afresh to the receptor situation. However, the key issue is still the form-content debate. How much freedom should the contextualizer have in transforming the biblical command? Larkin argues strongly that the biblical form as well as its meaning is normative unless the scriptural text explicitly points in the other direction.[9] Otherwise, he says, we are in danger of disregarding biblical content as "form," since there are no criteria for separating the two with any precision. Therefore, Larkin continues, we do not need principles for normativeness but for nonnormativeness; that is, we assume that the command is intended for all cultures unless there is specific evidence otherwise. While

I deal with this further in the next section, it is at the heart of the contextualization process and must be discussed here. I would argue that often the form as well as the content (such as baptism or the eucharistic celebration) is inviolate, but I disagree that no criteria exist for separating the two. In a very real sense I am not that far from Larkin, as he admits,[10] because the criteria are indeed found in the text itself. However, the starting point is quite different. Larkin and McQuilkin assume normativeness, while I seek to allow the text to tell me and in that sense assume nothing.

Two aspects support my contention that we dare not assume form as well as content to be normative. First, at every stage of the cultural development of Israel and the church, they had to contextualize biblical truths, often in terms of form. For instance, some forms of Israel's worship changed when they moved from the seminomadic tabernacle to temple worship. No longer were the tribes gathered in companies, and the day-by-day worship patterns altered dramatically. This was even more true during the exile after the temple had been destroyed and in the postexilic situation. The absence of centralized temple worship led to the development of the synagogue and a more democratic religion in which the priest increasingly exercised less control of the religious structure. Similarly, much of the New Testament chronicles the changing form of both worship and church government as they moved from a Jewish to a Jewish-Gentile amalgamation.

Second, the history of dogma demonstrates the changing forms in which theological truths have been presented. As I argued in chapter fourteen, systematic theology is a contextualization process that depends on the form-content distinction. In short, the distinction between form and content is essential to the contextualization process.[11] For instance, Hesselgrave and Rommen note that in Islamic areas it is viable to incorporate Muslim forms of worship like "sitting on the floor, removing one's shoes in the place of worship and bowing prostrate when praying" (1989: chap. thirteen). The content of worship and prayer is supracultural, but the form can be contextualized.

Cultural and Supracultural Norms in Scripture

The major difficulty in contextualizing Scripture is deciding exactly what are the cultural or time-bound elements in a passage and what are the supracultural or eternal principles. Some assert that the Bible, written in human language to specific cultural situations, is by nature culture-bound. Interpreters therefore must remove the time-bound (or, with Bultmann, the mythical) element before they can derive the normative principle underneath. Yet there is a vast distinction between affirming the circumstantial nature of Scripture—the fact that it was written to specific situations—and the belief that it is thereby culture-bound. In fact, one literary type of New Testament epistle, the "treatise" (for example, James, perhaps Hebrews or parts of Romans), is predicated on the premise that it is not written to answer specific problems but to center on theological truths meant for all.

James Olthuis argues that "misinterpretations" of the biblical text make any "certitudinal" authority on the surface level impossible (1987:24-26, 32-40). The issues of "semantic symbols" and "structural specificity" determine the "universe of discourse" against which the world of the interpreter must clash. Following Gadamer and the New Hermeneutic,

Olthuis states that we seek not the author's intended meaning (the "semantic" level of symbols) but the vision or world of the autonomous text (the level of "meaning"). Therefore, any certitudinal hermeneutic must take cognizance of the fact that true authority occurs at this visionary or macro-structure level. At this deeper level we encounter the true reality of God's revelation. However, Olthuis's assumption that all authoritative statements are found at the macro or deeper level of meaning fails to consider the strong probability that in many cases the surface structure itself states the deeper or normative truth. We cannot assume that biblical authority occurs only when Scripture is interpreted down to the "deep-level" principles of theological truth. It is clear that the Bible throughout claims authority for itself at the surface level (see Grudem 1983:19-59; McQuilkin 1983:39-41). When we distinguish cultural and normative aspects we are not doing so at the level of authority but rather of applicability.

Yet there are also situations in Scripture—slavery, footwashing, temple feasts, meat offered to idols and so on—that are first-century issues and seem to have little to do with us. While we want to avoid the reductionism and relativism of those above who give the Bible little authority at the surface level, we must know how to determine which passages are normative and which are not. McQuilkin and Larkin argue that only those passages which are explicitly overturned in the New Testament should be considered culturally relative.[12] Yet what do we do with the many passages that are implicitly tied to first-century culture (like slavery or meat offered to idols)? We must contextualize these at a secondary level, for such practices do not occur in our modern culture.[13]

Carson argues that attempts to distinguish supracultural from culture-bound content are misguided (1984:19-20). All biblical statements (even theological assertions like "God is holy") were written in cultural guise, that is, in human language, and attempts to distinguish some types from others are doomed to failure. Also, doing so leads to subjectivity, for the interpreter's grid and current cultural fads all too often determine what is "cultural" and no longer applies. While these are very real concerns, they do not obviate the attempt in this section. I am not establishing a canon within a canon (a set of superior commands) or distinguishing first-class from second-class passages. This is a matter of contextualization or application. The issue is not whether a passage is normative but whether the normative principle is found at the surface level (that is, supracultural) or at the principial level underlying the passage (with the surface situation or command applying mainly to the ancient setting). All biblical statements are authoritative; some, however, are so dependent upon the ancient cultural setting that they cannot apply directly to today since there are no parallels (such as footwashing or meat offered to idols). We need hermeneutical criteria to enable us to make such decisions on firm ground.

Few people assume that all biblical statements are normative for all time. Even those who come close, like denominations that still practice footwashing and the holy kiss, fail to demand cultural commands like many of the levitical laws. The problem is that few have sought hermeneutical criteria to distinguish the normative from the cultural. Denominations assume that their individual traditions will guide them, and ethno-theological anthropologists (such as Taber, Kraft) assume that individual cultures will somehow come up with the proper criteria.

Therefore, the major need is for hermeneutical rules that will aid the interpreter in demarcating the cultural from the supracultural within individual passages. First, we must answer the claim of many Third World theologians and anthropologists that our very criteria are culture-bound as the product of "Western thinking." This is erroneous, for if conceptual communication between cultures is to be possible at all, some means of detecting that communication must be attempted. While the Western mind can learn much from Eastern idealism or symbolism (which has many affinities with segments of biblical truth), the Eastern mind can also learn from the conceptual approach of Western thought. It is doubtful whether the "tradition" or "sound doctrine" so central to New Testament thought can be understood as anything other than conceptual or propositional in nature. In fact it is the job of hermeneutics to observe the generic type of any piece of literature and to interpret it properly on that basis (see further appendix two).

Kraft argues for a "dynamic equivalent" approach and believes that the key is the specificity of the command (1978:357-67). As the level moves to the more specific the command becomes more culture-bound as the product of "Western thinking." He proposes three levels of abstraction: (1) the basic ideal level, which is the most general category and therefore is true for all cultures; (2) the general principle level, which is true in all cultures but may be interpreted differently; and (3) the specific cultural form, which differs between cultures. The basic ideals would be those supracultural commands such as love for one's neighbor (Mt 22:39) or the need for proper order in church (1 Cor 14:40). The general principle would be the command not to steal, a sin against your neighbor. The specific cultural form would then be the command for women to pray with heads covered, a sin against proper church order. He illustrates this with the importance of polygamy for a "good reputation" in certain African cultures (in his case, the Higi culture of Nigeria), which would be allowed on the basis of 1 Timothy 3 (1979:323-27). Yet we would question whether passages against polygamy are not themselves supracultural in essence.[14]

Kraft's categorization model is inadequate, for it would demand that *any* general command be normative and *any* specific command be culture-bound. Yet the general commands (such as 1 Cor 14:40) derived their meaning from the cultural circumstances, and most specifics had their origin in general principles (such as the creation and Fall principles behind passages concerning women in the church).

With this in mind I would posit the following hermeneutical model for biblical contextualization, with the express purpose of providing "a series of covering laws to distinguish the eternal case from the cultural application in all the commands of Scripture."[15]

Hermeneutical Model

There are three basic steps in the process of deciding whether a particular command is normative or cultural, whether it applies at the surface or deep (principial) level. First, we note the extent to which supracultural indicators are found in the passage. We will use the passages on women in the church as a test case. The appeal to creation and the

Fall in 1 Timothy 2:13-14 (compare 1 Cor 11:8-9) would indicate that Paul is appealing to eternal principles in the passage. This points toward normative force, but in itself it does not solve the issue. The issue of meat offered to idols in 1 Corinthians 8—10 is linked to the principle of the stumbling block (8:7-13), and footwashing is linked to servanthood. This points to but is not proof of normative or supracultural force. We must consult the other two aspects before reaching a decision.

Second, we must determine the degree to which the commands are tied to cultural practices current in the first century but not present today. Both the head-covering (1 Cor 11:2-16) and speaking or teaching in public (1 Cor 14:34-35; 1 Tim 2:11-15) were closely linked to first-century customs regarding the woman's place in the home and in society. Whether the head-covering be a veil (the traditional view) or the hair piled on top of the head (Hurley), it was a sign of respectability; to allow the hair to flow loose signified a prostitute. For the Corinthian women to flaunt their freedom in this way was a scandal and was even grounds for divorce. In addition, women did not speak or teach in public; to do so broke cultural taboos in both Jewish and Greco-Roman worlds. Therefore, all three passages (1 Cor 11:2-16; 14:34-35; 1 Tim 2:11-15) were closely allied to cultural mores. However, this too is only a pointer and does not constitute proof that a passage is primarily cultural. We must consider a further aspect. These practices do not threaten the husband-wife relationship today.

Third, we must note the distance between the supracultural and cultural indicators. For instance, the Old Testament passages on creation and the Fall that Paul used relate to the wife's submission and are applied to the issues of the veil and speaking/teaching. This may favor the view that these commands are normative at the deeper level (submission) but cultural at the surface level (wearing the veil and teaching). In other words, distance may indicate that Paul himself was contextualizing a normative principle to address a current cultural problem. On the other hand the issue of authority in 1 Timothy 2:11-12 may indicate that the prohibition of teaching is normative. The interpreter must ask whether the distance between the supracultural and cultural indicators is sufficient to justify the decision that the surface command applied to the first century alone and only the underlying principle (in this case submission) is supracultural. If the distance is sufficient we would apply the surface command only in modern cultures that parallel the first-century situation. For example, women missionaries in Islamic cultures might well choose to go about with their heads covered.

These three criteria do work with other passages. The statements regarding homosexuality in Scripture (such as Rom 1:24-28; 1 Cor 6:9) are quite clear that it constitutes a serious moral sin. Furthermore, the eternal principle and its cultural application are one and the same; there is no "distance" between the cultural and supracultural aspects, indicating that the passages are normative. Also, as Fee and Stuart state,

> Since the Bible as a whole witnesses against homosexuality, and invariably includes it in moral contexts, and since it simply has not been proved that the options for homosexuality differ today from those of the first century, there seems to be no valid ground for seeing it as a culturally-relative matter. (1981:70)

In short, the criteria have helped us to apply properly two different sets of passages relating to current contextualization debates. Yet in and of themselves they do not provide enough depth for such momentous decisions. Other criteria are needed to supplement them, and I will divide these into general and specific categories.

1. General Principles.

a. *Didactic passages* should be used to interpret historical passages. It would be a mistake, for example, to assume that details describing Paul's missionary journeys in Acts were meant to guide missionary strategy today. The supracultural aspects occur under the surface of narratives detailing events, and they must be interpreted via teaching passages. Of course, recent approaches to the Gospels and narrative literature have shown that historical narratives do teach theological truths. Whenever the biblical story or saying has an intended theological point behind it, the interpreter should use that truth in didactic fashion. The difficulty, of course, is detecting when a passage has theological thrust and when it is primarily historical in character.[16] Nevertheless, we cannot teach urban evangelism as the missiological method from Paul's mission at Ephesus (Acts 19) as some in the past have attempted. In the same way, the mission of Jesus "only to the house of Israel" (Mt 10:56) has not been the church's pattern. When a historical narrative relates primarily to the past situation, the supracultural element is muted.

b. The *original setting and meaning* of the command must be understood before its significance can be determined. The application of a passage is closely connected to its textual and revelatory purpose. If we make a passage state something it does not indeed say, then our application is no longer tied to the Word of God. Gordon Fee provides an especially forceful discussion of this when he demonstrates how each different type of biblical genre must be applied according to its own set of rules (1976:105-27). The cultural setting is equally crucial, for we must first know the world behind the text before we can determine its relevance for our world (see A. Johnson 1976:128-61). This is perhaps the major error of many liberation theologians.

c. *Individual statements* must be placed within the broader context of Scripture as a whole. This principle is labeled *analogia scriptura* and means that we should not contextualize on the basis of a single context. This of course does not mean that we simply explain away the obscure or difficult text. Rather we first determine its message in its own context then place it within the larger teaching from the whole of Scripture. Only then may we apply it to our own day, for only then do we truly understand the exact meaning and principle underlying it. This applies, for instance, to the allusion to "baptism for the dead" in 1 Corinthians 15:29 where the absence of parallels makes any kind of normative status doubtful.

2. Specific Principles.

a. Try to determine the extent to which the underlying theological principle dominates the surface application. Julius Scott correctly stresses the need to isolate the salvific intention and relation of the command to the early church's faith and practice (1979:67-77). When we have ascertained the principle on which the command is based, we can delineate the extent to which they overlap. For instance, the command to greet "with a holy kiss" is based on the principle of mutual love. By separating the cultural practice of the command from the principle, we can reapply it today, greeting one another with Christian love and commitment, but not necessarily with a "holy kiss."

b. See when the writer depends on traditional teaching or on the other hand applies a temporary application to a specific cultural problem. These, of course, are not mutually exclusive. However, it is helpful to recognize when the author borrows from earlier teaching, which shows that the current situation does not entirely control the response. Paul's use of traditional teaching and Old Testament proof-texts must caution us before we too easily assume that the passages regarding women in the church no longer apply to our day. The same is true of Paul's arguments regarding long hair for women and short hair for men (1 Cor 11:14-15). There Paul uses cultural language ("it is a disgrace") but the key is "nature" ("does not the very nature of things teach you," v. 14), which George Knight interprets as the creation order rather than cultural practices (1984:247-50). However, this is not at all clear, and I agree with those who see "nature" in terms of cultural practices. Yet even if we accept Knight's interpretation, this does not mandate the command for us as well. Both tradition and culture interact, and we must turn to the other criteria to aid us in deciding whether the short hair—long hair passage transcends cultural differences.

c. When the teaching transcends the cultural biases of the author and readers, it is more likely to be normative. This is true regarding Galatians 3:28 and the issue of slavery, as well as regarding passages related to the universal mission. Clearly, they are not tied to any specific cultural situation and therefore are programmatic theological statements. Fee and Stuart state this another way (1982:68). When a writer agrees with a situation in which there is only one option, the passage is more likely to be culturally relative. They use slavery as an example. When Paul and the other writers fail to denounce slavery as evil, they simply reflect a situation in which there was no other possibility. The universality of the practice means that they had no basis for considering other options. In Galatians 3:28 they went as far as the larger situation allowed.

d. If the command is wholly tied to a cultural situation, it is not timeless in itself. However, as Cheryl Guth shows, it is not so easy to determine the extent of the cultural influence. She suggests four tests to do so:[17] (1) Does the author's language contain cultural indicators that lead one to search for the divine norm behind the temporal application? If the author himself states that it is not normative (such as Jn 13:15, which calls Jesus' footwashing an "example"), the decision is simple; if there is strong cultural language (such as "scandal," "disgrace," "no other practice" in 1 Cor 11:2-16 on the head covering), we have a pointer but not absolute proof of a time-bound assertion. (2) Does it point to a local custom or cultural institution? Again, we have to determine the extent of the connection. The wearing of the head covering was strongly connected to the first-century situation rather than to our own day, but is this enough to overcome the basis in the creation command? (3) Does the author address only a culture-specific situation or question? The instructions regarding meat offered to idols stemmed from the Corinthian situation as mentioned in Chloe's letter. Therefore, the principle of the strong and the weak applies but not the specifics (unless we have a similar cultural situation). (4) Would the command be an issue today if there were no mention of it in Scripture? This, of course, is more subjective but with the others can still be helpful. It is another pointer to the cultural basis of the head-covering command as well as footwashing or the holy kiss.

e. Commands that by nature are moral or theological will be closely tied to the divine will.[18] Commands dealing generally with such issues as adultery or prayer by nature transcend any particular cultural setting. Here we would note that the later prohibition of polygamy was not merely due to cultural change but was rooted in the progressive revelation of God's will.[19] In the same way, we must see the prohibition of homosexuality as normative, tied as it is to divinely established moral laws. Here too the answer to the question of baptism in Islamic lands is answered. It is a theological mandate with no cultural limits. Whether in Judaea or Rome, baptism was practiced. Anchored as it is in the Great Commission (Mt 28:19) and in God's will (1 Pet 3:20-21), it is mandated for all generations.

In sum, the major problem of dynamic-equivalent contextualization is the assumption that biblical authority occurs only at the "deep structure" level and not in the surface statements. As J. Robertson McQuilkin asks, "Does inspiration extend to all of Scripture or only to enduring religious principles?" (1980:114). I agree with McQuilkin's fear that such rules as espoused above may enable one to replace Scripture with culture as the truly authoritative norm. The criteria must be used together and never separately. For instance, the issue of women in the church can be solved only when one has compared the fact that Paul grounds it in the eternal norm of creation and the Fall with the further presence of cultural indicators within it. We must seek God's will for the present day rather than read our own will into the text.

It is important to emphasize that we are not arguing for a canon within the canon. We are not dealing here with meaning but with significance. The process of deciding supra-cultural/cultural does not entail the former having greater "authority" than the latter. Rather, we seek to delineate *how* a passage applies to us in our context, whether at the level of the surface command (if it is supracultural) or at the deeper level of the underlying principle (if the surface command is cultural, or meant for the first century but not applying literally to today). Both types are inspired and authoritative; the only question is in what way the command applies to our current context. We must remember that a culturally based command is still applicable today in any culture that parallels the first-century setting.

Finally, after determining the supracultural element, it is still difficult to inculturate it in the diverse situations of our day. As Buswell states, we must radically remove these principles from our own norms: "Only a supracultural message disengaged from any cultural context is free to be inculturated in another" (1978:103). In other words, the significance of a passage refers to the many different ways that principle can be applied in various contexts. Interpreters dare not demand their own contextualization but must allow the principle to live anew in other situations. That is the subject of the next section.

A Method for Contextualization

The key to contextualization is to seek a true fusion of the horizons of both the biblical text and the modern situation. This involves primarily a fusion of contexts, that behind the ancient text and that faced in the current context. Once more I will utilize Nida and Taber's useful diagram; only now I will switch from the original language and receptor language to the original context (OC) and receptor context (RC)—see figure 15.4.

Fig. 15.4. The Process of Contextualization.

There are two aspects of the biblical (original) context, the sociocultural situation behind the passage (discovered via background research) and the literary context that contains the passage (discovered via exegetical research). Both are essential. The cultural context determines the sphere of modern life addressed by the passage; the literary context determines the message addressed to the modern context. The interpreter must seek a consistent and significant overlap between the original and receptor contexts before true contextualization can occur. Failure at either level will result in an improper, if not false, contextualization that can have serious consequences. At the missiological level it will produce a syncretized religion that is only half Christian (called "christopaganism"), similar to that produced at Colossae or Ephesus (see Colossians, the Pastoral Epistles or 1 John). At the level of the Western church it can lead to serious distortions like positive confession, the gospel of prosperity or positive thinking. At the very least shallow contextualizing can undo much of the good that proper exposition has accomplished, since the congregation will carry into their daily lives an improper understanding as to how to put the elucidated truths into practice. Good contextualization is just as important as good exegesis in hermeneutics, since interpretation includes praxis as well as theoria. If the proper task of translation and exegesis is to ask how the original author would say it (that is, the truth presented in the passage) if he were speaking to my audience, the task of contextualization is to determine "how what was asked of the original audience (what the author asked them to do) can be relived by my audience."[20]

There should be contextual overlap or match in three areas for proper contextualization to occur, according to Hesselgrave and Rommen (1989: chap. twelve). There should be overlap first in the semantic field or at the level of meaning. If one alters the biblical message in order to establish communication or to apply the text to a specific need, truth can be sacrificed on the altar of relevance. The first priority is God's revealed message; the medium of communication must not only take second place, it must be selected entirely for the purpose of putting across that message. However, scholars fiercely debate the amount of freedom one has in choosing the correct term or idea. For instance, do we take a significant theological idea like "the lamb of God" and change it to "the pig of God" for certain African tribes that do not have lambs but raise swine instead? Many missiologists say no because there is not sufficient linguistic overlap and it will inevitably clash with Old Testament passages on pigs as unclean animals. The arguments for retaining the unknown figure is that the missionary can explain important concepts, and the process will deepen the understanding of the tribes. This is certainly valid in areas where there are teachers; however, it will not work in bush regions where there are none.

One solution might be to contextualize a figure like the lamb if the translation is for evangelistic purposes and is intended for areas devoid of Christian teachers. Elsewhere such important theological images, even if unknown, would be retained. However, one must wonder whether the new metaphor would be much better. For instance, the function of pigs in African societies is scarcely the same as lambs in ancient Judaea. Therefore, perhaps it is better to keep the term *lamb of God* and add a brief explanatory note.

The second area of overlap or match is that of context. The goal is to enable the modern hearer to actualize that revealed message with as much practical validity as did the original audience for whom it was intended. I will expand this in the next chapter, but must introduce the concept here as well. Interpreters/proclaimers must note the situation behind the passage—that is, the circumstances that led the original author to emphasize his point—and then they must seek a *parallel* situation in the lives of the receptor audience. The passage will then be applied to and address that parallel modern situation.

Finally, contextualization should seek to match the biblical message with the "internal template" of the hearer, namely one's internal bank of world view, knowledge about the world and memory system. Hesselgrave and Rommen assert that good contextualization will expand the internal memories to include the data being presented (1989: chap. 12). In other words the truths will be internalized and personalized to the extent that they become part of the individuals, transforming the very way they look at the world and react to it. In this sense contextualization includes not only interpretation and application but persuasion and motivation (see pp. 352-53). This is certainly correct, for praxis involves acting upon the data, not merely understanding how it applies.

The Willowbank Report calls for a fusion of the horizons that takes "with due serious-ness the original historical and cultural context" and at the same time speaks to our time. This is accomplished when the reader from his or her cultural background establishes a "dialogue" with the text:

> As we address Scripture, Scripture addresses us. We find that our culturally condi-tioned presuppositions are being challenged and our questions corrected. In fact, we are compelled to reformulate our previous questions and to ask fresh ones. So the living interaction proceeds. (Coote and Stott 1980:316-17)

In this sense contextualization is the second half of a unitary hermeneutical journey from meaning to significance as the Word of God is actualized in human, cultural experience.

This does not mean that the interpreter can move behind his own preunderstanding to meaning, as if we can leave our own cultural history and move solely into the biblical world to objective knowledge. As Dietrich asserts, "Any theology is necessarily contex-tual. Therefore it will be more honest the more it becomes *conscious* of its context" (italics his).[21] Within a proper hermeneutical spiral, the biblical world view highlights our own and enables us consciously to place our belief system in front of the context for challenge or (if need be) correction. Certainly, once we have explained the "meaning" of the text, we have already contextualized it to an extent. However, if the process of backward and forward transformation diagrammed above works (as I believe it does), we can discover that transcultural meaning which bridges from the text to our context without violating the original meaning. In this way we bracket and transcend our preunderstanding, yet communicate properly to our own cultural context.

In backward transformation the interpreter detects the transcultural element in the passage, that basic content which transcends the biblical context and addresses the church in every age. Some passages cross over intact, such as commands against pride and dissension (Phil 2:1-4, 14-18). Others must be transferred at a deeper level, such as Paul's diatribe against the Judaizers (Phil 3:1-6, 18-19), which would be applied to false teachers in general. Some are debatable, such as passages dealing with persecution (Heb 12; 1 Pet 3:13—4:19). Many believe these should be contextualized only in terms of specific persecution today while others think they are applicable to general trials as well (see Jas 2:2-4; 1 Pet 1:6-7).

The backward transformation yields universal truths that apply to all cultures. These can then be forward transformed to address particular issues in the receptor culture. The goal is to seek those parallel situations that the biblical writers would address if they were present today. For instance, the passage on the "traditions of the elders" (Mk 7:1-20) makes no sense in our modern context, for ritual uncleanness is not found in many societies today. Therefore, we must seek the universal truth embedded in the story. The issue is human tradition versus God's rules. The law requiring washing before eating was not a part of the Law of Moses; it was only found in the "oral tradition." Therefore, Jesus argued that the Pharisees set up extra rules that actually resulted in obviating the true intentions of God. This is the deep structure principle or universal truth. In contextualizing it in a receptor culture we would look for other legalistic regulations that become "yokes" around the believer's neck (compare Acts 15:10). Some might have certain dress codes or behavioral demands (such as "Sunday dress" or certain acts of piety) that stem from the near past rather than Scripture and can become barriers to the proclamation of the gospel. Such should be opposed in ways similar to Jesus in Mark 7. Similarly, worship patterns in oriental cultures should be built upon their own ways of expressing praise to God rather than upon Western modes.

Liberation theology provides a good case study. Its theologians' evaluation of context is certainly correct—the economic oppression of the poor, the misuse of Scripture by the wealthy to keep the poor content to wait for their reward in heaven and so forth. They also correctly note the strong emphasis on care for the poor in the Torah, the prophets, Jesus' teaching and the Epistles. However, when they give this context hermeneutical control over Scripture and turn even the cross into a protest against economic exploitation, they go too far. To define salvation as the liberation of the poor and to identify a guerilla fighter like Che Guevara as a Christ-figure are serious errors.

Scripture is just as opposed to economic oppression as is the liberation theologian, but not to the virtual exclusion of the spiritual sphere of salvation, which clearly is the central issue throughout the Bible. When liberation theologians reinterpret passages on spiritual salvation as demanding economic revolution, they ignore the meaning of the text and are guilty of serious hermeneutical error. Evangelical "liberationists" like Orlando Costas, René Padilla or Emilio Nuñez are in the process of developing an alternative model that seeks a balance between the temporal (the necessity of prophetic opposition to social injustice) and the spiritual (reaching the unbeliever with the gospel message of spiritual salvation in Jesus the Christ), between the *already* (liberation in the present) and the *not yet* (final liberation only at the Eschaton). Most important, evangelical contextualizers wish to operate from the whole counsel of God, to make the biblical voice central over the voice of the modern context, to achieve a true fusion of horizons in which all the intended transcultural truths of the Bible are actualized in the lives of Christians today. Opposition to social evils will not cease but rather will take its proper place not at the top but within the matrix of Christian praxis as one aspect of (but not the whole of) Christian reaction to the world (see, for example, Padilla 1979:63-78; Nuñez 1984:166-94).

Paul Hiebert calls for a "critical contextualization" that avoids the ethnocentrism of the past or the relativism and syncretism that too often results from dynamic equivalence approaches.[22] His three steps provide a good summary of the forward transformation process. First, one must study the receptor culture via an uncritical analysis of beliefs and customs; that is, a search for understanding and appreciation of their total world view and of the customs that result. Second, the preacher guides the people in a study of Scripture as it speaks to the "cognitive, affective, and evaluative dimensions" of their culture. In so doing, the people will be led from the intended meaning of the biblical text to its significance for their situation. Both aspects are necessary. Third, the people themselves evaluate critically their beliefs and customs in light of the biblical truths. Discovery leads to evaluation and then to response. At times this will result in a positive assessment as they integrate scriptural truth into their cultural assessment. At other times they will have to modify or radically change their customs. New rituals will be developed that express these contextualized truths.

Conclusion

A six-stage process may best describe the task of contextualization as it moves from the biblical text to our modern context, from original meaning to current significance. Simply stated, the method blends theoria and praxis, with the goal of enabling the church in diverse cultures to affirm and live out biblical truths with the same dynamic power as did the early church (see figure 15.5).

1. *Determine the surface message.* Using the exegetical tools elucidated in the first section of this book, the interpreter should determine the original intended message of the passage. Moreover, this should be done with contextualization in mind, that is, the way the biblical author addressed his original readers. Biblical books were situational in nature; they were written with a specific message addressed to a particular situation in the life of Israel or the church. The preacher/interpreter wants to distinguish both aspects: the original message and the way it was communicated to the reader.

2. *Determine the deep structure principle behind the message.* This is the larger biblical-theological truth utilized by the author in addressing the readers. The surface message

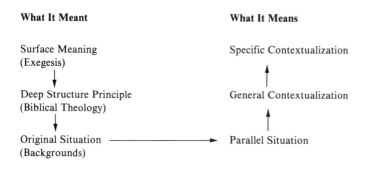

Fig. 15.5. The Six-Stage Process of Contextualization.

often contextualizes the deeper principle in order to address a specific problem in the original audience. For instance, the "alien" and "sojourner" passages in 1 Peter (1:1, 17; 2:11) build upon the early church's teaching on home or citizenship in heaven (such as Phil 3:20; Eph 2:19; Heb 12:22). Also, the passage on the head-covering for women (1 Cor 11:2-16) contextualizes the principle of submission (vv. 3, 7-9) for the problem of women praying with their heads uncovered. The "covering" was a sign of submission. Paul and the other sacred authors would stress one aspect of a larger theological truth in order to speak to a particular issue. It is helpful for the interpreter to discover the biblical theology behind the point of the text and to see exactly what issue is being addressed. As noted above, this is a critical aspect in delineating cultural from supracultural passages. It is also important as part of the process of contextualization. As I will note below, the passage can be applied to the modern context at either the surface or deep structure level.

3. *Note the original situation.* The situation behind the text determined why the author chose the particular aspect to stress in the surface message. However, this is also the most difficult of the three levels (surface message, biblical theological principle and the situation addressed) to determine. The Epistles and the prophets are more direct in stating the situation than is narrative literature, but nevertheless it is often very complex even there. For instance, what are the exact identities of the false teachers in the Pastorals, the heresy in Colossians, or the super-apostles in 2 Corinthians? However, we can still determine the situation in a general sense,[23] and so long as we do not assume more certainty than we possess, it is a helpful tool. In narrative books, there are two types, the historical situation depicted in the text and the *Sitz im Leben* ("situation in the life" of Israel and the church) behind the text. The latter is very speculative, and out of twenty-five articles by scholars on a passage, there will often be twenty-five different opinions. Therefore, the situation in the story itself is more valuable. For instance, it is almost impossible to detect the *Sitz im Leben* behind the Jacob-Esau conflict (Gen 27), but the situation in the text (rivalry over the blessing but God's unseen hand in the background) provides tremendous contextualization opportunities.

4. *Discover the parallel situation in the modern context.* Most scholars recognize the importance of applying a text in the same way it was used in the original setting (see Fee and Stuart 1981:60-61; Liefeld). This means that we should contextualize it in terms of parallel situations in our current context. It does little good to spend a great deal of time and energy exegeting a text properly only to throw it all away when we apply the text. If God's Word is any indicator, knowledge is inadequate unless it leads to action. As in Joshua 1:8, we study the text not just to increase our cognitive understanding (though that is certainly true of many passages) but more "to *act* according to all that is written in it." Proper contextualization is just as important as proper exegesis.

5. *Decide whether to contextualize at the general or the specific level.* Missiologists must decide whether to retain a specific image or message (such as the "lamb" in cultures that know nothing about sheep) or substitute a dynamic equivalent. For instance, should evangelism and conversion be direct and individual in cultures that are not? Many missiologists are turning to networking and "web relationships" (reaching the nuclear family as a whole) in oriental cultures. As another example, what form should baptism take and how public should it be in Muslim cultures? Issues like this provide great difficulty for contextualizers who wish to remain true to Scripture yet produce a relevant, dynamic Christianity in the diverse cultural settings around the world. Flexibility between general and specific levels has distinct limits (see the discussion of dynamic equivalence above).

In the sermon one can often choose to apply the message of the text generally (so long as it is tied to the biblical-theological principle behind the text, as in the diagram above) or specifically. For instance, passages dealing with persecution (such as Jas 1:2-4; 1 Pet 1:6-7) apply theology dealing with "trials of the faith" (note the "various trials" and "test of your faith" in Jas 1:2-3; 1 Pet 1:6) to persecution. The preacher is free to apply the principle in both directions; for the early church persecution was a specific type of trial. In many cases one can apply it only on the general level. Fee and Stuart note two types (1981:61-65): "extended application" (such as the application of "unequally yoked" in 2 Cor 6:14 to marriage with nonbelievers) and "particulars that are not comparable" (such as the "meat offered to idols" in 1 Cor 8—10). In both cases, choosing a comparable but general parallel is valid (in the latter it is mandatory). In the instance of meat offered to idols, the pastor could refer to issues that are not critical to God but matter to many Christians and can become stumbling blocks to weak believers (Fee lists women's slacks, movies, cards, dancing and mixed swimming). In such situations participation may not be biblically wrong, but if it will become a "stumbling block" (8:7-13), one should avoid doing so. More will be said on this in the following chapter.

16

H omiletics II:
The Sermon

S STATED IN THE INTRODUCTION, THE TRUE GOAL OF HERMENEUTICS IS NOT THE COMMEN-
tary but the sermon. The commentary performs an important task in opening up
the original intended meaning of the biblical passage. However, the true purpose
of the Bible is not static (as an object of study) but dynamic (as a life-changing mechanism). Therefore, contextualization is a necessary goal of interpretation. Meaning and
significance unite in the hermeneutical process, and it is the sermon that best brings the
two aspects together.

The sermon is a bridge-building mechanism that unites the ancient world of the biblical
text with the modern world of the congregation. Contextualization is the mortar that
binds these two worlds together, as the preacher attempts to help the congregation
understand the relevance of the text for their own lives. The sermonic process is a
continual bridging enterprise in which the preacher helps the audience to relive the drama
and spiritual power of the text for its original audience and then to understand how that
original message relates to similar situations in their own lives. Moreover, this is done
point by point as the passage develops. My basic principle is that any point worth
developing is a point worth applying—on the spot. Thus, the preacher travels back and
forth from the text to the modern context, developing the superstructure of both the text
and its contextualization for our day.

Rommen describes three stages in this process (1989:chap. 20): communicators first
seek to understand the text (meaning-intended) then to "decontextualize" or divest themselves of culturally conditioned understandings of the text (meaning perceived) and finally to contextualize the passage for the listeners' context (meaning-applied). I would
break the latter into two stages: personal appropriation (devotional study) and sermonic
application. Communicators must apply the text to their own lives before considering
how it touches the congregation's lives. Moreover, each stage is governed not just by the
science of hermeneutical procedures or by the art of pastoral experience but by spiritual
empowering from the Holy Spirit.

The Place of the Holy Spirit

There is a "theology" of contextualization, for this aspect of Bible study is also meant to be controlled by the power of God. The Holy Spirit was behind the biblical books (2 Tim 3:16; 2 Pet 1:21) and led the disciples to reproduce those aspects of Christ's life which God knew were necessary for the needs of the church (Jn 14:26; 15:26). The Holy Spirit alone can empower the preacher so that his message exemplifies not "persuasive words of [human] wisdom" but rather demonstrates "the Spirit and the power" of God (1 Cor 2:4-5).

Spurgeon delivered a well-known address titled "The Holy Spirit in Connection with our Ministry" (1877:1-23). His basic thesis was that our very ministries depend for their viability and power on the presence of the Holy Spirit, who gives knowledge and wisdom to those who seek him. The Spirit anoints the utterances of the preacher. "Oh, how gloriously a man speaks when his lips are blistered with the live coal from the altar—feeling the burning power of the truth, not only in his inmost soul, but on the very lips with which he is speaking!" (p. 7). The sermon must be forged in a spirit of dependence and devotion, that the strength may be of the Spirit rather than of the flesh. The effects of the gospel are entirely the result of the Spirit rather than of our skill. Finally, Spurgeon discusses the ways in which we can "lose this needful assistance" (pp. 17-22), namely through insensitivity to his prompting, dishonesty, lack of grace, pride, laziness and the neglect of prayer. The person of God must strive for the Holy Spirit in exegeting and proclaiming the Word of God.

In his *Institutes* Calvin speaks of the "internal witness of the Spirit" in bringing us to salvation and enabling us to understand God's Word (1:93-95). Frame calls this an "intimate participation in God's own self-knowledge" (1986:23). Although for many modern theologians (such as Barth) this inner testimony replaces the traditional view of inspiration, for the evangelical the Spirit's witness provides a means for appropriating the inspired Word of God. In other words the Spirit enables the reader to hear God's sovereignly chosen message found in his Word (Jn 16:13; 1 Thess 1:5; 2:13). As Frame points out, the Word provides the objective authority, the witness of the Spirit provides the subjective authority (that understood by us) of the divine revelation.

The "illumination" of the interpreter is one aspect of the larger ministry of the Holy Spirit in bringing people to regeneration and daily growth in their Christian life. It is that portion of the "internal testimony" which relates to understanding and applying God's revealed Word. Technically, the *testimonium spiritus sancti internum* relates to our conviction regarding Scripture's authority, and illumination refers to understanding that Word. As Klooster points out (1984:460), "Paul repeatedly prayed that the believers might grow in understanding and knowledge through the illumination of the Holy Spirit (1 Cor. 2:2; 2 Cor. 4:4-15; Eph. 1:17-19; Phil. 1:9-11; Col. 1:9-13; cf. also 1 John 2:20-27)." Klooster uses the term "organic illumination" to describe the relation of the Spirit to the process of interpretation. This means that the Spirit works through the mind and study of the interpreter. However, there is no guarantee that the person will "automatically" comprehend the intended meaning of the passage. The hermeneutical tools all provide grist for the Spirit's will in the act of interpretation.

While the Spirit enables the reader to gain insight into the Word, he does not provide that information for the reader. We still must utilize our rational capacity to draw inferences from the data. As Frame states, the Spirit allows us to overcome the effects of sin on the rational process. "The Spirit does not whisper to us special reasons which are not otherwise available; rather, he opens our eyes to acknowledge those reasons which *are* available" (Frame 1986:234). In other words, the Spirit makes it possible for the reader to use every faculty to discern the Word and apply it. How does this explain the fact that equally spiritual scholars interpret the same passage quite differently? The Spirit makes it possible to overcome our preunderstanding in order to discern the Word, but he does not guarantee that we will do so. On difficult passages we must use every tool we can muster and still will often read a text the way our experience and theological proclivities dictate. Some passages are so ambiguous that more than one interpretation is possible. We must make our hermeneutical choice but remain open to further leading from the Spirit and challenge from our peers. The Spirit enables us to free our minds to the text but does not whisper to us the correct answer.

Moreover, the Bible does not state that the unbeliever cannot intellectually interpret it quite accurately. As Larkin says, "Paul locates the barrier in the area of evaluation rather than cognition" (1988:289). In passages like 1 Corinthians 2:14 (to the "natural man" spiritual truths are "foolishness") and 2 Corinthians 4:4 ("the god of this world" has "blinded" unbelievers so they cannot "see the light of the gospel"), the non-Christian cannot understand the truth of the gospel. Such passages do not state that unbelievers cannot understand the *meaning* of the text but rather that they will reject the *implications* of it. The Holy Spirit deals in this latter realm, enabling readers to separate truth from falsehood and to apply the Word properly to their lives.

Connected with this theme is John's theology of the "chain of revelation" (see Osborne and Woodward 1979:9-10), which describes the Christian's authority and responsibility in sharing the Word. One of the major christological emphases in the Fourth Gospel is that of Jesus as the "sent one," a concept stemming from the Jewish idea of the *šālîaḥ,* the "representative" who reveals and embodies the will of the sender (Jn 14:6; 17:3, 6). In the Farewell Discourse of John 14—16 Jesus passes this authority on to the Holy Spirit, twice "sent," or "given," by the Father (14:16, 26) and twice by the Son (15:26; 16:7). The final stage is seen when the disciples/ believers themselves are described as "sent ones" (17:18; 20:21). In the latter passage this is accomplished via the coming of the Spirit (20:22) and involves a participation in Jesus' work as Judge (20:23; compare 5:22; 8:15-16; 9:39). Indeed, the Triune Godhead is incorporated within our ministry of the Word and empowers us as we share its message.

A Devotional Experience

On the way home from a sabbatical in Germany in 1985, we had a stopover in Iceland and took a tour through the lava fields and hot springs of that fascinating island. As we were passing through the desolate countryside the tour guide pointed to a series of stone cairns, erected in the last century to direct travelers to the firmer pathways over the soft ground. "We call these cairns 'priests,' " she said, "because they point the way but never go there themselves." This is all too often true, for preachers often do not "practice what they preach" and seem to proclaim an irrelevant, unworkable gospel message. The Word of God claims our allegiance and obedience before it asks us to minister to others.

There are three reasons why the preacher must give priority to personal application. First, the Word of God itself demands that our lives be changed before we partake of mission. This is seen in the oft-repeated condemnation of the "hypocrite" who gives the appearance of piety but lacks the inward transformation of character that God demands (Mt 6:2, 5, 16). True love and wisdom are characterized by an absence of hypocrisy (Rom 12:9; Jas 3:17), and the latter can be accomplished only when the gospel message we proclaim has first claim on our own lives. The truths we share are an "I-thou" summons from God, first to our own selves and then to our congregations. Sermon preparation therefore must be a devotional exercise first (a first-person encounter) and a proclamation event second (a second-person encounter). No one should ever preach a passage that has not first reached into the depths of his or her own heart.

The second reason for the centrality of the devotional experience is that we cannot ask someone to do that which we have been unwilling to do ourselves. If a congregation hears a preacher inveigh against losing one's temper and knows him to be continually irritable and cantankerous, they will lose respect for both messenger and message. Simple logic demands that we earn the right to be heard before we take leadership in the church. This is true not merely in general terms but specifically applies to every message we share. As stated in the introduction, we move from the meaning of the text to its implications for our own life and then to its significance for the situations of those whom God has committed into our care.

The final reason for the importance of a devotional experience is practical: when our lives have been touched by the message we are proclaiming, that message will be preached with an excitement and urgency it would not have otherwise. The best salesman is one who is personally convinced that the item is the answer to everyone's need. The person who does not pray can seldom provoke interest in a sermon on prayer. The message may be accurate and academically correct but lacks power. We must be convinced of the importance of an action if we are to persuade others to do it. As Spurgeon says above, such dishonesty can never experience the power of the Holy Spirit. On the other hand, when one moves from the prayer closet to the pulpit, when the passage studied that week has aroused the soul of the preacher, the message will demonstrate a presence and power it could never otherwise attain.

Mickelsen notes five goals in personal Bible study (1963:345-66): (1) fellowship with God as believers listen to what God has to say in the text; (2) directions from God for daily decisions, as Christians respond to the significance of the Word for the problems of life by maintaining an awareness of God's presence and an openness to his will; (3) the commands of God for modern situations, as the saints obey the injunctions of the Bible; (4) the counsel of God for interpersonal dialogue, as believers share their faith with others; and (5) the message of God for public preaching, as the pastor or Bible teacher confronts others with the biblical truths that have gripped his or her own life. The crucial point is that Scripture is dynamic, imparting life-changing principles that demand to be lived out in daily experience, rather than static, imparting only knowledge to be discussed and debated. Preachers ignore the personal dimension of the Word only to their peril.

From Text to Sermon

The hermeneutical process culminates not in the results of exegesis (centering on the original meaning of the text) but in the homiletical process (centering on the significance of the Word for the life of the Christian today). Modern scholars in fact often restrict the meaning of *hermeneutics* to significance and use *exegesis* for the process of detecting the intended meaning. While I cannot agree with this restricted meaning (see my introduction above) and believe that *hermeneutics* covers both meaning and significance, this definition does point to the importance of contextualization for the hermeneutical process.

There are four steps in proper sermonic development (see the six stages in the conclusion of the previous chapter—pp. 336-38).

First, one should study the original situation behind the message of the text. In other words, how was the biblical author contextualizing or applying biblical truths to the situation behind the text? This is discovered by applying background material to the problems addressed in the passage. For instance, some interpreters hold that the parable of the shrewd steward (Lk 16:1-13) uses the laws of usury to describe the actions of the steward (vv. 5-7), as he removed the interest from the loans—and perhaps his own commission as well (see Derrett and Fitzmyer). The "dishonesty" (v. 5), according to this view, occurred in verses 1-2 not in verses 5-7. If this is correct, Jesus contextualized his shrewdness (vv. 9-13) to demonstrate how the believer should use his worldly resources shrewdly to benefit the kingdom.

Second, the interpreter should determine the underlying theological principle behind the text. Every passage addresses a surface situation and applies a deeper argument to that situation! In the case of Luke 16, this is found in verses 8b-13, which use teaching on "treasures in heaven" (compare Lk 12:33; see vv. 22-34) to address a wise use of one's monetary resources to aid the poor and produce two heavenly rewards.

Third, the student of the Word must meditate on the biblical and theological truths studied. It takes time to think through the issues involved and the relationship between the surface or cultural aspects and the deeper or theological truths elucidated. Looking again at Luke 16:1-13, it is obvious that social concern is mandated for the believer. One's rewards in heaven are closely linked with helping the needy (compare Jas 2:13-17). These cultural overtones make it easier to think through the two spheres and to note how Jesus is arguing. We can then separate those elements which belong to the contextualized situation of the first century (such as the laws of usury) and those which transcend the time of writing and apply to every era of the church age. Here we focus the mind on God and his revelation, asking how these spiritual truths address the church.

Fourth, the reader seeks to discern parallels between the original situation addressed by the sacred writer and the contemporary experiences of the Christian and the church. Application built on the significance of the text will occur at this level. It is crucial to remember that the parallels should be genuine rather than contrived. The preacher/

teacher should ask, If the biblical writer were exhorting my congregation/class on this subject, what aspects of church life would he address? It would be hermeneutically weak, for instance, to rail against short hair or loose-flowing hair on women on the basis of 1 Corinthians 11:2-16, because how one wears her hair is no longer a sign of submission (see p. 331). We could address, however, the situation of overbearing husbands or demanding wives today (although one must at all times keep in mind Eph 5:25-33 here).

Principles for Determining Application

The most important thing (as stated in chap. fifteen) is to base the application/contextualization on the intended meaning of the text.[1] We want the passage to live anew in our own current situation, but it must be the inspired message which is relived rather than our subjective manipulation of the text. Therefore, we determine what the text says before we apply it. Our basic question is, If Paul (or Jeremiah and so forth) were preaching *this* principle to my congregation, what issues would he address? The original point of the passage is re-expressed in the thought modes of the receptor culture, whether our own or a further culture within which we are ministering at present.

As stated above, sermon preparation must be a devotional exercise (a first-person encounter) before it becomes a proclamation event (a second-person encounter). Preachers continually must place themselves before the text rather than merely place themselves behind the text in order to direct it to this or that situation in the church. The latter will result first in a barren message devoid of personal interaction and second in a misdirected message that often will derive from the needs of the congregation rather than from the message of the text. The goal is to wed the text with the current context of the congregation. However, the problem of distanciation (the cultural gap between biblical times and today) cannot be solved easily. Many erroneous methods have been devised:[2] (1) Literalistic preaching assumes God automatically bridges the gap and preaches the text as if it were written for today. Normally this is accompanied by a lack of serious effort to understand the text, resulting in shallow, subjective sermons. (2) Allegorizing began in Alexandria with Philo and then Origen, dominating the church in the Middle Ages. It assumes that beneath the literal, surface meaning lies the "real" meaning, such as the Song of Solomon as a picture of Christ and the church. The problem is that this normally ignores the intended meaning of the text and degenerates into eisegesis (reading into the text whatever you wish). (3) Spiritualizing takes historical passages (such as the David and Jonathan story, 1 Sam 20) and uses it as a parable illustrating a spiritual reality (such as earthly friendship). While there is some validity in this it too often ignores the historical context and fails to do justice to the intended theological meaning of the text. (4) Moralizing looks on all texts as providing examples of virtues (or vices) to be imitated (or avoided) by the Christian. Greidanus says, "Unfortunately, in overemphasizing virtues and vices, dos and dont's, and in not properly grounding the ethical demands in the Scriptures, they trivialize them and turn them into caricatures" (1988:163-64). This is often seen in biographical preaching, with Esau exemplifying the carnal Christian and Jacob the Christian with proper priorities. The problem again is that the actual message of the text is ignored, and often a message contrary to the intended meaning results. How then are we to determine the actual meaning and significance of a text?

First, we must recapitulate the steps to contextualization and apply them to sermonic application. Determining the situation behind the text is a major factor in differentiating the cultural from the supracultural elements in the text (see p. 329). While in many cases we cannot ascertain the exact situation with precision (especially in narrative portions; see p. 327), what we can discover is very helpful. This decision affects contextualization or application and provides the basis for the other principles below. By noting the situation behind the surface command, the interpreter can see how the author has contextualized his underlying theological principle (stage two) and can seek parallel situations in the life of his current congregation (stage three). For instance, the situation behind the prayer of Ephesians 3:16-19 (see pp. 112-17) is the disunity between Jewish and Gentile factions in the Ephesian church (see Eph 2:11-12). Each element of the prayer for love and discernment was addressed to that situation. Through this preachers or teachers can address similar factions in their own community, such as a rampant denominationalism that refuses to cooperate with other evangelical churches or internal squabbles in the church.

Liefeld notes several aspects in reviewing the "life setting" of the passage (1984:95-98). At the outset, one will study the circumstances or needs addressed. This will help both the preacher and the congregation to immerse themselves in the original situation and better understand how the text can address itself anew in the current context. Also, one will ask what purpose the text originally served. Simply put, one asks why the sacred writer emphasizes the particular points. For instance, why does Luke retell the story of Paul's conversion three times (Acts 9; 22; 26) rather than summarize the event the latter two times? What theological purpose led Luke to repeat such a lengthy event? Also, why does the book of Revelation repeat such similar judgments in the seals, trumpets and bowls? These are clues to the theology behind the text.

Further, the interpreter will ask what immediate results the author sought. This will make the purposes more specific as one asks how the text addressed the reader's situation and what it sought to accomplish in terms of concrete action. The interpreter will then describe this purpose or function in a single word or phrase. Liefeld (1984:99-107) suggests the following categories: Is the text motivational, convicting, comforting, proclaiming the Gospel, leading to worship, setting standards, setting goals, dealing with doctrinal issues, dealing with problems, showing cause-effect relationships, laying a foundation for faith or action, giving perspective on life, or teaching ethics? These will help specify the proper application.

The second stage in moving from text to context is to delineate the underlying theological principle (the "deep structure," see chap. fifteen) beneath the surface message of the text. Zuck calls this the "principalizing bridge," because the theological principle "spans the gulf between the past and the present, with a truth that is relevant to both" (1982:27-28). It bridges meaning or interpretation to significance or application. In fact it is inherent within both. For didactic passages this is relatively simple. Paul's command to "pray without ceasing" (1 Thess 5:17) is relevant for all times. Even passages like the head-covering on women (see pp. 329-32) are not too difficult once one has determined the supracultural core: women are to dress in such a way that they reflect their submission to their husbands (the supracultural element; see Eph 5:22-24) and should not flaunt their freedom in ways that bring shame to the gospel. In historical passages the core is more difficult, for it involves the thread of narrative theology (see chap. six) that ties together the message of that book. For instance, the narrative flow of John 9 dramatically contrasts the progressive coming to sight of the man born blind with the growing blindness of the Pharisees. In the encounter theology of the gospel as a whole the reader is being forced to come to terms with the gospel's demands. Jesus as the "light of the world" (Jn 8:12) causes every person to encounter the divine demands; will we come to sight or blind ourselves to the light?

McQuilkin names three ways we can determine the "generic principle," a biblical standard that applies to later situations (1983:258-65): (1) it might be stated directly in the text, as in "You shall love your neighbor as yourself" (Lev 19:18; Mk 12:31); (2) in historical portions it might be implied on the basis of the text's explicit interpretation of the event, as when Scripture itself commends the occurrence (such as the "thesis paragraph" on early church life and worship in Acts 2:42-47); (3) it may apply indirectly in terms of general principles rather than the specific situation if the cultural/supracultural indicators so dictate (such as the holy kiss being the same as the loving greeting in Christ). Many historical passages, especially Old Testament stories, apply only indirectly to us. For instance, the Sampson narratives hardly call for aggressive conduct on the part of the believer, nor do the Holy War passages justify all wars. Rather, they show that God can use even unworthy individuals (like Sampson) and that God alone can call a "holy war." In such cases we must search for the parallels or "implications" for us today.

The third stage entails a search for parallel situations in the current life of the congregation. The original situation behind the text (step one) led the sacred writer to employ certain theological principles (step two) to solve a certain problem or address a certain aspect in the life of the original readers. Now the interpreter tries to elucidate similar aspects in modern life to which the underlying biblical principle might also apply. This entails what Perry calls a "life-situation" analysis of the congregation's needs (1973:104-25). The preacher in a very real sense must become a sociologist analyzing the social and ethical needs of the flock before applying the text to meet those needs. In some ways it is as important to analyze the congregation's needs accurately as it is to exegete the text correctly. If one spends a great deal of time expounding the text's original meaning but applies it such that few lives are touched, or the wrong conduct results, the sermon has still failed to accomplish its God-given purpose.

One current theory that fails to accomplish this is found in some large churches. So-called super-pastors at times believe that their major calling is to feed their flock and so spend all their time in the study preparing their message(s), leaving the day-by-day ministry to their staff. The problem is they never get to know their flock, its needs and interests. At best they receive it secondhand from the staff or board. As a result they preach to modern America as a whole, often with a radio or television ministry. However, the specific needs of the congregation remain untouched—at least in the pastor's pulpit ministry. Pastors and missionaries must know their flock and take time to discover their specific situation in life. This will lead to a sermon style that eschews technical jargon as well as generalizations. The reason that in-depth preaching sometimes seems dry and uninteresting is not due to the content but to the style of the sermon. A proper contextualization will cause the preacher/teacher to become practical and specific. Application will not be dry or cliché-laden but will zero in on the people's specific needs, suggesting ways to make the text meaningful in the concrete situations encountered in the days following.

Primarily, the application should be specific rather than general. It does little good to say, "Pray more." The congregation already knows that. Center not just on the "what" but on the "why" and the "how." Be concrete, telling the overworked doctor and professional how prayer can help them in their daily struggles.[3] Give the high-school student practical advice as to how to face the unbelievable pressures on the modern teenager, or tell the housewife how to cope with an inattentive husband or rebellious children. In other words, address the individual needs of the congregation via the truths of the text. This can best be done by suggesting specific areas that the text can address and by giving examples at certain points in the message as to how the point can apply to the lawyer or the factory worker. By spreading these throughout the sermon all the various groups can be addressed specifically.

For instance, in expounding on Zephaniah 3:14-17 (see pp. 109-12) the preacher would first note the biblical principle and the situation to which it was directed. Zephaniah was addressing a nation that had become apostate and was no longer worthy to be called Israel. The enemies of Israel (Moab, Edom, Assyria) were assembling on her borders and divine judgment was about to fall. In this tense situation of 3:14-17 the remnant who remained true to God were comforted with respect to the divine love and protection God would extend to them. The parallel in the Western world today would be fairly direct. In the midst of our own apostate nations the believer faces many trials. In some senses these are "judgments" (v. 15) that humankind faces as a result of sin. They do not have to be military as in the surface of the Zephaniah text, for at the principial level trials often have the same function. In the midst of these trying situations believers today can be assured that God will vindicate his people and that his power and love are ever theirs. For instance, schoolteachers with parents or principals on their backs could rest in God's love and protection (see Col 3:3) and the elderly with children who have deserted them can know that God never will do so. The preacher could also contextualize this by asking the congregation to note areas in their lives over the past year in which God "delivered" them from previous trials, confirming that "all things work together for good" (Rom 8:28).

Practical Methods for Applying a Text

It is crucial to apply a text with sensitivity and tact. When we strike at the "cherished sins" of a person (long rationalized), we must pray for a divine wisdom so that the person will know we speak with love and understanding. We should not overly personalize the application, and those who are convicted by the sermon need to feel our compassion. As

Bauman says (1972:245-46), we must appeal to "shared values," to the common interests of the audience (the positive side) rather than to the differences that distinguish, for instance, the "spiritual" from the "carnal" (negative preaching). The latter causes a defensive reaction in the sinner/hearer. Above all, preachers need to share themselves, to be honest in showing how they have handled similar temptations. The audience can identify far more with a "human" person behind the pulpit. I have found personal illustrations to have a far greater impact than "cutesy" stories. This does not mean that we "hang out our dirty linen" in the sermon. We share not just problems but rather the solutions we have discovered as we have faced the problems addressed in the text. This will keep the congregation from concluding that we are "attacking" them and better demonstrate our own "devotional" study of the text we are preaching.

There are three types of application (see Broadus), and it is good to use these as a control list to ensure a variety of techniques in our sermons.

1. Focusing the Claims of the Truth. The modern audience cannot automatically apply biblical truths, for the teachings of Scripture were given in an ancient culture and address problems alien to our culture. Moreover, people today, as in ancient times, do not easily change their patterns of living. Rather, pet faults are rationalized away, and people (including preachers!) must be persuaded to change. Here we must steer a middle ground between Broadus, who says the application should normally be direct; and Bauman, who warns against insulting the audience by spelling out the obvious. The key is to maintain a balance between the direct and the labored. We should apply a text only when there is a need to drive home the point, rejecting the oblique, academic sermon in which the lesson itself is lost but at the same time refusing to belabor the obvious by wordy explanations of what the audience already knows or moralizing mini-sermons that break the flow of thought.

Direct application is a useful tool when used properly. There are several types: (1) Elucidation is a direct remark that states succinctly but precisely what the audience is to do; this is especially useful in evangelistic or parenetic (ethical exhortation) sermons. (2) Inference is an application in which the basic interpretation is itself the significance for today. Broadus (1944:212-13) insists that it must flow from the text and be practical rather than abstract (such as critical issues or philosophical/theological debates). (3) Lessons are more elaborate discussions in which the application is spelled out in detail. This should be done only when the audience analysis points to a particularly important need. (4) Hyperbole or overstatement is a powerful tool for driving home a point (such as Jesus' use of hyperbole in the Sermon on the Mount) but must be used with care, lest the audience take it as a literal application (such as feeling they have to have a prayer life like "Praying Hyde" or faith like George Mueller to be spiritually mature). (5) Interrogation bridges from direct to indirect application, since the rhetorical question demands a response (direct) yet does not specify the exact form that response should take (indirect). The preacher will look at both the message of the text and the needs of the congregation and see where one or another of these methods can best contextualize a particular point.

2. Suggesting Ways and Means. This is Broadus's title (1944:213). It is in essence indirect application and has great value in helping the audience to participate in the process of application. Direct application does not involve the mind but gives the congregation a task to accomplish. Indirect application forces the hearer to decide how to contextualize the point for oneself. Several psychological studies have shown that behavioral changes occur best in a context that induces the audience to participate in the process, to change themselves. While Bauman tends to overstate its importance, it is true that many situations and audiences favor an indirect approach (1972:249-50).

The average preacher or teacher lives in an idealistic world of "what" or "why," simply pointing to the theological principle behind a text and directly addressing the audience with it. However, the average congregation or class lives in a different world, with many obstacles providing a barrier between the realization of need and the achievement of practical change in their lives. Every person needs to discover not only "what" but "how"! The preacher therefore should suggest practical ways by which the individual can discover the application and put it to work in concrete daily situations.

The danger with a preponderance of direct application is the common "delusions of grandeur" fallacy: the preacher/teacher seems to believe he or she is an expert in all fields and can analyze exactly what the flock should do in every circumstance. For instance, preachers often lecture on politics or economics as if they know what politicians should do. This does not mean that ministers should remain uninvolved; they do have a prophetic responsibility to proclaim Christ's message of social concern (this is a major theme of Luke's Gospel). Rather, in doing so a pastor/teacher needs humility, to realize that he or she does not have all the answers. At times they must simply state, "We need to mobilize experts in this area." Churches would do well to sponsor key dialogues and to take action in such things as the ghetto landlord problem or urban injustice. However, they should seek good advice before acting in too precipitate a manner. In the sermon the pastor would highlight the problem and suggest some courses of action but avoid shallow demands. Here a dialogue sermon is helpful; in such a message the audience participates and suggests possible solutions.

There are four types of indirect application (see Bauman 1972:250-51):

a. *Illustrations* actually function as one type of application if they are done well. Literally, *illustrate* means to "throw light" on a topic; therefore, this type of application should explain the underlying principle of the text. A well-chosen illustration is one of the best methods because it attracts attention, arouses the emotions and often gives relief in an intense sermon by introducing a bit of humor and interest into an otherwise serious discussion. Moreover, an illustration will help the audience retain the point far longer. Stott shows that illustrations have played a central role throughout the history of preaching (1982:237-39). From the biblical use of metaphors to Jesus' parables, Scripture itself teems with examples. The Dominican friars in the Middle Ages even developed an "exempla" or collection of illustrations similar to the modern "treasury of sermon illustrations." The problem in the Middle Ages (as occasionally today) was that the "exempla" became ends in themselves and were used to "prove" erroneous theology. Therefore, the Reformers eschewed them and stressed preaching from the Bible. The Puritans returned to a rich use of imagery (such as Bunyan's *Pilgrim's Progress)* and illustrations have formed an essential part of the sermonic presentation ever since.

On the positive side, the illustration should match the point made by the text. If the illustration is chosen well, the audience will be moved to accept the argument. As Robinson states, "Logically, of course, examples cannot stand as proof, but psychologically they work with argument to gain acceptance. . . . The analogy wins as much agreement as the reasoned argument" (1980:149-50). Since they are experiential and closer to life they show a congregation how the truth can be practically useful in addressing current problems. When drawn from life situations they are especially relevant. For this reason it is best to make the illustration as close to the daily life of the congregation as possible.

Buttrick lists three criteria for judging an illustration: it must be analogous to the point made in the sermon (text); the shape of the illustration should match the structure of the content; and the illustration should be "appropriate" to the sermon content (1987:133-36). Furthermore, there should not be more than one illustration per point. Multiple examples will weaken the power of the point, for they will draw attention to the metaphor rather than to the message. The choice of illustration is critical, for it will center on the modern relevance of the point made. Finally, the illustration should be concise. A lengthy anecdote draws attention to itself and overwhelms the biblical point.

There are several sources for such illustrations. The most popular, of course, is the pastor's file of stories culled from *Reader's Digest,* the newspaper and so forth. While I use the former, I prefer two other sources that provoke greater interest. First, I like personal illustrations drawn from my own experiences. When I share my own struggles, the audience identifies me as a human being with the same problems they have. Two caveats are necessary on this topic: I must not just share my problems but must show how God has led me to answers. If the congregation sees only my struggles, they will lose respect for my authority. On the other hand, I must avoid the opposite extreme, painting myself almost as a saint who always comes out the hero. When the two sides are balanced—problems and solutions—the illustration will have power because I have proven the point in my own life.

A corollary of this is the illustration drawn from everyday life. The whole world surrounding you is a treasure-house of metaphors, examples and illustrations. The purpose of an illustration is to awaken the senses of the audience so they can feel the point of the text in a fresh, evocative way. You are building a word picture in their minds, turning their senses into a rich canvas onto which you are painting a portrait of the biblical truth involved. Therefore, you must be creative, spontaneous and colorful as you draw them into your illustration. For instance, when preaching on Yahweh the "victorious warrior" who "loves" his people (Zeph 3:17; see pp. 111-12) you can use the imagery of the military hero who returns victorious to claim his bride. As you paint the picture of the joy, beauty and pageantry of such a wedding (with the parallel of Israel and the church as a bride) the audience will listen!

The second source comes from historical research into the meaning of the text. The background behind a word or passage not only opens up its meaning but also provides some of the most interesting illustrations. I used to be afraid to teach Hebrews 8—10 because of its heavy dependence on Jewish ritual. However, I have discovered that people are fascinated by the explanation of the Old Testament background to Hebrews and become very interested in its message. The very explanation is a first step toward contextualization, for the hearer can see how the writer addressed the ancient situation and then can better identify parallels in modern life. Moreover, word studies often provide very interesting background material. I remember one sermon when I explained the military background behind the word *equip* in Ephesians 4:12. When I described the pastor-teacher (v. 11) as a "drill instructor" the audience's interest was immediately evident. Weeks later some still mentioned it. The background of a passage or term opens up the richness of its meaning and is an illustration in itself.

At the same time there are several cautions to note regarding possible misuses of illustrations. The first is the corollary of the discussion above: the illustration must fit the point of the text. The proverbial story of the speaker who used the same cute example in ten different sermons is tragically all too often the case. If the story does not center on the point of the passage it will detract from the power of the text and confuse the congregation. Second, the illustration must point to the message and not become an end in itself. If the story or example is too elaborate and lengthy, the audience will forget the point of the message and get caught up in the drama or humor of the narration. The result will be entertainment rather than conviction. As W. E. Sangster has said, illustrations are not to be "like pretty drawingroom lamps, calling attention to themselves" but rather "like street lamps, scarcely noticed, but throwing floods of light upon the road" (Stott 1982:241). The story or analogy must draw attention to the point of the text and not just to itself.

Illustrations also should be clear and easily understood. One should not have to belabor the explanation or exegete the illustration. If a story does not convey its point easily, it should not be used. It must be simple and yet interesting. We should not expand peripheral details or add unnecessary characters. Robinson calls for a dramatic simplicity: "A skillful storyteller cuts away surplus details that fail to contribute to the punch line of his story. . . . The story should be told as dramatically as possible so that the audience enters into the illustration and feels, as well as understands, the point being made."[4]

Moreover, the preacher must be honest when using illustrations. Many present fictional accounts as if they actually happened to them. In any ethical sense this is a lie, and many is the pastor whose reputation has been hurt when people discovered the stories he or she used had not really occurred. The sad thing is that the point would be just as relevant if the pastor presented it as a fictional story. On a related matter, pastors should not use personal illustrations involving family or friends unless they has received permission to do so. This should be done whether or not the person is named; great harm has been done when people realized suddenly that their experiences or problems were being used publicly to make a point.

b. *Multiple choice* can help a congregation realize possible applications of a point. The options are listed, and the congregation is asked to choose the best one. This can be used two ways: all but one can be negative or even humorous, used to point to the proper choice; or all can be relevant and the audience encouraged to note the one that best applies to their individual situations. The value of this type of application is that it treats the congregation as mature adults who can see the relevance of the text and make their own decisions. The difficulty is that unless the preacher works with skill the point can be unclear and the people confused. If multiple choice is used properly, the audience is subtly taught how to find their own sources of information. Indirect guidance is often superior to direct lecture. If used improperly, however, this tool can lead to confusion. I had a professor who would always list options and never give answers. Two kinds of students resulted: scholars who knew how to find answers on their own and agnostics who were never certain that there were answers! The preacher/teacher must guide the hearers to the answers and not leave them without tools for discovering those answers.

c. *Narration* is used most often in biographical sermons but can refer to an extended illustration in a message that calls for such. All the points made about illustrations apply to this except the demand for brevity and simplicity. The preacher in a sense is either retelling a biblical story or centering on a personal (or historical) event. The story must be told in dramatic fashion with extensive background material. For instance, parables or biblical stories can be expanded and explained in terms of their original meanings. For biblical stories this can be invaluable, for it immerses the congregation in the original setting of the text and helps them both to understand and to relive it. This enables them to discover parallels in their own lives with much greater facility.

Extended narration of personal anecdotes or current stories is much more difficult. As stated above in the discussion of illustrations, a lengthy story can detract from the power of the biblical message and can prove to be entertaining rather than motivational. In some instances, however, a lengthy story on a difficult point may be useful. For instance, if the point is particularly challenging or controversial, an extended story will help the audience understand and accept the argument. Nevertheless, if the lengthy illustration is to maintain its persuasive power, one must hold peripheral details to a minimum and include only those aspects which move the hearer to respond.

3. Persuasion and Motivation. While secular hermeneutics concludes with the impartation of meaning and significance, biblical hermeneutics is not finished until the hearer is persuaded of the relevance and truthfulness of the message and motivated to act accordingly. Actually, three separate steps build on the meaning of the text. The audience is told how to apply the message to their lives, persuaded with respect to its importance and motivated to change their lives accordingly—that is, to put the points into practice. Many preachers simply assume that people will be persuaded when the truth is placed in front of them. However, this ignores the ability of human nature to rationalize away the truth.

Persuasion dare not be attempted too quickly or too directly. It cannot be accomplished in a moment, and it is a common error of preachers to expect instant acquiescence to their arguments. It takes time and patience to help people alter the direction of their lives. Most of all, preachers/teachers dare not attempt persuasion in their own strength; they must realize that the Holy Spirit is the only one who can change lives. Therefore, persuasion and motivation have both a passive and an active aspect. Passively, Christian leaders depend on the Spirit and must spend much time in prayer seeking divine guidance and empowering for the message. Actively they seek wisdom to choose the proper techniques that will provide a channel for the Spirit to do his work.

The key is to persuade through the dynamic of the text itself. The pastor should lead people to agreement slowly, showing empathy for the difficulty experienced by many as they confront an area of their life that needs to be changed. In critical areas, such as doctrinal error or moral/ethical issues, the preacher will institute change over a period of time, perhaps through a series of messages. I prefer a "dialogue sermon" in which I lead them through a text and discuss with the congregation its meaning and implications when dealing with issues like materialism or abortion. The answers thereby come from them as they are led to the truth. This enables the pastor to show the congregation the value of the message and help them see the truth rather than just to confront the people with that point. It is a positive rather than a negative approach.

Motivation involves an appeal to the will or emotions, showing how the truth can fulfill the audience's basic needs or desires. On this topic I must begin with an important caveat: biblical ethics demands that the pastor be cautious, for unscrupulous preachers have bilked many people out of money or led them astray by misusing this aspect. Motivation research has demonstrated that a strong appeal to basic desires literally can force people to do anything. The television industry is the best example: by creating advertisements that appeal to basic drives they have proven that people can be led to buy virtually anything. When the pastor uses these (potentially dangerous) techniques, the motivation must be balanced and based on the actual meaning of the text.

Emotional appeals must be made carefully; many prefer logical argumentation because of the misuse of emotional appeals in some circles. However, we must remember that our Lord and Paul often utilized emotional arguments (see Sunukjian 1982:292-97). The key lies in the use of emotive, well-chosen language that leads the people to react. Most important, the appeal must be carefully tied to the truth content and never go beyond it. We must contextualize the passage properly before motivating the hearers to action. Speak positively and glowingly about the results that accrue from such action, but be certain that the results are both true and biblically based, derived from the text rather than from subjective experiences that may or may not be correct. Hyperbole is a common error when motivating an audience, for the stronger the argument the better the results. However, in such cases the speaker can replace content with emotion and is in danger of destroying the eternal truth in favor of temporary results.

Conclusion

A misconception has existed for some time that hermeneutics or the rules of interpretation begin and end with the "meaning" of the text. It is doubtful that Scripture itself would agree with this, for there is no hint there that a mere intellectual grasp of divine precepts is sufficient. Rather, one must be a doer and not merely a hearer (Jas 1:19-27). Application, therefore, is crucial to the task of biblical interpretation and must be as exacting as the process of determining the meaning. Contextualization refers to the attempt to translate the religious principles of Scripture for the different "contexts" or cultural heritages of our own day. We must make Scripture relevant for our time and understandable in cultures alien to the time of the Bible. Therefore, we must make a careful distinction between form and content, making certain that the latter remains the focus of our proclamation, unless the form itself is indispensable to its meaning (such as baptism or the eucharist).

The hermeneutical task has three levels: meaning—considering the intended message of the text; interpretation—asking to what extent its message is determinative for our own day; and contextualization—seeking the form that will best communicate that normative message and lead to concrete application to people's daily lives. At each level, however, we must stress and remain fully cognizant of both our complete dependence on the Holy Spirit and our human tendency to insert ourselves into the process of understanding/ theory and action/praxis that constitutes the task of interpretation.[5]

The following points will serve to conclude not only this chapter but the whole book proper.

1. Level I: Meaning/Interpretation.

a. Look at the *whole*. This is done on two levels. First, we chart the book itself, noting the ebb and flow of its thought-development. Second, we determine its biblical theology, that is, the major emphases the author seeks to stress. Through this the pastor/teacher develops both understanding of the whole message of the book/paragraph and a preliminary thesis statement.

b. Look at the *genre*. We must determine the genre or type of literature before interpretation can begin. The pastor will preach apocalyptic quite differently than poetry or narrative. As we know from chapters six through twelve, we must study and proclaim each biblical genre differently, according to its own purposes and rules, lest we proclaim a message alien to the divine intention in the text.

c. Look at the *grammar, semantics and syntax*. When we move from the whole to the parts, it is important to see how individual statements fit together, to note the major and minor clauses and to study the interrelationships of the units of thought. We must look at the whole statement and ask the author's intended meaning in the context before applying it to our context. Above all, we dare not declare our belief in an inspired, inerrant Scripture when by our treatment of the text we demonstrate a lack of concern for the inspired meaning. God couched his revelation within human language, and any study of linguistics demands that we note the relation of each word to its context. Word study must be wed with grammar and syntax to allow the divinely inspired message to shine through the text.

d. Look at the *historical/cultural background*. We need to understand the passage and book within their historical context as well. It is amazing how much more meaningful the Bible becomes when viewed in this light. Moreover, this often highlights a contextualizing situation in the history of Israel or the early church and provides a helpful step in leading the congregation to note the significance of the passage for their own lives. Finally, this aspect can lead us to highly meaningful illustrations as we recreate the "world" behind the text and draw parallels with our own world.

e. Look at the *analogia scriptura*. While the above steps recognize the diversity of Scripture, here we consider the unity of the Bible, asking what parallel passages help to clarify the true point of the text. Primarily, we need to realize that individual statements must be understood within the broader context of Scripture as a whole. We tend to overly dogmatize single passages when the author was only stressing one aspect of the larger truth for the sake of the problem he was addressing. We must consider several levels: the passage, the theology of the writer and the theology of Scripture as a whole. Each must be applied before we can understand the exact meaning of the passage.

f. Look at the interpretation of the passage throughout *church history*. Many modern errors of interpretation could be avoided if we were aware of similar mistakes in the past. On individual passages the better commentaries will often list the possible interpretations, and this can be of great benefit, lest we force a reading on a passage that does not really best fit the context. Moreover, the history of dogma also supplies the pastor with excellent examples of contextualization to use in the sermon.

2. Level II: Interpretation/Relevance. At this stage we determine the extent to which a passage is normative for all times or applies an underlying eternal command to a specific cultural situation. We all recognize that portions of Scripture are not meant to be followed today, such as historical narrative or purely cultural commands. That Paul made urban evangelism his approach at Ephesus (Acts 18—19) does not mean that the village evangelism of our time is wrong. Nor do we have to "greet one another with a holy kiss" (Rom 16:16 and others). However, we must evangelize and greet one another in love. Therefore, before we can contextualize a passage we must determine the extent to which it is meant for our day.

a. Note when the argument is anchored in *prior revelation*. If a statement is grounded in the Old Testament proof-text or a saying of Jesus or a canonical creed (such as 1 Cor 15:3-5), it may demonstrate that the author is not merely dealing with a current cultural situation but rather in the revealed, eternal counsel of God.

b. Determine the *circumstances* and the *underlying theological/ethical principle*. We must always search for the theology behind the statement as well as the historical situation that occasioned the emphasis. If the principle is prescriptive rather than descriptive, it will more likely be normative. Also, we must determine the distance between that underlying principle and the explicit statement in the text. If there is distance it will perhaps support a cultural application, and we will apply the passage at the principial level (deep theological structure) rather than at the surface level (see also points c-e below).

c. Determine whether the teaching transcends the *cultural biases* of the age. If it does transcend those norms of society, it will provide a clear signpost for the supracultural relevance of the command. If it does not, we must consider the other principles, for we may then need to contextualize it within the new situation.

d. Determine whether a teaching is primarily *cultural or theological/moral* in essence. If the former, it is usually applied at the principle level, such as those concerning slaves and their master (labor-management) or the holy kiss (Christian greeting). If the latter, it is supracultural and therefore normative for all ages and cultures.

e. Recognize that the *supracultural content of Scripture is eternal/universal* and cannot be altered, while cultural forms may be changed depending on the context. This of course provides a transition to the final section. The major point is that our decision regarding eternal norms is binding on all cultures. Pragmatic considerations should not be allowed to overrule biblical demands. At the same time, however, if we decide that the command is cultural, it is still binding in subcultures (such as many fundamentalist and evangelical groups) that are similar to the first century in this area.

3. Level III: Contextualization/Application. The purpose of contextualization/application is to make clear and readily available to persons in any culture the good news of God's love in Jesus Christ and the abundant life he provides. Further, the Bible demands that we challenge all persons and societies with the supracultural norms of Scripture.

a. Add to our exegesis of the Word an *exegesis of our world*. Before we can properly apply any biblical statement to our culture or another, we must seek a deeper understanding of the specific cultural environment. This is just as true of our society as it is of one overseas. Many pastors have lost touch with the professional, the factory worker and others. In another culture it is even more crucial and should involve both library research and participant observation. Busy pastors, too, need to function as a sociologist, constantly doing the type of life-situation study that will enable them to meet the needs of their congregation.

b. Allow the *Word to encounter the world*. At times this will involve a positive confirmation of the world and at other times a negative confrontation with it. Missionaries and pastors should seek redemptive analogies that will allow them to make the Word relevant and understandable within the given culture. Of course, this process may also have to distinguish cultural form from content, accepting the content but replacing the form in a culture that would not understand it. This positive or negative pull will be determined by a trialogue between text, interpreter/contextualizer and recipient culture. The Word first addresses the interpreter who must internalize it before seeking to apply it to the culture. The interpreter becomes contextualizer when he or she participates both in the Word and in the world. In this process the Word challenges then transforms first the interpreter and then the receptor culture.

c. Take account of the scriptural teaching regarding the *eschatological end of this age*. Jesus taught that the kingdom "has come" in his first advent and that we are now living in a state of tension between this age and the age to come. Jesus has bound Satan by the Incarnation and the cross (Mk 3:27), yet Satan is still the god or prince of this age (2 Cor 4:4; Eph 2:2). We now exist in the heavenlies (Eph 1:3 and others) where Satan operates (Eph 3:10; 6:10-12) and must manifest Jesus' victory in our lives. Many issues facing the church are of a global, even apocalyptic, nature. The church ignores these at her peril. We must avoid irrelevant or even deceitful speaking on these issues (such as social injustice, arms escalation and so forth) yet at the same time maintain a balance between evangelism (which is primary) and social concern (which in the end should not be radically separated from it).

d. Note the *priority of authority.* Too often preachers' and teachers' interpretations and even their applications are given an *ex cathedra* authority. We need to remember that only the inspired text is inerrant. Our interpretation is dependent on the Spirit's illumination and its authority depends on the amount of effort we put into studying the passage. Our finite understanding and human perspective too easily control our interpretation. Therefore, our delineation of a passage's message carries authority only to the extent that it conforms to its intended meaning. The contextualization is even further removed and is also dependent on the Spirit's illumination and is still another step removed from the text, since it depends on the interpretation and our own decision as to the text's normative content and applicability to the receptor culture. Therefore, our task in contextualization is to shape our response to the results of levels one and two.

e. Finally, realize the *necessity of praxis.* Proper contextualization recognizes that right understanding ideally results in right practice. The Bible seeks not just correct thinking or understanding but more the correct action that results. The same Hebrew and Greek words mean both "hear" and "obey." Therefore, changed lives are the intended results of the enculturation of the Word.

4. Level IV: Preparing the Sermon.

a. Rework the *outline.* The Bible study outline that resulted from the exegesis is presented in descriptive language and simply summarizes the meaning of the parts of the passage. In the sermon these points will be reworked in dynamic language in order to challenge the hearer to respond to the point.

b. Decide how to *contextualize the points.* The pastor or missionary will work through the sermon points on the basis of a life-situation analysis of the audience. Certain aspects will be emphasized to meet those needs and the pastor or teacher will then decide what type of contextualization (such as illustration, suggesting ways and means, direct confrontation of issues) will best serve the purpose at each point of the passage.

c. Work on *packaging the sermon.* The preacher must remove pedantic language and seek a smoothly flowing sermon. The wording should be worked carefully to maintain interest and grip the hearts of the hearers. The speaker will want to plan carefully the proper rhetorical techniques for the various parts of the sermon. The Holy Spirit is the one who actually persuades and motivates the listener, but the speaker must utilize methods that will form a channel rather than a barrier for the Spirit's work.

In conclusion, one cannot "rightly divide the Word" (2 Tim 2:15) until it has been interpreted and contextualized so that the same voice of God speaks today as spoke in biblical times. Of course, God is strong and wise enough to speak through erroneous interpretations. However, at the same time it is incumbent on each of us to speak with as clear a voice as possible, to seek to say, "God worked in my ministry because of (and not 'in spite of') the interpretation and contextualization that I was led to present today." Paul states, "How beautiful are the feet of those who bring good news" (Rom 10:16, from Isaiah 52:7). There is no greater privilege than to be the proclaimer of divine truth within the desperate situation of our world today. May we be careful to make certain (through the leading of the Holy Spirit and our own hard work) that it is indeed God's voice speaking through us as we contextualize his Word for our world.

Excursus on Preparing the Sermon

In many ways a detailed study of the sermonic process goes beyond the subject of this book. However, several aspects touch on the hermeneutical spiral from text to context and are helpful in communicating the significance of the passage.

1. Develop a Thesis (Propositional) Statement. After concluding the exegesis of the passage, the pastor/teacher should summarize the message as a whole and determine the single point the writer has been trying to develop. This is easiest when one preaches by paragraphs (using a paragraph Bible like the New International Version), for often a message changes themes slightly from one paragraph to another. The purpose is to center on the message as a whole rather than the isolated parts. Homileticians continually castigate biblical scholars for developing so many points in a message that the congregation is confused as to what areas they should develop in their lives. Moreover, the biblical writers saw their message as a single whole rather than as a series of disjointed parts. Therefore, we are true to Scripture only if we develop the "big idea" (Robinson's term) that the author intended. The details of the text or main points of the sermon will actually develop aspects of this thesis statement. Each main point will be one part of the larger whole, much like pieces of a pie (see figure 16.1).

2. Outline the Sermon. This is the third step in determining the structural development of the passage. In the basic survey of the context (chap. one above) the Bible student does a preliminary outline and in the detailed exegesis reworks that to its final form. In preparing the sermon the pastor takes that final outline and contextualizes each main point to speak dynamically to the congregation. Some (such as Adams, *Pulpit Speech)* have said that the sermon outline stems from the congregation's needs and not necessarily from the outline of the text. In other words, a sermon on prayer from Ephesians 3:14-21 (see chap. four) might have only two points, one on "strength" and the other on "love" if that were the perceived need of the hearers. The pastor would omit the other points and save them for another time. However, I find that problematic and unnecessary. It is problematic because the busy pastor could easily skew the meaning of the passage and thus of the words *strength* and *love* by ignoring the context from which they come. Adams is not saying that one should neglect exegesis, but on the pragmatic level this would occur. Further, such a method is unnecessary because the pastor could do the same thing by following the *text's* outline and contextualizing specifically at those points. The outline of the text must provide a control on the common tendency to analyze a text subjectively (from the congregation's needs) rather than objectively (from the author's meaning).

The technical exegetical outline is rephrased to communicate the dynamic message of the text. The goal is to speak the original message to the needs of our day. Therefore, it is a conscious contextualization of the text. For instance, the three points of Ephesians 3:16-19 could be reworked:

I. Petition God for Power (3:16-17a)

II. Petition God for Insight (3:17b-19a)

III. Petition God for Fullness (3:19b)

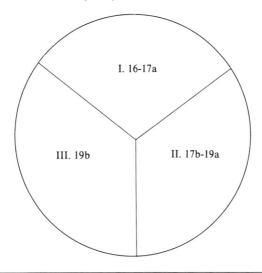

Fig. 16.1. The Pieces of a Sermon on Ephesians 3:16-19.

Alliteration has been much maligned of late, due to misuse on the part of many. We need to remember, however, that it is a technique used often in Scripture. For instance, Psalm 119 is an acrostic on the Hebrew alphabet, and Matthew organized his material in groups of threes, fives and sevens. So long as one does not skew the meaning of the passage, alliteration can be a valuable device for helping a congregation remember the points. One should not use this method constantly, however, lest the congregation tire of it. Variety is the primary goal. If one were to use alliteration on the Ephesian passage, the three "petitions" could be for power, perception and perfection (the latter is the title for v. 19b in Markus Barth's Ephesians commentary). Most important, the titles for the major sections should share two characteristics: (1) they should constitute parts of the thesis statement (see above); (2) they should ask the audience to participate in the application of the text to their own lives.

Let us employ Zephaniah 3:14-17 (see chap. four) as a further example. Developing the Bible study outline of the passage gives us the following:

I. We can respond joyfully to trials (3:14-15)

II. We can confess our hope in the midst of trials (3:16-17)

In this passage I have presented it as possibility rather than command because I want the hearers to respond with anticipation rather than with guilt, positively rather than negatively.

Liefeld mentions three functions of a good sermon outline: (1) it groups the data in order to facilitate comprehension; (2) it focuses attention on those parts which the text (or preacher) wants to emphasize; (3) it moves the sermon along toward its goal

(1984:115). I would add a fourth: it challenges the congregation to implement the major point(s) in their lives. An outline is like a good lawyer who not only assembles the facts but does so in such a way that the jury (the congregation) is moved to respond to the truths of the message. It establishes rapport and helps the audience desire to attain the goals presented in the message.

3. Rework the Body of the Sermon.   This must be done in keeping with the life-situation analysis of the congregation and the propositional statement. Choose those aspects of the message you wish to highlight and apply, then work carefully through the proper contextualization of those parts. With a proper balance between explanation, persuasion and motivation, the preacher will develop a message that immerses the congregation in the ancient situation and message and then in its relevance for their own lives.

Transition statements between points of the text are crucial, for they are the mortar that binds together the idea-blocks of the edifice of the sermon. Transitions should be natural, leading the congregation from one point to another and enabling the listeners to see the relationship and progression between the ideas. There are three elements here: the concise summary of the previous section ("We have seen how Jesus taught that God's forgiveness is conditional on our willingness to forgive"), a transitional phrase ("and now we will turn to the Epistles") and the introduction of the next point ("in order to see what they say about forgiveness"). The key is brevity and simplicity, making certain that the audience understands the development of the message.

Another critical element is sermonic flow. The preacher must remove all pedantic, unnecessary parts and rework the points so that the audience's interest will be maintained. The goal is to transmit not merely information about the text but the spiritual power of the text. Each element must flow into the next and details should be paired down so that the hearers are not bored by needless data that adds little or nothing to the real message of the text.

4. Prepare the Introduction and Conclusion.   These are the last elements of the sermon proper to be developed. One needs to know exactly what the passage teaches and how it should be developed for the congregation before deciding how to introduce and conclude the passage. Both aspects are tailored to fit the propositional statement. The introduction is written to catch the interest of the congregation and prepare them for the sermon proper. It should be about 10 per cent of the message and consists of three parts: (1) an interesting anecdote that will both capture the imagination of the listeners and lead into the propositional statement; (2) the propositional statement itself; and (3) a brief note of the context that situates the message in the larger framework of the biblical author's developing message, connects it with previous sermons in the expository series and leads naturally into the main points of the body of the message. This will help the audience note the larger context within which the passage occurs and will function in a sermon the same way a book chart (see chap. one) works in Bible study.

The conclusion ties together the points of the sermon and its contextualization, motivating the congregation to live out those points concretely in the days following. It should also be concise (no more than 10 per cent of the sermon) with well-phrased sentences built around a personal appeal that contextualizes the propositional statement. The goals are to sum up the message, drive home the main point and motivate the audience to act on it. The listeners should feel that the conclusion is addressed to them personally, and so it should be phrased in positive terms, centering on action (what to do) rather than guilt (what to avoid). Finally, the conclusion must be forceful, direct and urgent, demanding immediate response and giving the audience something to act on immediately (if they can put it off they will forget the point). I prefer concrete suggestions rather than generalities. Give them a "homework assignment" that asks them to put the sermon to work in specific ways in the days to follow. For instance, one could concretize the message above on Zephaniah 3:14-17 by asking each hearer to list three trials that he or she is experiencing currently and then to note specific ways in which God confirms his love (v. 17) to them in the midst of each trial during the coming week.

Excursus on Style

1. Story Preaching. The tendency in current homiletic theory is to reject the propositional form of preaching espoused in this section in behalf of "story preaching," an "event" approach that narrates a plot or tells a story rather than presents in didactic fashion a series of theological assertions. The problem of traditional preaching, it is argued, is its basis in Aristotelian rhetoric, which has controlled Western logic and communication from the start. As a result, preaching has always tended to be didactic, trying to convince the congregation of the truth of the propositional points made in the message. However, the homiletical version of reader-response criticism (pp. 377-80) argues that the Bible consists not of propositional assertions but of religious metaphors. As Buttrick says, "Revelation is associated with the symbols through which we interpret life. Thus preaching, as it forms faith-consciousness, is a means of God's self-disclosure and saving grace now" (1987:115-16). For story theology, preaching is not assertive but suggestive, not propositional but symbolic. Metaphor and self-awareness are the names of the game. Proclamation has given way to sharing, and truth-orientation has been replaced by life-centeredness. It is not so much content as shared experience that characterizes story preaching.

Steimle states that there are three "stories" in preaching (1980:41-42): the biblical story (the basis), the preacher's own story (the example) and the congregation's story (the occasion for the sermon). The "authority" of the sermon is derived from the extent to which it touches on and interweaves these three elements. According to Steimle, the "story sermon" must be "secular" from start to finish, addressing the needs of people today in the same way that biblical writers chose their redemptive metaphors (for example, "redemption" was derived from the slave market) from the secular world (pp. 165-67). For him the "timeless sermon," which is just as relevant today as it was a century ago, is not a good sermon, for it does not touch lives. A truly "biblical" sermon establishes a dialogue with the daily needs of the hearers, and the best way to do this is to structure the sermon around a plot or story that draws the audience into the suspense and life-relatedness of its message.

We can commend much in the emphasis on life-oriented metaphors and relevance. However, it ignores the fact that the Bible is indeed theological and propositional at the core (see appendix two). Moreover, redaction criticism has shown that behind even biblical narrative is a theological core. Proposition and metaphor are not opposed to one another. Narrative preaching has an important place in the preacher's arsenal, but it is a supplement to and not a replacement for the more didactic form. I agree with Greidanus that the text and subject matter should dictate sermon form (1988:148, 154). The textual form should be reflected in the sermon form. Moreover, relevance and relatedness can result from a judicious use of application and illustration in a didactic sermon as well as from a story sermon. However, authority is found not in the relevance of the contextualization but in the centrality of the revealed Word of God in the message. In one sense the three "story" elements (text, preacher, audience) is an excellent summary of the hermeneutical enterprise as developed in this book. In another sense, when it depends on a symbolic rather than a propositional approach to theology and the sermon, it turns the Word into word and Christian truth into relativism. We must adopt the "story" form only in two instances: when preaching biblical narrative, in which case it is the best way to preach the material; and as a method for applying and illustrating the point of the text.

2. The Style of Presentation.   A Bible study and a sermon differ markedly in presentation. The former is didactic while the latter is rhetorical and dynamic. Style in a Bible study maintains interest via dialogue as the original message is taught while sermonic style involves and grips the audience in more dynamic fashion. Style is the instrument by which the sermon becomes memorable. The great preaching stylists (such as Edwards, Barnhouse, Swindoll) have all worked as hard on presentation as they have on exegesis. Unfortunately, in many circles style has replaced content. Many spend far more time on packaging than on determining the truth content. The reason is obvious: poor content with good style will satisfy many, while good content with poor style will satisfy few. Yet style must always remain a supplement to the message of the text rather than an end in itself.

Preachers should develop their own style. By definition "style" denotes that which characterizes a person. It is unnecessary and wrong to copy the great rhetoricians of our day like Billy Graham or Haddon Robinson. All preachers and teachers must find their own manner of expression. It seldom comes easily; no great writer or speaker has ever failed to struggle in developing an individual style. The best way is to notice how you speak in formal situations, to discover what comes naturally. Building on this, work on vocabulary and experiment with various combinations of phrases. Rework sentences until they have that "ring" which feels comfortable. Roget's *Thesaurus* will help one find the correct words and avoid redundancy.

There are several qualities to seek in a good style.

a. *Clarity* enables the audience to understand the message easily. A common mistake of young seminary graduates is phrasing a sermon or lecture in language familiar to them (usually the technical language of the classroom) but unknown to their hearers. Actually, clarity is difficult to achieve, for most conceive of "style" as denoting flowery language and thus they sacrifice meaning for rhetoric. Bauman argues for precision and economy, the ability to find the exact expression and avoid "fuzzy" expressions like "fast travel" or "expensive meal" (1972:161-62). To do this well the speaker must work hard at developing a good vocabulary and learning how to use it.

b. *Energy and forcefulness* demonstrate enthusiasm. The audience will feel that the pastor is convinced of the importance of the message and will be more easily persuaded themselves. We cannot overstate the danger of a dry, uninteresting presentation. Speakers must make their hearers feel the excitement of the message if they are to catch their interest. Of course animate, passionate expression comes only when the speaker is fascinated with the message. Once more the devotional approach must be the starting point. We must study the message first for ourselves; after it has spoken to us, we can feel personally the value of the message and can communicate an aura of excitement. When the passion of the text is felt by the audience, they too will conclude that the truth is crucial for them.

c. *Vivid language* (Adams calls it "sense appeal" or utilizing "evocative language")[6] causes interest and paints word pictures in the minds of the hearers. Jesus constantly used rich metaphors. In our television generation people expect imagery and seldom develop interest without it. A television executive recently defended the industry's preoccupation with visual over content-oriented news: "A good story with poor pictures will always fail; a poor story with good pictures will never fail." The speaker must avoid overused, common expressions (dead metaphors) such as "sleeping like a log" and seek fresh images—for instance, "his repose seemed as peaceful as the slumbering oak, swaying gently in the breeze." Rhythm or alliteration can also be helpful, so long as it is not strained. An overly worked phrase can ruin a statement, but good metaphors will draw attention to the truth content.

d. *Fluency and elegance* add an air of poetry to good prose. It would be well for a speaker to write a manuscript sermon once in a while (many do nothing else!) to work on this. I do not wish to eschew simplicity (see the first point above); a well-written sentence will find that subtle balance between precision and elegance. The two are not mutually exclusive. Consider Albert Schweitzer's marvelous prose as he denied the validity of the "old quest for the historical Jesus" school:

> Formerly it was possible to book through-tickets at the supplementary-psychological-knowledge office which enabled those travelling in the interests of Life-of-Jesus construction to use express trains, thus avoiding the inconvenience of having to stop at every little station, change, and run the risk of missing their connexion. This ticket office is now closed. There is a station at the end of each section of the narrative, and connexions are not guaranteed. (1948:330-31)

We would do well to study great writers and expositors of the past, to see how they phrased their ideas. Also we should learn to think in terms of impressions, to seek that which will reach both the eyes and ears of our listeners. Paint pictures that will capture the imagination and help motivate the congregation in the direction of the sermonic goal.

3. Rhetoric and Delivery. One cannot easily summarize these aspects in a paragraph; the Greeks among others spent generations developing them.[7] However, I must mention several aspects because they are part of that final stage of the hermeneutical process, proclamation.

a. *Posture* can help tremendously when one seeks to project the positive image of one who is relaxed yet enthusiastic and confident. Studies have shown that posture communicates a great deal of information to an audience. If one is too stiff the audience becomes tense; if one is draped over the podium the audience assumes the content will not be strong. A good posture is an effective communicator.

b. *Tonal inflection and variety of pitch* sustains an audience's interest. Effective use of pauses will point to a particular emphasis. One should be animate in vocal tone as well as in gestures. A monotone or too-rapid delivery will cause the listener's attention to wander. I have often struggled with speed of delivery. Once after a sermon a woman asked in amazement, "Did you ever take a breath?" Since that time I have worked at pauses and rate of delivery but still do poorly at pacing my sermons. Most people cannot handle an unremitting flow of rhetoric. The rhythm or flow of speech is an important aid to the speaker. One should note the syllables to accent and keep the pace even through each sentence, not trailing off at the end of sentences.

c. *Gestures* should be direct and emphatic, well paced and moderate. Those which are overly dramatic will impress in the wrong way, detracting from the message and drawing attention to the speaker rather than to the text. Perry states that good gestures grow out of the speech (are natural) rather than are tacked onto the speech: it is important to seek both variety and precision, so that the hearers gain the impression of an earnest, relaxed and sensitive speaker (1973:186-87).

d. *Eye contact and facial expression* should also be direct and appropriate to the mood of the point. A proper use of these will convince the congregation of the speaker's sincerity and help lead them into the content of the message. In fact the only way to impart one's feeling of excitement for the message is to demonstrate it via pitch, rate, gestures and facial expression. Lack of animation hinders the audience's confidence in the speaker and turns them indifferent toward the message.

These are important supplements to the study of both text (the original meaning) and context (ways to apply the passage to the congregation). However, the external packaging must always be dependent on (rather than productive of) the interpretation of the text. These techniques are instruments for communication and dare never take precedence over the meaning and significance of the text. The average person reacts more to the packaging than to the content, and that makes it all the easier to spend most of one's time on the external aspects. The gifted preacher frequently depends on techniques rather than on the study of the text. Unfortunately, only a few listeners may even notice the difference. All of us must be ever cognizant that we do not just preach *to people;* more important, we preach *for God.* While people may not notice, God always does, and he alone is the final judge! Therefore, these rhetorical tools *must* be kept subservient to the overriding task of determining God's revealed message to his people of all ages and of its significance for this day.

However, I do not mean here that only "expository" sermons can be biblical. In an important recent debate Robinson says, "Topical preaching common in American pulpits flirts with heresy" (1984:804). Lutzer correctly responds that while there is an inherent danger, topical preaching, when done "effectively and with biblical integrity," is a valuable ally to expository preaching (1984:833). Many modern issues can be addressed better topically, such as theological or ethical subjects. The key is to make certain that every passage used in a topical message is preached in accordance with its context and intended meaning. When that is done the topical message is "biblical."

Appendix 1
The Problem of Meaning:
The Issues

OST READERS OF THE BIBLE ASSUME THAT IT IS POSSIBLE TO DISCOVER ITS INTENDED meaning. However, an extensive debate rages today over both the possibility and the importance of a critical examination of Scripture (or any other text) in order in order to ascertain its original message. These challenges have thrown the hermeneutical enterprise into disarray, for they have appeared from every side. Does "hermeneutics" mean principles of interpretation or the act of appropriating a text's "meaning" for one's own situation? What is the meaning of "meaning"? These questions form the topic of this appendix.

The process of discovering the "meaning" of a written utterance has three foci: the author, the text and the reader.

AUTHOR $\longrightarrow$ TEXT $\longleftarrow$ READER

The author "produces" a text while a reader "studies" a text. Yet which of the three is the primary force in determining its meaning? As we will see, the focus has shifted from one to another of these as various theories of meaning have been propounded. Since an author is no longer present to explain the meaning of the text once it is written, is the text "autonomous" from the author? And since the reader provides the grid by which the text is interpreted, what place does the text itself have in the process of understanding? These are valid questions that demand answers.

In 1967 the literary critic Paul de Man spoke of a similar "crisis" in criticism: "Well-established rules and conventions that governed the discipline of criticism and made it a cornerstone of the intellectual establishment have been so badly tampered with that the entire edifice threatens to collapse" (1971:3). In defining this crisis, he spoke of "the incredible swiftness with which conflicting tendencies succeed each other," the extensive appearance of books inaugurating "a new kind of novelle nouvelle critique," and the replacement of philosophy by the social sciences at the helm of literary criticism (pp. 3-4). There is no sign that this incredible productivity is waning, and one is bewildered to discover that by the time news appears regarding a "new" school, someone is already writing that the movement is passé. In these appendices I hope to make sense of the scene and to attempt a possible map for finding our way out of the maze to the kind of "field approach" that J. D. Crossan suggested a few years back when things seemed so much simpler (1977:39-49).

The problem is indeed a serious one. Some have charged proponents of a reader-oriented criticism with undue skepticism, but the difficulties of objective interpretation are far too great for such a charge to be valid. The simple fact is that all of us read a text on the basis of our own background and proclivities. It is not only impossible but dangerous to put our knowledge and theological tradition aside as we study a biblical text. That very knowledge provides categories for understanding the text itself. At the same time, however, these traditions have potential for controlling the text and determining its meaning. This constitutes reader-response interpretation—meaning produced by the reader rather than by the text. As Jeanrond says, texts are not so much objectively understood as they are read anew in each situation, a dynamic process that is often open-ended and produces a new image of reality in the act of reading (1987:11-12).

The point I wish to argue is not whether this is ever the case; any observer has to admit that it is usually so. But I do challenge whether this *must* or even *should* be the case. This is the task of hermeneutics, not only to determine principles for interpretation, but also to delineate the proper goal(s) of interpretation. The thesis of these appendices will support the priority of determining the author's intended meaning as the true core of biblical interpretation.

Hermeneutics originated as a biblical discipline. Yet many fields of study have provided input. Until recent decades, the primary influence was always philosophy. Then with structuralism linguistics came to the fore, and at the present time literary criticism has seemingly assumed the throne. Of course, no single force is behind the hermeneutical enterprise, and each of the above as well as sociology, anthropology, psychology and so forth are important. Jane Tompkins provides a helpful summary of the historical development in literary criticism (1980:ix-xxvi). She describes the evolution of the focal center of interest from text to reader to response, and it is illuminating to discover the parallels between literary critical thinking and biblical hermeneutics. We will trace this basic pattern below.

The Problem of the Reader and the Text

The problem of interpretation begins and ends with the presence of the reader. How does one get back to the perspective and message of an ancient text? The problem is difficult enough when we try to interpret one another in oral communication, for each of us has a slightly different perspective, and we use the same terms but with different content. Often my wife and I will discuss an issue for some time before we realize that we are looking at the problem from quite different vantage points. Only when we align our perspectives do we actually begin to communicate. When we multiply this by 2,000 years of development from biblical times to the current period, the problem becomes almost insurmountable. The tendency is to read modern issues back into the text, and a purely "objective" approach that re-creates the original situation without recourse to the modern preunderstanding is exceedingly difficult, indeed impossible.[1] The act of interpretation itself is done from within a cultural and theological framework. In fact, this framework is both positive and necessary if understanding is to take place. Yet where does that leave the text?

Hans Frei has shown most persuasively that this issue is hardly new to the twentieth century.[2] Biblical scholars throughout history have struggled with the difficulty of literal or text-oriented and nonliteral or cultural/theological approaches to the Bible. Nevertheless, the issue has surfaced in a new way in the last three decades. Frei states that the apologetic cast of hermeneutics has until recently eclipsed a realistic approach to narrative because "the historical-critical method was a powerful antidote to a serious consideration of narrative interpretation in its own right" (1974:141; see 124-54). In short, a true hermeneutics was rendered impossible by an approach that failed to let the text speak for itself. The hermeneutical switch from the text to the individual resulted from a switch of focus from the accessibility of the text (in terms of methodology for interpreting a text) to inquiry into the structure of understanding itself.[3] The focus of interest has thus shifted from the text to the self, and the significance of this shift is still being explored.

1. Author-centered Hermeneutics. Friedrich Schleiermacher (1768—1834) is the father of modern hermeneutics. For him the purpose of interpretation is the reconstruction of the author's original message. Interpreters, through historical and critical reflection on the text, align themselves with that intended meaning. Schleiermacher wedded the spirit of the Enlightenment to the process of interpretation by eschewing a dogmatic approach and treating the Bible like any other book. A German pietist and Lutheran preacher, Schleiermacher nevertheless refused to allow his philosophical system to triumph over his religious consciousness. His response was to wed idealism (which teaches that reality is determined by the rational process) with romanticism, which led Schleiermacher to say that religious faith is grounded in the feeling of absolute dependence upon God. Yet for Schleiermacher this "feeling" was a function of the intellect, and his hermeneutical system reflects this. The key to interpretation, according to Schleiermacher, is a common ground of understanding between subject and object, between reader and text.[4]

Schleiermacher's system has two major factors, the grammatical and the psychological, which correspond to the two spheres of knowledge—the external linguistic codes and the internal consciousness. Grammatical inquiry attempts to develop the linguistic dimension by demarcating the meaning of individual concepts on the basis of the surrounding words. Schleiermacher was ahead of his time in demanding that meaning be seen in the whole, not in isolated parts. Yet he is best known for the psychological aspect. Schleiermacher taught that the interpreter should align himself with the mind of the author and re-create the whole thought of the text as part of the author's life. The interpreter's task then is to reconstruct not only the text but the whole process of creating the thought on the part of the author.

Wilhelm Dilthey (1833—1911) takes this psychological approach to its logical conclusion. Interpretation for him involves the union of subject and object in a historical act of understanding. Dilthey called this the "rediscovery of the I in the Thou," by which he meant that one discovers one's self in the act of reading (1969:235). For this reason

Dilthey wrote his *Critique of Historical Reason* as a corrective to Kant by developing a system that united science and life, theory and praxis. The process of understanding is a historical process that seeks objective knowledge of an author's meaning. From Schleiermacher he borrowed the idea of readers identifying with authors but went further by positing the possibility that readers are in a position to understand the meanings of texts better than the authors themselves. Since readers intersect authors' minds from outside and bring to bear many techniques, they can recreate meanings that go deeper than the authors themselves realized (see Bleicher 1980:19-26 for a good discussion).

This approach has obvious weaknesses, and few have followed Schleiermacher or Dilthey this far. By making the author, more than the text, central to the hermeneutical process, they have moved beyond the possible bounds of hermeneutical theory. They have been guilty of reductionism by simplifying a complex process of understanding into a psychologistic study of the author.

2. The Movement Away from Author-Text: Gadamer. However, with the rise of the dialectical movement via Barth and especially Bultmann, this historical approach increasingly came under attack. Here I will attempt to chronicle the attack from a two-pronged perspective, the phenomenology of Heidegger and Gadamer and the semiotics of the poststructuralist school.

It would be instructive before I begin, however, to compare with this the parallel but distinct evolution of literary criticism. Similar to Schleiermacher's influence at the turn of the century, the school of New Criticism dominated from 1930—1960. With an emphasis upon the form and texture of the text rather than upon its historical dimensions, the New Critics took an intrinsic approach to the text that failed to consider adequately the subjective involvement of the interpreter. The onset of phenomenological and structuralist concerns appeared later on the scene than in biblical studies but accomplished a reorientation of the literary discipline much more quickly, to the extent that literary criticism has now moved further along the path of reader-oriented dynamics than has biblical hermeneutics (see Detweiler 1980:3-23). This is not to say that the school of New Criticism has been replaced. Indeed, it has spawned a number of off-shoots, such as the neo-Aristotelian "Chicago School" with its stress on a philosophically grounded "mimesis," or "imitation." Yet the scene today is controlled by the reader, rather than by text-oriented approaches.

In recent criticism we must begin with Hans-Georg Gadamer, whose magisterial *Truth and Method* typified the word-event theologians of the post-Bultmannian school. What Fuchs and Ebeling (founders of the "New Hermeneutics" school) label the "hermeneutical circle" is seen by Gadamer as the "fusion of horizons"; namely, the horizon of the text and that of the interpreter. Building upon the thought of the later Heidegger, Gadamer argues that language is grounded in our very "Being" rather than just in our thought-life, and thus both language and text are autonomous entities with a life of their own (see Thiselton 1980:327-56 for an excellent survey). The act of interpretation does not so much unlock the past meaning of the text as establish a dialectic with the text in the present. The psychologistic attempt (of Dilthey and others) to ascertain the author's intention is not a part of this, Gadamer argues, for in the act of writing "meaning has undergone a kind of self-alienation" and must be "stated anew" or reawakened to spoken language by the reader (1965:354-55).

In other words, when I study those passages where Paul reflects on his past life—such as Romans 7 and Philippians 3—I do not study Paul but the texts he wrote, and the texts speak to me in my present situation rather than re-create the original author's past situation. Gadamer states, "To understand it does not mean primarily to reason one's way back into the past, but to have a present involvement in what is said" (p. 353). This is because "texts do not ask to be understood as a living expression of the subjectivity of their writers. . . . What is fixed in writing has detached itself from the contingency of its origin and its author and made itself free for new relationships" (pp. 356-57). The language of the text as presently constituted is determinative for meaning.

Yet at the same time, Gadamer insists, interpretation is not an "action of one's subjectivity" but a historical act, a "placing of oneself within a process of tradition, in which past and present are constantly fused" (p. 258). The key is the "temporal distance" between subject (interpreter) and object (text); this allows one to sift the preunderstanding or historical tradition so as to select only those aspects which prove meaningful in understanding the text. Contrary to the Enlightenment's negative appraisal of preunderstanding as a barrier to interpretation, Gadamer makes it a positive factor, indeed the key to true understanding. Here Gadamer's use of "preunderstanding" is similar to Schleiermacher's: it is the common ground between the interpreter and the world of the text, that store of knowledge which allows one to grapple with the ideas in the text. The interpreter's prejudgments interrogate the text and are interrogated in turn by the text. Thereby subjectivity and objectivity merge together, and interpretation becomes application as new horizons of possibility are opened.[5] In short, both text and interpreter take part in the historical process of interpretation. The openness of the text is paralleled by the openness of the reader and the historically conditioned horizons of both merge in the act of coming-to-understanding. Most importantly for Gadamer this process occurs in the present and cannot be controlled by the past subjective component of authorial intention.

Gadamer follows Heidegger in orienting all understanding to language: understanding comes not so much through the "methods" of interpretation (as in the classical schools of hermeneutics) as in the act of "disclosure" (or "truth") within communication. Furthermore, it is an aesthetic experience and occurs more readily in oral than in written speech. In the former one has a ready-made context within which to interpret the communication. With a "text," however, the past thought-world is missing, and the message is open to the subjective perspective of the reader. The only solution is the universal basis of language. The interpreter comes to the text aware of his preunderstanding and utilizes it to ask questions of it. The thought-world of the text opens itself up and in the dialogue that follows reshapes the questions of the interpreter. This is Gadamer's version of the hermeneutical circle, called the "fusion" of horizons. The past (the text) and the present (the interpreter) merge.

It is important to realize here that Gadamer never denies the place of objective or scientific method. Rather, he argues that it can provide only a degree of certainty and can never truly re-create the "intended" or "original" meaning of the text. There are not two (interpretation and understanding) or three (with application) separate aspects in the hermeneutical enterprise but rather one single act of "coming-to-understanding." Past and present are fused together. One cannot interpret "God so loved the world" merely from the Johannine perspective; John 3:16 is always considered from the perspective of one's present experience of divine love.

In sum, Gadamer's aesthetic hermeneutic moves from the author and the text to a union of text and reader, with roots in the present rather than in the past. Yet there are several weaknesses inherent to this theory. As is true also of the New Hermeneutic, it is not so clear how Gadamer avoids the danger of subjective interpretation. For him there are two controls against subjectivity—the past horizon of the text and the present community of the interpreters (the "tradition" that challenges subjective interpretations). However, there are no clear criteria for avoiding subjectivism. In fact, each moment of reading can produce a new and innovative understanding.

Also, Gadamer does not develop a methodology for distinguishing true from false interpretation. As Jeanrond points out, "systematically distorted communication" can twist the meaning of the text (1987:14-16, 22-37; see also Thiselton 1980:314-16), but Gadamer develops no criteria for noting inadequate understandings. Furthermore, he has an uncritical view of the role of the reader in interpretation. It is difficult to see how he can avoid polyvalence (multiple meanings), since each present situation or perspective is free to guide the text wherever it wishes. Anarchy could easily be the result. Finally, Gadamer gives tradition an uncritical role in the act of coming-to-understanding. As Hirsch points out, "The reader who follows the path of tradition is right, and the reader who leaves this path is wrong" (1967:250). However, there is no stability in this approach, for tradition is ever developing and changing depending on the community and the data.

Moreover, this results in a radical change in the definition of truth since it would differ depending on the tradition that develops it. Truth would have no universal or absolute basis that would bridge from one community to another. While this may indeed be the case, it does not have to be so, and in these appendices I will attempt to establish the viability of seeking the original intended meaning of a text.

3. Structuralism.[6]   In France structuralism filled the vacuum left by a growing disenchantment with Sartrian existentialism; in biblical studies it filled a similar void caused by the disenchantment of many scholars with the results of form and redaction criticism. Current biblical criticism, proponents of structuralism argue, is preoccupied with the historical traditions rather than with genre and plot development and as a result has produced an impasse in which the interpreter is unable to cross the chasm between meaning and significance. Historical truth *(Geschichte)* is sacrificed on the altar of history *(Historie).* Structuralism takes the opposite pole and argues that such diachronic (historicist) interests are a barrier to true meaning and that the interpreter must consider only the synchronic (literary) presence of the text as a whole.

A movement further away from the priority of the author and text occurs within structuralism, or more accurately the poststructuralist school of semiotics.[7] Claude Levi-Strauss was the true "father of structuralism" (Kurzweil's term). Although he was more the popularizer than the creator of the school, he developed the system that we know today. Two primary sources influenced him. First, Ferdinand de Saussure (1915) distinguished between *langue* (the language system) and *parole* (the individual speech-act) and between the signifier (the image) and the signified (the concept behind it) in language. A term like "love," for instance, means quite different things not only in various cultures but even to individuals within the same culture. It is not easy to move from the signifier (love) to the signified (sacrificial giving, strong affection or lust) in a given speech-act.

Second, Roman Jacobson's formal system of binary opposites argues that a polarity exists between metaphor (the vertical relationship or association between a term and its literal meaning) and metonymy (the horizontal or sequential relationships between linguistic concepts, which lead to word-combinations). To use the same illustration ("love"), there is a tension between the semantic range of the metaphor and its specific use in the individual set of word-combinations within a speech-act. One must decipher the code behind the surface relationships of the words, and often these are contradictory. Only then can one "understand" the "meaning."

From this base Levi-Strauss forged his theory that linguistic phenomena must be understood not in the sense of "conscious" but "unconscious" meaning determined not by individual terms but by the unconscious "systems" within which they are encoded or found (1963:1:32-34). A structuralist will not be interested in the surface message of Romans 5:8 but in the underlying codes of Romans 5 and the hidden message behind the surface text. The interpreter must apply "general laws" to this closed system of signs in order to determine the deep structure or unconscious (mytho-poetic) meaning underlying the surface structure.

For structuralists the human mind structures thought via a closed system of signs or codes that are organized according to universal patterns in the brain. These patterns bridge from one culture to another and basically determine the writer's view of reality (world view). Therefore, this system subsists at the subconscious level. Meaning has both horizontal (syntagm) and vertical (paradigm) aspects, with the syntagm representing the thought-development within the surface context and the paradigm the thought-world to which each idea corresponds. The interpreter studies the structure of all the elements in the work taken as a whole; these elements become the clue or "code" that points to the deeper meaning-structure behind the writer's surface words.[8] In the many books and *Semeia* articles devoted to an application of these principles, the story as a whole is first of all decomposed or broken up into its basic narrative units (called "actants"). Then these units are examined in terms of the structural codes or narrative sequence in the actantial (narrative sequence) units; this yields the composition or structure of the configuration of the codes. Finally, the structure is recomposed on the basis of transformational rules (following Chomsky), from which the underlying message for today is determined.

This school is very confusing to the general reader (indeed to most scholars!). Perhaps an illustration—again from John 3—would help. The structuralist would deny that the surface statement from John 3:16 can impart the text's "meaning" to the individual. Rather one must consult the entire dialogue between Jesus and Nicodemus in 3:1-15, in particular the binary codes of the above (Jesus) and the below (Nicodemus), then further apply these to the editorial addition of 3:16-21, with its own codes of sending-receiving, judgment-salvation, believe-reject, light-darkness and truth-evil. These symbols are then deciphered to discover the deep structure or underlying message and then transformed on the basis of the codes of our own day. The background or the surface grammar does not speak, but rather the oppositions within the text itself communicate meaning. These, moreover, speak directly to every reader.

For structuralists one cannot utilize a diachronic approach to the text in order to delineate what it "meant" in the past but must take a synchronic approach in order to decipher what it "means" in the present. Therefore, this method (like phenomenological approaches) is unconcerned with the author's intended meaning and seeks only to uncover the structure behind the writer's expressed thought, the "common world" of the underlying codes that address us directly. Since appearances do not lead to reality, the interpreter can enter this common world only by uncovering the structures behind the whole rather than behind the parts, the plot development and plurisignification (many meanings) of the text rather than the past meaning of the surface statements.

In addition, structuralism opposes the stress on the subject or self proposed by phenomenology or existentialism. Humankind is seen as a whole rather than as individuals, and the universal laws of the mind are said to structure reality in such a way that the individual "is automatically devalued insofar as human thought functions everywhere according to the same logic" (Harari 1979:20). Experience and reality are no longer continuous but must be reordered or structured in terms of a deeper meaning, hidden from one's perception of phenomena. Thus one constructs models or code-structures that go beneath the perceived world to its underlying true nature. "There is, therefore, a discontinuity, a break between the diversity of the real and the formal abstraction of the structure that signifies it, the movement from one to the other implying a *passage* from diversity to simplicity, from the concrete to the abstract" (p. 22).

A dissatisfaction with basic structuralist concerns arose quite quickly, and inherent weaknesses in the system led to what is now called "poststructuralism." In fact, it is now often stated that structuralism per se has been superseded or is even "dead,"[9] replaced first by semiology (the early Barthes) and then by semiotics (Derrida and the later Barthes). It would be helpful here to summarize the weaknesses of the earlier structuralism that led to this shift:[10]

1. A preoccupation with linguistics and a failure to lay a secure philosophical foundation: this is considered to be one of the major distinctions between the old structuralism and the poststructuralists; all the other difficulties below are connected.

2. A denial of history: many poststructuralists realize that a radical denial of history leads to the dissolution of meaning. The progress of ideas dare not be replaced by a concern only for the moment, lest understanding itself be lost.

3. The loss of human freedom: if individuality is replaced by a closed system of codes, determinism results. There is no meaning in the individual, understanding adheres only

in the group mindset. This is too great a price to pay.

4. Overstatement of the place of a closed system of sign-codes and of binary dualism: they have extended partial truths to covering laws. Most today reject rigid views of a closed or universal system of laws and recognize that while the human mind does at times employ semantic opposition (such as good-evil, light-darkness), thought-structures cannot be forced into so limited a category.

5. A reductionistic tendency: the system forces the ideas and plots of a text into artificial theoretical constructs and ignores the complexities of individual surface expressions. Today poststructuralists realize that the school is more an ideology than a science and that it yields tentative classifications (what Barthes calls a "hypothetical model") rather than covering laws.

6. Failure to recognize the necessary link between deep narrative syntax and surface structure semantics: the surface structure determines the underlying principles, and usually the deep structure is based upon conscious rather than unconscious meaning. There is inadequate evidence for the separate existence of "deep structures" in the mind.

7. The difficulty of the quest for a text's world-representation: it is not so easy to determine how universal truths can be discovered by means of the sign-system, since the normal hermeneutical principle of mimesis or imitation is ignored in favor of the synchronic moment. The results of structuralist interpretation are even more subjective and diverse than those of historical criticism.

8. The radical denial of intentionality: the refusal to consider a text's historical horizon or context actually denies the synchrony of the text itself, since it arose in a past era, not out of the modern era. Saussure's distinction between *langue* and *parole* hardly demanded so radical a step.

4. Poststructuralism. There is a growing realization that structuralism itself can discuss only how a text communicates meaning, not what or why it does (see Perpich 1984; Harari 1979:22-23). The lack of a rigorous methodology has thereby led to a reappraisal. One of the first attempts has been to wed poststructuralist concerns and phenomenology, primarily aligned with the work of Paul Ricoeur. This movement has been influential to the extent that Norman Petersen concluded his article "Literary Criticism in Biblical Studies" by coining the term "phenomenological semiotics" (1980:42) to cover what I will label "the new literary criticism."

Detweiler (1978), Petersen (1978) and McKnight (1978) simultaneously attempted to bring together these formerly opposed disciplines. They correctly perceived the difficulties of both (1) the purely diachronic approach of tradition-critical study, which ignores the poetic function of the narrative, and (2) the purely synchronic approach of structuralism, which fails to appreciate the distance between interpreter and text. The hermeneutical problem relates both to extrinsic concerns (relating the text to other similar texts) and to intrinsic methods (dealing with the text itself). In so doing, all three deny both the structuralist view of language as a closed system of signs and the lack of concern with conscious meaning. Since language is a direct semantic system and the meaning of the surface level determines the deep structure message, the "intentionality" of the consciousness as defined by phenomenology is essential. Only by "bracketing" or considering the surface or conscious meaning can one get at the reality behind it.

The phenomenological perspective dealing with man's existence and perception of the world is wedded to the poetic dimension (Jacobsen). The resultant interaction with the text as text is made possible by the perspective of Ricoeur's "second naivete," a "post-critical" attitude that allows one to enter the imaginative thought-world of the aesthetic work. The biblical writer(s) and original readers are bracketed, and the interpreter speaks only of the "implied author" and the "implied reader" (see pp. 154-55, 162-63). Further-more, the new literary concern for the text itself leads to a refusal to psychologize by trying to distinguish the mind behind the text. The text speaks for itself. The author and reader cannot be known with certainty. One has only the text and the author provides only glimpses of himself, primarily via the "narrator" who becomes the presence behind the story and the actual source of information. He is the visible element in the text.

A further result is "polyvalence," or "plurisignification" ("multiple meanings"). Since the perspective of the reader is crucial for the interpretation, polyvalence naturally results when various contemporary world views are employed to examine the grid of the text. Susan Wittig's programmatic essay, "A Theory of Multiple Meanings," follows the post-structuralist essays in *Semeia* 9 interpreting the parable of the prodigal son from the perspectives of Freudian psychoanalysis, Jungian archetypes and strict structuralism. She argues that the situation as it is (that readings of a text by different individuals produce a multiplicity of meanings) demands a theory to explain the phenomenon (1977:84-92). She then suggests a semiotic approach to both reader and text and states that this demonstrates that ultimate significance is derived not merely from the interplay of the linguistic text but from a "second-order system." This system involves an "unstated" significance that compels the interpreter to complete it. Since readers complete the mean-ing of the text within the constraints of the surface structure itself, their mind or belief-system determines the unstated signified (the meaning of the text) more than the signifier/text itself. The analytic system employed "generates" or reshapes the interplay of text and interpreter, and plural meanings result—meanings determined not by the text but by its dialogue with various faith-communities.

J. D. Crossan follows Wittig's article with his "Metamodel for Polyvalent Narration" (1977:119-21, 133-34). Following Derrida (see below) he applies the Nietzschean concept of "play," arguing that "freeplay" in the text removes the possibility of any final or ultimate deciphering of its meaning. Since all sign-systems have their origin in play, all interpretation is ludic rather than mimetic, open-ended rather than representative. The text as a sign-system is in this light an arena open to many games, and each interpreting community is free to "play" on that field according to its own rules. Different "games" in a text lend themselves to different meanings. Crossan applies this theory to the two textual aspects of plot and metaphor, asserting that "plot manifests story as play," and that metaphor becomes allegory and therefore is plurisignificant at the core. All literature is read on different levels depending upon the "perceived perceivers" (the readers) and their perspectives. Since all language is metaphor, and since metaphor is "dead of mean-ing at its core," language is characterized by "absence" (the absence of literal meaning and of hermeneutical constraints). Therefore, multiple meaning necessarily results, as the perceiver provides the content for the autonomous and empty metaphor.

Wittig and Crossan would argue that each person will interpret the message of John 3, for example, on the basis of his or her own belief system. Moreover, each one's interpretation will be a valid "truth" from within these different perspectives. There is something to be said for this. For instance, Calvinists and Arminians often interpret "God so loved the world" quite differently, especially in comparison to other Johannine passages (such as Jn 6:37-40; 15:1-6). Some Calvinists stress 6:37-40 and emphasize the sovereign side of divine predestination in salvation; the *world* becomes the elect. Arminians emphasize 1:4, 7, 9; and 15:1-6 and the individual responsibility in faith-decision. Every person in the "world" is given a charge to respond to God's love. The debate is whether both sides are equally correct and whether or not an extended dialogue between the various systems (in this case between Calvinists and Arminians) can help the interpreter to "bracket" the systems and allow the text to speak for itself. I would argue that this latter is indeed the case.

With structuralism and poststructuralism we have moved even further from the object/text to the subject/reader. Barthes states, "As an institution, the author is dead: his civil states, his biographical person have disappeared; disposed, they no longer exercise over his work the formidable paternity whose account literary history, teaching, and public opinion had the responsibility of establishing and renewing."[11] The key is the autonomy of the text. Modern literary critics believe that the text as an entity becomes independent from the author as soon as it is written down, and therefore it cannot be restricted to the original author or readers. The proper place of the reader/perceiver/interpreter in the hermeneutical task introduces an epistemological and ontological dimension that distances the reader from the historical situation of the original writer. The hermeneutical circle thus established between text and reader involves the constant intrusion of the reader's own interpretation. Indeed, the autonomous nature of the text demands that the reader enter its common world and complete its meaning. This interaction between perceiver (reader) and perceived (text) opens the text to endless interpretive possibilities.

We are again at the heart of the problem. You, the reader, do not know me, the author. The text of this book does not truly reflect my personality. That is, of course, obvious; the question, however, is whether it adequately reflects my thoughts on the possibility of meaning. Can you as reader understand my opposition to polyvalence, or is this text autonomous from my views? At this moment I am writing in the library of the theology faculty of the University of Marburg. Certainly many of the professors here, schooled in the existential or historical-critical approaches and having grown up in the German culture, will read these arguments from a quite different perspective. The question is not whether they will agree but whether they can understand my arguments. I will not be around to clarify my points, so certainly this written communication lacks the dynamics of oral speech. Moreover, those readers without the necessary philosophical background will definitely struggle with the concepts herein.

However, does this mean that no amount of clarification can impart the meaning that I seek to communicate in these paragraphs? I think not. This issue has two aspects: can we know what another person meant in a written account, and is it important to know that original intended meaning? Both questions must be considered.

Most poststructuralists look at the Text as "art" rather than as "work," since art has a life of its own after it is completed while work is merely "displayed" (Barthes 1979:74-75). The old relationships between author, reader and observer have experienced what Barthes calls an "epistemological shift." With respect to this, he provides seven propositions (pp. 74-81): (1) The Text is experienced only as activity, as the production of a work that does not stop. (2) The Text is paradoxical or even subversive with respect to attempts to classify it generically; it cuts across all hierarchical distinctions and so is open-ended. (3) The field of the Text is that of the signifier, which has an infinite number of possible meanings; as such the Text is radically symbolic and without closure. (4) The irreducible plurality of meaning possibilities centers upon difference and intertextuality;[12] that is, the Text contains within itself other texts in terms of its multiple meanings. (5) Unlike a work of art, the Text is not linked to "the Father's signature," that is, the author's intentions; the author comes back, if at all, as a "guest" who is no longer necessary in the interpretive task. (6) The distance between writing and reading is removed when reader and Text are linked "in a single signifying process" in which the reader is asked to collaborate in producing a *new work* with the Text. (7) The Text participates with the reader in producing aesthetic pleasure via the "transparency of language relations"; at the moment of reading the interpreter makes it his or her own work.

5. Reader-Response Criticism.   Two final schools remain (reader-response and deconstruction), and each in quite distinctive fashion culminates the movement away from the author/text to the reader.[13] Reader-response criticism goes beyond the poststructuralists by positing not only the autonomy of the text but the veritable union between text and reader at the moment of response. Several essays in *Reader-Response Criticism* (Tompkins 1980) demonstrate this. Norman Holland argues that response involves a merger between author (note the presence of "author"!) and reader as the latter "mingles" his or her basic self with the text (pp. 70-100). This act is reader-centered rather than text-centered. David Bleich goes further, positing a subjective criticism in which even the autonomy of the text is denied and replaced by individual identity (pp. 134-63). The text is an object only in a physical sense; as meaning it exists only in the mind of the reader. Therefore, "response" unites the person with the text and is a subjective act, a process in which the whole community of interpreters produces "meaning" via a dialogue regarding the text. Note that with reader-response criticism subjectivity in interpretation is no longer something to be avoided but is to be welcomed and encouraged.

Stanley E. Fish defines meaning itself via phenomenological categories (1980:177). Understanding does not arise via experience; there is no epistemological choice between alternate meanings but an ontological union between the reader and the text. In other words, the text disappears and the reader "creates" meaning. Formal features such as style and authorial intent interpenetrate the reader's awareness, leading to Fish's basic thesis "that the form of the reader's experience, formal units, and the structure of intention are one, that they come into view simultaneously, and that therefore the questions of priority and independence do not arise." His major question is how one begins. If the text has no existence apart from interpretation, what does one interpret? Fish answers the dilemma by pointing to the prior existence of "interpretive strategies" that stem from the community of interpreters. The reading strategy, developed within an interpretive community (similar to Gadamer's "tradition"), unites with the text and produces meaning (see further below).[14]

Yet there are important differences between the proponents of reader-response criticism.[15] Some, like Wolfgang Iser, center more upon the text and maintain links with the formalism of the text-centered New Criticism. For Iser the themes of the text bridge to the readers and guide as well as correct their interpretation. Iser speaks of the "indeterminacies" or gaps in the text that force the reader to become involved in its textual "world." Thus it is in the dialectic between the indeterminate signs of the text and the perspective supplied by the reader that "understanding" occurs (1978:24-25). However, for Iser the text provides the impetus, engaging readers and drawing them into its narrative world. It does this via a textual "repertoire" or configuration that provides an internal sequence (plot, dialogue and so forth) perceived by the reader. The actantial units or developing sentence structure sets up a series of anticipations that involve the readers in the plot line and force them to complete its textual meaning. The readers do this on the basis of their reading strategy and experience, and therefore the text is plurisignificant at the core; nevertheless, for Iser the text controls the reading process (pp. 93-111). The modern readers in this way align themselves with the implied reader (see pp. 162-63 above) to grasp the reading strategy of the text.

Most biblical studies of the reader-response type (such as Culpepper, Fowler, Rosseguie) fit into this category. These latter scholars seek to blend reader-response with historical-critical perspectives and study how "the author of the gospel has undertaken to direct and control the reader's experience and reading" (Fowler 1981:149; quoted in Porter 1990).

Yet many literary practitioners of reader-response fit a second type, exemplified in Stanley Fish. For Fish the reading strategy is not *a* component in the production of meaning but *the* component. The reading situation dominates the text, which guides but has no identity outside the mind of the reader. The text supplies only potential meanings (note the stress on the plural, "meanings"), and these are then actualized by the readers, who select those meanings which fit their interpretive strategies. It is not a text's intention but "readers performing acts" that produce meaning (1980a:11-14). In fact for Fish the text as a formal entity does not exist apart from the reader's interpretive act. Preexistence belongs to the community that shapes the reader's experience.

"The relationship between interpretation and text is thus reversed: interpretive strategies are not put into execution after reading; they are the shape of reading and because they are the shape of reading, they give texts their shape, making them rather than, as is usually assumed, arising from them."[16] In other words, the Sermon on the Mount as a text is called into being as the reader experiences it. Moreover, there is no objective interpretation of Matthew 5—7 but rather a subjective act as the reader chooses a reading strategy and approaches the text accordingly. For this reason readers may experience a text differently each time they read it.

For Fish dialogue and critical inquiry can proceed only from within a set of reading interests with shared assumptions. Therefore, debate and understanding are possible only within a literary community. Those from differing communities use the same words or symbols but assign them differing meanings; there is no literal meaning, only a plurality of meaning possibilities that are actualized in the act of reading (pp. 356-76). The goal is not to discover what the text is saying but first to experience what it does and then to persuade others regarding the validity of your perspective on the text (pp. 303-21). The synchronic or present moment of reading alone can be called "interpretation." The past act of interpretation (that of the original readers) belongs to a community that remains forever lost and cannot be recovered. So for Fish the reader can exult in the present moment of discovery and creative experience in reconstructing the text.

In sum, neither text nor interpreter has autonomy, for both fuse at the moment of reading and cannot exist apart from the other. As Tompkins states, we should not separate the "formalist theory" of the New Criticism from the "institutional praxis" of the reader-response school (1980:201-32). Since both actually identify criticism/interpretation with issues of explication/meaning, they partake of the same rules. At the same time, however, their radical denial of the text and espousal of its autonomy places them further along the spectrum away from author-text and toward the reader/community as the generating force in hermeneutics.

Much can be commended in reader-response criticism, especially among those following Iser. Hermeneutical theory has not dealt sufficiently with the place of the reader and of the interpretive community in the act of coming-to-understanding. Similarly the influence of preunderstanding or the reading strategy upon so-called objective interpretation must be considered more carefully after interacting with this school. In fact the basic approach in chapter six (on narrative analysis) stems in large part from this school.

Nevertheless, there are several serious drawbacks. Primarily, there is a reductionism in saying that the reader rather than the author or text produces meaning. Not all reader-response critics posit this radically. Edgar McKnight says that "a literary approach to the Bible in the context of contemporary literary study, however, allows—even requires—a view of the text as both an ancient document with original meaning and a living message with contemporary significance" (1988:107). He would see continuity between the message for the original readers and for modern readers. At the same time, however, he would deny any necessary link between those meanings. The modern reader is free to find his or her own meaning in the text apart from considerations of historical or original "meaning."

Further, there is a radical and unnecessary skepticism inherent in the approach. While this is manifest more in Derrida than in Fish, it is nonetheless present in some degree in all these adherents. McKnight defines "postmodern" reading as one that challenges the assumption that a text has an objective or referential meaning. Rather, meaning is found in the reader (pp. 14-15). However, when these critics posit radical discontinuity between text and reader, they are guilty of disjunctive thinking. Text and reader are not completely autonomous. Rather they address one another (the hermeneutical circle) as the reader seeks understanding. While I the reader perceive the meaning of a text like the Sermon on the Mount from the standpoint of my preunderstanding, I can still allow the text to address, challenge and if necessary change that perspective. In other words, there is a dialogue, indeed a trialogue, between author, text and reader, leading to the "meaning" of the text. The exact place the author and text have in this system will be the subject of appendix two; here I want to make the simple point that both have a place in the process of discovering meaning.

Moore takes a similar approach to the naive reader-response assumption regarding the original readers.[17] These critics treat the text as if it were intended to be read by uninformed or casual readers who bring little knowledge to the text and are reading it for the first time. Therefore, the unfolding plot determines the "meaning" rather than the intertextual dimension (such as seeing the eucharistic aura of the Last Supper in the feeding of the 5,000). Yet this was hardly the case for the Gospels, which were written for the church and not just for the pagan. Along these lines I would bridge from the ancient informed or ideal reader to the modern counterpart. We, like the original readers, can also approach the text via a close or informed reading, discerning the intertextual and historical dimensions of the stories as well as the unfolding plot.

Moreover, while reader-response critics like Fish have a skeptical attitude toward the author and the text, they have an uncritical and docetic attitude toward interpretive communities and reading strategies. No critical apparatus exists for a critical dialogue between communities, only for dialogue within a community. Fish has created a system that has free play but never the type of "truth" that can bridge between communities. In the infinite possibilities within a text it is difficult to see how he escapes relativism.[18] Controls exist only within a reading community, and there are no controls to guard against relativizing communities, especially since the relativized reader is free to choose from an infinite number of communities. The kind of community envisaged by reader-response critics is at one and the same time too large (a macro-community encompassing a language system or culture as a whole) and too small (micro-communities with infinite combinations from which readers are free to choose any number at any time). It is hard to see how there is any cohesion with so indistinct and confused a concept of community.

6. Deconstruction. Jacques Derrida has developed an approach that takes the most radical tack thus far, for he questions the very possibility of theological or philosophical criticism as we currently define it. Derrida is the product of a direct line of continuity from structuralism to poststructuralism to deconstruction. Each school built upon the strengths and sought to correct the weaknesses of its predecessor. Poststructuralism (Barthes) reacted against the structuralist assumption that the linguistic codes provide a direct line to the meaning of a language or a text, arguing that every language, even the second-order discourse of structuralism, is open to another metalanguage behind it. Deconstruction then goes further to challenge the communicative power of language itself. It is indeed difficult to describe the thought of so complex a thinker in a few paragraphs, yet the very number of works that have recently appeared testifies to Derrida's impact upon theological studies (Detweiler 1982; Altizer et al. 1982; Culler 1982).

In fact, it is indeed strange that it has taken so long to "discover" Derrida, due to his impact upon the scene of structuralism since the mid-1960s, especially after the simultaneous publication in 1967 of three major works: *De le grammatologie, L'écriture et la différence* and *La voix et le phénomène.*[19]

Derrida attacks the very foundation of Western philosophical thinking, arguing that philosophy no longer holds an unassailable, privileged place as the overseer of truth. He builds upon Friedrich Nietzsche (1844—1900) in arguing for a rhetorical rather than a philosophical approach to epistemology. At its heart deconstruction attempts to free language and rhetoric from the constraints of philosophical thought. Here Nietzsche is essential as the precursor to Derrida. Nietzsche takes a skeptical look at Western metaphysics, arguing that it stemmed from the Socratic rejection of the metaphorical basis of language. Since Socrates and Plato, Nietzsche and Derrida assert, rational thinking has maintained a tyrannical hold over human understanding. Since all logic pretends to be rational but is actually metaphorical, attempts to determine meaning are doomed to failure, and truth is radically relative. This can be exemplified in Nietzsche's definition of truth:

> What, then, is truth? A mobile army of metaphors, metonyms, and anthropomorphisms—in short, a sum of human relations, which have been enhanced, transposed, and embellished poetically and rhetorically, and which after long use seem firm, canonical and obligatory to a people: truths are illusions about which one has forgotten that this is what they are: metaphors which are worn out and without sensuous power; coins which have lost their pictures and now matter only as metal, no longer as coins.[20]

Derrida coined the term *logocentrism* to describe philosophical reasoning; this term refers to the "myth" that the spoken word or rationality provides the central fulcrum behind the quest for understanding. Derrida deconstructs this presupposition. In "Violence and Metaphysics," Derrida argues that encounter with the text must always be defined by "negativity," for "the infinitely-other cannot be bound by a concept, cannot be thought of on the basis of a horizon; for a horizon is always the horizon of the same" (1978:92-109). Encounter can only transcend and separate itself from negativity via interrogation, that is, the reader's "play" in the text. The Platonic logos (the rational communication of meaning) is negated by the inside-outside superstructure of metaphor and the unity of thought and speech. In other words, metaphor controls both the internal meaning and the external sign-system behind language. One can never differentiate any distinct "meaning" in philosophical discourse, and so the latter becomes nonphilosophy, seen in "the inability to justify oneself, to come to one's own aid as speech" (p. 152).

Derrida defines deconstruction as a "decentering" process in which the central locus of a structure, that which gives it meaning, coherence and presence, has been disrupted and has become "a nonlocus in which an infinite number of sign-substitutions come into play" (p. 280). The metaphysics of "presence" in Western thought has been deconstructed by the dual concepts of sign (with the signified both identified with and "expelling its signifier outside itself") and of play as the Nietzschean destroyer of metaphysics by way of discourse (pp. 280-81). Derrida means that there is no actual "presence" of meaning in a text, because the symbols can no longer be identified with their original meaning. In the act of writing the author's intention (indeed his very presence) has been "expelled" from the autonomous text, which now "plays" in whatever interpretive playground the reader brings to it. A text like the resurrection narrative of Mark 16:1-8 no longer has any connection with the original author or readers. It consists of a series of signs that draw the reader into "freeplay" in its textual arena.

Derrida specifically attacks the concept (from Saussure) of "presence" in spoken language, arguing that "writing" has priority over speech, and that "absence" and "difference" characterize language. He is especially opposed to "closure," the search for a central meaning, because according to him the text becomes locked up in the single meaning and ceases to exist as text. Moreover, for Derrida, closure is impossible because when we unlock the door to the signs, we find the room empty: there is no central or original meaning. Rather, a text is "open" or free to be reproduced in the reader's experience.

"Difference" arises from Derrida's attack on the priority of spoken over written language in philosophy as seen in Saussure's theory of the speaker's "presence" behind speech. For Derrida the tension between speech *(parole)* and "language as system" *(langue)* is deconstructed in writing, which substitutes a depersonalized sign system for the so-called presence in speech. Writing introduces a freeplay that displaces meaning; in this sense the spoken word is a kind of "generalized writing," a writing-in-the-mind. Thus writing precedes speech and determines speech; this then disrupts the Western approach to language. "Difference" for Derrida is the result; this concept signifies an interplay between the French terms "differ" (pointing to the basic opposition between signifier and signified, which breaks down the concept of meaning) and "defer" (pointing to the fact that meaning is "deferred" by the endless play between text and reader). Since language *(parole)* can never yield complete access to the "self-presence" or thoughts *(langue)* that lay behind it, absence characterizes the search for meaning.[21]

For Derrida and his followers, there is never and cannot be any true transfer of meaning or the signified. Rather, the signified is transformed in the act of reading, and difference is conceived both in spatial (lack of contiguity) and temporal (meaning as deferred or excluded from the present) categories. Derrida states that one cannot know the "original meaning" of any text. The meaning derived by the interpreter differs radically from that of the author. The latter simply cannot be transferred. Here the outside-within tension comes to the fore in Derrida's thought:

> Writing is the outlet as the descent of meaning outside itself within itself: metaphor-for-others-aimed-at-others-here-and-now, metaphor as the possibility of others here-and-now, metaphor as metaphysics in which Being must hide itself if the other is to appear. . . . For the fraternal other is not first in the place of what is called inter-subjectivity, but in the work and peril of interrogation; the other is not certain within the place of the *response* in which two affirmations *espouse each other,* but is called up in the night by the excavating work of interrogation. Writing is the moment of this original Valley of the other within Being. The moment of depth as decay. Incidence and insistence of inscription.[22]

Deconstruction is not a formal school (though it is a "form") but a perspective on discourse and reading. Harari describes the system by relating it to Derrida's later article, "The Supplement of Copula." For Derrida the sign is a "supplement" (the written word) to discourse but as such never completes itself: "the supplement is added to make up for a deficiency, but as such it reveals a lack, for since it is in excess, the supplement can *never* be adequate to the lack . . . a supplement to the supplement is *always* possible" (1979:34; italics his). For instance, metaphysics is a supplement to the concept of presence in Descartes' *Cogito* ("I think, therefore I am") and as such must be deconstructed and recast apart from its historical referent (original intended meaning). Harari labels the task a "desedimentation"—not a deconstructing and restructuring of a text but the exposure of "forgotten and dormant sediments of meaning which have accumulated and settled into the text's fabric."[23] A text is neither past nor present; it has no father-author but is a "fabric of grafts" that is "always already: repositories of a meaning which was never present, whose signified presence is always reconstituted by deferment" (p. 37; quoted from 1972:92).

In sum, Derrida seeks to "decenter" or deconstruct Western metaphysical reasoning by pointing out its radically metaphorical nature. Philosophy, like language in general, is characterized by "absence" of meaning. However, writing precedes spoken language because it expresses the true sign-system behind speech and language. There is no "presence" in writing, and therefore none in language as a whole. Rather, there is "difference," the absence of any literal meaning signified behind the codes of language. As a result the interpreter must deconstruct meaning and engage in a sort of freeplay with the signs in the text. Moreover, readers deconstruct not only the original author-text referent but also all "understandings" of the text throughout history. Only then will the "field" of the text be open for the readers to "construct" their own understanding. There is no extratextual referentiality, for texts simply point to other texts (intertextuality) and words point to other words (metaphoricity), not to any external world behind the text. Yet it must be stressed that proponents do not consider deconstruction a negative movement that destroys any possibility of communication. They are not hermeneutical anarchists but seek to free the reader/interpreter from the "false" constraints of Western thinking and from the search for final meaning in a text. From their viewpoint, they are liberationists!

John P. Leavey describes a two-step process or strategy for the interpretive side of deconstruction, stemming from the view that "writing according to the latter wants-to-say-nothing, means-nothing . . . at the point where meaning runs out of breath" and that one must thereby "enter into the play . . . of difference" (1982:50; quoted from Derrida 1981:14). First, "reversal" overturns the hierarchy of the text and its intertexts on behalf of the concepts suppressed in the speech/writing opposition. Second, "reinscription" displaces or dislodges the new hierarchy so that a continual openness results. Displacement occurs though "undecidables" (concepts that do not fit philosophical oppositions and demand a new reading of the text) and "paleonymy" (the use of the old term for the new concept), involving the erasure of the term, the transformation of the old concept and the intervention of the new. This then constitutes the act of writing, which itself is characterized by absence and difference (pp. 50-55).

Deconstructionists would do two things to Mark 16. First, they would radically reject the historical referent that ties the text to first-century Christianity and would look for codes that unlock the narrative to new meanings. Second, they would delineate the multiplicity of new concepts that lay under the surface codes. At the level of original meaning they would detect nothing but "absence" and therefore would stress only the present interaction of the reader, who re-creates the text in newness.

What then are we to make of this movement? Its importance, both as challenge and as possibility, cannot be overstated. It does little good to react with anger or contempt as so many have done. Such is often the result more of ignorance than of knowledge. The problems in developing an architectonic schematic (a blueprint for understanding) for the interplay of author-writing-interpretation are very real and must be considered carefully. There are no glib answers, and scholars from the traditional and the postmodern camps must avoid labeling. Detweiler argues that the legacy of Derrida (1980:11) and the other poststructuralists is not "critical bankruptcy," for one

> plays with the text to draw in other dimensions and expand its significance. . . . Rather, I think that it recalls for us the delight . . . that literature and its interpretation should inspire. . . . One takes perverse joy in uncovering, or creating, a meaning for the text that is original, at the boundary line of credibility, and yet compelling. Through intertextuality Derrida's vision of a metaphoric criticism finds incipient realization.

I might note that a great deal of what the deconstructionist argues actually occurs in some modern preaching and Bible study groups. The tendency has often been to ignore the historical dimension of biblical texts and to ask directly, "How does this relate to my situation?" The difference of course is that Derrida denies the historical referent while many evangelicals merely are unaware of it. However, the result (namely, subjective interaction with the text) is quite similar.

Deconstruction has many strengths. The metaphorical nature of language is for the most part correct. While I would not give such a radical definition in terms of its closure and the absence of literal meaning (see pp. 300-301 and the discussion of Ricoeur below), there is little doubt that any valid hermeneutic must deal with the metaphorical and rhetorical dimensions of language. The process of deriving a core of meaning in a text is every bit as complex (though not so impossible) as Derrida asserts. The question is whether we are forever locked out of the external reference behind an utterance or whether the attainment of original meaning, though difficult, is indeed a possible goal. I would argue that it is, and the second appendix will center upon my reasons for this position. Here I will restrict myself to some tentative concerns with respect to deconstruction.

Derrida's views have been hammered out largely in interaction with Nietzsche, Husserl, Saussure and Heidegger. A central core of his polemic regarding these figures is his theory that writing precedes speech and disrupts the presence of *langue* in *parole*. Yet one wonders if this is entirely true. Is thinking merely a "writing in the mind" and does this demand a view that asserts the absence of meaning at the core of thought? I think not. The removal of the Kantian subject-object distinction is not nearly so easily accomplished. Certainly the hermeneutical circle blends subject and object. Derrida has taken a half-truth (an inconsistency or problem in epistemology) and elevated it into a covering law. Each step is problematic. Does writing really have ontological priority over speech and thought? Is the subject (the Cartesian "I") really missing in the act of language? Does the metaphorical nature of *langue* actually decenter the referential dimension behind *parole?* My argument is that so-called inconsistencies need not imply error. These are all viable problems but do not necessarily lead to so skeptical a view of literal meaning.

Derrida is correct if one posits a first reading of the text. His problem is his demand for complete and immediate access to the meaning that lies behind speech. It is a question as to whether one stresses the lack of completeness and time-span necessary to grasp meaning (thus "difference") or the resultant meaning achieved. If one is optimistic rather than skeptical, Derrida's critique fails to convince. A "close" reading can overcome these difficulties.

"Difference" is indeed true in essence, for there is often a great gap between signifier and signified. The question is whether it is as insurmountable a gap as Derrida argues. Here the pragmatic or commonsense argument is helpful. We all communicate in speech and writing as if the hearer/reader can decode the signs of that individual communication. The key is the context. Many deconstruction examples look at metaphor apart from context. If I say, "I love the big apple," you do not know whether I mean New York City or a large apple. But in a proper context you will know exactly what I mean. When the average Christian reads a passage of Scripture, he or she often deconstructs its meaning, for there is often no search (or even cognizance that one should search) for the "original meaning." However, this is not the issue. The question is whether one could (or should) search and discover its meaning. This introduces the ethical question. I agree with Vanhoozer that the reader has an ethical responsibility to consider the intended meaning of a text, especially if that text in essence asks us to do so (1987). As I will show in appendix two, this is certainly true of the Bible. Now, if deconstruction and reader-response critics are correct that such is an impossible dream, the ethical aspect would not be quite so strong a case. However, the absence of meaning has been claimed but (in my estimate) not proven.

Finally, the concept of "freeplay" in the infinite number of sign-potentials or meaning-possibilities must come under the same scrutiny. Again I would agree that this is usually the case, especially with a casual reading, but it does not have to be the case with a close reading. While scholars will disagree regarding interpretive details, usually a 70-80 per cent consensus regarding the basic parameters of a passage exists. Moreover, I will argue below that the very conflict of communities regarding the meaning of a text can and should drive scholars to a re-examination of that text and thereby closer to its "meaning." In other words, "difference" does not demand freeplay.

7. Conclusion. In this first major section I have attempted to trace a line of continuity away from the traditional concept of hermeneutics as a historical search for authorial intention.[24] On the basis first of phenomenology and then of structuralism the emphasis has shifted further and further from any such possibility to a stress first on preunderstanding and then on an ontological displacement of original meaning by the reader's encounter with the text. This has culminated in reader-response criticism, in which the reader recreates his own text, and in deconstruction, in which reader and text are deconstructed in the openness resulting from "difference."

The attack on objective interpretation has a certain validity. Hermeneutic theorists in the past have all too easily ignored the central importance of the reader in the interpretive process. Thiselton finds four levels at which the "illusion of textual objectivism" becomes apparent (1982:1-4): (1) Hermeneutically, the phenomenon of preunderstanding exerts great influence in the interpretive act. This subjective element cannot be denied. (2) Linguistically, communication demands a point of contact between the sender and the recipient of a message, and this distanciation provides a major barrier to recovering a text's meaning. The differing situations of the hearers remove any possibility of a purely objective interpretation. (3) These problems are magnified at the level of literary communication, where other factors such as narrative-time, plot development, characterization and dialogue enter the picture. Before one can interpret, one must note the literary conventions operative in the communication; this is the heart of the debate: whether it is possible to re-create the original literary context behind a text. (4) Philosophically, meaning is never context-free but is based on a large list of unconscious assumptions between sender and receiver. When these connecting links are not present, "literal meaning" becomes extremely difficult if not impossible, for meaning can never be context-free. We dare not ignore either the subjective "life-world" of the reader or the "inter-subjective social world" of the text.

Mediating Positions

Robert M. Polzin provides an excellent overview of the situation (1980:99-114). Recognizing many of the problems of structuralism enumerated above (problems I do not believe have been adequately solved in poststructuralism), Polzin correctly realizes that neither diachronic nor synchronic methods by themselves can properly be called scientific disciplines. The two are complementary and interdependent. Polzin's three assertions lead into this section: (1) A historical-critical analysis is necessary for "an adequate scholarly understanding" of what a text means; the extralinguistic context cannot be obviated on the basis of the "intentional fallacy." (2) A competent literary analysis is necessary "for even a preliminary scholarly understanding"; most historical-critical failures stem from a lack of acquaintance with proper literary analysis. In fact, the two (historical-critical and literary-critical) should form a type of hermeneutical circle in which they continually refine one another. (3) Both disciplines uncover lacunae that dispute the supposition that either is hermeneutically scientific, or that either interprets the Bible in the way it interprets itself. This latter point is where Polzin believes the "crisis" exists.

Like Polzin, many other modern scholars are trying to forge a middle ground or mediating position in which all three elements—author, text and reader—play a role.[25] Foremost in terms of influence would be Paul Ricoeur.

1. Paul Ricoeur.   Ricoeur has been central to all of these poststructural enterprises. His opposition to structuralism per se is well known, and the development of Ricoeur's own "poetics of the will" has prepared him for this enterprise. As Ricoeur chronicles his own development (1971:xiii-xvii), he moved from eidetics *(Freedom and Nature)* to phenomenology *(Fallible Man)* to his current preoccupation with hermeneutics *(The Symbolism of Evil, Freud and Philosophy, The Conflict of Interpretations)* and semantics *(The Rule of Metaphor)*. Recently he has moved into narrative criticism as well and has applied all of these areas to the task.[26]

Ricoeur agrees with phenomenologist thinkers that language forms the core of being. Therefore, the act of reading or understanding the symbolic expression of a text is a moment of self-understanding, and the experience of a meaning-event in the act of reading allows one to rise above finitude (1980:234-48). In his still-developing "poetics of the will" he revives the Aristotelian view of metaphor as mimesis *(contra* Derrida) and argues for a dialectic between metaphor and text. His "semantics of metaphor" redefines the normal rhetorical definition (metaphor as displacing literal meaning with figurative or second-level meaning) in an ontological direction: metaphor takes place at the level of statement rather than word; that is, it deals with the whole statement rather than with the individual term (1975:75-78). For Ricoeur metaphor bridges the gap between "reference" (the objective content of the text) and "sense" (the interpreter's response to the text) by becoming a living entity, a "semantic event." The hermeneutical circle thereby is not an interpenetration of author and reader but an ontological "dialectic between disclosing a world and understanding oneself in front of this world" (1974b:107-8; 1975:81-88).

This world-referential aspect of hermeneutics is Ricoeur's answer to the conflict between objective and subjective tendencies in interpretation. Theoretical history (objective) and contemporary relevance (subjective) are essential aspects of interpretation but are inadequate when considered separately. Since the text/discourse is a "work," it contains composition, genre and style; this syntactical configuration causes the author's intention to come to the fore, but in a world-referential sense, not as an end in itself or as a hermeneutical text. As a discourse-event, a work is also distanced from the author and surpasses itself in the act of coming-to-understanding. "Distanciation" (the distance between the historical text and the present reader) becomes a barrier between reader and author, but in the text the worlds or horizons come together. Therefore, interpretation is text- and not author-centered. Even though the speaker-hearer relationship is missing in written works, one can still share the world of the text. So while objective determination of authorial intent remains always a theoretical construct, the referential world, created by the author, grasps the reader (Ricoeur 1973a:135-41; 1975a:14-17).

Ricoeur stresses the text rather than the author. As Prickett says (1986:70), Ricoeur centers upon the poetic function of the text, with three basic functions: the autonomy of the text, the textual work as an external force, and the world of the text as a transcendental reality that draws the reader into its "multiple worlds."

At the same time, however, metaphor as a discursive process contradicts normal interpretation by establishing a semantic incongruence, that is, a new world of meaning that challenges the reader. The literal meaning of the term is disrupted by the metaphor, which forces the hearer/reader out of the normal channels of meaning and draws him or her into the new textual world created by the metaphor. Imagination provides the key to this extratextual new world, assimilating the symbol and reorienting the meaning in a "reality-shaping" mode (Ricoeur 1978:8-10). The role of hermeneutics is to discover this new world, experience it and thereby unite objective meaning with existential relevance by pointing toward the world of the text and the world of the self at the same time. Metaphor disengages readers from their own world and re-engages them at the focal point of interpretation.

For Ricoeur the key is to place oneself in front of the text rather than behind it, to allow the textual world to control the hermeneutical process. The interpreter dare not ignore the historical dimension, for the latter draws the reader into the world of the text, forging a unity between the two. To utilize John 3 once again, the historical dimension of the Christ-Nicodemus discourse and of John's editorial clarification forces the readers out of their preconceived world and into union with the message of the text on the "new birth" as an act of divine love. Moreover, the metaphors themselves control the readers' reaction. To this extent Ricoeur would agree with Gadamer. Both accept a limited version of the autonomy of the text from the author.

For Ricoeur interpretation is the appropriation of a text's meaning for current understanding. The internal world of the text is a self-contained entity that has priority over the reader, who is drawn into its sign-world and by critical reflection gains understanding (see Bleicher 1980:229-34). Interpretation in this way is a dialectic between two levels of understanding: a preliminary naive understanding and a deepening comprehension. The decomposition of the segments of the text (here Ricoeur follows structuralism) leads to observation of its symphonic arrangement. This leads to self-understanding, as a new event of textual criticism and self-criticism develops and merges (see Jeanrond 1987:49-52).

2. David Tracy. In a series of probing essays Tracy provides a "revisionist model" borrowed from process thought to solve the pluralist context of modern theological speculation. Since the problem of polyvalence has brought theology to a crisis, a good place to begin would be his interaction with Crossan. Crossan attempts to differentiate "religious" parables (which are polyvalent) from nonreligious or theological parables (which are not) and believes that a deconstruction of parable is necessary (see above). Tracy, however, prefers Wayne Booth's criterion of "relative adequacy," which by means of a "critical pluralism of readings" within "articulated critical understandings of the text" seeks a proper understanding (Tracy 1980:69-74). This means that one can determine critically the relative merits of potential meanings to delineate the best of the many possible interpretations.

In his *Blessed Rage for Order* Tracy blends Ricoeur and analytic thought when he states that New Testament "limit-language" parallels the "limit-experience" of our common humanity (1975:120-36). In other words, the "address" of biblical expression links the "limit of language by such strategies as intensification and transgression" with the similar "mystery" of authentic human experience (p. 132). If this is correct there is indeed an existential connection between the biblical world and that of the interpreter. While revisionist in essence, he argues, the "mode-of-being-in-the-world" discloses a "limit-referent" that promises a life of wholeness and total commitment. Within these categories Tracy believes that we can cognitively predicate the "truth" of the biblical assertions (p. 136). This existential link gives a transcendental aspect to the biblical message. Readers can consciously recognize the distance between themselves and the text and jump the gap in a critical reading.

Finally, in *The Analogical Imagination* Tracy articulates the need for a unity-in-difference stance within the pluralistic traditions based upon the Christian symbol-system (1981:446-55). This calls for a dialectic between traditions and an interdisciplinary approach. The self-exposure generated from such conversations (made possible by an "analogical imagination") will allow each to learn from the others in a healing act caused by a relaxed pluralism. Note that Tracy affirms the public status of biblical claims. The theologian's faith-stance allows him or her to enter the referential world of the text and to dialogue with it. The resultant interpretation is tested by one's interaction with the history of interpretation and the current theological community. Aspects then may be added or discarded on the basis of adequacy, "unfolding as cognitively disclosive of both meaning and truth and ethically transformative of personal, social and historical life" (1981:132; see pp. 99-135).

However, Tracy's "critical realism" does not share my own concern for discovering the intended meaning of a text. Like Ricoeur, Tracy accepts a degree of textual autonomy and a pluralism of reading strategies as the text and reader engage in a dialectical process of discovery on the basis of the interaction of reading communities. Tracy's strength is his development of the "classic text" that transcends cultural contexts and discloses truth via concrete interpretations that are publicly verifiable via a critical interaction between communities. However, as Jeanrond has said, Tracy needs a more explicit theory that can demonstrate the interaction between text (style, genre, plot) and reader (1987:135-42). Does critical reflection demand textual autonomy and a radical distance between sense and reference in a text? I think not and will develop this below. I will argue that the critical interaction between communities enables the individual interpreter to re-examine the text anew and approximate closely the intended original meaning.

3. Canon-Critical Approaches. Many recent biblical scholars are wrestling with the proper interdependence between the diachronic and synchronic aspects of the textual interpretation task. Certainly, we must agree with Bernard B. Scott that the "critical essay defining the proper relation between historical and literary criticism has yet to be written" (1982:314). At the same time, there have been great strides forward; Bernard Anderson traces the historical development of a critical perspective, arguing for a "post-critical" stance that remains aware of the results of traditio-historical criticism but deals with the canonical text as a unity. Following Brevard Childs he calls for a "transhistorical" approach that anchors the text in "the concrete particularity and historical referents" of the life of the original community yet recognizes its relevance for future generations. Canon criticism as clarified by rhetorical criticism provides the means for accomplishing this (Anderson 1981:5-21; compare 1974:ix-xviii).

There is no need here to describe the process of canon criticism; rather, I will note its implications for the author-text-reader problem. One of Childs's essays in this respect is "The Sensus Literalis of Scripture," in which he discusses the difficulty of discovering the literal sense of the text in light of the separation between the literal sense and its historical referent in historical-critical research (1977: 90-93). For Childs, four problems demand a new approach: (1) Identifying literal with historical meaning would destroy the integrity and significance of the former, since it would depend on historical research alone. (2) This preoccupation with origins is highly speculative, controlled by innumerable theoretical reconstructions. (3) The community of faith that shaped the traditions is lost. (4) The gap between historical reference and modern relevance cannot be bridged, for the text has been completely anchored in the past. The solution, Childs says, is to recognize that the canonical shaping of the biblical text is the hermeneutical key to later interpretations as one moves from past to present.

One important difference between Childs and Sanders is apropos our purpose (see pp. 271-73). Sanders agrees that one must study a passage in terms of its full literary or canonical context rather than merely its original historical context (1977:157-62) but argues that the "historical context that is really important is that of the present (whenever) reader" (1980:180). Sanders would thereby give equal weight to the current community of faith, while Childs stresses more the past community of faith as decisive for the present interpretation. Sanders believes that canon is dynamic, not just static, involving all the communities that took part in the shaping of tradition (including the current interpretive community), while Childs means that the literary form of the text itself as the final stage of the process must have priority. Thus Sanders stresses the historical shaping as well as the multivalent recontextualizing of the message for today (he calls this "resignification"; 1980:192-93). Childs demurs, arguing that this "does not do justice to the theological role of canon" (1980:201). As a result, Sanders is much more reader-oriented in his hermeneutic.

Gerald Sheppard contends for a "canon conscious redaction" on the part of the biblical writers and rabbis, who unified the diverse traditions "by creating explicit interpretive contexts between books or groups of books" and by collecting the books into larger units, such as Torah, Prophets, Wisdom (1982:25). According to Sheppard, parallels in the New Testament and early church tendencies toward a consensus canon (which united disparate traditions under the common rubric of "Gospel" and synthesized these diverse teachings under ecumenical confessions and magisterial creeds) calls for "a historical deconstruction of the canonical context in a manner which sustains and even vitalizes that context for the purposes of contemporary theological exegesis" (p. 33; see also Achtemeier 1980:118-34). A key to this is the view that "the modern intentionality theory of meaning," characteristic of the biblical theology movement, was "alien to Judaism," due to "the shift in both the context and meaning" of the canonical works (pp. 32-33; 1974:3-17). A tradition-critical understanding of canonical development, according to Sheppard, means that the terms and stories changed in meaning as the community of faith and its needs changed. Thus there was no "single meaning" for Israel or the church. This pluralism in the ancient books must lead to a plurality of reading in our day.

Raymond E. Brown, in a chapter entitled "What the Biblical Word Meant and What

It Means," builds upon his earlier contention that the Bible is "a divine communication in human words" (1981:23-44; compare 1968:606-10). As such the literal meaning (though not completely aligned with authorial intention) is a valid quest of historical criticism. At the same time, he asserts, one must note several aspects of "meaning": (1) the literal sense it had when it left the author's pen; (2) the sense it took on when later redactors modified it; (3) the sense it had when codified into a canonical relationship with other books; (4) the sense it has for members of later communities. Brown transforms the "canonical sense" into the sum total of these aspects of meaning. This involves a modicum of the autonomy theory, but Brown believes that historical criticism should maintain a controlling force. Nevertheless, the stages of church interpretation from then to now are also formative of meaning. Brown makes three observations to this effect: (1) the church's interpretation might differ greatly from the literal meaning; (2) the role of church authority concerns more what the Bible means than what it meant; (3) the tension produced is a proper one. The church speaks to its own time, but the literal meaning must be in constant dialogue as a control over exaggerations (1981:35-43).

This dichotomy is further demonstrated in David Kelsey's discussion of biblical authority. He argues for a "conceptual discontinuity" between textual meaning and theological formulation, since "translation" is a dynamic act that transforms the "semantic structure" of Scripture first into the church's affirmation and then into the further semantic structure of the contemporary world. It is the "aptness" rather than the accuracy of theological transformations that really count (1975:186-87, 192-93). Exegesis is thus not decisive for theology, although it is relevant. The decisive factor is one's "imaginative" judgment, which controls the perspective and thereby the creative use of Scripture as normative.[27]

4. Wittgenstein and His Followers.   The scholars above are united in the view that while intended meaning is possible and a legitimate goal of historical-critical investigation, such an enterprise cannot be the primary goal of hermeneutics, since the contemporary world must construct its own meaning. A group of scholars who apply insights garnered from the later Wittgenstein move closer to the centrality of the author/text for meaning.

An interesting bridge to this level of interpretation theory is Mary Gerhart's attempt to set Ricoeur and Hirsch side by side via Ricoeur's "Diagnostics," which describes the dialogue between empirical/object language and common sense/subject language in the pursuit of knowledge, in other words, a hermeneutical circle: objective knowledge is attained through subjective experience and yet provides the data by which that experience is understood. Gerhart notes three stages in text-interpretation: (1) a reflective and critical awareness of the text and its literary meaning; (2) a sifting process by which potential meanings are analyzed via the text, thereby reconstructing a model of the text by judging the adequacies of particular possibilities within its multiple "meanings"; (3) the determination of new vistas of meaning, as the "self" (subject pole) and "world" (object pole) encounter existential significance and the text becomes a model not behind but "in front of" (Ricoeur's concept) the reader (1976:137-56). While one could dispute the validity of Gerhart's attempt to blend Ricoeur's phenomenological concerns with Hirsch's distinction between meaning and significance (see further below), her system itself does mediate between the two, adding an important dimension to the developing dialectical approach to hermeneutics.

The towering figure behind much of the current debate is Ludwig Wittgenstein. As with Heidegger, there is considerable debate regarding the development between the early and later Wittgenstein, between his *Tractatus* and *Philosophical Investigations*. The former can be described as having a "picture" view of language, the latter a "game" theory.[28] The logical positivism of the early period gave way to semantic pluralism, yet with continuity in Wittgenstein's concern to elucidate the limits of language, to define what may be said (objective reality) and what can be "shown" or stated indirectly (subjective experience). In his *Investigations* Wittgenstein argued the priority of particular descriptions over general observations. The multifaceted character of language causes it to speak differently in various semantic situations or "games"; therefore, it cannot be expanded to abstract principles or universals but can be applied only to specific contexts (1953:sec.11). To distinguish the two phases of Wittgenstein's thinking, we might link his early "picture" theory with the referential aspect of meaning and his later "game" theory with the functional aspect of meaning. The actual use of language in various contexts came to be the key to communication.

A. C. Thiselton emphasizes two aspects of Wittgenstein's theory: (1) language games occur in a dynamic, changing context subject to historical and temporal change; (2) the meaning of a concept depends upon its utilization in specific contexts and so is not fixed or universal (1980:376-78). From this Thiselton develops three "classes" of grammatical utterances. Class one comprises "universal" or "topic-neutral" statements that do not provide information but clarify the concept as a whole, pursuant to the reader's understanding. Class two describes foundation statements that act as "the scaffolding of our thoughts" (Wittgenstein), that is, they are unshakable axioms, theological (for biblical interpretation) rather than cultural or rational in origin. Class three speaks of "linguistic recommendations" that apply "institutional facts" to force a reappraisal of one's views. An example of the latter is the "paradigm case," the shifts in Jewish categories within the universal church of Jew and Gentile. As a result, Thiselton argues, we can no longer maintain a monolithic view of metaphor; it functions differently depending on the language game (pp. 386-407).

While Wittgenstein spoke primarily of current language games in oral communication, Thistleton applies the same principles to past language games in written texts. Thistleton's generic categories help one to elucidate the kind of statement found in Scripture and thereby to determine its meaning. In a later section Thiselton applies this to the concept of biblical authority. Applying class two and class three utterances to biblical claims— for instance, the New Testament use of the Old Testament—the propositional content of Scripture is experienced in "the dynamic and concrete speech acts of particular language games" (p. 437). The objective content of Scripture is not obviated but is upheld by experience language, yielding positive models by which current theories may be identified or denied in terms of their Christian adequacy.[29] In other words, Wittgenstein's concept of language games provides a covering model by which oral speech or a written text can guide a hearer or reader into its intended meaning.

5. The Return of the Author—Betti, Hirsch, Juhl.   Thus far we have moved ever closer to the centrality of author-text in the hermeneutical process. For those who wish to anchor meaning specifically in authorial intention, Emilio Betti and E. D. Hirsch have provided the philosophical and methodological underpinning. Betti, the Italian legal historian, challenges the assumptions of Gadamer by calling for a distinction between objective interpretation or exposition *(Auslegung)* and subjective interpretation or bestowing meaning *(Sinngebung)*. He believes that hermeneutical rules can control the latter and lead to the former. The text as object can still be a valid goal, for both text and reader share a common transcendental, suprahistorical world (Gadamer 1962: chap. 1; see Palmer 1969:54-60).

E. D. Hirsch takes a similar tack. He separates "meaning" (the act of comprehending a text on the basis of the whole semantic field) and "significance" (the act of inserting that meaning into different contexts, such as modern culture). Meaning for Hirsch is grounded in the author's choice of language and so is unchanging, while significance applies that meaning to different situations or needs and so does change. While relativists (he calls them "cognitive atheists") deny such a distinction, Hirsch finds support in Husserl's concept of "brackets." The mind "brackets" alien information until it can work back to it. In this way, Hirsch argues, one can move behind preunderstanding to the text and discover the author's intended meaning (1967:101-26; 1976:1-13).

Every text, according to Hirsch, contains "intrinsic genres" similar to Wittgenstein's concept of "family utterances" that link language games. Genre is defined in ontological terms as the "type of utterance" that narrows down the "rules" that apply to a particular speech. Since understanding is itself genre-bound, verbal meaning depends upon isolating the particular genre. In answer to Gadamer, who states that the writer's original generic intention is altered by the interpreter's interaction with the text, Hirsch believes that intrinsic genre provides "that sense of the whole by means of which an interpreter can correctly understand any part in its determinacy" (1976:86).

The reader, according to Hirsch, must sift through potential interpretations by understanding the "implications" of each possibility. These implications depend upon understanding the intrinsic language game behind the choice of terms. These rules, he believes, are inherent in the context; and though several implications are possible, the "purpose" of the genre tells how the writer intended to use the statement. Since generic elements are "historical and culture bound," interpreters align themselves with the author's intended message by refusing to force their own rules upon the text (pp. 89-126). Hirsch argues that the "intentional fallacy" of Wimsatt and Beardsley was never meant to deny verbal meaning, and that this latter is the proper goal of literary criticism. While one can never be certain about the author's intended meaning, one can consider the possible interpretations and choose that which has the greatest probability or "validity" (the title of his book). Apart from the author's meaning, there is no way to achieve consensus.

The problem is that Hirsch does not have a developed methodology for validating the interpretation chosen or for choosing one particular meaning possibility over others. For

Hirsch one selects a possible meaning and then checks it over against the "intended" meaning. However, it is not clear how one goes about finding that elusive author's meaning. Once the choice is made, Hirsch has four criteria to "verify" it (1967:236; see 235-44): legitimacy (permissible within normal language rules), correspondence (accounts for all textual components); generic appropriateness (follows the rules of the particular genre, such as science or history); and coherence (the interpretation chosen is more plausible on the basis of the above criteria than are other possibilities). These are all viable principles of interpretation but in themselves do not constitute a verification principle. It is difficult to conceive how this can overcome the problem of preunderstanding or the influence of a reading strategy. Hirsch never quite solves these problems. He needs a much more complex validating procedure and more sophisticated reasoning. Hirsch can lead to possible meaning but it is difficult to ascertain whether his method produces probable meaning (as he claims).

Further, it is by no means clear how one adjudicates between meaning and significance. Here Hirsch is at his weakest. Since the very act of determining meaning is done from the standpoint of one's preunderstanding (as Gadamer points out), there is no objectively discernible "meaning"; the very act of interpretation has already become "significant." Therefore, how can one separate the two? I will discuss possible solutions to these two problems first in relation to Juhl and then in relation to Kaiser.

P. D. Juhl agrees with Hirsch's purpose but does not agree that one should separate authors from their texts. He asserts "that there is a logical connection between statements about the meaning of a literary work and statements about the author's intention." Therefore, when one determines the intended meaning of the text, one discovers the author's intended meaning (1980:12-15). In a lengthy critique of Hirsch, Juhl argues that Hirsch's definition of authorial intention is a recommendation rather than an analytical claim and therefore is not open to falsification. Its rigid objectivity could lead to a distortion of the true meaning of literary works and cannot actually resolve interpretive disagreements since it is a presupposition rather than a method (pp. 16-44). Juhl overcomes this problem by centering interpretation on the text rather than on the author. Nevertheless, he does not deny the centrality of the author. If one removes the author, the text floats in a historical sea of relativity, open to multiple meanings. The author anchors the text in history and makes interpretation of its original meaning possible. Yet Juhl notes that one knows the author only to the extent that the text reveals him. We do not know the John behind his Gospel, only what he has said within its pages. In this way Juhl avoids the weaknesses of Hirsch and magnifies his strengths.

When interpreting a text, Juhl continues to say, we must apply the criterion of coherence or complexity, since as we judge various theories regarding the meaning of a work, we move closer to the author's "likely" intention: "Even an appeal to the rules of language in support of a claim about the meaning of a work is an implicit appeal to the author's intention" (p. 113). In fact, Juhl states, even aesthetic considerations, such as poetic devices, gain meaning only insofar as the evidence they provide bears on the intended meaning. Therefore, each work does have a correct interpretation, and it is the critic's responsibility to sift through alternate readings and select that interpretation that is the most likely one (pp. 114-52, 196-238).

Walter Kaiser addresses the second problem, Hirsch's distinction between meaning and significance (1981:33-36; see also 1978:123-41). He argues that the latter rightly makes significance the secondary act but has not sufficiently developed it along the lines of contemporary application. Kaiser identifies significance with the literary question, Can we understand the author better than he understood himself? Kaiser narrows the question from the author's psychological make-up to the written text itself. The first step is a comprehensive understanding of the text, which is theoretically achievable if the author expresses himself with sufficient clarity. Since we cannot go beyond this, an interpreter cannot gain "better understanding" by creating new meaning but only by going deeper into the subject matter, primarily in terms of its significance for other cultures or situations. Most important for Kaiser, this application gains authority only in the extent to which it is derived from the author's original, intended meaning. Therefore, Kaiser would first ferret out the intended meaning in its original context and then would base its derived "meaning" or significance for today upon that "single meaning."

Thiselton goes a step further, noting four models for this tension (1985:109-11): (1) The historical-critical school has discussed "past" (the re-creation of the historical referent) and "present" (theology) meaning, but that leaves an "unbridgeable gap" between exegesis and theology and never develops the relation between the two (as in Kelsey above). (2) Hirsch's meaning-significance separation is not developed sufficiently. (3) Gadamer (and reader-response critics) go to the other extreme and posit an ontological unity between meaning and significance. Yet they leave the interpreter with no guidelines for a responsible interpretation that avoids relativism. (4) Thiselton posits an "action model" developed from Searle's "speech act" theory (see p. 399). Such an approach allows the text itself to guide. Assertive or propositional texts tend to carry their messages across intact while nonassertive or exhortatory passages need to be recontextualized. I would blend Kaiser and Thiselton. I am not so skeptical as Thiselton about the possibility of delineating the author's intended meaning and then recontextualizing that meaning for the contemporary context. At the same time his action model provides the basis for doing so. This will be the subject of the next appendix.

Summary

In the first two sections, I have taken a deliberately synthetic approach in order to demonstrate the two directions in which narrative hermeneutics is moving. On the one hand, a growing number of avant-garde interpreters are taking a "probing approach" in which they seek to break new ground in developing a reader-oriented hermeneutic. The basic argument of all these schools is simple: the theory that it is possible to discover the author's intended meaning in a text is a self-deluding myth. All the philosophical or literary systems have produced is a series of arguments or interpretations that have satisfied their own adherents; no "covering laws" have been forthcoming. In other words, they prove the existence of reading strategies but not of objective or intended meaning. Therefore, these critics argue, we must stop pretending that there is any first-order system that will unlock the meaning of texts. Rather, all works are aesthetic productions that are open to one extent or another (depending on the school) to the reader's "freeplay" on the playground of the text, and polyvalence (multiple meanings) is the necessary result.

On the other hand, many others, somewhat in reaction to the extent of the disappearance of the author-text, take a more cautionary approach as they seek both to bring the author-text back into the hermeneutical process and to interact positively with the results of the former, that is, to modify the purely diachronic methods of historical criticism. Furthermore, while the concerns of both groups are similar (to combat the artificial and static results of purely objective historical criticism), they are moving in opposite directions simultaneously. We might diagram the two in terms of author-text and text-reader (see figure 17.1).

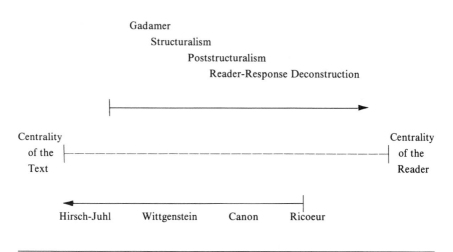

Fig. 17.1. The Place of Text and Reader in Recent Hermeneutical Study.

Appendix 2
The Problem of Meaning: Toward a Solution

I
T IS INTERESTING TO NOTE HOW AMERICAN LITERARY CRITICISM HAS BECOME VERY INFLU-
enced by continental poststructuralism while American philosophy has been strongly
affected by British analytical philosophy. This is true in both the social sciences and
religion. In addition, the two all too rarely engage in fruitful dialogue. Attending a
philosophical conference and a literary colloquium in successive weeks is almost like
walking into different worlds or dimensions of reality. However, there are growing signs
of rapprochement, especially between phenomenology and analytical philosophy. In this
section I would like to continue the dialogue and use it to suggest a solution for the
author-text-reader dilemma.

Meaning and Reference: The Contribution of Analytical Philosophy
The analytical philosophy school developed out of the logical positivism of Bertrand
Russell, the early Wittgenstein and their followers in three stages. First, A. J. Ayer built
upon Carnap and the Vienna circle in developing the verifiability principle (1946:34-37,
114-20). For Ayer language is a formal set of syntactical relationships and must be
"analyzed" to discover its logical validity. Further, a statement can be "verified" only by
empirical data from the physical world. This, of course, rules out both metaphysics and
theology. The problem is that the verification principle itself cannot be verified, and a
view limiting language to the merely syntactical or contextual is inadequate (see Weitz
1967:1:103-4). As a result of such criticism, Ayer modified his principle in the preface to
the second edition. Nevertheless, metaphysics as God-talk was still viewed as meaningless
because it belonged to the noncognitive realm.

The second stage came with the falsification principle of Antony Flew (1955:96-99).
He posited that no truth-statement can claim veracity unless it can be falsified, that is,
unless one can prove that the reverse cannot be true. If claimants can provide no criteria
that could theoretically force them to change their minds, the assertion has no meaning.
Once more, religious statements are placed in the noncognitive realm, and the theist is
commanded to be silent.

The gauntlet had been thrown, and proposed solutions flowed quickly. Several appeared in the same volume with Flew's essay. R. M. Hare agreed that God-talk is non-

cognitive but noted that life is built on such unverifiable "bliks." While not "assertions" as such, they are a "world-view" and thus are meaningful (1955:99-103). Basil Mitchell argued that theological statements are falsifiable but faith keeps them from being ultimately so. For instance, the fact of evil counts against the goodness of God, but faith overcomes the problem (1955:103-5). On the other hand, I. M. Crombie posited that theological assertions can be decisively falsified, but such a final test can occur only after death. Only then will the full picture be known (1955:109-30). All the responses argue that religious assertions are meaningful, though not cognitively meaningful. Nevertheless, they can be verified. On the basis of his radical separation between the cognitive and noncognitive realms, Flew stated in response that these attempts are falsified by their own subjectivity (1955:106-8).

Frederick Ferré represents the third stage, arguing that the more developed verification principle is still too narrow in limiting the concept of "fact" to empirical data (1961:42-57). "Paradox," when used of nonscientific explanations, does not mean "logical contradiction" but simply points to a reality beyond empirical reach. One cannot separate cognitive statements from value content. Further, Ferre asserts that God-talk centers upon ontological reality rather than upon pure empirical logic, and thereby can be accorded "meaning." Therefore, empiricism proves itself wrong "either in verbal rules (if the proposition is analytic) or in equivalent statements referring to actual or possible sense-perception (if the proposition is synthetic)" (p. 53). The answer is to ground "reality" in rational thinking rather than in mere sense-perception. Analogy, not picture-language, is the basis of an interpretive description of reality. Ferre points to imperative, performative and interrogative functions of speech as equally valid for analytical thinking (p. 55).

We might call this "interpretive realism" or "functional analysis" (with Ferre), which means that the verifiability test accords with the "use" of language in its own context (Wittgenstein's "language game"). It is important to note that this in no way denies the basic validity of the verifiability principle. Instead, analytical philosophy restricts it to its own realm or language game, namely the cognitive realm of sense data. Empirical verification is valid for scientific experimentation but does not render metaphysics meaningless. Since religious language belongs to a metaphysical world view, it is analogical (symbolically interpreting a wide range of experience), interpretive (presenting the intrinsic meaning of the facts) and confessional (resulting from personal beliefs). Thereby it is personal rather than scientific language. Arthur Holmes calls this the "language of mystery" (1971:155-62) and Ian Ramsey labels it "odd-talk" (1963:11-54). Since it delves into deep-seated paradoxes and truths beyond purely cognitive reasoning, the criteria for verification must be structured accordingly.[1]

With J. L. Austin's important *How to Do Things with Words,* analytical philosophy entered the hermeneutical arena. Austin argues that language has a performative function as well as an assertive dimension. He develops this in terms of three aspects of speech acts (1962:101-19): the *locutionary* act is what a sentence means at the propositional level; the *illocutionary* act is what the sentence accomplishes (assertion, promise, prediction); the *perlocutionary* act looks to the intended effects of the speech act (teaching, persuasion). Most actual utterances, according to Austin, contain all three components to one degree or another, and the truth content of the utterance is judged at all three levels.

John Searle's influential *Speech Acts* deepens and expands Austin's position. Searle argues that a false equation of meaning with use has given rise to several fallacious positions on the part of analytical philosophers.[2] Therefore, the basis of analytical theory should be language as referential rather than performative. His basic thesis is: "speaking a language is engaging in a (highly complex) rule-governed form of behaviour" (1969:77, 80). By nature speech partakes of "expressibility" and therefore enables us to judge individual statements by established rules for linguistic meaning. For Searle the sentence is an intentional device whereby one brings hearers into the proper arena so that they might apply the correct rules and recognize the meaning.

Searle builds the bridge from utterance to meaning via three "axioms" of reference (pp. 19-21, 42-50, 77-80): (1) the axiom of existence, which assumes that the object referred to exists in the rules of the language game (such as in the real world or in fiction); (2) the axiom of identity, which assumes that the predication is true of an object if it is true of anything identical with that object "regardless of what expressions are used to refer to that object"; (3) the axiom of identification, which assumes that "the utterance of that expression must communicate to the hearer a description true of, or a fact about, one and only one object, or if the utterance does not communicate such a fact the speaker must be able to substitute an expression, the utterance of which does" (p. 80). The context of the "illocutionary act" will provide preparatory conditions or presuppositions as well as "excluders" that help the listener to identify the referential meaning on the basis of the linguistic relationships (pp. 44-56).

Searle's theory provides an important basis for reflecting upon the relationship between sender and receiver or (in a historical act of communication) between text and reader. While a referential act of understanding (such as the recovery of the original meaning of John 3) is difficult, it is not impossible. The debate again is whether the identification of an utterance in the way Searle argues is indeed a possible enterprise.

Yet the basic difficulty is that Austin and Searle are dealing with spoken language while the issue here is written texts. Can the gap between the two be bridged? Does speech act theory cover biblical texts? Several respond affirmatively. Donald Evans applies Austin's insights to biblical assertions (1963:158-64). The alien-ness or odd-ness of biblical assertions is vitiated by this new view of language as a performative act. This is especially true when one adds the "self-involvement" of the reader. The believer's faith becomes an "onlook" that opens up new logic possibilities for accepting scriptural statements according to their own rules. The statement's commissive/performative force correlates with the theory of revelation as self-involving at heart. When we clarify this via Searle's reformulation of utterance as referential in essence, we can no longer radically separate biblical assertions from the possibility of meaning.

Kevin Vanhoozer, building upon Searle, sees four illocutionary factors in biblical literature: proposition (the data communicated); purpose (the reason for the propositional content); presence (the genre or form of the author's message); and power (the illocutionary force of the message). By noting these factors, Vanhoozer argues, we can interpret a text's intended meaning (1986:91-92).

Finally, I will note the "action model" of Lundin, Thiselton and Walhout, which seeks to "reclaim the importance of reference and the nonlinguistic world" from deconstruction theory (Lundin 1986:42). Three principles form the core of their approach (pp. 43-49, 107-13). First, written texts are objects as well as instruments. As objects they are not autonomous for they are produced by action. Thus they can be understood only via a theory of action that recognizes them as objects resulting from action and instruments producing action. Second, the meaning or sense of a text depends not just upon the semantic development of the terms but also upon the action or functioning purpose (illocutionary force) of the sentence in its context. Third, we must identify the temporal sequence of the actions in the text as a whole that defines the function of the particular sentence in its context. The result of these factors leads to the "intention" of the text. However, for these authors, there are multiple functions of a text, and these can lead to one type of "multiple meanings." Yet these are not free renderings but are based upon what the text itself intends to do (again its illocutionary purpose). For instance a parable narrates but also informs, directs, challenges and persuades. In short, a text itself performs speech acts and is open to questions of intentionality. Nevertheless, while the author is an important component of the text, he provides only one aspect of textual interpretation.

One major objection to the use of analytical philosophy from poststructuralist concerns is the dichotomy between speech and writing. Since writing codifies speech and removes it from the arena of dialogue, the performative or referential dimensions may no longer apply. However, I do not believe that this is the case.

Most current studies about the relationship between mind and language assume that there is no conceptual gap between them. Frege's work on sense and reference has argued forcefully for this essential unity by showing that concepts which are critical to a description of language are integral to mental acts (1980:56-78). Frege's theory of truth contains three basic maxims: (1) The meaning of individual terms depends upon their contribution to the meaning of sentences in the language. (2) The meaning of sentences depends upon recognizing the conditions under which the sentences are true; this meaning determines the truth value of the sentence. (3) Propositional attitudes such as belief, knowledge or assertion depend upon one's assigning senses to words and sentences. Sense is the meaning value assigned to the terms within the sentence, reference to the real world behind the sentence. Sense relates to the meaning of a term in its relation to other terms in the context.

As Cotterell and Turner explain, this occurs at several levels, each more complex (1989:78-82). At the sentence level, "sense" concerns the semantic relationship of the words to one another. At the paragraph level we must discern the complex relationship of the propositions to one another (the structural development of the paragraph). This structural development is even more difficult to determine at the discourse level. Here rhetorical criticism comes into play, as we trace the developing argument of the entire discourse. Naturally, at each level the task of delineating the original or literal sense becomes more complex, and scholars become more doubtful as to the possibility of discovering such.

Reference provides even greater problems. It is one thing to "understand" a description of the Holy of Holies (Ex 25), quite another to know what the "cherubim" at the two ends of the mercy seat (vv. 17-22) denote. Since "reference" refers to the exact thing signified by the term, there is no way to know the reference of "cherubim." Similarly, it is impossible to know the referential reality behind apocalyptic symbolism such as the many-headed beasts or the locust plague in the book of Revelation, or of certain biblical towns like Emmaus in Luke 24:13, of which no known evidence exists regarding its exact location. On the other hand, in many passages the referential dimension is essential. For instance, is Jesus using "Son of man" about himself (most critics) or another figure (so Bultmann)? Does the term denote a circumlocution for *I* or a Danielic glorified figure, or both? In the same way, scholars are constantly trying to identify the opponents in such epistles as 2 Corinthians, Galatians, Colossians or 1 John. In a very real sense all historical questions are questions of reference. Moreover, they are valid questions.

Postmodernists center upon the uncertainty and inconclusiveness of historicist issues and deny the validity of seeking the referential reality behind a statement. In fact many like Fish and Ricoeur have redefined the terms. The sense is the meaning of the terms but no longer is connected to the original situation, and reference denotes the world of the text rather than the extratextual reality behind the text. This, however, is an anti-realist position, and the realist (one who accepts the viability of a real world behind assertions) rightfully questions the viability of such skeptical assertions. Sense and reference are essentialist components of any theory of meaning, and more than that they are viable and possible goals of research. At times one can go no further than the sense, but both aspects must be considered in exegetical study.

Here I have sought to demonstrate the validity of religious language (both oral and written) as well as other types of discourse as employing sense and reference and therefore as open to verification analysis via criteria of adequacy. The importance of the community of scholars is crucial for the latter and also for analytical philosophy. However, we would argue that this does not entail the fusion of reader and text into a single entity but that the distanciation between reader and text provides a perspective for viable interpretation. Readers are both part of the referential world (by means of commitment) and separate from it (by means of historical distance). As a result they stand both within and outside the text and engage it in a meaningful dialogue. However, I admit that this does not yet allow us to go so far as to posit intentionality. That is the subject of the ensuing sections.

The Sociology of Knowledge, Paradigm Structure and Intentionality

1. Sociology of Knowledge. An essential aspect of hermeneutics is the effect of cultural heritage and world view on interpretation. The sociology of knowledge recognizes the influence of societal values upon all perceptions of reality. This is a critical factor in coming to grips with the place of preunderstanding in the interpretive process. Basically, sociology of knowledge states that no act of coming-to-understanding can escape the formative power of the background and the paradigm community to which an interpreter belongs. The tremendous changes in the philosophy of science in recent years have forced all the sciences (social science as well) to rethink the entire process of theory formulation and change.

The "critical hermeneutics" of Karl-Otto Apel and Jürgen Habermas are instructive here (see the description in Bleicher 1980:146-80). Both take an anthropological and sociological approach to knowledge. Apel accepts Gadamer's historicality of knowledge but goes one step further, arguing that the sociology of history makes genuine communication extremely difficult. Apel means that communication theory must concern itself with a "critique of ideology," that is, the tendency of individuals to manipulate or control others via the act of communication. The social environment is a critical factor that Gadamer and his successors tend to overlook. As a result the interaction between text and interpreter is not idealistic, for the text itself is the product of a social world and seeks to force the reader to enter into and emulate that world view. Apel demands cognizance of these factors and suggests a dialectic between basic hermeneutics and the sociology of knowledge, with the latter transcending the what to the why. When the interpreter becomes involved in this interplay of forces, the text and its thought-world are seen in a new light. Apel turns to psychoanalysis for a model, especially its stress upon a heightened self-understanding via a critical interaction between subject and object (1971:7-44, especially 41-44).

Habermas goes even further with the importance of a sociologically aware hermeneutics. He argues for three fields of knowledge: science, which utilizes technical information derived directly or analytically from the sense world; history, which interprets language along the lines of Gadamer; and the social sciences, which use reflection to free or "emancipate" people from the domination of historical forces. The third type provides the solution for Habermas, who weds Marx and Freud to overcome the control of interpretation by ideologies derived from the struggle between the classes. Therefore, Habermas must counter Gadamer's claim that hermeneutics has a universal thrust because it centers upon language, arguing that language itself is dominated by social forces, and that the only answer is a "critique of ideology" at the heart of hermeneutics. Like Apel, he finds his model in psychoanalysis. In the same way that Freudian psychoanalysis isolates "systematically distorted communication," so must hermeneutics liberate understanding from ideology. This is accomplished by "scenic understanding," which analyzes then explains the previously inaccessible forces behind a particular language game. One can then critique these forces in terms of their competence and viability.[3]

Habermas has indeed noted one of the basic weaknesses of Gadamer, his Heidegerrian assumption that language encompasses all meaning and that therefore hermeneutics has universal implications. At the same time, Habermas's critique of ideology is a good introduction to the importance of the sociology of knowledge as an interpretive tool. Although his Marxist-Freudian basis must be challenged, his basic thrust is important.

Ideological forces do indeed control hermeneutics for most of us. Whether Calvinist or Arminian, reformed or dispensational, process or liberation theologian, each faith community has given us certain ideological proclivities that guide our interpretation. Larkin notes four challenges from the sociology of knowledge for biblical interpretation (1988:67-69): (1) Divine revelation itself is culturally conditional since it was communicated to diverse cultures and comes to us with the indelible stamp of those cultures. (2) To understand the Bible we must comprehend the "categories of meaning" behind the messages; these are fragmentary and often assumed by the biblical writers, so they are difficult to unearth. (3) Our contemporary social context is also multiplex and changing, which affects our interpretations. (4) No unified world view or preunderstanding can lead to a fusion of horizons, so often the normative message of a text is the product of our perspective rather than of the texts themselves.

Sociology of knowledge highlights the distanciation between the biblical author's intended meaning and the modern reader's act of interpretation. Yet it is not entirely a negative factor, for it allows interpreters to identify with precision their cultural and religious heritage. This conscious identification is a critical factor in placing one's presuppositions in front of rather than behind the text, in allowing the text rather than ideological factors to guide the interpretive process. So long as we assume the absolute validity of these beliefs, they do indeed control interpretation. Only by identifying them for what they are—theological and cultural approximations of truth—can we keep them in perspective. The further problems of identifying the societal factors of the text and of uniting our perspective with that of the text have been dealt with in the body of this book (see chaps. five and fifteen).

2. Paradigm Change and Paradigm Communities. The major issue, of course, is the validity of the theories of the sociology and philosophy of science for the social sciences. While a final answer is almost impossible,[4] we must begin with Thomas Kuhn's *The Structure of Scientific Revolutions*. At the outset, it is a sociological and historiographical study rather than a philosophical treatise. Kuhn rejects the traditional view that science develops via inductive research and posits that scientific "paradigms" or supertheories control in the scientific community. A "paradigm" designates the set of beliefs and assumptions shared by a particular scientific community. His view is that paradigms shift more due to inadequacies in existing models than to the superiority of the new model. The reason is that scientific communities engage in problem-solving more than path-breaking enterprises. Change occurs when the community of scholars with their shared values comes to consensus on the validity of the new paradigm (Kuhn 1970).[5]

Garry Gutting states that the social sciences have no grounds for placing themselves within Kuhn's system, since they never demonstrate the universal consensus that is necessary to qualify for paradigm shifts (1980:2-15). On the other hand, as Gutting (pp. 15-19) and Frederick Suppe admit, a proper "philosophy of science must come squarely into contact with the basic issues in epistemology and metaphysics; and the attempt to do epistemology or metaphysics without regard to science is dangerous at best" (Suppe 1977:728). Furthermore, while complete consensus is seldom if ever achieved, the type of scholarly agreement that results in paradigm shift for the majority has often occurred, such as in recognizing that Jewish and Hellenistic backgrounds must be considered together in New Testament research. Few today (after Hengel and others) would consider only Judaism or Hellenism applicable to Paul. This is indeed a paradigm shift for History of Religions research. Many doubt Kuhn's pessimism about truth-seeking in philosophy and science as well as his resultant claim that science and art unite in their primary concern with puzzle-solving. In reality, both science and art/social sciences consider and evaluate truth-claims.

For our purposes we will center upon Ian Barbour's attempt to apply Kuhn's concept of theory choice to religious paradigms. He agrees with the importance of the shared paradigm within a community (note the parallels with reader-oriented criticism and analytical philosophy) and that observations are paradigm-dependent (parallels with phenomenological preunderstanding) but believes that the categories are too simplistic. There is a continual dialogue between paradigm communities and more often "microrevolutions" rather than full paradigm shifts result. Most important, competing claims are critically examined and discarded for rational reasons. Kuhn admits in his second edition that communication or critical dialogue can and does take place between competing paradigm groups. However, the problem of individual judgment from within a paradigm does not rule out purely rational decision making.

Barbour himself constructs a "model" for theory construction based upon observation, theoretical models, research traditions and metaphysical assumptions. He argues that (1) although all data are value-laden, rival theories are not incommensurable; (2) though paradigms resist falsification, observation maintains some control; (3) while no rules for paradigm shift exist, there are independent criteria of assessment. Therefore, even metaphysical assumptions are not immune to change. When applied to religious paradigms, several crucial aspects must be noted, such as the importance of the community (note similarities to Fish) and of the formational historical events (similar to Gadamer), which Barbour calls "revelatory" events. Most important, he stresses that religious commitment can and must be combined with "critical reflection" based upon such noncognitive criteria as social or psychological needs, ethics and simplicity or coherence. While the subjective features in the act of interpretation (influence of preunderstanding, resistance to change, absence of rules for paradigm choice) predominate over objective features (common data between disputants, cumulative effect of evidence, criteria that are not paradigm-dependent) in distinction from scientific theory, the objective features are still present (1980:223-45, see also Mitchell 1981:75-95).

In other words, while the act of interpreting the truth content or validity of a statement is difficult, it is not impossible. If the attempt is sophisticated and aware, the objective features above can enable one to decide between competing theories.

The primary barrier to a valid interpretation is, as already stated, one's preunderstanding. On the basis of differing presupposed systems, one interpreter may see coherence and adequacy in a particular theory of meaning while another may reject it. Is there any way out of the impasse? In many cases there is not, for the competing preunderstandings are often not open to a critical dialogue. In this case the original meaning can never be recovered. However, this need not be the case. Carson notes a semantic shift between two types of preunderstanding (1984:12-15): (1) A "functional non-negotiable" is an accepted position that remains open to the evidence; if Scripture should so dictate, the position will change. (2) An "immutable non-negotiable" is not open to correction but twists the data to cohere with the preconceived theory. I would add another category: a "negotiable" that seeks challenge and, if necessary, correction in order to ascertain truth.

All these categories are valid, depending on the issue. Moreover, these are not self-contained units. For instance, few would say they remain closed to the corrective force of Scripture itself, but they may be closed to the corrective impact of other paradigm communities. The critical interaction between competing systems is essential for a pluralistic approach to truth, for preunderstanding makes it quite difficult to identify weak points in one's own system. The criticisms of others highlight these anomalies and enable one to move closer to the text. The key is to create within one's self an attitude of openness to truth that allows us to welcome challenge from other interpretive communities because we know that "they may be right" and "this will drive me back to the text to discover the 'truth.' "

3. Intentionality. The paradigm communities described here share several common features, especially the centrality of the community, the issue of preunderstanding and the possibility of dialogue in a pluralistic setting. The question to which I turn now is whether polyvalence is the natural result or whether some view of intentionality is not only possible but necessary to the interpretive task. As I noted in the survey of mediating positions, a growing number would like to combine the two, either under "what the Bible meant—what it means" categories or under a distinction between meaning (the text's intended/original meaning) and significance (what the text means, or polyvalence). To summarize the arguments thus far, I believe that philosophy works functionally in terms of reference rather than empirically in terms of sense data and so we must consider religious statements in terms of a metaphysical world view rather than in terms of positivistic empiricism. This metaphysical world view is fact-oriented rather than logic-oriented and proceeds on the basis of ontology rather than on logical necessity. Paradigm communities critically interact on the basis of the criteria of adequacy and coherence, testing their truth claims. The Bible, seen as a revelatory communication from God, makes all this possible, for it provides the objective data for judging these truth claims. Let us apply this to the basic debate on intentionality.

The modern debate on intentionality began with the classic essay "The Intentional Fallacy" by W. K. Wimsatt and M. C. Beardsley. They argued "that the design or intention of the author is neither available nor desirable as a standard for judging the success of a work of literary art" (Wimsatt 1976:1). The problem of deriving the author's intention, especially if that is not effective in the written work, causes intentionality to repudiate itself. The highly negative cast of this theory has led to a great deal of acrimony and attempts at reformulation, to the extent that Graham Hough states, "This critical movement has by now disintegrated, as a result of its own internal contradictions, of direct assaults upon it, and of more philosophical consideration of meaning and intention in a non-literary context."[6] Yet it has not led to the demise of the problem of getting back to intention, and if anything the intensity of the denial has increased today, as evidenced in appendix one.

Analytical philosophers, such as J. L. Austin, have continually addressed the problem of intentionality. The classical statement is G. E. M. Anscombe's *Intention,* which addresses the issue through the thought of her own teacher, Ludwig Wittgenstein. She took a phenomenological approach, arguing that intention is a form of description that answers the question Why? Therefore, it is connected to practical knowledge and deals with actions (Anscombe 1963:83-89). Several recently have extended this to textual interpretation, taking a position similar to Juhl above. They assert: "Illocutionary acts are intentional, so in interpreting a text we are recovering the author's intention."[7]

I would like to extend this discussion in two directions: the issues of genre and probability (see section four below). Genre determines the extent to which we are to seek the author's intention. For instance, the French "new novel" (Derrida's major proof-text) demands that the interpreter break the normal bounds of established reading and interact on a new level.[8] Of course, I am cognizant of the debate regarding the validity of genre as a classificatory device rather than as an epistemological or ontological tool. However, as I have argued in my essay on "Genre Criticism—Sensus Literalis" (1984:1-27), these are not mutually exclusive categories. Thus, I believe that generic considerations determine the rules of the language game (see the discussion of Wittgenstein and Hirsch above) and therefore help one to discover the author's intention. In many types of poetry and narrative the text itself is multi-layered in terms of meaning, but that in itself is the author's intended message.

4. Probability Theory.   This is another complex issue. It has increasingly come to the fore in discussions of meaning transference and truth claims. My thesis is that any delineation of criteria for meaning depends upon adequacy, coherence or synonymy (Dummett 1975:97-122), and demands some theory of probability.

In separate articles in the 1967 issue of *Philosophy Review,* R. Firth (1967:3-27) and J. L. Pollock (1967:55-60) argue for the priority of probability theory over the quest for necessary knowledge. They state that the demand for certitude negates the quest for knowledge before it can even begin. Further, Ernest W. Adams provides an extremely relevant study of the connection between truth and probability in terms of one of the most difficult types of utterances, the conditional statement (1965:69-102). He argues that the pragmatic criterion of adequacy can be met only by probability theory.[9]

W. V. Quine's study of "The Nature of Natural Knowledge" attempts to refine knowledge theory in similar ways. He asserts that "similarity structures" stand behind both inductive and deductive logic. The starting point of theory formulation is the "observation sentence," stating an occasion that is both "subjectively observable" and "generally adequate . . . to elicit assent" from the witnesses present (1975:73; see 67-74). This occasion sentence becomes a theoretical or standing sentence via query and evidence, as reference leads to predication (note the similarities to Searle at this point). While Quine recognizes the "formless freedom for variation" in theory formulation, at the same time he concludes that they function within "a narrow spectrum of visible alternatives" that interact to revise a theory and thereby make for "the continuity of science." The basis of such is "refutation and correction" (p. 81; see 74-81). Moreover, the very process of refutation depends upon a recognition of probability as the basis for decisions.[10]

James Ross applies these theories to "Ways of Religious Knowing." His basic thesis is that no actual "infirmities" prevent religious knowledge. Religious discourse is inherently intelligible and accessible because there is continuity "from one meaning-differentiated occurrence to another" via analogy, relatedness and semantic contagion (1983:83-87). Ross believes that the content of religious discourse is indeed "craft-bound," internal to the life of the community and not fully accessible to those who will either study or immerse themselves into the community. Furthermore, faith and reason are not incompatible, and criteria for the proof of truth claims does exist alongside faith. Ross, along with Plantinga and others, believes that such criteria are accessible to the philosopher by the analogy theory of meaning and by participation in the community. Truths can be demonstrated and theories can be formed.[11]

I would go one step further. As the believing communities interact and debate truths, the same criteria of coherence and adequacy enable them to challenge and correct one another. Systems are not self-contained and mutually exclusive. If this were the case, "truth" would be relative, and Buddhist, Islamic and Christian claims would all be "true." While such is indeed the case *within* the various systems, this is not true in any final sense. David Wolfe denies the adequacy of relativism and calls for a critical "testing" of truth claims (1982:43-69). The criteria utilized of course depend upon the nature of the project, but there must be internal consistency (lack of contradiction), coherence, comprehensiveness (enveloping all experience) and congruity (the theory fits the evidence) in any general formulation of theory. These are utilized to test systems from within (self-criticism) and without (debate). The interrelations between internal (consistency and coherence) and external (comprehensiveness and congruity) criticism is critical, for these allow one to move beyond multiple meaning. Many interpretations are possible and fit the four criteria above, but not all are as probable. Through a critical openness to truth, based upon probability theory, a person within one system can allow the evidence to challenge and then change the interpretive scheme.

In similar fashion Keith Yandell argues for "reasonable belief" that can be "epistemically justified," that is, shown to be adequate by rational assessment (1984:152-55). The key is to recognize first that adequacy does not depend upon certain knowledge (pp. 130-44) but rather upon its ability to meet such criteria as mentioned above.[12] Both Wolfe and Yandell center upon the more general topic of religious knowledge or "God talk," but the principles adduced apply as well to the more specific question here of understanding the intended meaning and assessing the truth value of religious texts.

G. B. Caird provides an excellent discussion of "The Meaning of Meaning" (1980:37-61). He states that intentionality allows one to separate sense from reference, public meaning (the linguistic aspect, dealing with definition, etymology, sound and feeling) from private (the user's) meaning (that aspect of speech dealing with context, tone, referent and intention). With respect to intention, Caird argues that (1) words have the sense the speaker or writer intended them to have; (2) the speaker's intention determines the type of language used and therefore the rules of the game; and (3) a word has the referent that the speaker intended it to have. It is at the referent level that Caird allows a meaning beyond the author's intention, for statements in Scripture vary between non-transferable specifics (such as historical detail) and universally transferable generalities (axioms, proverbs). The issue is whether we are to connect the original meaning with the later meanings (similar to Hirsch's "meaning" and "significance"). Is there continuity or discontinuity between sense and reference? We will turn back to this shortly.

I would posit to Ross and Caird the likelihood that these meaning theories are based upon probability, and that even nontransferable specifics can be deciphered in terms of their original meaning. In part, later redefinitions and development of themes highlight the original intent by showing change or development. Certainly faith can give theories an aura of certitude, but within the community even the most established views are open to clarification and reformulation. A good example would be the recent summit on inerrancy within the evangelical camp, which resulted in a series of "affirmations" and "denials" intended to clarify and in some cases alter particular definitions (Radmacher 1984:881-87). The point is that religious theories are open to all the probability arguments adduced in criteria for verification. Although admittedly this occurs primarily within the community, I would agree with David Tracy that the growing pluralism and dialogue between communities is opening up many formerly closed groups to fruitful interaction. This I believe is a major step toward solving the problem of intertextuality by driving us back to the text and its meaning.

Probability theory has enormous potential for breaking the impasse between competing theories regarding intentionality. The conclusion of this study thus far would indicate that the theory of knowledge based upon sense and reference would make possible the goal of deriving the intended or original meaning of a work, depending upon generic considerations as noted above. My argument would proceed in this fashion: since one can detect the probable intention of a text, and if internal considerations within particular texts make it important to do so, then it is critical to seek the intended meaning.

Propositional Truth and the Logic of Narrativity

It remains to consider whether intratextual factors within the Bible demonstrate the need for intentionality. In this regard we must consider the possibility of assertive sentences and propositional truth claims in Scripture. It is increasingly popular today to deny that the Bible contains such, undoubtedly as a reaction to the rigid historicizing of many who build upon its supposedly propositional content. At the same time, we must note the presence of indicative and imperative sentences in the Scriptures and grapple with its didactic content even in narrative portions. An extremely interesting paper read at the Northwestern Conference on Semiotics (1982) was John Morreall's "Religious Texts and Religious Beliefs." He argued that the semiotic disregard for questions of reference to reality in the Bible undermines the very nature of religious belief. The extra dimensions of religious faith derive from assent to propositions, and without propositional content would be without meaning or faith content. While the language of the Bible is indeed the speech-act, the central speech-act is assertion, which entails reference to facts about this world and God's relation to it. If the autonomy thesis applies, no referential dimension and no set of assertions call for belief. Belief in the Bible demands that Scripture makes assertions and that they are true.

Of course, this does not mean that all speech-acts in Scripture take propositional form.

In fact, biblical narrative often goes the other direction, using a fictive type of genre to draw the reader into a narrative world of plot, dialogue and characterization. However, the reader should note the positive contribution of redaction criticism, which demonstrates the link between this narrative world and the intended theological assertions of the individual authors. In other words, the plot and structure of biblical narrative do indeed function at the level of assertion.

A. C. Thiselton notes the "unhelpful polarization in the debate" and points out that the question of dynamic versus static concepts of biblical truth-claims is not an either-or (1980:411-15, 433). His valuable discussion of the variety of language games within which "truth" occurs in Scripture is a case in point (1978:874-90). On the basis of our previous discussion we must allow the text to decide how we are to interpret its statements. Caird notes four explicit clues that point to nonliteral meaning (1980:183-97): (1) descriptive terms that label the narrative a parable or similitude or allegory; (2) the alternation of metaphor with simile to draw attention to its use; (3) the use of a genitive or other defining term to demonstrate the referent of a metaphor ("sword of the Spirit," "good fight of faith"); (4) the use of a qualifying adjective ("heavenly Father," "true bread"). Implicit pointers to figurative discourse would be: an impossible literality (a clear metaphor); low correspondence with the sense (such as anthropomorphic language about God); high development (poetically expanding the language on a topic); juxtaposition of images (Hebraic style); originality (live metaphors are more easily detected). The major point here is that the text itself often intends and points to figurative meaning. Metaphors often disrupt.

Figurative speech does not of itself entail polyvalence (see the discussion of metaphor and referentiality on pp. 300-302). Redaction criticism should teach us that. Even the parable was placed within its context for a purpose. Most polyvalent interpretations fail to consider the context, and I must say that the multiple meanings of parables like the prodigal son still have an amount of specificity in their canonical context. Of course, I recognize the tradition development within that context, as Sanders points out. However, this does not obviate original meaning, for we can distinguish levels of meaning, for instance, the hymn of Philippians 2:6-11 in its original creedal context (Christology) and in its setting in Philippians 2 (paradigm for humility). The point is that the broader definition of original/intended meaning covers such aspects as tradition-development in a canonical context. Further, I would not wish to deny out of hand a sense of propositional content for the nonliteral statements of Scripture. The parables were meant to elicit particular responses from their hearers and on the basis of probability theory we can approximate the contextual message and emphases. We can delineate static (propositional assertion) and dynamic (active or parenetic) material from one another.

In *The Word of God and the Mind of Man* (1982:43-54) Ronald Nash documents the assault on what he calls "propositional revelation." While he does not interact with the more recent literature, he presents a cogent case for propositional statements in the Bible. Applying Aristotle's Square of Opposition, he states that the true evangelical position is not that all revelation is propositional but that some is propositional. Historical events, for instance, are not propositional. Nash defines "propositional" as cognitive information that demands personal commitment. Further, this revelation is both personal and cognitive, both divine act and discursive language. Nash concludes by asserting that a proper dynamic/static balance in Scripture as propositional revelation does not entail bibliolatry or reductionism. The multiple uses of biblical language within both event (salvation history) and content (didactic and kerygmatic elements) form the objective and subjective poles of revelation. However, I must clarify Nash in one important respect. As I have just stated above, even historical narrative contains propositional content (theological truths that demand commitment and action) though that is not presented in propositional form. Nash fails to distinguish form from content.

Paul Achtemeier takes this a step further (1980:124-34). He posits that inspiration resides in a confluence of tradition (God's presence in past events, which gave revelational communities hope and self-identity), situation (the way God worked in new situations, which forced a recasting of old traditions) and respondent (anyone who contributed to the reformulation of tradition). Behind all is the developing (and canonical) community of faith. In drawing out some implications for hermeneutics he argues: (1) The biblical witness must be addressed anew to the contemporary community of faith in a way similar to the confluence of tradition, situation and respondent in biblical times. (2) This contemporary witness must remain "faithful to the intention of that original witness" and must "discern what that intention was 'in order to' comprehend the significance of the changed emphases in the witness to the new situation" (1980:150; see 149-54).

While I cannot agree with Achtemeier's dynamic approach to inspiration, his hermeneutics does not differ markedly from that espoused herein. There are two aspects to the single act of interpretation, and the latter (significance) must flow out of the former (intended meaning). In short, we must fuse our exegesis of the Word to an exegesis of our world. I do not wish to quibble terminology, to differentiate too radically between the phrase "meaning and significance" and the phrase "what it meant—what it means." The major point I would stress is that the latter in each pair should be connected to the former.[13]

It is now time to apply this to the issue of hermeneutics. Since narrative provides the most difficult example for general laws of hermeneutics, we will use it as a test case. Christopher Morse argues that "historical knowing takes, indeed requires, narrative form" (1979:98; see 97-108). It gains historical meaning as it expresses following (as organization/scheme, which moves toward a goal), interest (speaking to human needs) and conclusion (a definable outcome or goal). A narrative qualifies as history rather than fiction or myth when it meets four criteria: the picture is located in space and time; it is consistent with itself; it is related to evidence; and it has an emphatically public character. Morse with Moltmann believes that the resurrection, for instance, becomes historical narrative because it "generates" or makes history. As "hope sentences" rather than "descriptive sentences," the resurrection narratives employ "the self-involving logic of a promise" (1979:106).

While the nearly insurmountable problem of theology and history is beyond the scope of this discussion, a few remarks may be made. First, the empirical foundation of the criterion of analogy proposed by Troeltsch[14] and still present in many today can be debated. If we follow the analytical concept of sense and reference, we must allow the biblical claim some credence, and there is no question that the Bible intends to portray the acts of God within history. If philosophy, including a philosophy of history, works functionally rather than empirically, we would agree with Marc Bloch that history is known by the "tracks" or effects it has on people. Since the past progressively changes as people reflect upon it, the evidence must be sifted and categorized.[15]

Arthur Holmes calls for a realistic metaphysical historiography based on three factors (1971:78-84): (1) It will aid the historian in avoiding both historical skepticism and idealistic optimism, since no possibility will ever be "closed." (2) It will provide a rational (built on coherence and self-criticism) and properly empirical (demanding functional and actual adequacy) control on both metaphysical schemes and the subjectivity of the historian. (3) It will explicate its a priori principles and ground them in rational coherence and empirical adequacy. For us this will involve an "action" or "speech-act" model for intended meaning (including the historical veracity and theological truths embedded in narrative material).

The same arguments apply to other types of biblical genre. We can indeed test interpretational schemes for scriptural material on the basis of adequacy and coherence. The intended meaning of the text is not only possible but on the basis of the propositional intent of Scripture is a necessary goal. As Vanhoozer argues, there is an ethical mandate that we consider the intended meaning of a text. This is especially true of texts that demand to be understood on the propositional level. The Bible demands assent and goes to great lengths to insist that the reader understand its assertions (such as Paul in Romans). We do not have to take one of the extreme positions: the autonomy position, which studies "the text and nothing but the text"; or the historicist position, which wants only "what it meant" and psychologizes back to the author's (or authors') mind. Any proper hermeneutics must study the text both diachronically and synchronically, in terms of the past, present and future dimensions.

I agree with the call for a recognition of the "realistic character" of biblical narrative on the part of Frei (1974:10) and others, though I do not agree with their assertion that a referential theory of meaning is to account for the demise of realistic narrative (see Silva 1983:103-8). In my opinion, an improper use of a tool should not lead to the denigration of the tool itself. The basic solution is a trialogue between the author, the text and the reader. The author has produced the text and given it certain meanings that are intended to be understood by the reader. The text then guides the reader by producing certain access points that point the reader to the proper language game for interpreting that particular illocutionary act. The reader thereby aligns himself or herself with the textual world and propositional content, thus coming to understand the intended meaning of the text. It remains now to demonstrate how this works out in detail.

A Field Approach to Hermeneutics

Before attempting to integrate the various arguments of this appendix into a theoretical construct for hermeneutics, I must reintroduce the problem of the reader, so crucial to the negativism of postmodern scholars. All of the research I have done has tried to come to grips with the whole issue of reader and text. Several considerations point to a solution that will integrate the major aspects of the trialogue, author-text and text-reader. The polarities that have clouded the hermeneutical debate—dynamic versus static views of inspiration, propositional versus encounter theology, word versus sentence versus discourse models of communication, assertive versus poetic approaches to literature, the author versus the text versus the reader as the generating force of meaning—are not contradictory but are interdependent parts of a larger whole. Disjunctive thinking has created the crisis. Propositional content, sense and reference, intended meaning—all are viable, indeed necessary, components of the hermeneutical enterprise. It remains now to provide a hermeneutical grid for demonstrating this, to add praxis to theoria.[16]

1. A close reading of the text cannot be done without a perspective provided by one's preunderstanding as identified by a "sociology of knowledge" perspective. Reflection itself demands mental categories, and these are built upon one's presupposed world view and by the faith or reading community to which one belongs. Since neutral exegesis is impossible, no necessarily "true" or final interpretation is possible. There will always be differences of opinion in a finite world. However, as I have already stated, this does not demand polyvalence. Probability theory allows critical interaction and movement toward the intended meaning, however elusive it may prove at times, so long as the communities are open to critical dialogue. Here I want to stress that preunderstanding is primarily a positive (and only potentially a negative) component of interpretation. Preunderstanding only becomes negative if it degenerates into an a priori grid that determines the meaning of a text before the act of reading even begins.

2. I must distinguish "presupposition" from "prejudice." The key is to follow Ricoeur's suggestion and place ourselves "in front of" rather than "behind" the text, so that the text can have priority. This allows us to determine which types of preunderstanding are valid and which are not, as the text challenges, reshapes and directs our presuppositions. The fact-value dichotomy, as many philosophers have noted, cannot be used too stringently in assessing adequacy of criteria. Presuppositions can be external (philosophical or theological starting points) or internal (personality, pressure to publish) but must be recognized and taken into account when studying the text. My basic point is that they *can* be identified. When prejudices become subconscious and are taken for granted, the interpreter never examines them and they become the major hermeneutical tool, determining the meaning of the text. While this often happens and does indeed obfuscate the possibility of discovering the original meaning of a text, this is not a necessary occurrence. The text can address and if necessary change a presupposed perspective.

3. We must seek controls that enable us to work with presuppositions (the positive) rather than to be dominated by prejudices (the negative).

a. We must be open to new possibilities. Positivistic theologians interestingly were open on dogmatic issues but closed to new philosophical insights. Stuhlmacher calls for an "openness to transcendence" from his vantage point as a German historico-critical scholar. I would expand this to include all possible perspectives. We need a polyvalent attitude, an openness to many meaning possibilities, allowing the text and new critical ideas to interact as they challenge our perspectives. We must desire truth rather than confirmation of our pre-existing ideas.

b. We must understand the dangers of merely assuming our presuppositions. Stanton, Childs and Sheppard provide good examples from the history of exegesis. The "Rule of Faith" in the Middle Ages developed out of the patristic desire to gain control over subjective exegesis, then became a victim of its own ascendancy! Stuhlmacher speaks of an "effective-historical consciousness," by which he means the realization that we must consciously differentiate between the original "locale of interpretation" (the *Sitz im Leben*), the historical development of dogma and hermeneutics (these lie between us and the text, shaping our approach) and our own interpretative stance within both culture and our specific community of faith.

c. The interpreter must not only address the text but must allow the text to address him or her (the hermeneutical circle). In exegesis, our presuppositions/preunderstanding must be modified and reshaped by the text. The text must have priority over the interpreter. At the same time, the text must address the reader's contemporary *Weltanschauung*. The commissive force of Scripture must never be lost. The task of hermeneutics is never finished with original meaning but can only be complete when its significance is realized.

4. Polyvalent interpretations per se are unnecessary, but a pluralistic or polyvalent attitude is crucial. Again, my approach is an "interpretive realism" that is in constant dialogue with the various communities of faith in order to refine and reformulate theories on the basis of further evidence or more coherent models. Pure polyvalence lacks this rigorous dialectic because it tends to relativism, that every theory is as good as the next. There is little possibility for the growth of the store of knowledge when rugged individualism is in control of the theoretical process! Of course, we want to be open to the possibility that the polyvalent school is describing "the way it is" (to use Gadamer's expression). However, I have attempted to demonstrate why I do not believe this is the case.

5. We must allow good hermeneutical principles to shape our exegesis and to control our tendency to read our prejudices into the text. Critico-historical exegesis will make us aware of the need to consider biblical backgrounds and data (the historical dimensions); grammatico-historical exegesis allows the original or intended meaning to be the focus (the semantic dimension); and literary criticism keeps the text itself central (the literary dimension). All three integrate to allow preunderstanding to be a positive rather than a negative tool, to guide us to the original meaning of the text rather than to form a barrier to meaning. Stuhlmacher demands "methodological verifiability." The subjectivity of much of modern exegesis must be brought under control, lest "truth" be forfeited.

a. Consider the genre or type of literature (chaps. six to twelve above) and interpret each according to the proper rules of their particular language game. This is where the propositional and illocutionary aspects come into play. If the biblical statement is informative, we give it intellectual assent; if commissive, we react with obedience. A good example of this is Vanhoozer's distinction between infallibility and inerrancy: "Logically . . . infallibility is prior to inerrancy. God's Word invariably accomplishes its purpose (infallibility); and when this purpose is assertion, the proposition of the speech act is true (inerrancy)." In other words, each passage guides the interpreter in its intended direction, whether belief/assent or action.

b. The structural development of the passage (chap. one above) provides a control against artificial atomistic exegesis (the error of most historical approaches). Rhetorical and narrative approaches have moved away from the parts to the whole. Meaning (the author's intended meaning) results from the symmetry of the passage as a whole and not from the isolated parts. Moreover, the context of the whole controls the meaning of the parts and adjudicates between competing interpretations. The passage as a whole provides parameters so that the interpreter can choose between alternative proposals.

c. Semantic research (chap. three above) further helps the reader to discover the sense and reference of the passage. In the past linguistic word studies centered upon etymology and linguistic roots. Today, however, all recognize that semantics is based upon synchronic and structural considerations. The background of a word is a valid aspect only when this is a deliberate allusion to a past use, as in the New Testament use of the Old Testament. Meaning is determined on the basis of the congruence of two factors, semantic field (the number of possible meanings at the time of writing) and context (which tells you which of the possible meanings is indicated in the passage). We select the meaning that best fits the context.

d. A judicious use of background information (chap. five above) helps us avoid the opposite error, namely ignoring the historical aspect in favor of the poetic. Postmodernists so stress the intratextual dimension that they deliberately "deconstruct" the passage from its historical moorings and thus twist its meaning in an internal direction. The tendency is to say, "The text contains all the meaning there is," or to assert, "The reader's response is the meaning." The problem with these, however, is that the biblical author shared certain assumptions with his readers, and these are often open to the interpreter. In fact, background along with the author provides a major access point to the historical dimension of the text. The interpreter needs to discover these underlying "givens" for properly understanding the text.

e. The implied author and the implied reader in the text (chap. six) provide an indispensable perspective for the intended meaning of a text.[17] While postmodernists separate the real author from the implied author, I would not. The implied author is the conscious representation of the real author in the text. As such it provides an access point to the historicality of the text and its message, anchoring interpretation in the ancient period. The implied reader was the focus of the conscious direction of the text and as such provides the access point to the fusion of horizons. The original author had a certain audience in mind, and the text addresses itself to these implied readers. The real reader, by uniting with this textual configuration, can contextualize the text to discover the significance of the text's message for today (see chaps. fifteen and sixteen). Thereby the intended meaning of the text (the historical aspect) and the multiple significances of the text for today (the contemporary aspect) are fused in the act of interpretation.

f. The question of verification of competing interpretive possibilities is essential for any system such as the one espoused herein. In a very real sense, every chapter of this book is part of the verification process. My argument is that this is a threefold process: (1)

Inductively, the interpretation appears not from an inspired "guess" but from the structural, semantic and syntactical study of the text itself; in other words, it emerges from the text itself, which guides the interpreter to the proper meaning. (2) Deductively, a valid interpretation emerges by testing the results of the inductive research via a comparison with other scholars' theories and historical or background material derived from sources outside the text. One deepens, alters and at times replaces his or her theory on the basis of this external data, which is tested on the basis of coherence, adequacy and comprehensiveness. (3) Sociologically, this proceeds via a "critical realism" that governs an ongoing dialogue between the paradigm or reading communities. The continual challenge and critique from opposing communities drives the individual reader back to a re-examination of the text and his or her reading strategy. As a result the text continues to be the focus and leads one to the true intended meaning.

The reader is a positive, not negative, force in interpreting a text. I have argued here that the original meaning of a text is not a hopeless goal but a possible and positive and necessary one. A text invites each reader into its narrative world but demands that the person enter it upon its own terms. The creation of a new text is of course often (perhaps even usually) the result, but it is not a necessity. Throughout this book I have elucidated principles for determining the intended meaning of a text, specifically of the Bible. These principles apply to other texts besides Scripture, but my purpose is to restrict the discussion to the one body of literature which above all demands to be understood in terms of its original intended meaning. I agree with R. T. France's call for

> the priority in biblical interpretation of what has come to be called 'the first horizon,'
> i.e. of understanding biblical language within its own context before we start exploring its relevance to our own concerns, and of keeping the essential biblical context
> in view as a control on the way we apply biblical language to current issues. (1984:42)

This task is not merely a possible goal but is a necessary one. In short, in these two appendices I have tried to lay the philosophical foundation for the spiral from text to meaning; this book as a whole attempts to show how the spiral may lead to understanding.

Notes

Introduction:

[1]I am aware of the debates as to whether Mark 13 or 2 Thessalonians 2 are actually apocalyptic but am using the traditional consensus for illustrative purposes.

Chapter 1: Context

[1]In some ways the delineation of the historical context first may defeat the purpose of the logical or inductively derived context, since it immerses the student already in other people's ideas. The key is to keep this information at the preliminary stage rather than to assume its validity. The purpose of this approach is to remind the student from the start of the ancient situation behind the book and to ensure that one seeks always the original intended meaning rather than the significance of the passage only from a modern perspective.

[2]Of course, we recognize that paragraph divisions differ widely from version to version. However, for the purpose of this preliminary method, such decisions can await the deeper level of exegesis. Here we want only to chart the basic structural development of the book as a whole.

[3]Here I am adapting the earlier outline in Osborne and Woodward 1979:29.

[4]Of course, the beginning student will naturally take longer, while the experienced one will take less time. The time mentioned here denotes a median level.

[5]In the summer of 1983 I taught a doctor of ministry course on the book of Revelation. In the audience were pastors and denominational heads from quite different persuasions, with dispensational, historical premillennial and amillennial positions represented. I faced the course with much fear, wondering if the chemistry of the group would cause an explosion. Instead, we discovered a common area of agreement at this very level of theological theme. In spite of our hermeneutical and perspectival disagreements, we could unite at the level of theological meaning. It was one of the most satisfying experiences I have had in teaching!

[6]In addition to clauses, I would indent important prepositional or participial phrases. I have two criteria for deciding whether or not to indent phrases: (1) Is it important enough to be a separate main heading in my sermon outline? (2) Is it lengthy and complicated? Both criteria make these two prepositional phrases worthy of indentation here.

[7]When I encounter pastors who no longer use their Greek in the pulpit, most tell me that time was the crucial factor in their surrender. Exegesis professors are too idealistic, giving their students too many time-consuming steps to accomplish before the practical results of using their Greek can be realized. One of the major sources of discouragement is diagramming. The average pastor has seven to ten hours (if he spends twenty hours a week in study for two to three messages—Sunday morning, evening and perhaps midweek) to prepare, and diagramming can take up to two hours of that time if the passage is of any length.

[8]Some inductive Bible study methods allow the student to alter the order of the text and to place all subordinate clauses under the main clause. I prefer to maintain the order of the text (in order to avoid confusion later) and to utilize arrows to show which clause they modify. The student of course is free to choose which method seems more comfortable.

[9]The last three can also introduce a minor clause. We must examine the context and ask whether the

conjunction introduces a parallel or subordinate idea. Kaiser (1947:80-86) provides a good breakdown of coordinating conjunctions into connective conjunctions (and, or, nor, for, but, neither—nor, either—or, both—and, not only—but also), adversative conjunctions (but, except), emphatic conjunctions (yea, certainly, in fact), inferential conjunctions (therefore, then, wherefore, so) and transitional conjunctions (and, moreover, then). See also Traina (1952:49-52), Jensen (1963:39-42), Osborne and Woodward (1979:68-72) and Liefeld (1984:60-72). These lists are more extensive and do not attempt to collapse the classification into basic units.

[10]Apposition (v. 10) and content clauses (v. 11) do not modify and therefore are indicated by a bar rather than by an arrow.

[11]I am aware of the attempts to deny the incarnational setting of Philippians 2:6-8 (see Dunn 1980:114-21). However, the arguments are not convincing, and Hawthorne (1984:81-84) is certainly more correct in affirming the traditional interpretation.

[12]Muilenberg's justly lauded SBL presidential address of 1968, "Form Criticism and Beyond" (1969:1-18) looked to rhetorical criticism as the wave of the future. Indeed, it has proven to be so. However, in many studies (as noted by Kessler) it is linked with genre criticism, and that confuses the issue.

[13]Meyer and Rice (1982:156-57) and Nida (1983:22-45). In addition, see the discussions in Kuist (1947:80-86), Traina (1952:49-52), Jensen (1963:39-42), Osborne and Woodward (1979:68-72) and Liefeld (1984:60-72). These lists are more extensive and do not attempt to collapse the classification into basic units. Of the two, the former is more syntactically correct, but the latter cannot easily be subsumed under it, so the best solution is to combine them (the first four belong to Meyer and Rice).

[14]Many believe (see Longenecker 1975:175-80) that it is based on the similar set in 4 Q Florelegium, one of the scrolls from Qumran. There the Essenes collected 2 Samuel 7:10-14; Psalms 1:1; 2:1-2, while the rest of the text in 4 Q Florelegium has been lost.

[15]Meyer and Rice separate these two relationships, but since they are syntactically similar I will bring them under a single rubric. The one distinction is that the latter has "some overlap in topic content between the problem and the solution" (Meyer and Rice 1982:157).

[16]I prefer this translation to "apprehend" as more fitting to the theme of light-darkness in John.

Chapter 2: Grammar

[1]Jeanrond is absolutely opposed to any possibility of objective interpretation but argues that the interpreting community continually interacts and discovers "ever new interpretations of the text of Christian tradition" (1988:130). I would argue that these developing understandings are not "ever new" but must be anchored in the text's own statements. In other words, our interpretations spiral upward toward the intended meaning of the text.

[2]See Würthwein 1981:12-15 and Aland 1987:48-71 for the history of the transmission of the Old Testament and New Testament texts, respectively.

[3]Most Old Testament text critics would avoid the terms "text-types" or "text families" for Old Testament manuscripts, preferring "major textual traditions" or some such.

[4]In addition, some Septuagint books (for example, the Pentateuch, portions of Isaiah) are more accurate than others and have greater weight in text-critical decisions.

[5]Aland 1987:67 states unequivocally that only the Alexandrian, Koine (Byzantine) and D (Codex Bezae) texts are "incontestably verified." Western, Caesarean and Jerusalem text-types are "purely theoretical."

[6]Aland in fact goes so far as to say, "The primary authority for a critical textual decision lies with the Greek manuscript tradition. . . . Furthermore, manuscripts should be weighted, not counted, and the peculiar traits of each manuscript should be duly considered" (1987:275-76). Again, the New Testament external evidence is somewhat stronger and more clearly defined than that of the Old Testament, but on the whole scholars are optimistic with both.

[7]Würthwein states (in order of relative value) that after the Masoretic Text one should consult: the Samaritan Pentateuch, the Septuagint, Aquila's translation, Symmachus' version, Theodotian's revision of the Septuagint, the Peshitta, the Targums, the Vulgate, the Old Latin versions, and so forth.

[8]A new commentary series by Murray Harris (published by Eerdmans) is trying to remedy the imbalance by addressing grammatical issues more directly. The first volume on Colossians and Philemon (1990) exemplifies the promise of this series.

[9]I would recommend using these better grammars as reference tools. Look in the Scriptural indices and

find where your passage is discussed, then use these as mini-commentaries on your text.

[10]However, there is enough truth in the statement to justify an overhaul of exegesis courses. We need less grammar and a more balanced approach, particularly emphasis on holistic syntax and historical-cultural backgrounds. The instructor must always have in mind the seven to ten hours maximum that the average pastor can spend on a single sermon.

[11]A new approach to the verb system, exemplified by Stan Porter (1989) and D. A. Carson, challenges this and stresses aspect, which looks at the verbal "action" from the standpoint of the writer's subjective perspective rather than from the standpoint of the action itself (see Porter 1989:88). It remains to be seen how this will be received.

[12]See also Moule 1959:39-40, who adds that the subjective genitive also tends to merge indistinguishably with the genitive of possession. "The wisdom of God" might refer to that wisdom which God exercises or that which belongs to God. I would add that a descriptive force is also very viable, such as "divine wisdom."

[13]An excellent article on "Prepositions and Theology in the Greek New Testament" by Murray Harris (1978:1171-1215) will help immensely and provide a valuable resource tool in a proper delineation of the preposition in the New Testament.

[14]Barr himself admits that his critique is addressed not so much against the characteristics themselves as against the linguistic basis for such. The evidence must be drawn from the theology of the biblical books and from Greek philosophy rather than from the respective languages. My studies lead me to affirm the first and third but doubt the second. While the Old Testament does not contain as much stress on ethics, the abstract qualities of love, trust, and so forth are seen in the vertical dimension (such as the human's relationship to Yahweh), especially in the poets and prophets. The horizontal dimension (ethics) is seen in preliminary form in the Wisdom literature (such as Proverbs). Both abstract and concrete are found in Hebraic thought.

Chapter 3: Semantics

[1]For a more detailed discussion, see esp. Gibson 1981:47-96; Nida 1964:70-99; Louw 1982:50-60; and Thiselton 1978:1127-29.

[2]See also Gibson 1981:42-44, 165-75, where he challenges the absolute distinction between sense and reference posited by Caird (1982:9). Gibson argues, for instance, that proper nouns do have an aspect of sense and that predicates do have reference. See also Nida 1964:70-82, where he uses referential meaning in a more dynamic way, which would include our sense and reference. Gibson would argue for a more strict usage of the terms.

[3]For sources on synonyms in the Old Testament, see Girdlestone 1897; and in the New Testament see Trench 1880; Berry 1897 or Custer 1975.

Chapter 4: Syntax

[1]Jeanrond (1987:121-23) criticizes evangelical/fundamentalist hermeneutics at exactly this point, the tendency to provide meaning at the word or sentence level without determining its place in the whole of the context.

[2]For other examples, see Beekman and Callow 1974:342 (on Philemon 4-7); Liefeld 1984:51-52 (on Rom 5:1-11); and for comparative purposes see Louw 1982:84-87 (on Phil 1:3-5).

[3]For more extensive discussion of the sources of figures of speech, see Bullinger 1898: passim; Mickelsen 1963:179-81; and Caird 1980:156-59.

[4]Although Lincoln (1981:139-68) has made an excellent and provocative case for the literal meaning of this term, I remain convinced that the figurative sense fits the context better.

[5]In this section I am discussing only the positive side of Ricouer's theory. For his presupposition of polyvalence (multiple meaning) and the metaphorical force of all language, see appendix one. For excellent discussions of Ricoeur's theory of metaphor, read Perpich 1984:130-33 and Vanhoozer 1990.

[6]Caird (1980:136-37) discusses this as a type of metonymy (above, 5a), but it has a different rhetorical function so we are considering it separately.

[7]Following the chiasm of vv. 14-17 (discussed under v. 16 below) another outline is possible, keeping the middle pair together: I. Command to Rejoice (v. 14); II. Reasons for Rejoicing (vv. 15-16); III. God's Promise and Love (v. 17).

[8]This prophecy was probably given before the sudden cessation of Assyria as a world power after Ashurbanipal died in 626 B.C.

[9]The reader will note the absence of contextualization or application in this discussion, but that is the subject of a later chapter. Our purpose here is to illustrate how the exegetical techniques unite in the study of individual passages.

[10]Only Romans has as many and no other book contains it more than twice.

[11]At the moment I have been reading through the psalms using Peter Craigie's commentary (Word) and have enjoyed it tremendously. In fact I am editing a New Testament commentary series for InterVarsity Press that will add contextualization to the exposition of the text (see also the Bible Speaks Today Series).

[12]Some may be asking why we should worry about exegetical exactness in a devotional experience. However, as chaps. 15-16 will argue, contextualization in the sermon (or devotional experience) needs to be based upon *God's* message rather than our own. A lack of concern for the divinely inspired message has led many Christians astray. Moreover, studying deeply is like mining for gold. There are treasures under the text just waiting to be dug out!

[13]In addition to the works by Chomsky already mentioned, one can find excellent summaries of his thought in Lyons (1968:247-69; 1980:124-29; 228-35, 242-47) and Arens (1975:500-510). The latter goes beyond Chomsky to describe the school that he began and provides a valuable integration of the syntactical and semantic components.

[14]For excellent discussions of this, see Golden, Berquist and Coleman 1983:35-92; Foss, Foss and Trapp 1985:1-10; and Mack 1990:25-48.

[15]Mack (1990:34-35) notes that the Greeks developed two subtypes under each major category. Judicial rhetoric concerned either accusation or defense, deliberative consisted of persuasion or refutation, and epideictic concerned praise or blame. All six types are found in the New Testament, often several of them brought to bear on an issue simultaneously. Most recent rhetorical study centers on tracing the patterns in a given passage.

[16]Rhetorical criticism in this sense from an Old Testament perspective is a more difficult perspective, due to the much longer period envisaged and consequent multiplicity of cultural influences. However, a recent paper by David Howard, "Is Biblical 'Rhetorical Criticism' Really Rhetorical Criticism?" (forthcoming) argues cogently for the switch from style to persuasion in Old Testament rhetorical study as well.

[17]What follows is discussed in Kennedy (1984:23-25); Watson (1988:20-21); and Mack (1990:41-48).

[18]In this section I am interacting with Kennedy's discussion of the Sermon on the Mount as a deliberative speech (1984:39-72) as well as Mack's outline (1990:82-85).

[19]Kennedy (1984:55, 57) considers this to be the second half of the "proof" of the proposition, with 5:21-48 constituting the first half. According to him, 5:21-48 is characterized by ethos and pathos (emotional appeal) while the second (6:1-18) is a series of enthymemes with supporting argument. A similar outline (but more likely) is Mack's. He finds two theses in 5:17-20, with 5:21-48 supplying examples for the first (Jesus fulfilling the law) and 6:1-18 examples for the second (demanding a more perfect piety). However, 6:1-18 is more central to the entire sermon than this, and I believe it is better to see it as the *partitio*.

[20]Within this section, 6:19-24 states the major thesis (seek treasure in heaven); 6:25—7:6 provides a series of prohibitions (don't worry, judge or share truth with those unworthy); 7:7-14, two injunctions (on prayer and entering the narrow gate); and 7:15-23, two warnings (against false prophets and trying to enter heaven unworthily).

[21]The *refutatio* here is not a separate section but is found in virtually every paragraph from 5:21—7:27.

[22]There is a distinct tendency among many practitioners to take rhetorical criticism in a postmodern direction (see appendix one). For instance, Wuellner (1987:460-61) says it "takes us away from a traditional message- or content-oriented reading of Scripture to a reading which generates and strengthens ever-deepening personal, social, and cultural values." The emphasis is no longer on propositional truth but upon the "dynamics of personal or social *identification* and *transformation*" (p. 461). He sees in this an alignment of the new rhetorical criticism with feminist and non-Western modes of criticism.

[23]I am in the process of doing a major commentary on Mark and am quite discouraged by the unbelievable plethora of suggestions regarding the outline of the book. I am even more discouraged over how many of them sound plausible!

[24]There is no such detailed program developed for Old Testament rhetorical criticism, undoubtedly because the rhetorical techniques were developed primarily by the Greeks. No such patterns were available from

Akkadian, Sumerian, Egyptian, Babylonian or Persian sources. However, the steps above are still generally applicable to Old Testament texts. After finishing this excursus, I received an excellent Old Testament counterpart to Kennedy and Mack: Dale Patrick and Allen Schult, *Rhetoric and Biblical Interpretation* (Sheffield: The Almond Press, 1990). They present a good general program for going beyond stylistics to the rhetorical power of the text of the Old Testament.

Chapter 5: Historical and Cultural Backgrounds
[1]Much of the illustrative material is drawn from my forthcoming book tentatively titled *A Social History of Biblical Customs,* which will trace the development of these customs through the biblical period.
[2]Ayers 1983:135-36 and Neusner 1983:99-144 agree that the Hillel school of the Pharisees was the precursor of the second-century rabbis.
[3]Kee would add other types of study: social dynamics and social roles, tracing leadership roles within societal structure; anthropological analysis and group identity, which studies the symbol system behind the social organization; and sociology of knowledge, which analyzes internal and external social pressures on the belief system (1989:32-64). These add further detail to the broad category of "sociological interpretation."

Part 2: Genre Analysis
[1]For a more detailed discussion of the criteria for genre identification, see Horst 1978:122-23; Baird 1972:387-88; Osborne 1983:6-7, 24-25; and Longman 1985:61-67.

Chapter 6: Narrative
[1]John J. Collins (1982), 47-48, denies this, saying:
> The rediscovery of biblical narrative has been largely a consequence of the negative results of historical research. This point has theological importance. Many conservative biblicists have invoked literary criticism as a way of avoiding unwelcome historical conclusions. . . . It should be clear that such evasions will not work. . . . "Story" is not "history." It is essentially fiction, material which in some measure has been invented.

However, this is clearly a biased statement, for many literary critics do in fact combine the historical and the "fictive" dimensions of literary analysis (as I will argue below).
[2]See Marshall 1970, Martin 1972, Smalley 1978 and R. T. France 1989.
[3]Berlin 1983:13. Ryken argues that a literary approach is a supplement rather than a replacement for more traditional disciplines (1984:12, 131).
[4]Krieger 1964:3-70. Krieger argues that the historical (windows) and the literary (mirrors) are interdependent aspects of literary analysis.
[5]See Pratt 1983:158-59. Culpepper provides a more critical use of the imagery to suggest that we view the text as a mirror more than a window, since the latter is open only to the specialist who can separate tradition from redaction (1983:3-4). Yet a historical approach does not demand only a reconstruction of the event, and historical background provides a valid aspect of literary interpretation. Moreover, the historical data is available through the better commentaries and books on background. Thus it is readily accessible to the nonspecialist. On the text as "portrait" see Guelich 1982:117-25.
[6]Berlin says that "poetics is to literature as linguistics is to language. That is, poetics describes the basic components of literature and the rules governing their use" (1983:15).
[7]See Sternberg 1985:89; compare 89-91. However, I must demur from Sternberg's language, "choice to devise." This is part of his argument that Old Testament narrative is ideological rhetoric designed as propaganda for an omniscient God. I would explain the biblical language as due to the author's awareness of divine inspiration rather than as deliberate rhetoric.
[8]However, I disagree with those critics who string together these "seams" and asides into what amounts to a "subtext" behind the surface text. This results from the radical separation of the implied author from the real author, a theory that I reject (see further below). Instead, the editorial comments provide the author's commentary on the significance of the story he is narrating. These two elements—story and commentary—stand together in the narrative.
[9]See Culpepper 1983:20-34; Petersen 1978: 97-121; Kingsbury 1986:32-36; Rhoads and Michie 1982:36-44. From the side of pure literary criticism see Uspensky 1973:8-100; Genette 1980:161-86; and Chatman

1958:151-58.

[10]The nonevangelical considers the "inside" information an artistic creation of the author, while the evangelical believes that divine inspiration is behind the material, and that the information was gleaned in many different ways but is historically accurate.

[11]Lundin, Thiselton and Walhout 1985:69. Walhout develops four criteria for detecting a historical work (pp. 72-76): (1) the world in the text is factually accurate; (2) the point of view taken by the author often contains indicators of a historical perspective; (3) the use of the text by its readers and the circumstances behind its production point to its genre (whether history or fiction); (4) the uses of the text by the author himself (Is he making claims of an actual situation in the world behind the text?) point to a real or fictive world in the text.

[12]For a good narrative analysis of John 9 see Resseguie 1982:295-303.

[13]Culpepper 1983:161, from Aristotle's *Poetics* 1454a. Most make a distinction between "flat" (characters with only a single trait) and "round" (many traits) characterization. I prefer Berlin's categories (1983:23-24): a "type" (a static character with only a single trait), an "agent" (a mere functionary with no trait at all) and a "full-fledged" character (a realistic personage upon whom the action turns).

[14]See Chatman 1978:107-388 and Kingsbury 1986:9-10 for more detailed discussion.

[15]See Osborne 1984:108-10. For further discussion of the settings in Mark, see Rhoads and Michie 1982:64-72. Interestingly, they consider only geographical settings.

[16]Sternberg 1985:186-89. Fowler calls this "the rhetoric of indirection" (1983:53). The text provides the clues to help the readers discover the proper path through the story but uses these gaps to involve them in the author's actual message.

[17]Many scholars separate the implied reader from the "narratee" (see figure 18 in the text). The narratee corresponds to the narrator and is the literary figure to whom the text is explicitly directed. For instance, Luke-Acts is directed to Theophilus (Lk 1:3; Acts 1:1). Most of the time, the narratee is designated by specific asides or explanations in the text, guiding his or her understanding. The implied reader would be the implicit audience, "that set of values that is capable of bringing this work to its aesthetic completion" (Keegan 1985:101). However, I agree with Kingsbury that for all intents and purposes the narratee and implied reader are synonymous in biblical narrative. We could separate Theophilus (the narratee) and the church of Luke's time (the implied reader), but such would be artificial, for the explanations and summaries are addressed to both simultaneously.

[18]Fowler 1983:32-49 provides a helpful discussion of the issue as to whether the "implied reader" is ensconced in the text (so Wayne Booth) or created by the real reader from the text (so Wolfgang Iser). Fowler uses the phrase "ideal reader" (Stanley Fish) as the better term for the latter and develops this in his *Semeia* article (1985:5-21), in which he gives priority to the ideal reader and identifies the latter with an informed real reader. I would give priority to the implied reader of the text, since the ideal reader leads to a reader-response orientation in which the readers create their own meaning rather than discover the author's intended meaning (see the appendices to this book for further discussion).

[19]Reader-response critics argue that polyvalence (multiple meanings) controls the interplay between text and reader. This assumption is challenged in the appendices of this book, which argue that it is not only possible but mandatory to recover the author's meaning.

[20]Culpepper 1983:209. Culpepper does not give "intended meaning" the central place that I do; nevertheless, his statement is applicable. Dewey shows how "point of view" helps one detect the "implied reader" in Mark and thus to discover the "double identification" with both Jesus and the disciples (as well as the tension in the actual reader that this creates) in Mark (1982:97-106). In other words, these techniques combine to guide the reader to the text's meaning.

[21]I would not isolate the "commissive" dimension from the other aspects (such as intended meaning) above. As stated elsewhere in this volume, meaning and significance (the static and dynamic sides of interpretation) are intertwined.

[22]A good example is Alter 1981:3-12, 107-12, whose excellent studies of Genesis 37—39 have almost gained the status of classic work.

[23]Most current biblical narrative specialists—like Sternberg, Berlin or Culpepper—see tradition and literary criticism as complementary rather than opposed. Nearly all, however, recognize the paucity of results (in terms of understanding the text) from tradition criticism. Form and redaction critics too often are more interested in reconstructing the history and theology of the early church than in understanding the text

itself. Source criticism is helpful as a supplement to narrative analysis. However, when the identification of sources becomes an end in itself it tends to be speculative (such as the many unbelievably complex theories on the Synoptic problem) and detracts from the text's meaning.

[24]Sternberg 1985:70. Modern literary critics take strong exception to Sternberg's statement here, and indeed it is true that the antihistorical position is alive and well. Nevertheless, I believe that Sternberg makes a good point, for the earlier "heyday" of this opposition to the historical element in a text is indeed a thing of the past.

[25]While Rhoads and Michie deny the validity of the former, they recognize the value of background material: "None of these considerations means that our general knowledge of the first century is not helpful in the interpretation of the story; indeed it is often crucial."

[26]See the summary in Gillespie 1986:199-203, who tries to walk a middle path between authorial intention and total textual autonomy. A degree of autonomy is required, Gillespie argues (following Ricoeur), by semantic ambiguity (the impossibility of seeking clarification from the author).

[27]Obviously, I do not agree with McKnight in rejecting "plot, technique, character development." However, his basic point, that we be wary of modern approaches, has some validity.

[28]Kingsbury 1986:9. In one sense this hardly needs to be stated, for as said above, the central theme of plot by definition is always conflict. However, in Matthew the conflict between God and the machinations of his enemies (who attempt to disrupt his redemptive plan) is particularly central.

[29]See Walker 1977:76-93; Osborne 1979:305-22 and 1991; and McKnight 1988:83-95, as well as the bibliography in these works, for further material on redaction techniques.

[30]There is considerable debate as to whether the Olivet Discourse can be classified as "apocalyptic." Many believe that the absence of esoteric symbolism and other apocalyptic features in Mark 13 makes it doubtful that Jesus was employing Jewish apocalyptic here.

[31]On misunderstandings in John see Carson 1982:59-91 and Culpepper 1983:152-65. Carson stresses the historical side, Culpepper the literary. I would see them as complementary rather than contradictory.

[32]Greidanus 1988:148-54. He points to four advantages: (1) It is closer to the biblical form and so is less likely to distort the biblical text. (2) It creates interest by keeping the sermon moving forward to a climax. (3) It involves the hearers more holistically, reaching the intuitive and emotional side as well as the cognitive and rational side. (4) It communicates with the hearers indirectly and obliquely and so engages them more deeply by getting around their defenses.

[33]For the differences between didactic and narrative sermons see Greidanus 1988:144-54.

Chapter 7: Poetry

[1]LaSor, Hubbard, Bush (1982:604-605) describe the types of love poetry: descriptive songs, in which each lover extols the other's beauty (4:1-7; 5:10-16; 6:4-7; 7:1-9); songs of admiration (1:9-11; 4:9-11; 7:7-9); songs of yearning (1:2-4; 2:5-6; 8:1-4, 6-7); search narratives, in which the woman passionately seeks her lover (3:1-4; 5:2-7); the game of love (5:8—6:1, following the search of 5:2-7); teasing songs that detail the banter between the lovers (2:14-15; 5:2-3); boasting songs praising the beloved (6:8-10; 8:11-12); invitations to love (2:5, 17; 4:16; 7:11-13; 8:14).

[2]Many scholars believe that this love poem originated in the marriage ritual and liturgy. While such cannot be proven, it has merit.

[3]Kaiser 1981: 215. Most scholars consider it a musical term, the meaning of which has been lost. Therefore, it has little value in structural considerations.

Chapter 8: Wisdom

[1]Zimmerli (1933:179) calls this the central concept in the appropriation of wisdom.

[2]Nel (1982:62-64) argues that even in cases without motivation clauses (he discusses Prov 23:12; 27:2; 31:8-9) the latter is implicit. However, I do not find the argument convincing. He finds the motivation in 20:18 in the first half ("Make plans by seeking advice") but on formal grounds that do not state a consequence but rather a general admonition applied specifically in the second half ("if you make war, seek guidance"). There is no true motivation clause in such statements (see also 17:14; 20:19; 24:27, 29).

[3]A form similar to the allegory, the fable, is frequent in Near East wisdom but not found in the Old Testament. Therefore I do not discuss it here.

[4]Crenshaw 1974:255-560. I do not wish to intimate that these are not historical. "Imagined speech" is a

formal category not a historical judgment.

[5]Note that the believer is commanded to "submit" both to government (Rom 13:1-7; 1 Pet 4:13-17) and parents (Eph 6:1-4; Col 3:20). The principle is the same.

[6]Kaiser (1979: passim; 1981:73) argues that the refrain "Eat, drink, and find enjoyment in your work, for this is the gift of God" (Eccles 2:24-25; 5:18-20; 8:15) marks the four sections of Ecclesiastes and embodies a basically positive outlook on life. However, it is debatable whether these indeed demarcate the four sections of the book, and while there are positive glimpses (note also God's omnipotence in 3:14 and the necessity of fearing God in 8:12) it seems more likely that much of the book intends to show the complete futility of a life centered only upon the things of this life.

[7]While many have argued that the epilogue is secondary (Sheppard; Gordis 1968:349-50) due to the third-person style, which does not occur elsewhere in the book, most of the terms are found elsewhere in the book and the switch in style could easily be calculated to draw attention to the importance of the concluding section.

[8]For the strongest arguments for a developed system from a wisdom perspective, see Hermissor 1968:97-136, and from a general perspective, see Riesner 1984:123-99.

[9]See Sheppard 1988:1077. Blenkinsopp (1983:11-14) posits a series of scribal schools built on the Egyptian mode to educate the elite in Israeli society. While such is certainly possible, there is insufficient evidence to support the likelihood of such an enterprise. Thompson (1986:243, 245) posits that children may have been taught to read, though not in formal schools but through the family (or private homes) and in some cases in scribal academies. For instance, Isaiah 10:19 speaks of trees as being "so few that a child can write them down" and Isaiah 28:9-10 may draw an analogy from children writing the alphabet. However, these are elusive and do not demand a very high degree of literacy in Israel.

Chapter 9: Prophecy

[1]Yet this too has become a source of vigorous debate. Fishbane (1985:435-40) examines the prophetic interpretation of the Torah and concludes that direct authority lies not in the prophetic oracle but in the legal "tradition" of Moses behind it. Since the prophets contextualized the thrust of the "authoritative text" (the Mosaic and Deuteronomic traditions), the prophets, according to Fishbane, developed on "Aggadic exegesis," a tradition that reflected upon the theological implications of the received tradition and applied them to new contexts and situations. However, the two (direct revelatory inspiration and Aggadic exegesis of the Torah) are not mutually exclusive. As I will develop below, the prophets called the people back to Torah and covenant. As such the prophetic exegesis of the sacred texts is indeed aggadic, but the theological contextualization they utilized came directly from God.

[2]Lindblom 1962:69-70; Sawyer (1987:18-19) posits prophetic guilds on the basis of Near Eastern parallels (such as the 450 prophets of Baal in 1 Kings 18).

[3]Clements 1975:37-39. Clements and others argue that the so-called Deuteronomic movement played the critical role in reshaping the prophetic-legal tradition. Against this see Smith 1986b:996.

[4]Clements (1975:88) doubts that any such role of "covenant mediator" or "law speaker" can be substantiated. However, this is largely due to his acceptance of redaction-critical conclusions regarding the secondary nature of the covenant passages discussed below. I find a certain circular reasoning in the whole process. For instance, Clements (1975:43-45) accepts H. W. Wolff's conclusion that Deuteronomic redactors added the covenant emphases in Hosea and Amos. At the same time Clements believes Hosea played a formative role in the development of the Deuteronomic tradition itself. Yet if Hosea himself developed the emphases there is no need to posit a lengthy redactional process behind the book. I concur with Craigie's criticisms (1986:140-43) regarding the basic theory of Deuteronomic redactors in the prophetic period.

[5]Contra Tucker (1985:339), who speaks for several (Wolff, Warmouth) when he says "the prophets functioned primarily to announce the future as the word of God; they were not first of all preachers of repentance."

[6]It is unfortunate that Tan (1974:201-2) calls Mickelsen "non-literal" and hints that he denies any historical link. I would not call myself a "literalist" but would argue that Mickelsen's cautions in fact are similar to Tan's, who agrees that prophecy should not be allowed to exceed "the limits of what present history can attest" (p. 206) and that it should never be used to set dates or to spiritualize the text (pp. 208-9).

[7]See the list in Kuenen 1977:98-275 and the shorter discussion in Crenshaw 1971:51-52. Crenshaw (pp. 14-

15) builds upon Hempel's influential essay (1930:631-60), which viewed unfulfilled prophecy as causing a crisis of faith when some failed to come to pass. This led the prophets to adapt their message to new situations, exemplified especially in "Deutero-Isaiah's" reworking of the Cyrus prophecy (Is 44:28; 45:1) into the servant songs when Cyrus refused to recognize Yahweh as the basis of his victory over the Babylonians. This and similar theses, however, are unnecessary and speculative. There is simply no textual evidence for such a transformation. There was a "crisis of faith," but it was caused by the growing apostasy of the nation and the signs of divine punishment that accompanied it.

[8]For a fairly complete list of formulas and passages in which they are found, see Mickelsen 1963:81-84.

[9]In fact, Sawyer (1987:25-29) considers both types under the general category of "oracle" and specifically "messenger speech."

Chapter 10: Apocalyptic

[1]Aune (1986:86-87) proposes three aspects: form, content and function. All of these, however, relate more to genre or formal features.

[2]For instance, Sanders posits an "essentialist" definition that attempts to find the "most striking point of Jewish apocalypses," which he argues is the "revelation which promises reversal and restoration" (1983:456-58). The other elements, such as transcendence or pseudonymity, Sanders finds predominant in other types of literature as well. However, the promise of restoration is also a revelatory feature of prophetic writing. Again, there is no pure genre and the identification of apocalyptic is dependent upon an accumulation of characteristics rather than on traits peculiar to this genre alone.

[3]For instance, I disagree with Morris (1971:35-36) that the prophet had the sense of "standing in the council of God" (Jer 23:18) while the apocalyptist did not. In many visions the apocalyptic writer is in the very presence of God (such as the throne vision of Rev 4—5), and the perspective in this sense does not differ appreciably from that of the prophet.

[4]Collins makes this category the basis of his breakdown of apocalyptic works into two types: those which include an otherworldly journey and those which do not (1979:12-13). Collins places three subtypes under each major category: those with a review of history and an eschatological crisis; those without such a review but still predicting a public triumph of God; and those with an emphasis upon a personal rather than corporate deliverance.

[5]Rowley goes so far as to state that Daniel established the pattern for pseudonymity in apocalyptic works (1963:40-42). However, others dispute this. On behalf of the traditional view of the authorship and date of Daniel, see Harrison 1969:1110-27.

[6]Russell 1964:132-39; Charles believes that this was due to the close of the canon (1914:38-46).

[7]Sanders 1983:456; Sanders lists passages where themes of reversal and restoration are found: Daniel 7—12; 1 Enoch 83—90; 91—104; Jubilees 23; 4 Ezra 11-12 and so on (pp. 456-57).

[8]See Russell 1964:308-23. The idea of a two-Messiah doctrine is very debated. Rowland accepts it (1982:263), but Higgins doubts that such a belief was held (1966-67:211-39). A balanced perspective can be found in Longenecker 1970: 63-66, who says that early in the life of Qumran such a view was held but that by the first century the lay Messiah became the sole repositor of the Messianic office.

[9]Hanson's larger thesis is more questionable. He argues that there is a development from "Second Isaiah" (chaps. 40—55) to "Third Isaiah" (chaps. 56—66); in the latter work a group of visionaries struggling with the priestly party for religious revival surrender all hope in present historical processes and turn to a cosmic vision of direct divine intervention in the future. However, the exegetical evidence for such a hypothesis is not strong, and I fail to see such major changes in the text.

Chapter 11: Parable

[1]Again the goal is to discover the intended meaning of the text, that is, those details which the *author* allegorized, rather than the desired meaning of the reader (see further appendices one and two on this).

[2]Jeremias argues for "unless" or "if perhaps" on the basis of rabbinic interpretation of Isaiah 6:9-10 (1970:17-18). However, two caveats are necessary: this is one way the rabbis interpreted Isaiah 6:9-10 but not the only way; and in any case the rabbinic interpretation yields only one *possibility,* and the immediate context is the final arbiter.

[3]Via points out how easily we can allegorize even when denying allegory, using Ernst Fuchs as an example (1967:19-21).

[4]However, Marshall 1978 and Fitzmyer 1983 believe that the "birds" refer to Gentiles coming into the church, on the basis of Jewish parallels where "birds" refer to Gentile proselytes. But the context of Mark 4, centering as it does upon Jesus' conflict with the Jewish authorities, makes such an interpretation unlikely. Blomberg points to the possibility that Ezekiel 17:23 (in which the birds [the peoples of the earth] rest in the branches of the cedar of Lebanon) is behind the imagery (1990:285). However, he cautiously states that there is no proof from context that Jesus intended such an allusion.

[5]Lambrecht detects a three-stages process (1981:16-17): (1) The future is made visible and a new authentic existence is offered. (2) The hearer must reverse his direction and break with the past. (3) A far-reaching decision must be made in the present, involving a total commitment to the new reality. This is the power of the parable.

[6]The question as to whether the parable refers to the nations' treatment of the disciples or to the disciples' treatment of others is not endemic to my point. The parable itself would favor the first; the context of Matthew 24—25, the second. Most scholars opt for the former.

[7]The double invitation is a common oriental practice, consisting of the sending of an invitation then of servants to fetch the guests. Interestingly, Matthew in his version (22:1-10) does not stress the double invitation but includes a double refusal. Luke adds a further double invitation to the surprise guests. Clearly Matthew stresses Jewish guilt and Luke divine benevolence. As Perkins says, Matthew highlights refusal, anger and judgment, Luke the offer of salvation (1981:95-96).

[8]Although many believe that the audience and historical settings of the parables in the Gospels are the work of the Evangelists, I do not believe such is necessary. See Blomberg 1990.

[9]For the historicity of the two settings see Carson 1984:123-26; Marshall 1978:243-45. I believe that Jesus used the same parable form (each given 10-5-1 with the last hiding his money) in these two situations and that each Evangelist chose that which best fit his needs.

[10]However, Bailey's attempts to find complicated chiastic structure in nearly all of Luke's parables greatly exceeds the limits of likelihood.

[11]Stein 1981:80. However, Greidanus adds an important critical cautionary note that the modern retelling can actually detract from the meaning of the text and draws attention only to the creative (and highly entertaining) re-creation (1988:226). It is usually easier (and hermeneutically better) to retell the original story, using background information to unlock misunderstood aspects.

[12]Tolbert 1979:83-89. Blomberg clusters the parables into "simple three-point parables," "complex three-point parables," "two-point and one-point parables" (1990).

[13]Contra Guelich, who characterizes a growing number who state that the internal structure of the parable centers on the seed rather than on the soil and that only the later interpretation (vv. 14-20) centers on the soil (1989:196-97). I would argue that the debate is disjunctive and we have a both-and situation, that is, both seed and soil are central.

Chapter 12: Epistle

[1]One such is the whole question of normative vs. cultural commands, an issue discussed in chap. fifteen below; Fee and Stuart devote a second chapter on the Epistles to this topic.

[2]See Doty 1966:411-51; White 1982:5-12; Knutson 1982:15-22; Fitzmyer 1982:25-40; Dion 1982:59-71, 77-84; Pardee 1978:321-44.

[3]See Deissmann 1909:146-232; Roller 1933; Doty 1966:51-62; 1973; White 1982:89-104; Blaiklock 1979:545-52; Longenecker 1983:101-2.

[4]Martin (1977:233-34) follows Sanders (1962:348-52) in asserting that Paul was following the patterns of the Qumran hymns and Jewish liturgical prayers. Thus his prayers are not spontaneous but were carefully crafted for the church.

[5]Aune notes that the term *sermon,* or *homily,* is inaccurate to describe the literary genre of such epistles as Hebrews, James, 1 Peter, 1 Clement or the Epistle of Barnabas (1987:197-204). He traces those Hellenistic features (forensic, deliberative and epideictic [praise and blame], diatribe) and Jewish types (synagogue homily) behind the Epistles.

[6]The passage on the Jerusalem decree in Acts 15:19-29, asking the Gentile Christians to respect the religious sensibilities of their Jewish brethren, does apply to this. However, 1 Corinthians 8—10 does not.

[7]I do not wish to specify which are and which are not allowable. Each believer must prayerfully decide that alone.

Chapter 13: Biblical Theology

[1]Contra Carson, who argues that the process of unifying themes belongs within the realm of systematic theology and thus biblical theology is primarily a descriptive discipline (1983:69-70). As I will argue below, the task of collating themes properly belongs under biblical theology, which seeks not only the theology of a book but also the theology of Israel and of the early church.

[2]Gaffin 1976:44-45, following John Murray. Guthrie argues similarly that intertextual considerations demand that the Bible be treated as more than merely another human work (1981:34-36). The tendency to exaggerate differences between biblical writers must be controlled by a more holistic consideration of the biblical material.

[3]This builds upon the fourfold scheme of Vos, who follows the classical division of exegetical theology, historical theology, systematic theology and practical theology (1958:12-13). He believes that exegesis and biblical theology belong to the same division, but I would argue that they are sufficiently distinct to warrant assigning them a separate place in the process of interpretation.

[4]I disagree with those who, like Achtemeier, extend inspiration to later interpretive communities as well as to the biblical authors. In no sense could competing theologies be said to be "inspired" of God in a canonical sense. This of course is the classical debate between Roman Catholic and Protestant ideas regarding the "magisterium" or authority of the church to establish dogma. I would use the term *illumination* (see pp. 540-41) for the dogma of the church, for it is a human approximation that attempts to collate and logically summarize scriptural truth for the believing community rather than to establish new canonical authority.

[5]Anderson assigns just this role to the commentary, stating that one should approach the text first and then use the commentary to gain an appreciation for the history of the interpretation of the text (1982:342-47). This will aid contemporary interpretation and application. Yet while this is true in theory, very few commentaries provide such a historical perspective (an excellent exception is Philip Hughes's commentary on Hebrews).

[6]On the basis of the Roman Catholic dialogue on tradition and exegesis, Blenkinsopp says that the exegete must "make his way between the Scylla of philology and semantics and the Charybdis of an (unconsciously) autonomous biblical theology. It is his job to provide his colleague with the material necessary for his synthesis" (1964:84).

[7]Gaffin argues that biblical theology, by focusing on God's revelation in history, forces systematic theology to be true to the process of revelation and thereby to the intended (historical) meaning of the text itself (1976:42-50). In this way biblical theology regulates the results of exegesis and controls the subjective tendencies of dogmatics.

[8]As Hughes remarks, Guthrie

is writing something more like a systematic theology of the New Testament than anything else. . . . Certainly the themes with which dogmatics and New Testament theology deal are similar, but this does not mean a New Testament theology has to be *structured* thematically. . . . By ignoring individual theologies in the New Testament, there is a sense in which some of the theological message has slipped through the cracks in Guthrie's topical grid. (1982:112-13; italics his)

[9]Barrett correctly notes that biblical theology "may be characterized by the word process," systematics "by the word result" (1981:5). Systematic theology is that discipline which "involves the relation between unchanging biblical truth and varying philosophical modes."

[10]Tate goes a step further and considers "biblical preaching" to be a path *toward* a proper biblical theology, since of necessity preaching demands a new appreciation for the whole of Scripture (1981:179-80). He especially lauds Childs's attempt to provide a canonical method for doing this.

[11]Walter Bauer produced the classical work on diversity, arguing that what is called heresy in the New Testament was actually considered orthodox originally but lost out to the stream of tradition developed by Paul and his followers. The modern work with the greatest impact is Dunn 1977, who accepts Bauer's thesis that "there was no 'pure' form of Christianity that existed in the beginning which can properly be called 'orthodox'. . . [but] only different forms of Christianity competing for the loyalty of believers" (p. 3). After tracing the myriad of competing theories regarding the different communities of the New Testament period, Dunn concludes that the only unifying strand was the continuity between the historical Jesus and the Christ of faith (pp. 369-72). It is indeed strange that the single source of unity is an issue that has arisen only in the last century!

[12]Aune states that the New Testament has a variety of viewpoints but no outright contradiction (1973:10-15). When we recognize the analogical nature of biblical language, we can recognize themes behind the diverse expressions.

[13]Dunn 1982:18-21 and Sanders 1972:17-20. Achtemeier makes tradition one of three key components (tradition, situation, respondent) that interrelate to form the locus of inspiration, stating that "the traditions are the building materials out of which the community continues to construct itself and to shape its present and its future" (1980:126; see 124-26). In each renewed situation divine inspiration was present and so theology must remain cognizant of the whole process as well as of the final form of the text.

[14]Gese 1981:15-25. Gese sees the centerpoint of biblical theology to be the process of divine revelation centering upon Sinai (Old Testament) and Zion (New Testament).

[15]See Hasel 1982:66-67; Hayes and Prussner 1985:244, 262; Reventlow 1986:150-54.

[16]Sanders 1980:187-91. See also *JSOT* 16 (1980), which is devoted to Childs's canon criticism.

[17]For other examples of canonical criticism, see Outler 1980:263-76, who applies it to the New Testament, and Brueggemann 1982:1-13, who uses it as a "model" for a similar traditioning process in church education.

[18]See also Childs 1977: passim. For a helpful critique of Childs along the lines proposed here, see McKnight 1987:23-24.

[19]Dunn 1982. See also Dunn 1977:374-78, where he argues that the very diversity that is "canonized" in Scripture allows this to occur. I would agree with Dunn that this approach to doctrine is normal in theological circles but disagree that it is appropriate. Indeed this whole chapter is intended to demonstrate the hermeneutical necessity of doing biblical theology from the whole of (a united) Scripture rather than from the perspective of a "canon within the canon."

[20]Carson 1983:91. He states, "Can we safeguard our exegesis from an untoward usage of systematic theology? The answer, I fear is, 'not entirely.' "

[21]Ebeling 1955:212-14. Fuller argues similarly that for the Reformers dogmatic "keys" from their "faith" formed the basic hermeneutic, and Reformation theology reverted "to a scholasticism not unlike the medieval sort" (1978:200).

[22]Barr 1974:282. Barrett uses the New Testament as a model for this crisis in authority, stating that the false claims of conservatives parallel the legalistic authority of the law that Paul countered with his doctrine of grace (1981:16). For Barrett biblical authority cannot be linked to rigid, unchallengeable ecclesiastical utterances or to a "formulated set of dogmatic propositions." Rather, it is creative, dependent not upon a static doctrine of inspiration but upon its "apostolic effectiveness" in accomplishing its task.

[23]Nineham 1976:257-71. Knight takes a tradition-critical approach, querying whether authority rests upon the literature or upon the community that shaped it and invested it with authority (1980:140-41). Social, political and economic factors gave rise to the religious aura that produced a sense of canon and therefore are a critical aspect of the text's authority.

[24]See Marshall 1970; Martin 1972; Smalley 1978; and France 1989 on history and theology in Luke, Mark, John and Matthew respectively. See also Meyer 1979 and Gruenler 1982 on the larger issue of detecting history in the Gospels. Stanton asserts that the Gospels were biographies to the same degree as were other ancient works (1972:191-204). The lack of interest in chronology, the scarcity of historical background and the failure to provide a personal portrait were common to all ancient historians. In fact, there is more interest in these aspects in the Gospels than in comparable Jewish writings of that period.

[25]Hermann 1981:142, 150-52. Pannenberg 1968:125-33 presents the strongest case for the centrality of history for revelation. By defining history as "the totality of reality," Pannenberg argues that it must be open to transcendence. In this he is correct, for the divine element must always be a possible part of history if history details the experiences of human beings. Nevertheless, I prefer to label the concept "revelation *in* history" rather than to accept Pannenberg's overly rational "revelation *as* history."

[26]Bultmann 1963:50-75 and Baumgartel 1983:134-59, who adds that the Old Testament has been abolished in Christ since its promise has been realized.

[27]For further discussion, see Hasel 1978:186-96 and Fujita 1981:107-8. Zimmerli similarly points out, "The fundamental faith of the Christian community necessitates a thoughtful correlation of individual biblical statements in view of the whole because it contends that the two testaments do not witness to two different gods, but to one single Lord" (1982:95).

[28]See Baker 1976, an excellent work that explicates this relationship in depth.

[29]For an excellent example of this, see Marshall 1969, who examines the doctrine of perseverance as it develops through all the strata of the Bible, thereby allowing the doctrine to emerge along lines of the progress of revelation.

Chapter 14: Systematic Theology

[1]Of course this hardly means that one should not appeal to Scripture in developing or "proving" a theological position. Rather, the resultant theological stance should take account of *all* the relevant texts, those which are used by the opposing side as well as those which support your own position.

[2]Kaufman (forthcoming). See also his *The Theological Imagination* (1981) for an elaboration of these themes.

[3]Farley and Hodgson 1985:72-80. Here they closely follow Kelsey (1975, 1980), who presents a functional model of biblical authority, that Scripture is used by God to transform human existence and to guide the community.

[4]See Tracy 1981:99-135, where he defines a theologian as "the interpreter of religious classics" (p. 130). While the Bible is the archetypal Christian "classic" (by which he means a literary work that transcends its own environment to transform existence in every culture and setting), the theologian works with the classics of every age in constructing a relevant modern theology.

[5]Some who see this proclamation to demons chained in the abyss can still repeat this aspect of the Apostles' Creed. However, I interpret the "prison" of 1 Peter 3:19 as this world to which God has restricted the fallen angels/demons who rebelled and were driven from heaven.

[6]Tradition critics like Achtemeier and others apply this same criterion to Scripture. However, the traditions behind Scripture dealt with revelatory events and were much more closely linked to the originating events than were the ecclesial traditions of the third and fourth centuries.

[7]This hardly means that a technical knowledge of tradition is necessary, as if only a Ph.D. scholar can do theology. Instead I am saying that everyone consciously or unconsciously is part of an ongoing tradition and interprets Scripture from that inherited perspective. As Gadamer has pointed out, theological reflection is by nature a historical act.

[8]We must distinguish the role of the community or context in determining the meaning of Scripture from its role in shaping the very questions asked in theological reasoning. Theoretically only Scripture should determine theological truth, but all too often not only the agenda but the results are determined by community needs. The former (question-shaping) is valid but the latter (theology-determining) is dangerous. See further below.

[9]For the best application of reader-response theory to theological construction I have found, see Jeanrond 1988:104-28.

[10]Tracy 1981:339-64. In one sense Tracy's discussion of the "situation" belongs under the rubric of "community." However, I include it here because Tracy is discussing the effect of context upon religious experience.

[11]See Holmes 1968:131-38; Montgomery 1970:276-79; Feinberg 1979:267-304.

[12]Paul Feinberg (forthcoming) gives six reasons for taking abduction as the most appropriate method for theological decision-making: (1) it more accurately describes how theologians do in fact practice their craft; (2) it retains the best aspects of both inductive and deductive reasoning; (3) it provides a broader evidential base for verifying a dogmatic formulation; (4) it strengthens the staying power of theological assertions by pointing out anomalies that need further study; (5) it maintains the distinction between biblical teaching and interpretations of it, thus producing humility in the theologian; and (6) it leaves open the possibility of better formulations of doctrine, thereby leading to a continual process of contextualization rather than the naive assumption that one's formulation is inerrant.

[13]Montgomery (1970:274) borrows this model from L. K. Nash, *The Nature of the Natural Sciences* (1963), to illustrate how knowledge is "generated by endless cyclical renewal."

[14]This hardly means that these are the *only* components in theological construction. Truth in any field is relevant for doing theology. Most of the disciplines (such as psychology for the doctrine of man or sociology for a theology on society and the world) are valid for constructing particular theological models. However, these five are the components classically noted.

[15]For instance, Barr says, "There is no 'the Bible' that 'claims' to be divinely inspired, there is no 'it' that has a view of itself. There is only this or that source, like 2 Timothy or 2 Peter, which makes statements

about certain other writings, these rather undefined" (1977:78).

[16]Among many others, see Grudem 1983:19-59; Ferguson 1988:47-66; and Marshall 1982:19-30.

[17]See, for instance, Marshall 1982; Carson and Woodbridge 1983 and 1986 as well as the many works on the issue of inerrancy. Fackre states that the issue is so important that rather than discuss revelation in volume two (his original intention) he plans to devote the entire third volume to that topic (1987:347).

[18]Soskice 1985:43-51. For instance, the aspects of a "bear" that relate to the man in the sentence above will differ depending upon whether the context is that of a wrestler or a Wall Street broker. The whole utterance controls the metaphor's meaning, not simply the interaction between subject and metaphor.

[19]McFague 1982:37-41. Following Black and Ricoeur she uses the example, "war is a chess game" to demonstrate the world-changing yet reality-depicting value of metaphor. The dissimilarity between war and chess leads the reader to a new understanding of war. Both concepts are altered by their interaction, and new meaning results.

[20]See Casenave, who argues that metaphor in this way becomes an indispensable part of "language as disclosure" (1979:21-24).

[21]One voice of opposition is Searle, who says that when using metaphors a speaker means something different than what he says (due to the semantic opposition established in the metaphor) and so the true meaning must be explicated in literal terms to be understood (1979:81-82). Therefore, three situations are necessary for communication via metaphors (p. 112): shared strategies so the hearer can recognize that the utterance is not intended literally; shared principles so the hearer can understand the possible uses of the metaphor; and shared knowledge to enable the speaker and hearer to communicate the actual use of the metaphor in the particular speech act.

[22]See also Miall 1982:xiii, xviii; Moore 1982:3-6; Tourangeau 1982:24-27.

[23]Binkley 1981:149. See also Soskice 1985:83-96. Binkley finds three distinctions between literal and metaphorical language: (1) The ability of a sentence to be understood does not depend on literal vs. metaphorical distinctions. (2) Metaphor is a poetic device but not exclusively so, since it is also employed in propositional statements. The terms *literal* and *metaphorical* refer to the *way* sentences mean not *whether* they mean. (3) One should not confuse the meaning of a metaphor with the explication of its meaning. Metaphorical language imparts information in its own right and is understandable *as* metaphor.

[24]See Gunton 1989:34-36. He argues further (pp. 37-38) that metaphor may well be a better device for communicating God and the world since both can be known best indirectly. As such metaphor takes its place in the referential process in helping us understand and address both the world around us and the presence of God in it.

[25]McFague 1983:39-41. See also Hazelton, who says that metaphorical statements about God are kept "as free and open as possible, rather than becoming locked into a particular theory" (1978:169). New images respond to and criticize each other and even replace one another when a better metaphor (more apt for a particular new situation) is created.

[26]McFague 1983:41-42. The example she uses for this "metaphorical" rather than literal theological truth is substitutionary atonement, which she obviously sees as viable for one stage of Christianity but not for all.

[27]Alston 1980:133-36, 145-48. He goes even further and says that metaphorical truth-claims *must* be translated to be verifiable. For him literal predictability is necessary for knowledge acquisition in a meaningful sense.

[28]John Feinberg goes in a different direction when he states that the very demarcation between metaphorical and literal language is misguided (1989:180-81). If metaphor is analogical then it is similar to literal communication, since an analogy is a literal link between two corresponding ideas. To say "God is love" goes beyond pure metaphor, for the assertion means that God is literally a loving God. Yet if one accepts the dynamic model of metaphor there is no need to find an analogical element. The metaphor communicates as metaphor and not as analogous to a literal statement. The metaphor on the incomprehensible divine love does not simply compare it to the finite human experience of love. God's love is in tension with and transcends the human experience, so that the very meaning of "love" is transformed by being used to describe God. In other words, the phrase does not just express a literal truth (God loves) via human metaphor (our concept of love); it dynamically pictures a God who "loves" perfectly and thus redefines the meaning of love as well as redescribes God. Yet it is not thereby a partial and incomplete image, for as a referential concept the metaphor is both binding and authoritative.

[29]Since Romans 9 is a diatribe, it is indeed possible to argue that Paul is not describing the divine process of salvation but rather is utilizing the Old Testament metaphor of predestination metaphorically to stress God's sovereignty. At this point I have not studied Romans 9 sufficiently to state unequivocally that this is indeed the case, but my preliminary study suggests that it may be so (see also p. 125).

[30]McFague 1987:34. Previously she defined a model as "a dominant metaphor, a metaphor with staying power" (1982:23).

[31]Soskice 1985:101-3. She notes two types of models: one in which the source and subject are identical (a model airplane); and one in which they differ (billiard balls utilized to model the properties of gases).

[32]I disagree with those who say titular models become dead metaphors. *Yahweh* maintains its rich metaphorical meaning throughout the biblical period.

[33]See Barbour 1974:34-38, for his excellent presentation of these approaches.

[34]On the basis of his book I do not believe that van Huyssteen himself intended his statement to be interpreted this way.

[35]Of course these models by necessity are general and representative rather than specific. Every step within each model is debated by scholars of that particular persuasion. I have attempted to reproduce areas of general consensus while recognizing that individuals may well differ at one point or another. In fact the very necessity of making this caveat is proof of the heuristic nature of theological models.

[36]Most would say that the two (regeneration and belief) are simultaneous but that God's act of regeneration is logically the causative agent that produces belief. Therefore, in the diagram regeneration is placed before belief.

[37]Note how the order is reversed from the Calvinist system.

[38]Tracy 1981:130-32. See also Jeanrond 1988:129-50 for a sympathetic redescription of Tracy's scheme.

[39]See van Huyssteen 1989:47-67 and Poythress 1988:39-63 for a positive assessment; and John Feinberg 1989:176-79 for a strongly cautionary assessment. See also my interaction in appendix two.

[40]As stated above this means not only collecting all the passages that support one's position but also including (with equal weight) those utilized to support competing positions.

[41]Erickson hypothesizes six levels of authority, each depending upon the degree of certitude one can expect from the scriptural underpinning: (1) those derived from direct statements of Scripture; (2) those stemming from direct implications of Scripture; (3) those coming from probable implications of Scripture; (4) inductive conclusions from Scripture; (5) conclusions derived from general revelation; (6) outright speculations, often derived from biblical hints (1983:79-80). Of course, even at the top level Erickson warns that we must be "certain that we are dealing here with the teaching of Scripture, and not an interpretation imposed upon it." The problem is that we can never be absolutely certain and so must always be open to further clarification and arguments. Nevertheless, we can make probability decisions and these have great authority; we need never retreat to a full-blown relativism.

[42]Obviously these percentages are based upon my own estimation of the clarity of the biblical teaching on each issue as well as upon my assessment of the viability of my opponents' challenges. My colleagues undoubtedly would have quite different percentages depending upon their own degree of sureness regarding these issues.

[43]This hardly means that it is impossible to attain a high degree of probability or even certainty (for cardinal doctrines) regarding which theological systems or doctrines are correct or to demonstrate this to others. However, I am calling for a "hermeneutics of humility" that leads the competing communities to listen and learn from each other. We do not decide doctrinal truth on the basis of consensus or majority but rather on the basis of which position best coheres with the whole of scriptural teaching. For that we all need opposing schools to drive us away from our own "logical" systems and back to the biblical text.

[44]I recognize that every doctrine that I label "cardinal" is probably denied by some group that labels itself Christian. As below, I would therefore define a cardinal doctrine as one clearly mandated in Scripture and adhered to by the church proper through the ages.

[45]For excellent discussions of the relationship of critical realism to theology, see Hiebert 1985a:5-10 and van Huyssteen 1989:142-97.

[46]For an excellent survey of the biblical and church historical data, see Tucker and Liefeld 1987.

[47]One such attempt is Lewis and Demarest 1987, but their *Integrative Theology* is more innovative in method (moving from the theological problem to church history to the biblical data to other relevant doctrines and competing models and finally to current life situations addressed; see pp. 7-13) than in actual organ-

ization and construction. It is a step in the right direction but not exactly what I am talking about.

[48]A good example is the current ongoing dialogue between covenant and dispensational scholars. A group of dispensational scholars has been meeting annually at the Evangelical Theological Society to redefine their approach. This is a very healthy development.

Chapter 15: Homiletics I: Contextualization

[1]Hesselgrave and Rommen 1989:chap. 11. Larkin relates three "roots" behind the crisis in biblical authority in nonevangelical missiology, following the World Council of Churches 1971 Louvain statement on "The Authority of the Bible": (1) modern society's rebellion against authority mitigates against acceptance of Scripture as a standard, and this is compounded by the tendency to treat the Bible like any other book; (2) the contradictions within Scripture (according to the historical-critical method) make it difficult to choose which aspect is authoritative; (3) the historical and cultural distances between the ancient text and the modern context cause many to doubt whether the Bible has any relevance whatsoever for our day (1988:136).

[2]See the discussion of this in Padilla 1979:90-91. These are positive cultural elements that are "analogous" to the gospel and can become the means for contextualizing the gospel in that culture. Padilla clarifies this in "The Contextualization of the Gospel" (1978:12-30).

[3]Nida and Reyburn say it is "essential to distinguish" not only form from content but also between various levels of form (1981:6). "Form" includes transliteration, morphological structures, phrase structure, rhetorical devices, poetry, figurative language, discourse structure and literary genre. The more optional (such as transliteration) can be changed easily. The more significant (such as genre) probably will not.

[4]See also Olthuis 1987:11-52, where he develops a "hermeneutics of ultimacy," arguing that "certitude" is found at the deep level of principial meaning rather than at the surface level of culture-bound symbols.

[5]Kraft lists: "the existence of God, human sinfulness, God's willingness to relate to humans on certain conditions, the necessity of a human faithfulness response to God as preconditional to salvation" (1979:189). Details for Kraft become "case-studies" that should be contextualized.

[6]See the excellent discussion of relativism in Larkin 1988:19-21. He separates radical relativism, which holds that truth is completely dependent upon cultural context and is never universal, from qualified or moderate relativism, which believes that there are absolutes but that knowledge of them is conditional upon cultural perspectives so that a "multi-perspectival" approach (looking at the situation from many vantage points) is necessary.

[7]See also Padilla 1979:84-102. He places four elements within the circle: the interpreter's historical situation, the interpreter's world-and-life view, his theology and Scripture. I would clarify this further by placing the first three under my category of "interpreter." It is too easy in Padilla's diagram (p. 99) for Scripture to be overwhelmed by the others. Instead, it must transform them; the true dynamic in the fusion process is provided by the text, which forces me out of my own situation in life.

[8]In actuality there is a reversal of roles. The preacher/missionary is the receptor in the first step but the source in the second step. See Nida and Reyburn 1981:20 for more on this topic.

[9]Larkin 1988:314-16. See also McQuilkin 1984:217-40, who provides the underpinning for Larkin's thesis.

[10]See p. 315 where he says that the two sides describe "the same application process but with different emphases."

[11]See also Johnson's critique of McQuilkin (1984:255-82), for further detailed argumentation along these lines.

[12]McQuilkin 1980 and 1984:230-40; 113-24; Larkin 1988:118-25, 314-15. McQuilkin develops seven criteria for detecting a scripturally limited command: (1) if the context of the passage limits the application (such as celibacy in 1 Cor 7:8); (2) if subsequent revelation limits it (as in such Old Testament laws as divorce, food laws and the sacrificial system); (3) if the teaching conflicts with other biblical passages, which limits both to their proper sphere (such as the Nazirite vow, Num 6:5 vs. the necessity of short hair on males, 1 Cor 11:14); (4) if the basis for the teaching is explicit and is treated as normative (such as woman's silence in 1 Cor 14:34); (5) if the specific teaching and the principle behind it are normative (such as sexual sins like homosexuality or adultery); (6) if the Bible treats the historical context as normative (such as the Logia Jesu); (7) if the Bible treats the cultural context as limited.

[13]See Alan Johnson's critique of McQuilkin (1984:255-82).

[14]See Conn's more responsible statement:

A belief in the validity of other cultures does not obligate one to approve of such practices as Cannibalism, widow burning, infanticide, premarital sex, polygamy, and the like. But it does insist that *one take such customs seriously within the cultural context in which they appear* and attempt to appreciate the importance of their function within that context. Understanding is not acceptance! (1984:329)

[15]See Osborne 1977:337-52. Below, I am updating the list found there with more recent literature. Here I must render my appreciation to Guth (1981: chap. 2), who has done a great deal of this for me.

[16]This is similar to differentiating "local color" from allegorical/theological truth in parables, and the hermeneutical principles are much the same (see pp. 237-38).

[17]See also Larkin 1988:334-56; McQuilkin 1984:230-40.

[18]See Fee 1976:113 and Scott 1979:75. This is similar to Kraft's distinction of general vs. specific categories, since moral truths by definition are nonspecific.

[19]Günter (1976:2:576, 578-79) points out that while polygamy is mentioned, it is not truly countenanced and monogamy "occupies the central position" (such as Gen 1:26-27; 2:18-24; Deut 17:17). Furthermore, polygamy was practiced among Jews even in New Testament times—Herod, for example, had ten wives—and it was common among the aristocracy. Interestingly, it was allowed only by the Jews and was not allowed in Greco-Roman society generally.

[20]In one sense contextualization could virtually be identified with hermeneutics, since the exposition of a text's meaning is also a "contextualization" of its message. This indeed is how the term is used in missiological circles. However, I am using it in a more restricted sense, that of determining the significance or application of the biblical meaning for this modern age.

[21]Dietrich 1981:30. However, his dialogue with popular religion and ideologies fails to meet his own criteria, for they are given prominence over the biblical world view.

[22]Hiebert 1987:109-10. See also Conn 1984:211-60, who argues for doing this in a covenantal context. Conn argues for six criteria: (1) a biblical-theological concept of "revelation-as-process"; (2) a covenantal dimension demanding faithfulness in word and deed; (3) a culture-specific theology; (4) theology as an ever-renewed evangelistic response to contextual needs; (5) the unity of the church in developing communal faith-statements; (6) a prophetic function in challenging cultures and ideologies.

[23]See the excellent discussion in Fee and Stuart 1981:46-49.

Chapter 16: Homiletics II: The Sermon

[1]Note the excellent and extensive discussion of the relation of the historical-grammatical and historical-critical methods to the sermonic process in Greidanus 1988:24-101.

[2]Here I am building upon the excellent discussion in Greidanus 1988:159-66.

[3]Bettler 1986:344-47 speaks of a "funnel," as preaching moves from the general ("pray") to the particular ("pray sincerely") to the concrete ("pray in secret").

[4]Robinson 1980:152-53. Adams adds four principles for a proper use of stories or illustrations (1986:361-65): (1) Make certain that the story is drawn from and appeals to the shared background of the congregation (e.g., agricultural allusions in a farming community). (2) If you utilize stories new to the congregation, explain them carefully and colorfully. (3) Tell the familiar example in a new, startling way (such as Jesus' "I am" sayings in John's Gospel). (4) Avoid trite, well-worn clichés. Above all, involve all the senses of the congregation as you open their eyes, ears and total being to the truth of the text.

[5]I must thank an ad-hoc committee that met at the Third Congress for Missions at Trinity in May 1982 for developing a preliminary form of this. The committee consisted of Alan Andres, Canadian Director of Navigators; Timothy F. Conklin, Grace Bible College; Roger S. Greenway, Westminster Theological Seminary; Robert H. Matzken, The Netherlands; Timothy Monsma, Reformed Bible College; Grant R. Osborne, Trinity Evangelical Divinity School; Edward C. Pentecost, Dallas Theological Seminary.

[6]Adams 1986:354-55. He calls for sense-oriented language that evokes emotional response as well as a vivid use of sounds and gestures to punctuate the points.

[7]For a good summary of the historical development of rhetoric with application to preaching, see De Koster 1980:303-30.

Appendix 1: The Problem of Meaning: The Issues

[1]See Gadamer 1965:460-91; compare Bleicher 1980:117-27.

²Hans Frei 1974: passim. See also the more succinct survey of Childs 1977:80-90.

³Frei 1974:323. Paul Ricoeur traces three stages in the development of hermeneutics (1973:112-41). The classical period depended upon a classification method that utilized a genre-based approach to the text. Then Schleiermacher and the neo-Kantian movement along with Dilthey erected an epistemological base for hermeneutics, characterized by a diachronic interest in history. Finally, Heidegger along with Gadamer took an ontological approach, centering on the synchronic problem of being. The search for meaning partakes of that "alienating distanciation" (Gadamer) that characterizes human reflection and so present hermeneutics faces a dilemma of understanding that demands a new approach.

⁴Thiselton 1980:103-5 aligns this with one's "preunderstanding."

⁵Gadamer 1965:258-78. Mark C. Taylor believes that this disclosure of futurity is Gadamer's major concern (1982:48-49). However, as he himself admits, this comes more from Heidegger than Gadamer. Nevertheless, while not explicated fully by Gadamer, it does emerge logically from his system. The text does open up future potentialities for appropriation.

⁶The number of works detailing this school can hardly be listed here. See Harari's bibliography (1979:443-63), which deals with nonbiblical areas, and Patte 1976. See also the introduction and conclusion of Kurzweil 1980 and Harari 1979:17-72. For conservative biblical critiques, see Thiselton 1978:329-35 and Stancil 1980:4-59. An excellent survey of the issue can be found in Perpich 1984.

⁷Edith Kurzweil provides an illuminating (to those of us more acquainted with its biblical counterpart) portrait of the early movement (1980:227-45). She distinguishes semiotics as a later development rejected, in fact, by Levi-Strauss, who derided its lack of social involvement and preoccupation with linguistics. Semiology developed with Barthes as a literary-critical movement and semiotics with Derrida as a philosophico-linguistic enterprise.

⁸Most biblical scholars also utilize V. I. Propp's functional analysis (he developed thirty-one basic "functions" or characteristic plot developments that determine all stories); A. J. Greimas's actantial analysis (performative features and disjunctive sequences by which the binary opposites interact in the story); and Todorov's theory of narrative discourse (which deconstructs the grammatical sequence and reconstructs the text in terms of its propositional sequence).

⁹See Kurzweil 1980:229-30, 240-45 and Detweiler 1978:166. Of course I do not pretend that it was ever a unified movement. However, the consensus has clearly shifted away from the earlier model.

¹⁰In addition to Tompkins 1980, Frei 1974 and Childs 1977, see Peterson 1978:24-26; Perrin 1976:168-81; Derrida 1979:82-120; Ricoeur 1974a:250-66.

¹¹Roland Barthes 1975:27 as quoted in Taylor 1981:47. I recognize, of course, the semantic difference between my use of *text* and Barthes's use of *author*. By text-related interpretation, I mean an act that is concerned with historical intentionality. Therefore, analysis of *text* in my system includes what Barthes means by the *author*.

¹²Intertextuality, as Detweiler points out, has become a major issue in the postformalist debate (1980:10-11). "The text is its own interpretation . . . and reveals itself as insufficient for *serious* analysis, so that one turns to playfulness with the text as a way of encountering it" (p. 11; italics his).

¹³Again, we are forced to juxtapose two different ways of considering *text*. The first of the two, "reader-response" criticism, uses *text* to distinguish the historical production of the author from his or her intended meaning. Poststructuralism, on the other hand, utilizes *text* to depict that autonomous entity which separates itself from the author and completes its meaning only in the act of reading.

¹⁴As Tompkins points out, the problem here is that the "self as an independent entity vanishes" (1980:xxiii).

¹⁵For good surveys of this, see Freund 1987:passim; Jeanrond 1987:105-15; and Porter 1990.

¹⁶Fish 1980a:13. For a good discussion of Fish's influence on biblical studies see Moore 1986:707-19.

¹⁷Moore 1988:147-52. Of course, this is a criticism more of Iser and his followers than of Fish, who sees no validity in the original reader as a hermeneutical tool.

¹⁸See Eagleton 1983:85-90 and Jeanrond 1987:111-15, both of whom recognize the problem of arbitrariness in this approach.

¹⁹English translations: *On Grammatology,* tr. G. Chakravorty (Baltimore: Johns Hopkins Press, 1976); *Writing and Difference,* tr. A. Bass (Chicago: University of Chicago Press, 1978); *Speech and Phenomena,* tr. D. Allison (Evanston: Northwestern University Press, 1973). Good discussions of his thought are found in the introductions. Derrida himself says that one should read the first half of *On Grammatology* (on the history of the notion of the sign) as an elaboration of themes scattered through *Writing and Difference*

(Bass 1978:x).

[20]Friedrich Nietzsche, "On Truth and Lie in an Extra-Moral Sense," *The Portable Nietzsche*, 46-47.

[21]See Norris 1982:24-32, 46-47, for an excellent discussion of this.

[22]Derrida 1978:29-30; italics his. Gayatri Spirak, in her preface to *On Grammatology*, states, "In Derrida's reworking, the structure preface-text becomes open at both ends. The text has no stable identity, no stable origin, no stable end. Each act of reading the 'text' is a preface to the next" (p. xii).

[23]Harari 1979:37. Derrida considers the "metaphysical opposition of calculus and genesis" (of intention and writing), which produces a "lever of disorganization" with respect to "the authority of an 'author' over his very 'own' corpus" (1980:47-49). In other words, the relationship between the author and his creation has been deconstructed or erased.

[24]Foucault argues that the individualization of the author and the separation of an author from his work is a product of modern culture (1979:141-60). Writing has "freed itself from . . . the confines of its interiority" and become "identified with its own unfolded exteriority" (p. 142). As a result, writing has become "its author's murderer" because "the writing subject cancels out the signs of his particular individuality" (pp. 142-43). The unity of author and writer effaces the former and transcends her, so that she disappears. All that remains is a name.

[25]See also Keck 1980:115-28, who argues that a plurality of methods, including historical-critical reconstruction, is necessary to the survival of the church's canon.

[26]See Vanhoozer 1990, for an excellent analysis of this development in Ricoeur's thought.

[27]Kelsey 1975:197-207. See also Lynn Ross-Bryant 1981, who argues that "imagination" creates possible "meanings" in the dialogue between reader and text.

[28]Thiselton shows that the *Tractatus* was a product more of the Viennese neo-Kantian school than of British empiricism and so should not be radically separated from his later work (1980:358-59).

[29]See his distinction between the two on pp. 379-85 and its application to biblical authority on p. 438.

Appendix 2: The Problem of Meaning: Toward a Solution

[1]Ramsey believes two aspects of religious language give it an empirical character: "odd discernment" and "total commitment." Most today, however, no longer claim an "empirical" foundation for God-talk.

[2]Searle 1969:131-56. These fallacies are: the naturalistic fallacy, which argues that descriptive statements cannot entail evaluative statements; speech act analysis, which depends upon an analogous relationship between words and performative verbs; and assertion, which confuses "the conditions for the performance of the speech act of assertion with the analysis of the meaning of particular words occurring in certain assertions."

[3]Habermas 1971:133-50, ET 190-203; see Gadamer's response in Apel 1971:283-317.

[4]For a good recent discussion see Poythress 1988.

[5]See Hocking 1980:1-5 and Poythress 1988:39-49.

[6]Graham Hough argues that "the presented surface of the text" and "the inferred intention of the author" are not mutually exclusive goals but are complementary (1976:224; see 222-23). See also Morse Peckham, "The Intentional Fallacy?" (1976:139-57) and Alastair Fowler, "Intention Floreat" (1976:242-55).

[7]Hough 1976:225. He mentions two who have proclaimed this: A. J. Close, "Don Quixote and the 'Intentionalist Fallacy,' " *Br. J. Aesthetics* 12/2 (1972) and Quentin Skinner, "Motives, Intentions and the Interpretation of Texts," *New Literary History* 3/2 (1972).

[8]It is interesting that Jacques Derrida uses one of the new novels (Maurice Blanchot's *La Folie du jour*) as a paradigm of genre mixture to prove his case that the intermixing of genre demonstrates that no genre-class can control the text and that thereby the nonclosure of the text declasses genre. See his "The Law of Genre," *Glyph* 7 (1980): 210-13. In actuality, this demonstrates the validity of genre because Blanchot's work was written to illustrate that very point. In other words, the argument is circular.

[9]See also A. J. Ayer 1972:54-88. For a defense of necessity, see Alvin Plantinga 1974, and for a recent attempt to present a modified version of logical empiricism centering upon "causal models," see Clark Glymour 1980.

[10]For an important work developing these themes, see Grover Maxwell and Robert M. Anderson 1975, especially the discussion of Bayesian methods by Hesse and Maxwell and the essay on probability and reference by Kyburg.

[11]Paul Helm argues that the major reasons for believing that the Bible is the Word of God are "religious,"

concerned with "a person's bounden allegiance to God" (1982:303-20). Further, the evidence one adduces to prove the point is "internal," the claims of the text itself, rather than external. On the basis of Jesus' own claims one takes a stand and views objections rationally from within that stand. This stance is further anchored in the life and experience of the one who takes that stand.

[12]Yandell 1984:272-84, where he expands the list of twelve "rules."

[13]I. Howard Marshall says,

> The point is that the meaning of a text is constant and objective, whereas its significance may vary for different readers. The significance depends upon both the text and the readers, and is a function of their mutual interaction. Change the context, and you change the significance. . . . (Yet) it is of special importance to recognize that the significance flows out of the meaning. There can be no by-passing of exegesis on the way to exposition and significance. (1980:5)

I find this article to be an excellent, concise study of the problems Caird considers at greater length.

[14]Troeltsch, on the basis of positivistic developments in historiography, argued that historical claims (such as miracles) could be accepted only if they were analogous or cohered to modern experience.

[15]Marc Bloch 1954:48-75. R. G. Collingwood states that the inductive approach and the formulation of general laws are crucial (1965:35-36). Only the examination of evidence according to previously determined guidelines can produce viable history.

[16]Stanton 1978:60-71; Stuhlmacher 1977:83-90. See also Carl A. Braaten 1966:50-52 and Rudolf Bultmann 1960:289-96. In this discussion I will interact with several scholars, especially Graham Stanton and Peter Stuhlmacher.

[17]While one could argue that these concepts are a twentieth-century product of literary criticism, I would respond that they fit ancient texts as well as modern ones.

Bibliography

Achtemeier, Paul J.
1980   *The Inspiration of Scripture: Problems and Proposals.* Philadelphia: Westminster.

Adams, Ernest W.
1975   *The Logic of Conditionals: An Application of Probability to Deductive Logic.* Boston: D. Reidel.

Adams, Jay E.
1975   *Pulpit Speech.* Nutley, N.J.: Presbyterian and Reformed.
1986   "Sense Appeal and Storytelling." In *The Preacher and Preaching,* ed. Samuel T. Logan, Jr., pp. 350-66. Phillipsburg, N.J.: Presbyterian and Reformed.

Adler, Mortimer J., and
Charles van Doren
1972   *How to Read a Book.* Rev. and updated. New York: Simon and Schuster.

Aland, Kurt
1961   "The Problem of Anonymity and Pseudonymity in Christian Literature of the First Two Centuries." *JTS* 12:39-49.

Aland, Kurt, and
Barbara Aland
1989   *The Text of the New Testament: An Introduction to the Critical Editions and to the Theory and Practice of Modern Textual Criticism.* Trans. E. F. Rhodes. Grand Rapids: Eerdmans.

Allen, Ronald J.
1983   "Shaping Sermons by the Language of the Text." In *Preaching Biblically: Creating Sermons in the Shape of Scripture,* ed. Don M. Wardlaw, pp. 29-59. Philadelphia: Westminster.

Alonso-Schökel, Luis
1960   "Die stilistische Analyse bei den Propheten." *Supplement to Vetus Testamentum* 7:154-64.

Alston, William P.
1978   "Semantic Rules." In *Semantics and Philosophy,* ed. Milton K. Munitz and Peter K. Unger, pp. 17-48. New York: New York University Press.
1980   "Irreducible Metaphors in Theology." In *Experience, Reason and God,* ed. Eugene Thomas Long, pp. 129-48. Washington, D.C.: Catholic University Press of America.

Alter, Robert
1981   *The Art of Biblical Narrative.* New York: Basic.
1985   *The Art of Biblical Poetry.* New York: Basic.

Altizer, Thomas J. J.
1980   *Deconstruction and Theology.* Chico, Calif.: Scholars Press.

Anderson, Bernhard W.

 1974 "The New Frontier of Rhetorical Criticism: A Tribute to James Mui-lenberg." In *Rhetorical Criticism: Essays in Honor of James Muilenberg,* ed. J. J. Jackson and M. Kessler, pp. ix-xviii. Pittsburgh: Pickwick.

 1981 "Tradition and Scripture in the Community of Faith." *JBL* 100/1:5-21.

 1982 "The Problem and Promise of Commentary." *Interpretation* 36/4:342-47.

 1985 "Biblical Theology and Sociological Interpretation." *TTod* 42:292-306.

Anscombe, G. E. M.

 1963 *Intention.* Ithaca, N.Y.: Cornell University Press.

Apel, Karl, et al.

 1971 *Hermeneutik und Ideologiekritik.* Frankfurt: Suhrkamp.

Applebaum, S.

 1976 "The Social and Economic Status of the Jews in the Diaspora." In *The Jewish People in the First Century,* vol. 2, ed. S. Safrai and M. Stern, pp. 701-27. Philadelphia: Fortress.

Archer, Gleason

 1964 *A Survey of Old Testament Introduction.* Chicago: Moody.

Arens, Hans, et al.

 1975 *Handbuch der Linguistik.* Munich: Nymphenburger Verlagshand-lung.

Armerding, Carl

 1979 "Structural Analysis." *Themelios* 4/3:96-104.

Aune, David

 1973 "The New Testament: Source of Modern Theological Diversity." *Direction* 2:10-15.

 1983 "The Influence of Roman Imperial Court Ceremonial on the Apoc-alypse of John." *Biblical Research* 28:5-26.

 1986 "The Apocalypse of John and the Problem of Genre." *Semeia* 36:65-96.

 1987 *The New Testament in Its Literary Environment.* Philadelphia: West-minster.

Austin, J. L.

 1962 *How to do Things with Words.* Oxford: Clarendon.

Ayer, A. J.

 1946 *Language, Truth, and Logic.* New York: Dover.

 1972 *Probability and Evidence.* New York: Macmillan.

Ayers, Robert H.

 1983 *Judaism and Christianity: Origins, Developments, and Recent Trends.* New York: University Press of America.

Bailey, Kenneth E.

 1976 *Poet and Peasant: A Literary-Cultural Approach to the Parables in Luke.* Grand Rapids: Eerdmans.

 1980 *Through Peasant Eyes: More Lucan Parables, Their Culture and Style.* Grand Rapids: Eerdmans.

Baird, J. Arthur

 1972 "Genre Analysis as a Method of Historical Criticism." *SBL Proceedings,* vol. 2, ed. Lane C. McGaughy, pp. 385-412.

Baker, David L.
1976   *Two Testaments, One Bible.* Downers Grove: InterVarsity Press.
Barbour, Ian G.
1974   *Myths, Models, and Paradigms.* New York: Harper and Row.
1980   "Paradigms in Science and Religion." In *Paradigms and Revolutions.* Ed. Gary Gutting. Notre Dame, Ind.: Notre Dame University Press.
Barbour, R. S.
1972   *Traditio-Historical Criticism of the Gospels.* London: SPCK.
Barker, Kenneth L.
1982   "False Dichotomies Between the Testaments." *JETS* 25/1:3-16.
Barr, James
1961   *The Semantics of Biblical Language.* Oxford: Oxford University Press.
1963   "Revelation through History in the OT and in Modern Theology." *Int* 17:193-205.
1966   *Old and New in Interpretation: A Study of the Two Testaments.* London: SCM.
1974   "Trends and Prospects in Biblical Theology." *JTS* 25:265-82.
1976a   "Revelation in History." In *IDB Supplement,* pp. 746-49. Nashville: Abingdon.
1976b   "Biblical Theology." *IDB Supplement,* pp. 104-11.
1977   *Fundamentalism.* Philadelphia: Westminster.
1980   *The Scope and Authority of the Bible.* Philadelphia: Westminster.
Barrett, C. K.
1981   "What is New Testament Theology? Some Reflections." *Horizons in Biblical Theology* 3:21-29.
Barth, Markus
1974   *The Epistle to the Ephesians.* 2 vols. Anchor Bible Series. Garden City, N.Y.: Doubleday.
Barthes, Roland
1975   *The Pleasure of the Text.* Trans. Richard Miller. New York: Hill and Wong.
1979   "From Work to Text." In *Textural Strategies: Perspectives in Post-Structuralist Criticism,* ed. Josué V. Harari, pp. 73-81. Ithaca, N.Y.: Cornell University Press.
Barton, John, et al.
1984   *Prophets, Worship and Theodicy.* Oudtestamentische Studien 23. Leiden: E. J. Brill.
Bass, Alan
1978   Introduction to *Writing and Difference* by Jacques Derrida. Trans. Alan Bass. Chicago: University of Chicago Press.
Bauer, Walter
1971 [1934]   *Orthodoxy and Heresy in Earliest Christianity.* Ed. Robert A. Kraft and Gerhard Krodel. Philadelphia: Fortress.
Bauer, Walter;
William F. Arndt;
F. Wilbur Gingrich; and
Frederick W. Danker
1979   *A Greek-English Lexicon of the New Testament and Other Early Christian Literature,* 2d ed. Chicago: University of Chicago Press.

Bauman, J. Daniel

1972   *An Introduction to Contemporary Preaching.* Grand Rapids: Baker.

Baumgärtel, Friedrich

1963   "The Hermeneutical Problem of the OT." In *Essays on OT Hermeneutics,* ed. Claus Westermann and James L. Mays, pp. 134-59. Richmond: John Knox.

Beekman, John, and
John Callow

1974   *Translating the Word of God.* Grand Rapids: Zondervan.

Beitzel, Barry J.

1980   "Exodus 3:14 and the Divine Name: A Case of Biblical Paranomasia." *TJ* 1/1:5-20.

1985   *The Moody Atlas of Bible Lands.* Chicago: Moody.

Beker, J. Christiaan

1968   "Biblical Theology in a Time of Confusion." *TTod* 25:194.

1968   "Biblical Theology Today." *Princeton Seminary Bulletin* 61/2:13-19.

1973   "The Function of the Bible Today." In *Commitment Without Ideology.* Charles Daniel Batson et al., pp. 22-42. New York: Pilgrim.

Bergman, Jan

1983   "Introductory Remarks on Apocalypticism in Egypt." In *Apocalypticism in the Mediterranean World and the Near East,* ed. David Hellholm, pp. 51-69. Tübingen: J. C. B. Mohr.

Berlin, Adele

1983   *Poetics and Interpretation of Biblical Narrative.* Sheffield: Almond.

1985   *The Dynamics of Biblical Parallelism.* Bloomington: Indiana University Press.

Berry, George R.

1979 [1897]   *A Dictionary of New Testament Synonyms.* Grand Rapids: Zondervan.

Best, Thomas F.

1983   "The Sociological Study of the New Testament: Promise and Peril of a New Discipline." *SJT* 36:181-94.

Bettler, John F.

1986   "Application." In *The Preacher and Preaching,* ed. Samuel T. Logan, Jr., pp. 331-49. Phillipsburg, N.J.: Presbyterian and Reformed.

Betz, Otto

1962   "History of Biblical Theology." In *Interpreter's Dictionary of the Bible,* pp. 432-37. Nashville: Abingdon.

Binkley, Timothy

1981   "On Truth and Probability of Metaphor." In *Philosophical Perspectives on Metaphor,* ed. Mark Johnson, pp. 136-53. Minneapolis: University of Minnesota Press.

Birch, Bruce C.

1984   "Old Testament Theology: Its Task and Future." *Horizons of Biblical Theology* 6:iii-viii.

Black, Matthew

1967   *An Aramaic Approach to the Gospels and Acts.* Oxford: Clarendon.

Black, Max

1981   "Metaphor." In *Philosophical Perspectives on Metaphor,* ed. Mark Johnson, pp. 63-82. Minneapolis: University of Minnesota Press.

Blaiklock, Edward M.
    1979   "The Epistolary Literature." In *The Expositor's Bible Commentary.* Vol. 1: *Introductory Articles,* ed. Frank E. Gaebelein, pp. 545-54. Grand Rapids: Zondervan.

Blass, Friedrich, and
Albert Debrunner
    1961   *A Greek Grammar of the New Testament and Other Early Christian Literature.* Trans. and rev. Robert W. Funk. Chicago: University of Chicago Press.

Bleicher, Josef
    1980   *Contemporary Hermeneutics: Hermeneutics as Method, Philosophy, and Critique.* Boston: Routledge and Kegan Paul.

Blenkinsopp, Joseph
    1964   "Biblical and Dogmatic Theology: The Present Situation." *CBQ* 26:70-85.
    1977   *Prophecy and Canon: A Contribution to the Study of Jewish Origins.* Notre Dame, Ind.: University of Notre Dame Press.
    1980   "A New Kind of Introduction: Professor Childs' *Introduction to the Old Testament As Scripture." JSOT* 16:24-27.
    1983   *Wisdom and Law in the Old Testament.* New York: Oxford University Press.
    1984   "Old Testament Theology and the Jewish-Christian Connection." *JSOT* 28:3-15.

Bloch, Marc
    1954   *The Historian's Craft.* Manchester: Manchester University Press.

Blomberg, Craig L.
    1982   "New Horizons in Parable Research." *Trinity Journal* 3/1:3-17.
    1987   *The Historical Reliability of the Gospels.* Downers Grove: InterVarsity Press.
    1990   *Interpreting the Parables.* Downers Grove: InterVarsity Press.

Bock, Darrell L.
    1985   "Evangelicals and the Use of the Old Testament in the New: Part 1." *BibSac* 142/567:209-23.
    1985   "Evangelicals and the Use of the Old Testament in the New: Part 2." *BibSac* 142/568:306-19.

Boers, Hendrikus
    1984   "Polarities at the Roots of New Testament Thought: Methodological Considerations." *PerspRelStud* 11/4:55-75.

Boman, Thorleif
    1960   *Hebrew Thought Compared with Greek.* Philadelphia: Westminster.

Boucher, Madeleine
    1977   *The Mysterious Parable.* Washington, D.C.: Catholic Biblical Association of America.

Boyer, James L.
    1983   "Third (and Fourth) Class Conditions." *Grace Theological Journal* 4:164-75.

Braaten, Carl A.
    1966   *History and Hermeneutics.* Philadelphia: Westminster.

Broadus, John A.
    1944   *On the Preparation and Delivery of Sermons.* New York: Harper and Brothers.

Brock, Bernard L., and
Robert L. Scott, eds.
1989   *Methods of Rhetorical Criticism: A Twentieth-Century Perspective.*
        3d ed., rev. Detroit: Wayne State University Press.

Brown, Francis;
S. R. Driver;
and C. A. Briggs.
1968   *A Hebrew and English Lexicon of the Old Testament.* Oxford: Clarendon.

Brown, Herbert
1965   "The Problem of a NT Theology." *Journal for Theology and Church*
        1:169-83.

Brown, Raymond E.
1955   *The Sensus Plenior of Sacred Scripture: A Dissertation.* Baltimore:
        St. Mary's University.
1966, 1970   *The Gospel According to John.* 2 vols. Anchor Bible. Garden City,
        N.Y.: Doubleday.
1968   "The Literal Sense of Scripture." In *The Jerome Biblical Commentary,* 2:606-10. Englewood Cliffs, N.J.: Prentice-Hall.
1981   *The Critical Meaning of the Bible.* New York: Paulist.

Brueggemann, Walter
1980   "A Convergence in Recent Old Testament Theologies." *JSOT* 18:2-18.
1982   *The Creative Word: Canon as a Model for Biblical Education.* Philadelphia: Fortress.
1984   "Futures in Old Testament Theology." *Horizons in Biblical Theology*
        6/1:1-11.
1985a   "A Shape for Old Testament Theology, I: Structure Legitimation."
        CBQ 47:28-46.
1985b   "A Shape for Old Testament Theology, II: Embrace of Pain." *CBQ*
        47:395-415.
1985c   *The New Testament as Canon: An Introduction.* Philadelphia: Fortress.
1988   *Israel's Praise: Doxology against Idolatry and Ideology.* Philadelphia: Fortress.

Bullinger, E. W.
1968 [1898]   *Figures of Speech Used in the Bible: Explained and Illustrated.*
        Grand Rapids: Baker.

Bultmann, Rudolf
1951, 1955   *Theology of the New Testament.* Trans. K. Grobel. 2 vols. New York:
        Charles Scribner's Sons.
1960   "Is Exegesis without Presuppositions Possible?" In *Existence and
        Faith,* trans. Schubert M. Ogden, pp. 342-51. New York: World.
1963   "Prophecy and Fulfillment." In *Essays on Old Testament Hermeneutics,* ed. Claus Westermann, pp. 50-75. Richmond: John Knox.
1984a   "Theologie als Wissenschaft." *Zeit Theol Kirch* 81/4:447-69.
1984b   *Theologie des Neuen Testaments.* Rev. O. Merk, Neue Theologische
        Grundrisse. 9th rev. ed. Tübingen: Mohr-Siebeck.

Burdick, Donald W.
1974   "*Oida* and *Ginōskō* in the Pauline Epistles." In *New Directions in
        New Testament Study,* ed. Richard N. Longenecker and Merrill C.

Tenney, pp. 344-56. Grand Rapids: Zondervan.

Buswell, James O., III
1974   "Contextualization Theory, Tradition, and Method." In *Theology and Mission,* ed. David J. Hesselgrave, pp. 87-111. Grand Rapids: Baker.

Buttrick, David G.
1987   *Homiletic: Moves and Structures.* Philadelphia: Fortress.

Caird, G. B.
1980   *The Language and Imagery of the Bible.* London: Duckworth.

Calvert, D. G. A.
1972   "An Examination of the Criteria for Distinguishing the Authentic Words of Jesus." *NTS* 18:209-19.

Carlston, Charles E.
1975   *The Parables of the Triple Tradition.* Philadelphia: Fortress.

Carson, D. A.
1979   *The King James Version Debate.* Grand Rapids: Baker.
1982   "Understanding Misunderstandings in the Fourth Gospel." *TynB* 33:59-91.
1983   "Unity and Diversity in the New Testament: The Possibility of Systematic Theology." In *Scripture and Truth,* ed. D. A. Carson and John D. Woodbridge, pp. 65-95. Grand Rapids: Zondervan.
1984a   "Reflections on Contextualization: A Critical Appraisal of Daniel von Allmen's 'Birth of Theology.' "*East African Journal of Evangelical Theology* 3/1:16-59.
1984b   "A Sketch of the Factors Determining Current Hermeneutical Debate in Cross-Cultural Contexts." In *Biblical Interpretation and the Church,* ed. D. A. Carson, pp. 11-29. Nashville: Nelson.

Carson, D. A., and
John D. Woodbridge, eds.
1983   *Scripture and Truth.* Grand Rapids: Zondervan.
1986   *Hermeneutics, Authority, and Canon.* Grand Rapids: Zondervan.

Casenave, Gerald W.
1979   "Taking Metaphor Seriously: The Implications of the Cognitive Significance of Metaphor for Theories of Language." *Southern Journal of Philosophy* 17: 19-25.

Cervin, Richard S.
1989   "Does *Kephalē* Mean 'Source' or 'Authority Over' in Greek Literature? A Rebuttal." *Trinity Journal* ns 1:85-112.

Charles, R. H.
1913   *The Apocrypha and Pseudepigrapha of the Old Testament in English, with Introductions and Critical and Explanatory Notes to the Several Books.* Oxford: Clarendon.

Chatman, Seymour
1978   *Story and Discourse: Narrative Structure in Fiction and Film.* Ithaca, N.Y.: Cornell University Press.

Childs, Brevard S.
1964   "Interpreting in Faith: The Theological Responsibility of an Old Testament Commentary." *Interpretation* 18:432-49.
1967   *Isaiah and the Assyrian Crisis.* London: SCM.
1970   *Biblical Theology in Crisis.* Philadelphia: Westminster.
1974   *The Book of Exodus: A Critical Theological Commentary.* Phila-

delphia: Westminster.

1977   "The Sensus Literalis of Scripture: An Ancient and Modern Problem." *Beiträge zur Alttestamentlichen Theologie. Festschrift für Walther Zimmerli zum 70. Geburtstag,* ed. H. Donner et al., pp. 80-93. Göttingen: Vandenhoeck und Ruprecht.

1980a   "A Response." *Horizons in Biblical Theology* 2:189-211.

1980b   "Response to Reviewers of *Introduction to the Old Testament As Scripture.*" *JSOT* 16:52-60.

1982   "Some Reflections on the Search for a Biblical Theology." *Horizons in Biblical Theology* 4/1:1-12.

Chomsky, Noam

1965   *Aspects of the Theory of Syntax.* Cambridge, Mass.: MIT Press.

1972   *Studies on Semantics in Generative Grammar.* The Hague: Mouton.

Clements, R. E.

1965   *Prophecy and Covenant.* London: SCM.

1975   *Prophecy and Tradition.* Oxford: Basil Blackwell.

1982   "History and Theology in Biblical Narrative." *HBT* 4:45-60.

Close, A. J.

1972   "Don Quixote and the Intentionalist Fallacy." *Br. J. Aesthetics* 12/2.

Collingwood, R. G.

1965   *Essays in the Philosophy of History.* Austin: University of Texas.

Collins, John J., ed.

1979   "Apocalypse: The Morphology of a Genre." *Semeia* 14. Missoula, Mont.: Scholars Press.

Conn, Harvie M.

1984   *Eternal Word and Changing Worlds: Theology, Anthropology and Mission in Trialogue.* Grand Rapids: Zondervan/Academie Books.

Coote, Robert T., and John Stott, eds.

1980   *Down to Earth: Studies in Christianity and Culture.* Grand Rapids: Eerdmans.

Corset, P.

1985   "Le théologien face au conteur évangélique. A la recherche d'une théologie narrative." *RechSciRel* 73/1:61-84.

Cotterell, Peter, and Max Turner

1989   *Linguistics and Biblical Interpretation.* Downers Grove: InterVarsity Press.

Cox, Harvey

1965   *The Secular City: Secularization and Urbanization in Theological Perspective.* London: SCM.

Craddock, Fred B.

1985   *Preaching.* Nashville: Abingdon.

Craigie, Peter C.

1983   *Psalms 1-50.* Word Biblical Commentary. Vol. 19. Waco, Tex.: Word.

Crenshaw, James L.

1969   "Method in Determining Wisdom Influence upon 'Historical' Writing." *JBL* 88:129-42.

1971   *Prophetic Conflict: Its Effect Upon Israelite Religion.* New York: Walter de Gruyter.

1974   "Wisdom." In *Old Testament Form Criticism,* ed. John H. Hayes, pp. 225-64. San Antonio: Trinity University Press.

1976   "Prolegomenon." In *Studies in Ancient Israelite Wisdom.* Ed. J. L. Crenshaw. New York: Ktav.

Crombie, I. M.
1955   "Arising from the University Discussion." In *New Essays in Philosophical Theology,* ed. Antony Flew and Alasdair MacIntyre, pp. 109-30. New York: Macmillan.

Crossan, John Dominic
1973   *In Parables: The Challenge of the Historical Jesus.* New York: Harper and Row.

1977   "A Metamodel for Polyvalent Narration." *Semeia* 9:105-47.

1980   *Cliffs of Fall: Paradox and Polyvalence in the Parables of Jesus.* New York: Seabury.

Culler, Jonathan
1982   *On Deconstruction: Theory and Criticism after Structuralism.* Ithaca, N.Y.: Cornell University Press.

Culpepper, R. Alan
1983   *Anatomy of the Fourth Gospel: A Study in Literary Design.* Philadelphia: Fortress.

Curran, Charles E., and Richard A. McCormick
1984   *Readings in Moral Theology No. 4: The Use of Scripture in Moral Theology.* Ramsey, N.J.: Paulist.

Custer, Stewart
1975   *A Treasury of New Testament Synonyms.* Greenville, S.C.: Bob Jones University.

Dahood, Mitchell J.
1976   "Poetry, Hebrew." In *The Interpreter's Dictionary of the Bible: Supplementary Volume,* ed. K. Grim, pp. 669-70. Abingdon: Nashville.

Daniel-Rops, Henri
1962   *Daily Life in the Time of Jesus.* Trans. P. O'Brien. Ann Arbor: Servant.

Davids, Peter H.
1982   *The Epistle of James.* New International Greek Testament Commentary. Grand Rapids: Eerdmans.

Davies, W. D.
1983   "Reflections about the Use of the Old Testament in the New in its Historical Context." *JQR* 74:105-36.

De Koster, Lester
1986   "The Preacher as Rhetorician." In *The Preacher and Preaching: Reviving the Art in the Twentieth Century,* ed. Samuel T. Logan, Jr., pp. 303-30. Phillipsburg, N.J.: Presbyterian and Reformed.

de Man, Paul
1971   "Crisis and Criticism." In *Blindness and Insight: Essays in the Rhetoric of Contemporary Criticism.* New York: Oxford University Press.

Deer, D. S.
1985   "Unity and Diversity in the New Testament." *Bulletin de Théologie Africaine* 7/13-14:91-105.

Deissmann, Adolf
1909   *Light from the Ancient East.* Trans. L. R. M. Stracham. London:

Hodder and Stoughton.

Dentan, R. C.
1963   *Preface to Old Testament Theology.* New York: Seabury.

Derrett, J. D. M.
1970   "The Parable of the Unjust Steward." In *Law and the New Testament,* pp. 48-77. London: Darton, Longman and Todd.

Derrida, Jacques
1976   *Of Grammatology.* Trans. G. Chakrovorty. Baltimore: Johns Hopkins University Press.
1978   "Structure, Sign and Play in the Discourse of the Human Sciences." In *Writing and Difference,* trans. Alan Bass, pp. 278-93. Chicago: University of Chicago Press.
1978a   "Violence and Metaphysics. An Essay in the Thought of Emmanuel Levinas." In *Writing and Difference,* trans. Alan Bass, pp. 79-153. Chicago: University of Chicago Press.
1979   "The Supplement of Copula: Philosophy *before* Linguistics." In *Textual Strategies.* Ed. Josué Harari. Ithaca, N.Y.: Cornell University Press.
1980   "The Law of Genre." *Glyph* 7:210-13.
1982   *Margins of Philosophy.* Trans. Alan Bass. Chicago: University of Chicago Press.

Detweiler, Robert, ed.
1982   "Derrida and Biblical Studies." *Semeia* 23.

Dewey, Joanna
1982   "Point of View and the Disciples in Mark." *SBL Seminar Papers,* pp. 97-106. Chico, Calif.: Scholars Press.

Dibelius, Martin, and
Heinrich Greeven
1976   *James.* Trans. M. A. Williams. Philadelphia: Fortress.

Dietrich, Gabrielle
1981   "Dialogue and Context." *Ecumenical Review* 33/1:29-36.

Dilthey, Wilhelm
1969   *The Essence of Philosophy.* Trans. Stephen A. Emery. New York: AMS.

Dion, Paul E.
1982   "The Aramaic 'Family Letter' and Related Epistolary Forms in Other Oriental Languages and in Hellenistic Greek." In *Semeia* 22, ed. John L. White, pp. 59-76. Chico, Calif: Scholars Press.

Dodd, C. H.
1952   *According to the Scriptures.* Fontana Books. London: Collins.
1961   *The Parables of the Kingdom.* New York: Scribner's.

Doty, William G.
1966   "The Epistle in Late Hellenism and Early Christianity: Developments, Influences and Literary Form." Ph.D. diss., Drew University.
1973   *Letters in Primitive Christianity.* Philadelphia: Fortress.

Dulles, Avery
1965   "Response." In *The Bible in Modern Scholarship,* ed James P. Hyatt, pp. 214-15. Nashville: Abingdon.

Dumbrell, William J.
1985   "Jericho." In *Major Cities of the Biblical World.* Ed. R. K. Harrison. Nashville: Nelson.

Dummett, M. A. E.
 1975 "What Is a Theory of Meaning?" In *Mind and Language,* ed. Samuel
  D. Guttenplan, pp. 97-138. Oxford: Clarendon.
Dunn, James D. G.
 1977 *Unity and Diversity in the New Testament: An Inquiry into the Character of Earliest Christianity.* Philadelphia: Westminster.
 1980 *Christology in the Making.* Philadelphia: Westminster.
 1982 "Levels of Canonical Authority." *Horizons in Biblical Theology* 4/1:26-27, 40-43.
Eagleton, Terry
 1983 *Literary Theory: An Introduction.* Minneapolis: University of Minnesota Press.
Ebeling, Gerhard
 1955 "The Meaning of Biblical Theology." *JTS* n.s. 6/2:218-25.
Edwards, O. C., Jr.
 1983 "Sociology as a Tool for Interpreting the New Testament: A Review Article." *Anglical Theological Review* 65:431-48.
Efird, James M.
 1984 *How to Interpret the Bible.* Atlanta: John Knox.
Eichrodt, Walther
 1961 *Theology of the Old Testament.* Trans. J. A. Baker. Philadelphia: Westminster Press.
Elliott, John H.
 1981 *A Home for the Homeless. A Sociological Exegesis of 1 Peter.* Philadelphia: Fortress.
Emslie, B. L.
 1981 "Contrary Opinions Regarding the Unity of the New Testament and the Formulation of a New Testament Theology." *TheolEvang* 14/3:18-21.
Erickson, Millard J.
 1983 *Christian Theology.* 2 volumes. Grand Rapids: Baker.
Ericson, Norman R.
 1976 "Implications from the New Testament for Contextualization." In *Theology and Mission,* ed. David J. Hesselgrave, pp. 71-85. Grand Rapids: Baker.
Evans, Donald
 1963 *The Logic of Self-Involvement: A Philosophical Study of Everyday Language with Special Reference to the Christian Use of Language about God as Creator.* London: SCM.
Fackre, Gabriel
 1987 *The Christian Story.* Vol. 2: *Authority: Scripture in the Church for the World.* Grand Rapids: Eerdmans.
Farley, Edward, and
Peter C. Hodgson
 1985 "Scripture and Tradition." In *Christian Theology: An Introduction to Its Traditions and Task.* Ed. Peter C. Hodgson and Robert H. King. Philadelphia: Fortress.
Fee, Gordon D.
 1978 "Textual Criticism of the New Testament." In *Biblical Criticism: Historical, Literary, and Textual,* pp. 129-55. Grand Rapids: Zondervan.
 1983 *New Testament Exegesis: A Handbook for Students and Pastors.*

Philadelphia: Westminster.

Fee, Gordon D., and
Douglas Stuart
1981   *How to Read the Bible for All Its Worth: A Guide for Understanding the Bible.* Grand Rapids: Zondervan.

Feinberg, John
1984   "Truth: Relationship of Theories of Truth to Hermeneutics." In *Hermeneutics, Inerrancy, and the Bible,* ed. Earl D. Radmacher and Robert D. Preus, pp. 1-50. Grand Rapids: Zondervan.
1989   "Review Article: Rationality, Objectivity, and Doing Theology: Review and Critique of Wentzel Van Huyssteen's *Theology and the Justification of Faith,"* *Trinity Journal* ns 2:161-84.

Feinberg, Paul
1979   "The Meaning of Inerrancy." In *Inerrancy,* ed. Norman Geisler, pp. 267-304. Grand Rapids: Zondervan.
forthcoming   *Systematic Theology.* Vol. 1 of 4 vols.

Ferguson, Everett
1987   *Backgrounds of Early Christianity.* Grand Rapids: Eerdmans.

Ferguson, Sinclair B.
1988   "How Does the Bible Look at Itself?" In *Inerrancy and Hermeneutic: A Tradition, A Challenge, A Debate,* ed. Harvie M. Conn, pp. 47-66. Grand Rapids: Baker.

Ferré, Frederick
1961   *Language, Logic, and God.* New York: Harper and Row.
1968   "Metaphors, Models, and Religion." *Soundings* 51:327-45.

Fiorenza, Elisabeth
Schüssler
1984   *Foundational Theology: Jesus and the Church.* New York: Crossroad.

Firth, Roderick
1967   "The Anatomy of Certainty." *Ph Rev* 76:3-27.

Fish, Stanley E.
1980   "Interpreting the Variorum." In *Reader-Response Criticism,* ed. Jane P. Thompkins, pp. 164-84. Baltimore: Johns Hopkins University Press.
1980a   *Is There a Text in This Class? The Authority of Interpretive Communities.* Cambridge, Mass.: Harvard University Press.

Fishbane, Michael
1985   *Biblical Interpretation in Ancient Israel.* Oxford: Clarendon.

Fitzmyer, Joseph A.
1964   "The Story of the Dishonest Manager (Lk. 16:1-13)." *TS* 25:23-42.
1982   "Aramaic Epistolography." *Semeia* 22, ed. John L. White, pp. 25-26. Chico, Calif: Scholars Press.

Flew, Antony
1955   "Theology and Falsification." In *New Essays in Philosophical Theology,* ed. Antony Flew and Alasdair MacIntyre, pp. 96-99, 106-30. New York: Macmillan.

Flusser, David
1976   "Paganism in Palestine." In *The Jewish People in the First Century: Historical Geography, Political History, Social, Cultural and Religious Life and Institutions,* vol. 1, ed. S. Safrai and M. Stern, pp. 1065-1100. Philadelphia: Fortress.

Fohrer, Georg
1971   "σοφία." In *Theological Dictionary of the New Testament,* ed. Gerhard Kittel, 7:476-96. Grand Rapids: Eerdmans.

Foss, Sonja K.
1989   *Rhetorical Criticism: Exploration and Practice.* Prospect Heights, Ill.: Waveland Press.

Foss, Sonja K.;
Karen A. Foss;
and Robert Trapp
1985   *Contemporary Perspectives on Rhetoric.* Prospect Heights, Ill.: Waveland Press.

Foucault, Michel
1979   "What Is an Author?" In *Textual Strategies: Perspectives in Post-Structuralist Criticism,* ed. Josué Harari, pp. 141-60. Ithaca, N.Y.: Cornell University Press.

Fowler, Robert M.
1981   *Loaves and Fishes: The Function of the Feeding Stories in the Gospel of Mark.* Chico, Calif.: Scholars Press.
1983   "Who is 'the Reader' of Mark's Gospel?" *SBL Seminar Papers,* pp. 31-53. Chico, Calif.: Scholars Press.
1985   "Who Is 'the Reader' in Reader Response Criticism?" *Semeia* 31:5-23.

Frame, John M.
1986   "The Spirit and the Scriptures." In *Hermeneutics, Authority, and Canon,* ed. D. A. Carson and John D. Woodbridge, pp. 213-35. Grand Rapids: Zondervan.

France, R. T.
1977   "Exegesis in Practice: Two Samples." In *New Testament Interpretation,* ed. I. Howard Marshall, pp. 252-81. Grand Rapids: Eerdmans.
1977   "The Authenticity of the Sayings of Jesus." In *Historicity, Criticism & Faith,* ed. Colin Brown, pp. 101-43. Downers Grove: InterVarsity Press.
1982   *Jesus and the Old Testament.* Grand Rapids: Baker.
1984   "The Church and the Kingdom of God: Some Hermeneutical Issues." In *Biblical Interpretation and the Church: The Problem of Contextualization,* ed. D. A. Carson, pp. 30-44. Nashville: Nelson.

Freedman, David Noel
1977   "Pottery, Poetry, and Prophecy: An Essay on Biblical Poetry." *JBL* 96/1:5-26.

Frege, Gottlob
1980   *Translations from the Philosophical Writings of Gottlob Frege.* Ed. Peter Geach and Max Black. Tatawa, N.J.: Bowman and Littlefield.

Frei, Hans W.
1974   *The Eclipse of Biblical Narrative: A Study in Eighteenth and Nineteenth Century Hermeneutics.* New Haven: Yale University Press.

Freund, Elizabeth
1987   *The Return of the Reader: Reader-response Criticism.* London: Methuen.

Fujita, Neil S.
1981   *Introduction to the Bible.* New York: Paulist.

Fuller, Daniel P.
1978   "Biblical Theology and the Analogy of Faith." In *Unity and Diversity in New Testament Theology,* ed. Robert A. Guelich, pp. 195-213. Grand Rapids: Eerdmans.

Funk, Robert
1966   *Language, Hermeneutic and Word of God.* New York: Harper and Row.

Gadamer, Hans-Georg
1982 [1965]   *Truth and Method.* Trans. Garrett Broden and John Cumming. 2d ed. New York: Crossroad.

Gaebelein, Frank E.
1975   "Poetry, New Testament." In *The Zondervan Pictorial Encyclopedia of the Bible,* ed. M. C. Tenney, 4:813-14. Grand Rapids: Zondervan.

Gaffin, Richard
1976   "Systematic Theology and Biblical Theology." In *The New Testament Student and Theology,* ed. John H. Skilton, 3:35-37. Nutley, N.J.: Presbyterian and Reformed.

Gager, John G.
1975   *Kingdom and Community. The Social World of Early Christianity.* Englewood Cliffs, N.J.: Prentice-Hall.
1982   "Shall We Marry Our Enemies? Sociology and the NT." *Interpretation* 36:256-65.

Gans, Eric
1981   *The Origins of Language: A Formal Theory of Representation.* Berkeley: University of California Press.

Gardner, Howard
1974   *The Quest for Mind: Piaget, Levi-Strauss, and the Structuralist Movement.* New York: Alfred A. Knopf.

Genette, Gérard
1980   *Narrative Discourse: An Essay in Method.* Trans. J. E. Lewin. Ithaca, N.Y.: Cornell University Press.

Gerhart, Mary
1976   "Paul Ricoeur's Notion of 'Diagnostics': Its Function in Literary Interpretation." *JR* 56:137-56.

Gerstenberger, Erhard S.
1985   "The Lyrical Literature." In *The Hebrew Bible and Its Modern Interpreters,* ed. Donald A. Knight and Gene M. Tucker, pp. 409-44. Chico, Calif.: Scholars Press.
1988   *Psalms, Part I, with an Introduction to Cultic Poetry.* FOTL 14. Grand Rapids: Eerdmans.

Gese, Hartmut
1970   "Erwägungen zur Einheit der biblischen Theologie." *ZTK* 67:417-36.
1977   "Tradition and Biblical Theology." In *Tradition and Theology in the Old Testament.* Ed. Douglas A. Knight. London: SPCK.
1981   *Essays on Biblical Theology.* Trans. Keith Crim. Minneapolis: Augsburg.

Gesenius, F. W.
1910   *Gesenius' Hebrew Grammar.* Ed. Emil F. Kautzsch. Rev. A. E. Cowley. Oxford: Clarendon.

Gibson, Arthur
1981   *Biblical Semantic Logic: A Preliminary Analysis.* Oxford: Basil

Blackwell.

Gilkey, Langdon B.
1961   "Cosmology, Ontology, and the Travail of Biblical Language." *JR* 41:194-205.
1981   "The New Watershed in Theology." *Soundings* 64/2:118-31.

Girdlestone, Robert B.
1897   *Synonyms of the Old Testament*. Reprint. Grand Rapids: Eerdmans.

Gloer, W. Hulitt
1983   "Unity and Diversity in the New Testament. Anatomy of an Issue." *BibTheolBull* 13/2:53-58.

Glymour, Clark
1980   *Theory and Evidence*. Princeton: Princeton University Press.

Goergen, Donald J.
1986   *A Theology of Jesus*. Vol. 1: *The Mission and Ministry of Jesus*. Wilmington, Del.: Michael Glazier.

Goldingay, John
1984   "Diversity and Unity in Old Testament Theology." *VT* 34:153-68.

Goldberg, Michael
1982   *Theology and Narrative. A Critical Introduction*. Nashville: Abingdon.

Golden, James L.;
Goodwin F. Berquist and
William E. Coleman
1976   *The Rhetoric of Western Thought*. 3d ed. Dubuque, Iowa: Kendall/Hunt.

Goppelt, Leonhard
1982   *Typos: The Typological Interpretation of the Old Testament in the New*. Trans. Donald H. Madvig. Grand Rapids: Eerdmans.
1982a   *Theology of the New Testament*. Vol. 2: *The Variety and Unity of the Apostolic Witness to Christ*. Trans. John E. Alsup. Ed. Jürgen Roloff. Grand Rapids: Eerdmans.

Gordis, Robert
1968   *Koheleth, The Man and His World: A Study of Ecclesiastes*. New York: Schocken.

Gottwald, Norman K.
1979   *The Tribes of Yahweh: A Sociology of the Religion of Liberated Israel*. Maryknoll, N.Y.: Orbis.
1983   "Sociological Method in the Study of Ancient Israel." In *The Bible and Liberation: Political and Social Hermeneutics*. Ed. Norman K. Gottwald. Maryknoll, N.Y.: Orbis.

Graffy, Adrian
1984   *A Prophet Confronts His People: The Disputation Speech in the Prophets*. Rome: Biblical Institute.

Grässer, Erich
1980   "Offene Fragen im Umkreis einer biblischen Theologie." *ZTK* 77/2:200-21.

Grassmick, John D.
1976   *Principles and Practice of Greek Exegesis: A Classroom Manual*. Dallas: Dallas Theological Seminary.

Greidanus, Sidney
1988   *The Modern Preacher and the Ancient Text: Interpreting and*

Preaching Biblical Literature. Grand Rapids: Eerdmans.

Gross, Heinrich, and
Franz Mussner
1974 "Die Einheit von altem und neuem Testament." *Int Kath Zeit/Communio* 3/6:544-55.

Grudem, Wayne A.
1982 *The Gift of Prophecy in 1 Corinthians.* Washington, D.C.: University Press of America.
1983 "Scripture's Self-Attestation and the Problem of Formulating a Doctrine of Scripture." In *Scripture and Truth,* ed. D. A. Carson and John D. Woodbridge, pp. 19-59. Grand Rapids: Zondervan.

Gruenler, Royce
1982 *New Approaches to Jesus and the Gospels: A Phenomenological and Exegetical Study of Synoptic Christology.* Grand Rapids: Baker.
1983 *The Inexhaustible God. Biblical Faith and the Challenge of Process Theism.* Grand Rapids: Baker.
1990 *Meaning and Understanding: The Philosophical Framework for Biblical Interpretation.* Grand Rapids: Zondervan/Academie.

Guelich, Robert A.
1982 "The Gospels: Portraits of Jesus and His Ministry." *JETS* 24:117-25.
1989 *Mark 1-8:26.* Word Biblical Commentary. Waco, Tex.: Word.

Günther, Walther
1976 "Marriage." In *New International Dictionary of New Testament Theology,* ed. Colin Brown, 2:575-81. Grand Rapids: Zondervan.
1978 "Sin." In *New International Dictionary of New Testament Theology,* ed. Colin Brown, 3:573-85. Grand Rapids: Eerdmans.

Gunton, Colin
1989 *The Actuality of Atonement: A Study of Metaphor, Rationality, and the Christian Tradition.* Grand Rapids: Zondervan.

Guthrie, Donald
1981 *New Testament Theology.* Downers Grove: InterVarsity Press.
1990 [1970] *New Testament Introduction.* Rev. ed. Downers Grove: InterVarsity Press.

Güttgemanns, Gerhardt
1976 "What Is 'Generative Poetics'? Theses and Reflections Concerning a New Exegetical Method" and "Narrative Analysis of Synoptic Texts." Trans. William G. Doty. *Semeia* 6:1-21, 127-79.

Gutting, Gary, ed.
1980 *Paradigms and Revolutions.* Notre Dame, Ind.: University of Notre Dame Press.

Hagner, Donald A.
1976 "The OT in the NT." In *Interpreting the Word of God: Festschrift in Honor of Steven Barnabas.* Ed. Samuel J. Schultz and Morris A. Inch. Chicago: Moody.
1985 "Biblical Theology and Preaching." *ExpTimes* 96/5:137-41.

Hanson, Anthony T.
1969 "Book Review of George W. Knight, *The Faithful Sayings in the Pastoral Letters.*" *JTS* 20:719.

Hanson, Paul D.
1971 "Old Testament Apocalyptic Reexamined." *Interpretation* 25:454-79.
1982 *The Diversity of Scripture. A Theological Interpretation.* Overtures

to Biblical Theology 2. Philadelphia: Fortress.

1984 "The Future in Biblical Theology." *Horizons in Biblical Theology* 6/11:13-24.

1985 "Biblical Apocalyptism: The Theological Dimension." *Horizons in Biblical Theology* 7/2:1-20.

Hanson, Paul D., ed.

1983 *Visionaries and Their Apocalypses.* Philadelphia: Fortress.

Harari, Josué V., ed.

1979 *Textual Strategies: Perspectives in Post-Structuralist Criticism.* Ithaca, N.Y.: Cornell University Press.

Hare, R. M.

1955 "University Discussion." In *New Essays in Philosophical Theology,* ed. Antony Flew and Alasdair MacIntyre, pp. 99-103. New York: Macmillan.

Harris, Roy

1981 *The Language Myth.* London: Duckworth.

Harrison, Roland K.

1969 *Introduction to the Old Testament.* Grand Rapids: Eerdmans.

Hartman, Lars

1966 *Prophecy Interpreted. The Formation of Some Jewish Apocalyptic Texts and of the Eschatological Discourse.* Lund: Gleerup.

1983 "Survey of the Problem of Apocalyptic Genre." In *Apocalypticism in the Mediterranean World and the Near East,* ed. David Hellholm, pp. 329-44. Tübingen: J. C. B. Mohr.

Hartman, Sven S.

1983 "Datierung der ugaritischen Apokalyptik." In *Apocalypticism in the Mediterranean World and the Near East,* ed. David Hellholm, pp. 61-75. Tübingen: J. C. B. Mohr.

Hasel, Gerhard F.

1975 *Old Testament Theology: Basic Issues in the Current Debate.* Grand Rapids: Eerdmans.

1978 *New Testament Theology: Basic Issues in the Current Debate.* Grand Rapids: Eerdmans.

1981a "A Decade of Old Testament Theology: Retrospect and Prospect." *ZAW* 93:165-84.

1981b "The Meaning of the Animal Rite in Genesis 15." *JSOT* 19:61-78.

1982 "Biblical Theology: Then, Now, and Tomorrow." *Horizons in Biblical Theology* 4/1:61-93.

1984 "The Relationship between Biblical Theology and Systematic Theology." *Trinity Journal* 5/2:113-27.

1985 "Major Recent Issues in Old Testament Theology 1978—1983." *JSOT* 31:31-53.

Hatch, Edwin, and Henry Redpath

1975 *A Concordance to the Septuagint and Other Greek Versions of the Old Testament.* 2 vols. Oxford: Clarendon.

Hawthorne, Gerald F.

1983 *Philippians.* Word Biblical Commentary. Waco, Tex.: Word.

Hayes, John H.

1976 *Understanding the Psalms.* Valley Forge, Pa.: Judson.

1979 *An Introduction to Old Testament Study.* Nashville: Abingdon.

Hayes, John H., and
Carl R. Holladay
1982   *Biblical Exegesis: A Beginner's Handbook.* Atlanta: John Knox.
Hayes, John H., and
Frederick Prussner
1985   *Old Testament Theology: Its History and Development.* Atlanta:
John Knox.
Hayter, Mary
1987   *The New Eve in Christ. The Use and Abuse of the Bible in the Debate
about Women in the Church.* London: SPCK.
Hazelton, Roger
1978   "Theological Analogy and Metaphor." *Semeia* 13:155-76.
Helm, Paul
1983   "Faith, Evidence, and the Scriptures." In *Scripture and Truth,* ed.
D. A. Carson and John D. Woodbridge, pp. 303-20. Grand Rapids:
Zondervan.
Hempel, Johannes
1930   "Von irrendem Glauben." *Zeitschrift für systematische Theologie*
7:631-60.
Hendry, George S.
1930   "Biblical Metaphors and Theological Constructions." *Princeton
Seminary Bulletin* n.s. 2/3:258-65.
Hengel, Martin
1974   *Judaism and Hellenism: Studies in Their Encounter in Palestine during the Early Hellenistic Period.* Trans. John Bowden. 2 vols. Philadelphia: Fortress.
1980   *Jews, Greeks, and Barbarians: Aspects of the Hellenization of Judaism in the Pre-Christian Period.* Trans. John Bowden. Philadelphia:
Fortress.
Henry, Carl F. H.
1976   *God, Revelation, and Authority.* Vol. 2: *God Who Speaks and
Shows.* Waco, Tex.: Word.
Henry, Patrick
1979   *New Direction in New Testament Studies.* Philadelphia: Westminster.
Hermann, Siegfried
1981   *Time and History.* Trans. James L. Blemins. Nashville: Abingdon.
Hermisson, Hans-Jürgen
1968   *Studien zur israelitischen Spruchweisheit.* Neukirchen: Neukirchener
Verlag.
1978   "Observations on the Creation Theology in Wisdom." In *Creation in
the Old Testament,* ed. Bernhard W. Anderson, pp. 118-34. Reprint
1984. Philadelphia: Fortress.
Hesse, Franz
1963   "The Evaluation and the Authority of Old Testament Tests." In *Essays on Old Testament Hermeneutics.* Ed. Claus Westermann and
James L. Mays. Richmond: John Knox.
Hesselgrave, David J.
1978   *Communicating Christ Cross-Culturally.* Grand Rapids: Zondervan.
Hesselgrave, David J., and
Ed Rommen
1989   *Contextualization: Meanings, Methods, and Models.* Grand Rapids:

Baker.

Hiebert, Paul
1985 "Epistemological Foundations for Science and Theology." *TSF Bulletin* 8/4:5-10.
1985a "The Missiological Implications of an Epistemological Shift." *TSF Bulletin* 8/5:12-18.
1987 "Critical Contextualization." *International Bulletin of Missionary Research*, pp. 104-12.

Hiers, R. H.
1984 "Ecology, Biblical Theology, and Methodology: Biblical Perspectives on the Environment." *Zygon* 19/1:43-59.

Higgins, A. J. B.
1966/67 "The Priestly Messiah." *NTS* 13:211-39.

Hirsch, E. D., Jr.
1967 *Validity in Interpretation.* New Haven: Yale University Press.
1976 *The Aims of Interpretation.* Chicago: University of Chicago Press.

Hocking, Ian, ed.
1980 *Scientific Revolutions.* New York: Oxford Unversity Press.

Hoffmann, Thomas A.
1982 "Inspiration, Normativeness, Canonicity, and the Unique Sacred Character of the Bible." *CBQ* 44/3:447-69.

Holland, Norman N.
1980 "Unity Identity Text Self." In *Reader-Response Criticism,* ed. Jane P. Tompkins, pp. 118-33. Baltimore: Johns Hopkins University Press.

Holmberg, Bengst
1978 *Paul and Power: The Structure of Authority in the Primitive Church as Reflected in the Pauline Epistles.* Philadelphia: Fortress.

Holmes, Arthur F.
1968 "Ordinary Language Analysis and Theological Methods." *JETS* 11:131-38.
1971 *Faith Seeks Understanding.* Grand Rapids: Eerdmans.

Hooker, Morna D.
1959 *Jesus and the Servant, the Influence of the Servant Concept of Deutero-Isaiah in the New Testament.* London: SPCK.
1972 "On Using the Wrong Tool." *Theology* 75:570-81.
1973 "Were There False Teachers in Colossae?" In *Christ and Spirit in the New Testament,* ed. Barnabas Lindars and Stephen S. Smalley, pp. 315-31. Cambridge: Cambridge University Press.

Horst, S. Daemmrich
1978 "The Aesthetic Function of Detail and Silhouette in Literary Genres." In *Theories of Literary Genre,* ed. J. P. Strelka, pp. 12-22. University Park: Pennsylvania State University Press.

Hough, Graham
1976 "An Eighth Type of Ambiguity." In *On Literary Intention.* Ed. David Newton-deMolina. Edinburgh: At the University Press.

Howard, David M., Jr.
forthcoming "Is 'Biblical Rhetorical Criticism' Really Rhetorical Criticism?"

Hübner, Hans
1981 "Biblische Theologie und Theologie des Neuen Testaments." *Kerygma und Dogma* 27/1:2-19.

1984 "Rudolf Bultmann und das Alte Testament." *Kerygma und Dogma* 30/4:250-72.

Hughes, John J.
1983 "Review of New Testament Theology by Donald Guthrie." *Trinity Journal* n.s. 3/1:112-13.

Hughes, Philip E.
1983 "The Truth of Scripture and the Problem of Historical Relativity." In *Scripture and Truth,* ed. D. A. Carson and John D. Woodbridge, pp. 173-94. Grand Rapids: Zondervan.

Hultgard, Anderes
1983 "Forms and Origins of Iranian Apocalypticism." In *Apocalypticism in the Mediterranean World and the Near East,* ed. David Hellholm, pp. 387-412. Tübingen: J. C. B. Mohr.

Hunter, Archibald M.
1953 *The Unity of the New Testament.* London: SCM.
1960 "The Interpreter and the Parables." *Interpretation* 14:70-84, 167-85, 315-32, 440-54.
1964 *Interpreting the Parables.* London: SCM.

Hurley, James B.
1981 *Man and Woman in Biblical Perspective.* Grand Rapids: Zondervan.

Iser, Wolfgang
1974 *The Implied Reader: Patterns of Communication in Prose Fiction from Bunyan to Beckett.* Baltimore: Johns Hopkins University Press.
1978 *The Act of Reading: A Theory of Aesthetic Response.* Baltimore: Johns Hopkins University Press.

Jeanrond, Werner G.
1987 *Text and Interpretation as Categories of Theological Thinking.* Trans. Thomas J. Wilson. Dublin: Gill and Macmillan.

Jensen, Irving L.
1963 *Independent Bible Study.* Chicago: Moody.

Jensen, Richard A.
1980 *Telling the Story: Variety and Imagination in Preaching.* Minneapolis: Augsburg.

Jeremias, Joachim
1967 *The Prayers of Jesus.* Trans. John Bowden et al. London: SCM.
1969 *Jerusalem in the Time of Jesus.* Trans. F. H. Cave and C. H. Cave. 3d ed. London: SCM.
1972 *The Parables of Jesus.* Trans. S. H. Hooke. 8th ed. London: SCM.

Johnson, Alan F.
1983 "The Historical-Critical Method: Egyptian Gold or Pagan Precipice." *JETS* 26/1:3-15.
1984 " 'Response' to J. Robertson McQuilkin." In *Hermeneutics, Inerrancy, and the Bible,* ed. Earl D. Radmacher and Robert D. Preus, pp. 255-82. Grand Rapids: Zondervan/Academie Books.

Johnson, Elliott E.
1990 *Expository Hermeneutics: An Introduction.* Grand Rapids: Zondervan/Academie.

Johnson, John F.
1973 "Analogia Fidei: Hermeneutical Principle." *Springfielder* 37.

Jones, Geraint V.
1964 *The Art and Truth of the Parables.* London: SPCK.

Judge, E. A.
1960   *The Social Pattern of Christian Groups in the First Century.* London: Tyndale.
1980   "The Social Identity of the First Christians: A Question of Method in Religious History." *Journal of Religious History* 11:201-17.
Juhl, Peter D.
1980   *Interpretation: An Essay in the Philosophy of Literary Criticism.* Princeton: Princeton University Press.
Kaiser, Otto
1975   *Introduction to the Old Testament: A Presentation of its Results and Problems.* Trans. John Sturdy. Oxford: Basil Blackwell.
Kaiser, Walter C., Jr.
1978   "The Single Intent of Scripture." In *Evangelical Roots,* ed. Kenneth Kantzer, pp. 123-41. Nashville: Nelson.
1978   *Toward an Old Testament Theology.* Grand Rapids: Zondervan.
1979   "Legitimate Hermeneutics." In *Inerrancy,* ed. Norman L. Geisler, pp. 117-50. Grand Rapids: Zondervan.
1981   *Toward an Exegetical Theology: Biblical Principles for Preaching and Teaching.* Grand Rapids: Baker.
1985   *The Uses of the Old Testament in the New.* Chicago: Moody.
Kantzer, Kenneth, ed.
1978   *Evangelical Roots.* Nashville: Nelson.
Karlberg, Mark W.
1985   "Legitimate Discontinuities between the Testaments." *JETS* 28/1:9-20.
Käsemann, Ernst
1964   "The New Testament Canon and the Unity of the Church." In *Essays on New Testament Themes,* trans. W. J. Montague, pp. 95-107. London: SCM.
1970   *Das Neue Testament als Kanon. Dokumentation und kritische Analyse zur gegenwärtigen Diskussion.* Göttingen: Vandenhoeck und Ruprecht.
1973   "The Problem of a New Testament Theology." *NTS* 19/3:235-45.
1984   "Differences and Unity in the New Testament." *Concilium* 17:55-61.
Kaufmann, Gordon D.
1988   "Models of God: Is Metaphor Enough?" *Religion and Intellectual Life* 5: 11-18.
forthcoming   "How Do Protestant Liberal Theologians Approach 'Doing Theology' Today?" In *Doing Theology in Today's World.* Ed. Thomas McComiskey and John D. Woodbridge. Grand Rapids: Zondervan.
Kautzsch, Emil F., ed.
1910   *Gesenius' Hebrew Grammar.* Oxford: Clarendon.
Keck, Leander E.
1980   "Will the Historical-Critical Method Survive? Some Observations." In *Orientation by Disorientation,* ed. Richard A. Spencer, pp. 115-27. Pittsburgh: Pickwick.
Kedar, Benjamin
1981   *Biblische Semantik.* Stuttgart: Kohlhammer.
Kee, Howard Clark
1989   *Knowing the Truth: A Sociological Approach to New Testament Interpretation.* Philadelphia: Fortress.

Keegan, Terence J.
1985   *Interpreting the Bible: A Popular Introduction to Biblical Hermeneutics.* New York: Paulist.

Keil, Carl Friedrich
1971   *Biblical Commentary on the Old Testament: The Twelve Minor Prophets.* Vol. 11. Reprint. Grand Rapids: Eerdmans.

Kelsey, David
1975   *The Uses of Scripture in Recent Theology.* Philadelphia: Fortress.

Kennedy, George A.
1984   *New Testament Interpretation through Rhetorical Criticism.* Chapel Hill, N.C.: University of North Carolina Press.

Kermode, Frank
1979   *The Genesis of Secrecy.* Cambridge, Mass.: Harvard University Press.

Kessler, Martin
1982   "A Methodological Setting for Rhetorical Criticism." In *Art and Meaning: Rhetoric in Biblical Literature,* ed. David J. A. Clines, David M. Gunn, and Alan J. Hauser, pp. 1-19. JSOT Supp 19. Sheffield: JSOT Press.

Kidner, Derek
1964   *The Proverbs: An Introduction and Commentary.* Chicago: Inter-Varsity Press.

Kingsbury, Jack Dean
1969   *The Parables of Jesus in Matthew 13: A Study in Redaction Criticism.* Richmond: John Knox.
1986   *Matthew as Story.* Philadelphia: Fortress.

Kistemaker, Simon
1977   "The Canon of the New Testament." *JETS* 20/1:3-14.

Klein, Hans
1983   "Leben-neues Leben, Möglichkeiten und Grenzen einer gesamtbiblischen Theologie des Alten und Neuen Testaments." *EvangTheol* 43/2:91-107.

Klein, Ralph W.
1974   *Textual Criticism of the Old Testament: From the Septuagint to Qumran.* Philadelphia: Fortress.

Klooster, Fred H.
1984   "The Role of the Holy Spirit in the Hermeneutic Process: The Relationship of the Spirit's Illumination to Biblical Interpretation." In *Hermeneutics, Inerrancy, and the Bible,* ed. Earl D. Radmacher and Robert D. Preus, pp. 451-72. Grand Rapids: Zondervan/Academie Books.

Knierim, Rolf P.
1984   "The Task of Old Testament Theology." *Horizons in Biblical Theology* 6/1:25-57.

Knight, Douglas A.
1980   "Canon and History of Tradition: A Critique of Brevard S. Childs' Introduction to the OT as Scripture." *Horizons in Biblical Theology* 2:127-49.

Knight, George W., III
1968   *The Faithful Sayings in the Pastoral Letters.* Kampen: J. H. Kok.
1984   " 'Response' to J. Robertson McQuilkin." In *Hermeneutics, Iner-*

rancy, and the Bible, ed. Earl D. Radmacher and Robert D. Preus, pp. 241-53. Grand Rapids: Zondervan/Academie Books.

Knutson, F. Brent
1982   "Cuneiform Letters and Social Conventions." *Semeia* 22, ed. John L. White, pp. 15-23. Chico, Calif.: Scholars Press.

Koch, Klaus
1972   *The Rediscovery of Apocalyptic.* Trans. Margret Kohl. London: SCM.
1983   "Von prophetischen zum apokalyptischen Visionsbericht." In *Apocalypticism in the Mediterranean World and the Near East,* ed. David Hellholm, pp. 413-46. Tübingen: J. C. B. Mohr.

Koehler, Ludwig
1967   *Hebräisches und Aramäisches Lexikon zum Alten Testament.* Rev. Walter Baumgartner. Leiden: E. J. Brill.

Kovacs, Brian Watson, ed.
1982   "A Joint Paper by the Members of the Structuralism and Exegesis SBL Seminar." In *Society of Biblical Literature 1982 Seminar Papers,* ed. Kent Harold Richards, pp. 251-70. Chico, Calif.: Scholars Press.

Kraft, Charles
1978   "Interpreting in Cultural Context." *JETS* 21/4:357-67.
1979   *Christianity in Culture: A Study in Dynamic Biblical Theologizing in Cross-Cultural Perspective.* Maryknoll, N.Y.: Orbis.

Krieger, Murray
1964   *A Window to Criticism: Shakespeare's Sonnets and Modern Poetics.* Princeton, N.J.: Princeton University Press.

Kuenen, Abraham
1969 [1877] *The Prophets and Prophecy in Israel: An Historical and Critical Enquiry.* Amsterdam: Philo.

Kugel, James L.
1981   *The Idea of Biblical Poetry: Parallelism and Its History.* New Haven, Conn.: Yale University Press.

Kuhn, Karl Georg
1960   *Konkordanz zu den Qumrantexten.* Göttingen: Vandenhoeck und Ruprecht.

Kuhn, Thomas S.
1970   *The Structure of Scientific Revolutions.* Chicago: University of Chicago Press.

Kuist, Howard T.
1947   *These Words Upon Thy Heart.* Richmond: John Knox.

Kümmel, Werner G.
1975   *Introduction to the New Testament.* Trans. Howard Clark Kee. From the 17th German ed. Nashville: Abingdon.

Küng, Hans
1970   "Der Frühkatholizismus im NT als Kontroverstheologisches Problem." In *Das NT als Kanon.* Ed. Ernst Käsemann. Göttingen: Vandenhoeck und Ruprecht.

Kurzweil, Edith
1980   *The Age of Structuralism: Levi-Strauss to Foucault.* New York: Columbia University Press.

Kysar, Robert
1970   "The Background of the Prologue of the Fourth Gospel: A Critique of Historical Methods." *Canadian Journal of Theology* 16:250-55.

Ladd, George E.
1957   "Why not Prophetic-Apocalyptic?" *JBL* 76:192-200.
1974   *A Theology of the New Testament.* Grand Rapids: Eerdmans.

Lambdin, Thomas O.
1971   *Introduction to Biblical Hebrew.* New York: Charles Scribner's Sons.

Lambrecht, Jan
1981   *Once More Astonished: The Parables of Jesus.* New York: Crossroad.

Larkin, William J., Jr.
1988   *Culture and Biblical Hermeneutics: Interpreting and Applying the Authoritative Word in a Relativistic Age.* Grand Rapids: Baker.

LaSor, William S.
1978   "The Sensus Plenior and Biblical Interpretation." In *Scripture, Tradition, and Interpretation.* Grand Rapids: Eerdmans.

LaSor, William S.;
David A. Hubbard; and
Frederic W. Bush
1982   *Old Testament Survey: The Message, Form, and Background of the Old Testament.* Grand Rapids: Eerdmans.

Le Roux, J. H.
1983   "A Confessional Approach to the Old Testament." *OTE* 114-29.

Leavy, John P.
1982   "Four Protocols: Derrida, His Deconstruction." *Semeia* 23:42-57.

Lemke, Werner
1982   "Revelation through History in Recent Biblical Theology: A Critical Appraisal." *Interpretation* 36/1:34-46.

Levi-Strauss, Claude
1963, 1976   *Structural Anthropology.* 2 vols. New York: Basic.

Lewis, Gordon R., and
Bruce A. Demarest
1987   *Integrative Theology.* Vol. 1: *Knowing Ultimate Reality—The Living God.* Grand Rapids: Zondervan.

Liefeld, Walter L.
1984   *New Testament Exposition: From Text to Sermon.* Grand Rapids: Zondervan.

Lincoln, Andrew T.
1981   *Paradise Now and Not Yet.* Cambridge: Cambridge University Press.

Lindblom, Johannes
1962   *Prophecy in Ancient Israel.* Oxford: Basil Blackwell.

Linnemann, Eta
1966   *Jesus of the Parables.* Trans. John Sturdy. New York: Harper and Row.

Lisowsky, Gerhard
1958   *Konkordanz Zum Hebräischen Alten Testament.* 2d ed. Stuttgart: Württembergische Bibelanstalt.

Lohse, Eduard
1975   "Überlegungen zur Aufgabe einer Theologie des Neuen Testaments." *Evangelische Theologie* 35:147-50.

1984   *Grundriss der neutestamentlichen Theologie.* Theologische Wissenschaft 5. 3d rev. ed. Stuttgart: Kohlhammer.

Long, Burke O.
1982   "The Social World of Ancient Israel." *Interpretation* 36:243-55.

Longenecker, Richard N.
1970   *The Christology of Early Jewish Christianity.* SBT 17. London: SCM Press.
1975   *Biblical Exegesis in the Apostolic Period.* Grand Rapids: Eerdmans.
1983   "On the Form, Function, and Authority of the New Testament Letters." In *Scripture and Truth,* ed. D. A. Carson and John D. Woodbridge, pp. 101-14. Grand Rapids: Zondervan.

Longman, Tremper, III
1983   "Fictional Akkadian Royal Autobiography: A Generic and Comparative Approach." Ph.D. diss., Yale.
1983   "The Divine Warrior: The New Testament Use of an Old Testament Motif." *Westminster Theological Journal* 44:290-301.
1985   "Form Criticism, Recent Developments in Genre Theory, and the Evangelical." *Westminster Theological Journal* 47:46-67.
1987   *Literary Approaches to Biblical Interpretation.* Grand Rapids: Zondervan/ Academie Books.
1988   *How to Read the Psalms.* Downers Grove: InterVarsity Press.

Louw, Johannes P.
1981   *Semantics of New Testament Greek.* Philadelphia: Fortress.

Lund, Nils W.
1942   *Chiasmus in the New Testament.* Chapel Hill, N.C.: University of North Carolina Press.

Lundin, Roger;
Anthony C. Thiselton; and
Clarence Walhout
1986   *The Responsibility of Hermeneutics.* Grand Rapids: Eerdmans.

Lutzer, Erwin W.
1984   "Response to Haddon W. Robinson, 'Homiletics and Hermeneutics.' " In *Hermeneutics, Inerrancy, and the Bible.* Ed. Earl D. Radmacher and Robert D. Preus. Grand Rapids: Zondervan.

Lyons, John
1968   *Introduction to Theoretical Linguistics.* Cambridge: Cambridge University Press.
1977   *Semantics.* 2 vols. Cambridge: Cambridge University Press.
1981   *Language and Linguistics.* Cambridge: Cambridge University Press.

Mack, Burton L.
1990   *Rhetoric and the New Testament.* Guides to Biblical Scholarship. Minneapolis: Fortress.

Malherbe, Abraham J.
1983   *Social Aspects of Early Christianity.* 2d ed. Philadelphia: Fortress.

Malina, Bruce J.
1981   *The New Testament World: Insights from Cultural Anthropology.* Atlanta: John Knox.
1982 [1897]   "The Social Sciences and Biblical Interpretation." *Interpretation* 36:229-42.
1983   "Why Interpret the Bible with the Social Sciences?" *American Baptist Quarterly* 2:119-33.

Mandelkern, Salomon
1969 [1897]   *Veteris Testamenti Concordantiae Hebraicae atque Chaldaicae.* Tel Aviv: Sumptibus Schocken.

March, W. Eugene
1974   "Prophecy." In *Old Testament Form Criticism,* ed. John H. Hayes, pp. 141-77. San Antonio: Trinity University Press.

Marsden, George
1980   *Fundamentalism and American Culture: The Shaping of Twentieth-Century Evangelicalism 1870-1925.* New York: Oxford.

Marshall, I. Howard
1963   *Eschatology and the Parables.* London: Tyndale.
1969   *Kept by the Power of God: A Study of Perseverance and Falling Away.* Minneapolis: Bethany Fellowship.
1970   *Luke: Historian and Theologian.* Grand Rapids: Zondervan.
1976-77   "Orthodoxy and Heresy in Earlier Christianity." *Themelios* 2/1:5-14.
1978   *The Epistles of John.* NICNT. Grand Rapids: Eerdmans.
1980   "How Do We Interpret the Bible Today?" *Themelios* 5/2:4-12.
1982   *Biblical Inspiration.* Grand Rapids: Eerdmans.

Martin, Ralph P.
1972   *Mark: Evangelist and Theologian.* Grand Rapids: Eerdmans.
1977   "Approaches to New Testament Exegesis." In *New Testament Interpretation: Essays on Principles and Methods,* ed. I. Howard Marshall, pp. 220-51. Grand Rapids: Eerdmans.

Mathers, Donald
1959   "Biblical and Systematic Theology." *Canadian Journal of Theology* 5:15-24.

Maxwell, Grover, and Robert M. Anderson, eds.
1975   *Induction, Probability and Confirmation.* Minneapolis: University of Minnesota Press.

Mayo, S. M.
1982   *The Relevance of the Old Testament for the Christian Faith. Biblical Theology and Interpretative Methodology.* Washington, D.C.: University Press of America.

Mays, James L.
1980   "What Is Written. A Response to Brevard Childs' *Introduction to the Old Testament as Scripture." Horizons in Biblical Theology* 2:151-63.

McComiskey, Thomas E.
1978   *Covenants of Promise.* Grand Rapids: Baker.
1980   "Review of *Introduction to the Old Testament as Scripture* by Brevard S. Childs." *Trinity Journal* ns 1/1:88-91.

McCurley, Foster R., and John Reumann
1986   *Witness of the Word. A Biblical Theology of the Gospel.* Philadelphia: Fortress.

McFague, Sallie
1982   *Metaphorical Theology. Models of God in Religious Language.* Philadelphia: Fortress.
1987   *Models of God: Theology for an Ecological, Nuclear Age.* Philadelphia: Fortress.

McKane, William
 1970   *Proverbs: A New Approach*. London: SCM.
 1985   "Is There a Place for Theology in the Exegesis of the Hebrew Bible?" *SEA* 50:7-20.

McKnight, Edgar V.
 1978   *Meaning in Texts: The Historical Shaping of a Narrative Hermeneutics*. Philadelphia: Fortress.
 1988   *Post-Modern Use of the Bible*. Nashville: Abingdon.

McKnight, Scot
 1988   *Interpreting the Synoptic Gospels*. Grand Rapids: Baker.

McQuilkin, J. Robertson
 1980   "Limits of Cultural Interpretation." *JETS* 23/2:113-24.
 1983   *Understanding and Applying the Bible*. Chicago: Moody.
 1984   "Problems of Normativeness in Scripture: Cultural Versus Permanent." In *Hermeneutics, Inerrancy, and the Bible*, ed. Earl D. Radmacher and Robert D. Preus, pp. 217-40. Grand Rapids: Zondervan/Academie Books.

Mead, David G.
 1986   *Pseudonymity and Canon: An Investigation into the Relationship of Authorship and Authority in Jewish and Early Christian Tradition*. Tübingen: J. C. B. Mohr.

Meeks, Wayne A.
 1982   "The Social Context of Pauline Theology." *Interpretation* 36:266-77.
 1983   *The First Urban Christians. The Social World of the Apostle Paul.* New Haven: Yale University Press.

Metzger, Bruce M.
 1964   *The Text of the New Testament: Its Transmission, Corruption and Restoration*. New York: Oxford University Press.
 1971   *A Textual Commentary on the Greek New Testament*. New York: United Bible Society.

Meyer, B. J. F., and G. E. Rice
 1982   "The Interaction of Reader Strategies and the Organization of Text." *Text* 2-1/3:155-92.

Meyer, Ben F.
 1979   *The Aims of Jesus*. London: SCM.

Miall, David S., ed.
 1982   *Metaphor: Problems and Perspectives*. Atlanta: Highlands Humanities Press, xi-xix.

Mickelsen, A. Berkeley
 1963   *Interpreting the Bible*. Grand Rapids: Eerdmans.

Mitchell, Basil
 1955   "University Discussion." In *New Essays in Philosophical Theology*, ed. Antony Flew and Alisdair MacIntyre, pp. 103-5. New York: Macmillan.
 1981   *The Justification of Religious Belief*. New York: Oxford University Press.

Montgomery, John W.
 1970   "The Theologian's Craft." In *The Suicide of Christian Theology*, pp. 267-313. Minneapolis: Bethany Fellowship.

Moo, Douglas
1983   *The Old Testament in the Gospel Passion Narratives.* Sheffield, England: Almond.
1983   " 'Law,' 'Works of the Law,' and Legalism in Paul." *Westminster Theological Journal* 45:73-100.
1986   "Paul and Israel in Rom 7:7-12." *NTS* 32/1:122-35.

Moore, F. C. T.
1982   "On Taking Metaphor Literally." In *Metaphor: Problems and Perspectives,* ed. David S. Miall, pp. 1-13. Atlanta: Highlands Humanities Press.

Moore, Stephen D.
1986   "Negative Hermeneutics, Insubstantial Texts: Stanley Fish and the Biblical Interpreter." *JAAR* 54:707-19.
1988   "Stories of Reading: Doing Gospel Criticism As/With a 'Reader.' " *SBL 1988 Seminar Papers,* pp. 140-68. Chico, Calif.: Scholars Press.

Morgan, Donn F.
1981   *Wisdom in the Old Testament Traditions.* Oxford: Basil Blackwell.

Morgan, Robert
1973   *The Nature of New Testament Theology: The Contribution of William Wrede and Adolf Schlatter.* London: SCM.

Morgan, Robert, and John Barton
1988   *Biblical Interpretation.* New York: Oxford University Press.

Morgan-Wynne, John
1983   "New Testament Theology." *Theological Educator* 14/1:10-21.

Morris, Leon
1986   *New Testament Theology.* Grand Rapids: Zondervan.

Morse, Christopher
1975   *The Logic of Promise in Moltmann's Theology.* Philadelphia: Fortress.

Moscati, Sabatino
1969   *An Introduction to the Comparative Grammar of the Semitic Languages.* Wiesbaden, West Germany: Otto Harrassowitz.

Moule, C. F. D.
1959   *An Idiom Book of New Testament Greek.* 2d ed. Cambridge: Cambridge University Press.
1981   *The Birth of the New Testament.* London: A. and C. Black.

Moulton, W. F., and A. S. Geden
1978   *A Concordance to the Greek Testament.* Edinburgh: T. & T. Clark.

Mounce, Robert W.
1977   *The Book of Revelation.* NICNT. Grand Rapids: Eerdmans.

Muilenberg, James
1969   "Form Criticism and Beyond." *JBL* 88:1-18.

Murphy, Roland E.
1980   "The Old Testament As Scripture." *JSOT* 16:40-44.
1981   *The Forms of Old Testament Literature.* Vol. 13: *Wisdom Literature: Job, Proverbs, Ruth, Canticles, Ecclesiastes, Esther.* Grand Rapids: Eerdmans.

Murray, John
1978   "Systematic Theology." In *The New Testament Student and Theol-*

ogy, ed. John H. Skilton, 3:18-31. Nutley, N.J.: Presbyterian and Reformed.

1976   "Greek in Palestine and the Diaspora." In *The Jewish People in the First Century,* ed. S. Safrai and M. Stern, 1/2:1040-64. 2 vols. Philadelphia: Fortress.

Nel, Philip S.
1982   *The Structure and Ethos of the Wisdom Admonitions in Proverbs.* New York: Walter de Gruyter.

Neusner, Jacob
1983   *Formative Judaism III: Religious, Historical, and Literary Studies.* Chico, Calif.: Scholars Press.

Newman, Robert C.
1984   "Perspectives on the Image of God in Man from Biblical Theology." *EvangJourn* 2/2:66-76.

Nicholl, Donald
1958   "A Historian's Calling." *Downside Review* 76/246:275-92.
1979   "Historical Understanding." *Downside Review* 97/327:99-113.

Nickelsburg, George W.
1983   "Social Aspects of Palestinian Jewish Apocalypticism." In *Apocalypticism in the Mediterranean World and the Near East,* ed. David Hellholm, pp. 641-54. Tübingen: J. C. B. Mohr.

Nicole, Roger
1978   "The Relationship between Biblical Theology and Systematic Theology." In *Evangelical Roots,* ed. Kenneth Kantzer, pp. 185-93. Nashville: Nelson.
1984   "Patrick Fairbairn and Biblical Hermeneutics as Related to the Quotations of the Old Testament in the New." In *Hermeneutics, Inerrancy, and the Bible,* ed. Earl D. Radmacher and Robert D. Preus, pp. 765-76. Grand Rapids: Zondervan/Academie Books.

Nida, Eugene A.
1964   *Toward a Science of Translating.* Leiden: E. J. Brill.
1972   *Signs, Sense, and Translation.* Pretoria, South Africa: Pretoria University.
1972   "The Implications of Contemporary Linguistics for Biblical Scholarship." *JBL* 91:73-89.
1974   *Componential Analysis of Meaning.* The Hague: Mouton.
1975   *Exploring Semantic Structures.* Munich: Fink.

Nida, Eugene A.; and Charles R. Taber
1974   *The Theory and Practice of Translation.* Leiden: E. J. Brill.

Nida, Eugene A.; S. P. Louw; A. H. Snuman; and J. v. W. Cronje.
1983   *Style and Discourse.* New York: Bible Society.

Nida, Eugene A.; and William D. Reyburn
1981   *Meaning Across Cultures.* Maryknoll, N.Y.: Orbis.

Nineham, Dennis
1976   *The Use and Abuse of the Bible.* New York: Macmillan.

Norris, Christopher
1982   *Deconstruction: Theory and Practice.* New York: Methuen.
1985   *The Contest of Faculties: Philosophy and Theory after Deconstruction.* New York: Methuen.

Nuñez, Emilio A.
1984   "The Church in the Liberation Theology of Gutierrez: Description and Hermeneutical Analysis." In *Biblical Interpretation and the Church: The Problem of Contextualization,* ed. D. A. Carson, pp. 166-94. Nashville: Nelson.

Obayashi, Hiroshi
1970   "Pannenberg and Troeltsch: History and Religion," *JAAR* 38:401-19.

O'Brien, Peter T.
1977   *Introductory Thanksgivings in the Letters of Paul.* Leiden: E. J. Brill.

Ogden, Schubert M.
forthcoming   "How Do Process Theologians Approach the 'Doing of Theology' Today?" In *Doing Theology in Today's World.* Ed. Thomas McComiskey and John D. Woodbridge. Grand Rapids: Zondervan.

Olthius, James
1987   *A Hermeneutics of Ultimacy: Peril or Promise.* New York: University Press of America.

Osborne, Grant R.
1977   "Hermeneutics and Women in the Church." *JETS* 20/4.
1978   "Traditionsgeschichte and the Evangelical." *JETS* 21/2.
1979   "The Evangelical and Redaction Criticism: Critique and Methodology." *JETS* 22/4.
1983   "Genre Criticism: Sensus Literalis." *Trinity Journal* 4:1-27, with an abbreviated version in *Hermeneutics, Inerrancy, and the Bible.* Ed. Earl D. Radmacher and Robert D. Preus. Grand Rapids: Zondervan, 1984.
1984   *The Resurrection Narratives: A Redactional Study.* Grand Rapids: Baker.
1984a   "Mind Control or Spirit-Controlled Minds?" and "Devotions and the Spirit-Controlled Mind." In *Renewing Your Mind in a Secular World,* ed. John D. Woodbridge, pp. 55-70, 95-114. Chicago: Moody.
1988   "Type, Typology." *ISBE,* ed. Geoffrey W. Bromiley, 4:930-32. Grand Rapids: Eerdmans.
1988a   "Interpreting the New Testament." In *The Proceedings of the Conference on Biblical Interpretation,* pp. 137-67. Nashville: Broadman.
1991   "Redaction Criticism." In *New Testament Criticism and Interpretation,* ed. David Alan Black and David S. Dockery, pp. 199-224. Grand Rapids: Zondervan.

Osborne, Grant R., and Stephen Woodward
1979   *Handbook for Bible Study.* Grand Rapids: Baker.

Osten-Sacken, Peter von der
1986   *Christian-Jewish Dialogue. Theological Foundations.* Trans. Margaret Kohl. Philadelphia: Fortress.

Outler, Albert C.
1980   "The 'Logic' of Canon-making and the Tasks of Canon-Criticism."
        In *Texts and Testaments: Critical Essays on the Bible and Early
        Church Fathers,* ed. W. Eugene March, pp. 263-76. San Antonio:
        Trinity University Press.

Packer, J. I.
1978   "An Evangelical View of Progressive Revelation." In *Evangelical
        Roots,* ed. Kenneth Kantzer, pp. 143-58. Nashville: Nelson.

Padilla, C. René
1979   "Hermeneutics and Culture: A Theological Perspective." In *Gospel
        and Culture,* ed. John Stott and R. T. Coote, pp. 63-78. Pasadena:
        William Carey Library.

Palmer, Richard E.
1969   *Hermeneutics, Interpretation Theory in Schleiermacher, Dilthey,
        Heidegger, and Gadamer.* Evanston, Ill.: Northwestern University
        Press.

Pannenberg, Wolfhart
1967   *History and Hermeneutics.* Ed. Robert W. Funk. New York: Harper
        and Row.

1968   *Revelation at History.* New York: Macmillan.

Pardee, Dennis
1978   "An Overview of Ancient Hebrew Epistolography." *JBL* 97/3:321-
        46.

1982   *Handbook of Ancient Hebrew Letters.* Chico, Calif.: Scholars Press.

Patte, Daniel
1976   *Early Jewish Hermeneutic in Palestine.* Missoula: Scholars Press.

Payne, J. Barton
1976   "Psalms, Book of." In *Zondervan Pictorial Encyclopedia of the Bi-
        ble,* 4:924-47. Grand Rapids: Zondervan.

Peckham, Morse
1976   "The Intentional Fallacy?" In *On Literary Intention,* ed. David New-
        ton-de Molina, pp. 139-57. Edinburgh: At the University Press.

Peisker, Carl Heinz
1978   "Prophet." In *New International Dictionary of New Testament
        Theology,* ed. Colin Brown, 3:74-84. Grand Rapids: Zondervan.

1978a   "Parable." In *New International Dictionary of New Testament
        Theology,* ed. Colin Brown, 2:743-49. Grand Rapids: Zondervan.

Perkins, Pheme
1981   *Hearing the Parables of Jesus.* New York: Paulist.

Perpich, Sandra Wackman
1984   *A Hermeneutic Critique of Structuralist Exegesis, with Specific Ref-
        erence to Lk. 10:29-37.* New York: University Press of America.

Perrin, Norman
1976   *Jesus and the Language of the Kingdom.* Philadelphia: Fortress.

1984   "Jesus and the Theology of the New Testament." *Journal of Religion*
        64/4:413-31.

Perry, Lloyd M.
1973   *Biblical Preaching for Today's World.* Chicago: Moody.

Peterson, David L.
1981   *The Roles of Israel's Prophets.* Sheffield: JSOT Press.

Peterson, Norman R.
1978   *Literary Criticism for New Testament Critics.* Philadelphia: Fortress.
1980   "Literary Criticism in Biblical Studies." In *Orientation by Disorientation: Studies in Literary Criticism and Biblical Criticism, Presented in Honor of William A. Beardslee,* ed. Richard A. Spencer, pp. 25-50. Pittsburgh: Pickwick.

Petzoldt, Martin
1984   *Gleichnisse Jesu und Christliche Dogmatik.* Göttingen: Vandenhoeck und Ruprecht.

Piatelli-Palmarini,
    Massimo, ed.
1980   *Language and Learning: The Debate Between Jean Piaget and Noam Chomsky.* Cambridge, Mass.: Harvard University Press.

Pinnock, Clark
1971   *Biblical Revelation: The Foundation of Christian Theology.* Chicago: Moody.

Piper, Otto
1957   "Biblical Theology and Systematic Theology." *JBR* 25:106-11.

Plantinga, Alvin
1974   *The Future of Necessity.* Oxford: Clarendon.

Pokorný, Petr
1981   "Probleme biblischer Theologie." *Theologische Literaturzeitung.* 106/1:2-8.
1985   *Die Entstehung der Christologie. Voraussetzungen einer Theologie des Neuen Testaments.* Stuttgart: Calwer.

Pollock, John L.
1967   "Criteria and Our Knowledge of the Material World." *PhRev* 76:28-60.

Polzin, Robert M.
1980   "Literary and Historical Criticism of the Bible: A Crisis in Scholarship." In *Orientation by Disorientation: Studies in Literary and Biblical Criticism, Presented to William A. Beardslee,* ed. Richard A. Spencer, pp. 99-114. Pittsburgh: Pickwick.

Porter, Stanley E.
1989   *Verbal Aspect in the Greek of the New Testament with Reference to Tense and Mood.* New York: Peter Lang.
1990   "Why Hasn't Reader-Response Criticism Caught On in New Testament Studies?" *Journal of Literature and Theology* 4/3:278-92.

Poythress, Vern
1978   "Structuralism and Biblical Studies." *ExpT* 89/11.
1988   *Science and Hermeneutics: Implications of Scientific Method for Biblical Interpretation.* Grand Rapids: Zondervan.

Pratt, Richard L.
1983   "Pictures, Windows, and Mirrors in Old Testament Exegesis." *Westminster Theological Journal* 45:156-67.

Prickett, Stephen
1986   *Words and the Word. Language, Poetics, and Biblical Interpretation.* Cambridge: Cambridge University Press.

Priebe, Duane A.
1983   "The Unity of the Testaments." *Word and World* 3/3:263-71.

Quine, W. V.
1975   "The Nature of Natural Knowledge." In *Mind and Language,* ed. Samuel Guttenplan, pp. 67-81. Oxford: Clarendon.

Rad, Gerhard von
1962-65   *Old Testament Theology.* Trans. D. M. G. Stalker. 2 vols. New York: Harper.
1972   *Wisdom in Israel.* New York: Abingdon.
1976 [1955]   "Job xxxvii and Ancient Egyptian Wisdom." In *Studies in Ancient Israelite Wisdom,* ed. J. L. Crenshaw, pp. 267-77. New York: Ktav.

Radmacher, Earl D., and Robert D. Preus, eds.
1984   *Hermeneutics, Inerrancy, and the Bible.* Grand Rapids: Zondervan/ Academie Books.

Rahner, Karl
1969   *Theological Investigations,* vol. 6. Trans. Karl- H. Kruger and Boniface Kruger. Baltimore: Helicon.

Ramm, Bernard
1970   *Protestant Biblical Interpretation.* 3d ed. Grand Rapids: Baker.

Ramsey, Ian T.
1963   *Religious Language: An Empirical Placing of Theological Phrases.* New York: Macmillan.

Resseguie, James
1982   "John 9: A Literary—Critical Analysis." In *Literary Interpretation of Biblical Narrative,* ed. Kenneth R. R. Gros Louis, 2:295-303. Nashville: Abingdon.
1984   "Reader-Response Criticism and the Synoptic Gospels." *JAAR* 52:307-24.

Reventlow, Henning Graf
1985   *Problems of Old Testament Theology in the Twentieth Century.* Philadephia: Fortress.

Rhoads, David, and Donald Michie
1982   *Mark as Story: An Introduction to the Narrative of a Gospel.* Philadelphia: Fortress.

Richter, Philip J.
1984   "Recent Sociological Approaches to the Study of the New Testament." *Religion* 14:77-90.

Richter, Wolfgang
1971   *Texegese als Literaturwissenschaft.* Göttingen: Vandenhoeck und Ruprecht.

Ricoeur, Paul
1971   "Foreword." In *Hermeneutic Phenomenology: The Philosophy of Paul Ricoeur,* ed. Don Ihde, pp. xii-xvii. Evanston, Ill.: Northwestern University Press.
1973   "The Hermeneutical Function of Distanciation." *PhTod* 17:112-41.
1974a   *The Conflict of Interpretations.* Evanston, Ill.: Northwestern University Press.
1974b   "Metaphor and the Main Problem of Hermeneutics." *New Literary History* 6/1:95-110.
1975   "Biblical Hermeneutics: The Metaphorical Process." *Semeia* 4:75-106.

1976   "Philosophy and Theological Hermeneutics: Ideology, Utopia, and Faith." *The Center for Hermeneutical Studies in Hellenistic and Modern Culture* 17, pp. 1-28. Berkeley: Graduate Theological Union.

1977   *Rule of Metaphor.* Toronto: University of Toronto Press.

1978   "The Narrative Function." *Semeia* 13:177-202.

1980   "Towards a Hermeneutic of the Idea of Revelation." In *Essays on Biblical Revelation,* trans. David Pellauer. Philadelphia: Fortress.

Ridderbos, Nicholas H., and Peter C. Craigie

1986   "Psalms." *ISBE,* ed. Geoffrey W. Bromiley, 3:1029-40. Grand Rapids: Eerdmans.

Riesner, Rainer

1984   *Jesus als Lehrer. Eine Untersuchung zum Ursprung der Evangelien—Überlieferung.* Tübingen: J. C. B. Mohr.

Ringgren, Helmer

1983   "Akkadian Apocalypses." In *Apocalypticism in the Mediterranean World and the Near East,* ed. David Hellholm, pp. 379-86. Tübingen: J. C. B. Mohr.

Robinson, Donald

1985   *Faith's Framework. The Structure of New Testament Theology.* Sutherland, Australia: Albatross.

Robinson, J. Armitage

1904   *St. Paul's Epistle to the Ephesians.* London: James Clark & Co.

Robinson, James M.

1976   "The Future of New Testament Theology." *Religious Studies Review* 2:17-23.

Robinson, James M., and John B. Cobb, Jr., eds.

1967   *Theology as History.* New York: Harper and Row.

Robinson, John A. T.

1963   *Honest to God.* Philadelphia: Westminster.

Robinson, Haddon W.

1980   *Biblical Preaching: The Development and Delivery of Expository Messages.* Grand Rapids: Baker.

1984   "Homiletics and Hermeneutics." In *Hermeneutics, Inerrancy, and the Bible.* Ed. Earl D. Radmacher and Robert D. Preus. Grand Rapids: Zondervan/Academie Books.

Rodd, Cyril S.

1981   "On Applying a Sociological Theory to Biblical Studies." *JSOT* 19:95-106.

Rogers, Jack, and Donald McKim

1979   *The Authority and Interpretation of the Bible: An Historical Approach.* New York: Harper and Row.

Roller, Otto

1933   *Das Formular der Paulinischer Briefe, ein Beitrag zur Lehre vom antiken Briefe.* Stuttgart: Kohlhammer.

Ross, James

1982   "Ways of Religious Knowing." In *The Challenge of Religion: Contemporary Readings in Philosophy of Religion.* Ed. Frederick Ferré et al. New York: Seabury.

Rowland, Christopher
    1982   *The Open Heaven: A Study of Apocalypticism in Judaism and Early Christianity*. London: SPCK.

Rowley, H. H.
    1963   *The Relevance of Apocalyptic.* 3d ed. London: Lutterworth.

Ruiz, Gregorio
    1985   "La hermeneutica biblica de la Teologia de la Liberación." *SalTerrae* 73:113-25.

Ruler, Arnold A. von
    1971   *The Christian Church and the Old Testament.* Trans. Geoffrey W. Bromiley. Grand Rapids: Eerdmans.

Russell, C. Allyn
    1976   *Voices of American Fundamentalism*. Philadelphia: Westminster.

Russell, David S.
    1964   *The Method and Message of Jewish Apocalyptic.* London: SCM.
    1978   *Apocalyptic: Ancient and Modern*. Philadelphia: Fortress.

Russell, Leslie R.
    1982   "Synergism in the New Testament." *Crux* 18/2:14-17.

Ryken, Leland
    1984   *How to Read the Bible as Literature.* Grand Rapids: Zondervan/ Academie Books.

Ryle, Gilbert
    1963   "The Theory of Meaning." In *Philosophy and Ordinary Language.* Ed. Charles E. Caton. Urbana: University of Illinois.

Sanders, E. P.
    1977   *Paul and Palestinian Judaism: A Comparison of Patterns of Religion.* Philadelphia: Fortress.
    1983   "The Genre of Palestinian Jewish Apocalypses." In *Apocalypticism in the Mediterranean World and the Near East,* ed. David Hellholm, pp. 447-59. Tübingen: J. C. B. Mohr.

Sanders, Jack T.
    1962   "The Transition from Opening Epistolary Thanksgiving to Body in the Letters of the Pauline Corpus." *JBL* 81:348-62.

Sanders, James
    1972   *Torah and Canon*. Philadelphia: Fortress.
    1976   "Adaptable for Life: The Nature and Function of Canon." In *Magnalia Dei: Essays on the Bible and Archaeology in Memory of G. Ernest Wright,* ed. Frank Moore Cross et al., pp. 531-60. Garden City, N.Y.: Doubleday.
    1977   "Biblical Criticism and the Bible as Canon." *USQR* 32:157-65.
    1980   "Canonical Context and Canonical Criticism." *Horizons in Biblical Theology* 2:173-97.

Sandmel, Samuel
    1962   "Parallelomonia." *JBL* 81:2-13.

Savage, Mary
    1980   "Literary Criticism and Biblical Studies: A Rhetorical Analysis of the Joseph Narrative." In *Scripture in Context: Essays on the Comparative Method,* ed. Carl D. Evans, William W. Hallo, John B. White, pp. 79-100. Pittsburgh: Pickwick.

Sawyer, John F. A.
    1972   *Semantics in Biblical Research: New Methods of Defining Hebrew*

Words for Salvation. London: SCM.

1976   *A Modern Introduction to Biblical Hebrew.* Boston: Oriel.

1987   *Prophecy and the Prophets of the Old Testament.* New York: Oxford University Press.

Schillebeeckx, Edward

1964   *Dogmatic vs. Biblical Theology.* Baltimore: Helicon.

Schnackenburg, Rudolf

1963   *New Testament Theology Today.* Trans. David Askew. New York: Herder and Herder.

Schoonhoven, E. Jansen

1980   "The Bible in Africa." *Exchange* 9:9-18.

Schubert, Paul

1939   *Form and Function of the Pauline Thanksgivings.* Berlin: Töpelmann.

Schweitzer, Albert

[1906] 1948   *The Quest of the Historical Jesus, a Critical Study of its Progress from Reimarus to Wrede.* Trans. W. Montgomery. New York: Macmillan.

Scobie, C. H. H.

1984   "The Place of Wisdom in Biblical Theology." *BibTheolBull* 14/2:43-48.

Scott, Bernard Brandon

1981   *Jesus, Symbol-Maker for the Kingdom.* Philadelphia: Fortress.

1982   "Review of *Orientation by Disorientation,* ed. Spencer." *INT* 37/2:314.

Scott, J. Julius, Jr.

1979   "Some Problems in Hermeneutics for Contemporary Evangelicals." *JETS* 22/1:67-77.

Scott, R. B. Y.

1953   *The Relevance of the Prophets.* New York: Macmillan.

1971   *The Way of Wisdom in the Old Testament.* New York: Macmillan.

Scroggs, Robin

1980   "The Sociological Interpretation of the New Testament: The Present State of Research." *NTS* 26/2:164-79.

Searle, John R.

1969   *Speech Aids: An Essay in the Philosophy of Language.* New York: Cambridge University Press.

1979   *Expansion and Meaning: Studies in the Theology of Speech Acts.* Cambridge: Cambridge University Press.

Setiloane, Gabriel

1979   "Where are We in African Theology Today?" *Africa Theological Journal* 8/1:1-14.

Sheppard, Gerald T.

1974   "Canon Criticism: The Proposal of Brevard Childs and an Assessment for Evangelical Hermeneutics." *Studia Biblica et Theologica* 4:3-17.

1977   "The Epilogue to Qohelet as Theological Commentary." *Catholic Biblical Commentary* 39:182-89.

1980   *Wisdom as Hermeneutical Construct.* New York: Walter de Gruyter.

1982   "Canonization: Hearing the Voice of the Same God through Historically Dissimilar Traditions." *Interpretation* 36/1:21-33.

1988   "Wisdom." *ISBE,* ed. Geoffrey W. Bromiley, 4:1074-82. Grand Rapids: Eerdmans.

Sigal, Phillip

1983   "Aspects of Dual Covenant Theology: Salvation." *Horizons in Biblical Theology* 5/2:1-48.

Silva, Moisés

1977-78   "Ned B. Stonehouse and Redaction Criticism." *Westminster Theological Journal* 40:77-88.

1980   "Bilingualism and the Character of New Testament Greek." *Biblical* 69:148-219.

1980a   "The Pauline Style as Lexical-Choice: Ginoskein and Related Terms." In *Pauline Studies: Essays Presented to Professor F. F. Bruce,* ed. Donald A. Hagner and Murray J. Harris, pp. 184-207. Grand Rapids: Eerdmans.

1983   *Biblical Words and Their Meaning: An Introduction to Lexical Semantics.* Grand Rapids: Zondervan.

1990   *God, Language and Scripture: Reading the Bible in the Light of General Linguistics.* Grand Rapids: Zondervan.

Skinner, Quentin

1972   "Motives, Intentions and the Interpretation of Texts," *New Literary History* 3/2.

Smalley, Stephen S.

1978   *John: Evangelist and Interpreter.* Exeter: Paternoster.

Smart, James D.

1979   *The Past, Present, and Future of Biblical Theology.* Philadelphia: Westminster.

Smend, Rudolf

1980   "Questions about the Importance of the Canon in an OT Introduction." *JSOT* 16:45-51.

Smick, Elmer B.

1983   "Old Testament Theology: The Historico-genetic Method." *JETS* 26:145-55.

Smith, Gary V.

1986   "Prophecy, False." *ISBE,* ed. Geoffrey W. Bromiley, 3:956-986. Grand Rapids: Eerdmans.

1986a   "Prophet, Prophecy." *ISBE,* ed. Geoffrey W. Bromiley, 3:986-1004. Grand Rapids: Eerdmans.

Smith, Morton

1983   "On the History of 'APOKALYPTO' and 'APOKALYPSIS.'" In *Apocalypticism in the Mediterranean and the Near East,* ed. David Hellholm, pp. 9-20. Tübingen: J. C. B. Mohr.

Smith, Ralph L.

1984   *Micah-Malachi.* Word Biblical Commentary. Waco, Tex.: Word.

Smith, Robert H.

1983   "Were the Early Christians Middle Class? A Sociological Analysis of the New Testament." In *The Bible and Liberation,* ed. Norman K. Gottwald, pp. 441-57. Maryknoll, N.Y.: Orbis.

Soskice, Janet Martin

1985   *Metaphor and Religious Language.* Oxford: Clarendon.

Sperber, Alexander

1966   *A Historical Grammar of Biblical Hebrew.* Leiden: E. J. Brill.

Spohn, William C.
1986   "The Use of Scripture in Moral Theology." *TheolStud* 47/1:88-102.

Sproul, R. C.
1980   "Biblical Interpretation and the Analogy of Faith." In *Inerrancy and Common Sense,* ed. Roger R. Nicole and J. Ramsey Michaels, pp. 119-35. Grand Rapids: Baker.

Spurgeon, Charles Haddon
1877   *To My Students: Being Addresses Delivered to the Students of the Pastor's College,* vol. 2. Grand Rapids: Associated Publishers and Authors.

Stagg, Evelyn, and
Frank Stagg
1978   *Woman in the World of Jesus.* Philadelphia: Westminster.

Stagg, Frank
1972   "The Abused Aorist." *JBL* 91:222-31.

Stambaugh, John E., and
David L. Balch
1986   *The New Testament in Its Social Environment.* Philadelphia: Westminster.

Stancil, Bill
1980   "Structuralism and New Testament Studies." *SWJT* 22:4-59.

Stanton, Graham N.
1972   "The Gospel Tradition and Early Christological Reflection." In *Christ, Faith, and History,* ed. Stephen W. Sykes and J. P. Clayton, pp. 191-204. Cambridge: Cambridge University Press.

Steimle, Edmund A.
1980   "By What Authority?" and "The Fabric of the Sermon." In *Preaching the Story,* ed. Edmund A. Steimle, Mornis J. Niedenthal, and Charles L. Rice, pp. 37-42, 163-75. Philadelphia: Fortress.

Stein, Robert H.
1980   "The 'Criteria' for Authenticity." In *Gospel Perspectives,* ed. R. T. France and David Wenham, 1:225-63. Sheffield: JSOT Press.
1981   *An Introduction to the Parables of Jesus.* Philadelphia: Westminster.

Stendahl, Krister
1962   "Biblical Theology." In *Interpreter's Dictionary of the Bible,* 1:419-22.
1965   "Method in the Study of Biblical Theology." In *The Bible in Modern Scholarship.* Ed. J. Philip Hyatt. Nashville: Abingdon.

Sternberg, Meir
1985   *The Poetics of Biblical Narrative, Ideological Literature and the Drama of Reading.* Bloomington: Indiana University Press.

Sterrett, T. Norton
1974   *How to Understand Your Bible.* Downers Grove: InterVarsity Press.

Stott, John R. W.
1964   *The Epistles of John.* TNTC. Grand Rapids: Eerdmans.

Stowers, Stanley K.
1986   *Letter Writing in Greco-Roman Antiquity.* Philadelphia: Westminster.

Strack, Hermann L., and
Paul Billerbeck
1961-65   *Kommentar zum Neuen Testament aus Talmud und Midrasch.* 6 vols. Munich: Beck.

Straub, Hans
 1984   "Theologie des Alten Testaments als Bestandteil einer biblischen
         Theologie." *BN* 24:125-37.
 1985   "Theologie des Alten Testaments als Bestandteil einer biblischen
         Theologie." *EvT* 45:20-29.

Stuart, Douglas
 1980   *Old Testament Exegesis: A Primer for Students and Pastors.* Phil-
         adelphia: Westminster.

Stuhlmacher, Peter
 1977   *Historical Criticism and Theological Interpretation of Scripture.*
         Philadelphia: Fortress.
 1979   "The Gospel of Reconciliation in Christ—Basic Features and Issues
         of a Biblical Theology of the New Testament." *Horizons in Biblical
         Theology* 1:161-90.
 1980   ". . . in verrosteten Angeln." *ZTK* 77/2:222-38.
 1986   *Reconciliation, Law and Righteousness. Essays in Biblical Theology.*
         Trans. E. R. Kalin. Philadelphia: Fortress.

Sundberg, A. C., Jr.
 1964   *The Old Testament of the Early Church.* Cambridge, Mass.: Harvard
         University Press.
 1975   "The Bible's Canon and the Christian Doctrine of Inspiration." *In-
         terpretation* 29/4:352-71.

Sunukjian, Donald R.
 1982   "The Preacher as Persuader." In *Walvoord: A Tribute,* ed. Donald
         K. Campbell, pp. 289-99. Chicago: Moody.

Suppe, Frederick, ed.
 1977   *The Structure of Scientific Theories.* Chicago: University of Illinois
         Press.

Taber, Charles R.
 1978   "Is There More than One Way to Do Theology?" *Gospel in Context*
         1:1-8.
 1979   "Hermeneutics and Culture: An Anthropological Perspective." In
         Gospel and Culture, ed. John R. W. Stott and R. T. Coote, pp. 109-
         31. Pasadena: William Carey Library.

Tan, Paul Lee
 1974   *The Interpretation of Prophecy.* Winona Lake, Ind.: Assurance Pub-
         lishers.

Tate, Marvin E.
 1981   "Promising Paths toward Biblical Theology." *Review and Expositor*
         78:179-80.

Taylor, Mark C.
 1982   *Deconstructing Theology.* Chico, Calif.: Scholars Press.

Terrien, Samuel
 1985   "Biblical Theology: The Old Testament (1979-1984). A Decade and
         a Half of Spectacular Growth." *BTB* 15:127-35.

Terry, Milton
 1964 [1890] *Biblical Hermeneutics: A Treatise on the Interpretation of the Old
         and New Testaments.* Grand Rapids: Zondervan.

TeSelle, Sallie M.
 1975   *Speaking in Parables.* Philadelphia: Fortress.

Theissen, Gerd
1978   *Sociology of Early Palestinian Christianity.* Trans. John Bowden. Philadelphia: Fortress.
1982   *The Social Setting of Pauline Christianity: Essays on Corinth.* Trans. John H. Schütz. Philadelphia: Fortress.

Thiselton, Anthony C.
1977   "Semantics and New Testament Interpretation." In *New Testament Interpretation,* ed. I. Howard Marshall, pp. 75-104. Grand Rapids: Eerdmans.
1978   "Language and Meaning in Religion." In *New International Dictionary of New Testament Theology,* ed. Colin Brown, 3:1123-46. Grand Rapids: Zondervan.
1980   *The Two Horizons: New Testament Hermeneutics and Philosophical Descriptions.* Grand Rapids: Eerdmans.
1985   "Reader Response Hermeneutics, Action Models, and the Parables of Jesus." In *The Responsibility of Hermeneutics,* by Roger Lundin, Anthony C. Thiselton, and Clarence Walhout, pp. 79-113. Grand Rapids: Eerdmans.

Thomas, J. C.
1982   "Faith and History: A Critique of Recent Dogmatics." *Religious Studies* 18/3:327-36.

Thomas, Robert L.
1980   "A Hermeneutical Ambiguity of Eschatology: The Analogy of Faith." *JETS* 25:45-53.

Tompkins, Jane P., ed.
1980   *Reader-Response Criticism: From Formalism to Post-Structuralism.* Baltimore: Johns Hopkins University Press.

Tourangeau, Roger
1982   "Metaphor and Cognitive Structure." In *Metaphor: Problems and Perspectives.* Ed. David Miall. Atlanta: Highlands Humanities.

Tov, Emanuel
1980   "Determining the Relationship between Qumran Scrolls and the LXX: Some Methodological Issues." *1980 Proceedings IOCS-Vienna: The Hebrew and Greek Texts of Samuel.* Ed. Emanuel Tov. Jerusalem: Academon.
1981   *The Text-Critical Use of the Septuagint in Biblical Research.* Jerusalem Biblical Studies. Jerusalem: Simon.
1982a   "A Modern Textual Outlook Based on the Qumran Scrolls." *Hebrew Union College Annual* 53:11-27.
1982b   "Criteria for Evaluating Textual Readings: The Limitations of Textual Rules." *Harvard Theological Review* 75/4:429-48.

Tracy, David
1975   *Blessed Rage for Order: The New Pluralism in Theology.* New York: Seabury.
1980   "Reflections on John Dominic Crossan's Cliffs of Fall." *Seminar Papers: SBL, 1980.* Chico, Calif.: Scholars Press.
1981   *The Analogical Imagination: Christian Theology and the Culture of Pluralism.* New York: Crossroads.

Traina, Robert A.
1952   *Methodical Bible Study.* New York: Ganis and Harris.

Trench, Richard Chenivix
1980 [1880]   *Synonyms of the New Testament.* Grand Rapids: Eerdmans.
Trudinger, L. Paul
1974   " 'Eli, Eli, Lama Sabachthani' A Cry of Dereliction or Victory?" *JETS* 17:235-38.
Tucker, Gene M.
1985   "Prophecy and the Prophetic Literature." In *The Hebrew Bible and Its Modern Interpreters,* ed. Douglas A. Knight, pp. 325-68. Chico, Calif.: Scholars Press.
Tucker, Ruth A., and
Walter Liefeld
1987   *Daughters of the Church: Women and Ministry from New Testament Times to the Present.* Grand Rapids: Zondervan.
Turner, Nigel
1963   *A Grammar of New Testament Greek.* Vol. 3: *Syntax,* by James H. Moulton and W. F. Howard. Edinburgh: T. & T. Clark.
1976   *A Grammar of New Testament Greek.* Vol. 4: *Style,* by James H. Moulton and W. F. Howard. Edinburgh: T. & T. Clark.
1980   *Christian Words.* Edinburgh: T. & T. Clark.
Tur-Sinai, N. H.
1967   "By What Methods and to What Extent Can We Establish the Original Text of the Hebrew Bible?" *Proceedings of the Israel Academy of Sciences and Humanities* 1/1:1-13.
Ullmann, Stephen
1964   *Semantics: An Introduction to the Science of Meaning.* Oxford: Blackwell.
Uspensky, Boris
1973   *A Poetics of Composition. The Structure of the Artistic Text and Typology of a Compositional Form.* Trans. V. Zavarin and S. Wittig. Berkeley: University of California Press.
van der Waal, C.
1981   "The Continuity between the Old and New Testaments." *Neotestamentica* 14:1-20.
Vanhoozer, Kevin J.
1986   "The Semantics of Biblical Literature: Truth and Scripture's Diverse Literary Forms." In *Hermeneutics, Authority, and Canon.* Ed. D. A. Carson and John D. Woodbridge. Grand Rapids: Zondervan.
1987   "A Lamp in the Labyrinthe: The Hermeneutics of 'Aesthetic' Theology." *Trinity Journal* ns 8/1:25-56.
1990   *Biblical Narrative in the Philosophy of Paul Ricoeur: A Study in Hermeneutics and Theology.* Cambridge: Cambridge University Press.
Van Huyssteen, Wentzel
1989   *Theology and the Justification of Faith: Constructing Theories in Systematic Theology.* Trans. H. F. Snijders. Grand Rapids: Eerdmans.
Vermes, Geza
1982   "Jewish Literature and New Testament Exegesis: Reflections on Methodology." *Journal of Jewish Studies* 33:361-76.
Via, Dan O.
1967   *The Parables—Their Literary and Existential Dimension.* Philadelphia: Fortress.

Vischer, Wilhelm
1949   *The Witness of the Old Testament to Christ.* 2 vols. London: Lut-
        terworth.

von Balthasar, Hans Urs
1983   "Unity and Diversity in New Testament Theology." *Communio*
        10:106-16.
1983   "Einheit und Vielheit neutestamentlicher Theologie." *IntKathZeit/*
        Communio 12:101-9.

Vos, Geerhardus
1948   *Biblical Theology: Old and New Testaments.* Grand Rapids: Eerd-
        mans.

Vriezen, Theodorus C.
1958   *An Outline of Old Testament Theology.* Trans. S. Neuijen. Wagenin-
        gen: H. Veenman.
1963   "Theocracy and Soteriology." In *Essays on Old Testament Herme-*
        neutics. Ed. Claus Westermann and James L. Mays. Richmond: John
        Knox.

Walker, William A.
1977   "A Method for Identifying Redactional Passages in Matthew on
        Functional and Linguistic Grounds." *CBQ* 39:76-93.

Walter, Nikolaus
1986   "Wie halten wir es mit der Eschatologie?" *Die Zeichen der Zeit* 40/
        7:158-62.

Walther, James A.
1969   "The Significance of Methodology for Biblical Theology." *Perspec-*
        tive 10/3:217-33.

Waltke, Bruce K.
1978   "The Textual Criticism of the Old Testament." In *Biblical Criticism:*
        Historical, Literary, and Textual, by Roland K. Harrison, Bruce K.
        Waltke, Donald Guthrie, and Gordon D. Fee, pp. 47-82. Grand Rap-
        ids: Zondervan.

Ward, Wayne E.
1977   "Towards a Biblical Theology." *Review and Expositor* 74/3:371-87.
1981   "New Testament Theology: Retrospect and Prospect." *Review and*
        Expositor 78/2:153-68.

Ware, J. H.
1983   "Rethinking the Possibility of a Biblical Theology." *PerspRelStud*
        10/1:5-13.

Warfield, B. B.
1932   "The Idea of Systematic Theology." In *Studies in Theology,* pp. 49-
        87. New York: Oxford University Press.

Watson, Duane F.
1988   *Invention, Arrangement, and Style: Rhetorical Criticism of Jude and*
        2 Peter. SBL Dissertation Series 104. Atlanta: Scholars Press.

Weber, Max
1952   *Ancient Judaism.* New York: Free Press.

Webster, Edwin C.
1982   "Pattern in the Fourth Gospel." In *Art and Meaning: Rhetoric in*
        Biblical Literature. Ed. David J. A. Clines, David M. Ginn and Alan
        J. Hauser. JSOT Supp 19. Sheffield: JSOT Press.

Weinberg, Christiane, and
    Ota Weinberg
        1979   *Logik, Semantik, Hermeneutik.* Munich: Beck.
    Weir, J.
        1982   "Analogous Fulfillment. The Use of the Old Testament in the New Testament." *Persp RelStud* 9/1:65-76.

Weitz, Morris
        1967   "Philosophical Analysis." In *Encyclopedia of Philosophy,* ed. Paul Edwards, 1:102-8. New York: Collier-Macmillan.

Wellek, Rene,
    and Austin Warren
        1956   *Theory of Literature.* New York: Harcourt, Brace and World.
Wells, David F., and John
    D. Woodbridge
        1977   *The Evangelicals.* Grand Rapids: Baker.
Wenham, John
        1965   *The Elements of New Testament Greek.* Cambridge: Cambridge University Press.

Werner, Eric
        1962   "Music" and "Musical Instruments." In *Interpreter's Dictionary of the Bible,* 3:457-76. Nashville: Abingdon.

Westermann, Claus
        1963   "Remarks on the Theses of Bultmann and Baumgärtel." In *Essays on Old Testament Hermeneutics,* ed. Claus Westermann and James L. Mays, pp. 123-33. Richmond: John Knox.
        1967   *Basic Forms of Prophetic Speech.* Trans. Hugh C. White. Philadelphia: Westminster.

White, John L.
        1982   "The Ancient Epistolography Group in Retrospect." *Semeia* 22, ed. John L. White, pp. 1-14. Chico, Calif.: Scholars Press.
        1982a   "The Greek Documentary Letter Tradition Third Century B.C.E. to Third Century C.E." *Semeia* 22, ed. John L. White, pp. 89-106. Chico, Calif.: Scholars Press.

Whitley, Charles F.
        1963   *The Prophetic Achievement.* Leiden: E. J. Brill.
Widengren, Gus
        1983   "Leitende Ideen und Quellen der iranischen Apokalyptik." In *Apocalypticism in the Mediterranean World and the Near East,* ed. David Hellholm, pp. 77-161. Tübingen: J. C. B. Mohr.

Wikgram, George V.
        1978   *The Word Study Concordance.* Pasadena: William Carey Library.
Williams, Ronald J.
        1967   *Hebrew Syntax: An Outline.* Toronto: University of Toronto Press.
Wilson, Robert R.
        1984   *Sociological Approaches to the Old Testament.* Philadelphia: Fortress.

Wimsatt, W. K., and
    Monroe C. Beardsley
        1976   "The Intentional Fallacy." In *On Literary Intention,* ed. David Newton-deMolina, pp. 1-13. Edinburgh: At the University Press.

Wink, Walter
1973   *The Bible in Human Transformation: Toward a New Paradigm for Biblical Study.* Philadelphia: Fortress.

Wittgenstein, Ludwig
1953   *Philosophical Investigations.* Trans. G. E. M. Anscombe. New York: Macmillan.

Wittig, Susan
1977   "A Theory of Multiple Meanings." *Semeia* 9:75-103.

Wolfe, David L.
1982   *Epistemology: The Justification of Belief.* Downers Grove: InterVarsity Press.

Wolff, Hans Walter
1974   *Anthropology of the Old Testament.* Trans. Margaret Kohl. London: SCM.

Wood, Leon
1979   *The Prophets of Israel.* Grand Rapids: Baker.

Woodbridge, John D.
1982   *Biblical Authority: A Critique of the Rogers/McKim Proposal.* Grand Rapids: Zondervan.

Woudstra, Marten H.
1983   "The Old Testament in Biblical Theology and Dogmatics." *CTJ* 18:47-60.

Wrede, William
1897   "The Task and Methods of 'New Testament Theology.' " Trans. in Robert Morgan, *The Nature of New Testament Theology: The Contribution of William Wrede and Adolf Schlatter,* pp. 68-116. London: SCM, 1973.

Wright, Christopher J. H.
1984   "The Use of the Bible in Social Ethics: Paradigms, Types and Eschatology." *Transformation* 1/1:11-20.

Wright, G. Ernest
1952   *God Who Acts: Biblical Theology as Recital.* London: SCM.

Wuellner, Wilhelm
1987   "Where Is Rhetorical Criticism Taking Us?" *CBQ* 49:448-63.

Würthwein, Ernst
1976   "Egyptian Wisdom and the Old Testament." In *Studies in Ancient Israelite Wisdom,* ed. James L. Crenshaw, pp. 113-33. New York: Ktav.

1979   *The Text of the Old Testament: An Introduction to the Biblia Hebraica.* Grand Rapids: Eerdmans.

Yamauchi, Edwin M.
1972   *The Stones and the Scriptures.* New York: J. B. Lippincott.
1984   "Sociology, Scripture and the Supernatural." *JETS* 27/2:169-92.

Yandell, Keith
1989   *Christianity and Philosophy.* Grand Rapids: Eerdmans.

Zerwick, Max
1963   *Biblical Greek Illustrated by Examples.* Rome: Biblical Institute.

Zimmerli, Walther
1963   "Promise and Fulfillment." In *Essays on Old Testament Hermeneutics.* Ed. Claus Westermann and James L. Mays. Richmond: John Knox.

1976 "Concerning the Structure of Old Testament Wisdom." In *Studies in Ancient Israelite Wisdom,* ed. James L. Crenshaw, pp. 175-207. New York: Ktav.

1982 "Biblical Theology." *Horizons in Biblical Theology* 4/1:95-130.

1984 "Biblische Theologie." *BerlinTheol/Zeit* 1/1:5-26.

Zuck, Roy B.

1982 "Application in Biblical Hermeneutics and Exposition." In *Walvoord: A Tribute,* ed. Donald Campbell, pp. 15-38. Chicago: Moody.

Subject Index

Author Index

Index to Scripture and Other Ancient Writings